The VRML Sourcebook

ANDREA L. AMES
DAVID R. NADEAU
JOHN L. MORELAND

John Wiley & Sons, Inc.
New York • Chichester • Brisbane • Toronto • Singapore

Publisher: Katherine Schowalter
Editor: Tim Ryan
Managing Editor: Micheline Frederick
Text Design & Composition: North Market Street Graphics, Dave Erb

This text is printed on acid-free paper.

Library of Congress Cataloging-in-Publication Data:
Ames, Andrea L.
The VRML sourcebook / Andrea L. Ames, David R. Nadeau, John L. Moreland.
p. cm.
Includes index.
ISBN 0-471-14159-3 (pbk. : alk. paper)
1. Hypertext systems. 2. VRML (Document markup language) 3. Virtual reality. I. Nadeau, David R. II. Moreland, John L. III. Title.
QA76.76.H94A52 1996
006—dc20 95–30080
CIP

Printed in the United States of America

10 9 8 7 6 5 4 3 2 1

Contents

Chapter 5 Positioning Shapes 57

Chapter 6 Rotating Shapes 77

Chapter 7 Scaling Shapes 101

Chapter 10 Shading with Materials 181

Chapter 11 Grouping Nodes 199

Chapter 12 Instancing Shapes 237

Chapter 13 Linking in Your Worlds 255

Chapter 14 Creating Shapes with Faces, Lines, and Points 277

Preface

The purpose of this book is to introduce you to the Virtual Reality Modeling Language (VRML) in a friendly, practical, and non-technical way. Our goal is to provide a book filled with useful and interesting examples so you can start building your own VRML worlds right away.

The book is practical and task-oriented in style and structure. In other words, we answer your "What if I want to . . . ?" questions rather than explaining how to use the syntax first. This way, you can find the information you want whether or not you know what a **MaterialBinding** node does.

Using VRML requires that you understand a little about computers and a little about computer graphics. We do not assume you understand either of these fields extensively, and we provide background concepts whenever necessary. The book is not meant to be a computer graphics primer nor a basic programming text, however.

Intended Audience

The VRML Sourcebook is written for a variety of people, and we structured the book to enable each portion of our audience to access the information they need quickly and easily.

Computer Hobbyist or Enthusiast

You may be a computer hobbyist or enthusiast. If so, we wrote this book primarily for you! You may have a computer at home or at school and enjoy using it to fiddle with interesting technology. Maybe you've taken a computer class; written some programs in Basic, Pascal, C, or C++; or written some DOS batch files, HyperCard/HyperTalk scripts, or UNIX shell scripts. You probably have Internet access and enjoy surfing the Web, reading Internet news, and conversing with your friends using E-mail. Maybe you've written your own HTML pages and have your own home page. Essentially, you are your own system administrator, maintaining your PC or Macintosh system software and enjoying the time you spend with your computer.

Technical or Non-Technical Artist

You may be a computer hobbyist or enthusiast *and* an artist, or just an artist looking for a new medium. As well as the knowledge of the hobbyist, you might also create two- and three-dimensional graphics on your PC or Mac with commercial software. You probably understand a little about lighting models, morphing, and paint programs. Even if VRML is your first foray into computer-based art, this book is for you.

Virtual Reality Hobbyist or Enthusiast

As a virtual reality (VR) enthusiast, you may have no computer background other than playing games. You probably keep up with the latest developments in cool VR games and other environments. You probably own all the latest CD-ROM games and hold the high scores at your house. Welcome! You can use this book with no prior technical knowledge to create your *own* VR worlds.

Technical Experts and Application Developers

Although we wrote this book primarily for a non-technical audience, we tried to include something for everyone. If you're interested in more syntax explanation than that provided in the VRML specification, you'll find it here. Although we've kept the language non-technical, the technical material is covered in detail.

How to Best Use This Book

As we've already stated, *The VRML Sourcebook* is written for a variety of people, and we structured the book to enable each portion of our audience to access the information they need quickly and easily. For each of our potential audiences, we've provided a pathway through the book.

Computer Hobbyist or Enthusiast and Technical or Non-Technical Artist

Depending on your understanding of 3-D graphics concepts, you may want to read thoroughly or only skim the conceptual graphics discussions. These are found in each chapter's "Understanding . . ." section. For example, positioning objects within your world (called "translation") is discussed in Chapter 5. The first section, "Understanding Translation," is a conceptual discussion about translation in general.

To get the best understanding of VRML, read carefully the larger sections containing syntax subsections. These are conceptual VRML and computer graphics discussions. For example, the **Translation** node's syntax is discussed in "Understanding the **Translation** Node Syntax." This is a subsection of "Positioning a Shape Using Translation," a VRML concepts discussion.

The examples in the "Experimenting with . . ." sections illustrate the 3-D, computer graphics, and VRML concepts discussed in the conceptual sections of each chapter. Not only do they reinforce the ideas you've just read, they give you templates for building your own worlds. The "Extended Examples" sections at the end of each chapter provide additional ideas and models for your worlds.

Virtual Reality Hobbyist or Enthusiast

If you want to get a solid understanding of the technical aspects of VRML, thoroughly read the "Understanding . . ." sections that discuss 3-D graphics concepts and the VRML and computer graphics conceptual sections which contain the syntax descriptions.

The examples in the "Experimenting with . . ." sections illustrate the 3-D, computer graphics, and VRML concepts discussed in the conceptual sections of each chapter. Not only do they reinforce the ideas you've just read, they give you templates for building your own worlds.

If you want to start building cool worlds right away, skim the conceptual information and start creating the example files in the "Experimenting with . . ." sections. Don't forget the extended examples at the end of each chapter.

Technical Experts and Application Developers

Skim the table of contents for the "Syntax:" sections of each chapter. In those sections, you will find the meat of VRML. For further explanation about how VRML has implemented particular computer graphics concepts and methods, see the conceptual discussions of which the syntax sections are a part.

For example, the **Rotation** node is discussed in the "Understanding the **Rotation** Node Syntax" section. That section is one part of a larger section called "Orienting a Shape Using Rotation." The larger section describes VRML's particular way of implementing rotation.

Some chapters cover more advanced, complex subjects. These are indicated by the word *Advanced* after the title in the table of contents, like this: "Performing Custom Shape Transforms (Advanced)." These chapters present more technical topics in a non-technical way.

Conventions

We've established some formatting and typographical conventions to help you better access and understand the information in this book.

Typographical Conventions

Bold type in the serif body typeface indicates syntax. For example, all node and field names and field values are bold. **Bold, sans serif type** indicates new items that are defined in the surrounding text. `Text displayed in a monospaced font` indicates VRML text, file names, and coordinates.

Formatting Conventions

We've developed the following formatting conventions to help you easily find specific kinds of information in the book.

Syntax

The default syntax is always presented in a syntax box, which lists the VRML node, its associated fields, the default values of those fields, and a comment about the type of data of each field value. Syntax boxes accompany detailed syntax discussions that thoroughly explain all the components within the box. This is an example of a syntax box:

SYNTAX **Translation node**

```
Translation {
   translation 0.0 0.0 0.0      # X, Y, Z distance
}
```

Examples, Diagrams, and Images

For every concept and task, we provide a variety of examples. We provide diagrams to help visually illustrate conceptual discussions, and we include images showing the results of example VRML text files.

Example VRML files are presented as figures. We assume you are trying some of these by typing them and displaying them with your browser on your computer. We reuse example text in later chapters so you have to type as little as possible. (You can also get all example text from the John Wiley & Sons ftp site at: `ftp.wiley.com/public/computer_books/vrml`.)

Images resulting from example VRML files are presented with black backgrounds. That is the default background color for most VRML browsers and these images look most like what you'll see on your screen when you try the examples.

Diagrams appear throughout the book, singly and in series. The series provide a behind-the-scenes look at what your browser is doing when it loads your VRML files. Normally, the series illustrate a breakdown of complex changes occurring as a result of your VRML text. In each diagram series:

- *Grayed axes indicate the original axes of the scene.*
- *Black axes indicate the "new" axes or origin resulting from the current translation, rotation, scale, etc. (the center[s] of the object[s] under discussion). These axes provide a visual contrast to the gray axes, making it more apparent what changes have taken place from one step in a series to another.*
- *Arrows are provided to indicate changes in specific directions.*

For example, the diagram series in Figure P.1 illustrates what happens when you position a cylinder.

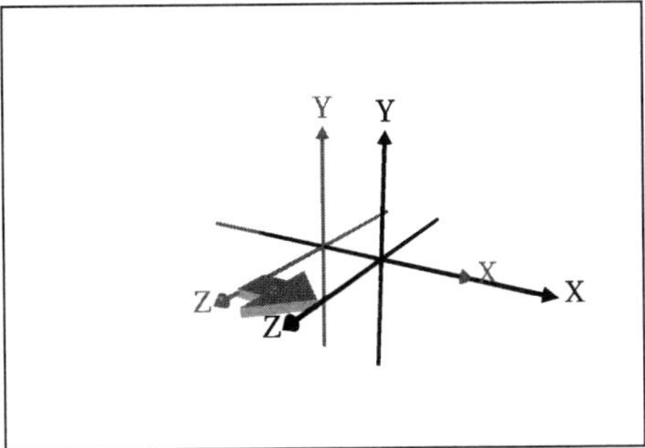

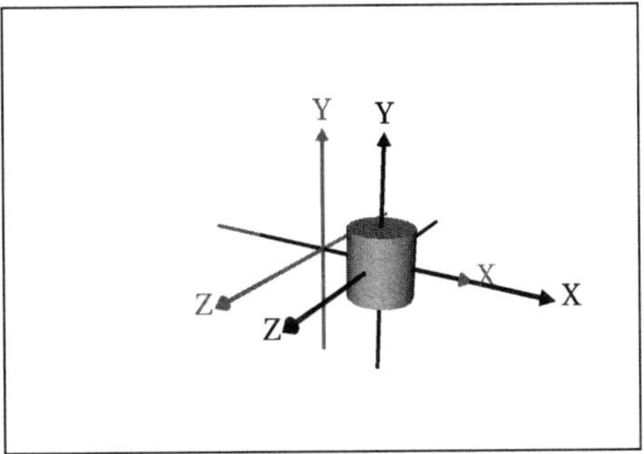

Figure P.1 *Translating +2.0 units along the X axis and drawing a cylinder*

In the first diagram, the "new," or current, black axes are positioned to the right of the original gray axes. This movement is indicated by the gray arrow. In the second diagram, the cylinder is drawn at the new position, indicated by the black axes.

Tips

Tips are special notes, techniques, and cautions that appear throughout the body text of the book. They are separated from the main discussion by extra white space and indicated by the word *Tip* in a small, black box. They are also presented in an italic sans serif typeface that differs from the body text of the book.

TIP *This is an example of a tip. Tips describe interesting, additional, and important information relating to the current discussion.*

Colophon

An inspirational note: All of the images in this book (except one—can you guess which one?) were created with VRML. This book was drafted and produced with a variety of computers and computer-based tools, from PCs and Macintoshes to UNIX workstations.

Drafts were produced using Macintosh computers, FrameMaker, and Microsoft Word. Images were created on UNIX workstations and converted with SDSC's ImageTools and DeBabelizer. Drafts were edited on a PC using Microsoft Word. Final pages were produced using Macintosh computers and QuarkXPress software.

Acknowledgments

We thank everyone who supported us while this book was in progress, especially SDSC (the San Diego Supercomputer Center) for providing computer and information resources without which this book would not be. Special thanks to a few at SDSC who provided exceptional support for our efforts: Ann Redelfs, Sid Karin, Regan Moore, Anke Kamrath, and Mark Sheddon.

Thanks to our stalwart technical reviewers and "explainers"—we are not worthy!—Mike Bailey, Len Wanger, and Robert Russ. And to our brave usability testers: Rich Toscano, Jayne Keller, and Noah Heldman. Thanks to Charles Eubanks for providing some of the extended examples. Thanks to the third-floor sanity checkers who spot-tested a number of examples and explanations: Allan Snavely, Shawn Strande, Liz Smith, and Gina Caputo. And to the other reviewers who gave of their time to make this a better quality product: Dru Clark, Roman Ginis, and Jason Rogers.

Thanks to our families for their understanding and support—even when we dropped out of sight for four months and didn't call home. Thanks to our friends for helping to relieve some of the stress. And special thanks to Jon Jenkins and Paul Lackey, whose talent on their inspirational *Continuum* CD kept the words flowing.

Finally, very special thanks to Tim Ryan, our editor at Wiley, who patiently put up with three newbie authors and made published professionals of us—you're a saint! And to all the people at Wiley who helped us and made us look great in print, especially Micheline Frederick.

CHAPTER 1

Introduction to VRML

VRML is an acronym for the **Virtual Reality Modeling Language**. Using VRML you can craft your own three-dimensional virtual worlds. You can build your own virtual rooms, buildings, cities, mountains, and planets. You can fill your virtual worlds with virtual furniture, cars, people, spacecraft, or anything else you can dream up. Your imagination is the only limit.

Perhaps the most exciting feature of VRML is its ability to link virtual worlds together on the **World Wide Web** (WWW or **the Web**). Using linking, you can connect a door in your world to another VRML world described elsewhere on the Web. Doors in *that* world can link back to your world or to other worlds on the Web. VRML linking puts the entire Internet at your fingertips, enabling you to explore the network as if wandering through a vast universe, stepping between worlds through door after mouse hole after gateway after mirror after portal after worm hole.

Understanding the Internet and the World Wide Web

The **Internet** is an international network of computers connecting together universities, companies, research laboratories, homes, and government offices. You can think of the Internet as a giant, electronic highway system.

The **World Wide Web** is a complex spider's web of information available via the Internet. You can think of Web information as one kind of traffic on the electronic highway. Other kinds of Internet traffic include electronic mail (E-mail), audio and video broadcasts, electronic news (called *net news*), and all the data traffic necessary to manage the Internet itself.

Browsing the Web

You can travel the Internet using a wide variety of applications, the most common of which are **Web browsers**. These applications enable you to browse through the incredible amount of information available on the Web.

Common Web browsers include Netscape, Mosaic, and the browsers offered by America Online and Microsoft Network services. All of these Web browsers primarily display formatted text documents and any images embedded within them. The text formatting is controlled with a language called **HTML**, which stands for the **HyperText Markup Language**. HTML commands are embedded within the text to achieve various page designs.

Using HTML, you can author your own text documents for the Web. For instance, many companies have Web documents describing their products and services, pricing, organizational structure, and company policies. Individuals may have Web documents for their clubs, scout troops, or school activities.

Within an HTML document you can embed **links** that connect your document to other documents on the Web. Each link is **anchored** to a word, phrase, or line of text in your document. Most Web browsers display these links by underlining the anchor text on the page.

Clicking on anchor text directs the Web browser to follow a link and retrieve the Web document to which the link connects. That retrieved Web document may also contain links, which lead you to more documents, and their links, and so on. By following links in an HTML document, you can browse the vast spider's web of information on the Internet.

Figure 1.1 shows the Netscape Web browser displaying a text document which provides information about VRML. Each of the underlined words and phrases in the document are anchors for links to other documents.

Browsing the Web in 3-D

When a Web browser follows a link, it retrieves a file from the Web and checks the type of information the file contains. If it contains text, HTML, or images, the Web browser displays the document itself. To present other types of information, such as sounds, movies, and 3-D VRML worlds, the Web browser passes that information to a **helper application**.

To view VRML documents, you need a VRML helper application called a **VRML browser**. The list of available VRML browsers is growing rapidly. Some of the more common VRML browsers available when this book was printed include NAVFlyer, WebFX, WebSpace, WebView, Whirlwind, and WorldView.

Figure 1.2 shows Silicon Graphics' WebSpace VRML browser displaying the dungeon example from a later chapter in this book.

In VRML you can create links that are anchored to shapes in the VRML world. Typical anchor shapes include doors, windows, books, and maps. Clicking an anchor shape directs the VRML browser to follow the link and retrieve the VRML docu-

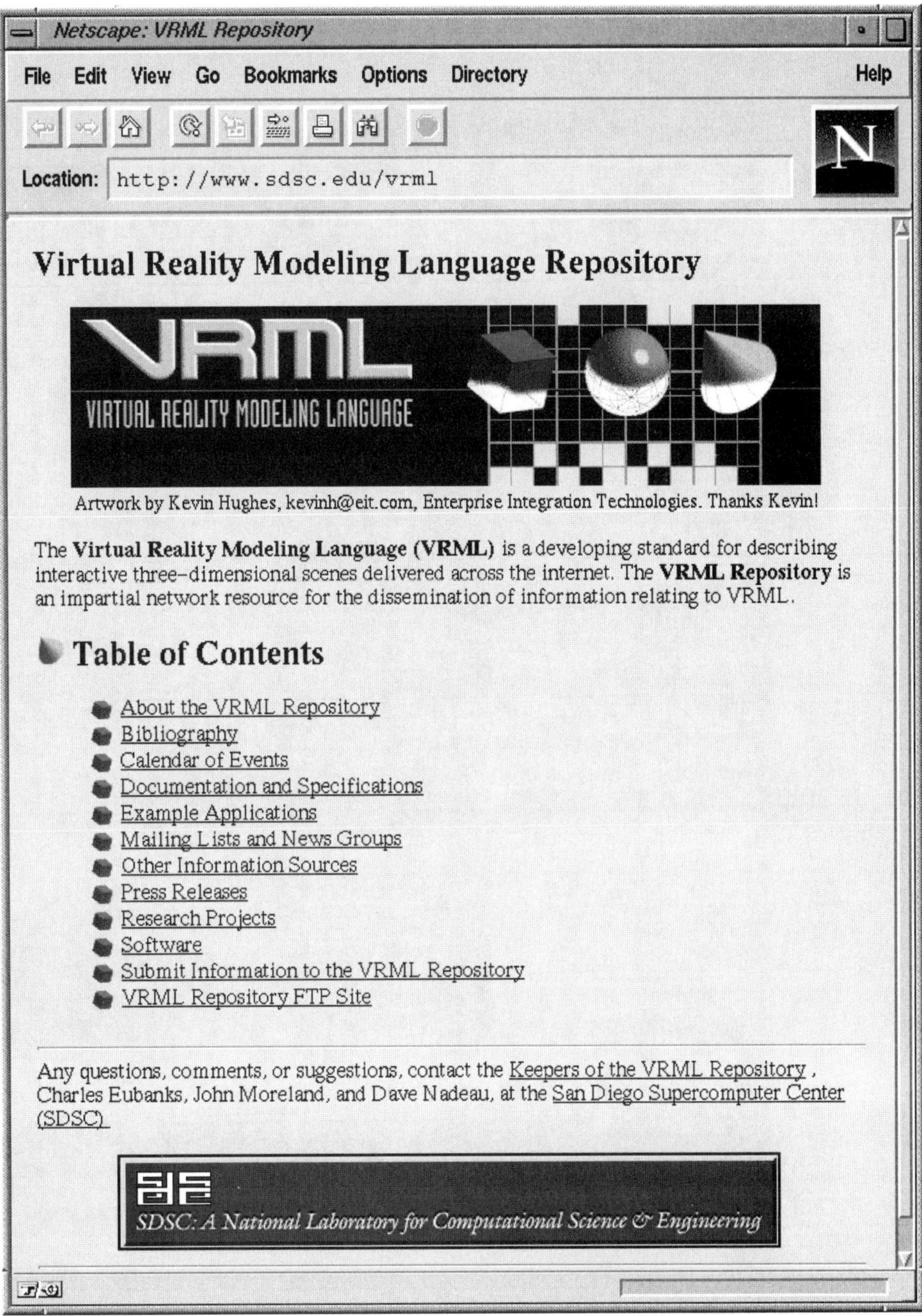

Figure 1.1 *A Web page displayed with the Netscape Navigator Web browser.*

Figure 1.2 *A VRML page displayed with the WebSpace VRML browser.*

ment to which the link connects. That document may also contain links for you to follow, and so on. By following links in a VRML document, you can browse the Web in 3-D, stepping from virtual world to virtual world as you travel the Internet.

Configuring Your Web Browsers

Because HTML and VRML Web browsers are typically purchased separately, you must configure your HTML Web browser so that it knows about your VRML Web browser and can automatically start the VRML browser when needed. Check both your HTML and VRML browser manuals to see how to configure them. Look for sections discussing *helper applications* and *mime types.*

Understanding URLs

A link in an HTML or VRML document is the address of a document on the Web, similar to a street address for a house. Web document addresses are specified with **URL**s, which stands for **Universal Resource Locator**.

A URL Web address is made up of three main parts:

- *The name of the communications scheme necessary to retrieve a file*
- *The name of the computer, or* **host**, *on the Internet*
- *The directory path and file name for the file to be retrieved from the host*

For instance, the following URL is the Web address for an HTML document describing *The VRML Repository,* the principal Internet site for information on VRML:

```
http://www.sdsc.edu/vrml
```

The string `http:` in this URL is the name of the **hypertext transfer protocol** communications scheme used by most Web browsers. Most URL Web addresses use this scheme. Other communications schemes include `ftp:` for the **file transfer protocol** and `file:` to refer to a file on your own hard disk.

The string `//www.sdsc.edu` in the preceding URL is the name of a host on the Internet. This particular host is the World Wide Web host at SDSC, the San Diego Supercomputer Center on the campus of the University of California in San Diego. The `.edu` at the end of the host name designates SDSC as an educational site on the Internet. Such a designation is reserved for universities, schools, and other educational organizations. Other common designations include `.com` for commercial companies, `.org` for non-profit organizations, and `.gov` for government sites.

Finally, the string `/vrml` at the end of the preceding URL is the name of a file to retrieve from SDSC. In this case, this is the name of an HTML document describing The VRML Repository.

Using any Web browser, you can enter a URL, like the one just cited, and the browser will retrieve the file from the Internet and display it on your screen. Any of several Internet books in the style of telephone yellow pages are available that give lists of URLs for interesting information on the Internet.

Important Web Sites

There are two important Web sites to know about for VRML: *The VRML Repository* and *John Wiley & Sons.*

The VRML Repository is the principal Internet site for up-to-date information on VRML software, example worlds, documentation, and more. The repository also maintains a list of all of the VRML browsers currently available and how to get more information about them. The URL for the VRML Repository is:

```
http://www.sdsc.edu/vrml
```

The second important Web site to know is the John Wiley & Sons Web site. This site includes all of the VRML examples in this book, as well as additional examples that didn't make it into the book. Also included at the Wiley Web site is the errata list for this book, as well as notes on additions and changes made to the VRML specification after this book went to press. The URL for the Wiley site is:

```
http://www.wiley.com/compbooks/
ftp.wiley.com/public/computer_books/vrml
```

The VRML Specification

VRML's features are defined by a public VRML specification document available at the VRML Repository. VRML is a rapidly evolving standard with a tremendous amount of support from the software community. As VRML evolves, so will the VRML specification document. You are encouraged to check the VRML Repository for the latest information on the VRML specification.

Creating Your Own Worlds with VRML

To create your own virtual world with VRML you'll need your VRML browser and any word processor. VRML files are text files that give your VRML browser instructions about how to draw 3-D shapes for your world.

Starting in your word processor, you'll type VRML instructions, such as those given in the examples throughout this book. Next, you'll save your file as a text file, then load it into your VRML browser to view it in 3-D. To add more to your world, return to the word processor, type in a few more VRML instructions, save the file, and read it back into your VRML browser. Repeating this sequence of operations enables you to gradually construct your own virtual worlds.

Three-dimensional drawing applications are also being developed to help you create VRML files. Using these applications, you can quickly create VRML files that you can then view using your VRML browser and edit further with your word processor.

Summary

The Internet is a vast electronic highway linking together educational, commercial, and government institutions throughout the world. The World Wide Web links together one type of information traffic on the Internet.

Web browsers enable you to travel the Web, browsing through archives of shareware, sounds, movies, and documents on any topic. Text documents are described using HTML (HyperText Markup Language). Three-dimensional virtual worlds are described using VRML (Virtual Reality Modeling Language).

To view VRML worlds, use a VRML browser, typically configured as a helper application for your HTML Web browser. Once configured, VRML information received by your HTML Web browser is automatically displayed by your VRML browser.

A document on the Web is addressed using its URL (Universal Resource Locator). A URL names the communications scheme to use when retrieving the document (typically `http`), the Internet host from which to retrieve the document, and the name of the document.

CHAPTER 2

Understanding Key VRML Concepts

In construction, houses and office buildings are built using blueprints that specify the building materials and layout of the building. Your VRML file serves as the blueprint for building the virtual world you create. It specifies and organizes the structure of your VRML world.

Understanding the VRML File

A VRML file is a textual description of your VRML world. It is a file containing text that you create with any text editor or word processor. It can also be created using applications that let you edit worlds in three dimensions or utilities that translate other graphics file formats to VRML. Your VRML file describes how to draw shapes, where to put them, what color to make them, and so on.

TIP *VRML file names end with* `.wrl` *(sometimes pronounced* dot world*) extension, which indicates that the file contains a VRML world. We often refer to your VRML files as worlds in this book.*

The Parts of a VRML File

VRML files have four main components, as shown in Figure 2.1. Type the text in this figure *exactly* as it's shown, view it with a VRML browser, and you've created your first VRML world.

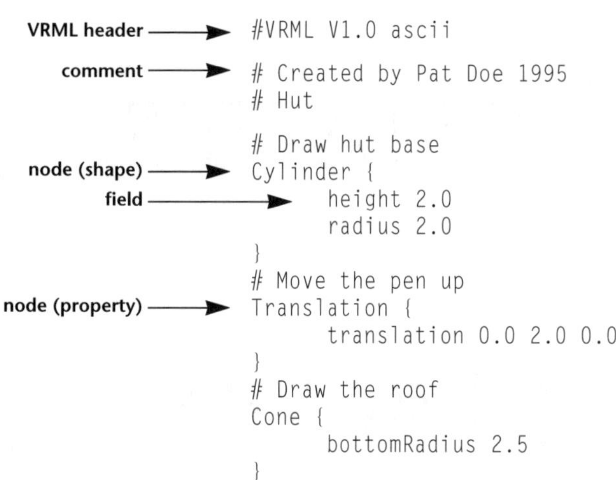

Figure 2.1 *Your first VRML world.*

TIP *For now, don't worry about the details of nodes like **Cylinder, Translation,** and **Cone.** We'll discuss them in detail later in the book.*

The main components of a VRML file are:

- *The VRML header (required)*
- *Nodes (required)*
- *Fields (optional)*
- *Comments (optional)*

TIP *Browsers skip spaces, tabs, and blank lines in VRML files. You can format your file in any way you like, including any number of spaces and blank lines within your file. Browsers do not ignore case, however, as VRML understands the difference between uppercase and lowercase letters. Note the use of uppercase letters in examples and syntax boxes.*

The VRML Header

Notice that the VRML file in Figure 2.1 starts with this line:

```
#VRML V1.0 ascii
```

This is the **VRML header**, which is required in any VRML file. It must be the first line of the file, and it must contain the exact text shown in the VRML header syntax box.

SYNTAX **The VRML header**

```
#VRML V1.0 ascii
```

The header describes to the browser that this file is:

- *A VRML file*
- *Compliant with version 1.0 with the VRML specification*
- *An ascii file*

TIP *In version 1.1 of VRML, the header text may be updated to the next revision and use a different file type indicator in order to support international character sets, like this:*

```
#VRML V1.1 qft8
```

Nodes

A VRML file contains **nodes** that describe shapes and their properties in your world. These are the building blocks of VMRL. Individual nodes describe shapes, colors, lights, cameras, how to position and orient shapes, and so on. Nodes generally contain:

- *The type of node (required)*
- *A set of curly braces (required)*
- *Some number of* **fields** *(optional) that define attributes of the node within the curly braces*

TIP *Fields are optional within nodes because each field has a* ***default value*** *that is used by your VRML browser if you don't specify a value. For example, a* default *VRML cube has a width of 2.0 VRML units, a height of 2.0 units, and a depth of 2.0 units. (We describe VRML units in more detail later in this chapter.) You can change these sizes in the* ***Cube*** *node's fields, but if you omit the fields completely from the text of your VRML file, the browser* defaults *automatically to a 2.0-unit by 2.0-unit by 2.0-unit cube. The syntax boxes throughout the book contain each shape node and its corresponding default field values.*

The **Cylinder** node in Figure 2.1 contains all of these items:

```
Cylinder {
   radius 0.75
}
```

Curly braces group all of the field information within the node. The fields grouped between the curly braces *belong to* the node. The shape defined by the node and its related fields are then considered a single entity in your world.

Curly braces are required in nodes, but they need not be on separate lines. We show examples in this format so they are easier to read. A default shape node might also look like this:

```
Cone {}
```

Or like this:

```
Cone
{}
```

Fields

The example in Figure 2.1 contains a field within the **Cylinder** node:

```
radius 0.75
```

Fields define the attributes of a node. In the preceding field, the **radius** field defines the radius of the cylinder to be 0.75 units. Other nodes have fields to set colors, orient shapes, and set the brightness of lights.

TIP *VRML units are not bound to any real-world unit of measurement, such as inches, centimeters, or picas. They describe a size or a distance within the context of your VRML world. You can think of a unit as an inch, a kilometer, an angstrom, or a light-year—whatever unit of distance is most convenient for you.*

Field values define attributes like color, size, or position, and every value is of a specific type. In the **Cylinder** node's **radius** field, the radius is specified with a floating-point value. These and other **field value data types** are described in detail in Appendix D.

TIP *The order of fields within a node is not important. You can specify fields within a node in any order you wish.*

Comments

VRML comments allow you to include extra information in your VRML file that doesn't affect the appearance of your world. This allows you to add notes to the file about who created it, when it was created, why it was created, and what it contains. You can also include notes to yourself describing what different parts of the file draw. When you work on that file months or years later, you'll have your notes to help you remember your intentions.

Comments begin with a pound sign (#) and end at the end of a line. Anything you type on a line following a pound sign will be skipped by the VRML browser.

The file in Figure 2.1 contains many comments—for example, the text describing what the file draws and who wrote it:

```
# Created by Pat Doe 1995
# Hut
```

Understanding Ordering within a VRML File

As we discussed at the beginning of this chapter, a construction blueprint specifies the building blocks—materials and layout—of a house or office building. You now know what the building blocks of a VRML file are: nodes with their accompanying fields.

Just as it is important to know *what* materials to build your VRML file with, it is also important to know *when* to use each node to obtain desired effects in your worlds. Order is very important in VRML. If you want the house in your scene to have its roof above the walls (not below), for example, you have to be specific about it by the order of the nodes in your VRML file.

Giving Drawing Directions

Your VRML file describes how to draw a three-dimensional world. Nodes and their fields define what shapes are drawn, where each is drawn, what color each shape is, and so on. This is all defined in a particular order, making your file a series of directions for the VRML browser that describes what to draw.

Similarly, if you give a friend directions for drawing a square, they might look something like this:

1. Get out your pen, and get ready to draw.
2. Put the pen down on the paper, and drag it along to your right two inches.
3. Without lifting the pen, drag it up the paper, away from you, two inches.
4. Without lifting the pen, drag it to the left two inches.
5. Still without lifting the pen, drag it down the paper, toward you, two inches.
6. Stop drawing, and lift the pen off the paper.

Now your friend has a square drawn on the paper.

VRML works very much like this. VRML nodes are drawing instructions. Your browser reads your VRML file and follows the drawing instructions described by the nodes to create a three-dimensional world on your screen.

Ordering Your Drawing Directions

As in the drawing directions to your friend, order is critical in VRML drawing instructions. If you told your friend to perform the instruction in step 4 before step 3, would the directions still result in a square? No, they would produce a capital letter L. The same is true with VRML. To get the results you expect, you must carefully order the directions within your VRML file.

For example, if you decide to make a hut, and you know that VRML has predefined instructions for drawing cylinders and cones, you can use a cylinder for the hut and put a cone on top for its roof. The VRML file to do this, shown in Figure 2.2, looks like your first VRML file from Figure 2.1.

```
#VRML V1.0 ascii

# Created by Pat Doe 1995
# Hut

# Draw hut base
Cylinder {
        height 2.0
        radius 2.0
}
# Move the pen up
Translation {
        translation 0.0 2.0 0.0
}
# Draw the roof
Cone {
        bottomRadius 2.5
}
```

Figure 2.2 *Your first VRML file: a hut.*

Imagine that your VRML browser uses a virtual drawing pen to display your worlds. A **Cylinder** node instructs the browser to draw a cylinder (the walls of the hut), a **Translation** node tells the browser to move its virtual drawing pen, and a **Cone** node tells the browser to draw a cone (the hut roof). When you view this file, you give these directions to your browser. If your browser understood English instead of VRML, the directions might look something like this:

1. Get out your pen, and get ready to draw. In VRML, that is:

   ```
   #VRML V1.0 ascii
   ```

2. Put the pen down, and draw a cylinder with a radius of 0.75 units. In VRML, that is:

   ```
   Cylinder {
      radius 0.75
   }
   ```

3. Lift the pen, and move it up the page 2.0 units (inches, meters, etc.). In VRML, that is:

```
Translation {
   translation 0.0 2.0 0.0
}
```

4. Put the pen down, and draw a cone. In VRML, that is:

```
Cone {
}
```

5. Stop drawing, and lift the pen.

After following these instructions, your browser will draw a hut like the one in Figure 2.3.

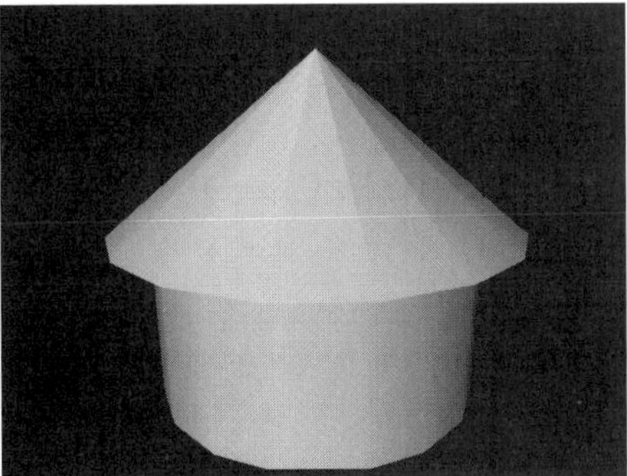

Figure 2.3 *A hut.*

Understanding VRML Space

Up to this point, we've given loose drawing instructions, like "Put the pen down on the paper, and drag it along to your right two inches." Loose instructions like these can be confusing if you try to describe more complicated shapes, like the silhouette of a person's head or the curves of a car body. For these kinds of shapes, you need more precise drawing instructions.

Giving precise drawing instructions means giving precise measurements. Remember that your worlds are measured in **VRML units**, and you can consider them to be any unit of measurement that is useful for you. Those units must be *consistent*, however. If you measure the size of shapes (cubes, cylinders, text, etc.) in inches, you must also measure the properties of those shapes in inches. For example, one property of a shape is its position. A two-inch cube can be positioned three *inches* from a cylinder, but it can't be positioned three *feet* from the cylinder. In this case, it must be positioned 36 *inches* from the cylinder to keep the units consistent.

TIP *It may be easiest to think of VRML units as just that: generic units. Don't assign any real-world unit of measurement to them. Then you'll know that your measurements are always consistent.*

Drawing in Two Dimensions

You may recall learning about the **X axis** and **Y axis**, **coordinates,** and the **origin** in school. Picture a set of X and Y axes on a piece of graph paper, like those in Figure 2.4.

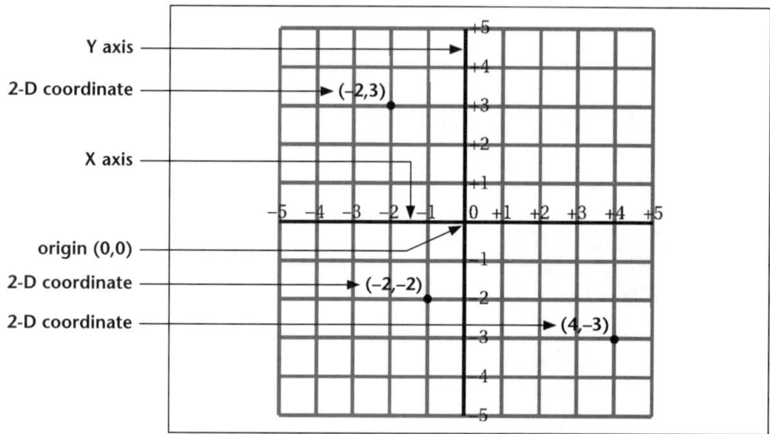

Figure 2.4 *X and Y axes, coordinates, and the origin on graph paper.*

These are the key things to understand about this two-dimensional system:

- *The point at which the axes cross is called the* origin, *and is labeled (0.0,0.0).*
- *The coordinates shown in Figure 2.4 are made up of an X value and a Y value. X values correspond to the numbers along the X axis, and Y values correspond to the numbers along the Y axis. The shorthand used for describing a 2-D coordinate is* (x,y), *where* x *is the X value and* y *is the Y value.*
- *Numbers increase from left to right along the X axis and from bottom to top along the Y axis. Negative X values appear to the left of the origin and the Y axis, and negative Y values appear below the origin and the X axis.*

Using this system, you can give precise drawing instructions to your friend by specifying coordinates in terms of X and Y values. To draw the previous square on your graph paper, you might give your friend these instructions.

1. Get out your pen, take off the cap, and get ready to draw.
2. Put the pen down on the paper at (–2.0,–2.0) and drag it to (2.0,–2.0).
3. Without lifting the pen, drag it up the paper to (2.0,2.0).
4. Without lifting the pen, drag it to the left to (–2.0,2.0).
5. Still without lifting the pen, drag it down the paper to (–2.0,–2.0).
6. Stop drawing, and lift the pen off the paper.

Your friend drew the square shown in Figure 2.5 exactly the way you wanted it with the help of precise instructions.

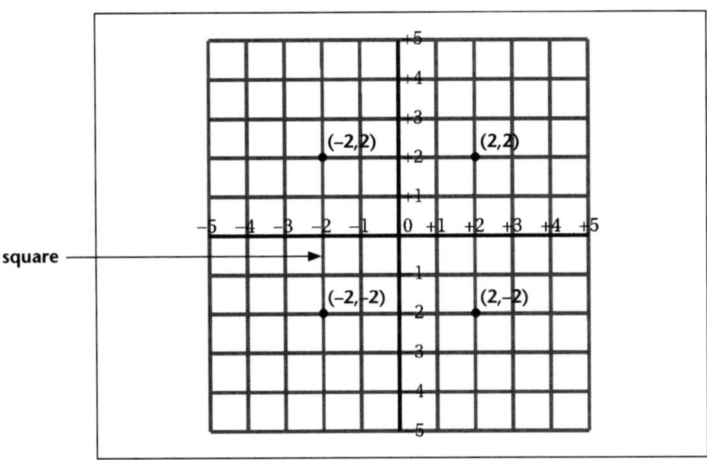

Figure 2.5 *The square your friend drew.*

Adding a Third Dimension

Using a piece of graph paper, you can draw precisely any 2-D shape. VRML, however, draws shapes in three dimensions. You can extend your 2-D graph paper to create a 3-D drawing space by using a second piece of graph paper. Tape the first piece of graph paper to the wall, and place a second piece on the floor against the wall.

The left edge of the second piece of graph paper forms a third axis, the **Z axis**, with numbers increasing as they proceed toward you and away from the wall. Three-dimensional shapes placed at higher values along the Z axis are closer to you. Shapes placed at lower values are farther away from you. Shapes placed at negative Z-axis values are on the other side of the wall from you. In the 3-D space, X is positive to the right, Y is positive upward, and Z is positive toward you in the space.

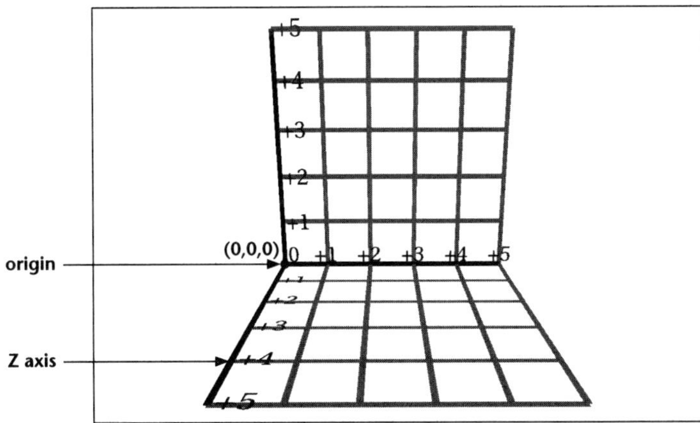

Figure 2.6 *Graph paper in three dimensions.*

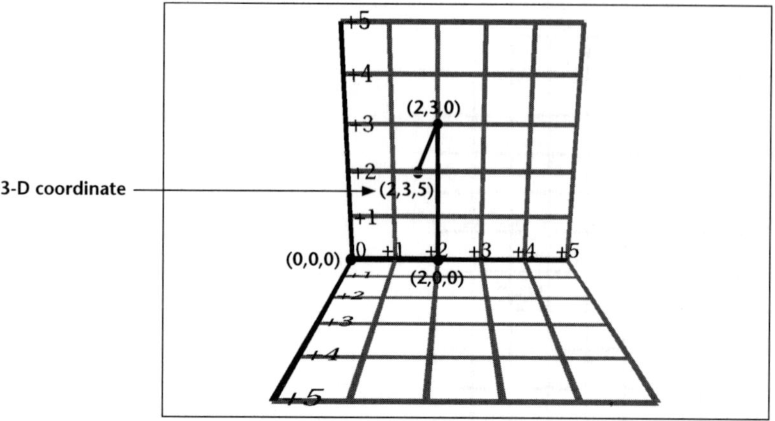

Figure 2.7 *The (2.0, 3.0, 5.0) coordinate in 3-D space.*

Your graphed space now looks like the one in Figure 2.6.

The graph paper on the floor gives you a third drawing direction. Now, you can move your virtual pen up and down, left and right on the wall graph paper and toward you and away from you along the floor graph paper.

To position your 3-D virtual pen, first move it to the desired X and Y values of the graph paper on the wall. Then, lift your pen off the paper, and align it in the air over the desired Z value of the graph paper on the floor. This midair pen location is described by the X,Y coordinate of the paper on the wall, and the Z value of the paper on the floor. For example, positioning your virtual pen at an X value of 2, a Y value of 3, and a Z value of 5 looks like Figure 2.7.

The midair point at the X value of 2, the Y value of 3, and the Z value of 5 can be written as (2.0,3.0,5.0), extending the 2-D coordinate shorthand used earlier. Such a trio of numbers is called a **3-D coordinate**. The special coordinate at (0.0,0.0,0.0) where the X, Y, and Z axes all cross is called the **3-D origin**, or more commonly, just the *origin*.

Right-Hand Rule for Three-Dimensional Axes

You can more easily remember how the Z axis is positioned in relation to the X and Y axes that you already know by using the right-hand rule for 3-D axes. Position your right hand like the hand in Figure 2.8, with your thumb pointing in the positive X direction and your index finger pointing in the positive Y direction.

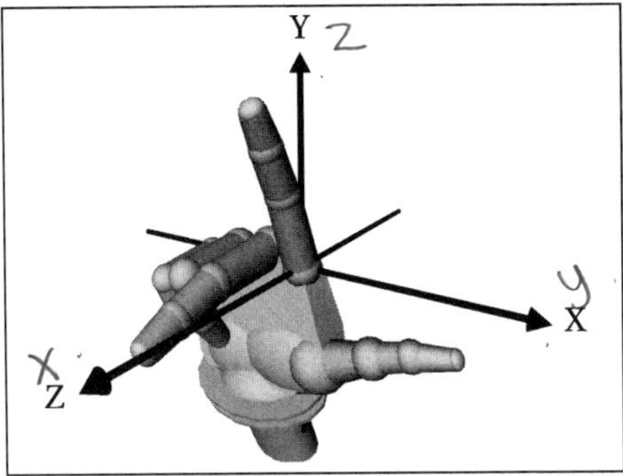

Figure 2.8 *The right-hand rule for three-dimensional axes.*

Now, your middle finger points in the positive Z direction.

Summary

A VRML world is created by a browser reading and displaying a VRML file. The VRML file contains nodes. Files must also contain the VRML header, and they may contain comments. The nodes describe the shapes to be drawn and the properties of those shapes, like color and position. A node may contain fields which describe attributes of that node, like height and radius.

The ordering of nodes in your VRML file determines the order in which your world is constructed. VRML reads the nodes in your file from top to bottom, and follows the nodes' drawing instructions in that order. As the nodes in the file direct the VRML virtual pen, it moves, draws, moves again, and draws again (depending on the actual nodes in your file).

The VRML drawing space is three-dimensional, described by an X axis from left to right, a Y axis from bottom to top, and a Z axis from the back of the space (away from you) forward (toward you). X is positive to the right, Y is positive upward, and Z is positive toward you in the space. You can navigate the pen around in this space using X, Y, and Z values to construct 3-D coordinates.

CHAPTER 3

Using Predefined Shapes

VRML's predefined shapes are the cube, the sphere, the cylinder, and the cone. These shapes are called **primitive shapes**, or **primitives**.

You can use a cube to make a box or a building. If you stretch or flatten the cube, you can create a skyscraper, a tabletop, a book, a wall, and many more items. Spheres make shapes such as balls, balloons, and planets, and you can use a cylinder to create a Greek column, a castle tower, a car wheel, a pencil, or a tree trunk. A cone can easily become the roof of a castle tower, the point of a pencil, a funnel, a lamp shade, and more.

Understanding How Primitive Shapes Are Drawn

Recall from Chapter 2 that VRML nodes are drawing instructions describing shapes to be drawn and the properties of those shapes (like color, position, etc.). Your browser reads your VRML file and follows the drawing instructions described by the nodes to create a 3-D world on your screen.

Recall also that fields within nodes define the **attributes** of shapes and properties (like width, radius, rotation amount, etc.). Attributes are shape and property features that you control each time you create a new shape. Typically, shape attributes are features that you want to be different for each shape.

VRML's primitives are created with **Cube, Sphere, Cylinder,** and **Cone** nodes. Each of these nodes is an instruction to the VRML virtual pen to draw one of the primitive shapes. Each primitive shape node has one or more fields that allow you to specify attributes like a cube's width, a sphere's radius, or the height of a cylinder or cone.

VRML's primitive shapes are *always* drawn centered at the tip of the VRML virtual pen. The tip of the virtual pen is a representation of the origin. When you instruct the VRML virtual pen to draw primitive shapes, they are always drawn centered around the origin. To illustrate this, each shape in this chapter is depicted by a figure containing an example VRML file and a diagram. Each diagram shows the origin and the X, Y, and Z axes of the VRML world and the shape created by the example file.

TIP *Primitive shapes are hollow and appear dark inside. We'll explain why shape interiors appear dark in a later chapter.*

Drawing Cubes

To create a cube using the default field values, type the VRML file in Figure 3.1.

```
#VRML V1.0 ascii

Cube {
}
```

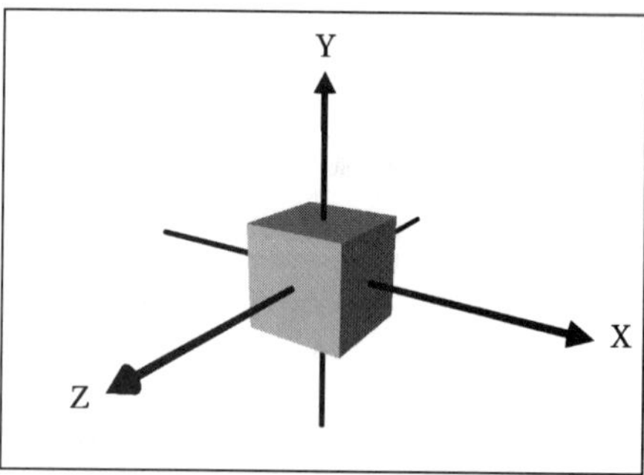

Figure 3.1 *Default cube.*

Understanding the **Cube** Node Syntax

The VRML virtual pen draws the default cube 2.0 units high, 2.0 units wide, and 2.0 units deep. Cubes are always drawn centered around the origin, as are all primitive shapes.

You can use the **Cube** node to make rectangular blocks of any size by setting the node's width, height, and depth fields. The cube's width is its size along the X axis. The height is the cube's size along the Y axis. The depth is its size along the Z axis.

SYNTAX **Cube node**

```
Cube {
  width   2.0     # floating point value
  height  2.0     # floating point value
  depth   2.0     # floating point value
}
```

Experimenting with Cubes

You can create a tall block that you might use as a city skyscraper by typing the VRML file in Figure 3.2.

```
#VRML V1.0 ascii

Cube {
      height 4.0
}
```

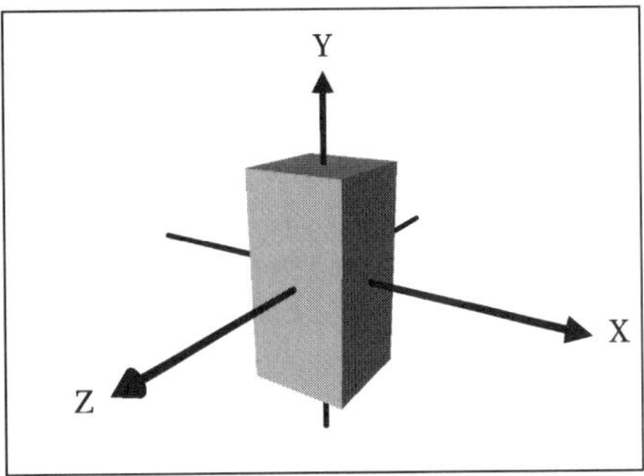

Figure 3.2 *A tall block, like a city skyscraper.*

In this example, the **Cube** node's **height** field is set to 4.0 units, but we've not set values for the **width** or **depth** fields. Because they weren't specified, your browser uses the default values of 2.0 units wide and 2.0 units deep. The virtual pen still draws the tall block centered around the origin, even though its width, height, and depth are not equal.

You can set one, two, or all three **Cube** node fields at once to create blocks of any size. You can create a flattened pizza box by specifying a small height, such as 0.25 units. You can make a wall for a room by setting the **width** and **height** fields to the room's dimensions and the **depth** field to the thickness of a wall.

You can create a block with any dimensions by setting all three **Cube** node fields at once by typing the VRML file in Figure 3.3.

```
#VRML V1.0 ascii

Cube {
      width 1.0
      height 3.0
      depth 5.0
}
```

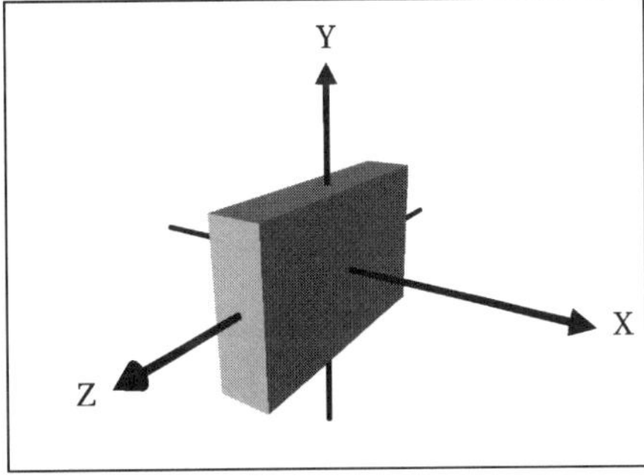

Figure 3.3 *A block with a small width, a medium height, and a large depth.*

Drawing Spheres

To create a default sphere, type the VRML file in Figure 3.4.

```
#VRML V1.0 ascii

Sphere {
}
```

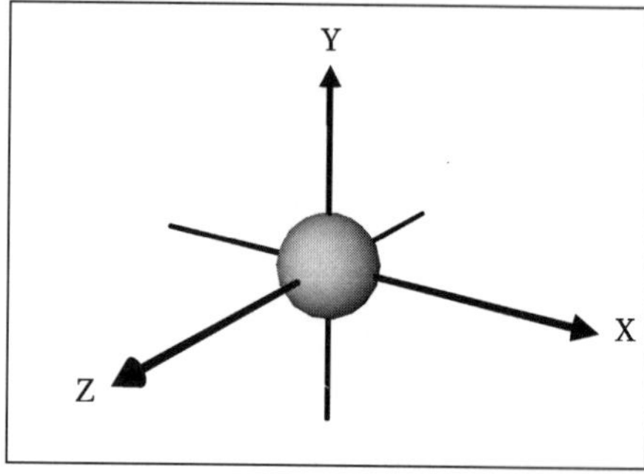

Figure 3.4 *Default sphere.*

TIP *Notice that the sphere is not perfectly smooth. It's faceted, because it is created with many small triangles. We'll explain why in a later chapter.*

Understanding the **Sphere** Node Syntax

The virtual pen draws the default sphere with a radius of 1.0 unit and always centers it at the origin. You can use the **Sphere** node to create a ball of any size by setting the node's **radius** field. A sphere's radius is its size from the origin to the surface of the sphere in any direction.

SYNTAX **Sphere node**

```
Sphere {
  radius 1.0        # floating point value
}
```

Experimenting with Spheres

You can create a larger sphere, such as a planet, by typing the VRML file in Figure 3.5.

```
#VRML V1.0 ascii

Sphere {
      radius 2.0
}
```

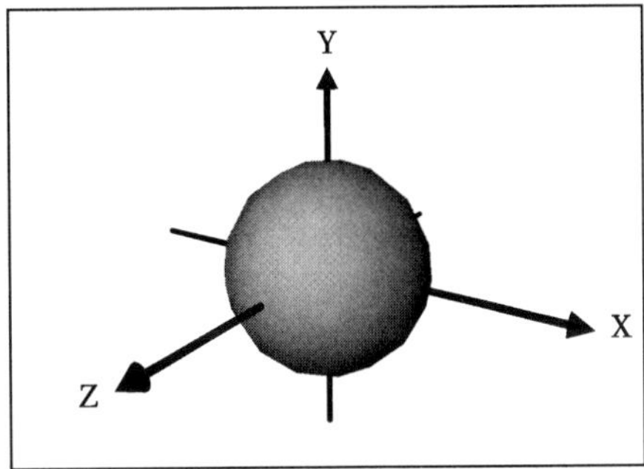

Figure 3.5 *A larger sphere, such as a planet.*

Drawing Cylinders

To create a default cylinder, type the VRML file in Figure 3.6.

```
#VRML V1.0 ascii

Cylinder {
}
```

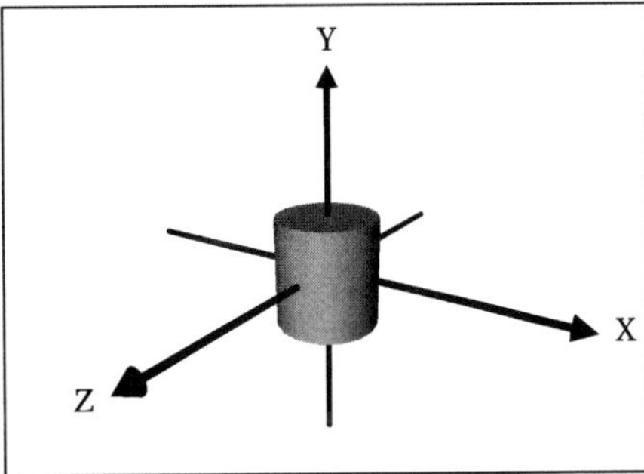

Figure 3.6 *Default cylinder.*

TIP *Notice that the sides of the cylinder are not perfectly smooth. The sides are faceted, because they are created with many small triangles. We'll explain why in a later chapter.*

Understanding the **Cylinder** Node Syntax

The VRML virtual pen draws the default cylinder with a radius of 1.0 unit, a height of 2.0 units, and always centers it around the origin. The default cylinder's axis lies along the Y axis. (A cylinder's axis is the imaginary line that runs through its center from bottom to top.)

SYNTAX Cylinder node

```
Cylinder {
  height  2.0      # floating point value
  radius  1.0      # floating point value
  parts   ALL      # parts list
}
```

You can use the **Cylinder** node to create tall pipes, flat pedestals, or Greek columns by setting the node's **radius** and **height** fields. The cylinder's height is its size along the Y axis, and its radius is the cylinder's size from the origin in the X and Z directions.

You can also specify what **parts** of the cylinder you want the virtual pen to draw. A cylinder's parts are the individual pieces that make up the whole cylinder shape.

- *The **SIDES** are the tube-shaped part.*
- *The **TOP** is the circular, top part.*
- *The **BOTTOM** is the circular, bottom part.*

Using the **parts** field, you can also specify that **ALL** the parts are drawn: the **SIDES,** the **TOP,** and the **BOTTOM** parts.

The **parts** field syntax calls for the field name (**parts**) and one or more **parts** field values. If more than one part is specified, the parts must be separated by a vertical bar (|) and enclosed in parentheses, like this:

```
Cylinder {
   parts (TOP|BOTTOM)
}
```

TIP *Although parentheses in the **parts** field are not required when specifying only one part, you may want to use them all the time. This will help you remember to include them when you specify more than one part. Throughout the rest of the book, we include parentheses in the **parts** fields of all the examples.*

If you turn off the cylinder's **TOP** or **BOTTOM** parts, you can see inside it. When you turn off both ends, you can see straight through it, as you can through a pipe or tube. When you turn off the **SIDES** part of the cube, the **TOP** and **BOTTOM** parts remain, one floating above the other.

Experimenting with Cylinders

You can create a ring by setting the **Cylinder** node's height to a small value and the radius to a large value; then draw only the sides of the cylinder, like the cylinder in the VRML file in Figure 3.7.

```
#VRML V1.0 ascii

Cylinder {
      radius 3.0
      height 0.5
      parts (SIDES)
}
```

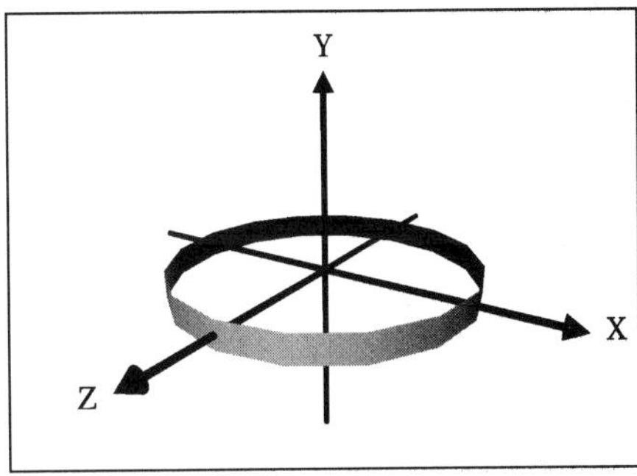

Figure 3.7 *A ring, created by drawing only the sides of a cylinder.*

You can create a tube by using a larger height value to draw a taller ring. You can also create a disk using only the top of the cylinder by typing the VRML file in Figure 3.8.

```
#VRML V1.0 ascii

Cylinder {
      radius 3.0
      height 0.5
      parts (TOP)
}
```

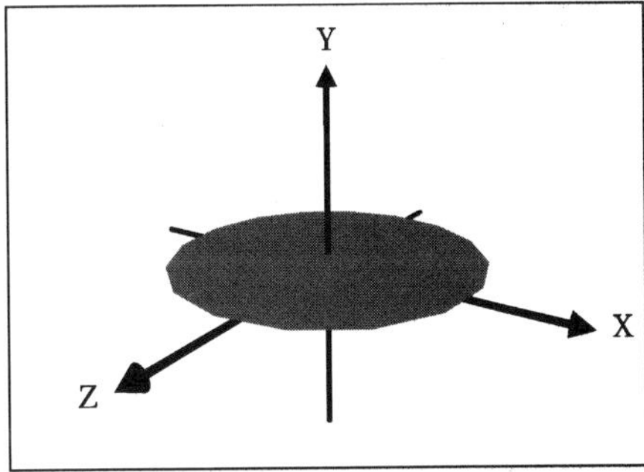

Figure 3.8 *A disk, created by drawing only the top of a cylinder.*

TIP *Notice that on your screen you can barely see the disk. This is because the top of a cylinder is thin and you are viewing it edge-on. If you rotate the world on your screen with your browser, you'll see the white top of the disk. The underside of the disk appears dark. We'll explain why in a later chapter.*

You can also create a disk using the bottom of the cylinder.

Now, put the ring and the disk together and create a cup or a can, like the one shown in Figure 3.9, by drawing both the sides and bottom of the cylinder, but not the top.

```
#VRML V1.0 ascii

Cylinder {
      radius 3.0
      height 0.5
      parts (SIDES|BOTTOM)
}
```

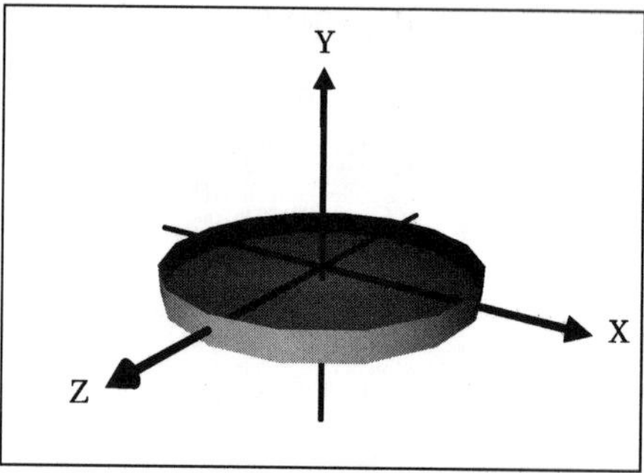

Figure 3.9 *A cup or can, created by drawing the bottom and sides of a cylinder.*

Drawing Cones

To create a default cone, type the VRML file in Figure 3.10.

```
#VRML V1.0 ascii

Cone {
}
```

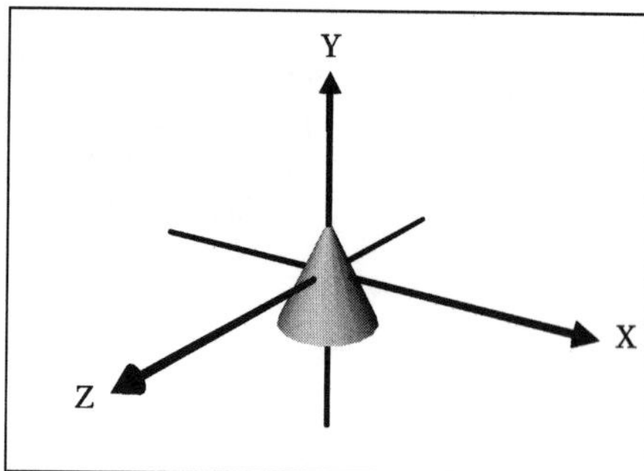

Figure 3.10 *Default cone.*

TIP *Notice that the sides of the cone are not perfectly smooth. The sides are faceted, because they are created with many small triangles. We'll explain why in a later chapter.*

Understanding the **Cone** Node Syntax

The VRML virtual pen draws the default cone with a bottom radius of 1.0 unit and a height of 2.0 units, and always centers it around the origin. The default cone's axis lies along the Y axis. (A cone's axis is the imaginary line that runs through its center from bottom to top.)

SYNTAX Cone node

```
Cone {
  height        2.0      # floating point value
  bottomRadius  1.0      # floating point value
  parts         ALL      # parts list
}
```

You can use the **Cone** node to create tall teepees or short, squat lamp shades by setting the node's **radius** and **height** fields. The cone's height is its size along the Y axis, and its radius is the cone bottom's size from the origin in the X and Z directions.

You can also specify what parts of the cone you want the virtual pen to draw. Similar to cylinders, the cone's parts are the individual pieces that make up the whole cone shape.

- *The* ***SIDES*** *are the sloping part.*
- *The* ***BOTTOM*** *is the circular, bottom part.*

Using the **parts** field, you can also specify that **ALL** the parts are drawn: the SIDES and the BOTTOM parts. The **parts** field syntax calls for the field type (**parts**) and one or more **parts** field values.

TIP *It doesn't make much sense to specify two parts in the* ***Cone*** *node's* ***parts*** *field, since cones have only two parts. If you want both the bottom and sides of the cone drawn, specify* ***ALL*** *in the parts field. Even more efficient, don't include a* ***parts*** *field in the node at all, since* ***ALL*** *is the default value of the* ***parts*** *field.*

If you turn off a cone's BOTTOM part, you can see inside it. When you turn off the SIDES part of the cone, the flat, disk-shaped BOTTOM part remains.

Experimenting with Cones

You can create a bullhorn by drawing only the sides of the cone, like the one shown in Figure 3.11.

```
#VRML V1.0 ascii

Cone {
        parts (SIDES)
}
```

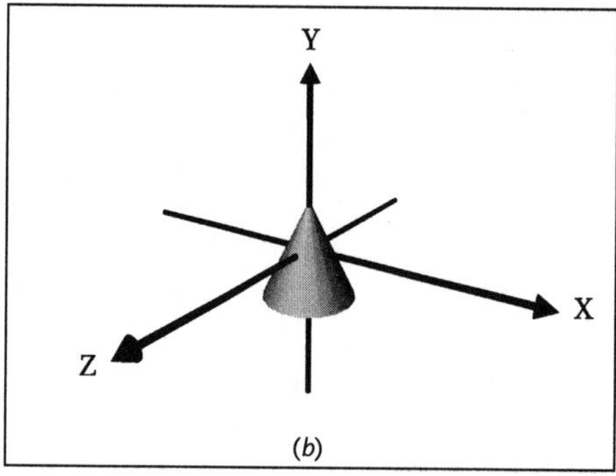

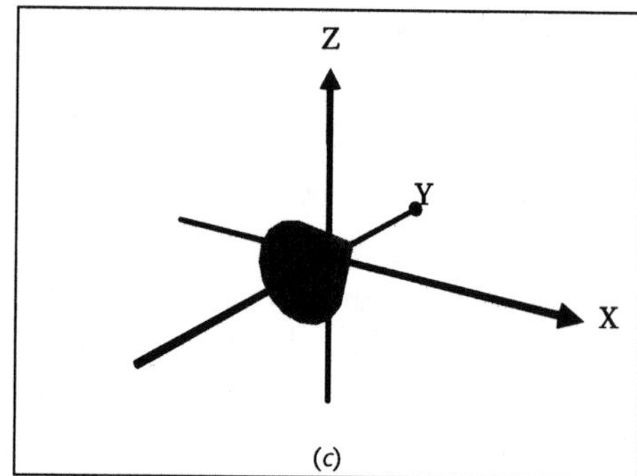

Figure 3.11 *A bullhorn, created by drawing only the sides of a cone.*

If you rotate the world on your screen with your browser, like Figure 3.11*c*, you can see that the cone has no bottom.

You can also create a disk using just the bottom of the cone by typing the VRML file in Figure 3.12.

```
#VRML V1.0 ascii

Cone {
        parts (BOTTOM)
}
```

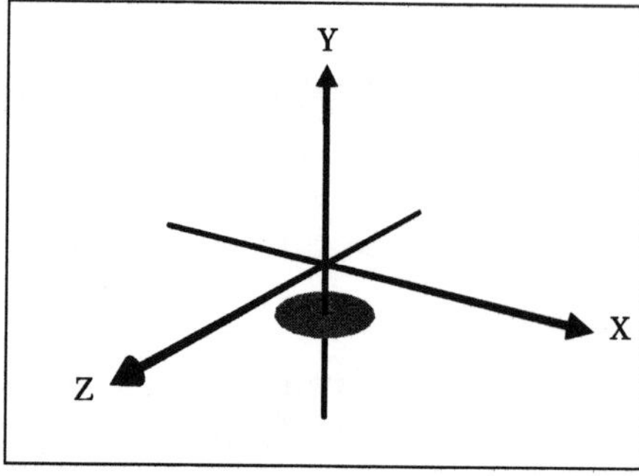

Figure 3.12 *A disk, created by drawing only the bottom of a cone.*

Drawing Overlapping Shapes

You can direct the virtual pen to draw more than one shape, and the shapes can overlap. This is an important ability for creating complex shapes. The VRML text in Figure 3.13 creates a 3-D plus sign.

```
#VRML V1.0 ascii

Cube {
      width 25.0
}
Cube {
      height 25.0
}
Cube {
      depth 25.0
}
```

Figure 3.13 *A 3-D plus sign.*

The three **Cube** nodes in this example create the three long poles of the plus sign. All three cubes cross in the middle, overlapping each other.

You can create more complicated shapes, for example, the space station shown in Figure 3.14, by combining different shaped nodes.

```
#VRML V1.0 ascii

Cube {
      height 10.0
      width 10.0
      depth 10.0
}
Sphere {
      radius 7.0
}
Cylinder {
      height 0.5
      radius 12.5
}
Cylinder {
      height 20.0
      radius 4.0
}
```

Figure 3.14 continues

```
Cylinder {
      height 30.0
      radius 3.0
}
Cylinder {
      height 60.0
      radius 1.0
}
```

Figure 3.14 *A space station.*

Extended Examples

The following examples build on the concepts we present in this chapter. They illustrate the worlds you can create using only VRML's primitive shapes. Try them on your own.

TIP *All of the VRML text in the extended examples throughout this book are available via anonymous ftp from John Wiley & Sons at* `ftp.wiley.com/public/computer_books/vrml` *and from the VRML Repository at* `http://www.sdsc.edu/vrml`.

The Planet Saturn

The VRML file in Figure 3.15 creates the planet Saturn.

```
#VRML V1.0 ascii

Sphere {
      radius 2.0
}
Cylinder {
      height 0.1
      radius 5.1
      parts (SIDES)
}
Cylinder {
      height 0.1
      radius 5.2
      parts (SIDES)
}
Cylinder {
      height 0.1
      radius 5.3
      parts (SIDES)
}
```

Figure 3.15 continues

```
Cylinder {
      height 0.1
      radius 5.4
      parts (SIDES)
}
Cylinder {
      height 0.1
      radius 4.1
      parts (SIDES)
}
Cylinder {
      height 0.1
      radius 4.2
      parts (SIDES)
}
Cylinder {
      height 0.1
      radius 4.3
      parts (SIDES)
}
Cylinder {
      height 0.1
      radius 4.4
      parts (SIDES)
}
Cylinder {
      height 0.1
      radius 4.5
      parts (SIDES)
}
Cylinder {
      height 0.1
      radius 4.6
      parts (SIDES)
}
Cylinder {
      height 0.1
      radius 4.7
      parts (SIDES)
}
Cylinder {
      height 0.1
      radius 4.8
      parts (SIDES)
}
Cylinder {
      height 0.1
      radius 3.3
      parts (SIDES)
}
```

Figure 3.15 continues

```
Cylinder {
      height 0.1
      radius 3.4
      parts (SIDES)
}
Cylinder {
      height 0.1
      radius 3.5
      parts (SIDES)
}
Cylinder {
      height 0.1
      radius 3.6
      parts (SIDES)
}
Cylinder {
      height 0.1
      radius 3.7
      parts (SIDES)
}
Cylinder {
      height 0.1
      radius 3.8
      parts (SIDES)
}
```

Figure 3.15 *The planet Saturn.*

A Pointy Shape

The VRML file in Figure 3.16 creates a cool pointy shape. There are many things you can use this for: a futuristic building, a lamp shade or hanging light fixture, a flower, a space probe, and so on.

```
#VRML V1.0 ascii

Cone {
      height 10.0
      bottomRadius 1.0
}
Cone {
      height 9.0
      bottomRadius 2.0
}
Cone {
      height 8.0
      bottomRadius 3.0
}
Cone {
      height 7.0
      bottomRadius 4.0
}
```

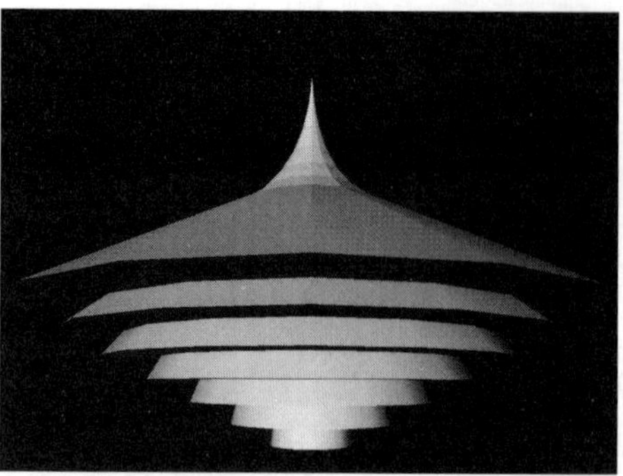

Figure 3.16 continues

```
Cone {
        height 6.0
        bottomRadius 5.0
}
Cone {
        height 5.0
        bottomRadius 6.0
}
Cone {
        height 4.0
        bottomRadius 7.0
}
```

Figure 3.16 *A pointy shape you can use for many things.*

Summary

VRML's four primitive shapes are the cube, the sphere, the cylinder, and the cone. Each shape's node contains fields which allow you to specify shapes of different sizes. Cylinders and cones have parts which can be turned on and off: the **TOP,** the **BOTTOM,** and the **SIDES** of a cylinder and the **BOTTOM** and the **SIDES** of a cone. All of the primitive shape node fields are optional.

Default primitives are drawn centered around the origin. Cylinders' and cones' axes lie along the Y axis.

CHAPTER 4

Using Text

Using VRML's text and font features, you can add 3-D text shapes to your world. You can make street and building signs, label world features, add dimension labels to a 3-D design, and include notes and help information for other users of your world.

VRML text capabilities enable you to specify the text the VRML virtual pen draws, as well as the text's line spacing, width, and how it is justified (left- or right-justified or centered) with the **AsciiText** node. You can also control the font family, style, and size of the text with the **TextStyle** node.

VRML's text features are similar to those found in any 2-D word processor. However, unlike 2-D text, VRML text shapes are drawn in three dimensions. You can create 3-D text shapes and move around in your world with your browser, viewing the text from different angles: edge on, from the front, from the back, and so on.

Understanding VRML Text

Recall from Chapter 2 that VRML nodes describe the shapes within and the properties of your VRML worlds. Properties are VRML features that you control globally so that you don't have to specify them every time you create a shape. For instance, you can set the font style once, and use that style over and over again. You can think of properties as changing the way the VRML virtual pen moves and draws.

Text pen properties affect how all subsequent text shapes are drawn, and these properties remain in effect until you change them. As in shape nodes, if you don't specify values for the fields within property nodes, your VRML browser uses the default values for those fields.

TIP *In later chapters we'll discuss additional properties that control drawing position, orientation, color, and so on.*

Text Shape Attributes

Text shapes are created with the **AsciiText** node. The attributes of the **AsciiText** node include:

- *The **text string**, or series of characters, for the VRML virtual pen to draw*
- *The vertical line spacing of the text*
- *The horizontal spacing, or width, of the text*
- *The justification of the text*

You can use any letters in the Ascii character set within a VRML text string. This includes all of the characters found on a typical computer keyboard, including the alphabet, numbers, and punctuation.

TIP *Ascii stands for American Standard Code for Information Interchange. It is an important standard that defines the character set used by American computers. The ascii character set includes all of the characters found in the English language. It does not, however, include many of the characters and symbols found in other languages, such as the Greek letters (α β ψ), umlauts (ü), accents (é), or many mathematical symbols ∞ ≥ ± ≠. Ascii also does not include many of the graphic characters found in some computer character sets (↑ ↓ → ←). As a general rule, if the character is shown on a key on your computer keyboard, then it is in the ascii character set.*

You can create a single line or multiple lines of text. You can justify lines of text so that they line up on the left, the right, or are centered one above the other. You can also control the vertical spacing between lines of text, and the horizontal width of each text line.

Like the primitive shape nodes you used in Chapter 3, all of the text shape attributes have default values. The default justification, for instance, is left-justified text.

Also like the primitive shapes, VRML text is always created at the tip of the virtual pen. The tip of the pen is a representation of the origin. So when you instruct the VRML virtual pen to draw default text shapes, they are always drawn at the origin.

Text Properties

Some VRML nodes describe properties that change the way the VRML virtual pen moves and draws. The **FontStyle** node, for instance, controls pen properties. The fields of the **FontStyle** node control these attributes:

- *The font family in which the text is created*
- *The font style of the text*
- *The font size of the text*

VRML provides three font families for text shapes: **serif**, **sans**, and **typewriter**. The serif font family is similar to the Times Roman font family found on most computers. Likewise, sans is similar to Helvetica, and typewriter is similar to Courier.

The serif and sans font families both use variable-width characters in which an "i," for example, takes up less space than a "W." Variable-width characters like these are used by word processors in order to make blocks of text have a more uniform appearance.

The typewriter font family uses fixed-width characters in which an "i" takes the same amount of space as a "W." Fixed-width characters like these are typically used in computer command windows, such as those on DOS or UNIX computers.

Unlike some computer font families, all three VRML font families can be drawn at any font size without any degradation in quality. Font sizes specify the character height in units, just like those used to set a cube's height or a sphere's radius.

All three font families can be used to draw normal, bold, italic, or bold and italic styles of text.

Like the **AsciiText** shape node, the field values of the **FontStyle** property node have default values. The default font size, for instance, creates 10.0-unit-tall characters.

Creating Text

To create a text shape using the default field values, type the VRML file in Figure 4.1.

```
#VRML V1.0 ascii

AsciiText {
      string "Qwerty"
}
```

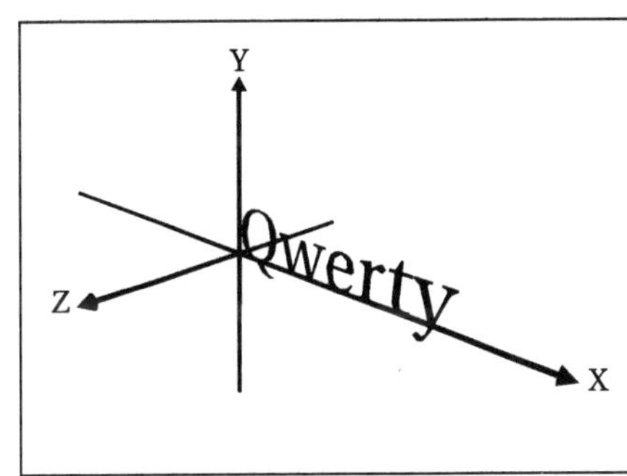

Figure 4.1 *Default "Qwerty" text shape.*

The **AsciiText** node directs the virtual pen to draw the 3-D text string "Qwerty."

Understanding the **AsciiText** Node Syntax

The **AsciiText** node has four fields: **string**, **justification**, **width**, and **spacing**.

SYNTAX **AsciiText node**

```
AsciiText {
   string          ""        # string
   justification   LEFT      # justification type
   width           0.0       # floating point value
   spacing         1.0       # floating point value
}
```

The **string** field specifies one or more lines of text to draw. Each line of text is enclosed within quotation marks. To create more than one line of text, list the text strings enclosed by square brackets and separated by commas. For example, the following are all valid **string** field values:

```
string "Pat's Cafe"

string [ "Standard Deviation", "42.0" ]

string [ "For I dipt into the future, far as human eye could see,"
         "Saw the Vision of the world, and all the wonder that would be.",
         "- Locksley Hall, Lord Tennyson" ]
```

Carriage returns between or within quoted strings are skipped by the VRML browser. For instance, the following two **string** field values produce identical results:

```
string "Make it so."

string "Make
it so."
```

The **AsciiText** node always draws flat text characters with a Z-axis depth of 0.0. Text characters in a string are drawn from left to right along the X axis, and from top to bottom down the Y axis.

The **justification** field values shown in Table 4.1 determine how lines of text will be placed along the X axis from left to right. The default justification is left-justified text.

The **AsciiText** node's **width** field enables you to control the width of each line of text. When drawn, each line of text is compressed or expanded to fill the specified width. A **width** field value of 0.0 directs the VRML browser to draw a line of text at its default width by neither compressing nor expanding the string letter size and spacing. The default width varies when using a proportional font.

Table 4.1 Justification Field Values and the Resulting Text Placement

Justification	*Placement*
LEFT	The left edge of each string is placed at an X coordinate of 0.0
RIGHT	The right edge of each string is placed at an X coordinate of 0.0
CENTER	The center of each string is placed at an X coordinate of 0.0

TIP *Some VRML browsers compress the character shapes of a string in order to make it fit within the given width. Others compress only the spacing between the characters.*

You can control the width separately for each line of text by including multiple width values within square brackets and separated by commas. For instance, the following are all valid text-width specifications:

```
width 0.0
width 100.0
width [ 100.0, 140.0, 83.0 ]
```

In the last **width** field example, the first value corresponds to the first line of text specified in the **string** field of the node, the second value corresponds to the second line in the string, and so on. For example, note the following **AsciiText** node's **string** and **width** field values:

```
AsciiText {
   string [ "ABCDEFG,"
            "HIJK",
            "LMNOP" ]
   width [ 100.0, 14.0, 83.0 ]
}
```

In this example, "ABCDEFG" is displayed with a width of 100.0 units, "HIJK" is displayed with a width of 14.0 units, and "LMNOP" is displayed with a width of 83.0 units.

The first line of text in an **AsciiText** node's **string** field is always drawn resting on the X axis at a Y coordinate of 0.0. The **spacing** field specifies a **spacing factor** that determines how subsequent lines of text are placed below the X axis, moving down along the Y axis.

The spacing factor is just a multiplication factor. For instance, if the current font is 10.0 units tall, then a spacing factor of 2.0 places the second line of text 20.0 units *down* the Y axis ($2.0 \times 10.0 = 20.0$). The third line of text is placed 40.0 units down the Y axis, the fourth is placed 60.0 units down the Y axis, and so on. The default spacing factor is 1.0.

Negative spacing factors direct the virtual pen to move *up* the Y axis to position and draw subsequent lines of text, instead of *down* the Y axis as with positive spacing factors.

TIP *The current font and its character height are controlled by the **FontStyle** node discussed in the next section. When you don't specify a **FontStyle** node, the default font creates text shapes with a character height of 10.0 units.*

Selecting a Font

You can set properties that control the way subsequent **AsciiText** nodes will draw text with the **FontStyle** node. For instance, the VRML text in Figure 4.2 sets the pen's font family property, then the pen draws text using that font family.

```
#VRML V1.0 ascii

FontStyle {
      family SANS
}
AsciiText {
      string "Qwerty"
}
```

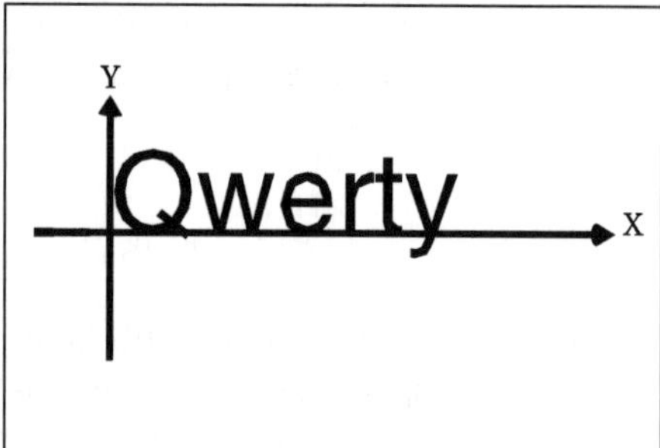

Figure 4.2 *The "Qwerty" text shape using the sans font family.*

Notice the structure of the VRML file in Figure 4.2. Reading the VRML file from the top to the bottom, the **FontStyle** node sets the virtual pen's font family to use the sans font family, and then the **AsciiText** node directs the pen to draw text using that font family.

Understanding the FontStyle Node Syntax

The **FontStyle** node has three fields: **family, style,** and **size.**

SYNTAX **FontStyle node**

```
FontStyle {
   family  SERIF      # font family
   style   NONE       # font style
   size    10         # floating point value
}
```

The **family** field specifies which of the standard VRML font families to use. The three **family** field values are:

- ***SERIF****—A variable-width, serif font like Times Roman*
- ***SANS****—A variable-width, sans-serif font like Helvetica*
- ***TYPEWRITER****—A fixed-width font like Courier*

The default **family** field value is **SERIF.**

TIP *Different VRML browsers will use different internal fonts to implement the serif, sans, and typewriter font families. For instance, while Times Roman is the typical font family used for serif, other possibilities include font families such as New York and Palatino. The font family actually displayed depends on your VRML browser.*

The **style** field selects the text style to use. The **style** field values are:

- *NONE—Normal text*
- *BOLD—Bold text*
- *ITALIC—Italic, or slanted, text*

The **style** field syntax calls for the field name (**style**) and one or more **style** field values. If more than one style is specified, the styles must be separated by a vertical bar (|) and enclosed within parentheses, like this:

```
FontStyle {
   style (BOLD|ITALIC)
}
```

TIP *Although you can specify any combination, it doesn't make sense to specify combinations other than (**BOLD|ITALIC**), since (**NONE|BOLD**) and (**NONE|ITALIC**) create normal text. The most efficient way to create normal text is to omit the **style** field, since **NONE** is the default value of the **style** field.*

The **size** field controls the height of the text, measured in units. The default size for text is 10.0 units. Text can be any height without any degradation in drawing quality. The text height also affects how lines of text are spaced. (Remember that the spacing factor specified in the **AsciiText** node's **spacing** field is multiplied by the height of the font to determine vertical spacing.)

TIP *In Chapter 3, you created a default cube 2.0 units wide, high, and deep. The default sphere, cylinder, and cone have similar default sizes. Note, however, that the default font size creates 10.0-unit-high characters. So, when mixing primitive shapes and text in the same world, you may want to adjust the font or primitive shape size to give primitive and text shapes compatible sizes.*

Experimenting with Text

The following examples provide a more detailed examination of the ways in which the **AsciiText** and **FontStyle** nodes can be used and how they interact with nodes we've discussed in previous chapters.

Using Text Justification

Figures 4.3 through 4.5 illustrate how you can left- and right-justify and center a text string.

```
#VRML V1.0 ascii

AsciiText {
      string [ "Qwerty",
               "0123" ]
      justification LEFT
}
```

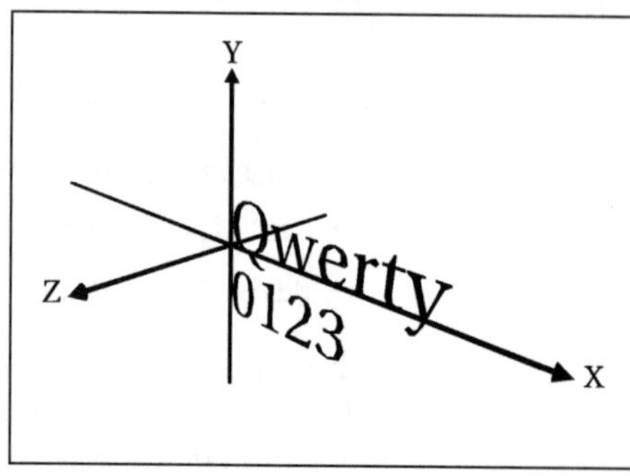

Figure 4.3 *A left-justified, two-line text string.*

```
#VRML V1.0 ascii

AsciiText {
      string [ "Qwerty",
               "0123" ]
      justification RIGHT
}
```

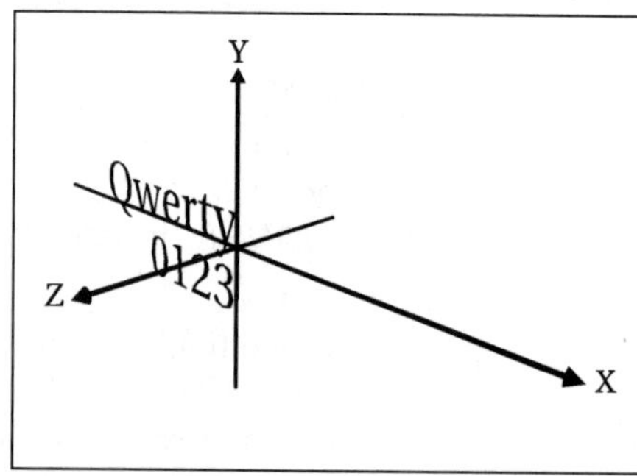

Figure 4.4 *A right-justified, two-line text string.*

```
#VRML V1.0 ascii

AsciiText {
      string [ "Qwerty",
               "0123" ]
      justification CENTER
}
```

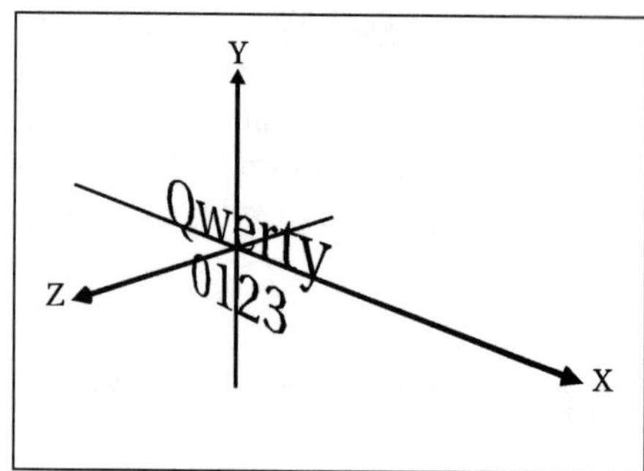

Figure 4.5 *A centered, two-line text string.*

Using Text Line Spacing

Using the **spacing** field, you can vary the vertical spacing between text, as shown in Figures 4.6 and 4.7.

```
#VRML V1.0 ascii

AsciiText {
	string [ "Qwerty",
	         "0123" ]
	spacing 1.0
}
```

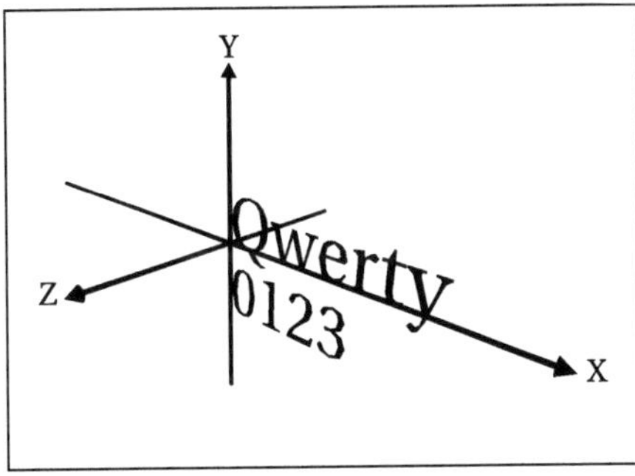

Figure 4.6 *A two-line text string with vertical spacing of 1.0.*

```
#VRML V1.0 ascii

AsciiText {
	string [ "Qwerty",
	         "0123" ]
	spacing 2.0
}
```

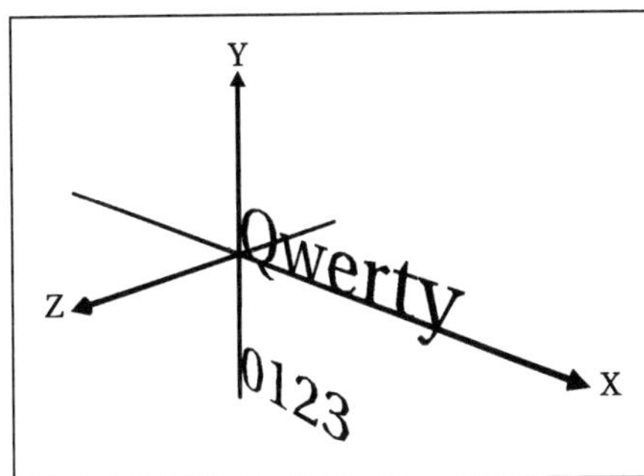

Figure 4.7 *A two-line text string with vertical spacing of 2.0.*

You can also use spacing factors that reduce the spacing between lines, as shown in Figure 4.8.

```
#VRML V1.0 ascii

AsciiText {
	string [ "Qwerty",
	         "0123" ]
	spacing 0.5
}
```

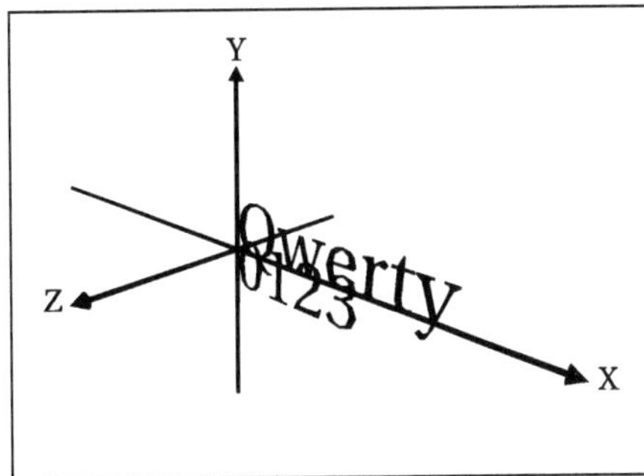

Figure 4.8 *A two-line text string with vertical spacing of 0.5.*

Figure 4.9 shows text that uses a spacing factor of –1.0.

```
#VRML V1.0 ascii

AsciiText {
      string [ "Qwerty",
               "0123" ]
      spacing -1.0
}
```

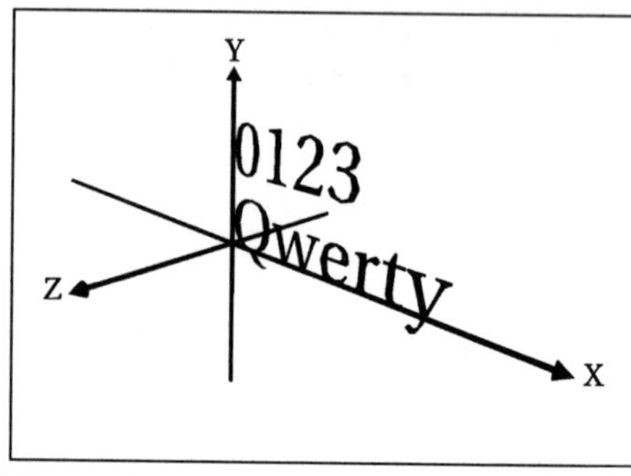

Figure 4.9 *A two-line text string with vertical spacing of –1.0.*

Using Text Width

Using the **AsciiText** node's **width** field, you can vary the horizontal spacing and expand or compress text lines. Figure 4.10 shows a text string using the default width.

```
#VRML V1.0 ascii

AsciiText {
      string "Qwerty"
      width 0.0
}
```

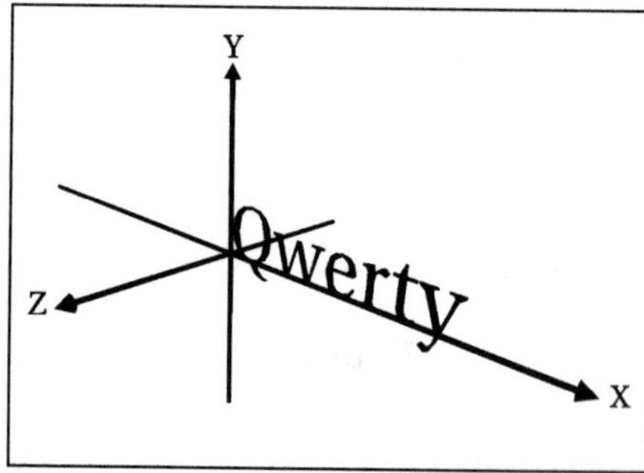

Figure 4.10 *A two-line text string with a width of 0.0.*

If you specify a two-line text string but use only *one* width value, the specified width is applied only to the *first* line of the text string. In Figure 4.11, the first line of the text string is 20.0 units wide, as specified in the **width** field, but the second line of the string is the default width.

```
#VRML V1.0 ascii

AsciiText {
      string [ "Qwerty",
               "Qwerty" ]
      width 20.0
}
```

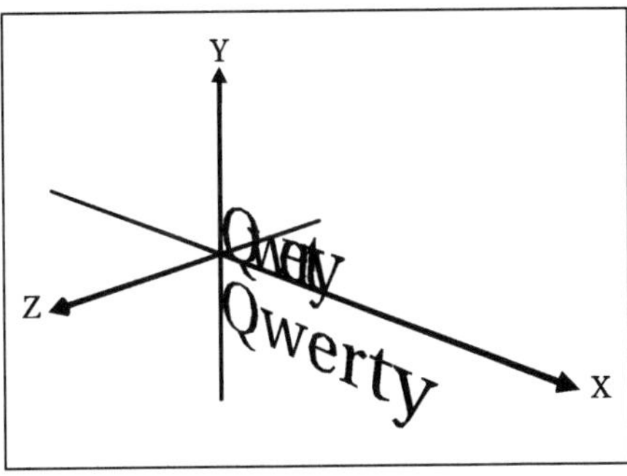

Figure 4.11 *A two-line text string with one width value specified, affecting only the first line of the text string.*

Using a *list* of widths, you can override the default width and control each text line's width independently. For example, the VRML text in Figure 4.12 compresses the first line, but expands the second.

```
#VRML V1.0 ascii
AsciiText {
      string [ "Qwerty",
               "Qwerty" ]
      width [ 30.0, 40.0 ]
}
```

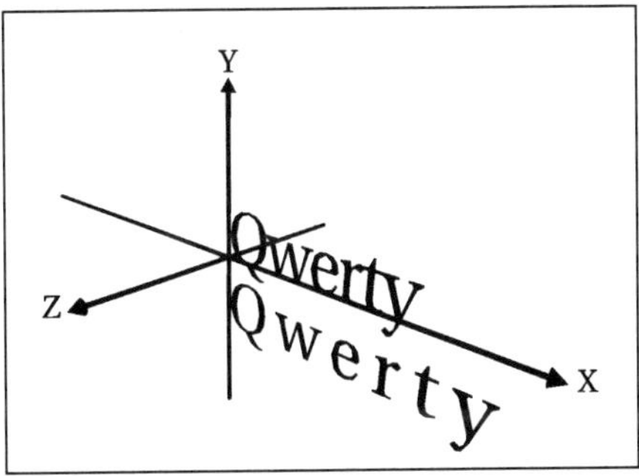

Figure 4.12 *A two-line text string, the first line with a width of 30.0 and the second with a width of 40.0.*

Using Text More Than Once

You can include any number of **AsciiText** nodes within the same VRML file. Figure 4.13 for instance, creates two blocks of text. The first is right-justified at the origin and the second is left-justified.

```
#VRML V1.0 ascii

AsciiText {
      string "First "
      justification RIGHT
}
AsciiText {
      string "Second"
      justification LEFT
}
```

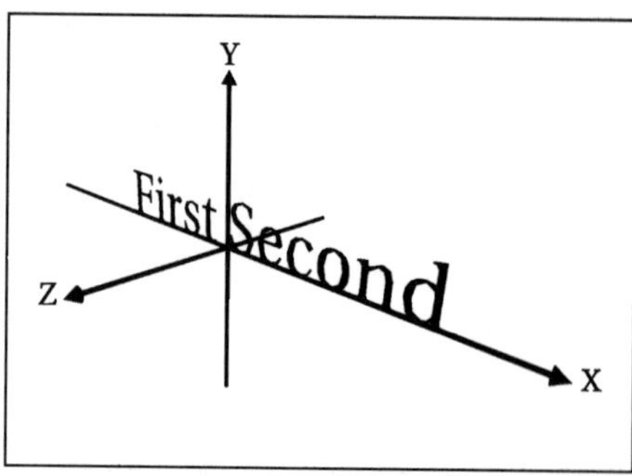

Figure 4.13 *Two text strings, one left-justified and one right-justified.*

In the preceding example, different **justification** field values are specified in the two **AsciiText** nodes to ensure that the string shapes don't overlap. If you remove the **justification** fields, the text shapes are drawn overlapping each other, as shown in Figure 4.14.

```
#VRML V1.0 ascii

AsciiText {
      string "First "
}
AsciiText {
      string "Second"
}
```

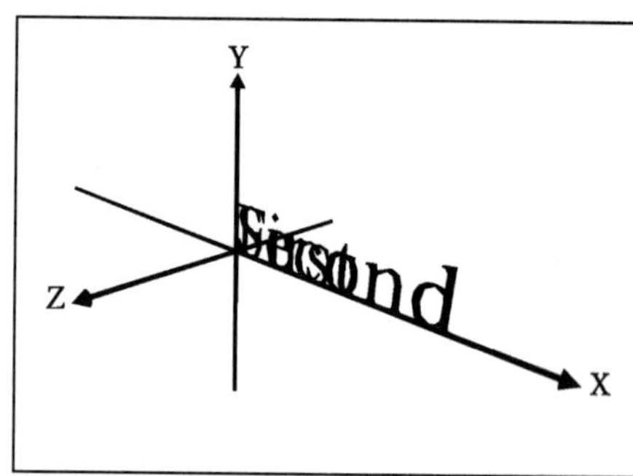

Figure 4.14 *Two overlapping shapes.*

Using Font Families

Using the **family** and **style** fields of a **FontStyle** node, you can select the font family and style for subsequent text shapes. Figures 4.15 through 4.17 illustrate bold serif, italic serif, and normal sans text. Figure 4.24 shows all combinations of the four styles (**NONE**, **BOLD**, **ITALIC**, and **BOLD|ITALIC**) and the three VRML font families (**SERIF**, **SANS**, and **TYPEWRITER**).

```
#VRML V1.0 ascii

FontStyle {
      family SERIF
      style BOLD
}
AsciiText {
      string "Qwerty"
}
```

Figure 4.15 *Bold serif text.*

TIP *Notice that the edges of the rounded letters like the "Q" and the "e" are not perfectly smooth. The edges are faceted, because they are created with many small triangles. We'll explain why in a later chapter.*

```
#VRML V1.0 ascii

FontStyle {
      family SERIF
      style ITALIC
}
AsciiText {
      string "Qwerty"
}
```

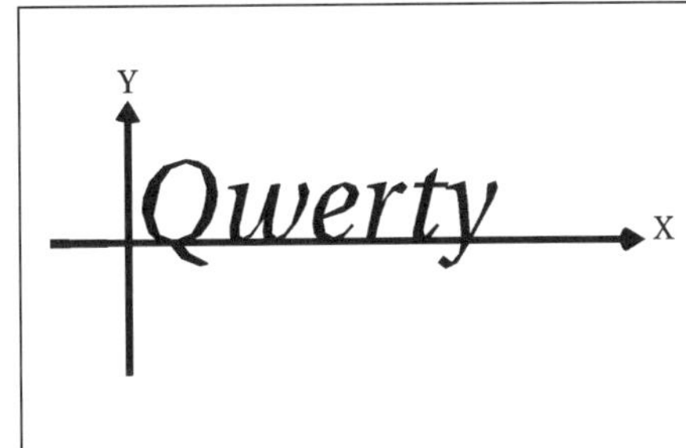

Figure 4.16 *Italic serif text.*

```
#VRML V1.0 ascii

FontStyle {
      family SANS
      style  NONE
}
AsciiText {
      string "Qwerty"
}
```

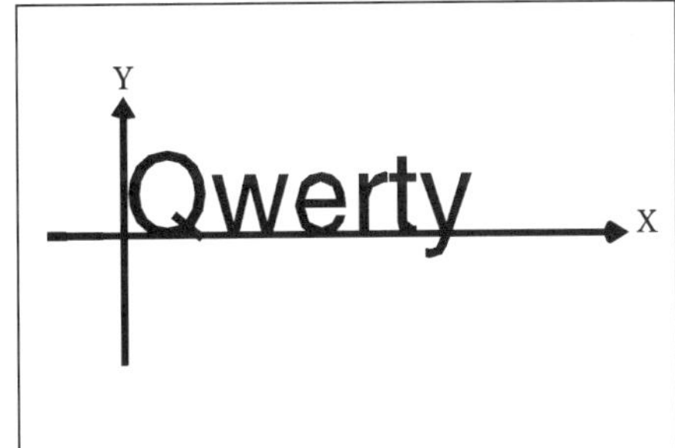

Figure 4.17 *Normal sans text.*

Using Font Size

Using the **FontStyle** node's **size** field, you can create large or small text. Changing the size of the font changes the size of individual characters and the spacing between lines of text. For instance, you can reduce font size to 5.0 units, as in Figure 4.18.

```
#VRML V1.0 ascii

FontStyle {
      size 5.0
}
AsciiText {
      string "Qwerty"
}
```

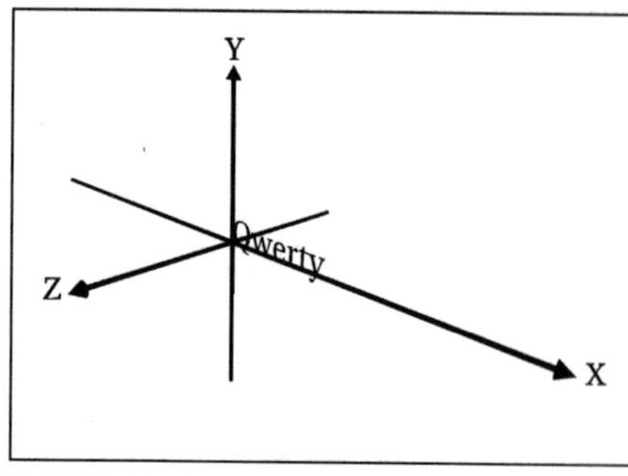

Figure 4.18 *Five-unit-high text.*

For comparison with the 0.5-unit-high text, Figure 4.19 illustrates 10.0-unit-high text.

```
#VRML V1.0 ascii

FontStyle {
      size 10.0
}
AsciiText {
      string "Qwerty"
}
```

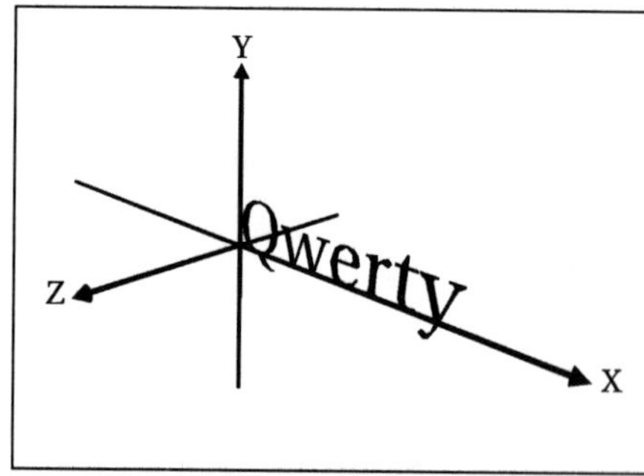

Figure 4.19 *Ten-unit-high text.*

You can also use negative sizes to flip text upside down and create a mirror effect, as shown in Figure 4.20.

```
#VRML V1.0 ascii

FontStyle {
      size -10.0
}
AsciiText {
      string "Qwerty"
}
```

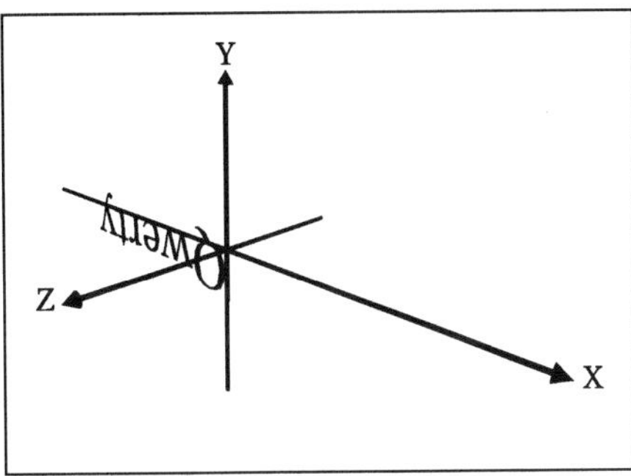

Figure 4.20 *Text flipped upside down using a negative size.*

Using Font Style More Than Once

You can change the pen's text properties more than once in the same VRML file. Each time you change text properties with a **FontStyle** node, the new properties affect all subsequent **AsciiText** nodes until the text properties are changed again with another **FontStyle** node.

Figure 4.21 draws two text nodes, each using a different font family, style, and size.

```
#VRML V1.0 ascii

FontStyle {
      family SERIF
      style  ITALIC
      size   8.0
}
AsciiText {
      string "One"
      justification RIGHT
}
FontStyle {
      family SANS
      style  BOLD
      size   15.0
}
AsciiText {
      string "Two"
      justification LEFT
}
```

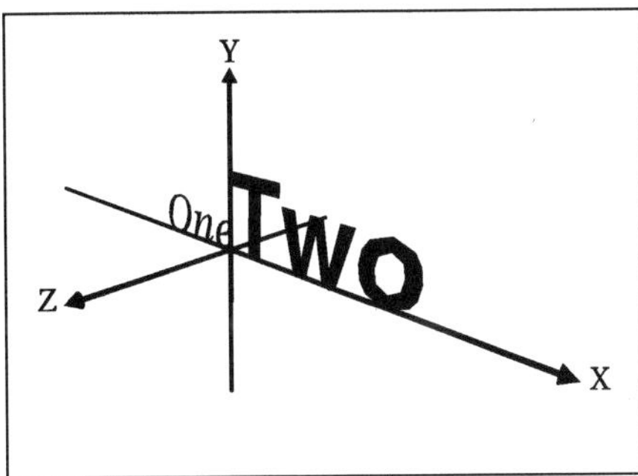

Figure 4.21 *Two text strings with different properties created using two **FontStyle** nodes.*

Reading the VRML text in Figure 4.21 from top to bottom, the VRML virtual pen is instructed to:

1. Change the text property to 8.0-unit, italic serif text.
2. Draw the right-justified string "One."
3. Change the text property to 15.0-unit, bold sans text.
4. Draw the left-justified string "Two."

Combining Text and Primitive Shapes

You can combine text with the primitive shapes. Figure 4.22 draws two lines of text with a flattened cube between them.

```
#VRML V1.0 ascii

AsciiText {
      string [ "Above", "Below" ]
      justification CENTER
}
Cube {
      height 0.1
      width 50.0
      depth 20.0
}
```

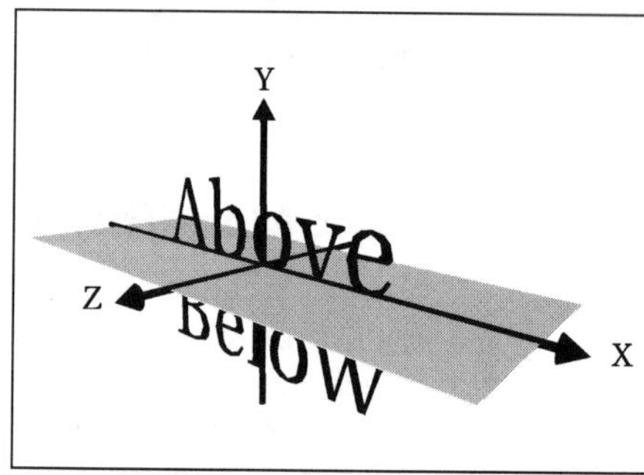

Figure 4.22 *Two lines of text with a flat cube between them.*

Reading the VRML text in Figure 4.22 from top to bottom, the VRML virtual pen is instructed to:

1. Draw a centered, two-line text string at the origin.
2. Draw a wide, flat, deep cube at the origin.

Extended Examples

The following examples build on the concepts we present in this chapter. They illustrate the worlds you can create using only VRML's text shapes. Try them on your own.

TIP *All of the VRML text in the extended examples throughout this book are available via anonymous ftp from John Wiley & Sons at* `ftp.wiley.com/public/computer_books/vrml` *and from the VRML Repository at* `http://www.sdsc.edu/vrml`*. For anonymous ftp instructions, see the Preface.*

An Eye Chart

Figure 4.23 shows text shapes in the format of an eye chart. If you read it closely, you may see a message. Notice the use of blank lines within text strings.

```
#VRML V1.0 ascii

FontStyle {
	family SERIF
	style  NONE
	size   20
}
AsciiText {
	string ["","","B K"]
	justification CENTER
	spacing -1
}
FontStyle {
	size   14
}
AsciiText {
	string ["","","Q Z O"]
	justification CENTER
	spacing -1
}
FontStyle {
	size   9
}
AsciiText {
	string ["","","M P S B R"]
	justification CENTER
	spacing -1
}
FontStyle {
	size   5
}
AsciiText {
	string ["","","J K Q W V D U I Y"]
	justification CENTER
	spacing -1.2
}
FontStyle {
	size   3
}
AsciiText {
	string ["","","A S C I I T E X T H T M L N E T"]
	justification CENTER
	spacing -1.2
}
FontStyle {
	size   1.5
}
```

Figure 4.23 continues

```
AsciiText {
      string ["","","V R M L I S C O O L B R O W S E T H E W E B I N 3 D"]
      justification CENTER
      spacing -1.5
}
```

Figure 4.23 *An eye chart.*

A List of Font Styles

Figure 4.24 illustrates the font styles available for VRML text. Again, notice the use of blank lines within text strings.

```
#VRML V1.0 ascii

FontStyle {
      family SERIF
      style  NONE
}
AsciiText {
      string ["Serif Normal"]
}
FontStyle {
      family SERIF
      style  BOLD
}
AsciiText {
      string ["","Serif Bold"]
}
FontStyle {
      family SERIF
      style  ITALIC
}
AsciiText {
      string ["","","Serif Italic"]
}
FontStyle {
      family SERIF
      style  (BOLD|ITALIC)
}
AsciiText {
      string [ "","","","Serif BoldItalic"]
}
FontStyle {
      family SANS
      style  NONE
}
AsciiText {
      string [ "","","","", "Sans Normal"]
}
```

Serif Normal
Serif Bold
Serif Italic
Serif BoldItalic
Sans Normal
Sans Bold
Sans Italic
Sans BoldItalic
Typewriter Normal
Typewriter Bold
Typewriter Italic
Typewriter BoldItalic

Figure 4.24 continues

```
FontStyle {
      family SANS
      style  BOLD
}
AsciiText {
      string [ "","","","","","Sans Bold"]
}
FontStyle {
      family SANS
      style  ITALIC
}
AsciiText {
      string [ "","","","","","","Sans Italic"]
}
FontStyle {
      family SANS
      style  (BOLD|ITALIC)
}
AsciiText {
      string [ "","","","","","","","Sans BoldItalic"]
}
FontStyle {
      family TYPEWRITER
      style  NONE
}
AsciiText {
      string [ "","","","","","","","", "Typewriter Normal"]
}
FontStyle {
      family TYPEWRITER
      style  BOLD
}
AsciiText {
      string [ "","","","","","","","","","Typewriter Bold"]
}
FontStyle {
      family TYPEWRITER
      style  ITALIC
}
AsciiText {
      string [ "","","","","","","","","","","Typewriter Italic"]
}
FontStyle {
      family TYPEWRITER
      style  (BOLD|ITALIC)
}
AsciiText {
      string [ "","","","","","","","","","","","Typewriter BoldItalic"]
}
```

Figure 4.24 *A VRML font style chart.*

Summary

VRML's **AsciiText** node enables you to create single- or multiline blocks of text, control vertical line spacing, text width, and left- or right-justify or center text.

Using the **FontStyle** node, you can set text pen properties that apply to all subsequent **AsciiText** nodes. You can choose a font family from the three families supported by VRML: serif, sans, and typewriter. For each family you can select whether text should be drawn bold, italic, both, or neither. You can also control the font size, which in turn affects the vertical line spacing of multiline blocks of text.

CHAPTER 5

Positioning Shapes

You can position shapes anywhere in your world. You can stack them on top of each other, inside each other, or hang them in midair. You can arrange multiple cubes as buildings along a city street, or make a row of Greek columns with cylinders. You can also position text shapes anywhere you want in your world to create signs on buildings, label items, and include notes in your worlds. You can position one shape or a group of shapes.

In Chapters 3 and 4, we drew primitive shapes and text shapes using VRML's virtual pen. In Chapter 4, we also used the **TextStyle** node to change the virtual pen's properties prior to drawing text. In this chapter, we'll use the **Translation** node to position the virtual pen in a new location before drawing. The **Translation** node changes the pen's *position* property prior to drawing shapes.

TIP *Positioning in VRML is called* **translation**. *The word* translation *has many meanings, like the conversion of text or speech from one language to another. It also means moving or transporting something from one place to another, which describes the function of the* ***Translation*** *node.*

Understanding Translation

In VRML, translation directs the positioning of VRML's virtual pen. Each time you change the position property of the virtual pen with a translation, it comes to rest in a new location at which you can draw any VRML shape.

After drawing a shape, you can change the position property of the pen again, draw another shape, and so on. You use sequences of positioning and drawing instructions to gradually build a complicated world in VRML.

Imagine drawing a model of a city street lined with buildings. You can draw this street using the virtual pen and a series of instructions like these:

1. Start with the pen at the end of the street you want to draw.
2. Draw a wide, flat square for the downtown area of the city.
3. Position the pen on the left side of the street.
4. Draw a tall building.
5. Position the pen on the right side of the street.
6. Draw a short building.
7. Position the pen down the street past the short building.
8. Draw a skyscraper.
9. Continue in this way until your street is populated with buildings.

Each new instruction either positions the virtual pen or draws a new building at the pen's new position. Notice that each building is drawn *relative to* the pen's current position.

The ordering of your instructions is very important in VRML. If you swapped steps 5 and 6 in these instructions, what would the street look like? Step 5 positions the pen across the street, and step 6 draws the short building. If you draw the building before positioning the pen, the short building is drawn overlapping the tall building drawn in step 4.

TIP *The tip of the VRML virtual pen is a representation of the origin. When you position the virtual pen to draw a shape in a new location, you are positioning* the origin and its associated X, Y, Z axes *in a new location. To position shapes in various locations within your world, you must* first move the origin and axes, *and* then draw the shape.

In the preceding drawing instructions, the VRML browser positions the origin and axes each time a translation instruction is given, like this:

1. Start with the origin and axes at the end of the street you want to draw.
2. Draw a wide, flat square for the downtown area of the city.
3. Position *the origin and axes* on the left side of the street.
4. Draw a tall building.
5. Position *the origin and axes* on the right side of the street.
6. Draw a short building.
7. Position *the origin and axes* down the street past the short building.
8. Draw a skyscraper.
9. Continue in this way until your street is populated with buildings.

Notice that each building is drawn in a position *relative to* the previous building, because a translation preceding a drawing instruction positions the origin *relative to* the previous translations. To illustrate this relative positioning in VRML, each example file in this chapter is associated with a diagram or a series of diagrams. The diagrams show the origin's position at each point in the VRML file's drawing instructions. The starting origin position is included in each diagram in gray so that you can see the new origin's position (shown in black) in relation to the original position.

Positioning a Shape Using Translation

Figure 5.1 instructs VRML to draw the downtown area of the city and the street with the first building on it.

```
#VRML V1.0 ascii

# Draw the ground with a wide, deep, flat cube
Cube {
      height 0.1
      width 10.0
      depth 20.0
}
# Move to the left side of the street
Translation {
      translation -3.0 4.0 0.0
}
# Draw the tall building with a tall cube
Cube {
      height 8.0
}
# Move to the right side of the street
Translation {
      translation 6.0 -2.0 0.0
}
# Draw the short building with a short cube
Cube {
      height 4.0
}
# Move down the street
Translation {
      translation 0.0 4.0 -3.0
}
# Draw a skyscraper next to the short
# building using a tall cylinder
Cylinder {
      height 10.0
}
```

Figure 5.1 *Drawing the downtown area of a city and one building.*

Notice the structure and order of the VRML file in Figure 5.1. Starting at the top of the file, the VRML browser reads the **Cube** node and draws a flattened cube to use as the downtown area of the city. The **Translation** node then moves the origin (the tip of the virtual pen) to the left side of the street. Once there, the pen draws a cube. The list of nodes in this VRML file mimics the first four drawing instructions from the previous section.

Understanding the **Translation** Node Syntax

The **Translation** node has a single **translation** field containing three floating-point values. This field describes *a distance by which to move the origin* before it comes to rest in a new position. To enable the origin (and the tip of the virtual pen) to move in the X, Y, and Z directions individually, the **translation** field specifies three distances: the first in the X direction, the second in the Y direction, and the third in the Z direction. Any of these distances may be positive or negative values.

SYNTAX **Translation node**

```
Translation {
   translation 0.0 0.0 0.0       # X, Y, Z distance
}
```

Using the **Translation** node, you can position the origin before drawing any shape or text.

Experimenting with Translation

The following examples provide a more detailed examination of the ways in which the **Translation** node can be used and how it interacts with nodes we've discussed in previous chapters.

Translating in Different Directions

You can use the **Translation** node to move the origin any distance in any direction. Figures 5.2 through 5.7 show the origin moving along the X, Y, and Z axes in both positive and negative directions. In each case, the origin is moved *first*, then the cylinder is drawn. The diagrams in each figure illustrate the result of the VRML file preceding them.

```
#VRML V1.0 ascii

Translation {
      translation 2.0 0.0 0.0
}
Cylinder {
}
```

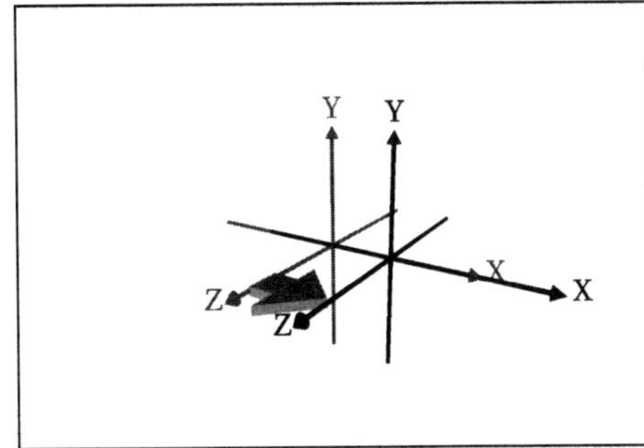

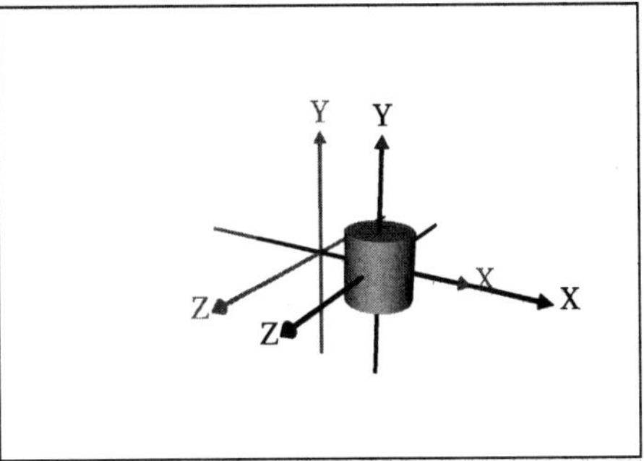

Figure 5.2 *Translating +2.0 units along the X axis and drawing a cylinder.*

```
#VRML V1.0 ascii

Translation {
      translation -2.0 0.0 0.0
}
Cylinder {
}
```

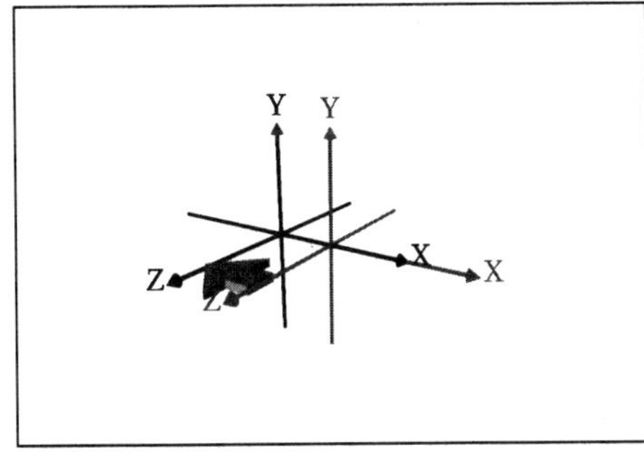

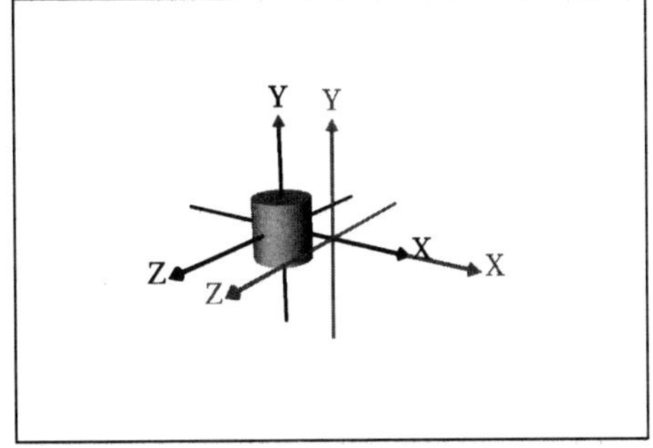

Figure 5.3 *Translating –2.0 units along the X axis and drawing a cylinder.*

```
#VRML V1.0 ascii

Translation {
      translation 0.0 2.0 0.0
}
Cylinder {
}
```

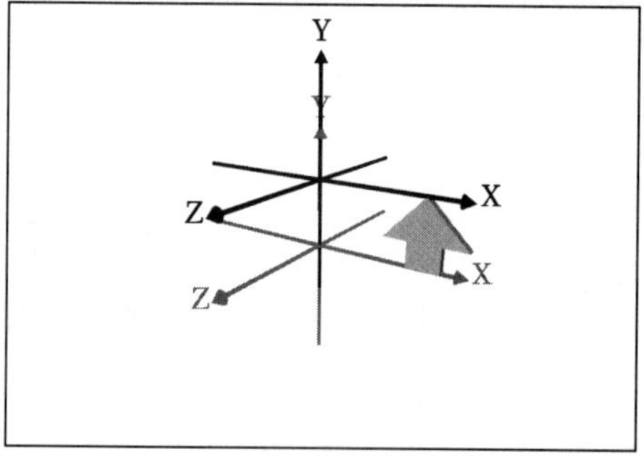

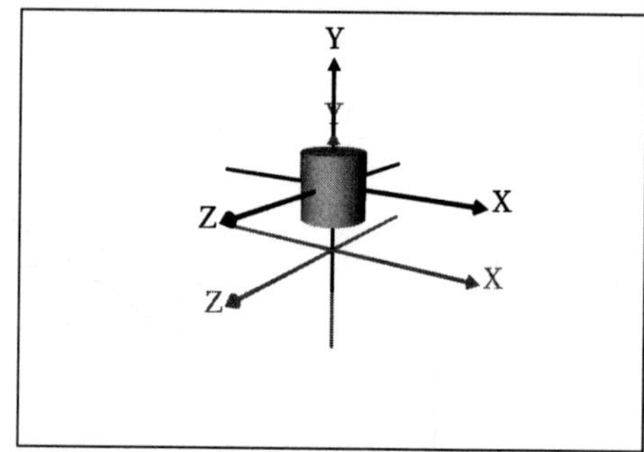

Figure 5.4 *Translating +2.0 units along the Y axis and drawing a cylinder.*

```
#VRML V1.0 ascii

Translation {
      translation 0.0 -2.0 0.0
}
Cylinder {
}
```

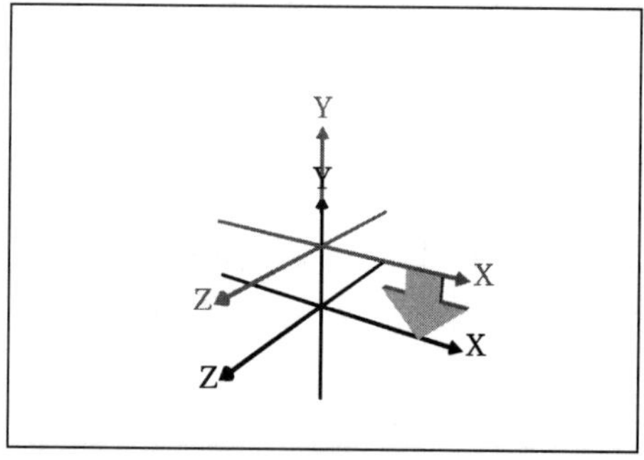

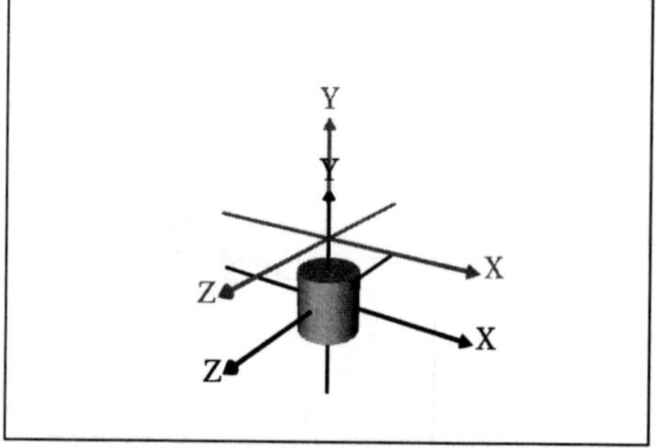

Figure 5.5 *Translating –2.0 units along the Y axis and drawing a cylinder.*

```
#VRML V1.0 ascii

Translation {
      translation 0.0 0.0 2.0
}
Cylinder {
}
```

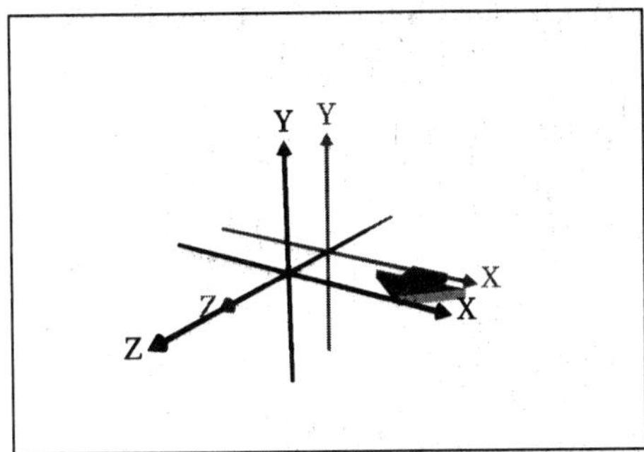

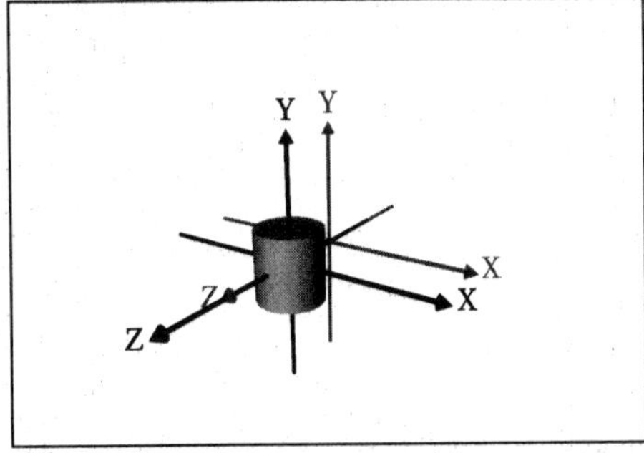

Figure 5.6 *Translating +2.0 units along the Z axis and drawing a cylinder.*

```
#VRML V1.0 ascii

Translation {
      translation 0.0 0.0 -2.0
}
Cylinder {
}
```

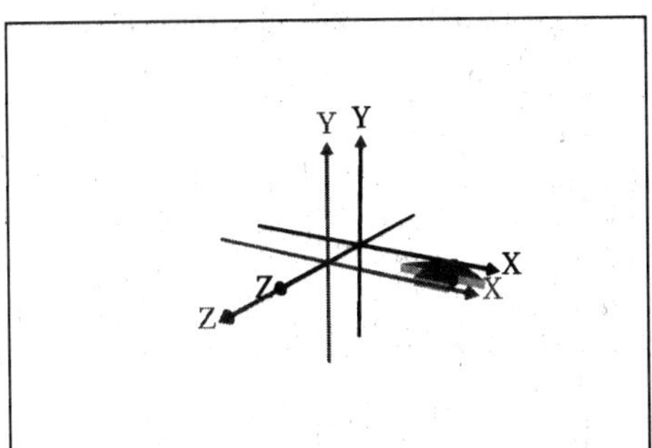

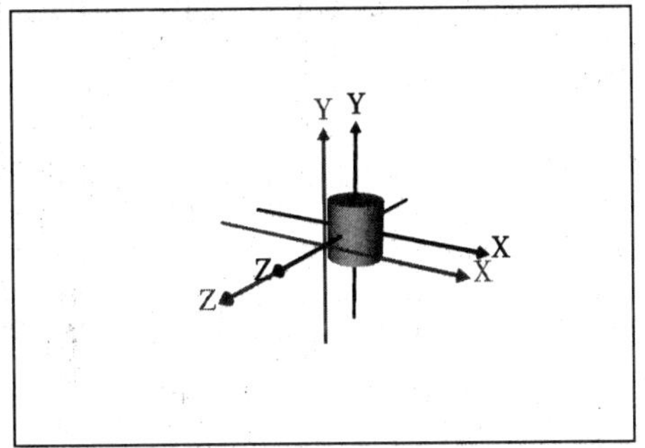

Figure 5.7 *Translating –2.0 units along the Z axis and drawing a cylinder.*

Figures 5.2 through 5.7 show the origin translating in only one direction at a time. The **translation** field in Figure 5.2, for example, set the X value to 2.0, and set the Y and Z values to 0.0. You can also set two or all three of the **translation** field values to translate the origin in diagonal directions.

The following example translates the origin in three directions at once: 6.0 units in the X direction, 1.0 unit in the Y direction, and 5.0 units in the Z direction. Again, the origin is translated *first,* then the cylinder is drawn. The diagrams illustrate the result of the VRML file in Figure 5.8.

```
#VRML V1.0 ascii

Translation {
      translation 6.0 4.0 5.0
}
Cylinder {
}
```

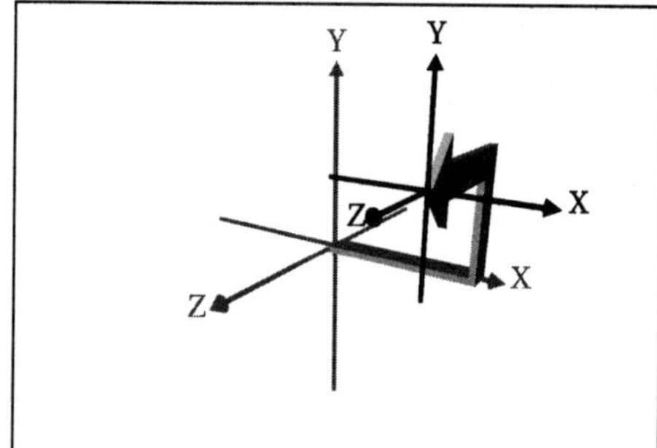

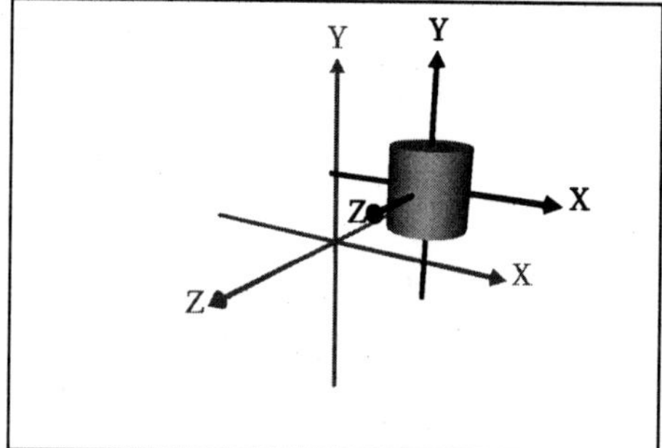

Figure 5.8 *Translating 6.0 units along the X axis, 1.0 unit along the Y axis, 5.0 units along the Z axis, and drawing a cylinder.*

Translating between Drawing Shapes

You can draw shapes before or after you translate the origin. For instance, you can build a hut (the same one we built in Chapter 2) using a **Cylinder** node, a **Translation** node, and a **Cone** node, like the one shown in Figure 5.9.

```
#VRML V1.0 ascii

# Draw hut base
Cylinder {
      height 2.0
      radius 2.0
}
# Move the pen up
Translation {
      translation 0.0 2.0 0.0
}
# Draw the roof
Cone {
      bottomRadius 2.5
}
```

Figure 5.9 *A hut.*

Reading the VRML file from top to bottom, the virtual pen is instructed to:

1. Draw a cylinder at the current origin position.

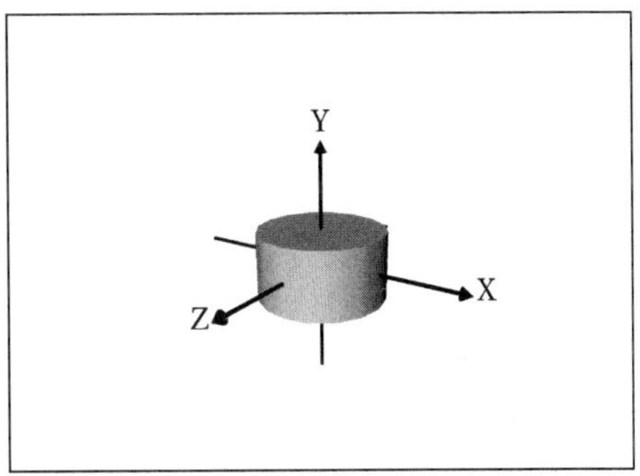

Figure 5.10 *Drawing a cylinder for the walls of the hut.*

2. Translate 2.0 units in the Y direction.

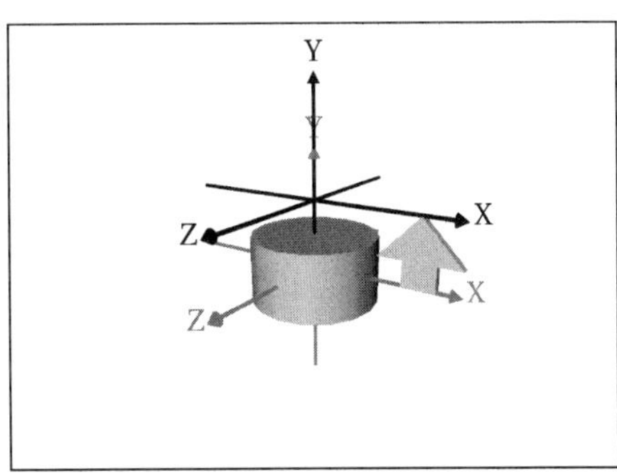

Figure 5.11 *Moving 2.0 units in the Y direction.*

3. Draw a cone at the current origin position.

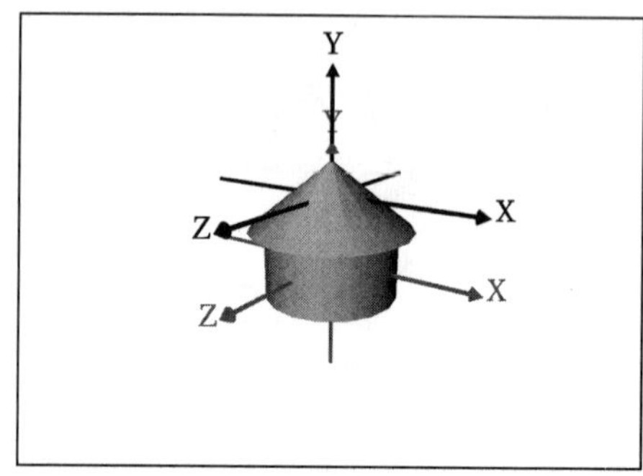

Figure 5.12 *Drawing a cone for the hut's roof.*

Translating More Than Once

Consider again the city street example from the beginning of this chapter. The text used to create the downtown area and one building looks like that in Figure 5.13.

```
#VRML V1.0 ascii

# Draw the ground with a wide, deep, flat cube
Cube {
   height 0.1
   width 10.0
   depth 20.0
}
# Move to the left side of the street
Translation {
    translation -3.0 4.0 0.0
}
# Draw the tall building with a tall cube
Cube {
    height 8.0
}
```

Figure 5.13 *The VRML text needed to draw the downtown area of a city and one building.*

Reading the VRML file from top to bottom, the virtual pen is instructed to:

1. Draw a cube at the current origin position.

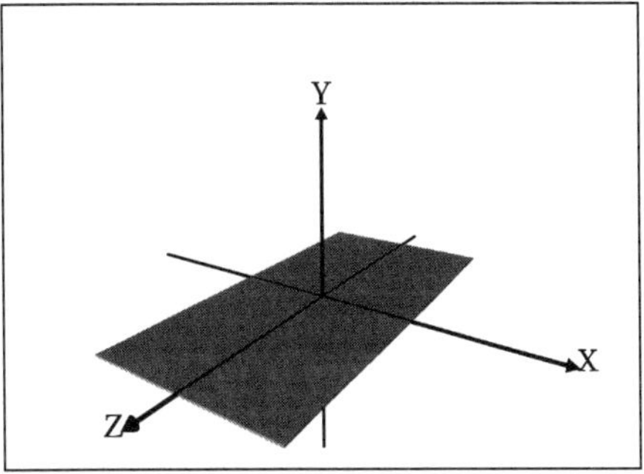

Figure 5.14 *Drawing a broad, flat cube.*

TIP *We've omitted the arrows indicating translation direction from the remaining diagrams in this chapter. (You should now be used to tracking translations from one diagram to another.) The rest of the diagrams in this chapter are complex enough that the arrows may clutter them and cause confusion.*

2. Translate –3.0 units in the X direction and 4.0 units in the Y direction.

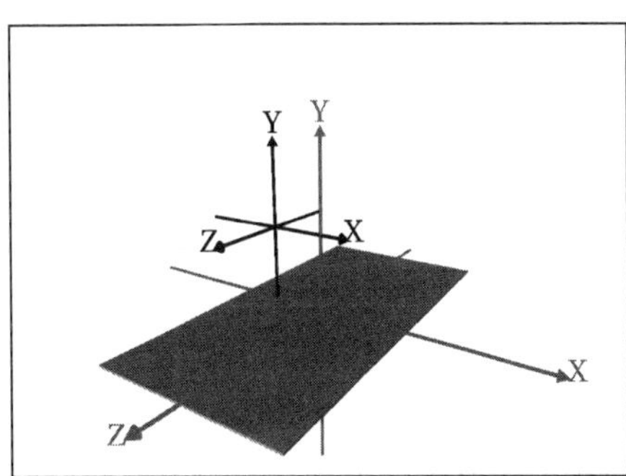

Figure 5.15 *Moving to the side of the street.*

TIP *The **Translation** node positions the virtual pen 4.0 units up the Y axis* in addition *to positioning it –3.0 units in the X direction. What happens if you don't move the origin up, but leave it at street level instead? When the virtual pen draws the 8.0-unit-high cube, it draws the cube* centered *around the current origin position. The resulting cube extends 4.0 units above the street level and 4.0 units* below *the street level. To ensure that the bottom of the cube is sitting on the ground, the **Translation** node positions the origin and the virtual pen 4.0 units above the ground before the cube is drawn.*

3. Draw an 8.0-unit-high cube at the current origin position.

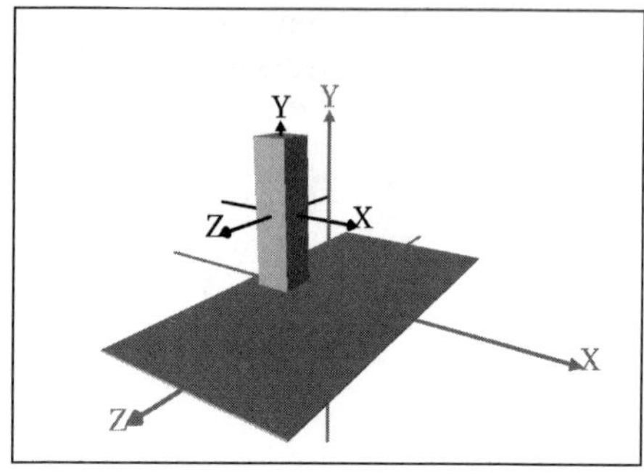

Figure 5.16 *Drawing a tall building.*

To add another building to the city street, add nodes to your VRML file to translate the origin to the other side of the street and draw a short building. Add the highlighted text shown in Figure 5.17 to the end of the VRML file started in Figure 5.13.

```
#VRML V1.0 ascii

# Draw the ground with a wide, deep, flat cube
Cube {
      height 0.1
      width 10.0
      depth 20.0
}
# Move to the left side of the street
Translation {
      translation -3.0 4.0 0.0
}
# Draw the tall building with a tall cube
Cube {
      height 8.0
}
# Move to the right side of the street
Translation {
      translation 6.0 -2.0 0.0
}
# Draw the short building with a short cube
Cube {
      height 4.0
}
```

Figure 5.17 *Adding another building to the city street.*

Continue reading the VRML file, beginning with the additional **Translation** node. The virtual pen is instructed to:

4. Translate 6.0 units in the X direction and –2.0 units in the Y direction. The origin is now 2.0 units down the Y axis so that the short cube is drawn sitting on the ground.

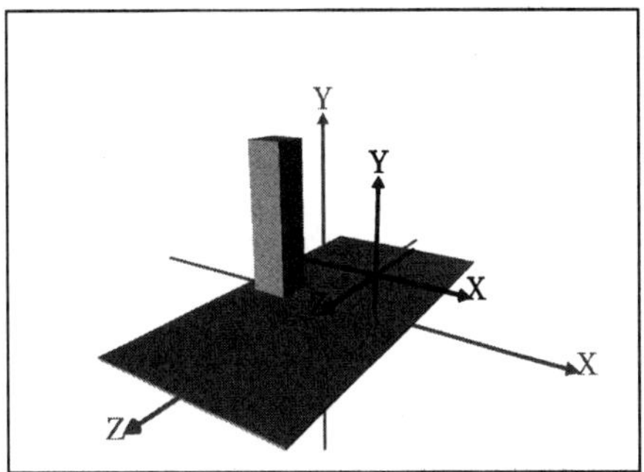

Figure 5.18 *Moving across the street and down a bit in preparation for drawing the short building.*

5. Draw a 4.0-unit-high cube at the current origin position.

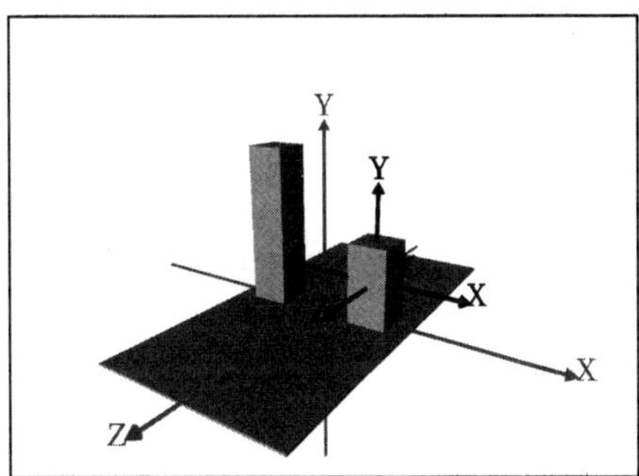

Figure 5.19 *Drawing a short building.*

You can use this same approach over and over as you add more buildings to your city street. To put a skyscraper beside the short building, add the highlighted **Translation** node and **Cylinder** node shown in Figure 5.20 to the end of the VRML file started in Figure 5.13.

```
#VRML V1.0 ascii

# Draw the ground with a wide, deep, flat cube
Cube {
      height 0.1
      width 10.0
      depth 20.0
}
```

Figure 5.20 continues

```
# Move to the left side of the street
Translation {
      translation -3.0 4.0 0.0
}
# Draw the tall building with a tall cube
Cube {
      height 8.0
}
# Move to the right side of the street
Translation {
      translation 6.0 -2.0 0.0
}
# Draw the short building with a short cube
Cube {
      height 4.0
}
# Move down the street
Translation {
      translation 0.0 4.0 -3.0
}
# Draw a skyscraper next to the short
# building using a tall cylinder
Cylinder {
      height 10.0
}
```

Figure 5.20 *Adding a third building to the city street.*

Continue reading the VRML file, beginning with the additional **Translation** node. The virtual pen is instructed to:

6. Translate –3.0 units in the Z direction and 4.0 units in the Y direction. The translation instruction positions the origin 4.0 units up the Y axis to ensure that the skyscraper sits on the ground and doesn't dangle 4.0 units below the ground.

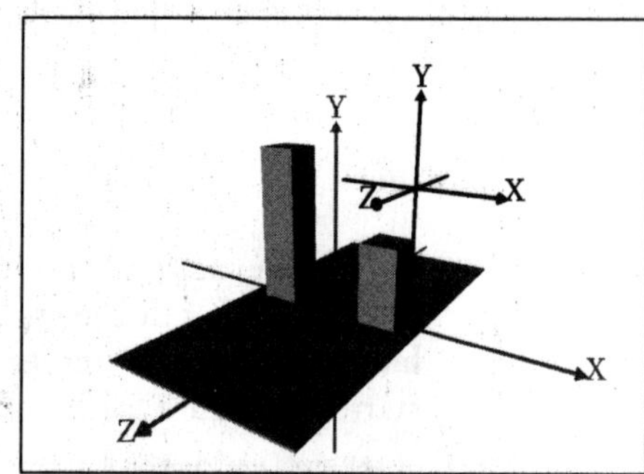

Figure 5.21 *Moving next to the short building and up a bit to prepare for drawing the skyscraper.*

7. Draw a 12.0-unit-high cylinder and the current origin position.

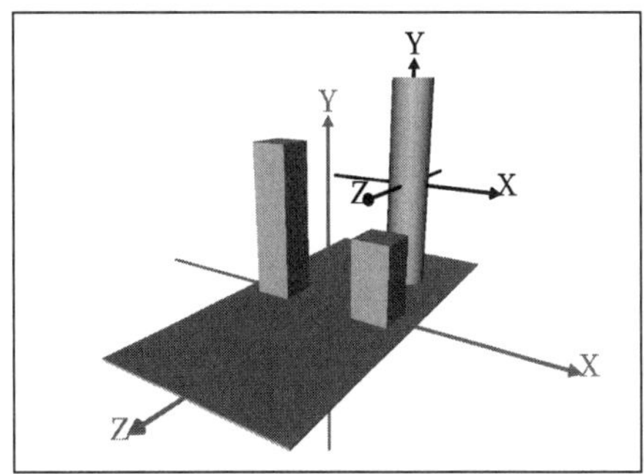

Figure 5.22 *Drawing a tall skyscraper.*

Extended Examples

The following examples build on the concepts we present in this chapter. They illustrate the worlds you can create by translating the origin and using only VRML's primitive shapes. Try them on your own.

TIP *All of the VRML text in the extended examples throughout this book are available via anonymous ftp from John Wiley & Sons at* `ftp.wiley.com/public/computer_books/vrml` *and from the VRML Repository at* `http://www.sdsc.edu/vrml`.

A Book

Figure 5.23 is a book created using only primitive shapes and translations.

```
#VRML V1.0 ascii

# Pages:
Cube {
      width 7.0
      height 10.0
      depth 2.0
}
# Front cover:
Translation {
      translation 0.125 0.0 1.0
}
Cube {
      width 7.25
      height 10.5
      depth .25
}
```

Figure 5.23 continues

```
# Back cover:
Translation {
      translation 0.0 0.0 -2.0
}
Cube {
      width 7.25
      height 10.5
      depth .25
}
# Spine:
Translation {
      translation -3.75 0.0 1.0
}
Cube {
      width .25
      height 10.5
      depth 2.0
}
Translation {
      translation 0.0 0.0 1.0
}
Cylinder {
      height 10.5
      radius .125
}
Translation {
      translation 0.0 0.0 -2.0
}
Cylinder {
      height 10.5
      radius .125
}
```

Figure 5.23 *A book.*

A Chair

If you look closely at the image of the chair in Figure 5.24, it looks very complex. The VRML text, however, is composed entirely of primitive shapes and translations.

```
#VRML V1.0 ascii
Cube {
      width 6
      height .5
      depth 6
}
Translation {
      translation 2.75 -1.5 2.75
}
Cylinder {
      radius .25
      height 9.0
}
Translation {
      translation 0.0 3.0 -5.5
}
Cylinder {
      radius .25
      height 15.0
}
Translation {
      translation -5.5 0.0 0.0
}
Cylinder {
      radius .25
      height 15.0
}
Translation {
      translation 0.0 -3.0 5.5
}
Cylinder {
      radius .25
      height 9.0
}
Translation {
      translation 0.0 4.5 -2.5
}
Cube {
      width .5
      height .5
      depth 6.0
}
Translation {
      translation 5.5 0.0 0.0
}
Cube {
      width .5
      height .5
      depth 6.0
}
```

Figure 5.24 continues

```
Translation {
      translation -2.75 4.0 -3.0
}
Cube {
      width 5.5
      height 2.5
      depth 0.5
}
Translation {
      translation -1.5 -4.0 0.0
}
Cylinder {
      radius .15
      height 6.0
}
Translation {
      translation 1.0 0.0 0.0
}
Cylinder {
      radius .15
      height 6.0
}
Translation {
      translation 1.0 0.0 0.0
}
Cylinder {
      radius .15
      height 6.0
}
Translation {
      translation 1.0 0.0 0.0
}
Cylinder {
      radius .15
      height 6.0
}
Translation {
      translation 1.25 6.0 0.0
}
Sphere {
      radius 0.5
}
Translation {
      translation -5.5 0.0 0.0
}
Sphere {
      radius 0.5
}
```

Figure 5.24 *A chair.*

Summary

Translation allows you to move the origin of your VRML world and precisely position it to draw shapes wherever you want them. All shapes are drawn *relative to* the current origin position.

The **Translation** node specifies the distance and direction the origin is moved. The node's **translation** field contains three values instructing the origin to move by a particular distance in each of the X, Y, and Z directions.

Translation can occur in the positive or negative direction, and you can translate the origin in one, two, or all three directions at once. You can translate more than once within a VRML file, and you can translate and then draw one shape or many shapes.

CHAPTER 6

Rotating Shapes

Rotation allows you to turn a cone upside down to make a funnel, turn a cylinder on its side to make a car wheel, or balance a cube on one corner. You can rotate one shape or a group of shapes to create sideways text, car wheels, opening doors, and more.

In Chapter 5, we used a **Translation** node to change the virtual pen's position property before drawing shapes. In this chapter, we'll use a **Rotation** node to change the virtual pen's *orientation* property and turn it to point in different directions before drawing.

Understanding Rotation

Think of **Rotation** and **Translation** nodes in your VRML file as directions for the driver of a car. You might give to the driver the following instructions to get to your house:

1. Start the car.
2. Drive straight three blocks.
3. Turn left.
4. Drive straight five blocks.
5. Stop at the second house on the left.

VRML nodes are like driving instructions for the VRML browser. The **Translation** node is similar to the "drive straight" instruction, and the **Rotation** node is similar to the "turn left" and "turn right" instructions. Unlike driving a car, a **Rotation** node can also specify a "turn up" or "turn down" instruction. In fact, the **Rotation** node can specify any combination of turning directions to cause your virtual pen to rotate in three dimensions.

Look again at the driving instructions. Step 2 states "drive straight," but so does step 4. If the driver was initially facing north, then "drive straight" in step 2 means "drive further north." Does step 4, which also states "drive straight," mean "drive further north," as well? No, because the driver turns left in step 3 and is no longer facing north. Instead, the car is facing west. We used exactly the same "drive straight" instruction in two places, but it caused the car to go north the first time and west the second time. The meaning of "drive straight" was changed because we turned, or *rotated*, between the two "drive straight" directions.

VRML's virtual pen also follows instructions in this way. Rotation changes the direction in which the virtual pen is facing *in relation to its current orientation.* When the virtual pen "moves straight ahead" after a rotation, the pen translates in a new direction relative to the current orientation of the pen.

TIP *The tip of the VRML virtual pen is a representation of the origin. When you rotate the virtual pen to draw a shape with a new orientation, you are actually* rotating the origin and the associated X, Y, Z axes *to a new orientation.*

If the driving instructions were a VRML file, the browser would orient the axes each time a *rotate* instruction is given, like this:

1. Start the car.
2. Drive straight (translate) three blocks.
3. Rotate *the origin and axes* 90.0 degrees about the Y axis.
4. Drive straight (translate) five blocks.
5. Stop at the second house on the left.

Notice that the rotation in step 3 is relative to the translation in step 2, and the translation in step 4 is relative to the rotation in step 3 *and* the translation in step 2. Each change in pen property is affected by the property changes occurring before it.

To illustrate the relative nature of property changes in VRML, each example file in this chapter is associated with a diagram or a series of diagrams. The diagrams show the axes' position and orientation at each point in the VRML file's series of instructions. The starting axes' position and orientation is included in each diagram in gray so that you can see the new axes' position and orientation (shown in black) in relation to the original position and orientation.

TIP *Files with many translations and rotations can get confusing, similar to getting lost driving in an unfamiliar neighborhood. When planning your VRML drawing instructions, try sketching X, Y, and Z axes, then step through your VRML file one node at a time. Move or rotate the axes at each step to determine their position and direction. See the series of diagrams throughout this chapter for an example of this.*

Orienting a Shape Using Rotation

Recall from Chapter 3 that you can create a cone shape using the **Cone** node. A cone is always created with its tip pointing upward. If you want to draw a funnel, you have to make the tip of the cone point downward. To do that, you rotate your virtual pen and the axes in your VRML world with a **Rotation** node, and then draw the cone, like the one shown in Figure 6.1.

```
#VRML V1.0 ascii

Rotation {
     #                  Z   +180 degrees
     rotation 0.0 0.0 1.0 +3.14159
}
Cone {
}
```

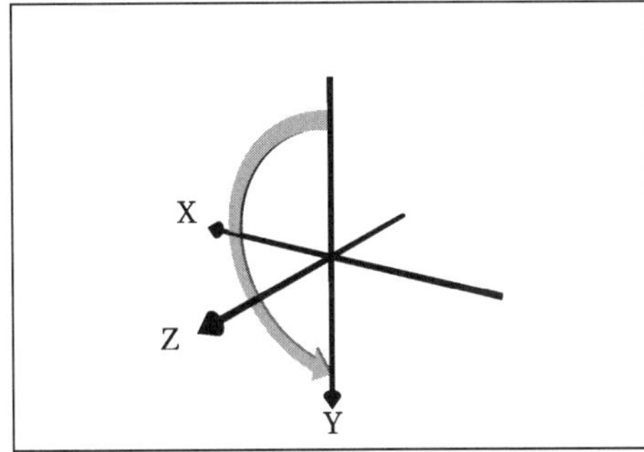

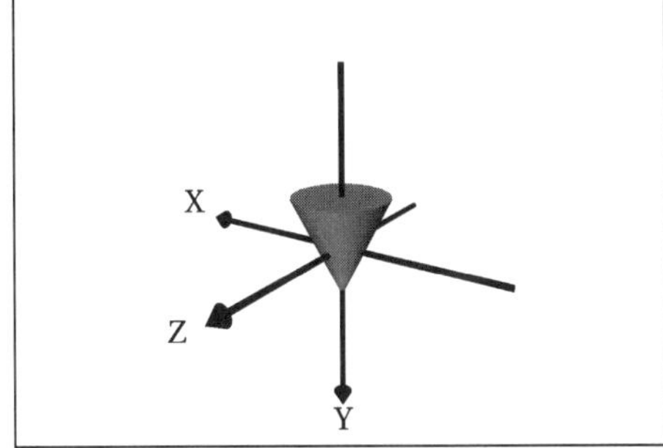

Figure 6.1 *A funnel created by rotating a cone +180.0 degrees.*

Notice the structure and order of the VRML file in Figure 6.1. Since the axes and the virtual pen were upside down when the pen drew the cone, the cone itself is drawn upside down.

This technique works for drawing cones, or any shape, sideways or at any other angle. First, use a **Rotation** node to turn the virtual pen and the axes, then draw the cone.

Understanding the **Rotation** Node Syntax

The **Rotation** node has a single **rotation** field containing four floating-point values. The first three of these values are called, collectively, the **rotation axis**. The fourth value is the **rotation amount** in radians.

SYNTAX **Rotation node**

```
Rotation {
   rotation 0.0 0.0 1.0 0.0       # rotation axis and amount}
```

Using the **Rotation** node, you can change the orientation property of the virtual pen and axes before drawing any shape.

Rotation Axis

The rotation axis is an imaginary line about which your shape is rotated. When you spin a toy top, for example, it spins around an imaginary line running vertically through its center. That imaginary line is the top's rotation axis. Similarly, the Earth rotates about an imaginary line running through the North and South Poles. That line is the Earth's rotation axis.

A rotation axis can point in any direction. The rotation axis of a car wheel, for example, points horizontally out of the center of the wheel. When rotating a shape in VRML, you must specify a direction for the rotation axis.

To define a direction for a rotation axis, imagine drawing a line between two coordinates in space. One coordinate is always the origin (0.0, 0.0, 0.0), the point where the X, Y, and Z axes cross. The origin is assumed when defining the rotation axis direction, so you don't have to specify it in the **rotation** field.

The second coordinate's location is defined in the first three values of the **Rotation** node's **rotation** field. The imaginary line drawn between these two coordinates is the rotation axis.

For example, to define a rotation axis for a toy top spinning about a vertical rotation axis, use an imaginary line that points straight up from the origin. The second coordinate defining the line must be directly above the origin for the top to spin straight up, such as (0.0, 1.0, 0.0).

TIP *The distance between coordinates in a rotation axis doesn't matter. Any point on the imaginary line is valid. To define a rotation axis that points straight up along the Y axis, (0.0, 2.0, 0.0), (0.0, 0.357, 0.0), and (0.0, 1.0, 0.0) are all equivalent, because they all point straight up.*

Most rotation axes lie to the right along the X axis, up along the Y axis, and out along the Z axis. While you can define a rotation axis in any direction, these are the most commonly used, shown in Table 6.1.

Table 6.1 Common Values for Common Rotation Axes

Direction	*Rotation Axis Values*
To the right along the X axis	`1.0 0.0 0.0`
Up along the Y axis	`0.0 1.0 0.0`
Out along the Z axis	`0.0 0.0 1.0`

Amount of Rotation

In addition to defining a rotation axis, you must also indicate how much you want a shape to rotate around that axis. This value is defined in the rotation amount, the fourth value of the **Rotation** nodes's **rotation** field. The rotation amount is specified by a rotation angle measured in radians.

TIP *The most common way to specify an angle is in units of degrees, not radians. In the body text of the book, we will discuss angles in terms of degrees but convert degrees to radians in VRML examples. We've provided a conversion table and an explanation of degrees-to-radians conversion in Appendix A.*

Again consider the example from Figure 6.1 that rotated the cone, now shown in Figure 6.2.

```
#VRML V1.0 ascii

Rotation {
      #                  Z   +180.0 degrees
      rotation 0.0 0.0 1.0 +3.14159
}
Cone {
}
```

Figure 6.2 *Rotating a cone +180.0 degrees.*

In the example, the rotation axis is `0.0 0.0 1.0`, creating an imaginary line that points straight out the Z axis. The rotation amount is 3.141 radians, or 180.0 degrees. In this example, the **Rotation** node turns the axes until the Y axis is pointing straight down; then the virtual pen draws a cone.

To turn the cone on its side, tip pointing left, use the same rotation axis with a smaller rotation amount. Instead of 180.0 degrees, rotate only 90.0 degrees, as shown in Figure 6.3.

```
#VRML V1.0 ascii

Rotation {
      #                   Z    +90.0 degrees
      rotation 0.0 0.0 1.0  +1.57079
}
Cone {
}
```

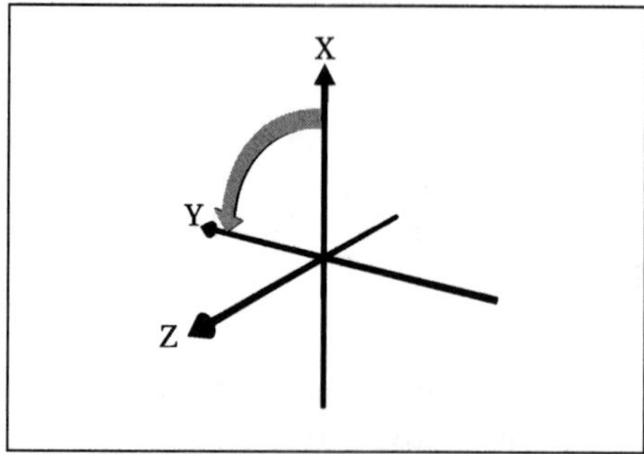

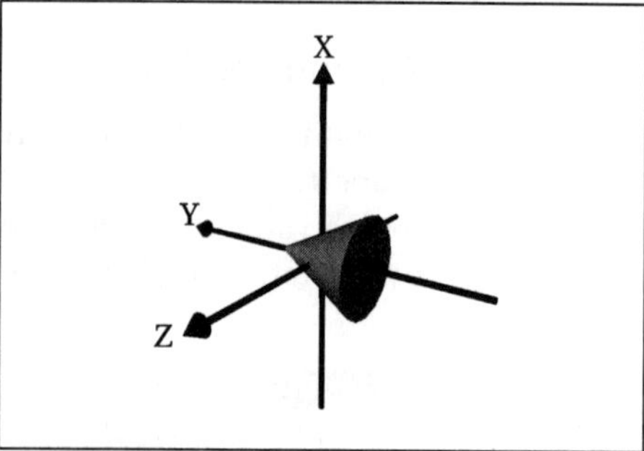

Figure 6.3 *Rotating a cone +90.0 degrees.*

To rotate the cone to point directly toward you, turn the virtual pen about a rotation axis that runs horizontally along the X axis, as shown in Figure 6.4.

```
#VRML V1.0 ascii

Rotation {
      #         X              +90.0 degrees
      rotation 1.0 0.0 0.0  +1.57079
}
Cone {
}
```

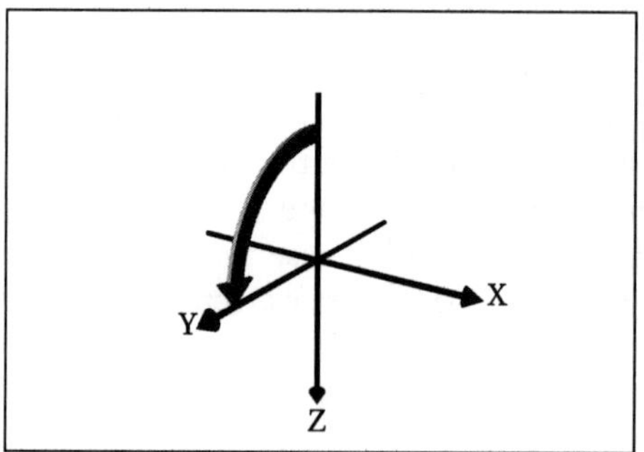

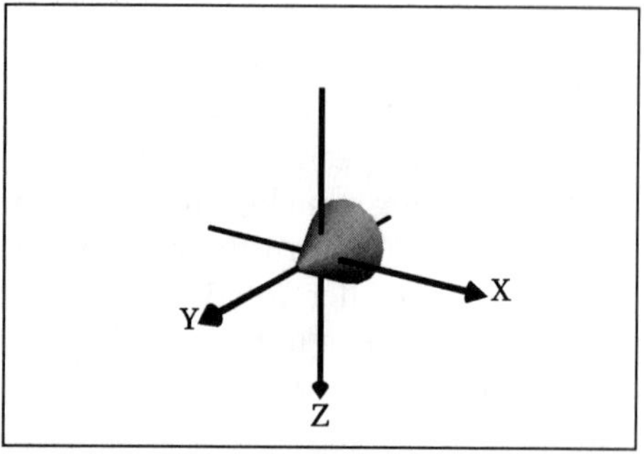

Figure 6.4 *Rotating a cone +90.0 degrees to point straight toward you.*

To rotate the cone by other angles or around other axes, experiment with different rotation amounts and axes.

Experimenting with Rotation

The following examples provide a more detailed examination of the ways in which the **Rotation** node can be used and how it interacts with nodes we've discussed in previous chapters.

Rotating Using Positive and Negative Rotation Amounts

All of the previous examples in this chapter illustrate positive rotation with the cone tip facing left along the X axis, down along the Y axis, or straight out the Z axis. To rotate the same cone to point to the right along the X axis or back along the Z axis, use negative rotation amounts.

The example in Figure 6.5 rotates the axes, and the virtual pen draws a cone that points to the right. The **rotation** field specifies a rotation amount of –90.0 degrees (–1.570 radians) about a rotation axis that lies along the Z axis.

```
#VRML V1.0 ascii

Rotation {
	#                 Z    -90.0 degrees
	rotation 0.0 0.0 1.0   -1.57079
}
Cone {
}
```

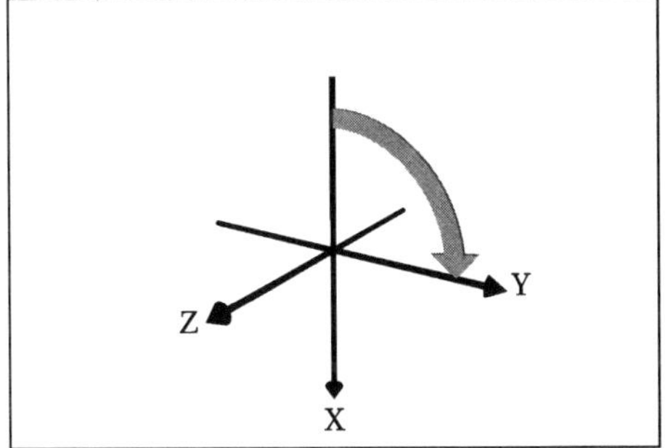

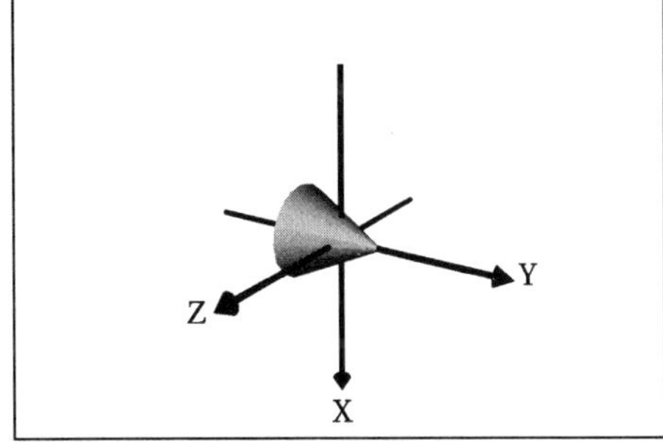

Figure 6.5 *Rotating a cone –90.0 degrees to point to the right.*

The example in Figure 6.6 rotates the axes, and the virtual pen draws a cone that points straight back. The **rotation** field specifies a rotation amount of –90.0 degrees (–1.570 radians) about a rotation axis that lies along the X axis.

```
#VRML V1.0 ascii

Rotation {
      #          X                    -90.0 degrees
      rotation 1.0 0.0 0.0   -1.57079
}
Cone {
}
```

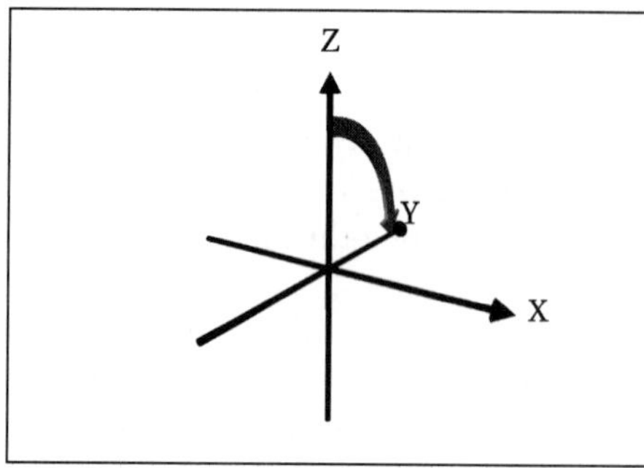

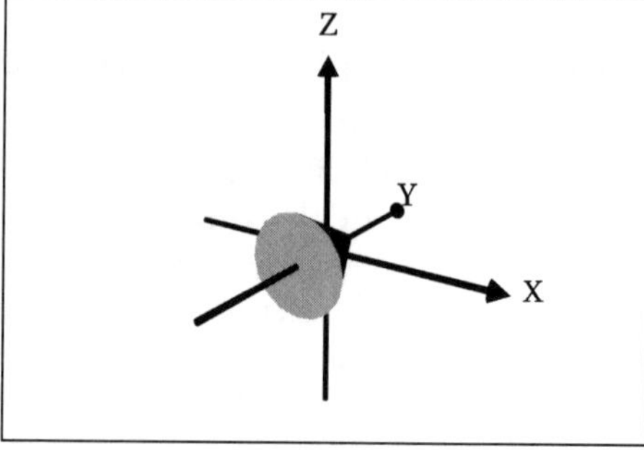

Figure 6.6 *Rotating a cone –90.0 degrees to point straight back.*

If you get confused trying to determine a positive rotation amount vs. a negative one, just remember the right-hand rule for rotation.

Right-hand rule for rotation: Determining positive and negative rotation amount in 3-D space

It is very easy to get confused about rotations and become unsure whether a positive or negative rotation amount turns shapes left or right, forward or back, up or down. The right-hand rule for rotation is a handy way to remember which way is which.

Imagine grabbing the rotation axis with your right hand, wrapping your fingers around the axis, and pointing your thumb in the positive direction of the axis as if you were hitchhiking. A *positive* rotation angle will rotate shapes around the axis in the same direction as the one in which your fingers are wrapped. A *negative* rotation angle will rotate shapes in the opposite direction. Figure 6.7 illustrates the right-hand rule around the X, Y, and Z axes.

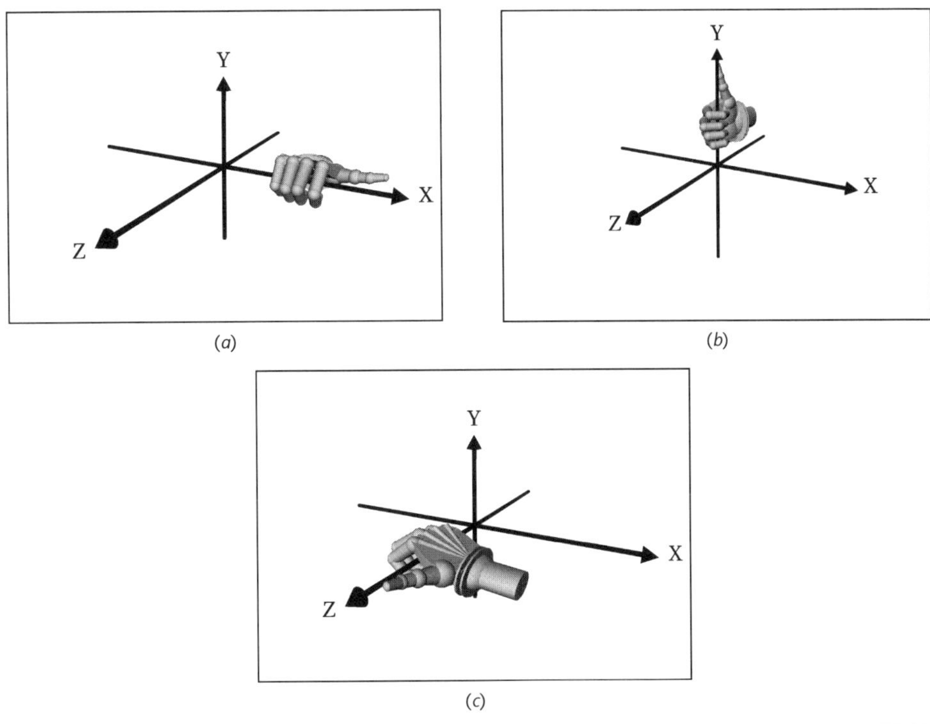

Figure 6.7 *The right-hand rule to determine a positive/negative rotation angle around (a) the X axis, (b) the Y axis, and (c) the Z axis.*

For example, if you define a rotation axis of `0.0 0.0 1.0` that points out the positive Z axis, and you want to know which way a positive rotation will turn a shape, grab the axis and point your thumb straight out in the positive Z direction as shown in Figure 6.7*c*. A positive rotation angle rotates around the axis in the same direction as you wrap the fingers of your right hand, and the axes tilt to the left. A negative rotation angle turns in the opposite direction and tilts the axes to the right.

If you define a rotation axis of `0.0 1.0 0.0` (pointing straight up the Y axis), grip the Y axis with your right hand and point your thumb upward, as if giving the thumbs-up sign. A positive rotation angle rotates around the axes in the same direction as that in which your fingers wrap. A negative angle rotates in the opposite direction.

Rotating a Shape around Different Axes

You can use the **Rotation** node to turn the axes any amount in any direction. Figures 6.8 through 6.13 show rotation of the axes in positive and negative amounts.

```
#VRML V1.0 ascii

Rotation {
      #          X                +45.0 degrees
      rotation 1.0 0.0 0.0  +0.78539
}
Cone {
}
```

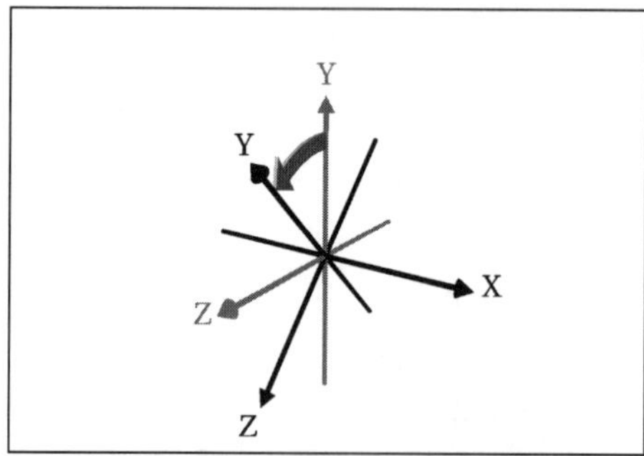

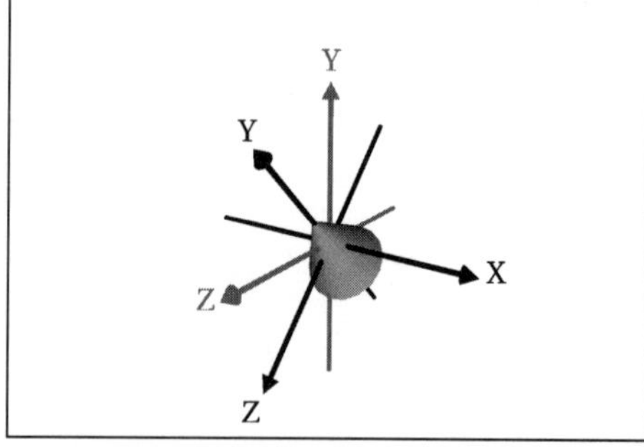

Figure 6.8 *Rotating +45.0 degrees about the X axis and drawing a cone.*

```
#VRML V1.0 ascii

Rotation {
      #          X                -45.0 degrees
      rotation 1.0 0.0 0.0  -0.78539
}
Cone {
}
```

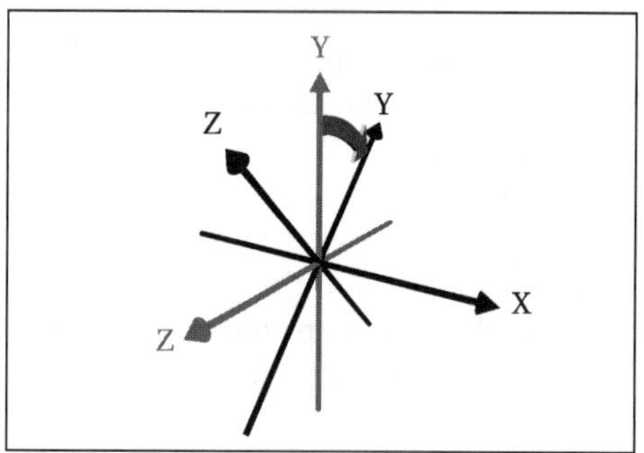

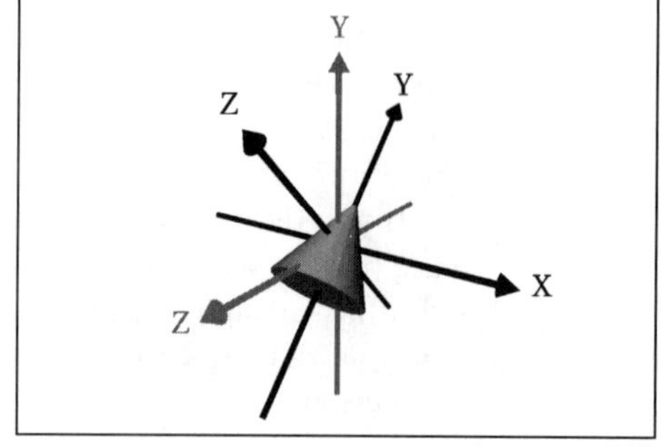

Figure 6.9 *Rotating –45.0 degrees about the X axis and drawing a cone.*

```
#VRML V1.0 ascii

Rotation {
      #              Y        +45.0 degrees
      rotation 0.0 1.0 0.0  +0.78539
}
Cone {
}
```

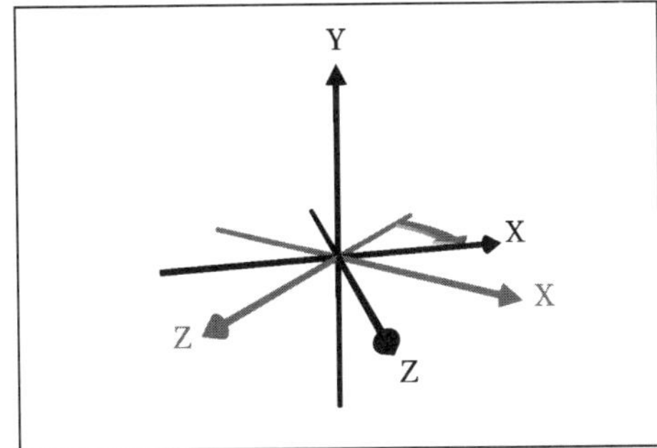

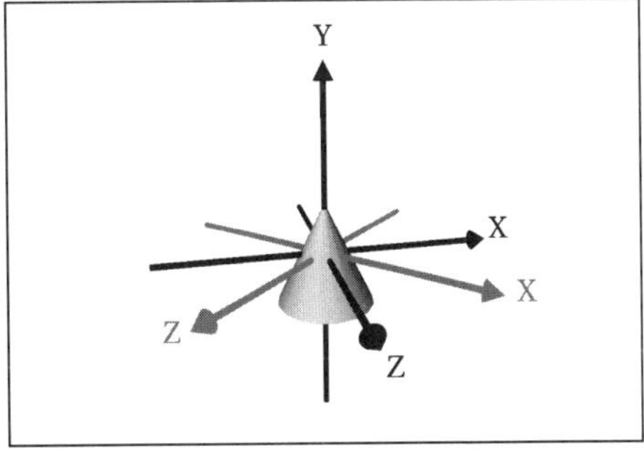

Figure 6.10 *Rotating +45.0 degrees about the Y axis and drawing a cone.*

```
#VRML V1.0 ascii

Rotation {
      #              Y        -45.0 degrees
      rotation 0.0 1.0 0.0  -0.78539
}
Cone {
}
```

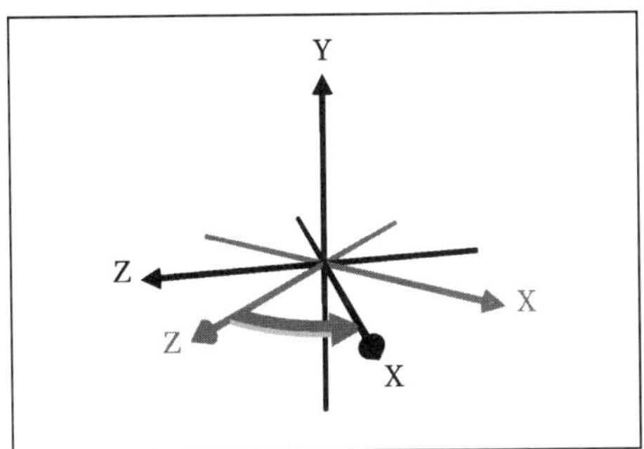

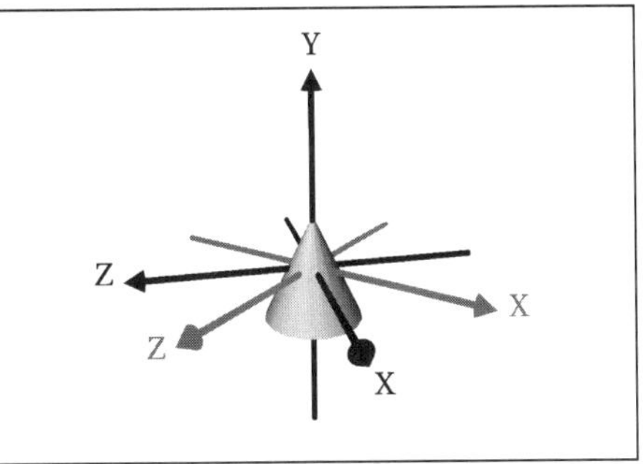

Figure 6.11 *Rotating –45.0 degrees about the Y axis and drawing a cone.*

```
#VRML V1.0 ascii

Rotation {
      #                  Z    +45.0 degrees
      rotation 0.0 0.0 1.0  +0.78539
}
Cone {
}
```

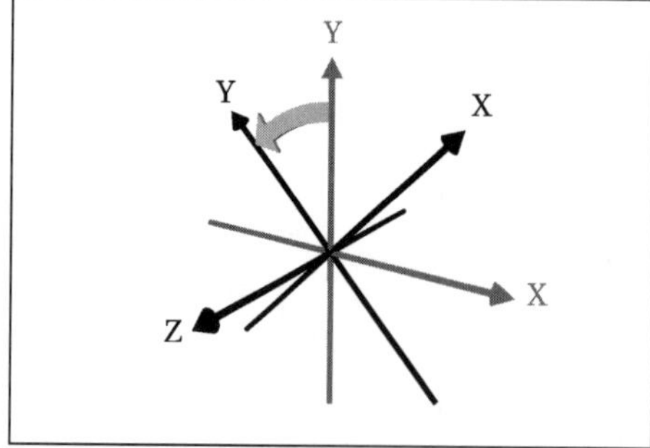

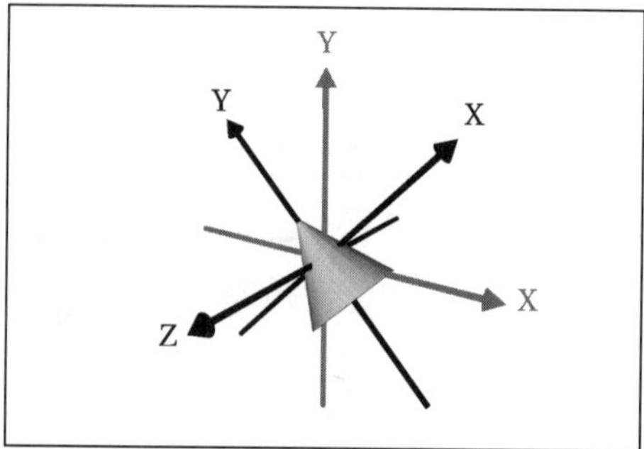

Figure 6.12 *Rotating +45.0 degrees about the Z axis and drawing a cone.*

```
#VRML V1.0 ascii

Rotation {
      #                  Z    -45.0 degrees
      rotation 0.0 0.0 1.0  -0.78539
}
Cone {
}
```

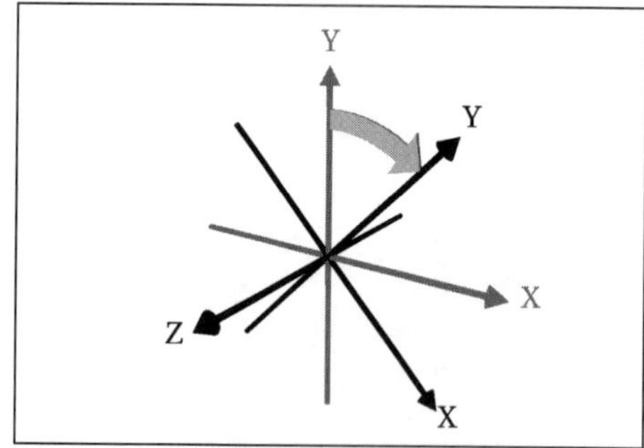

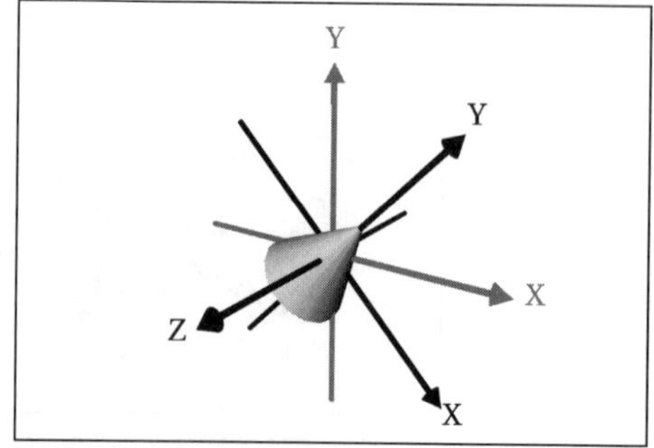

Figure 6.13 *Rotating −45.0 degrees about the Z axis and drawing a cone.*

Rotating and Drawing Multiple Shapes

You can draw shapes before or after you rotate the axes with a **Rotation** node. For instance, you can make a plus sign from **Cylinder** nodes, as shown in Figure 6.14.

```
#VRML V1.0 ascii

Cylinder {
      height 25.0
      radius 2.0
}
Rotation {
      #                   Z    +60.0 degrees
      rotation 0.0 0.0 1.0  1.0472
}
Cylinder {
      height 25.0
      radius 2.0
}
```

Figure 6.14 *A plus sign drawn with cylinders.*

Reading the file from top to bottom, the virtual pen is instructed to:

1. Draw a cylinder at the current origin position and with the current axes' orientation.

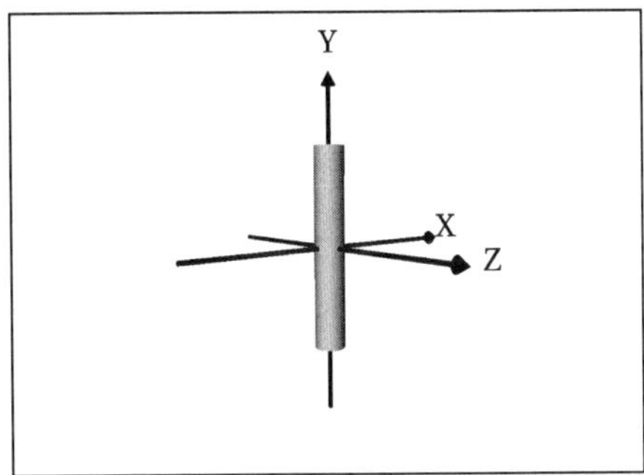

Figure 6.15 *Drawing a cylinder.*

2. Rotate +60.0 degrees about the Z axis.

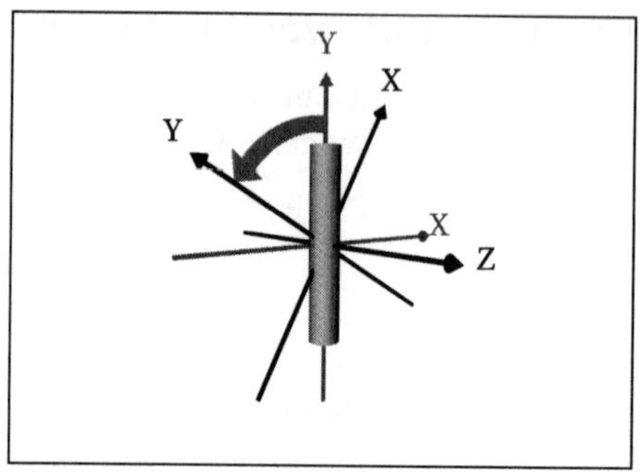

Figure 6.16 *Rotating the axes to prepare for drawing the next cylinder.*

3. Draw another cylinder at the current origin position and with the current axes' orientation.

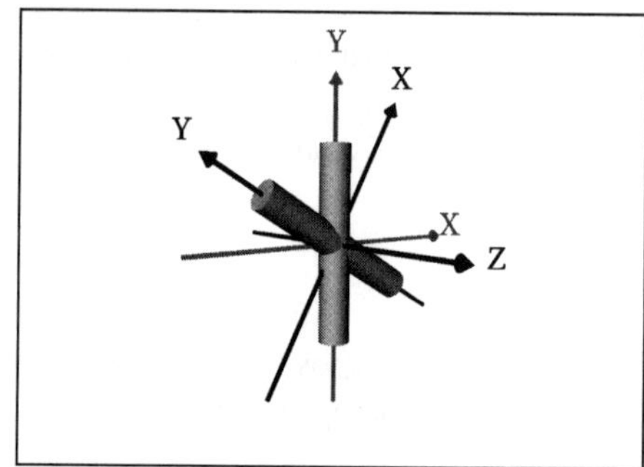

Figure 6.17 *Drawing another cylinder.*

Since the virtual pen and the axes are tilted to the left, the second cylinder is drawn tilted to the left.

Rotating More Than Once

You can rotate the axes more than once in a VRML file. Each time the VRML browser reads another **Rotation** node, it rotates the virtual pen *relative to* its current orientation.

For example, the plus sign of cylinders in Figure 6.14 can be extended to include a third cylinder pointing out from the middle of the shape with the highlighted text in the VRML file shown in Figure 6.18.

```
#VRML V1.0 ascii

Cylinder {
      height 25.0
      radius 2.0
}
Rotation {
      #                  Z    +60.0 degrees
      rotation 0.0 0.0 1.0  1.0472
}
Cylinder {
      height 25.0
      radius 2.0
}
Rotation {
      #                  Z    +60.0 degrees
      rotation 0.0 0.0 1.0  1.0472
}
Cylinder {
      height 25.0
      radius 2.0
}
```

Figure 6.18 *Adding another cylinder to the plus sign drawn with cylinders.*

Continue reading the file from top to bottom, beginning with the additional **Rotation** node. The virtual pen is instructed to:

4. Rotate +60.0 degrees about the X axis relative to the current axes' orientation, rotating *the entire orientation of the axes* an additional +60.0 degrees.

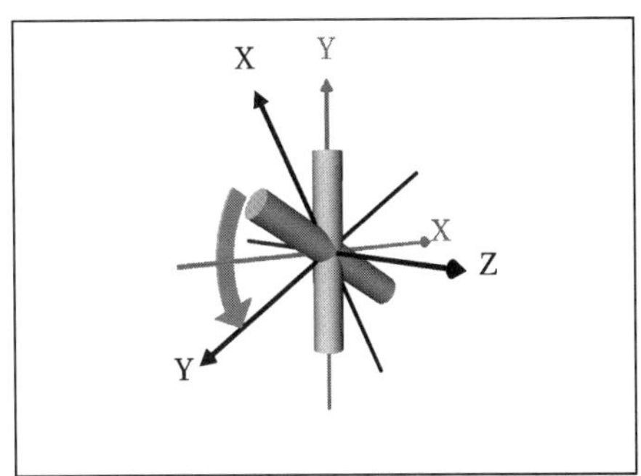

Figure 6.19 *Rotating the axes to prepare for drawing the next cylinder.*

5. Draw the third cylinder at the current origin position and with the current axes' orientation.

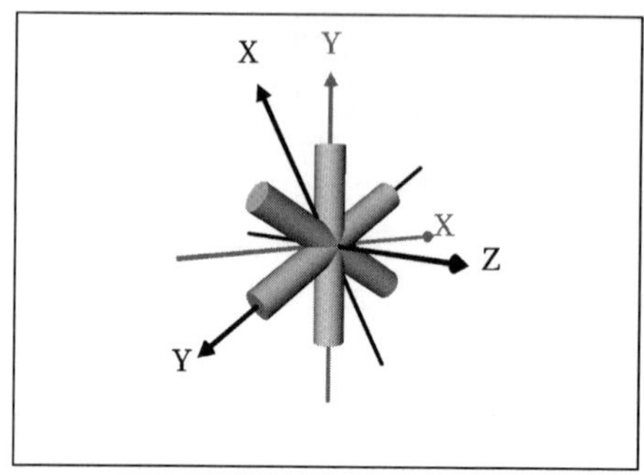

Figure 6.20 *Drawing the last cylinder.*

After drawing the second cylinder, the second **Rotation** node turns the virtual pen *relative to* its current orientation. Since the pen is tilted on its side, the X axis points straight up. An X axis rotation of `1.0 0.0 0.0` and a rotation amount of +90.0 degrees turns the pen to face out from the middle of the plus sign. When the last cylinder is drawn, it also points straight out from the middle of the plus sign.

Rotating and Translating Together

Rotation nodes can be used in combination with others, like **Translation** nodes. You can rotate the axes with a **Rotation** node, then position them with a **Translation** node. Each new node provides instructions for the virtual pen about how to change the orientation of the axes and how far away to position the origin before drawing something, like a cone or a cylinder. As we've mentioned before, *order is critical* to the resulting position and orientation of the shapes, and each translation and rotation is *relative to* the current origin position and axes orientation.

Translate, Rotate, Then Draw a Cylinder

The VRML text in Figure 6.21 positions the origin 3.0 units to the right, reorients the axes 30.0 degrees along the Z axis, then draws a cylinder.

```
#VRML V1.0 ascii

Translation {
      translation 3.0 0.0 0.0
}
Rotation {
      #                 Z    +30.0 degrees
      rotation 0.0 0.0 1.0  +0.52359
}
Cylinder {
}
```

Figure 6.21 *Translating, rotating, and drawing a cylinder.*

Reading the VRML file from top to bottom, the virtual pen is instructed to:

1. Translate 3.0 units along the X axis.

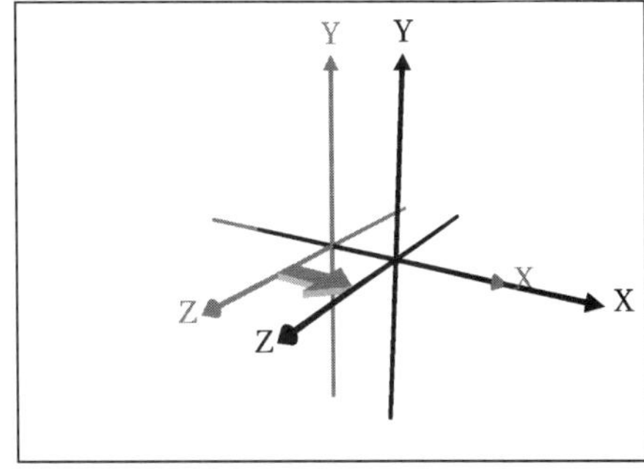

Figure 6.22 *Positioning 3.0 units to the right.*

2. Rotate +30.0 degrees about the Z axis.

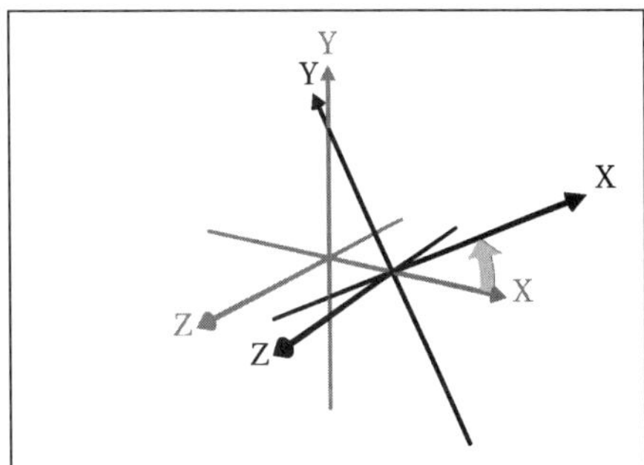

Figure 6.23 *Rotating +30.0 degrees about the Z axis.*

3. Draw a cylinder at the current origin position and with the current axes orientation.

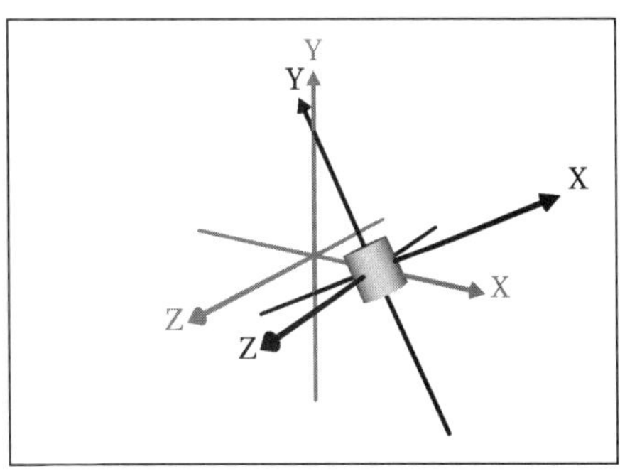

Figure 6.24 *Drawing a cylinder.*

Rotate, Translate, Then Draw a Cylinder

Consider the previous example but with the **Translation** and **Rotation** nodes swapped in order. In the new order, shown in Figure 6.25, the axes reorient *first, then* reposition to the right, then the pen draws the cylinder.

```
#VRML V1.0 ascii

Rotation {
      #                Z   +30.0 degrees
      rotation 0.0 0.0 1.0  0.52359
}
Translation {
      translation 3.0 0.0 0.0
}
Cylinder {
}
```

Figure 6.25 *Rotating, translating, and drawing a cylinder.*

Reading the VRML file from the top down, the virtual pen is instructed to:

1. Rotate +30.0 degrees about the Z axis.

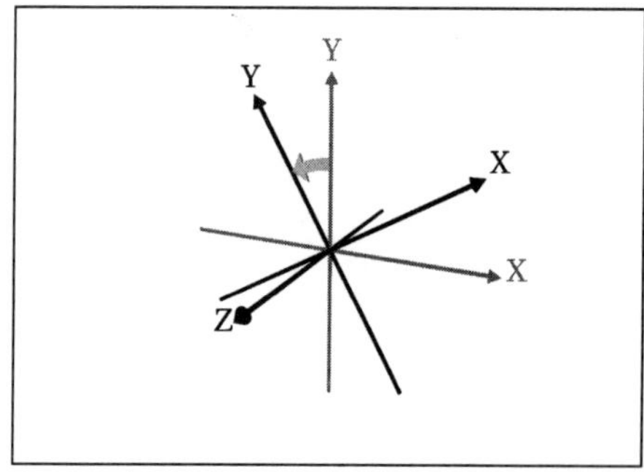

Figure 6.26 *Rotating +30.0 degrees about the Z axis.*

2. Translate 3.0 units along the X axis. Because the axes were rotated in step 1, the X axis now points upward and to the right. This translation occurs *relative to* the previous rotation.

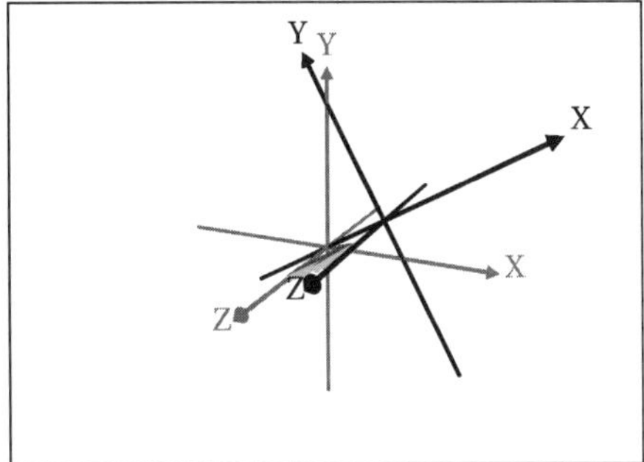

Figure 6.27 *Moving 3.0 units along the X axis.*

3. Draw a cylinder at the current origin position and with the current axes' orientation.

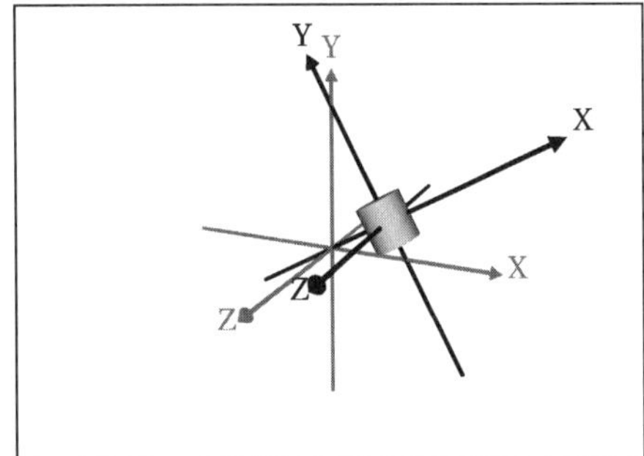

Figure 6.28 *Drawing a cylinder.*

The final location of the cylinder in this example is different from its final location in the last example. The order of the **Rotation** and **Translation** nodes made all the difference.

Extended Examples

The following examples build on the concepts we present in this chapter. They illustrate the worlds you can create by rotating, translating, and using only the VRML primitive and text shapes. Try them on your own.

TIP *All of the VRML text in the extended examples throughout this book are available via anonymous ftp from John Wiley & Sons at* `ftp.wiley.com/public/computer_books/vrml` *and from the VRML Repository at* `http://www.sdsc.edu/vrml`.

A Jet Turbine

The VRML text in Figure 6.29 constructs an interesting 3-D design that looks a bit like the fan blades of a jet turbine. The idea is simple: create a flattened cube, rotate a little, and repeat. Using the same two nodes, repeated over and over, you gradually build up a much more complicated shape.

The cube used in this example has a height of 0.6 units to create the turbine effect. Increasing the cube height changes the fan-blade size to create other interesting designs. Try these height values: 4.0, 7.0, and 10.0. You can also try changing the rotation axis and the rotation amount to create other interesting shapes.

TIP *We don't print all the nodes of the turbines in Figure 6.29. We include just enough nodes so that you get an idea of the structure of the file.*

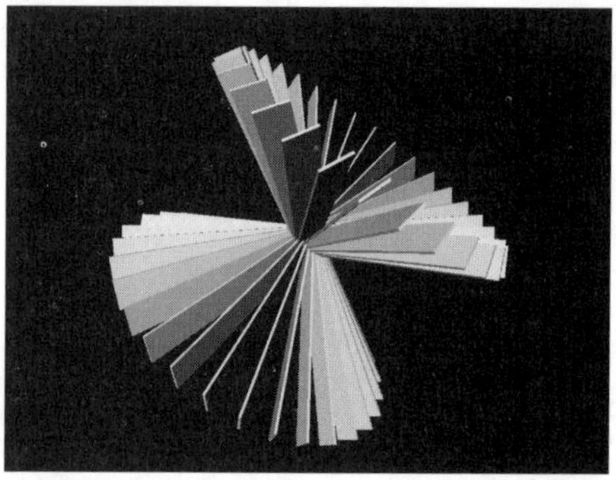

```
#VRML V1.0 ascii

# First blade
Cube {
      width 8.0
      height 0.6
      depth 0.05
}
Rotation {
      rotation 1.8 2.5 1.0 0.2
}

# Second blade - an exact copy
# of the first blade
Cube {
      width 8.0
      height 0.6
      depth 0.05
}
Rotation {
      rotation 1.8 2.5 1.0 0.2
}

# Third blade - an exact copy of the first blade
Cube {
      width 8.0
      height 0.6
      depth 0.05
}
Rotation {
      rotation 1.8 2.5 1.0 0.2
}

# and so on. . .
```

Figure 6.29 *A jet turbine.*

A Semi Truck and Trailer

The example VRML text in Figure 6.30 constructs a simple model of a semi truck and its trailer. You can extend this example to include an exhaust pipe, bumpers, wheel hubs, a spare tire under the trailer, and more.

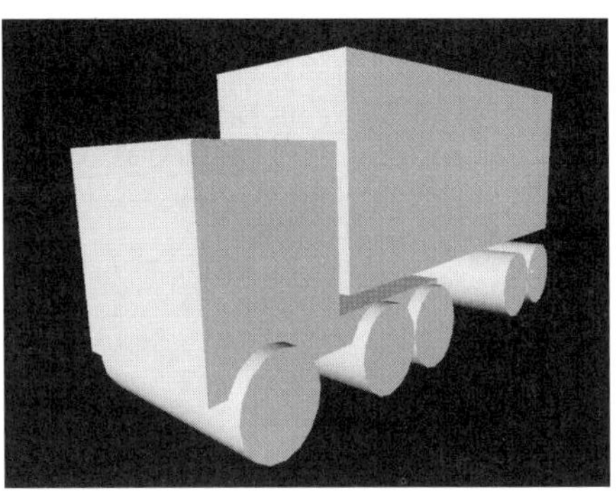

```
#VRML V1.0 ascii

# Truck cab
Cube {
      height 6.0
      width  5.0
      depth  6.0
}
# Truck trailer platform
Translation {
      translation 5.5 -2.5 0.0
}
Cube {
      height 1.0
      width  6.0
      depth  6.0
}
# Trailer hitch
Translation {
      translation 0.0 1.0 0.0
}
Cylinder {
      height 1.0
      radius 0.2
}
# Truck trailer
Translation {
      translation 6.5 3.5 0.0
}
Cube {
      height 7.0
      width 18.0
      depth 6.0
}
# Front wheels of cab
Translation {
      translation -12.5 -5.5 0.0
}
Rotation {
      #       X          +90.0 degrees
      rotation 1.0 0.0 0.0  1.57
}
Cylinder {
      height 7.0
      radius 1.5
}
```

Figure 6.30 continues

```
# Rear wheels under trailer hitch
Translation {
      translation 5.0 0.0 0.0
}
Cylinder {
      height 7.0
      radius 1.5
}
Translation {
      translation 3.0 0.0 0.0
}
Cylinder {
      height 7.0
      radius 1.5
}
# Rear wheels under trailer
Translation {
      translation 8.0 0.0 0.0
}
Cylinder {
      height 7.0
      radius 1.5
}
Translation {
      translation 3.0 0.0 0.0
}
Cylinder {
      height 7.0
      radius 1.5
}
```

Figure 6.30 *A semi truck and trailer.*

Summary

Rotation allows you to turn and tilt the VRML virtual pen to draw shapes with any orientation. All shapes are drawn *relative to* the orientation of the pen. As with translation, rotation occurs before the affected shape is drawn: The pen is rotated, then the shape is drawn.

The **Rotation** node specifies the rotation axis and rotation amount the pen is rotated with its **rotation** field. The rotation axis is an imaginary line, defined by the origin and a coordinate, about which the virtual pen and origin are rotated before a shape is drawn. The rotation amount is the number of radians the pen and origin are rotated. Commonly, rotation occurs around either the X, the Y, or the Z axis, but any rotation axis can be defined.

You can rotate using positive or negative rotation amounts, and the right-hand rule can be used to determine positive from negative rotation amounts. Using the right-hand rule, grab the rotation axis with your right hand, and wrap your fingers around it. Point your thumb in the positive direction of the axis. Positive rotation occurs in the direction in which your fingers are wrapped. Negative rotation occurs in the opposite direction.

You can rotate one shape or many, and you can rotate more than once within a VRML file. You can also combine rotation and translation to create different effects when orienting and positioning multiple shapes. Ordering of the **Rotation, Translation,** and shape nodes determines the resulting world.

CHAPTER 7

Scaling Shapes

Shapes can be any size in VRML. You can create shapes as large as planets in a solar system or as small as atoms in a molecule. You can create buildings, furniture, cars, yachts, and many other shapes in any size. Once you've created these shapes, you can change their size to put a bed on the yacht or shrink down the yacht to fit in a bathtub.

You can create your own library of cities, cars, trees, and furniture, all with different sizes. Then you can combine shapes to create new worlds, growing some shapes and shrinking others to make their sizes compatible. That way, even if you've created a car that's 1000.0 units long, you can shrink it down later to fit on a bookshelf only 3.0 units long.

In Chapters 5 and 6 we translated and rotated to change VRML's virtual pen's position and orientation properties. In this chapter, we'll use a **Scale** node to change the pen's scale property, changing its drawing size before drawing and the way it is translated and rotated before drawing.

Understanding Scaling

Playing with toy trains, model cars, or dollhouses are fun hobbies. Each of these involves carefully crafted, miniature models of much larger, real-life objects. A model car, for instance, is typically only one foot long, but the real car may be 20 feet long. The model car you play with is an exact replica of the real car, but it is shrunk, or scaled down, to be only one foot in size.

When something large, like a car, is scaled down to something small, like a model car, the size difference is called a **scale factor**. Similarly, when something small, like an ant, is scaled up to something large, like a monster, that size difference is also called a scale factor.

A scale factor is just a multiplication factor. For example, to create an object like a car at half its original size, use a scale factor of 0.5, and to create it at one-tenth its original size, use a scale factor of 0.1. Similarly, to create an object at twice its original size, use a scale factor of 2.0. To create it at ten times its original size, use a scale factor of 10.0.

Like translation and rotation, scale is a VRML property, and when the scale property is changed, that change affects subsequent shapes and properties. Scaling changes the drawing size of the VRML virtual pen and the size of the units within your VRML world, or space, so that subsequent shapes and properties are also scaled. For example, because scaling changes the size of the units within your VRML world, subsequent translation distances are larger or smaller depending on the scale factor.

Similarly, scaling is affected by previous changes. As with translations and rotations, scaling changes take place *relative to* the current origin position, the current axes orientation, and the current scale of your VRML units.

Changing the Size of a Shape Using Scale

Scaling enables you to combine two or more shapes together although they may be different sizes. For example, imagine you and a friend decide to create a virtual room using VRML. Your job is to create a table. Your friend's job is to create a chair. Figure 7.1 contains the VRML text of the table you might create.

```
#VRML V1.0 ascii

# Table base
Translation {
      translation 0.0 1.25 0.0
}
Cylinder {
      height 2.5
      radius 0.25
}
# Table top
Translation {
      translation 0.0 1.25 0.0
}
Cube {
      height 0.1
      width 5.0
      depth 7.0
}
Translation {
      translation 0.0 -2.5 0.0
}
```

Figure 7.1 *The table.*

Figure 7.2 shows the chair your friend might create.

```
#VRML V1.0 ascii

# Chair seat
Translation {
      translation 0.0 3.0 0.0
}
Cube {
      height 0.2
      width 3.2
      depth 4.0
}
# Chair front legs
Translation {
      translation -1.5 -1.5 0.0
}
Cube {
      height 3.0
      width 0.2
      depth 4.0
}
# Chair back legs and back
Translation {
      translation 3.0 2.5 0.0
}
Cube {
      height 8.0
      width 0.2
      depth 4.0
}
```

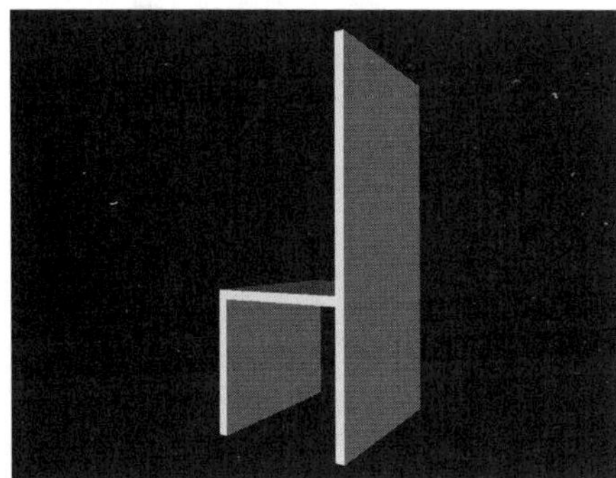

Figure 7.2 *The chair.*

When you are both finished, you put them together in the same VRML file and discover that your friend's chair is too big for your table. The table and chair are each fine. When combined, however, the chair is too big, as shown in Figure 7.3.

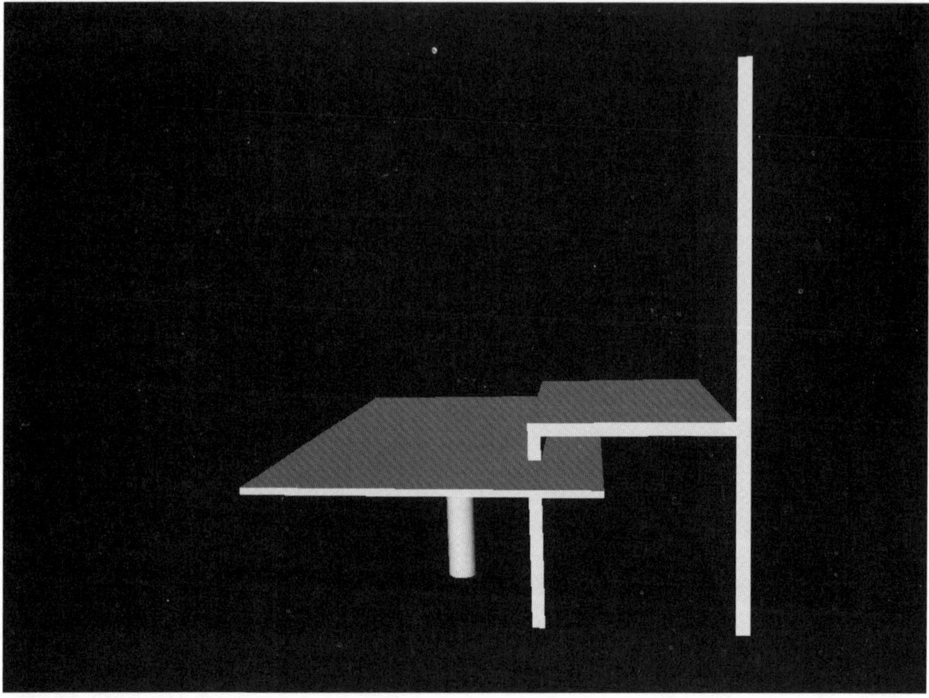

Figure 7.3 *The table and chair together.*

What should you do? You and your friend can fix this size problem by building the chair again from the beginning, this time at a smaller size. The chair in the preceding example would be easy to rebuild, but what if your friend's chair was very complex?

Starting over could take a lot of time. An easier way to solve this problem is to use a VRML **Scale** node to scale down the chair, as shown in Figure 7.4.

```
#VRML V1.0 ascii

######################
# Table base
Translation {
      translation 0.0 1.25 0.0
}
Cylinder {
      height 2.5
      radius 0.25
}
# Table top
Translation {
      translation 0.0 1.25 0.0
}
```

```
Cube {
      height 0.1
      width 5.0
      depth 7.0
}
Translation {
      translation 0.0 -2.5 0.0
}

# Move to where the chair should be placed
Translation {
      translation 3.0 0.0 0.0
}

# Scale down the chair to make it match the table
Scale {
      scaleFactor 0.5 0.5 0.5
}

######################
# Chair seat
Translation {
      translation 0.0 3.0 0.0
}
Cube {
      height 0.2
      width 3.2
      depth 4.0
}
# Chair front legs
Translation {
      translation -1.5 -1.5 0.0
}
Cube {
      height 3.0
      width 0.2
      depth 4.0
}
# Chair back legs and back
Translation {
      translation 3.0 2.5 0.0
}
Cube {
      height 8.0
      width 0.2
      depth 4.0
}
```

Figure 7.4 *The table and the scaled chair together.*

Notice how the **Scale** node is used in Figure 7.4. First, the browser reads the **Cylinder** and **Translation** nodes and draws your table. The next **Translation** node positions the virtual pen to the chair's location next to the table. The **Scale** node then scales down the units in your world and instructs the pen to draw all subsequent shapes smaller than normal.

As the VRML browser reads the nodes of your friend's chair, the virtual pen moves in the scaled down units and draws cubes that are shorter, thinner, and have less depth than normal. The result is your friend's entire chair is shrunk down to make its size compatible with your table, as shown in Figure 7.5.

Figure 7.5 *The table and the scaled chair together.*

Understanding the **Scale** Node Syntax

The **Scale** node has a single **scaleFactor** field with three floating-point values. This field specifies a scale factor for all of the VRML virtual pen's subsequent drawings. To enable you to scale the pen's drawing size in the X, Y, and Z directions individually, the **scaleFactor** field specifies three scale factor values: the first for scaling in the X direction, the second for scaling in the Y direction, and the third for scaling in the Z direction. Any of these values may be positive or negative.

SYNTAX **Scale node**

```
Scale {
    scaleFactor 1.0 1.0 1.0       # X, Y, Z scale factor
}
```

The X, Y, and Z values in the **scaleFactor** field are multiplication factors. For instance, to scale and draw a shape at twice its current size, use a scale factor of 2.0. To scale and draw a shape at half its current size, use a scale factor of 0.5. A scale factor of 1.0 leaves subsequent shapes and properties unchanged.

TIP *A scale factor of 0.0 instructs the virtual pen to draw shapes 0.0 times their original size. Since anything multiplied by 0.0 is always 0.0, scaling with a scale factor of 0.0 shrinks subsequent shapes down to nothing and makes them invisible.*

TIP *Negative scale factor values instruct the virtual pen to draw shapes turned inside out. Shapes drawn after scaling with negative scale factors may produce unexpected results.*

If you specify different scale factors for the X, Y, and Z values of the **scaleFactor** field, the virtual pen will stretch or compress shapes by different amounts horizontally, vertically, and from front to back. This warps the shape.

To increase or decrease a shape's size without warping it, specify the same scale factor for each of the **scaleFactor** field values. For example, in the table and chair example, the **Scale** node's **scaleFactor** field values are all the same. This scales down the entire chair to half its original size:

```
Scale {
    scaleFactor 0.5 0.5 0.5
}
```

The **Scale** node affects more than just the size of shapes drawn by the virtual pen. It also affects the *distance* the pen travels when later positioned by a **Translation** node. When you scale down the units of the VRML space, translation distances are scaled down by the same scale factor. Each unit in the VRML space is scaled by the **scaleFactor** field's values. Similarly, when you scale up the units in your VRML space, translations are scaled up as well.

For example, when you translate 3.0 units *before* scaling, the virtual pen repositions itself by 3.0 units and subsequent shapes are scaled and drawn 3.0 units in distance from the starting origin (represented by the gray axes in the diagrams in this book). If you translate 3.0 units *after* scaling by 0.5, the translation distance is scaled, so subsequent shapes are drawn at 3.0 × 0.5 = *1.5 units in distance* from the starting origin.

Each time the VRML browser reads a new **Scale** node, it increases or decreases the scale factor for virtual pen positioning, rotating, and drawing. If you include more than one **Scale** node in your VRML file, then the resulting growth or shrinkage specified in the second **Scale** node is *relative to* that specified in the first. A third **Scale** node scales relative to the second, and so on.

For example, a default cube is 2.0 units wide by 2.0 units high by 2.0 units deep. If you specify a scale factor of 3.0 before drawing a default cube, the cube is drawn scaled to three times its normal size to 6.0 units wide by 6.0 units high by 6.0 units deep.

If you scale up by 3.0 again, the cube is drawn scaled to three times its *current* size. It is now *six* times larger than the original cube. If you scale up the cube by 3.0 again, the cube is again scaled to three times its *current* size. It is now *nine* times larger than the original cube. Every scale change occurs *relative to* all the previous scale changes.

Experimenting with Scale

The following examples provide a more detailed examination of the ways in which the **Scale** node can be used and how it interacts with nodes we've discussed in previous chapters.

Scaling a Shape in Different Directions

The **Scale** node changes the proportions of the units in the VRML space, changing the proportions of the virtual pen's positioning and drawing size. You can use the same scale factors for the X, Y, and Z **scaleFactor** field values, or different scale factors for each. Using different values for X, Y, and Z warps subsequent shapes and can create interesting results.

Figures 7.6 through 7.11 show a sphere drawn after the scale property is changed. The units of the VRML space are scaled up and scaled down in first the X, then the Y, and finally the Z direction.

Each figure showing X-direction scaling specifies Y and Z **scaleFactor** field values of 1.0. Each figure showing Y-direction scaling specifies X and Z values of 1.0. Each Z-direction scaling example specifies X and Y values of 1.0. Using a scale factor of 1.0 in two directions allows you to scale up or down in only one direction at a time.

```
#VRML V1.0 ascii

Scale {
        scaleFactor 2.0 1.0 1.0
}
Sphere {
}
```

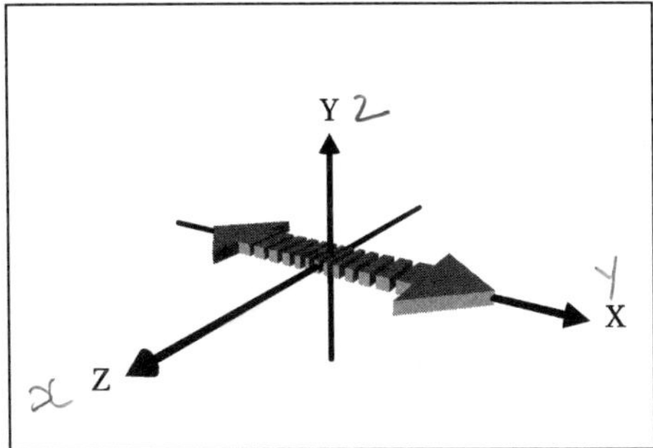

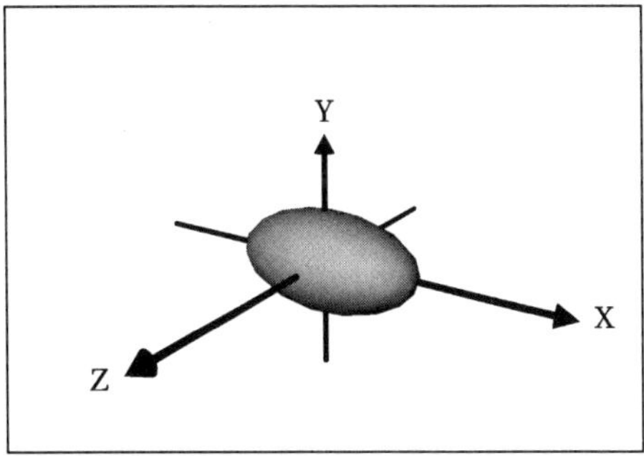

Figure 7.6 *Doubling scale in the X direction and drawing a sphere.*

```
#VRML V1.0 ascii

Scale {
        scaleFactor 0.5 1.0 1.0
}
Sphere {
}
```

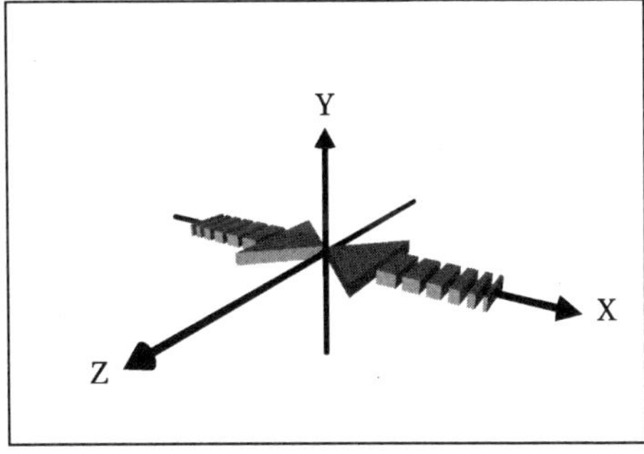

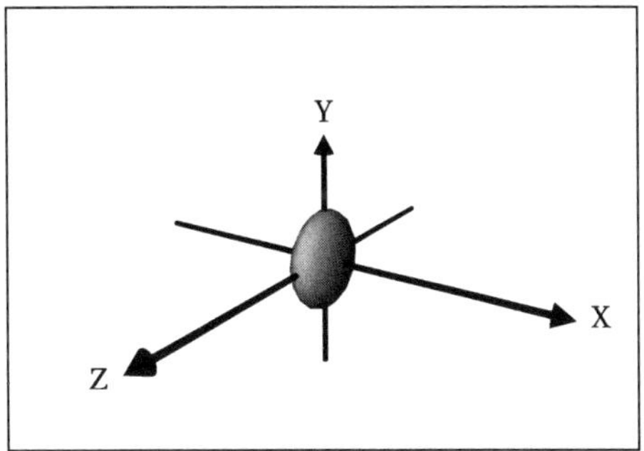

Figure 7.7 *Halving scale in the X direction and drawing a sphere.*

```
#VRML V1.0 ascii

Scale {
      scaleFactor 1.0 2.0 1.0
}
Sphere {
}
```

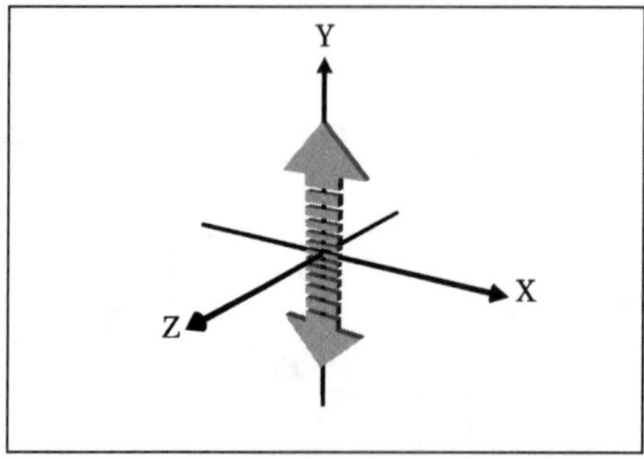

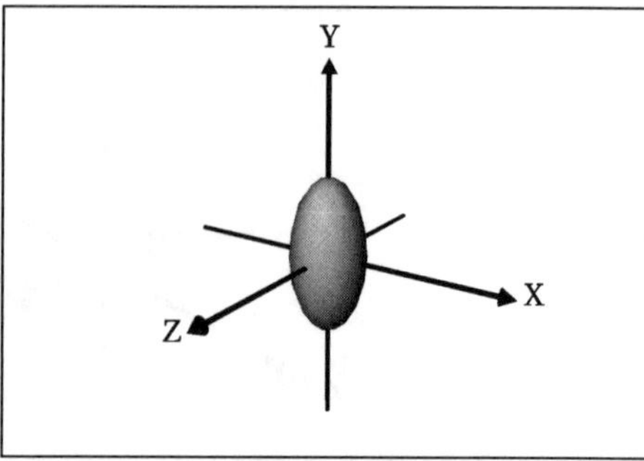

Figure 7.8 *Doubling scale in the Y direction and drawing a sphere.*

```
#VRML V1.0 ascii

Scale {
      scaleFactor 1.0 0.5 1.0
}
Sphere {
}
```

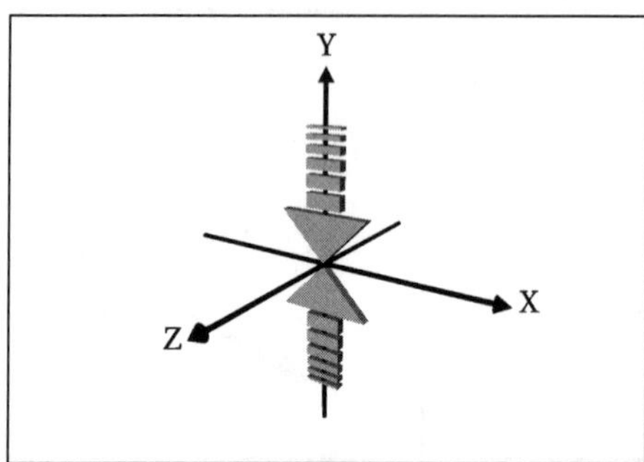

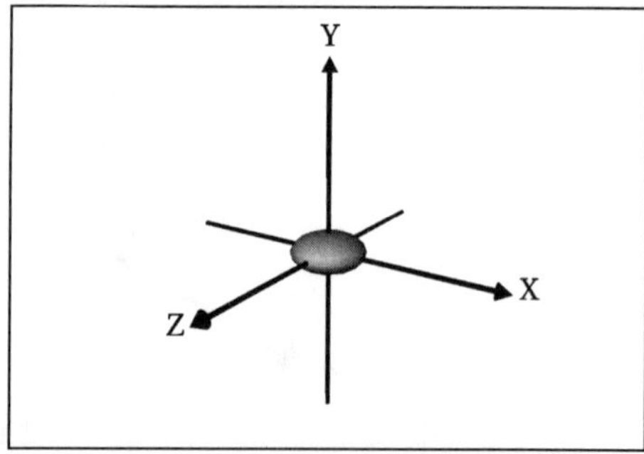

Figure 7.9 *Halving scale in the Y direction and drawing a sphere.*

```
#VRML V1.0 ascii

Scale {
      scaleFactor 1.0 1.0 2.0
}
Sphere {
}
```

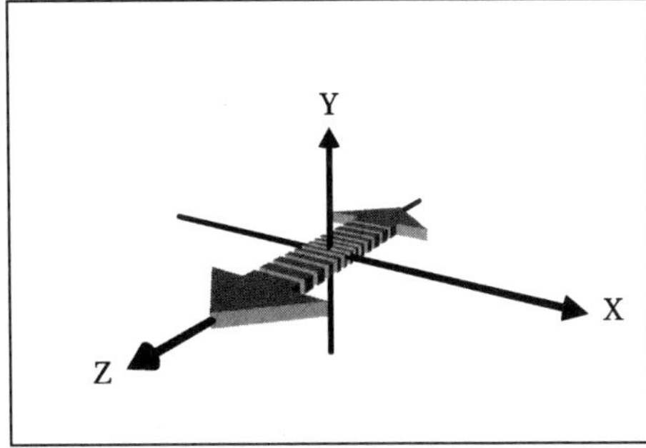

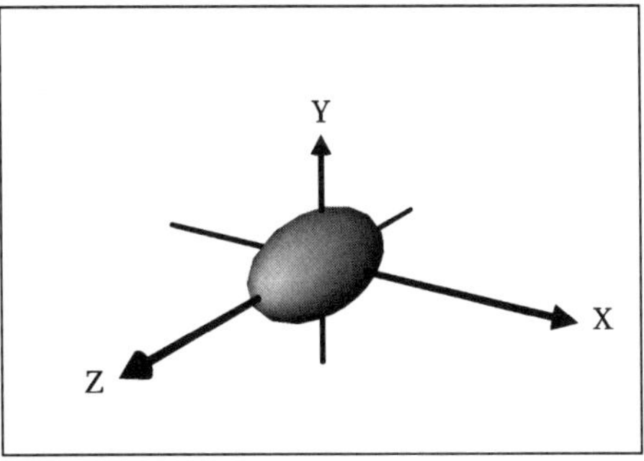

Figure 7.10 *Doubling scale in the Z direction and drawing a sphere.*

```
#VRML V1.0 ascii

Scale {
      scaleFactor 1.0 1.0 0.5
}
Sphere {
}
```

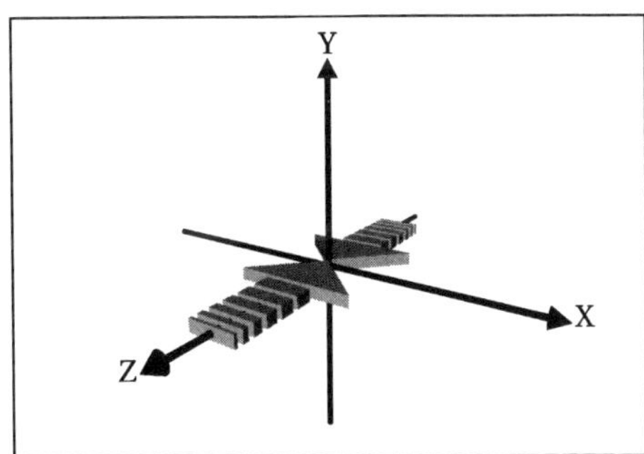

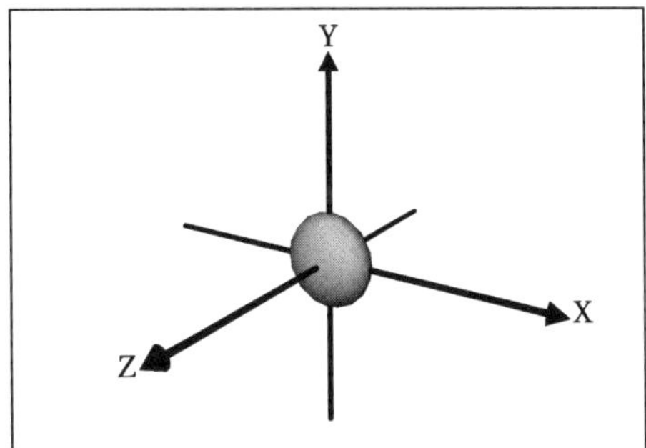

Figure 7.11 *Halving scale in the Z direction and drawing a sphere.*

You can scale and then draw other shapes, as well. For example, a cylinder drawn after scale is doubled in the X direction looks like the cylinder shown in Figure 7.12.

```
#VRML V1.0 ascii

Scale {
      scaleFactor 2.0 1.0 1.0
}
Cylinder {
}
```

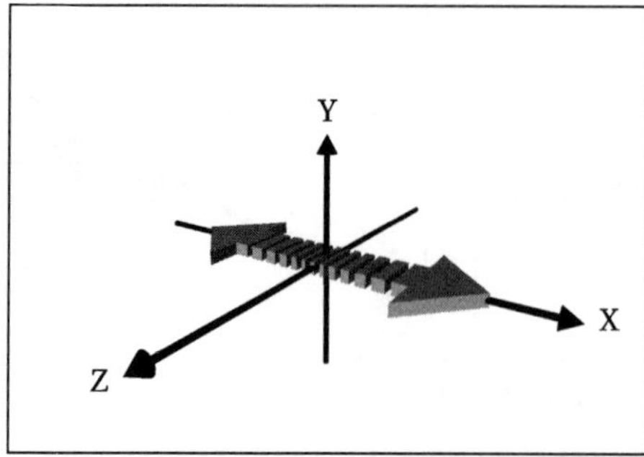

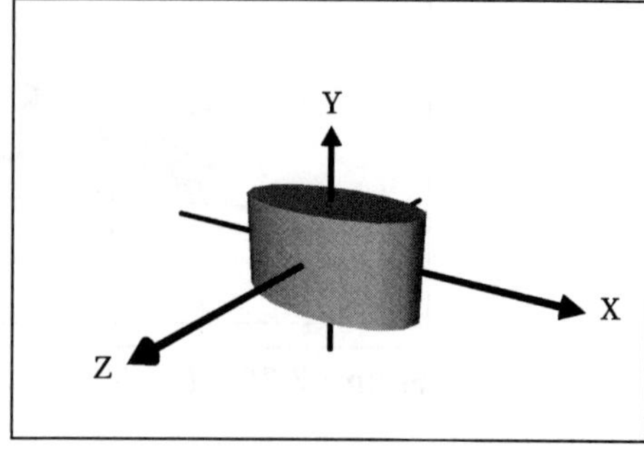

Figure 7.12 *Doubling scale in the X direction and drawing a cylinder.*

A cone drawn after scale is doubled in the X direction looks like the cone shown in Figure 7.13.

```
#VRML V1.0 ascii

Scale {
      scaleFactor 2.0 1.0 1.0
}
Cone {
}
```

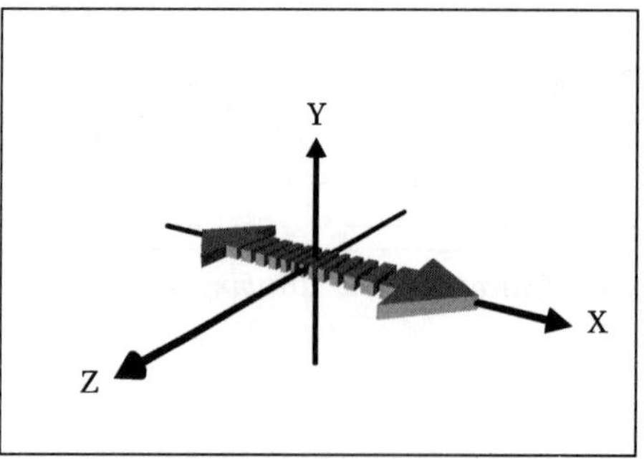

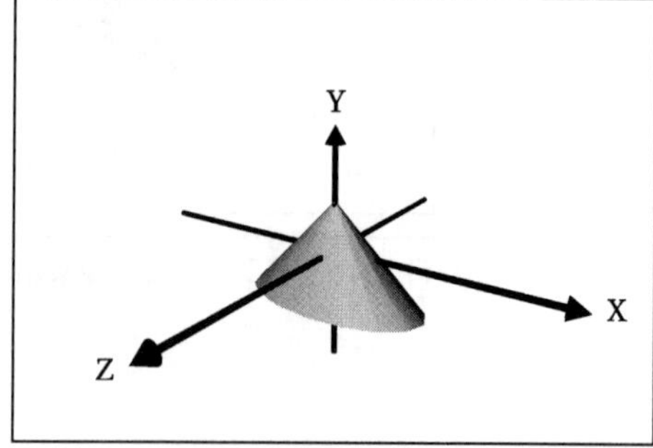

Figure 7.13 *Doubling scale in the X direction and drawing a cone.*

TIP *Scaling in X, Y, or Z and then drawing a cube has the same effect as changing the* ***height, width,*** *or* ***depth*** *fields within the* ***Cube*** *node. Similarly, scaling in the Y direction and then drawing a cylinder or a cone has the same effect as changing the* ***height*** *field in the* ***Cylinder*** *or* ***Cone*** *node. If you want to scale only a single shape, it is more efficient to change the field values within the shape's node than to scale it. The browser will draw your shapes faster if you change field values rather than scale one shape. Scaling is best for changing the size of complex shapes, such as the chair at the beginning of this chapter.*

Figures 7.6 through 7.13 show scaling in only one direction. You can also scale in two or all three directions at once. When you scale in more than one direction, the three **scaleFactor** field values may be the same or different. In this example, the virtual pen is instructed to scale up by 2.0 in the X direction, scale down by 0.5 in the Y direction, scale up by 4.0 in the Z direction, and draw a cylinder.

```
#VRML V1.0 ascii

Scale {
      scaleFactor 2.0 0.5 4.0
}
Cylinder {
}
```

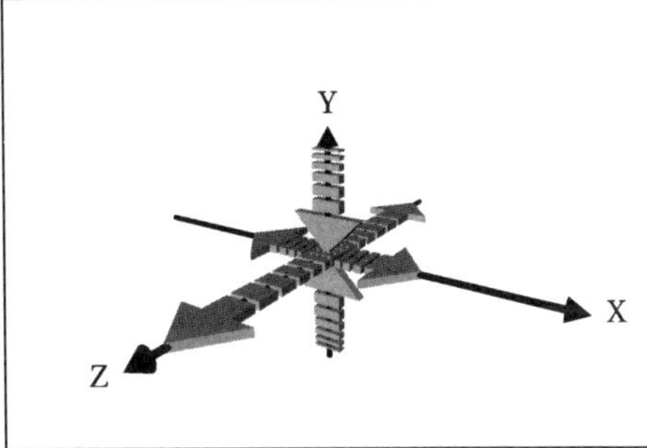

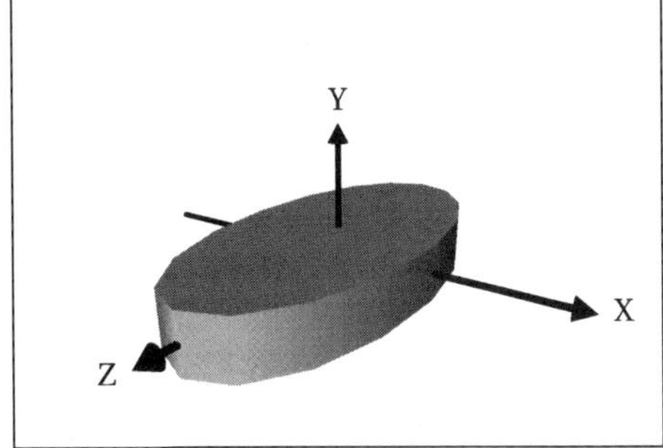

Figure 7.14 *Scaling up by 2.0 in the X direction, scaling down by 0.5 in the Y direction, scaling up by 4.0 in the Z direction, and drawing a cylinder.*

Scaling More Than Once

You can scale the virtual pen more than once in a VRML file. Each time the browser reads another **Scale** node, it increases or decreases the size of the units in your VRML space *relative to* the current size.

By scaling more than once, you can use the chair shape from the beginning of this chapter to build three different-sized chairs: a large chair, a medium chair, and a small chair, as shown in Figure 7.15.

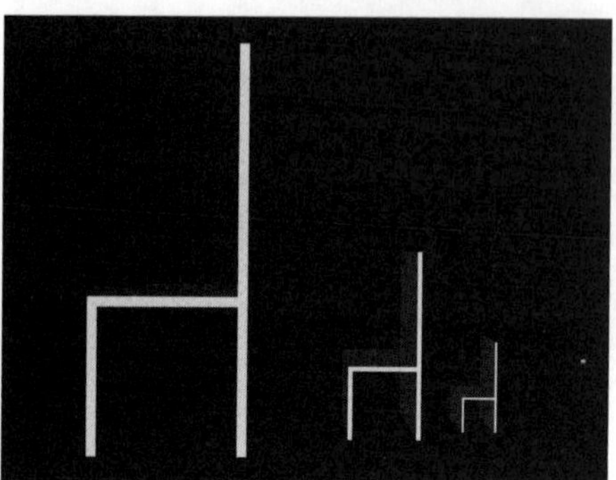

```
#VRML V1.0 ascii

# BIG CHAIR
# Chair seat
Cube {
      height 0.2
      width 3.2
      depth 4.0
}
# Chair front legs
Translation {
      translation -1.5 -1.5 0.0
}
Cube {
      height 3.0
      width 0.2
      depth 4.0
}
# Chair back legs and back
Translation {
      translation 3.0 2.5 0.0
}
Cube {
      height 8.0
      width 0.2
      depth 4.0
}
# Move to the base of the chair
Translation {
      translation 0.0 -2.5 0.0
}
# Move to the right and draw shapes smaller
Translation {
      translation 3.0 0.0 0.0
}
Scale {
      scaleFactor 0.5 0.5 0.5
}
# MEDIUM CHAIR
# Chair seat
Cube {
      height 0.2
      width 3.2
      depth 4.0
}
# Chair front legs
Translation {
      translation -1.5 -1.5 0.0
}
Cube {
      height 3.0
      width 0.2
      depth 4.0
}
```

Figure 7.15 continues

```
# Chair back legs and back
Translation {
      translation 3.0 2.5 0.0
}
Cube {
      height 8.0
      width 0.2
      depth 4.0
}
# Move to the base of the chair
Translation {
      translation 0.0 -2.5 0.0
}
# Move to the right and draw shapes smaller
Translation {
      translation 3.0 0.0 0.0
}
Scale {
      scaleFactor 0.5 0.5 0.5
}
# SMALL CHAIR
# Chair seat
Cube {
      height 0.2
      width 3.2
      depth 4.0
}
# Chair front legs
Translation {
      translation -1.5 -1.5 0.0
}
Cube {
      height 3.0
      width 0.2
      depth 4.0
}
# Chair back legs and back
Translation {
      translation 3.0 2.5 0.0
}
Cube {
      height 8.0
      width 0.2
      depth 4.0
}
```

Figure 7.15 *Scaling multiple times in one VRML file to produce a large chair, a medium chair, and a small chair.*

The first five nodes of the VRML text draw the chair in Figure 7.2. Following the nodes that draw the first chair, a **Translation** node translates the origin +3.0 units in the X direction, and a **Scale** node scales down the units of the VRML space by a factor of 0.5.

The original chair text follows the **Scale** node. Because the units of the VRML drawing space are scaled down, the drawing size of the virtual pen is also scaled down, and the chair is drawn at half the original size. This creates the medium-sized chair.

Following the VRML text creating the medium-sized chair, another **Translation** node translates the origin 3.0 more units in the positive X direction. Notice that the pen is positioned only *half* the distance of the last translation, however, because the **Scale** node scaled down the units of the VRML space by a factor of 0.5, and all translating occurs *relative to* the current scale.

A second **Scale** node scales down the drawing space *again* by a factor of 0.5. When the third chair is drawn, it is drawn at *half* the current drawing size, or *one-quarter* of the original drawing size.

The original drawing size is 1.0 (without scaling), and the first **Scale** node causes the pen to draw at one-half that size: $1.0 \times 0.5 = 0.5$ times the original drawing size. The drawing size after the first **Scale** node is 0.5, and the second **Scale** node causes the pen to draw at one-half *that* size: $0.5 \times 0.25 = 0.25$ times the original drawing size.

Using multiple **Scale** nodes, you can combine multiple shapes to fit together into one world at exactly the sizes you wish. You can scale down some and scale up others, and you can scale up and down within the same VRML file.

Scaling and Translating Together

Scale nodes can be used in combination with other nodes, like **Translation** nodes. You can put **Translation** nodes before or after **Scale** nodes. However, the order you choose can make a big difference in how the virtual pen draws your world. For instance, the VRML text in Figures 7.16 and 7.20 both draw a cube. The first example translates, then scales. The second example scales, then translates. As you read the examples, notice how the ordering of the nodes changes the image the virtual pen draws.

Translate, Scale, Then Draw a Cube

The example text in Figure 7.16 illustrates translating the origin 3.0 units to the right, then scaling up the pen's drawing size by a factor of 1.5, and finally drawing a cube.

```
#VRML V1.0 ascii

Translation {
      translation 3.0 0.0 0.0
}
Scale {
      scaleFactor 1.5 1.5 1.5
}
Cube {
}
```

Figure 7.16 *Translating, scaling, then drawing a cube.*

Reading the VRML file from top to bottom, the virtual pen is instructed to:

1. Translate 3.0 units along the X axis.

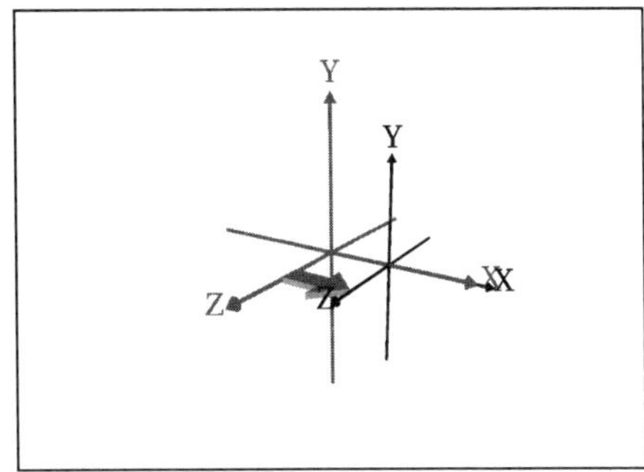

Figure 7.17 *Repositioning 3.0 units to the right.*

2. Scale by a factor of 1.5 in X, Y, and Z.

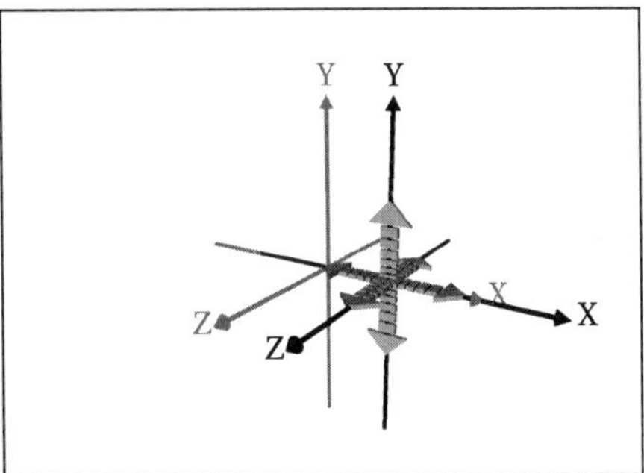

Figure 7.18 *Scaling to 1.5 times the current scale.*

3. Draw a default cube at the current origin, with the current axes' orientation, and at the current scale.

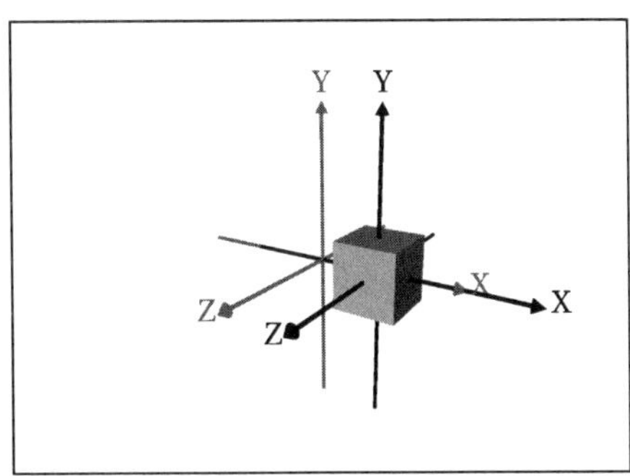

Figure 7.19 *Drawing a cube.*

With the **Cube** node, you specified a 2.0-unit-sized cube. The cube is drawn as a *3.0-unit-sized cube*, however, because the units of the VRML space are scaled with the **Scale** node to 1.5 times their normal size before the cube is drawn.

Scale, Translate, Then Draw a Cube

Consider the previous example but with the **Translation** and **Scale** nodes reversed in order. In the new order shown in Figure 7.20, the **Scale** node changes the virtual pen's drawing size *first*, then the **Translation** node translates to the right, and the pen draws the cube.

```
#VRML V1.0 ascii

Scale {
      scaleFactor 1.5 1.5 1.5
}
Translation {
      translation 3.0 0.0 0.0
}
Cube {
}
```

Figure 7.20 *Scaling, translating, then drawing a cube.*

Reading the VRML file from top to bottom, the virtual pen is instructed to:

1. Scale by a factor of 1.5 in X, Y, and Z.

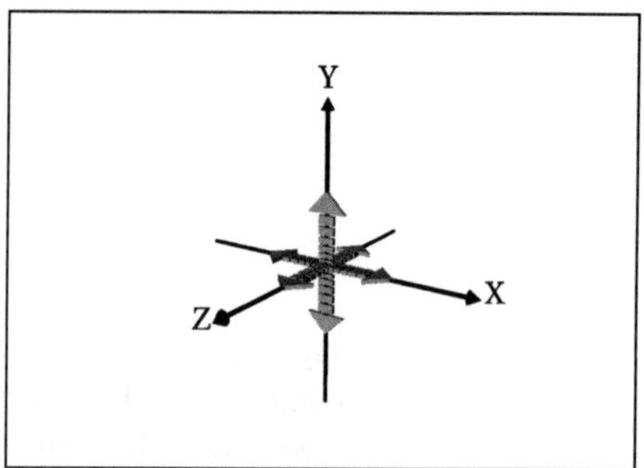

Figure 7.21 *Scaling to 1.5 times the current scale.*

2. Translate 3.0 units along the X axis.

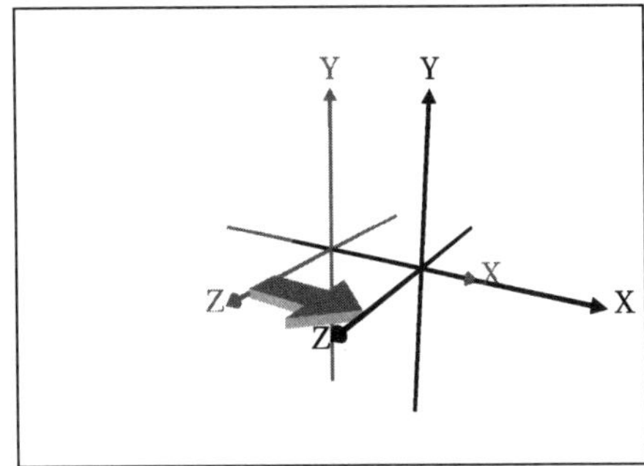

Figure 7.22 *Translating to the right.*

3. Draw a default cube at the current origin position, with the current axes' orientation, and at the current scale.

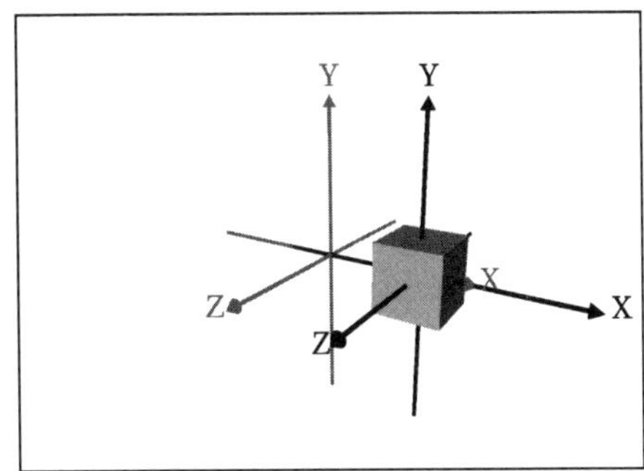

Figure 7.23 *Drawing a cube.*

With the **Cube** node, you specified a 2.0-unit-sized cube. However because the units of the VRML space are scaled with the **Scale** node to 1.5 times their normal size, the cube is drawn as a *3.0-unit-sized cube.* This is the same as the resulting cube shown in Figure 7.19, but there is a difference between the cubes' *positions* in the two examples.

The *order* of the **Translation** and **Scale** nodes affects where the cube is drawn in Figure 7.23 compared to where it is drawn in Figure 7.19. In both examples, you specify that the center of the cube be drawn 3.0 units in distance from the starting origin (shown with the gray axes), and in Figure 7.19 the cube is drawn as you specified. In Figure 7.23, however, the cube is drawn with its center *4.5 units* in distance from the starting origin. The shape is moved by the *scaled* translation distance farther away from the starting origin than you specified. By scaling *before* translating, the translation *distance* is scaled as well as the size of the cube.

Using Scale and Rotation Together

Scale nodes can be used together with **Rotation** nodes. You can put **Rotation** nodes before or after **Scale** nodes. Just like ordering **Translation** and **Scale** nodes, the order of **Rotation** and **Scale** nodes can also make a big difference in the appearance of your world.

For instance, the following two examples both draw a stretched cylinder. The first example rotates, then scales, and the second example scales, then rotates. As you read these examples, notice again how the order of nodes changes the image drawn by the virtual pen.

Rotate, Scale, Then Draw a Cylinder

In the example in Figure 7.24, you rotate around the Z axis by +90.0 degrees. Next, you scale the VRML units by 1.5 in the Y direction and in 1.0 in the X and Z directions. Finally, you draw a cylinder.

```
#VRML V1.0 ascii

Rotation {
	#                 Z    +90.0 degrees
	rotation 0.0 0.0 1.0   1.57
}
Scale {
	scaleFactor 1.0 1.5 1.0
}
Cylinder {
}
```

Figure 7.24 *Rotating, scaling, then drawing a cylinder.*

Reading the VRML file from top to bottom, the virtual pen is instructed to:

1. Rotate +90.0 degrees about the Z axis.

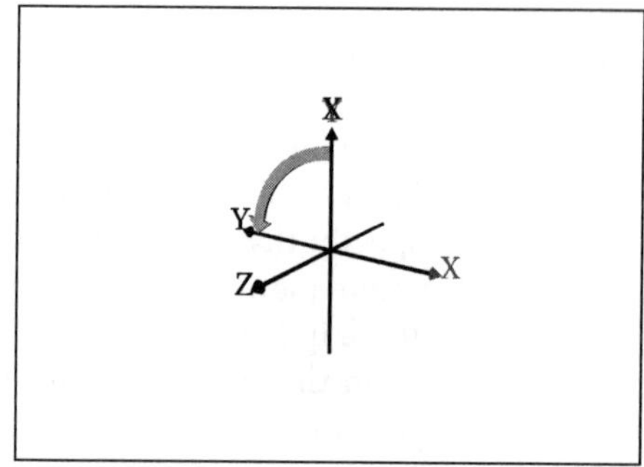

Figure 7.25 *Rotating to the left.*

2. Scale by a factor of 1.5 in the Y direction.

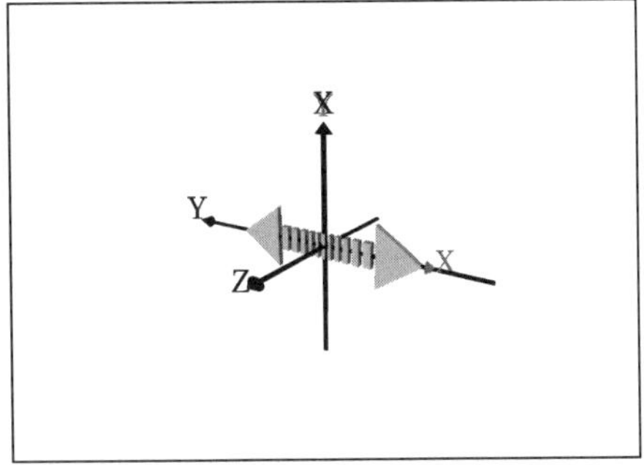

Figure 7.26 *Scaling by 1.5 times the current scale.*

3. Draw a cylinder at the current origin position, with the current axes' orientation, and at the current scale.

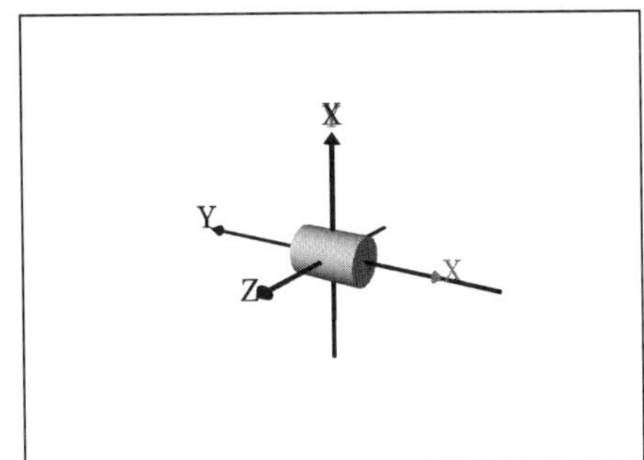

Figure 7.27 *Drawing a cylinder.*

With the **Cylinder** node, you specified a 2.0-unit-high cylinder with a 1.0-unit radius. However, because the units of the VRML space are scaled with the **Scale** node to 1.5 times their normal size, the cube is drawn as a *3.0-unit-sized cube.*

Scale, Rotate, Then Draw a Cube

Consider the previous example but with the **Rotation** and **Scale** nodes reversed in order. In the new order, shown in Figure 7.28, the **Scale** node changes the virtual pen's drawing size *first,* then the **Rotation** node rotates the axes and the pen, and the pen draws the cylinder.

```
#VRML V1.0 ascii

Scale {
      scaleFactor 1.0 1.5 1.0
}
Rotation {
      #                    Z    +90.0 degrees
      rotation 0.0 0.0 1.0  1.57
}
Cylinder {
}
```

Figure 7.28 *Scaling, rotating, then drawing a cylinder.*

Reading the VRML file from top to bottom, the virtual pen is instructed to:

1. Scale by a factor of 1.5 in the Y direction.

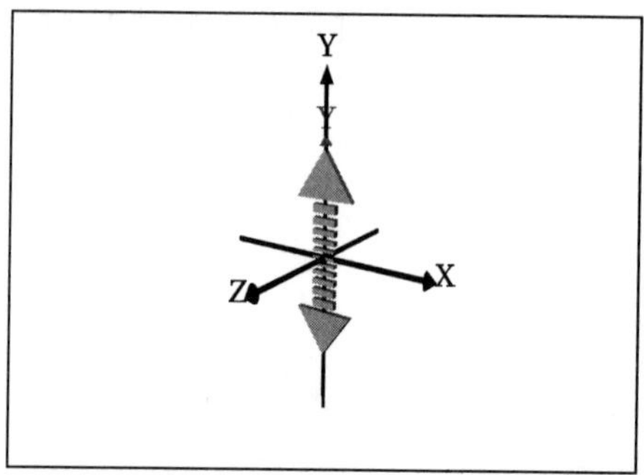

Figure 7.29 *Scaling by 1.5 times the current scale.*

2. Rotate +90.0 degrees about the Z axis.

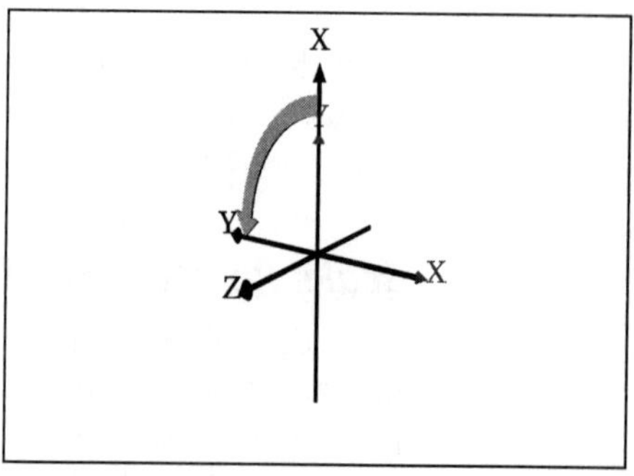

Figure 7.30 *Rotating to the left.*

3. Draw a cylinder at the current origin position, with the current axes' orientation, and at the current scale.

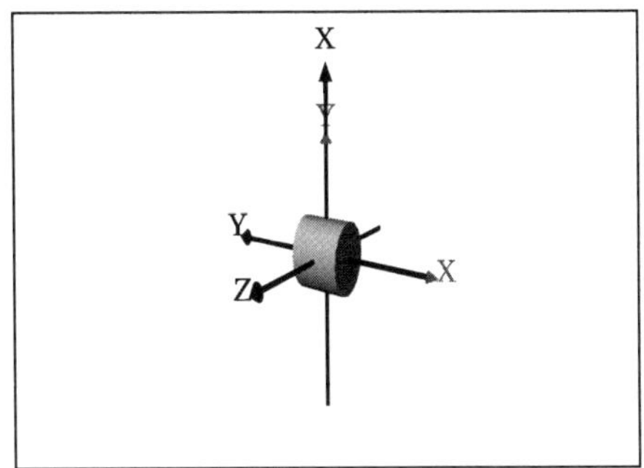

Figure 7.31 *Drawing a cylinder.*

The ordering of nodes in your VRML file makes a big difference in the drawing results. In this example, you first scale in *only* the Y direction. When you rotate *after* the scale, the orientation of the scale does *not* change. After the rotation occurs, your world is *still* scaled along the *old* Y axis or the *new* X axis. When your cylinder is drawn, it is lying on its side, so it is also scaled in the old Y (or the new X) direction.

Extended Examples

The following examples build on the concepts we present in this chapter. They illustrate the worlds you can create by scaling, rotating, translating, and using only the VRML primitives and text shapes. Try them on your own.

TIP *All of the VRML text in the extended examples throughout this book are available via anonymous ftp from John Wiley & Sons at* `ftp.wiley.com/public/computer_books/vrml` *and from the VRML Repository at* `http://www.sdsc.edu/vrml`.

A Submarine

The submarine in Figure 7.32 is created by squashing a sphere to create the body of the sub and warping a cylinder to create the base of the tower.

```
#VRML V1.0 ascii

# A Submarine

# Main circular tower and periscope mast
Cylinder {
      height 1.5
      radius 0.4
}
```

Figure 7.32 continues

```
Cylinder {
      height 3.0
      radius 0.05
}
# Move right and down to place the sub body
Translation {
      translation 1.0 -1.0 0.0
}
# Stretch in X everything drawn next
Scale {
      scaleFactor 4.0 1.0 1.0
}
# Use a stretched sphere as the sub body
Sphere {
      radius 1.0
}
# Move up and draw the tower base
Translation {
      translation 0.0 1.0 0.0
}
Cylinder {
      height 0.5
      radius 0.5
}
```

Figure 7.32 *A submarine.*

A Computer Monitor

The example in Figure 7.33 creates a computer monitor. When you create a keyboard and mouse to go with this monitor, you can scale any or all of the shapes to fit together within one world.

```
#VRML V1.0 ascii

Rotation {
      #        -X             +5.0 degrees
      rotation -1.0 0.0 0.0  0.087
}
Scale {
      scaleFactor 1.0 1.0 0.25
}
# Rounded screen:
Sphere {
      radius 2.0
}
Scale {
      scaleFactor 1.0 1.0 4.0
}
```

Figure 7.33 continues

```
Translation {
      translation 1.707 0.0 0.0
}
# Screen boarder:
Cube {
      width 0.586
      height 4.0
      depth 1.0
}
Translation {
      translation -3.414 0.0 0.0
}
Cube {
      width 0.586
      height 4.0
      depth 1.0
}
Translation {
      translation 1.707 1.707 0.0
}
Cube {
      width 4.0
      height 0.586
      depth 1.0
}
Translation {
      translation 0.0 -3.414 0.0
}
Cube {
      width 4.0
      height 0.586
      depth 1.0
}
Translation {
      translation 0.0 1.707 -1.914
}
# Body:
Cube {
      width 2.828
      height 2.828
      depth 2.828
}
Rotation {
      #        X              +5.0 degrees
      rotation 1.0 0.0 0.0  0.087
}
Translation {
      translation 0.0 -1.5 0.0
}
#  Base:
Cone {
      bottomRadius 1.5
}
```

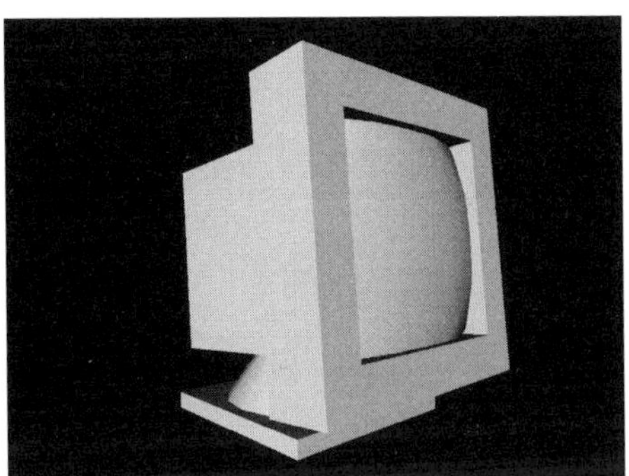

Figure 7.33 continues

```
Translation {
      translation 0.0 -0.875 0.0
}
Cube {
      width 3.0
      height .25
      depth 3.0
}
```

Figure 7.33 *A computer monitor.*

A Rocket

The example in Figure 7.34 creates a rocket. If you have planets created, but they are very small compared to this rocket, you can scale the rocket shape so that it will fit in a world with the planets.

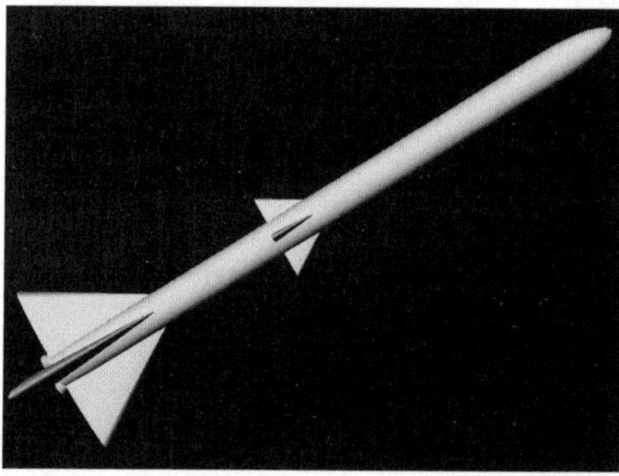

```
#VRML V1.0 ascii

Scale {
      scaleFactor 0.1 1.0 1.0
}
Cone {
      bottomRadius 5.0
      height 8.0
}
Scale {
      scaleFactor 10.0 1.0 0.1
}
Cone {
      bottomRadius 5.0
      height 8.0
}
Translation {
      translation 0.0 12.0 0.0
}
Cone {
      bottomRadius 2.5
      height 4.0
}
Scale {
      scaleFactor 0.1 1.0 10.0
}
Cone {
      bottomRadius 2.5
      height 4.0
}
Scale {
      scaleFactor 10.0 1.0 1.0
}
```

Figure 7.34 continues

```
Cylinder {
      radius 1.0
      height 32.0
}
Translation {
      translation 0.0 16.0 0.0
}
Scale {
      scaleFactor 1.0 4.0 1.0
}
Sphere {
}
Scale {
      scaleFactor 1.0 0.25 1.0
}
Translation {
      translation 0.75 -32.0 0.0
}
Cone {
      bottomRadius 0.5
      height 1.0
}
Translation {
      translation -1.5 0.0 0.0
}
Cone {
      bottomRadius 0.5
      height 1.0
}
Translation {
      translation 0.75 0.0 0.75
}
Cone {
      bottomRadius 0.5
      height 1.0
}
Translation {
      translation 0.0 0.0 -1.5
}
Cone {
      bottomRadius 0.5
      height 1.0
}
```

Figure 7.34 *A rocket.*

Summary

Scaling allows you to change the size of one or more shapes by changing the size of the VRML space and units. All virtual pen drawing, positioning, and orientation is affected by scaling.

The **Scale** node specifies three scale factors to increase or decrease the size of the space in the X, Y, and Z directions. To create a shrunken or grown shape without warping it, use the same scale factor for all three directions. To create a warped shape, use different scale factors for X, Y, and Z.

You can scale before drawing one shape or many, and you can scale more than once within a VRML file. You can also combine scaling with rotation and translation to create different effects when sizing, orienting, and positioning multiple shapes. The order of **Scale, Rotation,** and **Translation** nodes determines how the virtual pen draws an image.

CHAPTER 8

Translating, Rotating, and Scaling Shapes

Using sequences of the **Translation, Rotation,** and **Scale** nodes, you can position, orient, and change your drawing size before drawing shapes. Some sequences of **Translation, Rotation,** and **Scale** nodes are so common that VRML has a special **Transform** node to enable you to specify these actions more succinctly in your VRML files *and* to cause your browser to perform the actions more quickly. Using the **Transform** node you can translate, rotate, and scale all at once instead of using three separate nodes.

Understanding Transforms

In computer graphics, **transform** is the general term for translation, rotation, and scale operations. All three of these transforms affect the way the virtual pen draws subsequent shapes.

The **Transform** node is an efficient way of specifying common sequences of the translation, rotation, and scale transforms. Because the **Transform** node is designed specifically to perform these common sequences, your VRML browser draws your world more quickly when you use the **Transform** node in place of multiple **Translation, Rotation,** and **Scale** nodes.

Translating, Rotating, and Scaling by Combining Transforms

The **Transform** node efficiently combines three common sequences of **Translation, Rotation,** and **Scale** nodes:

- *Translate, rotate, then scale (in that order)*
- *Scale about an arbitrary center point*
- *Scale with a specific orientation*

It can also perform all three sequences at once. This enables you to scale about a center point, with a scale orientation, *and* rotate and translate a shape. If you try to perform all of these operations with individual **Translation, Rotation,** and **Scale** nodes, you must use *seven* nodes. Using the single **Transform** node instead, your VRML browser can perform all of these operations at once and do so more quickly than if you used the seven individual nodes.

Replacing a "Translate, Rotate, Then Scale" with a Transform Node

One of the most frequent sequences of transforms is this:

```
Translation {
   translation . . .
}
Rotation {
   rotation . . .
}
Scale {
   scaleFactor . . .
}
```

A sequence of these three nodes is used to position the origin and virtual pen to a location in your world, turn the axes and pen to face in a new direction, then scale the units of the space and the drawing size of the pen. Imagine that you are building a room in VRML using the chair and table from Chapter 7. To position the chair where you want it in your room, use a **Translation** node. To turn it to face a desired direction, use a **Rotation** node. Finally, to make it the right size in relation to your room, use a **Scale** node. After these three nodes, include the VRML text for your chair, as shown in Figure 8.1.

```
#VRML V1.0 ascii

######################
# Room floor
Cube {
      width 10.0
      height 0.1
      depth 10.0
}
Translation {
      translation 0.0 0.05 0.0
}
# Draw the chair to the left
Translation {
      translation -3.5 0.0 0.0
}
```

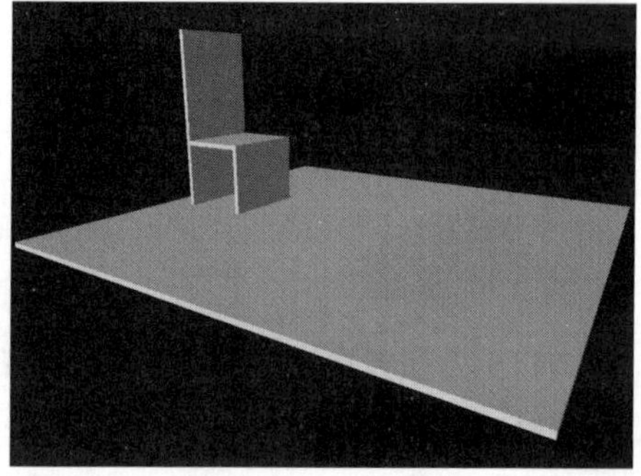

Figure 8.1 continues

```
# Turn so that the chair will be drawn facing right
Rotation {
      #            Y       +180.0 degrees
      rotation 0.0 1.0 0.0  3.14
}
# Scale down so that the chair will match the room's size
Scale {
      scaleFactor 0.5 0.5 0.5
}
#######################
# Chair from chapter 7
. . .
```

Figure 8.1 *Your chair in the room after positioning, rotating, and scaling.*

Next, to position the table in the room as shown in Figure 8.2, use another **Translation** node. To turn the table the way you want it, use a **Rotation** node. And to make the table the correct size in relation to the chair, use a **Scale** node.

```
#VRML V1.0 ascii

#######################
# Room floor
. . .
#######################
# Chair from chapter 7
. . .
Translation {
      # Draw the table to the right
      translation -9.5 0.0 0.0
}
Rotation {
      # Turn the table around
      #            Y       +90.0 degrees
      rotation 0.0 1.0 0.0  1.57
}
Scale {
      # Scale up so that the table will match the room size
      scaleFactor 2.0 2.0 2.0
}
#######################
# Table from chapter 7
. . .
```

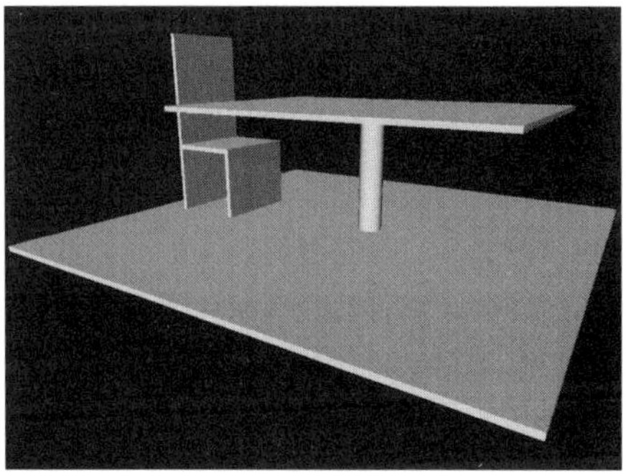

Figure 8.2 *Your table added to the room after positioning, rotating, and scaling again.*

To position, orient, and scale additional chairs, tables, desks, bookcases, and other furniture, use more **Translation, Rotation,** and **Scale** nodes, one set of three for each new piece of furniture. This particular sequence of three nodes is very handy, and occurs frequently in VRML files.

The **Transform** node enables you to perform a translation, rotation, and scale sequence all at once in one node. The chair and table can be placed in the room using **Transform** nodes like those shown in Figure 8.3.

```
#VRML V1.0 ascii

########################
# Room floor
. . .
Transform {
      # Draw the chair to the left
      translation -3.5 0.0 0.0
      # Turn so that the chair will be
      # drawn facing right
      #           Y        +180.0 degrees
      rotation 0.0 1.0 0.0  3.14
      # Scale down so that the chair
      # will match the room's size
      scaleFactor 0.5 0.5 0.5
}
########################
# Chair from chapter 7
. . .
Transform {
      # Draw the table to the right
      translation -9.5 0.0 0.0
      # Turn the table around
      #           Y        +90.0 degrees
      rotation 0.0 1.0 0.0  1.57
      # Scale up so that the table will match the room's size
      scaleFactor 2.0 2.0 2.0
}
########################
# Table from chapter 7
. . .
```

Figure 8.3 *Your chair and table in the room after positioning, rotating, and scaling twice using **Transform** nodes.*

Notice how the **Transform** node is used in Figure 8.3. The original **Translation, Rotation,** and **Scale** nodes are replaced with a single **Transform** node. The **translation, rotation,** and **scaleFactor** fields of the original three nodes are used in the same way in the **Transform** node.

When the VRML browser reads the **Transform** node, it instructs the virtual pen to translate, rotate, and scale just as if the original three nodes are used. The advantage is that the VRML browser can process the combined translation, rotation, and scaling instructions within a **Transform** node more quickly than it can process the three separate nodes.

Using the **Transform** Node to Scale about a Center Point

Another common sequence of **Translation** and **Scale** nodes is used to scale a shape about an arbitrary center point using a sequence of nodes like this:

```
Translation {
   translation . . .
}
Scale {
   scaleFactor . . .
}
Translation {
   translation . . .
}
```

This is most useful for scaling a complicated shape, like the table from Chapter 7. The table shape is composed of a **Translation** node, a **Cylinder** node, another **Translation** node, and a **Cube** node. Think of all four nodes as a single table shape.

Imagine that your friend created a table similar to the one in Chapter 7 and gave it to you. Your friend originally created the table as part of a room of furniture, and to fit into that room, the table must be centered at 3.0 in the X direction. Your friend *built into* the table shape a **Translation** node to center the table at 3.0 in the X direction, as shown in Figure 8.4.

```
#VRML V1.0 ascii

# Table
Translation {
      translation 3.0 0.0 0.0
}
# Table base
Translation {
      translation 0.0 1.25 0.0
}
Cylinder {
      height 2.5
      radius 0.25
}
# Table top
Translation {
      translation 0.0 1.25 0.0
}
Cube {
      height 0.1
      width 5.0
      depth 7.0
}
```

Figure 8.4 *The table your friend built, centered at +3.0 units in the X direction.*

When you include your friend's table in your room, you realize you need to scale it up to fit into your larger room. The following VRML text illustrates how you might accomplish this by copying the table text into the file describing your room and preceding it with a **Scale** node.

```
#VRML V1.0 ascii

########################
# Your room
. . .
# Scale the table up to fit into my room
Scale {
      scaleFactor 2.0 2.0 2.0
}
########################
# Your friend's table
. . .
```

Figure 8.5 *Scaling the table to fit into your room with the chair.*

The table is scaled to twice its original size, as you wanted, but it is now centered at a position that is farther away than you want it, as shown in Figure 8.6.

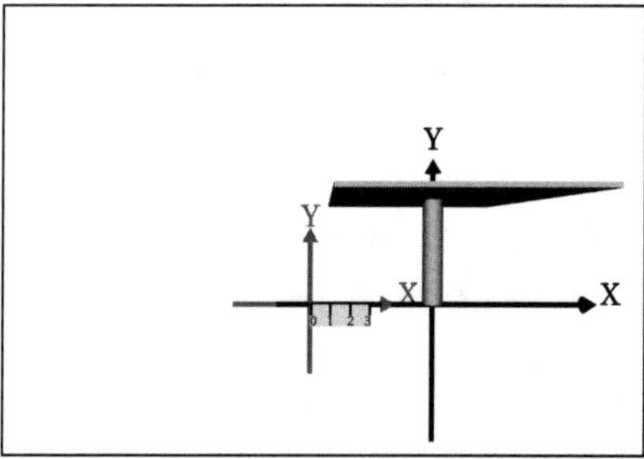

Figure 8.6 *The table your friend built, now positioned twice the original distance specified in the table shape's VRML text.*

TIP *We include in the next few diagrams a 3.0-unit ruler that starts at the origin and runs along the positive X axis. The right-hand end of the ruler is the point at which we want the table centered. We also omit the room shape to keep the diagrams uncluttered.*

The resulting positioning and center point of the table is predictable. Any shape or property following a **Scale** node is also scaled, so the **Translation** node built into the table shape that centers the table at 3.0 in the X direction is scaled. Instead of being positioned at the right-hand end of the ruler, the table ends up 3.0 units in distance *beyond* the right-hand end of the ruler.

Now you have a problem. You don't want the table scaled and positioned 3.0 units in distance *away from* the center point your friend specified. You want it scaled and positioned with its center *at* that center point.

For the preceding table shape, you can solve this problem by deleting the first **Translation** node in the table shape. That is the node your friend used to position the table at 3.0 units in the X direction. For more complicated shapes, however, the solution may not be that easy. It may be very difficult to figure out how to modify the shape to center it at the origin.

If you can't easily position a shape at the origin by deleting an extra **Translation** node, you may resort to using a sequence of nodes to undo your friend's centering and position and scale the shape the way you want it, like this:

```
#VRML V1.0 ascii

# Put the table where I want it
Translation {
        translation 3.0 0.0 0.0
}
# Scale the table up to fit into my room
Scale {
        scaleFactor 2.0 2.0 2.0
}

# "Undo" the table's built-in centering
Translation {
        translation -3.0 0.0 0.0
}

########################
# Your friend's table
. . .
```

Positioning the table where you want it and scaling it → (points to the Translation and Scale nodes)

"Undoing" your friend's centering → (points to the Translation -3.0 node)

Your friend's centering → (points to # Your friend's table)

Figure 8.7 *A series of nodes that enables you to position and scale the table the way you want it.*

Reading the file from top to bottom, you instruct the virtual pen to:

1. Translate 3.0 units in the X direction.

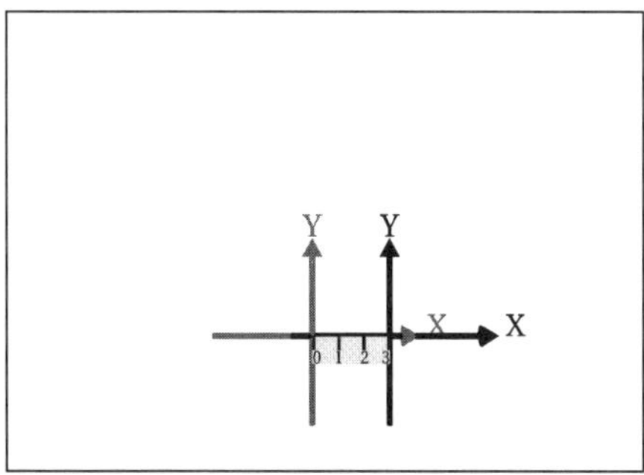

Figure 8.8 *Translating 3.0 units to the right.*

2. Scale by 2.0 in the X, Y, and Z directions. This changes the scale property of your virtual pen. Every movement and drawing action performed by the pen from this point on will be *doubled* in scale.

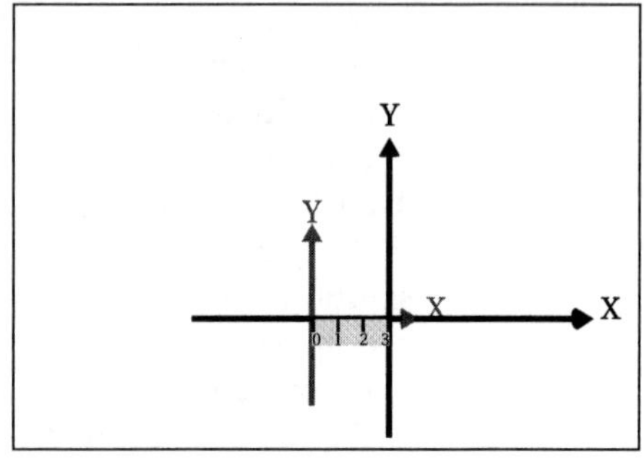

Figure 8.9 *Scaling by 2.0 in the X, Y, and Z directions.*

3. Translate –3.0 units in the X direction. Because everything is scaled by 2.0, this translation positions the pen 2.0 × –3.0, or –6.0, units in the X direction—*3.0 units to the left* of the left-hand end of the ruler.

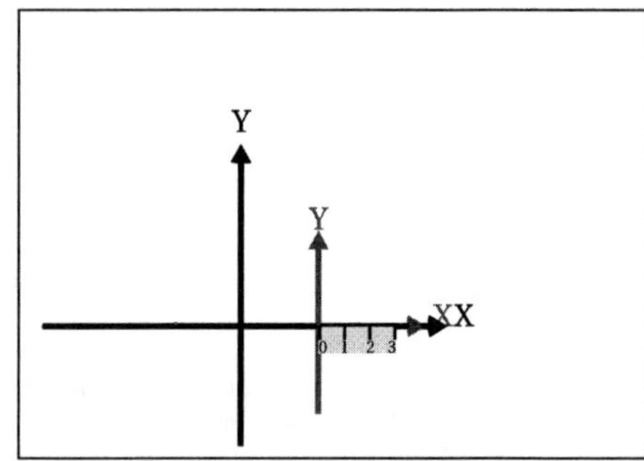

Figure 8.10 *Translating 3.0 units to the left.*

4. Draw the table.
   a. Translate 3.0 units in the X direction. Because the scale doubled all subsequent translations, this translation positions the pen at a 6.0-unit distance from the current pen position, which is where we want the table centered.

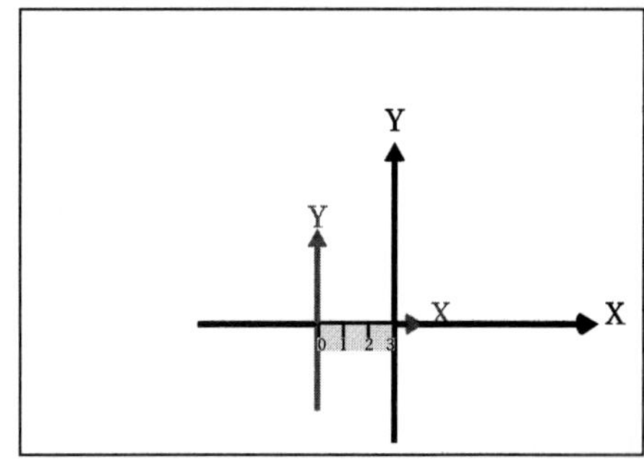

Figure 8.11 *Translating 3.0 units to the right.*

b. Translate 1.25 units in the Y direction (prepare to draw the table base).
c. Draw a cylinder (the table base).
d. Translate 1.25 in the Y direction (prepare to draw the table top).
e. Draw a cube (the table top).

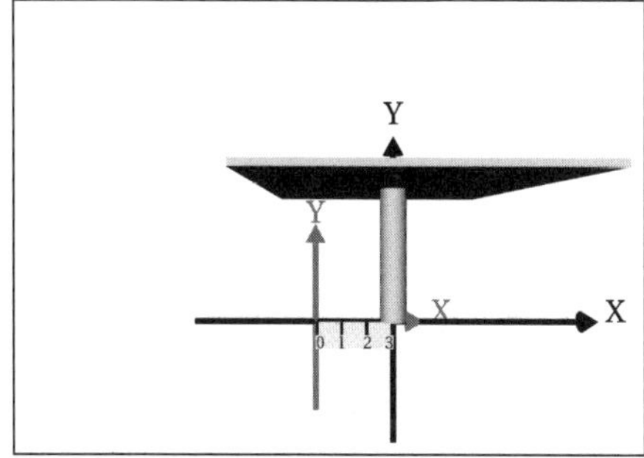

Figure 8.12 *Drawing the table.*

This sequence of nodes has the effect of *scaling about a center point* that is 3.0 units along the X axis. You can also scale about a center point using the scale center point feature of a **Transform** node like this:

```
#VRML V1.0 ascii

Transform {
      scaleFactor 2.0 2.0 2.0
      center 3.0 0.0 0.0
}
# Your friend's table
. . .
```

Figure 8.13 *Replacing the **Translation, Scale,** and **Translation** nodes with a **Transform** node.*

Notice how the **Transform** node is used in Figure 8.13. The **Transform** node replaces the first three nodes in Figure 8.7: the **Translation, Scale,** and **Translation** nodes. The **scaleFactor** field of the **Transform** node is the same as that of a **Scale** node. The **center** field, however, is a translation distance to the center point about which you want to scale.

This kind of problem can be avoided by designing your shapes with more natural center points in mind. For a table or a chair, that might be a point at the floor between the legs. For an airplane, that might be the middle of the fuselage. That way, when you use the shape, you can position it where you want it without being constrained by someone else's built-in positioning of the shape. Doing this makes your shapes much more reusable by you and by others.

Using the **Transform** Node to Control Scale Orientation

You may need to scale a shape in an arbitrary direction, but a **Scale** node lets you scale only in the X, Y, and Z directions. Using **Rotation** and **Scale** nodes in combination, you can scale in any direction like this:

```
Rotation {
   rotation . . .
}
Scale {
   scaleFactor . . .
}
Rotation {
   rotation . . .
}
# Your shape
. . .
```

Using this sequence you can warp how subsequent shapes are drawn by stretching or squashing them in any direction. The first **Rotation** node orients the axes to scale in the direction you want, the **Scale** node stretches or squashes, and the second **Rotation** node reorients the axes to their original orientation (before the first **Rotation** node) before drawing the shape.

You can accomplish this scale orientation using a single **Transform** node instead of the preceding three nodes, like this:

```
Transform {
   scaleFactor . . .
   scaleOrientation . . .
}
# Your shape
. . .
```

Notice how the **Transform** node is used in the preceding VRML text. The **Rotation, Scale,** and **Rotation** nodes have been replaced by a single **Transform** node. You specify in the **scaleOrientation** field of the **Transform** node a rotation axis and rotation amount like those you use in a **Rotation** node's **rotation** field. The **scaleOrientation** field performs the function of the first *and* second **Rotation** nodes, by rotating and then rotating back after scaling.

Understanding the **Transform** Node Syntax

A single **Transform** node typically takes the place of three nodes: a **Translation** node followed by a **Rotation** node followed by a **Scale** node. The special scale orientation and center features of the **Transform** node extend its capabilities so that it can replace as many as seven nodes.

SYNTAX **Transform node**

```
Transform {
   translation 0.0 0.0 0.0                 # X, Y, Z distance
   rotation 0.0 0.0 1.0 0.0                # rotation axis and amount
   scaleFactor 1.0 1.0 1.0                 # floating point value
   scaleOrientation 0.0 0.0 1.0 0.0        # rotation axis and amount
   center 0.0 0.0 0.0                      # X, Y, Z distance
}
```

The **Transform** node has five fields, three of which are already familiar to you. The **translation** field specifies an X, Y, Z distance exactly as it does in a **Translation** node. The **rotation** field specifies a rotation axis and rotation amount, exactly as it does in a **Rotation** node. The **scaleFactor** field specifies three scale factors, one each for the X, Y, and Z directions, exactly as it does in a **Scale** node.

The **Transform** node has two additional fields. The **scaleOrientation** field specifies a rotation axis and a rotation amount that enable you to scale as if oriented in a specific direction. The scale orientation is independent of the **rotation** field and does not permanently rotate the axes. The **center** field specifies a distance to a center point about which you want to scale or rotate. The scale center is independent of the **translation** field distances and does not permanently translate the origin. Neither the **scaleOrientation** field nor **center** field have a direct equivalent in the **Scale** node discussed in Chapter 7. Instead, they provide added functionality for certain uses of the **Transform** node.

The **Transform** node with all its associated fields, like this:

```
Transform {
   translation . . .
   rotation . . .
   scaleFactor . . .
   scaleOrientation . . .
   center . . .
}
```

is equivalent to this sequence of nodes *in this order:*

```
Translation {
   translation . . .
}
Translation {
   translation . . .
}
Rotation {
   rotation . . .
}
Rotation {
   rotation . . .
}
Scale {
   scaleFactor . . .
}
Rotation {
   rotation . . .
}
Translation {
   translation . . .
}
```

TIP *The **Transform** node always affects the virtual pen by first translating it, then rotating it, and finally by scaling it. You can order the fields within the **Transform** node in any order, but the transforms will always be applied in this order.*

Experimenting with Transforms

The following examples provide a more detailed examination of the ways in which the **Transform** node can be used and how it interacts with nodes we've discussed in previous chapters.

Translating, Rotating, and Scaling Using **Transform** Nodes

Transform nodes are convenient for performing a three-node set of directions including a translation, a rotation, and a scale. To show how you can use a single **Transform** node in place of the three individual nodes, the following examples translate, rotate, and scale a cylinder.

Translate, Rotate, Scale, Then Draw a Cylinder

The example text in Figure 8.14 uses **Translation, Rotation,** and **Scale** nodes to draw an enlarged cylinder tilted on its side.

```
#VRML V1.0 ascii

Translation {
      translation 3.0 0.0 0.0
}
Rotation {
      #                Z    +90.0 degrees
      rotation 0.0 0.0 1.0  1.57
}
Scale {
      scaleFactor 2.0 2.0 2.0
}
Cylinder {
}
```

Figure 8.14 *Translating, rotating, scaling, and drawing a cylinder.*

Reading from the top of the VRML file to the bottom, you instruct the virtual pen to:

1. Translate 3.0 units along the X axis.

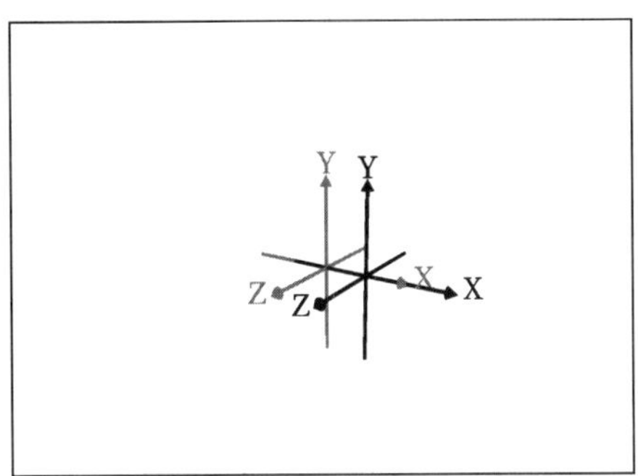

Figure 8.15 *Translating 3.0 units to the right.*

2. Rotate +90.0 degrees around the Z axis.

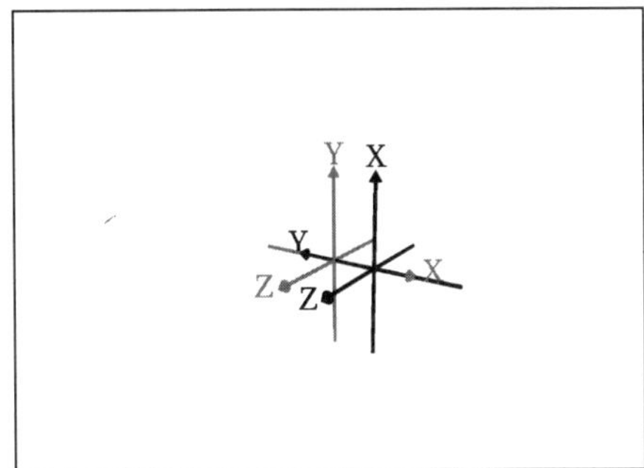

Figure 8.16 *Rotating the axis 90.0 degrees about the Z axis.*

3. Scale by a factor of 2.0 in the X, Y, and Z directions based on the pen's new orientation.

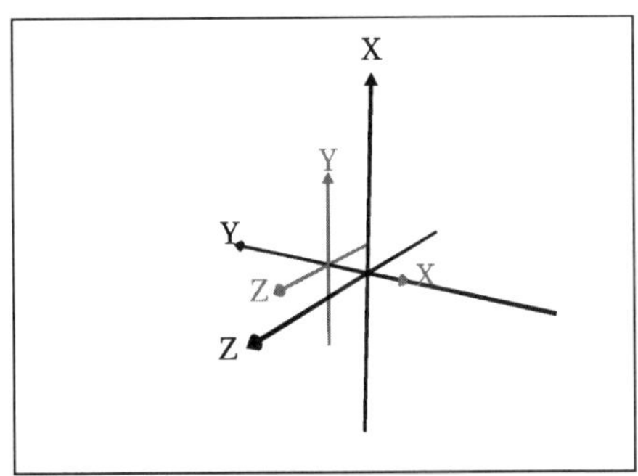

Figure 8.17 *Scaling by 2.0 in the X, Y, and Z directions.*

4. Draw a cylinder centered at the current origin, with the current axes' orientation, and with the current scale.

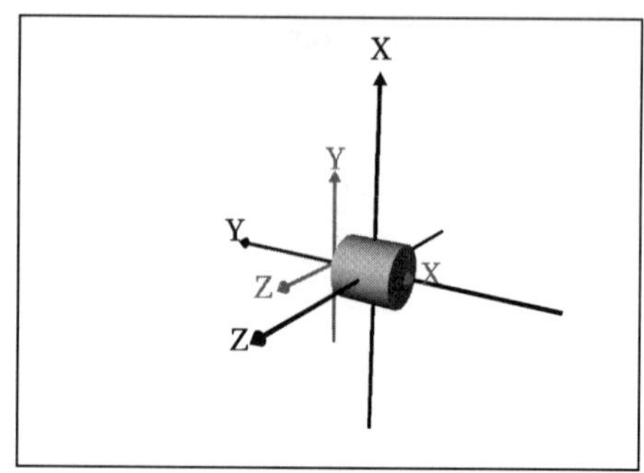

Figure 8.18 *Drawing a cylinder.*

The pen is rotated in step 2, and its drawing space is scaled up in step 3. The resulting cylinder is drawn sideways and at twice its normal size.

Transforming a Cylinder

Using a **Transform** node, you can translate, rotate, and scale all at once as shown in Figure 8.19.

```
#VRML V1.0 ascii

Transform {
        translation 3.0 0.0 0.0
        rotation 0.0 0.0 1.0 1.57
        scaleFactor 2.0 2.0 2.0
}
Cylinder {
}
```

Figure 8.19 *Transforming a cylinder.*

Reading from the top of the file to the bottom, the virtual pen is instructed to:

1. Transform all at once:
   a. Translate 3.0 units along the X axis.
   b. Rotate +90.0 degrees around the Z axis.
   c. Scale by a factor of 2.0 in the X, Y, and Z directions based on the axes' new orientation.

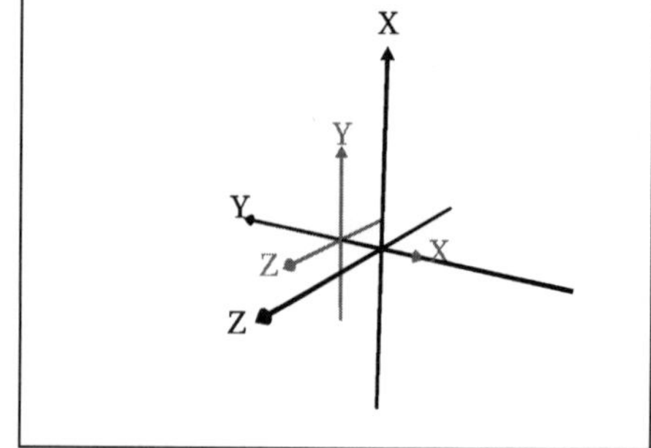

Figure 8.20 *Transforming the virtual pen.*

2. Draw a cylinder at the current origin, with the current axes' orientation, and with the current scale.

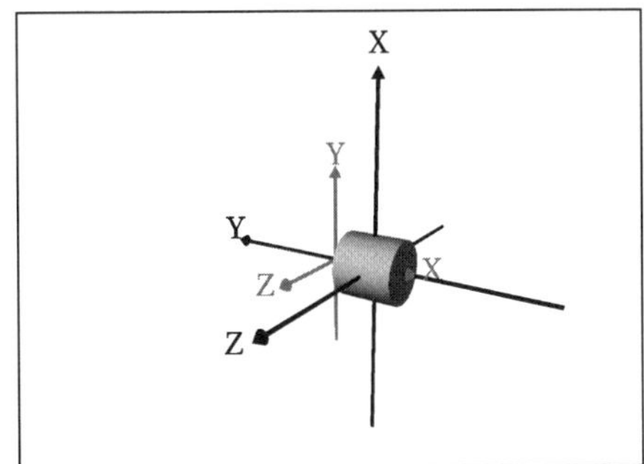

Figure 8.21 *Drawing a cylinder.*

The result is a large cylinder turned on its side. This is identical to the cylinder in Figure 8.18 produced using three separate nodes. The single **Transform** node, however, can be handled more quickly by your VRML browser than the three separate nodes of the first example.

Scaling about a Center Point

The center field of a **Transform** node enables you to direct the virtual pen to increase or decrease its drawing size relative to any point in space. The use of a scale center point in **Transform** nodes is somewhat complicated. When interpreting VRML text containing a **Transform** node using a scale center, it may help to mentally replace the **Transform** node with the following three nodes:

```
Translation {
   translation . . .
}
Scale {
   scaleFactor . . .
}
Translation {
   translation . . .
}
```

The example text in Figure 8.22 scales up an off-center cylinder by using a **Transform** node and a scale center point:

```
#VRML V1.0 ascii

Translation {
      translation 3.0 0.0 0.0
}
Scale {
      scaleFactor 2.0 2.0 2.0
}
```

Figure 8.22 continues

```
Translation {
      translation -7.0 0.0 0.0
}
# Your Shape, centered at +7.0 along the X axis
Translation {
      translation 7.0 0.0 0.0
}
Cylinder {
}
```

Figure 8.22 *Scaling an off-center cylinder.*

Reading the VRML file from the top to the bottom, you instruct the virtual pen to:

1. Transform all at once:
   a. Translate 3.0 units along the X axis.
   b. Scale by a factor of 2.0.
   c. Translate back to the left. Because the translation occurs after the drawing size is scaled by a factor of 2.0, the distance translated to the left is also scaled.

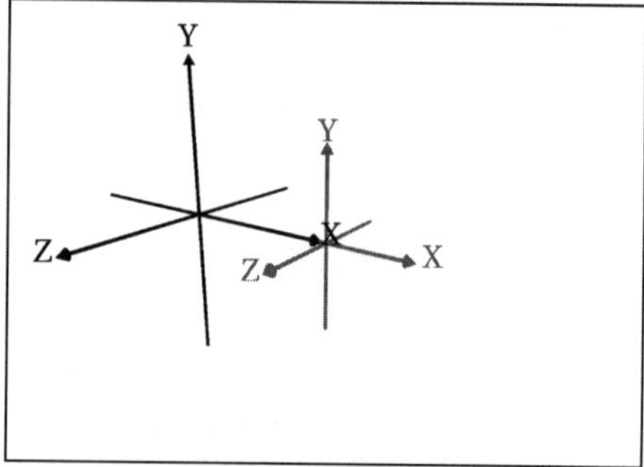

Figure 8.23 *Translating to the right, scaling, and moving the pen back to the left.*

2. Translate 3.0 units along the X axis. Because everything is scaled by 2.0, this translation positions the virtual pen 2.0 × 3.0, or 6.0, units along the X axis.

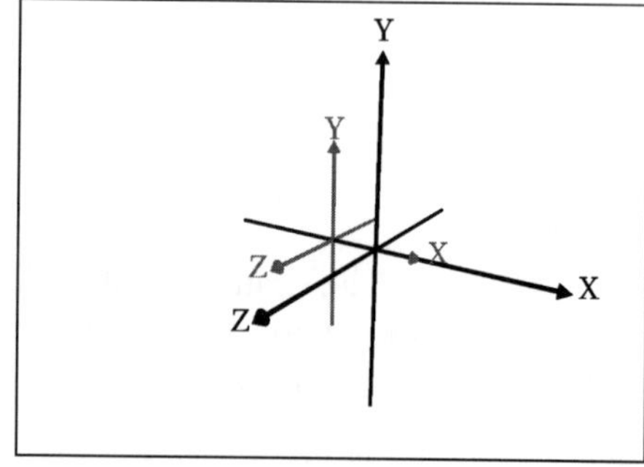

Figure 8.24 *Translating 3.0 units to the right.*

3. Draw the cylinder at the current origin, with the current axes' orientation, and at the current scale.

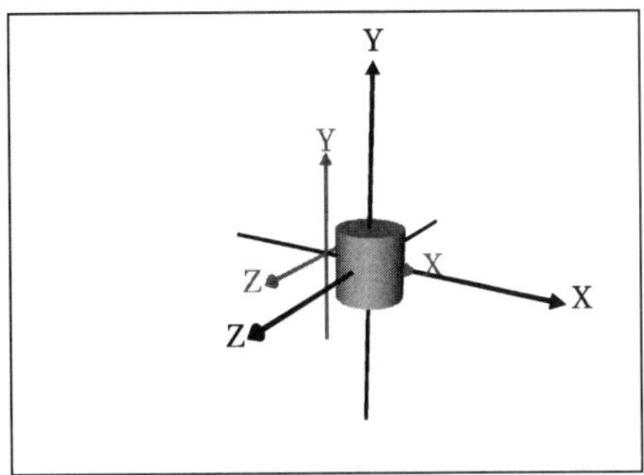

Figure 8.25 *Translating 3.0 units to the right.*

The result is a cylinder drawn twice normal size, centered 3.0 units along the X axis.

The **Transform** node in the previous example is equivalent to the following VRML text, but it's more efficient to use one node, as shown in Figure 8.26.

```
#VRML V1.0 ascii

Translation {
      translation 3.0 0.0 0.0
}
Scale {
      scaleFactor 2.0 2.0 2.0
}
Translation {
      translation -3.0 0.0 0.0
}
# Off-center cylinder
Translation {
      translation 3.0 0.0 0.0
}
Cylinder {
}
```

Figure 8.26 *The sequence of nodes equivalent to the* ***Transform*** *node.*

Scaling with a Scale Orientation

The **scaleOrientation** field of a **Transform** node enables you to specially orient the virtual pen before scaling the drawing size as directed by the **scaleFactor** field. The effect is identical to rotating the virtual pen first, then scaling, then rotating back again.

When interpreting VRML text with a **Transform** node using a **scaleOrientation** field, it may help to mentally replace the **Transform** node with the following three nodes:

```
Rotation {
   rotation . . .
}
Scale {
   scaleFactor . . .
}
Rotation {
   rotation . . .
}
```

The example text in Figure 8.27 uses a scale orientation to turn the axes +45.0 degrees around the Z axis before stretching the drawing space by a factor of 2.0 in the *new* Y direction.

```
#VRML V1.0 ascii

Transform {
      scaleFactor 1.0 2.0 1.0
      #                       Z    +45.0 degrees
      scaleOrientation 0.0 0.0 1.0  0.785
}
Sphere {
}
```

Figure 8.27 *Transforming a sphere.*

Reading the VRML file from the top to the bottom, the virtual pen is instructed to:

1. Transform all at once:
   a. Rotate +45.0 degrees around the Z axis.
   b. Scale by a factor of 2.0 in the virtual pen's *new* Y direction. This new direction is +45.0 degrees from the original Y-axis orientation.
   c. Rotate –45.0 degrees around the Z axis.

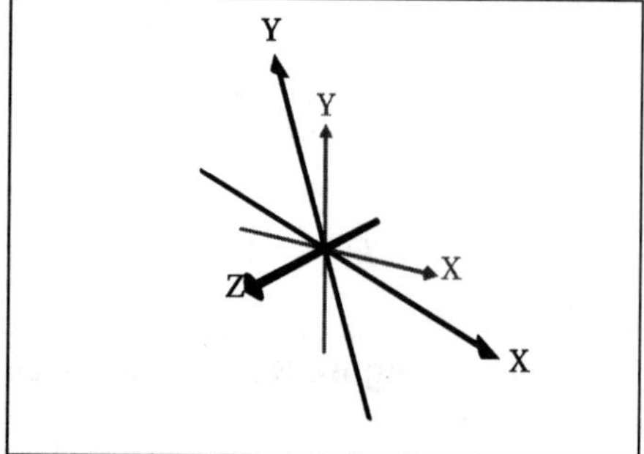

Figure 8.28 *Transforming the virtual pen.*

2. Draw a sphere at the current origin, with the current axes' orientation, and at the current scale.

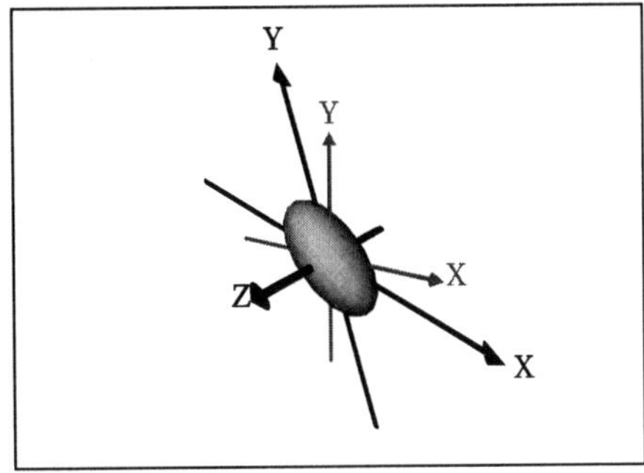

Figure 8.29 *Drawing a sphere.*

The sphere is drawn as an oblong pill shape, because the drawing size is stretched in the *new* Y-axis direction. This is +45.0 degrees from the original Y-axis direction.

The use of a **Transform** node in Figure 8.27 is equivalent to the **Rotation** and **Scale** nodes in Figure 8.30.

```
#VRML V1.0 ascii

Rotation {
      #                         Z    +45.0 degrees
      scaleOrientation 0.0 0.0 1.0  0.785
}
Scale {
      scaleFactor 1.0 2.0 1.0
}
Rotation {
      #                         Z    -45.0 degrees
      scaleOrientation 0.0 0.0 1.0  -0.785
}
Sphere {
}
```

Figure 8.30 *The sequence of nodes equivalent to the **Transform** node.*

Using **Transform** Nodes with Other Nodes

A **Transform** node can be used in combination with additional **Translation, Rotation,** and **Scale** nodes, either before or after the **Transform** node. The **Transform** node acts exactly like an equivalent sequence of **Translation, Rotation,** and **Scale** nodes. For instance, the following two sequence of VRML nodes are equivalent:

*Sequence using **Transform** node*	*Sequence* not *using **Transform** node*

`Rotation {`
`   rotation ...`
`}`
	`Rotation {`
	`   rotation ...`
	`}`

`Transform {`
`   translation ...`
`   rotation ...`
`   scaleFactor ...`
`}`
	`Translation {`
	`   translation ...`
	`}`
	`Rotation {`
	`   rotation ...`
	`}`
	`Scale {`
	`   scaleFactor ...`
	`}`

`Translation {`
`   translation ...`
`}`
	`Translation {`
	`   translation ...`
	`}`

You can also use more than one **Transform** node, one after another with, or without intervening shape, **Translation, Rotation,** or **Scale** nodes.

Extended Examples

The following examples build on the concepts we present in this chapter. They illustrate the worlds you can create using transformations and VRML's primitive shapes. Try them on your own.

TIP *All of the VRML text in the extended examples throughout this book are available via anonymous ftp from John Wiley & Sons at* `ftp.wiley.com/public/computer_books/vrml` *and from the VRML Repository at* `http://www.sdsc.edu/vrml`.

Place a Semi Truck on a City Street

Figure 8.31 uses the city street you built in Chapter 5 and the semi truck you built in Chapter 7. To position the truck on the city street, you need to translate it to the position where you want it, rotate it to face the correct direction on the street, and scale it down to fit on the street. Since this order of operations is exactly what the **Transform** node supports, you can use it to speed up drawing the scene.

Try changing the translation distances to move the truck up and down the street. Try changing the scale factors to make the truck bigger or smaller in relation to the city buildings.

```
#VRML V1.0 ascii

# City street from chapter 5

# Draw the ground with a wide, deep,
# flat cube
Cube {
      height 0.1
      width 10.0
      depth 20.0
}
# Move to the left side of the street
Translation {
      translation -3.0 4.0 0.0
}
# Draw the tall building with a tall
# cube
Cube {
      height 8.0
}
# Move to the right side of the street
Translation {
      translation 6.0 -2.0 0.0
}
# Draw the short building with a short cube
Cube {
      height 4.0
}
# Move down the street
Translation {
      translation 0.0 4.0 -3.0
}
# Draw a skyscraper next to the short
# building using a tall cylinder
Cylinder {
      height 10.0
}
# Position the truck on the street beside the first tall building
# Turn the truck around to face out the positive Z axis
# Scale down the truck so it looks right on the street
Transform {
      translation -4.0 -5.2 6.0
      #             Y      +90.0 degrees
      rotation 0.0 1.0 0.0  1.57
      scaleFactor 0.15 0.15 0.15
}
# Semitruck from chapter 7
# Truck cab
```

Figure 8.31 continues

```
Cube {
      height 6.0
      width 5.0
      depth 6.0
}
# Truck trailer platform
Translation {
      translation 5.5 -2.5 0.0
}
Cube {
      height 1.0
      width 6.0
      depth 6.0
}
# Trailer hitch
Translation {
      translation 0.0 1.0 0.0
}
Cylinder {
      height 1.0
      radius 0.2
}
# Truck trailer
Translation {
      translation 6.5 3.5 0.0
}
Cube {
      height 7.0
      width 18.0
      depth 6.0
}
# Front wheels of cab
Translation {
      translation -12.5 -5.5 0.0
}
Rotation {
      #        X            +90.0 degrees
      rotation 1.0 0.0 0.0  1.57
}
Cylinder {
      height 7.0
      radius 1.5
}
# Rear wheels under trailer hitch
Translation {
      translation 5.0 0.0 0.0
}
Cylinder {
      height 7.0
      radius 1.5
}
```

Figure 8.31 continues

```
Translation {
     translation 3.0 0.0 0.0
}
Cylinder {
     height 7.0
     radius 1.5
}
# Rear wheels under trailer
Translation {
     translation 8.0 0.0 0.0
}
Cylinder {
     height 7.0
     radius 1.5
}
Translation {
     translation 3.0 0.0 0.0
}
Cylinder {
     height 7.0
     radius 1.5
}
```

Figure 8.31 *Semi truck on a city street.*

Pointy, Abstract Shapes

The VRML text in Figure 8.32 creates a pointy, abstract shape. The shape can be used for a number of things, such as a futuristic building, the shell of a prehistoric arthropod, a thorn, or a bizarre hat.

```
#VRML V1.0 ascii

Scale {
     scaleFactor 1.0 1.0 0.3
}
Transform {
     translation 0.0 0.5 0.0
     scaleFactor 1.3 1.0 1.0
     scaleOrientation 0.0 0.0 1.0 0.392
}
Cone {
     height 5.0
     bottomRadius 6.0
}
Transform {
     translation 0.0 0.5 0.0
     scaleFactor 1.3 1.0 1.0
     scaleOrientation 0.0 0.0 1.0 0.392
}
```

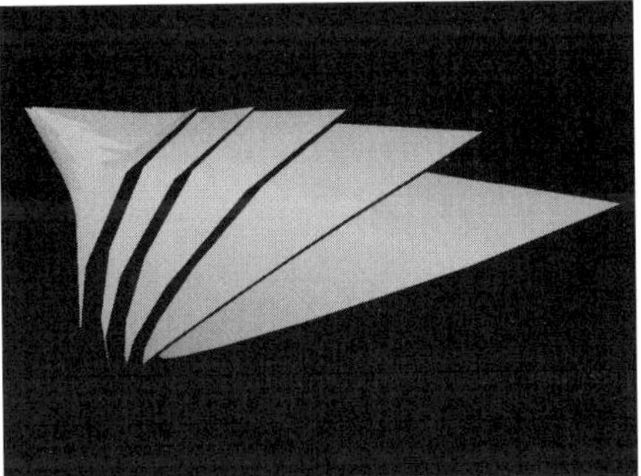

Figure 8.32 continues

```
Cone {
      height 6.0
      bottomRadius 5.0
}
Transform {
      translation 0.0 0.5 0.0
      scaleFactor 1.3 1.0 1.0
      scaleOrientation 0.0 0.0 1.0 0.392
}
Cone {
      height 7.0
      bottomRadius 4.0
}
Transform {
      translation 0.0 0.5 0.0
      scaleFactor 1.3 1.0 1.0
      scaleOrientation 0.0 0.0 1.0 0.392
}
Cone {
      height 8.0
      bottomRadius 3.0
}
Transform {
      translation 0.0 0.5 0.0
      scaleFactor 1.3 1.0 1.0
      scaleOrientation 0.0 0.0 1.0 0.392
}
Cone {
      height 9.0
      bottomRadius 2.0
}
```

Figure 8.32 *A pointy, abstract shape.*

Summary

Several sequences of three or more **Translation, Rotation,** and **Scale** nodes are common in VRML worlds. To speed up these common sequences, VRML provides a special **Transform** node.

You can combine the effects of a set of **Translation, Rotation,** and **Scale** nodes into a single **Transform** node using its **translation, rotation,** and **scaleFactor** fields. This sequence enables you to change the size of a shape, orient it, and position it all at once.

You can combine the effects of up to five **Translation, Rotation,** and **Scale** nodes into a single **Transform** node using its **center** and **scaleOrientation** fields. This combination enables you to scale shapes about a center point and stretch or compress them along arbitrary axis orientations.

Transform nodes may be used in combination with other nodes to create even more complicated effects.

CHAPTER 9

Performing Custom Shape Transforms (Advanced)

The **Translation, Rotation, Scale,** and **Transform** nodes perform standard shape transforms. While these are the most common types of shape transforms, they are not the *only* types. **Shear** and **taper** transforms, for instance, also exist and let you warp shapes in interesting ways.

Because shearing and tapering are not common transforms, VRML does not provide special shear and taper nodes. Instead, VRML has a generic **MatrixTransform** node which acts as a kind of mathematical back door into your browser's virtual-pen drawing mechanisms. Using the **MatrixTransform** node you can direct the virtual pen to shear, taper, and perform other custom shape warping.

Understanding Matrix Transforms

The **MatrixTransform** node enables you to set values in a four-row by four-column grid of numbers called a **transform matrix**. Such a matrix is the basis of the underlying math used by your VRML browser to draw shapes with its virtual pen.

TIP *The mathematical reasoning behind transform matrices is beyond the scope of this book. In this chapter we discuss how to use transform matrices with the* ***MatrixTransform*** *node, but we skip all of the math. Appendix C lists several good computer graphics textbooks that cover transform matrices in much more depth.*

A transform matrix directs the virtual pen to translate, rotate, and scale all subsequent shapes. In fact, the common **Translation, Rotation, Scale,** and **Transform** nodes are really just convenient ways to create transform matrices. Each of these nodes takes the field values you provide and, internally, produces a four-row by four-column transform matrix which is then used to direct the virtual pen.

Using the **Translation, Rotation, Scale,** and **Transform** nodes, you can avoid the mathematical details involved in creating transform matrices yourself. If you want to shear, taper, and perform other custom shape warping, you can compute your own transform matrix and instruct the virtual pen directly by using the **MatrixTransform** node.

TIP *As you might expect, when you start instructing the virtual pen directly using your own transform matrices, you risk giving it bad directions. Some transform matrices can crash your VRML browser.*

Transforming a Shape Using Matrix Transforms

A transform matrix has four rows and four columns of floating-point values, like this example matrix:

```
1.0 0.0 0.0 0.0
0.0 1.0 0.0 0.0
0.0 0.0 1.0 0.0
0.0 0.0 0.0 1.0
```

The values in each row and column control how the virtual pen transforms shapes. Some combinations of values rotate shapes, while others translate them, scale them, or warp them in interesting ways.

You can direct your browser's virtual pen with a custom transform matrix by using the **MatrixTransform** node. For example, the VRML text in Figure 9.1 uses a taper transform matrix which instructs the pen to draw a cylinder with its top smaller than its bottom.

```
#VRML V1.0 ascii

# Direct the virtual pen to taper shapes
MatrixTransform {
      matrix      1.0   0.0   0.0   0.0
                  0.0   1.0   0.0   0.5
                  0.0   0.0   1.0   0.0
                  0.0   0.0   0.0   1.0
}
Cylinder {
}
```

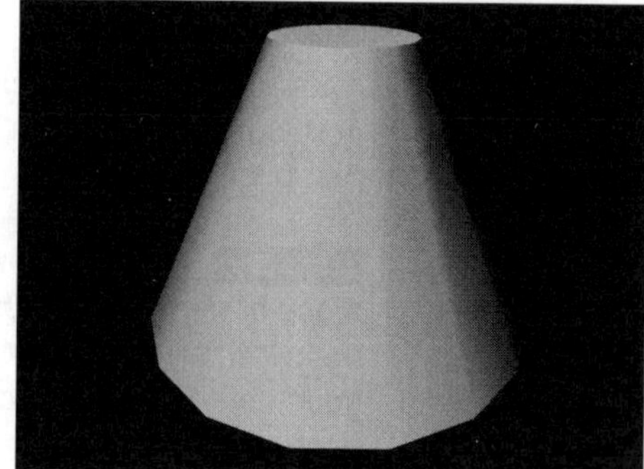

Figure 9.1 *Tapering a cylinder.*

Notice how the **MatrixTransform** node is used in Figure 9.1. The **MatrixTransform** node directs the actions of the virtual pen using a custom transform matrix. Depending on the actual values in the transform matrix, you can direct the virtual pen to translate, rotate, scale, or warp whatever shapes are subsequently drawn.

Understanding the **MatrixTransform** Node Syntax

The **MatrixTransform** node has a single matrix field with 16 floating-point values forming a transform matrix. The first four values are the first row of the matrix, the second four are the second row, and so on. Transform matrix values in any row or column may be positive, negative, or zero.

TIP *The last column in a transform matrix cannot be all zeros, because it causes browser problems.*

SYNTAX **MatrixTransform node**

```
MatrixTransform {
    matrix 1.0 0.0 0.0 0.0        # floating point values
           0.0 1.0 0.0 0.0        # floating point values
           0.0 0.0 1.0 0.0        # floating point values
           0.0 0.0 0.0 1.0        # floating point values
}
```

TIP *In version 1.1 of VRML, browsers may optionally ignore the fourth column in the matrix. With those browsers, you will be unable to perform tapering effects controlled by that column.*

Experimenting with Matrix Transforms

A transform matrix in a **MatrixTransform** node can be broken down into four parts like those shown in Figure 9.2.

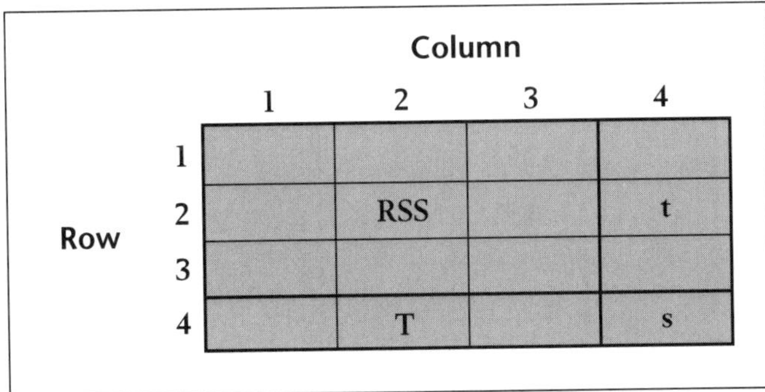

Figure 9.2 *The four parts of a transform matrix.*

Each of the four parts of the transform matrix (shown in Figure 9.2 as `RSS`, `T`, `t`, and `s`) control different types of virtual-pen shape transforms, as shown in Table 9.1.

Table 9.1 Transforms Controlled by Each Part of a Transform Matrix

Matrix Part	*Transforms*
RSS	Rotating, scaling, and shearing
T	Translating
t	Tapering
s	Global scaling

You can set values in one, two, three, or all four parts of a transform matrix at once. Some value positions in the matrix are used to create more than one effect.

When you don't wish to set values in a part of a matrix, you should set that part's values to its default values found in the identity matrix:

```
MatrixTransform {
    matrix 1.0 0.0 0.0 0.0
           0.0 1.0 0.0 0.0
           0.0 0.0 1.0 0.0
           0.0 0.0 0.0 1.0
}
```

If you direct the virtual pen with the identity matrix, no transform properties are changed. The identity matrix is a "do nothing" drawing instruction.

The primary purpose of the **MatrixTransform** node is to enable you to warp shapes and create custom effects. Understanding the standard transforms helps you create your own matrix transforms.

Translating Using the `T` Part of a Transform Matrix

To control translation within a transform matrix, set the three values in the `T` part of the matrix, as shown in Figure 9.3.

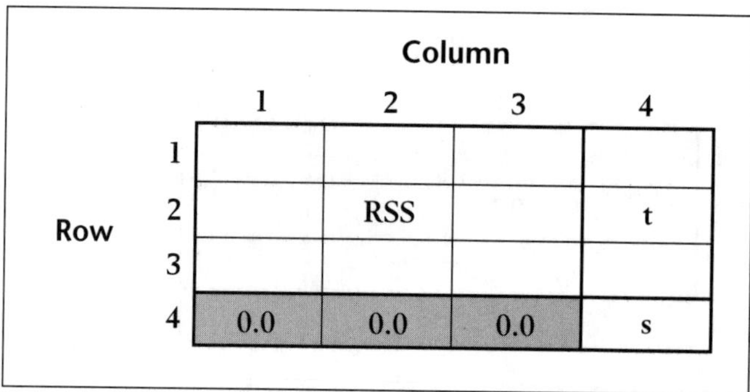

Figure 9.3 *The `T`, or translation, part of a transform matrix.*

The three values in the T part are X, Y, and Z translation distances exactly like those in a **Translation** node. For instance, the following transform matrix directs the virtual pen to translate by 3.0 units in X, –2.0 units in Y, and 5.0 units in Z:

```
MatrixTransform {
   matrix 1.0  0.0  0.0  0.0
          0.0  1.0  0.0  0.0
          0.0  0.0  1.0  0.0
          3.0 -2.0  5.0  1.0
}
```

In this example matrix, the remaining values in the RSS, t, and s parts are set to their default values from the identity matrix.

The following **Translation** node internally creates a transform matrix exactly like the preceding one:

```
Translation {
   translation 3.0 -2.0 5.0
}
```

Scaling Using the RSS Part of a Transform Matrix

You control scaling by specifying the three diagonal values in the RSS part of a transform matrix, as shown in Figure 9.4.

Row \ Column	1	2	3	4
1	1.0	0.0	0.0	
2	0.0	1.0	0.0	t
3	0.0	0.0	1.0	
4		T		s

Figure 9.4 *The RSS, or rotation, scale, and shear, part of a translation matrix.*

The three diagonal RSS values are X, Y, and Z scale factors exactly like those in a **Scale** node. For instance, the following transform matrix directs the virtual pen to scale up by a factor of 2.5 in the X direction, 5.0 in the Y direction, and 3.0 in the Z direction:

```
MatrixTransform {
   matrix 2.5 0.0 0.0 0.0
          0.0 5.0 0.0 0.0
          0.0 0.0 3.0 0.0
          0.0 0.0 0.0 1.0
}
```

In this example matrix, the remaining values in the `RSS`, `T`, `t`, and `s` parts are set to their default values from the identity matrix.

The following **Scale** node internally creates a transform matrix exactly like the preceding one:

```
Scale {
   scaleFactor 2.5 5.0 3.0
}
```

Scaling Using the `s` Part of a Transform Matrix

You can also control scaling by setting the single value in the `s` part of a transform matrix, as shown in Figure 9.5.

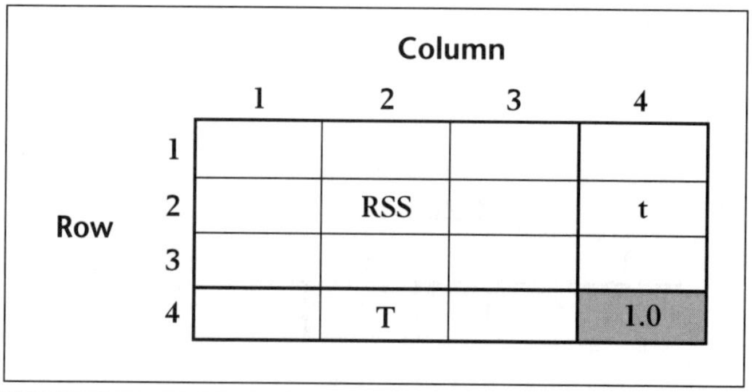

Row \ **Column**	1	2	3	4
1				
2		RSS		t
3				
4		T		1.0

Figure 9.5 *The* `s`*, or scale, part of a transform matrix.*

The **Translation, Rotation, Scale,** and **Transform** nodes all set this value to 1.0. Setting it to *smaller* values *increases* the drawing size of the virtual pen, while setting it to *larger* values *decreases* the pen's drawing size. For instance, you can scale by a factor of two by setting the `s` value to 0.5 like this:

```
MatrixTransform {
   matrix 1.0 0.0 0.0 0.0
          0.0 1.0 0.0 0.0
          0.0 0.0 1.0 0.0
          0.0 0.0 0.0 0.5
}
```

In this example matrix, the remaining values in the `RSS`, `T`, and `t` parts are set to their default values from the identity matrix.

Normally, you don't set the `s` value to scale. Using the `RSS` part for scaling gives you more flexibility and is more intuitive. When you scale by setting the `s` part of the matrix, a *smaller* value *increases* the pen's drawing size, and vice versa, which is not as intuitive a way to scale as the **Scale** node.

Rotating Using the `RSS` Part of a Transform Matrix

You control rotation by setting values in the `RSS` part of a transform matrix, as shown in Figure 9.6.

Column

Row		1	2	3	4
	1	1.0	0.0	0.0	
	2	0.0	1.0	0.0	t
	3	0.0	0.0	1.0	
	4		T		s

Figure 9.6 *The `RSS`, or rotation, scale, and shear, part of a transform matrix.*

Values in the `RSS` part of the matrix are usually set in groups of four and indicate a rotation angle around the X, Y, or Z axes.

X Rotation

The four values in the lower-right corner of the `RSS` part of a transform matrix specify rotation around the X axis, as shown in Figure 9.7.

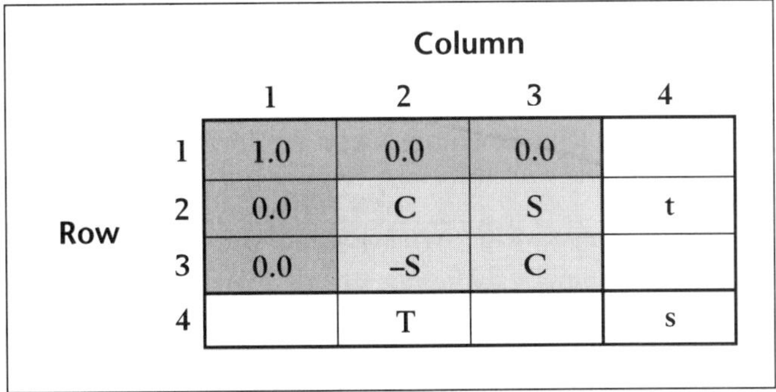

Column

Row		1	2	3	4
	1	1.0	0.0	0.0	
	2	0.0	C	S	t
	3	0.0	–S	C	
	4		T		s

Figure 9.7 *Transform matrix values specifying X-axis rotation.*

The C, S, and -S values used in the preceding matrix are abbreviations:

- *C—Cosine of the rotation amount*
- *S—Sine of the rotation amount*
- *-S—Negative of the sine of the rotation amount*

Many hand calculators and calculator programs for your computer can calculate sine and cosine values. They are often abbreviated on calculator buttons as COS for cosine and SIN for sine.

TIP *Some calculators require that the rotation amount used to compute sine or cosine values be in radians, while others require the use of degrees. Be sure to read your calculator manual to see which one your calculator uses. If it requires radians, be sure to convert from degrees to radians first, before computing a sine or cosine. Appendix A discusses how to convert between radians and degrees.*

For example, to rotate by 30.0 degrees (0.523 radians), the C, S, and -S values are as shown in Table 9.2. Using these values, the following transform matrix directs the virtual pen to rotate 30.0 degrees around the X axis:

```
MatrixTransform {
    matrix 1.0    0.0    0.0    0.0
           0.0    0.866  0.5    0.0
           0.0   -0.5    0.866  0.0
           0.0    0.0    0.0    1.0
}
```

In this matrix, the remaining values in the RSS, T, t, and s parts are set to their default values from the identity matrix.

The following **Rotation** node internally creates a transform matrix exactly like the preceding one:

```
Rotation {
  #        X            +30.0 degrees
  rotation 1.0 0.0 0.0  0.523
}
```

Table 9.2 Transform Matrix Values Used to Rotate by 30.0 Degrees

Matrix Abbreviation	*Description*	*Value*
C	Cosine of 30.0 degrees	0.866
S	Sine of 30.0 degrees	0.5
-S	Negative S (negative sine of 30.0 degrees)	–0.5

Y Rotation

The four values in the corners of the RSS part of a transform matrix specify rotation around the Y axis, as shown in Figure 9.8.

Row \ Column	1	2	3	4
1	C	0.0	–S	
2	0.0	1.0	0.0	t
3	S	0.0	C	
4		T		s

Figure 9.8 *Transform matrix values specifying Y-axis rotation.*

For example, the following transform matrix directs the virtual pen to rotate 30.0 degrees around the Y axis, using the same C, S, and -S as those values used in the previous example:

```
MatrixTransform {
    matrix 0.866  0.0   -0.5    0.0
           0.0    1.0    0.0    0.0
           0.5    0.5    0.866  0.0
           0.0    0.0    0.0    1.0
}
```

In this matrix, the remaining values in the RSS, T, t, and s parts are set to their default values from the identity matrix.

The following **Rotation** node internally creates a transform matrix exactly like the preceding one:

```
Rotation {
   #              Y        +30.0 degrees
   rotation 0.0 1.0 0.0  0.523
}
```

Z Rotation

The four values in the upper left corner of the RSS part of a transform matrix specify rotation around the Z axis, as shown in Figure 9.9.

	Column 1	Column 2	Column 3	Column 4
Row 1	C	S	0.0	
Row 2	-S	C	0.0	t
Row 3	0.0	0.0	1.0	
Row 4		T		s

Figure 9.9 *Transform matrix values specifying X-axis rotation.*

For example, the following transform matrix directs the virtual pen to rotate 30.0 degrees around the Z axis, using the same `C`, `S`, and `–S` values as those used in the previous examples:

```
MatrixTransform {
    matrix  0.866  0.5    0.0  0.0
           -0.5    0.866  0.0  0.0
            0.5    0.0    1.0  0.0
            0.0    0.0    0.0  1.0
}
```

In this matrix, the remaining values in the `RSS`, `T`, `t`, and `s` parts are set to their default values from the identity matrix.

The following **Rotation** node internally creates a transform matrix exactly like the preceding one:

```
Rotation {
   #                    Z    +30.0 degrees
   rotation 0.0 0.0 1.0  0.523
}
```

Tapering Using the `t` Part of a Transform Matrix

Using the three values in the `t` part of a transform matrix, you can control a shape-warping effect called a **taper transform**, as shown in Figure 9.10.

Column

Row	1	2	3	4
1				0.0
2		RSS		0.0
3				0.0
4		T		s

Figure 9.10 *The t, or taper, part of a transform matrix.*

A taper transform warps a shape by directing the virtual pen to draw one side of the shape bigger than its opposite side. For example, you can taper a cylinder by making the top of the cylinder smaller than the bottom, like the cylinder in Figure 9.11.

```
#VRML V1.0 ascii

MatrixTransform {
      matrix      1.0      0.0      0.0      0.0
                  0.0      1.0      0.0      0.5
                  0.0      0.0      1.0      0.0
                  0.0      0.0      0.0      1.0
}
Cylinder {
}
```

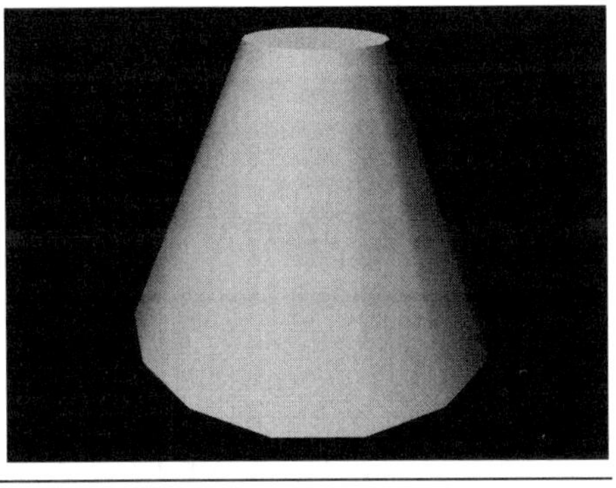

Figure 9.11 *A tapered cylinder.*

The three values in the `t` part of a transform matrix are, from the top down, X, Y, and Z taper factors. A *positive* taper value tapers a shape (*decreases* its size) in the *positive* axis direction, while a *negative* taper value tapers a shape in the *negative* axis direction.

X Taper

Using a positive X taper factor decreases a shape's size as the virtual pen draws farther to the right, and increases it as it draws farther to the left on the X axis. A negative X taper factor reverses this effect.

For example, Figure 9.12 shows a cube tapered in X by specifying a positive X taper factor of 0.5.

```
#VRML V1.0 ascii

MatrixTransform {
        matrix      1.0     0.0     0.0     0.5
                    0.0     1.0     0.0     0.0
                    0.0     0.0     1.0     0.0
                    0.0     0.0     0.0     1.0
}
Cube {
}
```

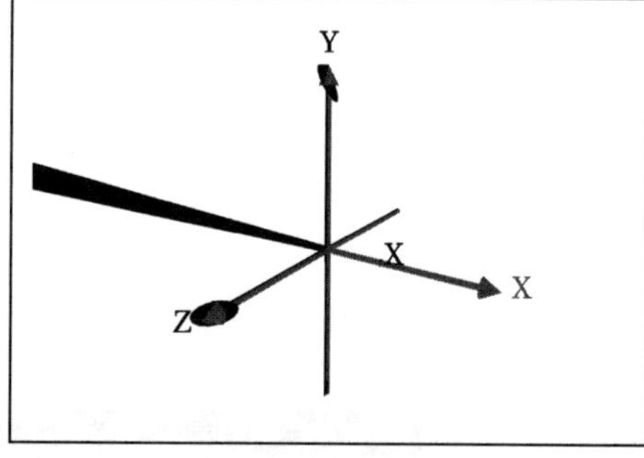

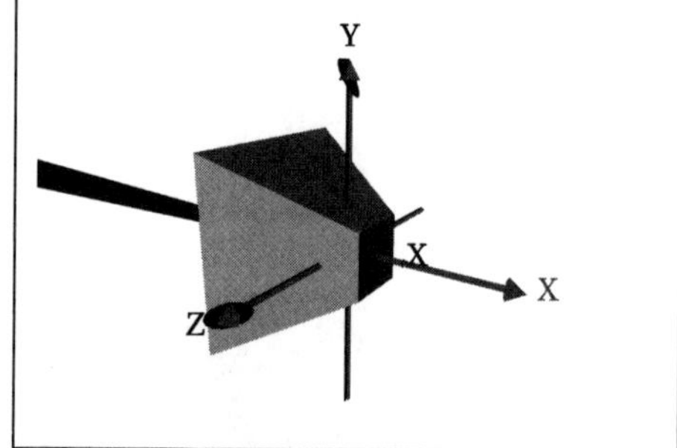

Figure 9.12 *A cube tapered in X.*

Y Taper

Using a positive Y taper factor decreases a shape's size as the virtual pen draws farther up and increases it as it draws farther down the Y axis. A negative Y taper factor reverses this effect.

For example, Figure 9.13 shows a cube tapered in Y by specifying a positive Y taper factor of 0.5.

```
#VRML V1.0 ascii

MatrixTransform {
        matrix      1.0     0.0     0.0     0.0
                    0.0     1.0     0.0     0.5
                    0.0     0.0     1.0     0.0
                    0.0     0.0     0.0     1.0
}
Cube {
}
```

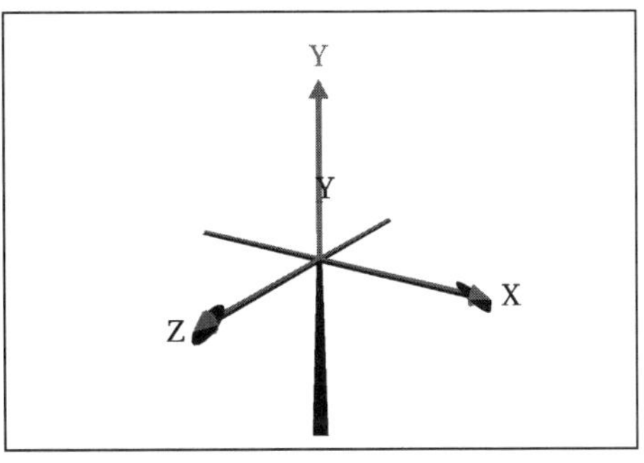

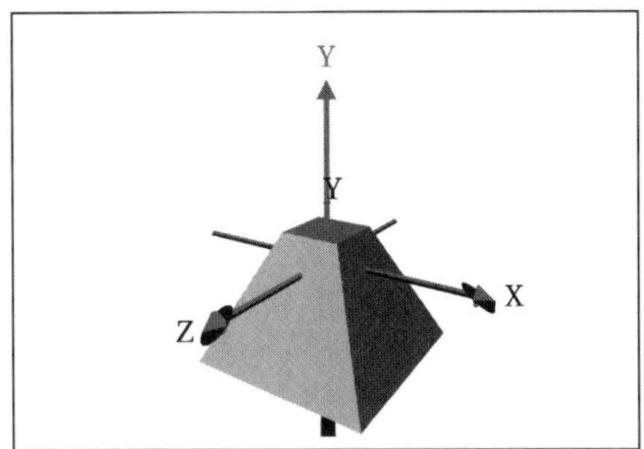

Figure 9.13 *A cube tapered in Y.*

Z Taper

Using a positive Z taper factor decreases a shape's size as the virtual pen draws farther forward and increases it as it draws farther back on the Z axis. A negative Z taper factor reverses this effect.

For example, Figure 9.14 shows a cube tapered in Z by specifying a positive Z taper factor of 0.5.

```
#VRML V1.0 ascii

MatrixTransform {
      matrix      1.0    0.0    0.0    0.0
                  0.0    1.0    0.0    0.0
                  0.0    0.0    1.0    0.5
                  0.0    0.0    0.0    1.0
}
Cube {
}
```

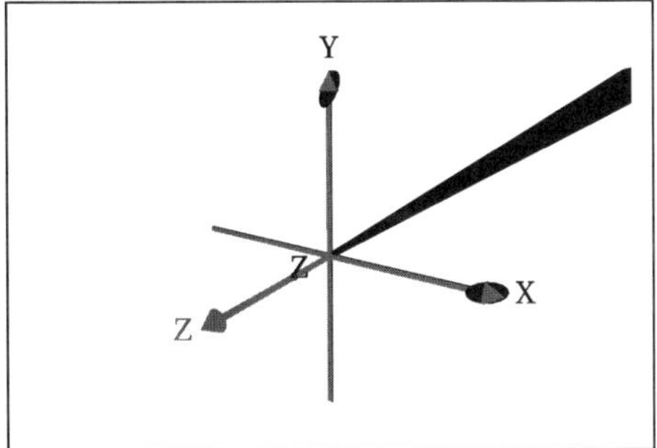

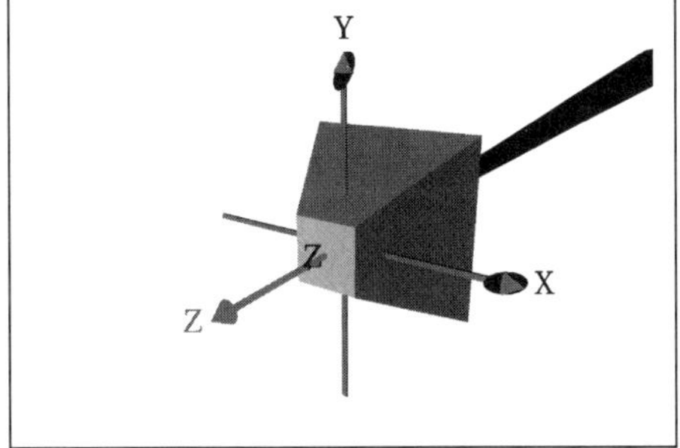

Figure 9.14 *A cube tapered in Z.*

You can taper in X, Y, and Z simultaneously by setting all three taper factors.

The effects of tapering become more pronounced the farther along an axis the virtual pen draws. The result is similar to drawing-size scaling but with a scale factor that gets smaller or larger the farther along an axis that a shape is drawn. This scaling effect squeezes the sides of a shape *and* compresses the shape lengthwise along the axis. Like squeezing, the lengthwise compression also becomes more pronounced the farther along an axis the pen draws.

The following two figures illustrate the lengthwise compression that occurs as a result of tapering. Figure 9.15 shows a stack of ten cylinders, piled up along the positive Y axis. Figure 9.16 shows the same stack of ten cylinders but tapered using a Y-taper matrix transform.

Figure 9.15 *A stack of ten cylinders.*

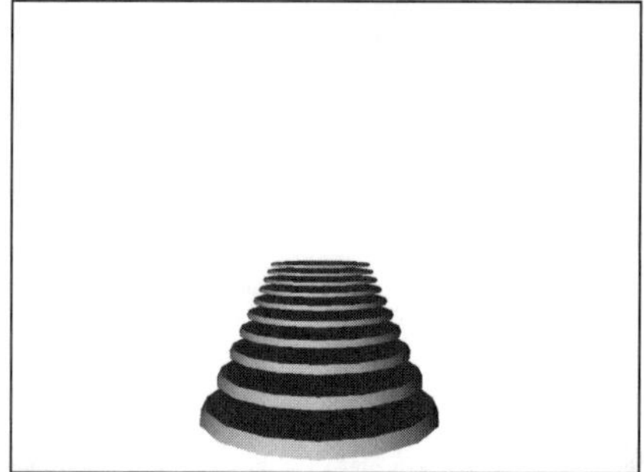

Figure 9.16 *A stack of ten cylinders, tapered using Y-axis tapering.*

Notice that as the stack in Figure 9.16 is tapered more and more dramatically up the Y axis, the individual cylinders in the stack and the spacing between them gets smaller and smaller. The lengthwise compression along the Y axis squashes the tapered shape. The resulting tapered stack of ten cylinders is shorter than the untapered stack.

TIP *Taper factors should always be between –1.0 and 1.0. Taper factors outside of this range create warped shapes with one side so large your VRML browser can't draw them. Good taper factor values are usually between –0.5 and 0.5.*

TIP *For each shape or group of shapes in your world, some VRML browsers internally create invisible cubes, called* **bounding boxes**, *that are computed to be just big enough to entirely contain the shape or group of shapes. The VRML browser uses such bounding boxes to speed up some drawing decisions. However, some VRML browsers do not consider shape warping when they compute bounding boxes. As a result, the bounding boxes they compute are too small and their drawing decisions based on those bounding boxes are wrong. The typical result is that worlds containing warped shapes at the edges of the world may not display properly.*

Shearing Using the RSS Part of a Transform Matrix

Using six of the values in the RSS part of a transform matrix, you can specify a shape-warping effect called a **shear transform**, as shown in Figure 9.17.

		Column			
		1	2	3	4
Row	1	1.0	0.0	0.0	
	2	0.0	1.0	0.0	t
	3	0.0	0.0	1.0	
	4		T		s

Figure 9.17 *Transform matrix values specifying a shear transform.*

A shear transform warps a shape by directing the virtual pen to slide one side of the shape in one direction along an axis, while sliding the opposite side of the shape in the opposite direction along the same axis. For example, you can shear a cube by making the top of the cube slide right, while the bottom slides left, like the cube shown in Figure 9.18.

```
#VRML V1.0 ascii

# X Shear on Y
MatrixTransform {
      matrix      1.0   0.0   0.0   0.0
                  0.5   1.0   0.0   0.0
                  0.0   0.0   1.0   0.0
                  0.0   0.0   0.0   1.0
}
Cube {
}
```

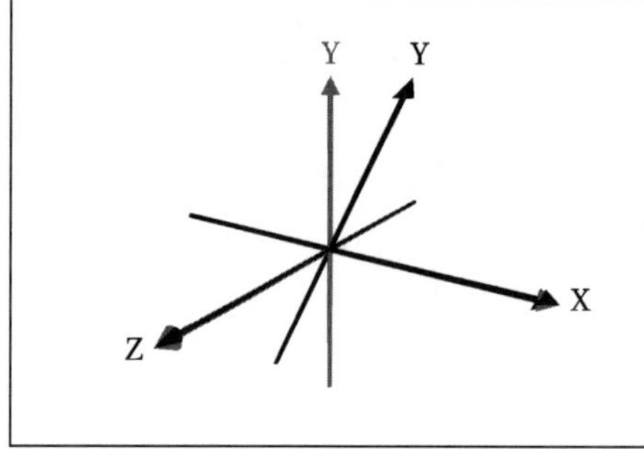

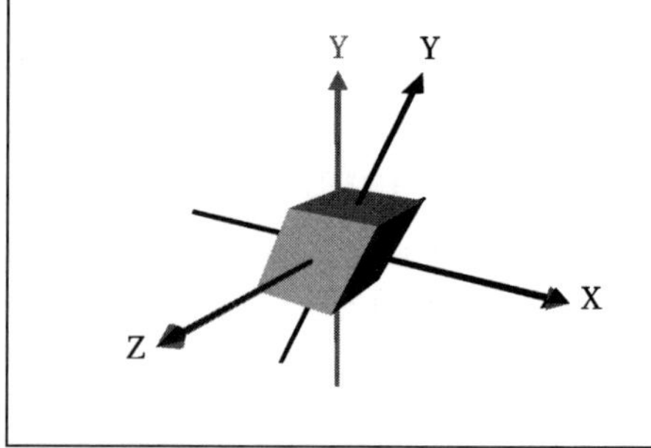

Figure 9.18 *X-shearing a cube by Y.*

By using a larger shear amount, you can skew the cube even more and create a car windshield, a ramp for a parking garage, or the sleek front of a race car. If you shear an entire car shape, you warp it like a cartoon car zooming at high speed.

Six values in the `RSS` part of a transform matrix are **shear factors**. Each one controls the amount of shearing for one of six shearing types (see Table 9.3).

Table 9.3 Shearing Values for the Six Shearing Types

		Matrix	
Shear Type	*Slide the sides of a shape along the . . .*	*Row*	*Column*
X shear	X axis, sliding most those sides that are farthest along the . . .		
by Y	Y axis	2	1
by Z	Z axis	3	1
Y shear	Y axis, sliding most those sides that are farthest along the . . .		
by X	X axis	1	2
by Z	Z axis	3	2
Z shear	Z axis, sliding most those sides that are farthest along the . . .		
by X	X axis	1	3
by Y	Y axis	2	3

X Shear

The following examples illustrate X shearing.

X Shear by Y An *X shear by Y* slides the top and bottom parts of a shape in opposite directions along the X axis. A *positive* shear factor causes shape parts farther *up* on the Y axis to be slid farther *right*, and parts farther *down* on the Y axis to be slid farther *left*. A *negative* shear factor reverses this effect.

For example, Figure 9.19 shows a cube sheared in X by Y by specifying a positive shear factor of 0.5.

```
#VRML V1.0 ascii

# X Shear on Y
MatrixTransform {
      matrix     1.0    0.0    0.0    0.0
                 0.5    1.0    0.0    0.0
                 0.0    0.0    1.0    0.0
                 0.0    0.0    0.0    1.0
}
Cube {
}
```

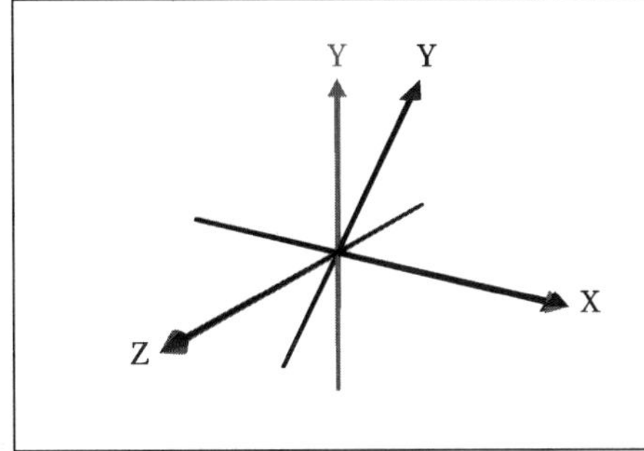

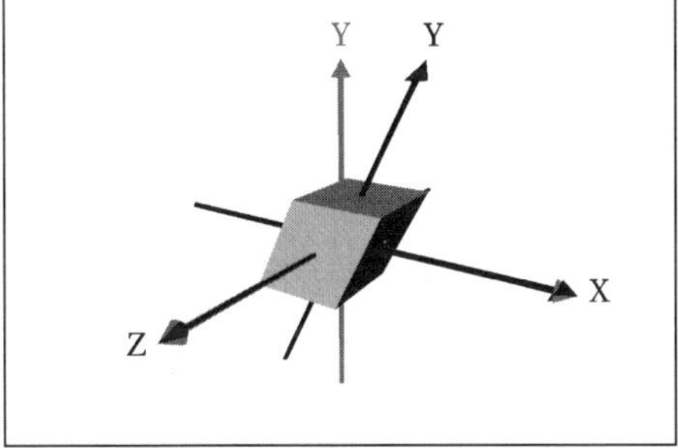

Figure 9.19 *X-shearing a cube by Y.*

X Shear by Z An *X shear by Z* slides the front and back parts of a shape in opposite directions along the X axis. A *positive* shear factor causes shape parts farther *forward* on the Z axis to be slid farther *right*, and parts farther *back* on the Z axis to be slid farther *left*. A *negative* shear factor reverses this effect.

For example, Figure 9.20 shows a cube sheared in X by Z by specifying a positive shear factor of 0.5.

```
#VRML V1.0 ascii

# X Shear on Z
MatrixTransform {
      matrix      1.0    0.0    0.0    0.0
                  0.0    1.0    0.0    0.0
                  0.5    0.0    1.0    0.0
                  0.0    0.0    0.0    1.0
}
Cube {
}
```

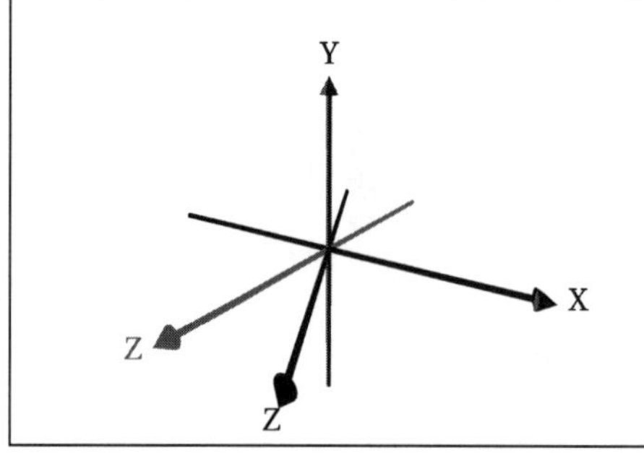

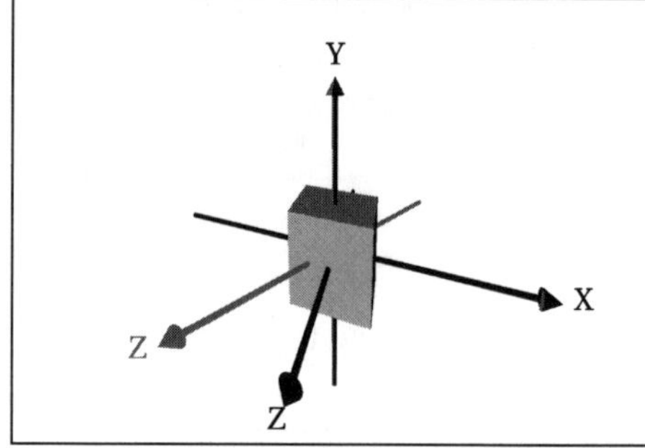

Figure 9.20 *X-shearing a cube by Z.*

Y Shear

The following examples illustrate Y shearing.

Y Shear by X A *Y shear by* X slides the right and left parts of a shape in opposite directions along the Y axis. A *positive* shear factor causes shape parts farther *right* on the X axis to be slid farther *up,* and parts farther *left* on the X axis to be slid farther *down.* A *negative* shear factor reverses this effect.

For example, Figure 9.21 shows a cube sheared in Y by X by specifying a positive shear factor of 0.5.

```
#VRML V1.0 ascii

# Y Shear on X
MatrixTransform {
      matrix      1.0    0.5    0.0    0.0
                  0.0    1.0    0.0    0.0
                  0.0    0.0    1.0    0.0
                  0.0    0.0    0.0    1.0
}
Cube {
}
```

Figure 9.21 continues

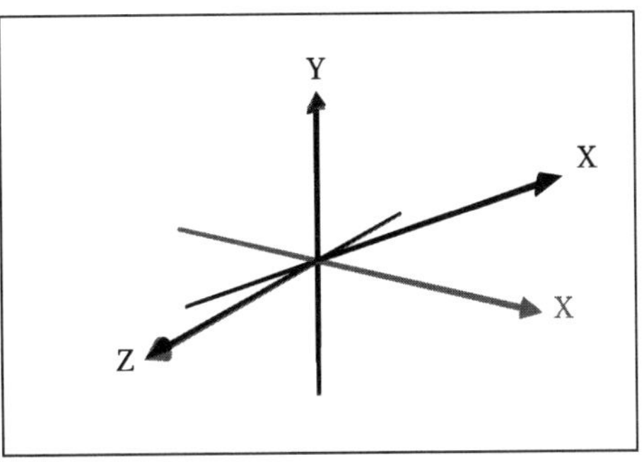

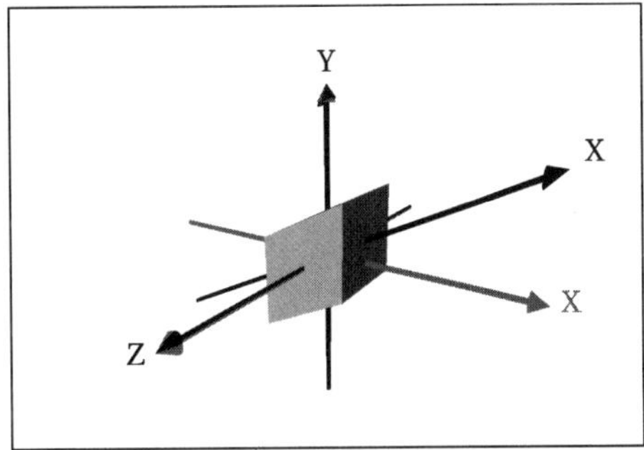

Figure 9.21 *Y-shearing a cube by X.*

Y Shear by Z A *Y shear by Z* slides the forward and back parts of a shape in opposite directions along the Y axis. A *positive* shear factor causes shape parts farther *forward* on the Z axis to be slid farther *up,* and parts farther *back* on the Z axis to be slid farther *down*. A *negative* shear factor reverses this effect.

For example, Figure 9.22 shows a cube sheared in Y by Z by specifying a positive shear factor of 0.5.

```
#VRML V1.0 ascii

# Y Shear on Z
MatrixTransform {
      matrix      1.0    0.0    0.0    0.0
                  0.0    1.0    0.0    0.0
                  0.0    0.5    1.0    0.0
                  0.0    0.0    0.0    1.0
}
Cube {
}
```

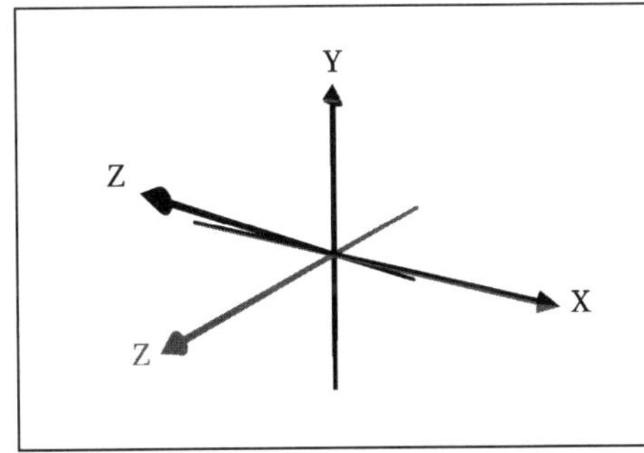

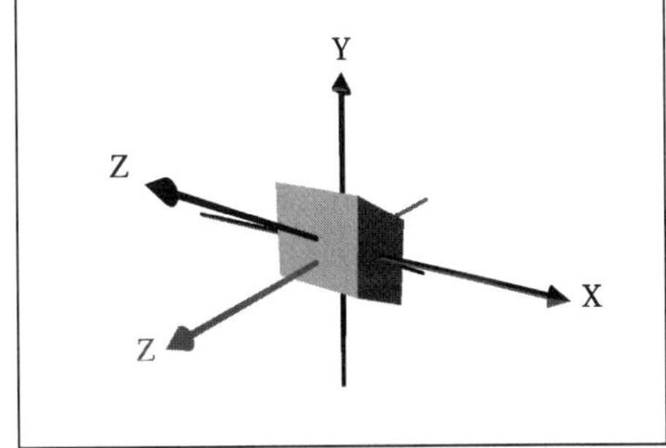

Figure 9.22 *Y-shearing a cube by Z.*

Z Shear

The following examples illustrate Z shearing.

Z Shear by X A *Z shear by* X slides the right and left parts of a shape in opposite directions along the Z axis. A *positive* shear factor causes shape parts farther *right* on the X axis to be slid farther *forward,* and parts farther *left* on the X axis to be slid farther *back.* A *negative* shear factor reverses this effect.

For example, Figure 9.23 shows a cube sheared in Z by X by specifying a positive shear factor of 0.5.

```
#VRML V1.0 ascii
# Z Shear on X
MatrixTransform {
        matrix      1.0     0.0     0.5     0.0
                    0.0     1.0     0.0     0.0
                    0.0     0.0     1.0     0.0
                    0.0     0.0     0.0     1.0
}
Cube {
}
```

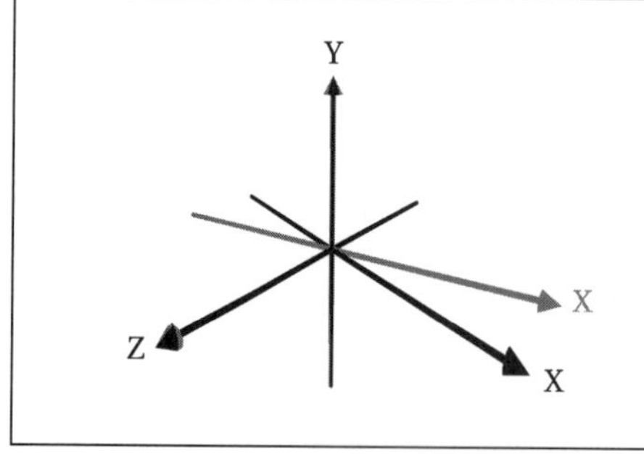

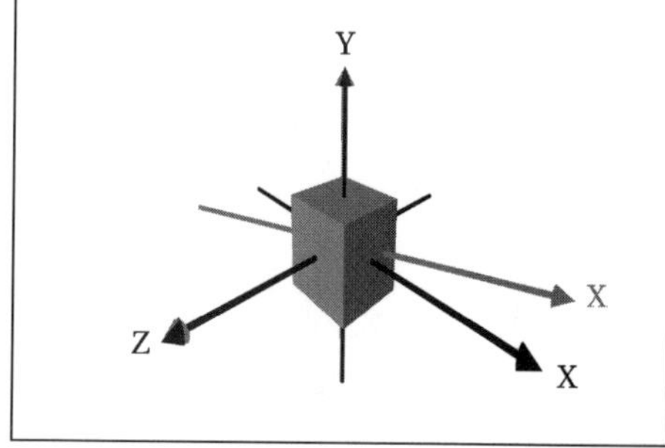

Figure 9.23 *Z-shearing a cube by X.*

Z Shear by Y A *Z shear by* Y slides the top and bottom parts of a shape in opposite directions along the Z axis. A *positive* shear factor causes shape parts farther *up* on the Y axis to be slid farther *forward,* and parts farther *down* on the Y axis to be slid farther *back.* A *negative* shear factor reverses this effect.

For example, Figure 9.24 shows a cube sheared in Z by Y by specifying a positive shear factor of 0.5.

```
#VRML V1.0 ascii

# Z Shear on Y
MatrixTransform {
      matrix      1.0    0.0    0.0    0.0
                  0.0    1.0    0.5    0.0
                  0.0    0.0    1.0    0.0
                  0.0    0.0    0.0    1.0
}
Cube {
}
```

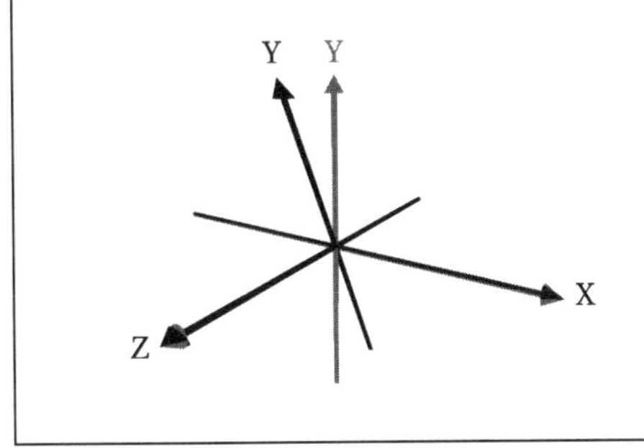

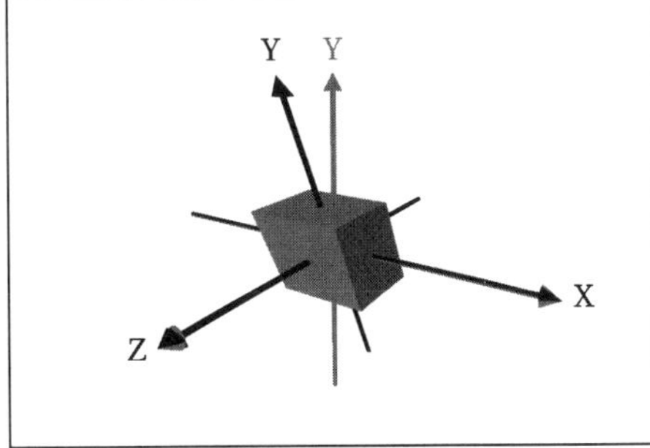

Figure 9.24 *Z-shearing a cube by Y.*

You can shear in more than one direction at a time by setting multiple shear factors in the RSS part of the transform matrix.

Setting Values in More Than One Part of a Transform Matrix

You can simultaneously set values in more than one part of the same transform matrix. This lets you combine shearing, tapering, rotating, translating, and scaling together in one transform matrix. For instance, the VRML text in Figure 9.25 directs the virtual pen to taper in the Y direction by 0.5, X shear by Y with a factor of 0.8, then draw a cylinder.

```
#VRML V1.0 ascii
MatrixTransform {
      matrix      1.0    0.0    0.0    0.0
                  0.8    1.0    0.0    0.5
                  0.0    0.0    1.0    0.0
                  0.0    0.0    0.0    1.0
}
Cylinder {
}
```

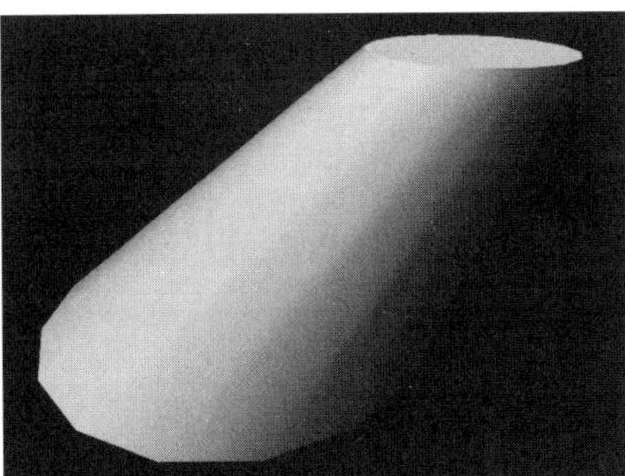

Figure 9.25 *Tapering, shearing, and drawing a cylinder.*

By combining shearing, tapering, and other transforms you can direct the virtual pen to warp shapes in very complex and interesting ways.

Using **MatrixTransform** Nodes with Other Nodes

You can use a **MatrixTransform** node in combination with additional **Translation, Rotation, Scale,** and **Transform** nodes, either before or after the **MatrixTransform** node. For instance, you can use a **MatrixTransform** node to direct the virtual pen to shear subsequent shapes, and follow it with a **Translation** node to move the virtual pen before drawing. Similarly, you can rotate the virtual pen first with a **Rotation** node, then instruct the virtual pen to taper shapes using a subsequent **MatrixTransform** node.

You can also use more than one **MatrixTransform** node. For instance, you could direct the virtual pen to shear using a **MatrixTransform** node with a shear transform matrix, and follow it later with a **MatrixTransform** node directing the virtual pen to taper by using a taper transform matrix.

Extended Examples

The following examples build on the concepts presented in this chapter. They illustrate the worlds you can create using VRML's primitive shapes and matrix transforms. Try them on your own.

TIP *All of the VRML text in the extended examples throughout this book are available via anonymous ftp from John Wiley & Sons at* `ftp.wiley.com/public/computer_books/vrml` *and from the VRML Repository at* `http://www.sdsc.edu/vrml`.

An Ancient City

The example text in Figure 9.26 builds an ancient city with a row of arches leading up to a flat-topped pyramid. The pyramid is built using a tapered cube.

A large flattened cube is used first for the ground of the city. To draw the pyramid, a **MatrixTransform** node tapers the virtual pen before drawing a cube. Since the remaining parts of the city should not be tapered, the cube is followed by another **MatrixTransform** that *untapers* the virtual pen by tapering in exactly the opposite direction (a –0.5 Y taper to undo the original +0.5 Y taper). The remainder of the VRML file draws a row of columns and arch blocks leading up to the pyramid.

```
#VRML V1.0 ascii
# Ground
Cube {
        height 0.1
        width 20.0
        depth 20.0
}
```

Figure 9.26 continues

```
# Central Pyramid
Translation {
      translation 5.0 2.2 0.0
}
MatrixTransform {
      matrix      1.0   0.0   0.0   0.0
                  0.0   1.0   0.0   0.5
                  0.0   0.0   1.0   0.0
                  0.0   0.0   0.0   1.0
}
Cube {
      height 2.1
      width 2.8
      depth 2.8
}
MatrixTransform {
      matrix      1.0   0.0   0.0   0.0
                  0.0   1.0   0.0   -0.5
                  0.0   0.0   1.0   0.0
                  0.0   0.0   0.0   1.0
}

# Two rows of columns
Translation {
      translation -14.0 -1.2 -2.0
}

# Front two columns
Cylinder {
      height 2.0
      radius 0.2
}
Translation {
      translation 0.0 0.0 4.0
}
Cylinder {
      height 2.0
      radius 0.2
}
Translation {
      translation 0.0 1.15 -2.0
            }
Cube {
      height 0.3
      width 0.6
      depth 5.0
}
Translation {
      translation 2.0 -1.15 -2.0
}

# Second two columns
Cylinder {
      height 2.0
      radius 0.2
}
```

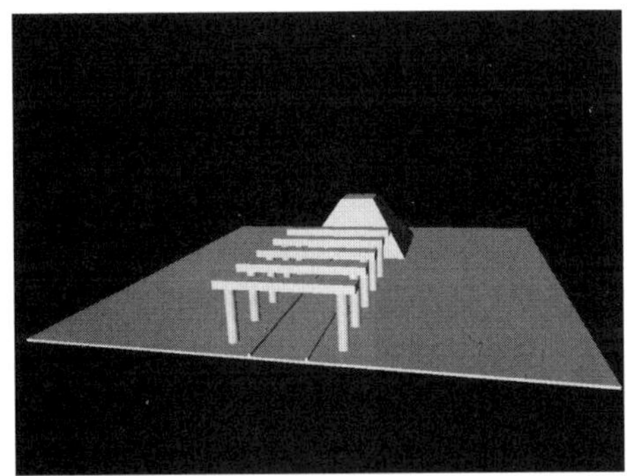

Figure 9.26 continues

```
Translation {
      translation 0.0 0.0 4.0
            }
Cylinder {
      height 2.0
      radius 0.2
}
Translation {
      translation 0.0 1.15 -2.0
}
Cube {
      height 0.3
      width 0.6
      depth 5.0
}
Translation {
      translation 2.0 -1.15 -2.0
}

# Third two columns
Cylinder {
      height 2.0
      radius 0.2
}
Translation {
      translation 0.0 0.0 4.0
}
Cylinder {
      height 2.0
      radius 0.2
            }
Translation {
      translation 0.0 1.15 -2.0
}
Cube {
      height 0.3
      width 0.6
      depth 5.0
}
Translation {
      translation 2.0 -1.15 -2.0
}

# Fourth two columns
Cylinder {
      height 2.0
      radius 0.2
}
Translation {
      translation 0.0 0.0 4.0
}
Cylinder {
      height 2.0
      radius 0.2
}
```

Figure 9.26 continues

```
Translation {
      translation 0.0 1.15 -2.0
}
Cube {
      height 0.3
      width 0.6
      depth 5.0
            }
Translation {
      translation 2.0 -1.15 -2.0
}

# Fifth two columns
Cylinder {
      height 2.0
      radius 0.2
}
Translation {
      translation 0.0 0.0 4.0
}
Cylinder {
      height 2.0
      radius 0.2
}
Translation {
      translation 0.0 1.15 -2.0
}
Cube {
      height 0.3
      width 0.6
      depth 5.0
}
Translation {
      translation 2.0 -1.15 -2.0
}

# Road to the pyramid
Translation {
      translation -4.0 -0.9 1.0
}
Cube {
      width 14.0
      height 0.1
      depth 0.1
}
Translation {
      translation 0.0 0.0 2.0
}
Cube {
      width 14.0
      height 0.1
      depth 0.1
}
```

Figure 9.26 *An ancient city.*

A Race Car

This example creates a sleek race car. The main body of the car is a sheared and tapered cube. Using two **MatrixTransform** nodes, the virtual pen is directed to draw the cube *X sheared by Y* and tapered in Y. This creates a sleek, swept-back body shape a little like a DeLorean sports car.

The car's wheels are drawn first, before warping the pen to draw the car body. After the car body, bubble windows are added, as well as a fin. Because the virtual pen is still drawing based on the shear and taper transforms applied to the car body, the bubble windows and the fin are also sheared and tapered. This helps the bubble windows fit with the front of the car and makes the fin look as swept back as the car body.

```
#VRML V1.0 ascii

# Front and back wheels
Rotation {
      #        X              +90.0 degrees
      rotation 1.0 0.0 0.0  1.57
}
Translation {
      translation -1.6 -0.35 0.0
}
Cylinder {
      height 2.5
      radius 0.2
}
Translation {
      translation 2.0 0.0 -0.1
}
Cylinder {
      height 2.6
      radius 0.3
}
Rotation {
      #        X              -90.0 degrees
      rotation 1.0 0.0 0.0  -1.57
}
Translation {
      translation -0.4 0.25 0.0
}

# Swept back race car body
Scale {
      scaleFactor 1.0 0.2 1.0
}
MatrixTransform {
      matrix      1.0    0.0    0.0    0.0
                  0.8    1.0    0.0    0.0
                  0.0    0.0    1.0    0.0
                  0.0    0.0    0.0    1.0
}
```

Figure 9.27 continues

```
MatrixTransform {
      matrix      1.0    0.0    0.0    0.0
                  0.0    1.0    0.0    0.2
                  0.0    0.0    1.0    0.0
                  0.0    0.0    0.0    1.0
}
Cube {
}

# Bubble windows
Translation {
      translation -0.35 0.05 0.0
}
Scale {
      scaleFactor 1.0 0.9 1.1
}
Sphere {
}
Scale {
      scaleFactor 1.0 1.11 0.91
}

# Swept back fin
Translation {
      translation 0.8 1.4 0.0
}
Cube {
      height 1.1
      width 0.6
      depth 0.2
}
Translation {
      translation 0.0 0.4 0.0
}
Cube {
      height 0.3
      width 0.7
      depth 2.2
}
```

Figure 9.27 *A race car.*

Summary

The **MatrixTransform** node enables you to give transform instructions directly to the virtual pen in the form of transform matrices. These are, in fact, the underlying mechanisms by which the standard **Translation, Rotation, Scale,** and **Transform** nodes direct the virtual pen.

Two common types of transform matrices are those used to taper and shear subsequent shapes drawn by the virtual pen. Using a taper transform matrix, you can direct the virtual pen to scale down one side of a shape while simultaneously scaling up the opposite side of the same shape. You can taper in the X, Y, and Z directions using X, Y, and Z taper factors set in the `t` part of a transform matrix.

Using a shear transform matrix, you can direct the virtual pen to slide one side of a shape in the positive direction of an axis, while simultaneously sliding the opposite side of the same shape in the negative direction of the same axis. There are six ways to shear, including: *X shear by Y*, *X shear by Z*, *Y shear by X*, *Y shear by Z*, *Z shear by X*, and *Z shear by Y*. For each type of shear you indicate the shear factor by setting a value in the `RSS` part of a transform matrix.

MatrixTransform nodes may be used singly, or in combination with other transform nodes or other **MatrixTransform** nodes.

CHAPTER 10

Shading with Materials

VRML shapes can be drawn in any color. You can create green lawns, blue skies, beige carpets, and orange sunsets. Shapes can be semitransparent, or they can glow. You can create see-through screen doors and glowing light bulbs.

You can direct the virtual pen to draw any shape, or any group of shapes, using any color and making the shapes as transparent or aglow as you like. All of the examples in the previous chapters have used the default virtual-pen color: white. Using the **Material** node, you can change the virtual-pen properties that control drawing color, glow color, and transparency amount.

Understanding Color

Imagine that you had to make a list of all the colors in the world: red, magenta, blue, mauve, purple, and so on. Color lists like this are not very precise. They are too vague and too limited. VRML has a more accurate way of describing color so that you can be as precise about color as you are, for example, about shape positioning, rotating, and scaling.

If you've taken an art class, you may remember experimenting with paint colors. Starting with just a few colors of paint, you can create a huge variety of colors by mixing them together in different proportions. To get orange you mix a dab of yellow paint with a dab of red paint. To get purple you mix a dab of red with a dab of blue. To make a color lighter you add white, and to make it darker you add black.

You can carefully measure the amount of each basic color you use to create a new color, then give the measurements to a friend. By mixing the same paints in the same amounts, your friend can create exactly the same color you did. Color measurements like this are used to create all the shades of paint you find in a paint store.

Similar to mixing colors of paint, you can also mix colors of light. To get orange light you can mix red light and yellow light. To get purple light you can mix red light and blue light. To make a light brighter, you turn up its intensity. To make a light darker, you turn down its intensity.

Imagine mixing together colors of light like this by using three flashlights aimed at a white wall in a darkened room. Figure 10.1 shows the three flashlights shining on the wall.

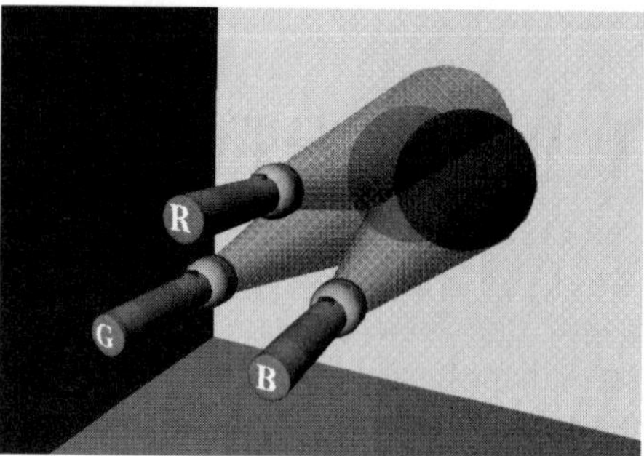

Figure 10.1 *Three colored flashlights shining on a white wall.*

The first flashlight has a red bulb, the second has a green bulb, and the third has a blue bulb. If you just turn on the flashlight with the red bulb, you'll see a red circle of light on the wall. Similarly, if you just turn on the flashlight with the green or blue bulb, you'll see only a green or blue circle of light on the wall.

If you turn on the flashlights with the green bulb and the blue bulb at the same time, you'll see a light bluish-green called *cyan*. If you on turn the flashlights with the red bulb and the blue bulb, you'll see a bluish-red called *magenta*. Finally, if you turn on all of them at once, you'll mix all three colors of light together, and you'll see white. Color plate 2*a* shows how this looks.

If you put dimmer knobs on each of the three flashlights, you can control their brightness. This lets you mix different amounts of red, green, and blue light to create a large variety of colors. Using just red, green, and blue lights, it is possible to create most of the colors the human eye can see.

If you carefully measure the dimmer-knob positions you used to create a new color, you can give those measurements to a friend. By adjusting dimmer knobs on their own three flashlights, your friend can use your knob measurements to create exactly the same color of light that you created.

VRML uses precise color measurements to specify the amount of red, green, and blue light to mix together to define virtual pen colors. These color measurements are called **RGB colors**, because they indicate how to combine amounts of red (R), green (G), and blue (B) light.

Table 10.1 Sample RGB Colors

Red	*Green*	*Blue*	*Description*
1.0	0.0	0.0	Pure red
0.0	1.0	0.0	Pure green
0.0	0.0	1.0	Pure blue
1.0	1.0	1.0	White
0.0	0.0	0.0	Black
1.0	1.0	0.0	Yellow
0.0	1.0	1.0	Cyan
1.0	0.0	1.0	Magenta
0.75	0.75	0.75	Light gray
0.5	0.5	0.5	Medium gray
0.25	0.25	0.25	Dark gray
0.5	0.0	0.0	Dark red
0.0	0.5	0.0	Dark green
0.0	0.0	0.5	Dark blue

RGB colors contain three floating-point values, each one between 0.0 and 1.0. The first value in an RGB color specifies the amount of red to use, the second specifies the amount of green, and the third the amount of blue. A value of 0.0 for a red, green, or blue amount means to turn that color off. A value of 1.0 for a red, green, or blue amount means to turn on that color completely. Values between 0.0 and 1.0 mean a color should be turned on partially. For example, Table 10.1 shows some sample RGB colors.

Using RGB colors, you can precisely create an enormous number of colors. Color plate 1 shows a sampling of colors you can create, and Appendix B lists the RGB color values used to create each one. To create a color of your own, start by looking for a similar color on the color plates, get the RGB color values from the appendix, and then adjust the individual red, green, and blue amounts up or down until you get exactly the color you want.

Understanding Shading, Glowing Effects, and Transparency

You can direct the VRML virtual pen to draw shapes in any color, make them glow, and make them semitransparent.

Shading

When light shines on a shape, such as the sphere in Figure 10.2*a*, the sides facing the light are bright, while the sides facing away are dark. Sides of the shape that partially face the light have an intermediate brightness that depends on how much they face the light. Artists call these variations in brightness **shading**.

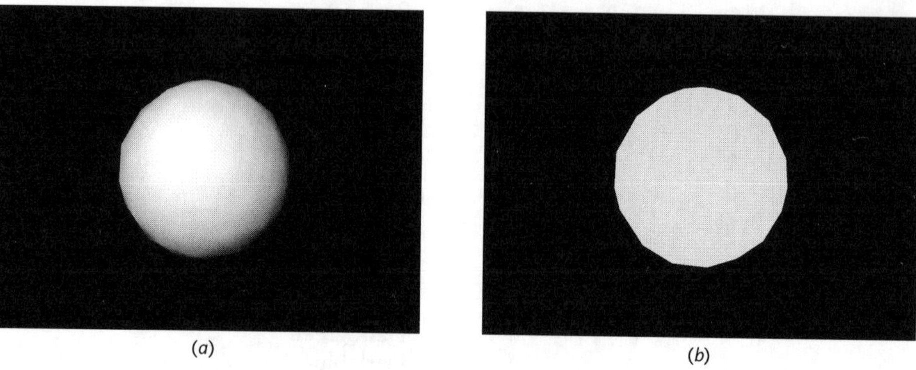

(*a*) (*b*)

Figure 10.2 *Comparing a shaded sphere with an unshaded one.*

Shading gives you the sense that a shape is three-dimensional. Compare, for instance, the shape in Figure 10.2*a* with the shape in Figure 10.2*b*. Both shapes have a circular outline, but one is clearly a sphere, while the other looks more like a flat circle. Actually, they are both drawn using a VRML **Sphere** node. The first sphere is shaded and looks three-dimensional. The second sphere is not shaded and looks flat.

The VRML virtual pen shades shapes by automatically computing the way a light brightens some sides of a shape while leaving other sides dark. To perform this shading, however, the virtual pen needs to know where the light is in relation to the shape. For instance, if the light is to the right of the shape, then the right sides are drawn bright, and the left sides drawn dark. If the light is to the left of the shape, then the left sides are drawn bright, and the right sides drawn dark.

Your VRML browser automatically includes a light for you in every world. This automatic light is positioned so that it shines on the world's shapes from the same viewpoint as you use to view your world. If you move to the right, so does the light. If you move to the left, so does the light. Because this light moves with you as your viewpoint changes, it is often called a **headlight**. You can imagine, in fact, that the headlight is attached to your head like a miner's light, like the one shown in Figure 10.3. As you look about your VRML world, the headlight always shines directly in front of you.

You can place additional lights in your world using the VRML lighting nodes: **PointLight, DirectionalLight,** and **SpotLight.** All three of these nodes are discussed in Chapter 21. Many users find that the headlight is all that they need to properly light their world.

Whether you use the headlight, or the lighting nodes, you control how shapes are shaded using the **Material** node. Material properties are like all other VRML prop-

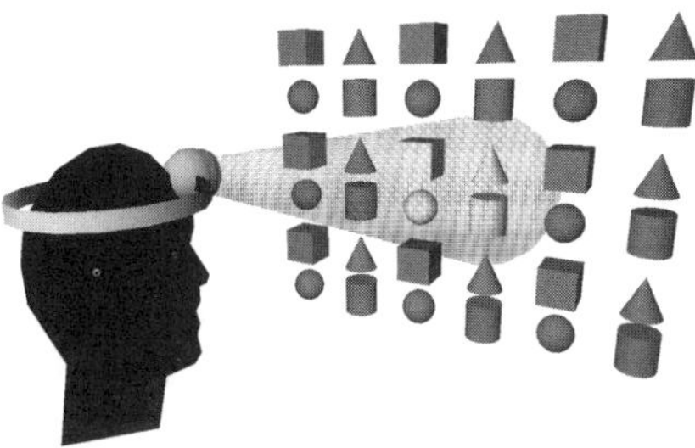

Figure 10.3 *Your headlight—think of it as a miner's headlight.*

erties. Once changed, the virtual pen is directed to use the new material properties for drawing all subsequent shapes.

Glowing Effects

Glowing shapes include light bulbs, computer screens, and neon signs. When a shape glows, it emits its own light. A brightly glowing shape, like a light bulb or the sun, appears simply as a mass of color. Shading effects on the shape are washed out by the shape's own glow.

For example, Figure 10.4 shows a VRML-generated image of a hanging light bulb. Figure 10.4*a* shows the light bulb turned off, and Figure 10.4*b* shows the light bulb turned on. The turned-off bulb is shaded by VRML's virtual pen and is clearly a sphere. The turned-on bulb glows so brightly that the shading is washed out. The bulb appears as a circular mass of light.

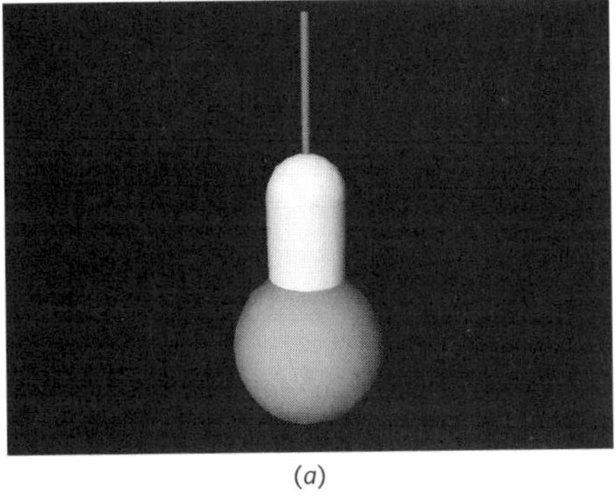

(*a*)

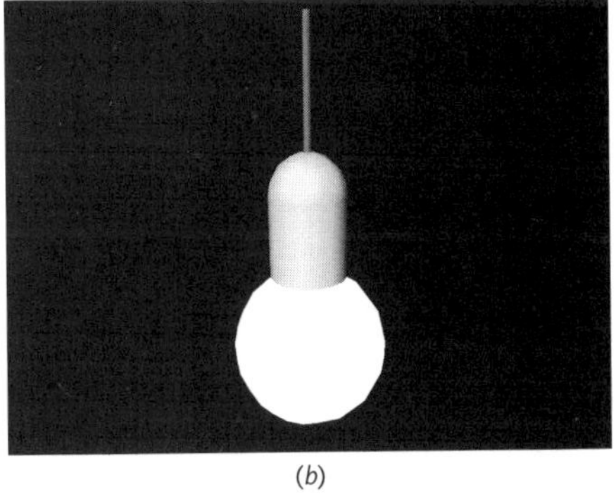

(*b*)

Figure 10.4 *Comparing shading of a light bulb when turned off vs. turned on.*

Using VRML's **Material** node, you can specify that a shape glows when drawn by the virtual pen.

Transparency

Opaque shapes block light, while transparent shapes let light pass straight through them. Semitransparent shapes block a little of the light while letting the rest through. Windows, for instance, are almost completely transparent. Screen doors are semitransparent, and walls are opaque.

Using VRML's **Material** node you can specify how transparent a shape is when drawn by the virtual pen.

Shading a Shape Using Materials

You can control how VRML's virtual pen colors and shades shapes by using a **Material** node. This node lets you specify the RGB color and the amount of glow and transparency of all subsequent shapes drawn by the virtual pen. For instance, the example text in Figure 10.5 directs the virtual pen to draw a red sphere.

```
#VRML V1.0 ascii

Material {
      diffuseColor 1.0 0.0 0.0
}
Sphere {
}
```

Figure 10.5 *A red sphere.*

Notice how the **Material** node is used in Figure 10.5. The **Material** node sets the virtual pen's drawing color to red. The **Sphere** node causes the pen to draw a red sphere.

The **Material** node can be used in the same way to direct the virtual pen to draw shapes partially transparent or to make them glow. In each case, fields in the **Material** node change the way the virtual pen draws subsequent shapes in your VRML file.

Understanding the **Material** Node Syntax

The **Material** node has six fields to control the material properties of the virtual pen, determining how the pen colors and shades shapes. The **ambientColor, diffuseColor, specularColor,** and **emissiveColor** fields each specify an RGB color consisting of three floating-point values. The **shininess** and **transparency** fields are shininess and transparency factors specified by floating-point values.

SYNTAX **Material node**

```
Material {
   diffuseColor  0.8 0.8 0.8          # RGB color
   emissiveColor 0.0 0.0 0.0          # RGB color
   transparency  0.0                  # transparency factor
   ambientColor  0.2 0.2 0.2          # RGB color
   specularColor 0.0 0.0 0.0          # RGB color
   shininess     0.2                  # shininess factor
}
```

The **diffuseColor** field specifies an RGB color for the virtual pen. The virtual pen automatically computes darker colors as it shades the sides of a shape, gradually darkening the shading color as it progresses from the lighted sides of a shape to the unlighted sides. The default **diffuseColor** is the medium-bright white we've used for all the examples in previous chapters.

The **emissiveColor** field selects the RGB glow color. Brighter emissive colors make shapes appear to *emit* more light and thus glow more brightly. The default emissive color is black, which directs the virtual pen to draw shapes so that they do not glow at all.

TIP *Glowing shapes will not light up shapes around them. The glow caused by using the **emissiveColor** field only directs the virtual pen to draw shapes brighter than usual,* as if *they emitted light. For example, if you turn off the default headlight of your VRML browser, shapes that are shaded with emissive colors are still visible. Other shapes are left shaded dark.*

You can set values in both the **diffuseColor** and **emissiveColor** fields to achieve the effect of a partial glow, like a dim light bulb.

The **transparency** field selects a transparency factor that controls how transparent the virtual pen draws subsequent shapes. A transparency factor of 0.0 creates shapes that are opaque, while a factor of 1.0 makes them completely transparent. The default transparency factor is 0.0.

The **ambientColor, specularColor,** and **shininess** fields are used in complex lighting situations where worlds contain one or more of the **PointLight, DirectionalLight,** or **SpotLight** nodes. The use of these three **Material** node fields is discussed in Chapter 21.

Experimenting with Shading

The following examples provide a more detailed examination of the ways in which the **Material** node can be used and how it interacts with nodes we've discussed in previous chapters.

Shading Shapes

Using a **Material** node, you can change the shading color of any shape drawn by the virtual pen. The example text in Figure 10.6 draws a table, and shades it brown by adding a **Material** node at the top of the VRML text.

```
#VRML V1.0 ascii

# Draw in brown
Material {
      diffuseColor 0.56 0.36 0.2
}
# Table top
Cylinder {
      height 0.1
      radius 2.5
}
# Table base
Translation {
      translation 0.0 -1.25 0.0
}
Cylinder {
      height 2.5
      radius 0.25
}
```

Figure 10.6 *A brown table.*

Reading from the top of the file to the bottom, the virtual pen is instructed to:

1. Change its color to brown.
2. Draw a brown cylinder.
3. Move to where the table base should be drawn.
4. Draw a brown cylinder.

The result is the brown table and base shown in Figure 10.6.

A VRML file may contain more than one **Material** node. Each one specifies new color, glow, and transparency properties that will continue to be used by the virtual pen until another **Material** node changes those properties. For instance, the example text in Figure 10.7 creates a pencil and colors each part of the pencil with a different color by using multiple **Material** nodes. The result is the yellow pencil shown in Figure 10.7.

```
#VRML V1.0 ascii

# Dark gray pencil lead
Material {
      diffuseColor 0.2 0.2 0.2
}
```

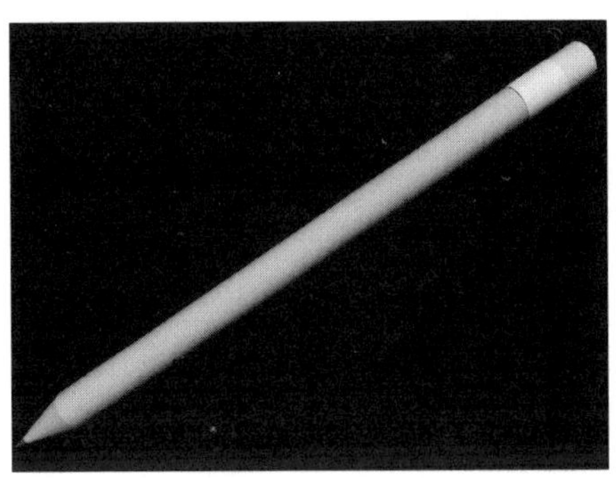

```
Cone {
      height 0.2
      bottomRadius 0.07
}
# Light brown wood tip
Material {
      diffuseColor 0.6 0.5 0.2
}
Translation {
      translation 0.0 -0.4 0.0
}
Cone {
      height 1.0
      bottomRadius 0.3
}
# Yellow shaft
Material {
      diffuseColor 0.7 0.65 0.0
}
Translation {
      translation 0.0 -4.5 0.0
}
Cylinder {
      height 8.0
      radius 0.3
}
# Silver erase holder
Material {
      diffuseColor 0.8 0.8 0.8
}
Translation {
      translation 0.0 -4.35 0.0
}
Cylinder {
      height 0.7
      radius 0.31
}
# Pink eraser
Material {
      diffuseColor 1.0 0.6 0.6
}
Translation {
      translation 0.0 -0.6 0.0
}
Cylinder {
      height 0.5
      radius 0.3
}
```

Figure 10.7 *A yellow pencil.*

Making Shapes Glow

The VRML text in Figure 10.8 builds the hanging light bulb in Figure 10.4*b*. The light bulb wire is drawn in a dark gray, the light-bulb socket in brass, and the light bulb itself glows a pure white.

```
#VRML V1.0 ascii

# Dark gray light bulb hanging wire
Material {
      diffuseColor 0.4 0.4 0.4
}
Cylinder {
      radius 0.05
      height 2.0
}
# Yellowish light bulb socket
Material {
      diffuseColor 1.0 1.0 0.4
}
Translation {
      translation 0.0 -1.0 0.0
}
Sphere {
      radius 0.5
}
Translation {
      translation 0.0 -0.5 0.0
}
Cylinder {
      radius 0.5
      height 1.0
}
# White light bulb
Material {
      diffuseColor  1.0 1.0 1.0
      emissiveColor 1.0 1.0 1.0
}
Translation {
      translation 0.0 -1.45 0.0
}
Sphere {
}
```

Figure 10.8 *A light bulb, turned on.*

The **Material** node just before the light bulb's **Sphere** node specifies an emissive color to cause the bulb to glow bright white. The **diffuseColor** field of the same node sets the shading color to black, which *turns off* shading and makes the shape have a more pure glow. The result is the glowing white light bulb shown in color plate 2*b*.

TIP *Glowing shapes will look better if you reduce or turn off shading. You can do this by setting the* ***diffuseColor*** *field to low values, or even* `0.0 0.0 0.0` *to turn off shading completely.*

You can use the **emissiveColor** field to cause any shape to be drawn as if it is glowing. This can be used to create neon signs, like that in Figure 10.9. This example creates the neon restaurant sign shown in Figure 10.9.

```
#VRML V1.0 ascii

# Glowing red sign letters
Material {
      diffuseColor  0.0 0.0 0.0
      emissiveColor 0.5 0.0 0.0
}
AsciiText {
      string "Pat's Cafe"
      justification CENTER
}
# Glowing red sign frame
Translation {
      translation 0.0 3.5 -0.5
}
Cube {
      height 16.0
      width  61.0
      depth   0.4
}
# Dark gray sign background
Material {
      diffuseColor 0.2 0.2 0.2
}
Cube {
      height 15.0
      width  60.0
      depth   0.5
}
# Brown sign post
Material {
      diffuseColor 0.56 0.36 0.2
}
Translation {
      translation 0.0 -24.0 0.0
}
Cylinder {
      height 32.0
      radius  4.0
}
# Green ground
Material {
      diffuseColor 0.0 0.4 0.0
}
```

Figure 10.9 continues

```
Translation {
     translation 0.0 -16.0 0.0
}
Cube {
     width 70.0
     height 0.4
     depth 70.0
}
```

Figure 10.9 *A neon sign.*

Making Shapes Transparent

The **transparency** field of the **Material** node enables you to control how transparent the virtual pen will draw shapes. The default value is 0.0, which makes shapes opaque. As you increase the transparency value, shapes are drawn more and more transparent. A value of 1.0 directs the virtual pen to draw shapes entirely transparent, which makes them invisible.

The example text in Figure 10.10 draws the text "Fade Away," but covers the word "Away" with a cube. The images that follow vary the transparency value of the cube, gradually changing from fully opaque (Figure 10.10*b*) to fully transparent (Figure 10.10*d*).

The **transparency** field value used in Figure 10.10*c* is 0.25.

TIP *You can use transparency to help you find and correct problems in complex VRML files. If you temporarily change the* ***transparency*** *field of* ***Material*** *nodes, you change some of your file's shapes to semitransparent. This reduces the clutter of a complex world and lets you see* inside *shapes to perhaps see where shapes aren't lining up correctly. After you've corrected your file, turn the semitransparent shapes opaque again by changing* ***Material*** *node* ***transparency*** *fields back to 0.0.*

TIP *Different VRML browsers use different techniques for drawing transparent shapes. Some browsers and graphics hardware use a* **screen-door effect** *that overlays a kind of screen-door mesh on transparent shapes. The* ***transparency*** *field controls the density of that screen so that a high transparency value creates a mostly see-through mesh, while a low transparency value makes the mesh mostly opaque. Other VRML browsers and graphics hardware use a transparency drawing method that actually computes how colors blend when colored shapes show through semitransparent colored shapes. Using this* **color-blending method,** *no screen meshes are used. Check your browser or graphics board manuals, or try the preceding examples to see which transparency method your browser uses.*

```
#VRML V1.0 ascii

AsciiText {
      string "Fade Away"
      justification RIGHT
}
Material {
      transparency 0.0
}
Translation {
      translation -12.0 3.5 1.0
}
Cube {
      height 16.0
      width  29.0
      depth   0.4
}
```

(*a*)

(*b*)

(*c*)

(*d*)

Figure 10.10 *The "Fade Away" text shape—images show various transparencies of the cube covering "Away."*

Extended Examples

The following examples build on the concepts presented in this chapter. They illustrate worlds you can create by applying material properties (color, transparency, and glow) to the VRML primitive shapes. Try them on your own.

TIP *All of the VRML text in the extended examples throughout this book are available via anonymous ftp from John Wiley & Sons at* `ftp.wiley.com/public/computer_books/vrml` *and from the VRML Repository at* `http://www.sdsc.edu/vrml`.

A Colorful Jet Turbine

You can add color to the jet turbine-like shape from Chapter 6. For each turbine blade, add a **Material** node before each **Cube** node to set the blade's color. You can create a variety of colorful designs by choosing different colors for individual blades or groups of blades, like the colors in Table 10.2 that are shown in Figure 10.11.

Table 10.2 Blade Colors

	RGB Color		
Blade	*Red Value*	*Green Value*	*Blue Value*
1	1.0	0.0	0.0
2	0.93	0.0	0.07
3	0.87	0.0	0.13
4	0.80	0.0	0.20
5	0.73	0.0	0.27
6	0.67	0.0	0.33
7	0.60	0.0	0.40
8	0.53	0.0	0.47
9	0.47	0.0	0.53
10	0.40	0.0	0.60
11	0.33	0.0	0.67
12	0.27	0.0	0.73
13	0.20	0.0	0.80
14	0.13	0.0	0.87
15	0.07	0.0	0.93
16	0.0	0.0	1.0
17	0.0	0.0	1.0
18	0.07	0.0	0.93
19	0.13	0.0	0.87
20	0.20	0.0	0.80
21	0.27	0.0	0.73
22	0.33	0.0	0.67
23	0.40	0.0	0.60
24	0.47	0.0	0.53
25	0.53	0.0	0.47
26	0.60	0.0	0.40
27	0.67	0.0	0.33
28	0.73	0.0	0.27
29	0.80	0.0	0.20
30	0.87	0.0	0.13
31	0.93	0.0	0.07
32	1.0	0.0	0.0

Color plate 2*c* and Figure 10.11 show the resulting colored turbine. We include enough VRML text in Figure 10.11 to get you started.

```
#VRML V1.0 ascii

# First blade
Material {
      diffuseColor 1.0 0.0 0.0
}
Cube {
      width 8.0
      height 0.6
      depth 0.05
}
Rotation {
      rotation 1.8 2.5 1.0 0.2
}
# Second blade
Material {
      diffuseColor 0.93 0.0 0.07
}
Cube {
      width 8.0
      height 0.6
      depth 0.05
}
Rotation {
      rotation 1.8 2.5 1.0 0.2
}
# etc. . .
```

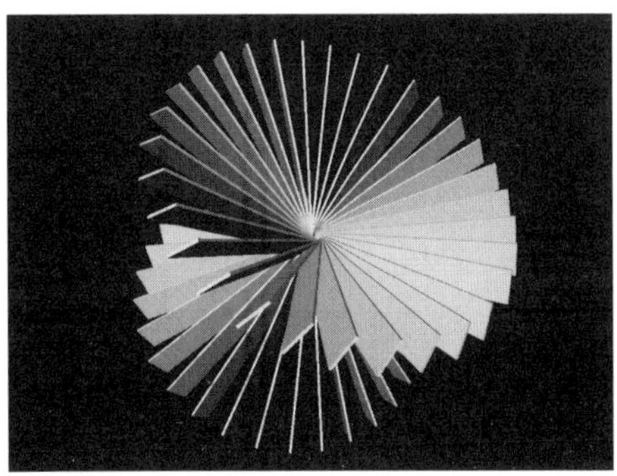

Figure 10.11 *A colored turbine.*

A Digital Clock

The digital clock in Figure 10.12 uses diffuse colors for all but the LED. The numbers of the LED are emissive red.

```
#VRML V1.0 ascii

# Body of digital clock
Material {
      diffuseColor 0.5 0.15 0.0
}
Cube {
      width  0.5
      height 0.15
      depth  0.3
}
# Bezel
Translation {
      translation 0.0 0.0 0.15
}
```

Figure 10.12 continues

```
Material {
     diffuseColor 0.7 0.7 0.7
}
Cube {
     width  0.5
     height 0.15
     depth  0.001
}
# Clock display background
Material {
     diffuseColor 0.0 0.0 0.0
}
Cube {
     width  0.45
     height 0.10
     depth  0.0015
}
# Glowing digital display
Translation {
     translation 0.04 -0.03 0.001
}
Material {
     diffuseColor 0.0 0.0 0.0
     emmissiveColor 1.0 0.0 0.0
}
FontStyle {
     family SANS
     style BOLD
     size 0.09
}
AsciiText {
     string "12:00"
     justification CENTER
     width 0.3
}
# Alarm indicator
Translation {
     translation -0.22 0.055 0.0
}
AsciiText {
     string "."
}
# AM/PM indicator
Translation {
     translation 0.0 -0.055 0.0
}
FontStyle {
     family SANS
     style BOLD
     size 0.02
}
```

Figure 10.12 continues

```
AsciiText {
     string "PM"
}
# Snooze bar
Translation {
     translation 0.18 0.105 -0.06
}
Material {
     diffuseColor 0.8 0.8 0.8
}
Cube {
     width  0.35
     height 0.01
     depth  0.05
}
# Alarm and time setting buttons
Translation {
     translation -0.16 0.0 -0.07
}
Cube {
     width  0.03
     height 0.01
     depth  0.03
}
Translation {
     translation 0.04 0.0 0.0
}
Cube {
     width  0.03
     height 0.01
     depth  0.03
}
# Fast and slow set buttons
Translation {
     translation 0.06 0.0 0.0
}
Cube {
     width  0.03
     height 0.01
     depth  0.03
}
Translation {
     translation 0.04 0.0 0.0
}
Cube {
     width  0.03
     height 0.01
     depth  0.03
}
```

Figure 10.12 continues

```
# Alarm on/off switch
Translation {
     translation 0.06 0.0 0.005
}
Cylinder {
     height 0.015
     radius 0.007
}
Translation {
     translation 0.0 0.0 -0.015
}
Material {
     diffuseColor 0.1 0.1 0.1
}
Cube {
     width  0.02
     height 0.001
     depth  0.05
}
```

Figure 10.12 *A clock with an emissive LED.*

Summary

A **Material** node changes the color the virtual pen uses to draw all subsequent shapes. You can use more than one **Material** node in a file to give each shape its own color.

Using the **Material** node's **diffuseColor** field, you can control the virtual pen's shading color. Colors are specified using RGB colors that specify the amount of red (R), green (G), and blue (B) light to mix together to achieve the desired color. The virtual pen automatically shades shapes based on what sides face towards, or away from, lights in the world.

VRML browsers provide all worlds with a headlight. The headlight is automatically positioned so that it always points in the same direction as the one in which you are looking in your VRML world.

By setting the **emissiveColor** field of the **Material** node, you can direct the virtual pen to draw shapes that appear to glow. The glowing color is specified using an RGB color. A **Material** node can have both the **emissiveColor** and the **diffuseColor** fields set, each with a different color.

Using the **transparency** field of the **Material** node, you can direct the virtual pen to draw semitransparent shapes. Transparency values vary from 0.0 (opaque) to 1.0 (fully transparent).

CHAPTER 11

Grouping Nodes

In VRML you can group together any number of nodes and then manipulate the group as a whole. For instance, you can group together nodes to create a complex building, then place the building group on a city block using a single translation. You can group together nodes to build a sofa, a desk, or a bookcase, then translate and rotate each group to place it within a room.

Grouping helps you organize large VRML files and makes it easier to build complex worlds. You can also put groups inside other groups. For example, you could put the nodes of a VRML building into a group, then multiple building groups into a city block group, multiple city block groups into a city group, multiple city groups into a state group, and so on. Using this kind of group hierarchy, you can manipulate large parts of a world at once.

VRML provides four different grouping nodes: **Group, Switch, TransformSeparator,** and **Separator.** You can use any of these nodes in any combination to help organize your VRML worlds.

Understanding Grouping

The VRML grouping nodes each collect together a list of nodes to be members of a **group**. A group's membership can include any number of nodes, of any type, including transformations, primitive shapes, text, font styles, materials, and even other groups.

Group member nodes in VRML are called **children** or **child nodes** of the group node. The group node managing the child nodes is called a **parent node** for the group.

You can have any number of groups within a VRML file. It is common to create a group for every complex shape in a world. To build a room, you can create a group for the nodes used to make a desk, another for the nodes used to make a table, and additional groups for each chair, bookcase, fireplace, lamp, sofa, and so on. You could then create groups of groups by combining a desk group and a lamp group, or several bookcase groups to create a row of bookcases for a library.

Grouping Shapes and Properties with Groups

The VRML **Group** node groups together a list of member nodes (children). When the VRML browser reads a **Group** node, the virtual pen is directed to follow the instructions within each of the group's children, in order, from first to last within the group. After finishing the last node in the group, the VRML browser continues by reading the node following the **Group** node in the VRML file.

The example text in Figure 11.1 groups the nodes used to build a table.

```
#VRML V1.0 ascii

# Table
Group {
      # Table base
      Translation {
            translation 0.0 1.25 0.0
      }
      Cylinder {
            height 2.5
            radius 0.25
      }
      # Table top
      Translation {
            translation 0.0 1.25 0.0
      }
      Cube {
            height 0.1
            width 5.0
            depth 7.0
      }
}
# Floor
Translation {
      translation 0.0 -2.5 0.0
}
Cube {
      height 0.1
      width 10.0
      depth 10.0
}
```

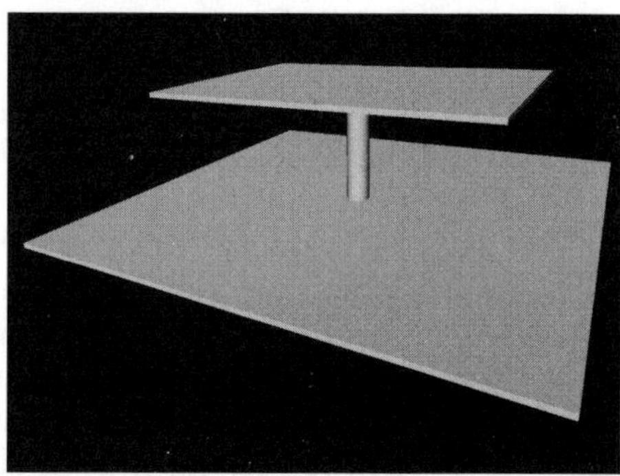

Figure 11.1 *Grouping the nodes used to build a table.*

Notice how the **Group** node is used in Figure 11.1. Nodes included in the group are placed within the curly braces of the **Group** node. Reading the VRML file from the top to the bottom, the virtual pen enters the group, draws the table (translate, cylinder, translate, cube), and exits the group. Following the group, the pen repositions, then draws the floor beneath the table.

Understanding the **Group** Node Syntax

The **Group** node has no fields. The curly braces of a **Group** node group together the list of child nodes that are contained within the group.

SYNTAX **Group node**

```
Group {
}
```

A **Group** node directs the virtual pen to follow the directions of each of the group's child nodes, in order, from top to bottom. Pen position changes, color changes, and so on, made by nodes within the group affect how the pen draws shapes following the **Group** node in the VRML file.

TIP *In version 1.1 of VRML, support for the **Group** node may be dropped.*

Grouping Shapes and Properties with Transform Separators

Similar to the **Group** node, the VRML **TransformSeparator** node groups together a list of child nodes. When the VRML browser reads a **TransformSeparator** node, the virtual pen is directed to:

1. Save its current pen position, orientation, and drawing size properties.
2. Follow the directions of each of the group's child nodes, in order, from first to last within the group.
3. Restore the transform properties saved in step 1.

After completing step 3, the VRML browser reads the nodes following the **TransformSeparator** node in the VRML file.

The way the virtual pen saves and restores its properties is similar to using a bookmark to save your place in a book. Later, when you return to the book, your bookmark indicates where you stopped reading. Similarly when the browser completes a **TransformSeparator** group, it restores the saved position, orientation, and scale properties.

Because the virtual pen restores its pen position, orientation, and scale after reading a transform separator group, any position or orientation changes you make using nodes *inside* the group do not affect how the pen draws nodes *outside* of the group. This *separates* parts of your world, building and refining each part independently, without causing changes later in the same file to nodes outside the group.

Figure 11.2 creates a simple fence and gate using three flattened cubes. A **TransformSeparator** node is used to separate the fence gate from the **Rotation** node used to open the gate. This prevents the **Rotation** node from rotating the rest of the fence, as well.

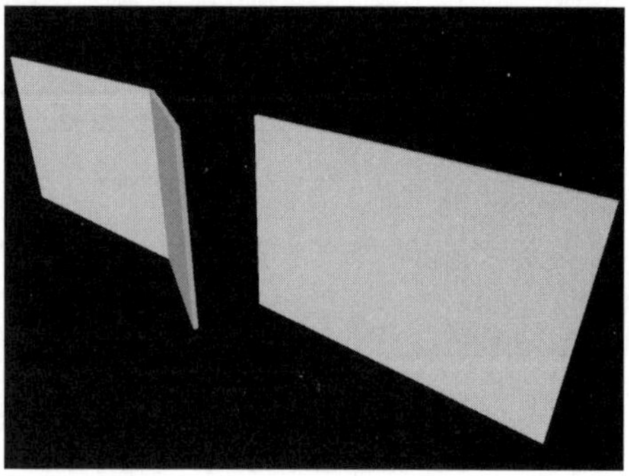

```
#VRML V1.0 ascii

# Fence - to the left of the gate
Cube {
      width 6.0
      height 4.0
      depth 0.1
}
Translation {
      translation 3.0 0.0 0.0
}
# Gate
TransformSeparator {
      # Open the gate
      Rotation {
            #             Y         -30.0 degrees
            rotation 0.0 1.0 0.0   -0.523
      }
      Translation {
            translation 1.5 0.0 0.0
      }
      Cube {
            width  3.0
            height 4.0
            depth  0.1
      }
}
# Fence - to the right of the gate
Translation {
      translation 6.0 0.0 0.0
}
Cube {
      width  6.0
      height 4.0
      depth  0.1
}
```

Figure 11.2 *A fence with a **TransformSeparator** node separating the rotation of the gate from the rest of the fence.*

Notice how the **TransformSeparator** node is used in Figure 11.2. Nodes included in the transform separator group are placed within the curly braces of the **TransformSeparator** node. Reading the VRML file from the top to the bottom, the virtual pen draws a cube to the left of the gate for the fence, enters the transform separator group, saves the transform properties, and draws a rotated cube for the fence gate. The pen then exits the group, restoring the transform properties, and draws a cube to the right of the gate for the fence. Because the **Rotation** node to open the gate is within the **TransformSeparator,** its effect applies only to the gate, and not to anything drawn after the group.

Understanding the **TransformSeparator** Node Syntax

The **TransformSeparator** node has no fields. The curly braces of a **TransformSeparator** node group together the list of child nodes contained within the transform separator group.

SYNTAX **TransformSeparator node**

```
TransformSeparator {
}
```

A **TransformSeparator** group node directs the virtual pen to save properties by transform nodes, such as the **Translation, Rotation, Scale, Transform,** and **MatrixTransform** nodes. Properties include those listed in Table 11.1.

After saving these properties, the virtual pen follows the directions of each of the group's child nodes, in order, from top to bottom. Following the last child node, the pen restores the saved properties. Position, orientation, and drawing size changes made by nodes within the transform separator group do *not* affect how the pen draws shapes that follow the **TransformSeparator** node in the VRML file.

TransformSeparator nodes may contain any other nodes as their children, including other **TransformSeparator** nodes.

Each **TransformSeparator** node has its own internal storage space in which the virtual pen saves the current properties just prior to entering that **TransformSeparator** node, and from which it restores the properties when exiting the **TransformSeparator** node. This ensures that properties aren't confused when a **TransformSeparator** node is included as a child within another **TransformSeparator** node.

Table 11.1 Properties Saved upon Entering, and Restored upon Exiting, the TransformSeparator Node

Property	*Nodes that change the property*
Position	**Translation, Transform, MatrixTransform**
Orientation	**Rotation, Transform, MatrixTransform**
Drawing size	**Scale, Transform, MatrixTransform**

For example, the following VRML text shows one **TransformSeparator** node included within another:

```
# Outer separator
TransformSeparator {
   ...
   # Inner separator
   TransformSeparator {
      ...
   }
   ...
}
```

Between its entry into the outer separator and its entry into the inner separator, the pen's properties can be changed. When the virtual pen enters the *outer* **TransformSeparator** node, it saves the *current* properties within that node. When it enters the *inner* **TransformSeparator** node, it saves the *current* properties again, but this time it saves them within the *inner* node.

When the pen leaves the *inner* node, it restores the properties to those saved within the *inner* **TransformSeparator** node. When it leaves the *outer* group, it restores the properties to those saved within the *outer* **TransformSeparator** node.

TIP *In version 1.1 of VRML, support for the **TransformSeparator** node may be dropped.*

Grouping Shapes and Properties with Separators

The VRML **Separator** node groups together a list of child nodes similar to the **Group** node. When the VRML browser reads a **Separator** node, the virtual pen is directed to:

1. Save *all* the current properties, including position, orientation, drawing size, color, font style, and so on.
2. Follow the directions of each of the group's child nodes, in order, from first to last within the group.
3. Restore the properties saved in step 1.

After completing step 3, the VRML browser reads the nodes following the **Separator** node in the VRML file.

The **Separator** node acts just like a **TransformSeparator** node, except that it saves and restores *all* of the virtual pen's properties, not just the transform properties of position, orientation, and drawing size. For instance, a **Separator** node will save and restore the pen's color and font style, while a **TransformSeparator** will not.

The example text in Figure 11.3 creates the same simple fence from the previous section, but uses a **Separator** node instead of a **TransformSeparator** node. **Material** nodes are added to color the fence tan and the gate white. The **Separator** node separates the fence gate so that the gate's color and rotation do *not* affect the rest of the fence.

```
#VRML V1.0 ascii

# Fence - to the left of the gate
Material {
      diffuseColor 0.5 0.3 0.1
}
Cube {
      width  6.0
      height 4.0
      depth  0.1
}
Translation {
      translation 3.0 0.0 0.0
}
# Gate
Separator {
      # Open the gate
      Rotation {
            #            Y          -30.0 degrees
            rotation 0.0 1.0 0.0  -0.523
      }
      Translation {
            translation 1.5 0.0 0.0
      }
      Material {
            diffuseColor 1.0 1.0 1.0
      }
      Cube {
            width  3.0
            height 4.0
            depth  0.1
      }
}
# Fence - to the right of the gate
Translation {
      translation 6.0 0.0 0.0
}
Cube {
      width  6.0
      height 4.0
      depth  0.1
}
```

Figure 11.3 *A fence with a **Separator** node separating the rotation and color of the gate from the rest of the fence.*

Notice how the **Separator** node is used in Figure 11.3. Nodes included in the separator group are placed within the curly braces of the **Separator** node. Reading the

VRML file from the top to the bottom, the virtual pen draws a tan cube for the fence to the left of the gate, enters the separator group, saves the current properties, and draws a white rotated cube for the fence gate. The pen then exits the group, restoring the saved properties, and draws a tan cube for the fence to the right of the gate. Because the **Rotation** node to open the gate and the **Material** node to make the gate white are both within the **Separator** node, their effects apply only to the gate and not to anything drawn after the group.

Understanding the **Separator** Node Syntax

The **Separator** node has a single **renderCulling** field that lets you fine-tune when the VRML browser will draw the separator's children. The curly braces of a **Separator** node group together the list of child nodes contained within the separator group.

SYNTAX **Separator node**

```
Separator {
   renderCulling AUTO       # culling type
}
```

A **Separator** group node directs the virtual pen to save all pen properties. Properties include those listed in Table 11.2.

TIP *Material binding, coordinate, lighting, normal, shape hints, and texture properties are discussed in later chapters.*

Table 11.2 VRML Properties

Property	*Nodes that change the property*
Position	**Translation, Transform, MatrixTransform**
Orientation	**Rotation, Transform, MatrixTransform**
Drawing size	**Scale, Transform, MatrixTransform**
Color	**Material**
Color use	**MaterialBinding**
Font style	**FontStyle**
Coordinates	**Coordinate3**
Lighting	**DirectionalLight, PointLight, SpotLight**
Normals	**Normal**
Normal use	**NormalBinding**
Shape hints	**ShapeHints**
Texture	**Texture2**
Texture position	**Texture2Transform**
Texture orientation	**Texture2Transform**
Texture size	**Texture2Transform**
Texture coordinates	**TextureCoordinate2**

TIP *In version 1.1 of VRML, lighting may no longer be treated as a property.*

After saving these properties, the virtual pen follows the directions of each of the group's child nodes, in order, from top to bottom. Following the last child node, the pen restores the saved properties. Property changes made by nodes *within* the separator group do *not* affect how the pen draws shapes that *follow* the **Separator** node in the VRML file.

Separator nodes may contain any other nodes as their children, including other **Separator** nodes. Like **TransformSeparator** nodes, each **Separator** node has its own internal storage space in which the current properties are saved.

For each **Separator** node, some VRML browsers create special imaginary boxes just large enough to hold all the shapes drawn by children of a separator group. These imaginary boxes, called **bounding boxes**, are used to determine if anything drawn by the separator is visible from the current viewing position. If the bounding box is visible from the current view, then the answer is yes. If the bounding box is *not* visible from the current view, then the answer is no. When the answer is no, the VRML browser skips any of the shapes within the separator, since none of them are seen anyway. This process of skipping shapes that can't be seen in the current view is called **render culling**.

The **renderCulling** field of the **Separator** node lets you control whether the VRML browser does, or does not perform render culling. When set to **ON,** the VRML browser always performs render culling using bounding boxes. When set to **OFF,** the VRML browser does *not* perform render culling and draws everything within a **Separator** node, even if some shapes are not seen from the current viewing position. Finally, when **renderCulling** is set to **AUTO,** the decision about whether to perform render culling or not is left up to the VRML browser.

TIP *We recommend that you always use the **renderCulling** field value of **AUTO.***

Grouping Shapes and Properties with Switches

Similar to the **Group** node, the VRML **Switch** node groups together a list of child nodes. When the VRML browser reads a **Switch** node, the virtual pen is directed to follow the directions of *only one* of the group's child nodes. The choice of which node's instructions are followed is up to you. After following the directions of the selected child node, the browser reads the nodes following the **Switch** node in the VRML file.

A switch group is similar to a multiposition dial, like the tuner knob on a stereo. Turning the tuner knob *switches* stations, letting you choose which one of many stations you'd like to listen to. A switch group is used in the same way. The group contains a list of nodes and lets you select which one the virtual pen uses. Later you can change your choice, and the pen will use a different node from your switch group.

You can use switch groups to collect together nodes that describe different variations on the design of your world. For instance, a **Switch** node can hold a selection of colors set by **Material** nodes. Changing the switch directs the virtual pen to use one or another of the colors, like choosing between different crayons in a crayon box.

The example text in Figure 11.4 creates a switch group from nodes to select the flavor color of a lollipop.

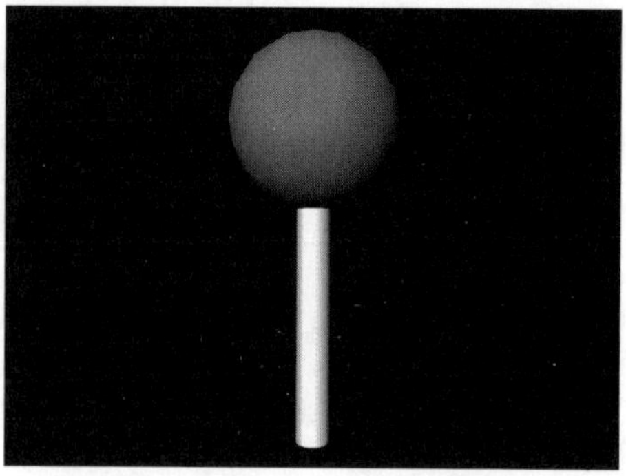

```
#VRML V1.0 ascii

# White stick
Translation {
      translation 0.0 3.0 0.0
}
Material {
      diffuseColor 1.0 1.0 1.0
}
Cylinder {
      height 8.0
      radius 0.6
}
# Candy
Translation {
      translation 0.0 7.0 0.0
}
Switch {
      whichChild 0
      # Grape
      Separator {
            Material {
                  diffuseColor 1.0 0.0 1.0
            }
            Sphere {
                  radius 3.0
            }
      }
      # Cherry
      Separator {
            Material {
                  diffuseColor 1.0 0.0 0.0
            }
            Sphere {
                  radius 3.0
            }
      }
      # Lemon
      Separator {
            Material {
                  diffuseColor 1.0 1.0 0.0
            }
            Sphere {
                  radius 3.0
```

Figure 11.4 continues

```
            }
        }
    }
```

Figure 11.4 *Using a **Switch** node to select between four flavors of a lollipop.*

Notice how the **Switch** node is used in Figure 11.4. Nodes included in the switch group are placed within the curly braces of the **Switch** node. Reading the VRML file from the top to the bottom, the virtual pen draws a white cylinder for the stick, moves up, then enters the switch. The virtual pen selects the 0th (first) child, changes its pen color to purple, exits the switch, then draws a purple sphere for the grape lollipop.

Understanding the **Switch** Node Syntax

The **Switch** node has one field, **whichChild,** whose value is an integer that determines which child node is used by the virtual pen. The curly braces of a **Switch** node group together the list of child nodes contained within the switch group.

SYNTAX **Switch node**

```
Switch {
   whichChild -1       # integer
}
```

The **whichChild** field indicates which child node is read by the browser and drawn by the pen. Child nodes are numbered starting with 0 for the first node and increasing by one for each subsequent node, in order, within the switch group.

TIP *Notice that the first child node in a group has a number of 0, not 1. If there are four children in a switch group, they will be numbered 0, 1, 2, 3. The last child node in a group, then, has a number one less than the size of the group.*

TIP *Some VRML browsers will quit or report an error if a **whichChild** field's value is too large.*

The **whichChild** field defaults to –1, which indicates that *no* child node in the switch group directs the virtual pen. Instead, the pen will skip over the entire **Switch** node and its contents, then continue by reading the nodes after the **Switch** node in the VRML file.

If the **whichChild** field is –3, the virtual pen follows the instructions within *all* of the child nodes in the switch group. The effect is identical to that of a simple **Group** node. Each node in the switch is read, in order, from top to bottom.

Pen position changes, color changes, made by nodes within the Switch group affect how the pen draws the shapes *following* the **Switch** node in the VRML file.

TIP *In version 1.1 of the VRML specification, the* ***Switch*** *node may be changed so that it saves and restores all properties upon entry into and exit from the group.*

Experimenting with Grouping

The following examples provide a more detailed examination of the ways in which the **Group, Switch, TransformSeparator,** and **Separator** nodes can be used and how they interact with nodes we've discussed in previous chapters.

Comparing the Four Types of Grouping

The four types of VRML grouping nodes are summarized in Table 11.3. To illustrate the differences, the following four examples all contain the same shape and property nodes. Because of the differences in the grouping nodes used, the resulting images differ in content, position, or color.

Table 11.3 A Comparison of the Four VRML Grouping Nodes

Node	*Members Drawn*	*Properties Saved*
Group	All	None
Switch	None, one, or all	None
TransformSeparator	All	Transform (position, orientation, drawing size)
Separator	All	All (transform, color, font style, etc.)

*Using a **Group** Node*

```
#VRML V1.0 ascii

Material {
      diffuseColor 0.0 1.0 0.0
}
Group {
      Material {
            diffuseColor 1.0 0.0 0.0
      }
      Cube {
      }
      Translation {
            translation 3.0 0.0 0.0
      }
      Sphere {
      }
}
```

Figure 11.5 continues

```
Cylinder {
      height 3.0
      radius 0.5
}
```

Figure 11.5 *Using a **Group** node.*

Reading from the top of the file to the bottom, the virtual pen is instructed to:

1. Change its color to green.
2. Draw the group.
   a. Change its color to red.
   b. Draw a cube using the current pen properties. The cube is drawn red.

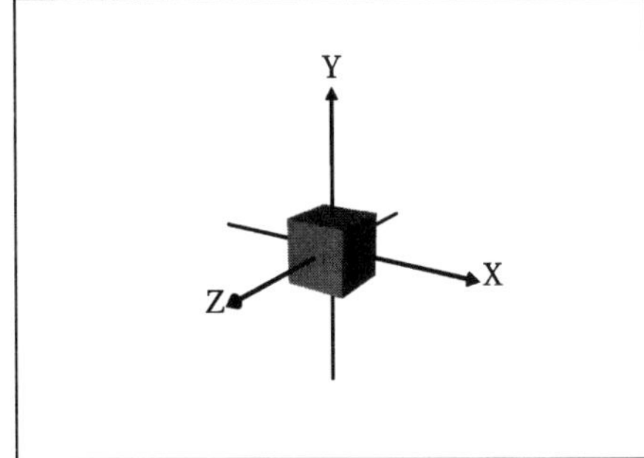

Figure 11.6 *Changing properties and drawing the group.*

   c. Translate 3.0 units along the X axis from the current pen position.

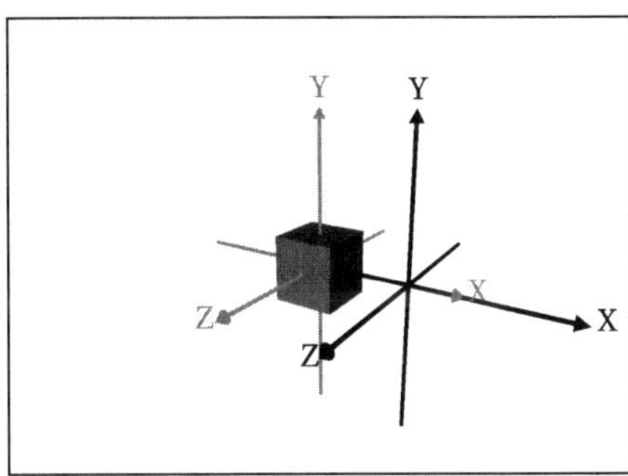

Figure 11.7 *Moving 3.0 units to the right.*

d. Draw a sphere using the current pen properties. The sphere is drawn red and 3.0 units to the right of the cube.

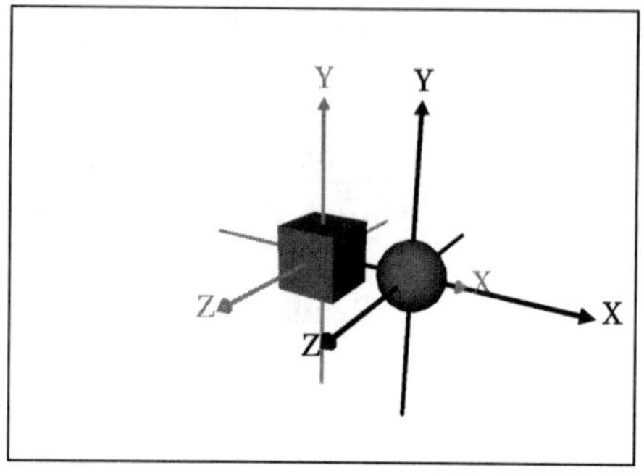

Figure 11.8 *Drawing the sphere.*

3. Draw a cylinder using the current pen properties. The sphere is drawn red and through the middle of the sphere.

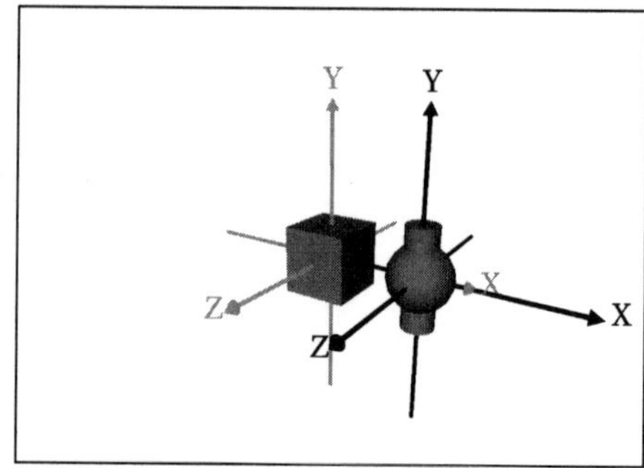

Figure 11.9 *Draw the cylinder.*

The virtual pen *always* draws *all* of the children of a **Group** node, and *doesn't* save or restore any pen properties. The result is a red cube, a red sphere to its right, and a red cylinder running through the center of the sphere.

*Using a **Switch** Node*

```
#VRML V1.0 ascii

Material {
      diffuseColor 0.0 1.0 0.0
}
Switch {
      whichChild 1
      Material {
            diffuseColor 1.0 0.0 0.0
      }
```

Figure 11.10 continues

```
        Cube {
        }
        Translation {
             translation 3.0 0.0 0.0
        }
        Sphere {
        }
}
Cylinder {
        height 3.0
        radius 0.5
}
```

Figure 11.10 *Using a **Switch** node.*

Reading from the top of the file to the bottom, the virtual pen is instructed to:

1. Change its color to green.
2. Draw the switch group, choosing only the second child node in the switch group. The second child is a cube.
   a. Draw a cube using the current pen properties. The cube is drawn green.

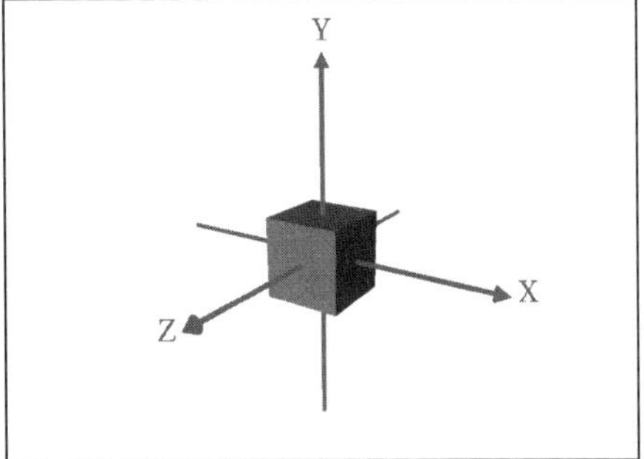

Figure 11.11 *Changing properties and drawing the group.*

3. Draw a cylinder using the current pen properties. The cylinder is drawn green.

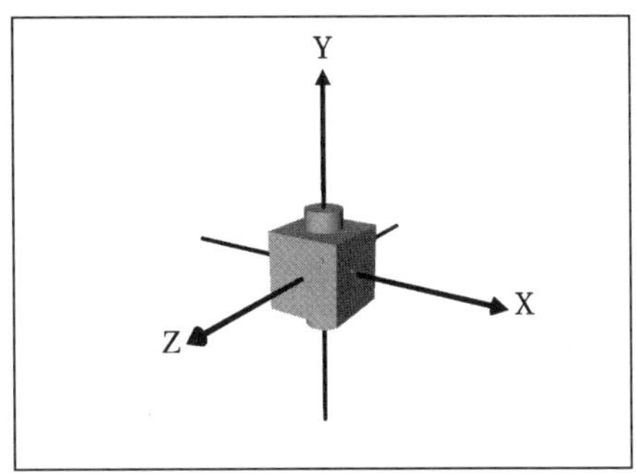

Figure 11.12 *Drawing the cylinder.*

The virtual pen draws only *one* of the children of a **Switch** node, and *doesn't* save or restore any pen properties. The result is a green cube with a green cylinder running through the center of the cube.

*Using a **TransformSeparator** Node*

```
#VRML V1.0 ascii

Material {
      diffuseColor 0.0 1.0 0.0
}
TransformSeparator {
      Material {
            diffuseColor 1.0 0.0 0.0
      }
      Cube {
      }
      Translation {
            translation 3.0 0.0 0.0
      }
      Sphere {
      }
}
Cylinder {
      height 3.0
      radius 0.5
}
```

Figure 11.13 *Using a **TransformSeparator** node.*

Reading from the top of the file to the bottom, the virtual pen is instructed to:

1. Change its color to green.

2. Draw the transform separator group.
   a. Save the pen position, orientation, and drawing size. The position at the origin is saved.
   b. Change its color to red.
   c. Draw a cube using the current pen properties. The cube is drawn red.

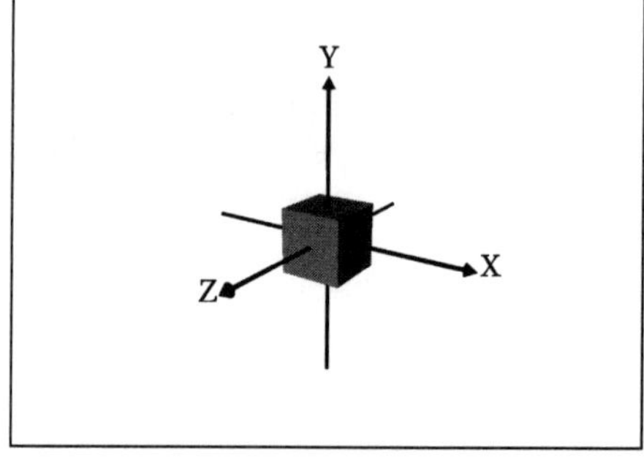

Figure 11.14 *Changing properties and drawing the group.*

d. Translate 3.0 units along the X axis from the current pen position.

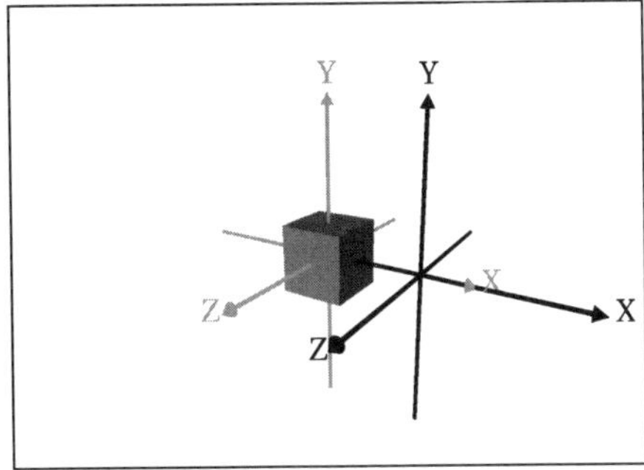

Figure 11.15 *Moving 3.0 units to the right.*

e. Draw a sphere using the current pen properties. The sphere is drawn red and 3.0 units to the right of the cube.

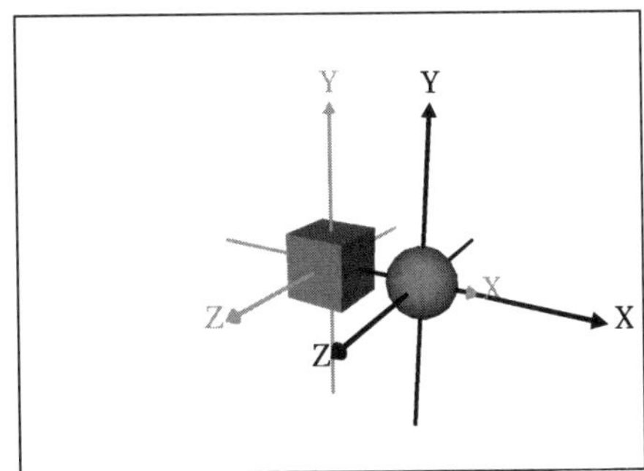

Figure 11.16 *Drawing the sphere.*

f. Restore the pen position, orientation, and drawing size. The pen is repositioned to the starting origin.

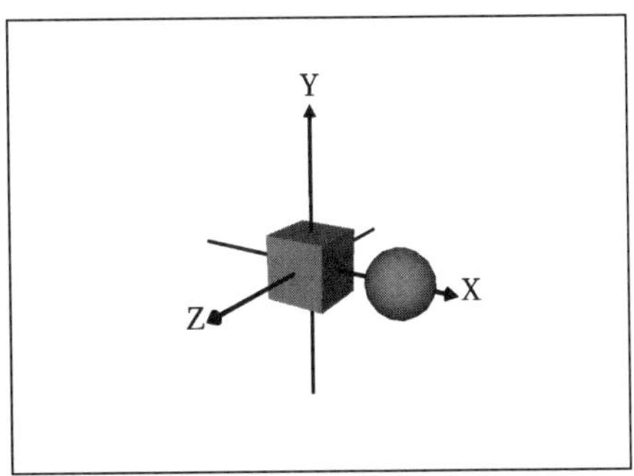

Figure 11.17 *Restoring the pen properties.*

3. Draw a cylinder using the current pen properties. The cylinder is drawn red and through the middle of the cube.

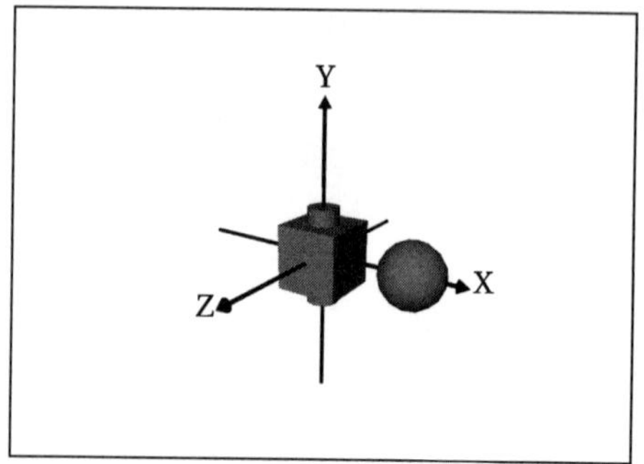

Figure 11.18 *Drawing the cylinder.*

The virtual pen *always* draws *all* of the children of a **TransformSeparator** node, *saving* the transform properties first, and *restoring* them when it exits the group. The result is a red cube with a red sphere to its right. After restoring the pen position to what it was before entering the group, a red cylinder is drawn running through the center of the cube.

*Using a **Separator** Node*

```
#VRML V1.0 ascii

Material {
      diffuseColor 0.0 1.0 0.0
}
Separator {
      Material {
            diffuseColor 1.0 0.0 0.0
      }
      Cube {
      }
      Translation {
            translation 3.0 0.0 0.0
      }
      Sphere {
      }
}
Cylinder {
      height 3.0
      radius 0.5
}
```

Figure 11.19 *Using a **Separator** node.*

Reading from the top of the file to the bottom, the virtual pen is instructed to:

1. Change its color to green.

2. Draw the separator group.
   a. Save all of the pen properties, including position and color. The green pen color and its position at the origin are saved.
   b. Change its color to red.
   c. Draw a cube using the current pen properties. The cube is drawn red.

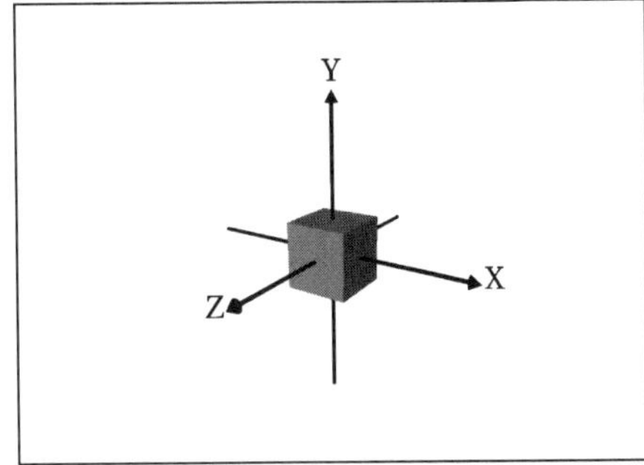

Figure 11.20 *Changing properties and drawing the group.*

   d. Translate 3.0 units along the X axis.

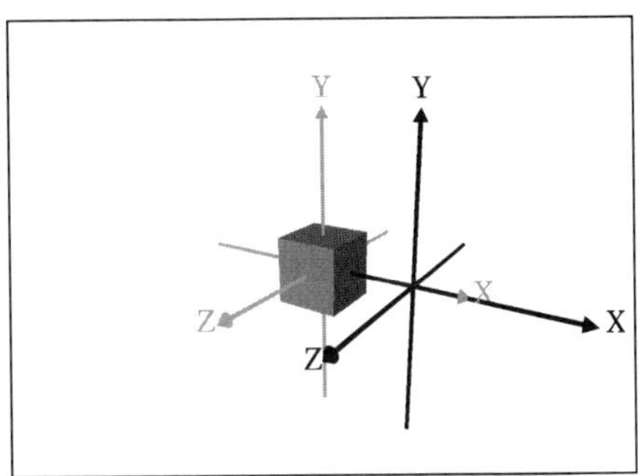

Figure 11.21 *Moving 3.0 units to the left.*

   e. Draw a sphere using the current pen properties. The sphere is drawn red and 3.0 units to the right of the cube.

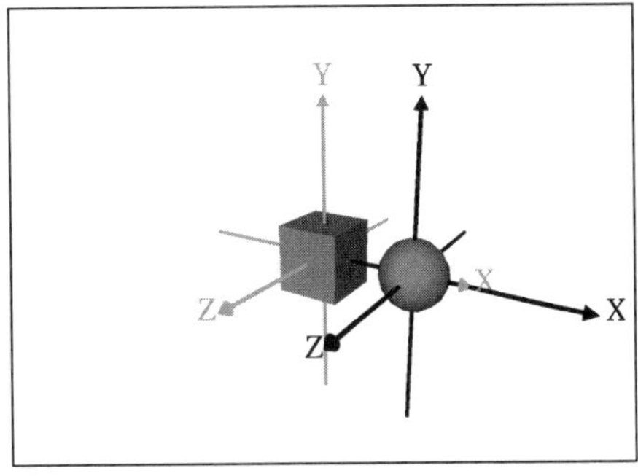

Figure 11.22 *Drawing the sphere.*

f. Restore all of the pen properties. The pen is repositioned to the starting origin and its color is changed back to green.

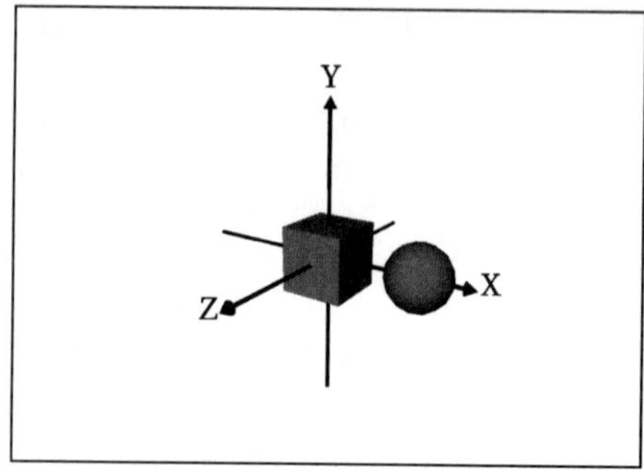

Figure 11.23 *Restoring the pen properties.*

3. Draw a cylinder using the current pen properties. The cylinder is drawn green and through the middle of the cube.

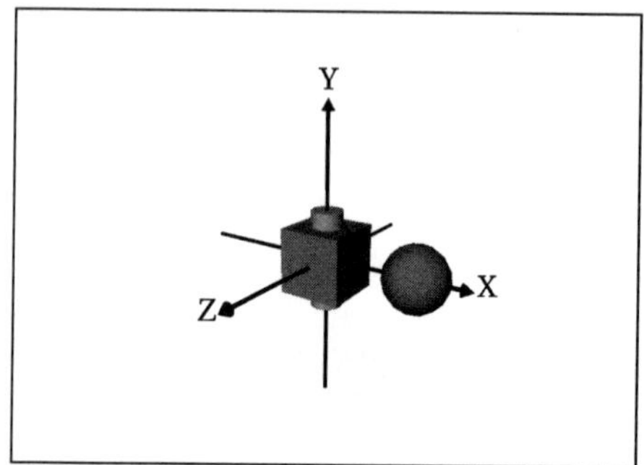

Figure 11.24 *Drawing the cylinder.*

The virtual pen *always* draws *all* of the children of a **Separator** node, *saving* all properties first, and *restoring* them when it exits the group. The result is a red cube with a red sphere to its right. After restoring the pen position and color to what they were before entering the group, a green cylinder is drawn running through the center of the cube.

Combining Shapes Using Separators

The principal use of **TransformSeparator** and **Separator** nodes is to separate different components of the same world. This lets you make changes to the position, orientation, size, and color of one component without those changes affecting later components of the same world.

Consider again the VRML text for the fence in Figure 11.3 now shown in Figure 11.25.

```
#VRML V1.0 ascii

# Fence - to the left of the gate
Material {
      diffuseColor 0.5 0.3 0.1
}
Cube {
      width  6.0
      height 4.0
      depth  0.1
}
Translation {
      translation 3.0 0.0 0.0
}
# Gate
Separator {
      # Open the gate
      Rotation {
            #             Y          -30.0 degrees
            rotation 0.0 1.0 0.0   -0.523
      }
      Translation {
            translation 1.5 0.0 0.0
      }
      Material {
            diffuseColor 1.0 1.0 1.0
      }
      Cube {
            width  3.0
            height 4.0
            depth  0.1
      }
}
# Fence - to the right of the gate
Translation {
      translation 6.0 0.0 0.0
}
Cube {
      width  6.0
      height 4.0
      depth  0.1
}
```

Figure 11.25 *The fence.*

Reading the VRML file from the top to the bottom, the virtual pen is instructed to:

1. Change its color to brown.

2. Draw a flattened cube using the current pen properties. The cube is drawn brown.

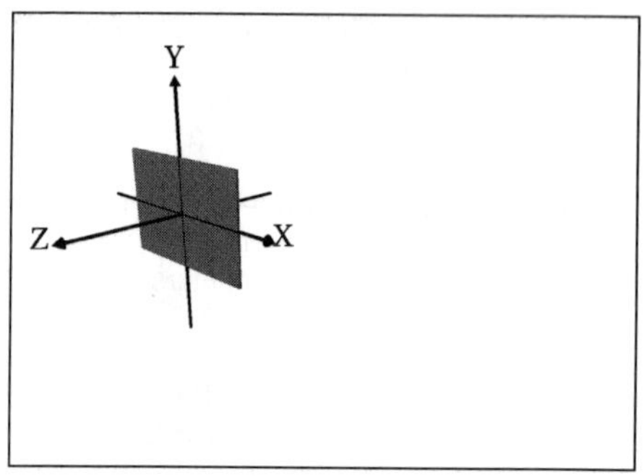

Figure 11.26 *Changing the pen color and drawing the fence to the left of the gate.*

3. Translate 3.0 units along the X axis.

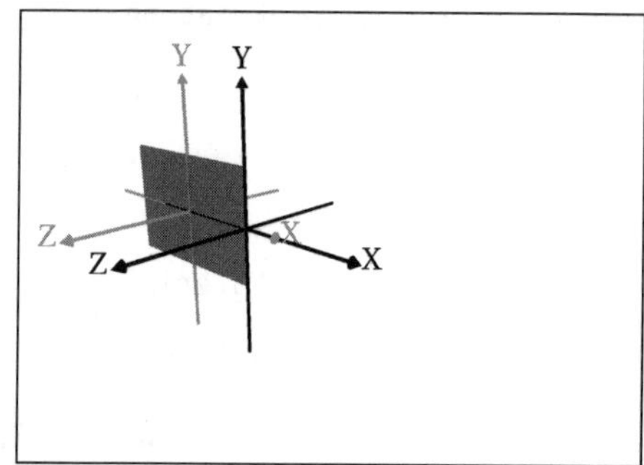

Figure 11.27 *Moving to the gate hinge.*

4. Draw the separator group.
   - **a.** Save all of the pen properties.
   - **b.** Rotate the pen –30.0 degrees around the Y axis.

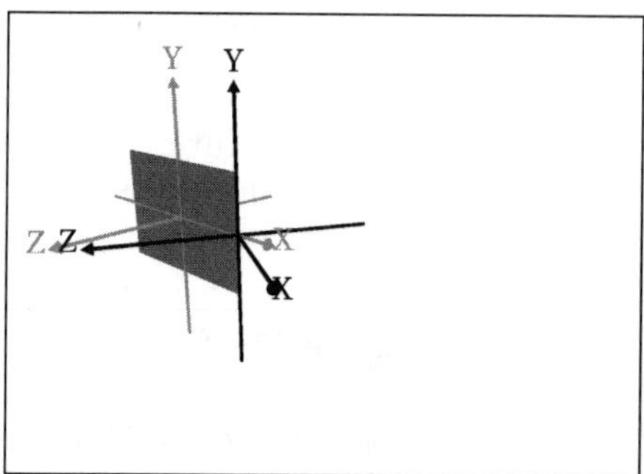

Figure 11.28 *Rotating the pen to prepare to draw the open gate.*

c. Translate 1.5 units along the X axis.

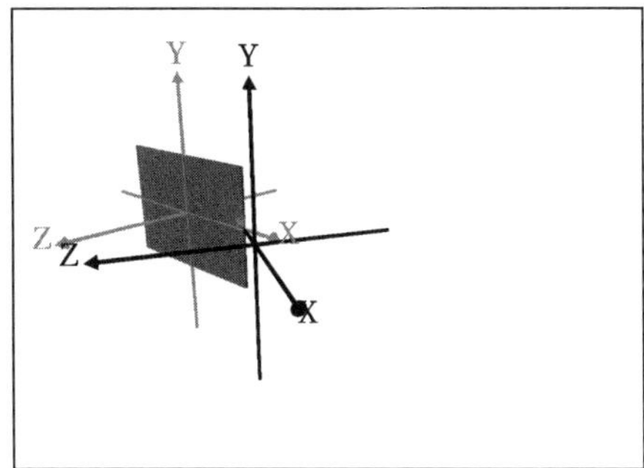

Figure 11.29 *Moving to the center of the gate to prepare to draw it.*

d. Change its color to white.
e. Draw a flattened cube using the current pen properties. The cube is drawn white, rotated, and to the right of the first brown piece of the fence.

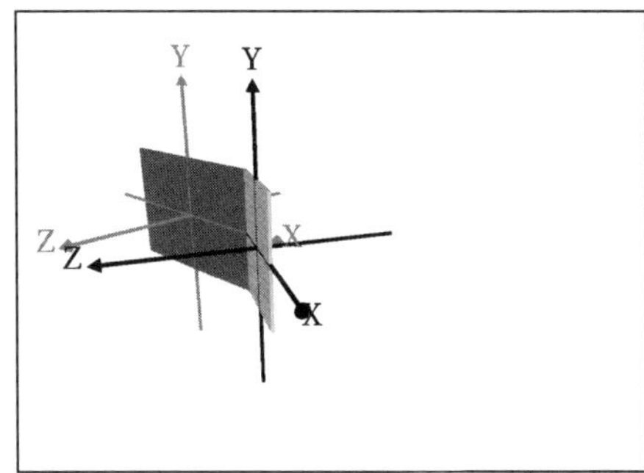

Figure 11.30 *Drawing the white gate.*

f. Restore all of the pen properties. The pen is repositioned to the gate hinge, the axes are reoriented to the starting axes' orientation, and the pen's color is changed back to brown.

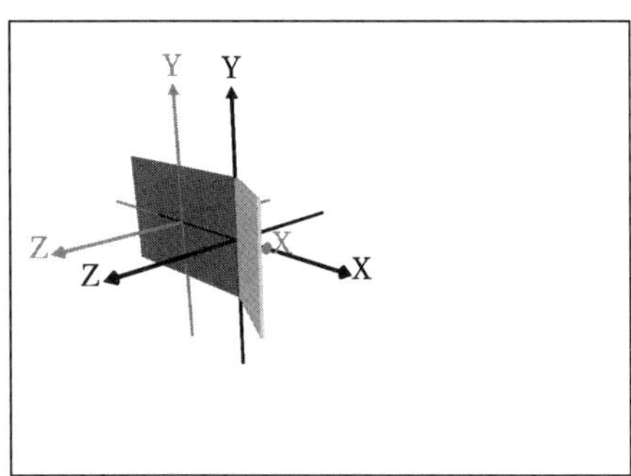

Figure 11.31 *Restoring the pen properties.*

5. Translate 6.0 units along the X axis.

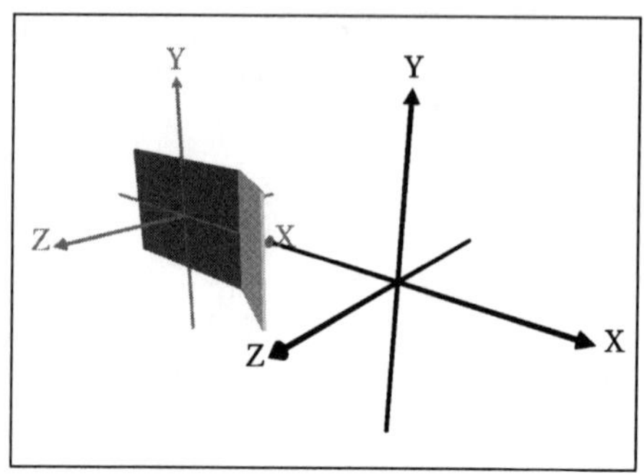

Figure 11.32 *Moving to the center of the next piece of the fence.*

6. Draw a flattened cube with the current pen properties. The cube is drawn brown and to the right of the gate.

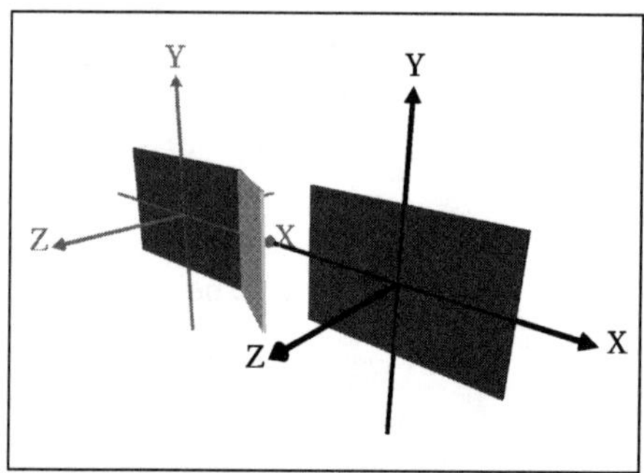

Figure 11.33 *Drawing the brown fence to the right of the gate.*

Notice that the gate's open angle and color are both isolated within the **Separator** node. You can change the gate rotation angle and its color without affecting anything drawn after the **Separator** node.

You can use **Separator** and **TransformSeparator** nodes like this to help isolate and separate parts of your world. This enables you to more easily build complex worlds.

Switching between Shapes

In the **Switch** node example shown earlier in this chapter, the switch group's children were all **Material** nodes used to set different flavor colors for a lollipop. You can also put other types of nodes in a **Switch** node. The example in Figure 11.34, for instance, switches between different primitive shapes.

```
#VRML V1.0 ascii

Switch {
      whichChild 0
      Cube {
      }
      Cylinder {
      }
      Cone {
      }
      Sphere {
      }
}
```

Figure 11.34 *Switching between primitives.*

When the **whichChild** field is set to 0, a cube is drawn; when the field is set to 1, a cylinder is drawn; and so on.

Imagine that the shapes you'd like to switch between are more complex. To use a **Switch** node to switch between complex shapes, group each complex shape in its own **Separator** node, and then group *those* **Separator** nodes in the **Switch** node's group. For instance, the example in Figure 11.35 switches among three different designs for a cafe sign.

```
#VRML V1.0 ascii

# Cafe sign designs for Pat's Cafe
Switch {
      whichChild 0
      # Design 0 - blue letters without a background
      Separator {
            # Blue sign letters
            Material {
                  diffuseColor 0.2 0.2 0.8
            }
            AsciiText {
                  string "Pat's Cafe"
                  justification CENTER
            }
      }
      # Design 1 - black letters on a rectangular white background
      Separator {
            # Black sign letters
            Material {
                  diffuseColor 0.0 0.0 0.0
            }
            AsciiText {
                  string "Pat's Cafe"
                  justification CENTER
            }
```

Figure 11.35 continues

```
            # White background
            Translation {
                  translation 0.0 3.5 -0.5
            }
            Material {
                  diffuseColor 0.8 0.8 0.8
            }
            Cube {
                  width  60.0
                  height 15.0
                  depth   0.5
            }
      }
      # Design 2 - red letters on a circular gray background
      # with a red frame
      Separator {
            # Red sign letters
            Translation {
                  translation 0.0 10.0 0.0
            }
            Material {
                  diffuseColor  0.0 0.0 0.0
                  emissiveColor 0.5 0.0 0.0
            }
            AsciiText {
                  string [ "Pat's", "Cafe" ]
                  justification CENTER
            }
            # Red sign frame
            Translation {
                  translation 0.0 -1.0 -0.5
            }
            Rotation {
                  #        X            +90.0 degrees
                  rotation 1.0 0.0 0.0  1.57
            }
            Cylinder {
                  height 0.4
                  radius 25.0
            }
            # Gray background
            Material {
                  diffuseColor 0.1 0.1 0.1
            }
            Cylinder {
                  height 0.5
                  radius 24.0
            }
      }
}
```

Figure 11.35 continues

(a)

(*b*) (*c*) (*d*)

Figure 11.35 *Switching among three complex shapes, all grouped with separators.*

The images in Figure 11.35 show the three sign designs controlled by the **Switch** node. Figure 11.35*b* shows the design when the **whichChild** field is set to 0. Figure 11.35*c* shows design 1, and Figure 11.35*d* shows design 2.

Using Separators inside Separators

Another key use of **Separator** nodes is to help build articulated mechanisms, such as an adjustable desk lamp, like those in Figure 11.36. Mechanisms like these have a component structure that is hierarchical.

The lamp consists of four main parts:

- *The lamp base*
- *The first lamp arm*
- *The second lamp arm*
- *The lamp shade*

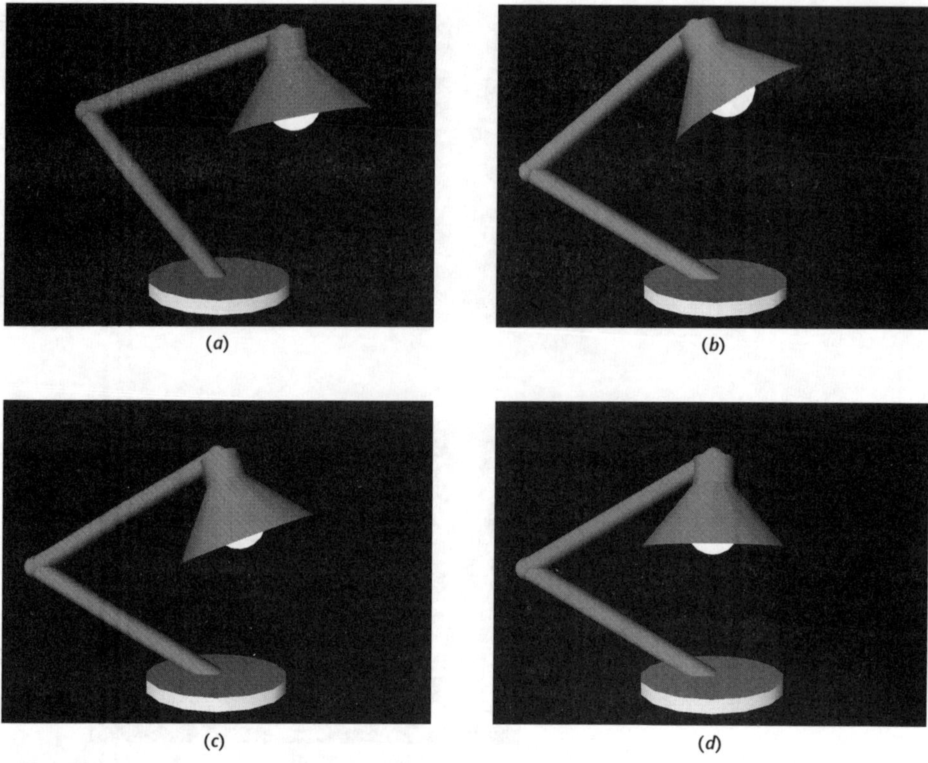

(a) (b) (c) (d)

Figure 11.36 *An adjustable desk lamp in various positions.*

The lamp is built by connecting the shade to the second arm, the second arm to the first, and the first arm to the base. Such a structure is sometimes written by indenting the parts in the list so that each part is beneath the part to which it connects, like this:

The lamp base
  The first lamp arm
    The second lamp arm
      The lamp shade

Because of this hierarchical structure, movement of one part only affects that part and the parts listed underneath it. For instance, movement of the lamp base moves the whole lamp. Movement of the first arm moves the second arm and the lamp shade as well, but leaves the base alone. Movement of the second arm moves the lamp shade, too, but leaves the first arm and base alone. Movement of the lamp shade does nothing to the rest of the lamp.

Figure 11.36*a* shows the desk lamp in an initial position. Figure 11.36*b* rotates the first arm forward. The second arm and the lamp shade follow. Figure 11.36*c* rotates the second arm down, bringing the lamp shade with it. Figure 11.36*d* rotates just the lamp shade down.

You can build hierarchical mechanisms, like the desk lamp, using **Separator** nodes for each part. Group into an outer **Separator** node the nodes necessary to build that part of the lamp, like the lamp base. Also group into that outer node a new child **Separator** node for each part that is connected to it, like the first lamp arm.

Those inner child **Separator** nodes in turn contain the nodes necessary to build *their* connected parts, like the second lamp arm. They also contain any child **Separator** nodes necessary to build parts that are connected to *them*, like the lamp shade. For instance, the desk lamp's structure would look like this:

```
# Whole Lamp
Separator {
   # The lamp base's nodes
   ...
   Separator {
      # The first lamp arm's nodes
      ...
      Separator {
         # The second lamp arm's nodes
         ...
         Separator {
            # The lamp shade's nodes
            ...
         }
      }
   }
}
```

Figure 11.37 shows the full VRML text for the adjustable desk lamp shown in Figure 11.36.

```
#VRML V1.0 ascii

# Whole lamp
Separator {
      # The lamp base
      Cylinder {
            height 0.08
            radius 0.5
      }
      Separator {
            # The first lamp arm
            Rotation {
                  #        X             -40.0 degrees
                  rotation 1.0 0.0 0.0  -0.698
            }
            Translation {
                  translation 0.0 0.75 0.0
            }
```

Figure 11.37 continues

```
Material {
      diffuseColor 1.0 0.0 0.0
}
Cylinder {
      height 1.5
      radius 0.07
}
Translation {
      translation 0.0 0.75 0.0
}
Sphere {
      radius 0.08
}
Separator {
      # The second lamp arm
      Rotation {
            #        X             +110.0 degrees
            rotation 1.0 0.0 0.0  1.918
      }
      Translation {
            translation 0.0 0.75 0.0
      }
      Cylinder {
            height 1.5
            radius 0.07
      }
      Translation {
            translation 0.0 0.75 0.0
      }
      Sphere {
            radius 0.08
      }
      Separator {
            # The lamp shade
            Rotation {
                  #        X              -80.0 degrees
                  rotation 1.0 0.0 0.0  -1.39
            }
            Translation {
                  translation 0.0 -0.15 0.0
            }
            Cylinder {
                  height 0.3
                  radius 0.15
                  parts (SIDES|TOP)
            }
            Translation {
                  translation 0.0 -0.15 0.0
            }
```

Figure 11.37 continues

```
                        Cone {
                              height 0.6
                              bottomRadius 0.5
                              parts (SIDES)
                        }
                        # Light bulb
                        Translation {
                              translation 0.0 -0.15 0.0
                        }
                        Material {
                              diffuseColor 0.0 0.0 0.0
                              emissiveColor 0.5 0.5 0.5
                        }
                        Sphere {
                              radius 0.2
                        }
                  } # end lamp shade
            } # end second arm
      } # end first arm
} # lamp base
```

Figure 11.37 *The hierarchical VRML text of the adjustable desk lamp.*

You can experiment with the desk lamp by adjusting the rotation angles for each of the two arms and the lamp shade. The four images shown in Figure 11.36, for instance, use the rotation angles listed in Table 11.4.

Extended Examples

The following examples build on the concepts presented in this chapter. They illustrate the worlds you can create by grouping VRML's primitive shapes. Try them on your own.

Table 11.4 Rotation Angles (in radians) Used to Produce the Desk Lamp Positions Shown in Figure 11.36

Figure	*First lamp arm*	*Second lamp arm*	*Lamp shade*
(*a*)	−0.698 (−40 degrees)	1.918 (110 degrees)	−1.39 (−80 degrees)
(*b*)	−0.523 (−30 degrees)	1.918 (110 degrees)	−1.39 (−80 degrees)
(*c*)	−0.523 (−30 degrees)	1.57 (90 degrees)	−1.39 (−80 degrees)
(*d*)	−0.523 (−30 degrees)	1.57 (90 degrees)	−1.05 (−60 degrees)

TIP *All of the VRML text in the extended examples throughout this book are available via anonymous ftp from John Wiley & Sons at* `ftp.wiley.com/public/computer_books/vrml` *and from the VRML Repository at* `http://www.sdsc.edu/vrml`.

Couch

The example text in Figure 11.38 creates a couch. Notice that each component of the couch is enclosed in a group node.

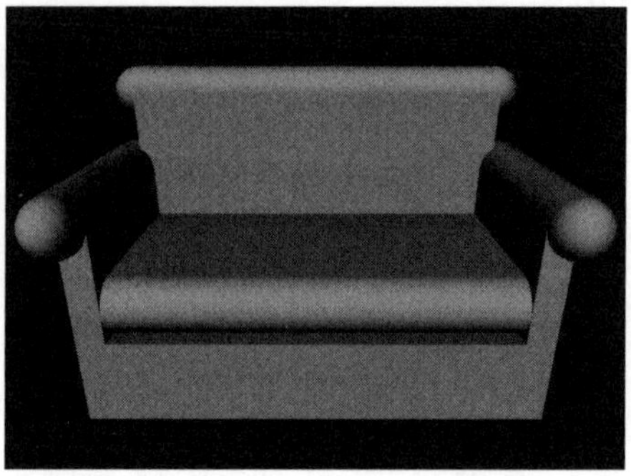

```
#VRML V1.0 ascii

Material {
      diffuseColor 0.0 0.2 0.0
}
# Right arm
Separator {
      Translation {
            translation 8.0 2.0 4.0
      }
      Sphere {
      }
      Transform {
            translation 0.0 0.0 -4.0
            #         X             +90.0 degrees
            rotation 1.0 0.0 0.0  +1.57
      }
      Cylinder {
            height 8.0
      }
}
# Left arm
Separator {
      Translation {
            translation -8.0 2.0 4.0
      }
      Sphere {
      }
      Transform {
            translation 0.0 0.0 -4.0
            #         X             +90.0 degrees
            rotation 1.0 0.0 0.0  +1.57
      }
      Cylinder {
            height 8.0
      }
}
# Sides
Separator {
      Translation {
            translation 7.5 -1.5 0.0
      }
```

Figure 11.38 continues

```
        # Right side
        Cube {
              height 7.0
              width 1.0
              depth 8.0
        }
        Translation {
              translation -15.0 0.0 0.0
        }
        # Left side
        Cube {
              height 7.0
              width 1.0
              depth 8.0
        }
  }
  # Bottom
  Separator {
        Translation {
              translation 0.0 -3.5 0.0
        }
        Cube {
              height 3.0
              width 14.0
              depth 8.0
        }
  }
  # Back
  Separator {
        Translation {
              translation 0.0 1.5 -3.5
        }
        Cube {
              height 7.0
              width 15.0
              depth 1.0
        }
        Translation {
              translation 7.5 3.5 -0.5
        }
        Sphere {
        }
        Translation {
              translation -15.0 0.0 0.0
        }
        Sphere {
        }
        Transform {
              translation 7.5 0.0 0.0
              #                Z    +90.0 degrees
              rotation 0.0 0.0 1.0  +1.57
        }
```

Figure 11.38 continues

```
        Cylinder {
              height 15.0
        }
  }
  # Cushions
  Separator {
        Translation {
              translation 0.0 -1.0 0.0
        }
        Cube {
              height 2.0
              width 14.0
              depth 6.0
        }
        Transform {
              translation 0.0 0.0 3.0
              #                   Z    +90.0 degrees
              rotation 0.0 0.0 1.0  +1.57
        }
        Cylinder {
              height 15.0
        }
  }
```

Figure 11.38 *A couch.*

Table

The example text in Figure 11.39 creates a table with a note on it. Notice that each component is enclosed within a group.

```
#VRML V1.0 ascii

Separator {
      Material {
            diffuseColor 0.25 0.15 0.1
      }
      Cylinder {
            radius 8.0
            height 0.5
      }
      Translation {
            translation 0.0 -1.0 0.0
      }
      Cylinder {
            height 1.0
      }
      Translation {
            translation 0.0 -0.5 0.0
      }
```

Figure 11.39 continues

```
		Sphere {
		}
		Translation {
			translation 0.0 -1.5 0.0
		}
		Sphere {
		}
		Translation {
			translation 0.0 -1.5 0.0
		}
		Sphere {
		}
		Translation {
			translation 0.0 -1.5 0.0
		}
		Sphere {
		}
		Translation {
			translation 0.0 -1.5 0.0
		}
		Cylinder {
			height 3.0
		}
		Translation {
			translation 0.0 -1.0 0.0
		}
		Cone {
			height 3.0
			bottomRadius 2.0
		}
		Translation {
			translation 0.0 -1.0 0.0
		}
		Cone {
			height 1.5
			bottomRadius 4.0
		}
		Translation {
			translation 0.0 -0.75 0.0
		}
		Cylinder {
			height 0.25
			radius 5.5
		}
	}
	Transform {
		translation 5.0 0.26 0.0
		#        X              -90.0 degrees
		rotation 1.0 0.0 0.0  -1.57
		scaleFactor 0.3 0.3 0.3
	}
```

Figure 11.39 continues

```
# Note
Separator {
      Rotation {
            #                 Z    +45.0 degrees
            rotation 0.0 0.0 1.0  +0.785
      }
      Material {
            diffuseColor 1.0 1.0 1.0
      }
      Cube {
            height 11.0
            width 8.5
            depth 0.01
      }
      Material {
            diffuseColor 0.0 0.0 0.0
      }
      Translation {
            translation -3.0 4.0 0.01
      }
      FontStyle {
            size 0.7
            family SERIF
            style ITALIC
      }
      AsciiText {
            string "Went to the computer"
      }
      Translation {
            translation 0.0 -1.0 0.0
      }
      AsciiText {
            string "store.  Be back soon."
      }
      Translation {
            translation 2.0 -1.5 0.0
      }
      AsciiText {
            string "-me"
      }
      Transform {
            translation 0.0 -3.0 0.075
            #                 Z    +45.0 degrees
            rotation 0.0 0.0 1.0  +0.785
            scaleFactor 0.2 0.2 0.2
      }
      Material {
            diffuseColor 1.0 1.0 0.0
      }
      Cylinder {
            height 20.0
      }
```

Figure 11.39 continues

```
        Material {
              diffuseColor 0.25 0.15 0.1
        }
        Translation {
              translation 0.0 11.0 0.0
        }
        Cone {
        }
}
```

Figure 11.39 *A table.*

Summary

To help you organize large VRML worlds, VRML has four grouping nodes: **Group, Switch, TransformSeparator,** and **Separator.** All four nodes group together a list of child nodes. Child nodes can be of any type, including grouping nodes. Using grouping nodes within grouping nodes, you can build up hierarchical structures.

Group nodes direct the virtual pen to draw each child node from the top of the group to the bottom. No pen properties are saved or restored upon entry into or exit from a **Group** node.

Switch nodes direct the virtual pen to draw a single child node selected by the **whichChild** field of the switch. No pen properties are saved or restored upon entry into or exit from a **Switch** node.

TransformSeparator nodes direct the virtual pen to draw each child node from the top of the group to the bottom. Pen transform properties (position, orientation, and size) are saved upon entry into the **TransformSeparator node,** and restored upon exit from the group. Each **TransformSeparator** node has its own storage space for these pen properties.

Separator nodes direct the virtual pen to draw each child node from the top of the group to the bottom. All pen properties (transform, color, font style, etc.) are saved upon entry into the separator, and restored upon exit from the group. Each separator has its own storage space for these properties.

CHAPTER 12

Instancing Shapes

When building worlds, it is common to use multiple copies, or **instances**, of the same shape. You might, for example, have multiple chairs around a table, multiple stop signs in a city, multiple piano keys on a piano keyboard, or multiple wheels on a car or truck. Each instance of the shape is identical to every other instance of the same shape. The instances typically differ only in their position, orientation, scale, color, and so on, in your world.

In VRML you can define a *name* for any node. Later in the same file, you can create instances of that same node by providing the node's defined name. Using this feature you can define a node, it's fields, and their values *once* in a VRML file, then use copies of the node over and over as many times as you need. This significantly reduces the effort it takes to make complex, repetitive worlds and reduces the size of your VRML files as well.

In this chapter, you'll use the DEF syntax to define names for nodes and the USE syntax to later use those names to create multiple instances of the named node.

Understanding Instancing

In VRML, you can *define* a name for any node in your world. Names can be any sequence of letters and numbers. Once a node has a name, you can use that name later in your file to make copies of that node. We say that the named node is the **original**, and that each of the copies is an **instance** of the original.

Only the original node sets field values or includes group children. Each of the instances *uses* the original's field values and children without change. This enables you to define *once* the node that makes up a chair, then later instance that chair multiple times around a table without repeating the chair's nodes and fields again for each chair. Additionally, if you make a change to the original chair, all of the instances are immediately changed as well. This makes it very easy to rapidly make changes throughout your world to change a chair, window, door, or sofa design, update all four wheels of a car to a new size, select a new tree species used throughout a landscape design, and so on.

Any VRML node can be defined as an original node for use in instancing. You can define names for shape nodes, such as cubes, cylinders, and text. You can also define names for property nodes, such as the **Material** and **FontStyle** nodes, and you can define names for grouping nodes, such as **Separator** nodes and **Switch** nodes.

Instancing by Defining and Using Shapes

The example text in Figure 12.1 defines a name for a flattened cube node used to make a single stair in a staircase. The same stair cube is then repeatedly instanced to build each of the remaining stairs in the staircase.

```
#VRML V1.0 ascii

# Original stair
DEF stair Cube {
      width  1.0
      height 0.1
      depth  3.0
}
# Second stair
Translation {
      translation -1.0 0.8 0.0
}
USE stair
# Third stair
Translation {
      translation -1.0 0.8 0.0
}
USE stair
# Fourth stair
Translation {
      translation -1.0 0.8 0.0
}
USE stair
```

Figure 12.1 *Instancing a stair to create a staircase.*

Notice the structure and order of the VRML file in Figure 12.1. Starting at the top of the file, the VRML browser reads the **Cube** node with a defined name of *stair*. The browser saves the *stair* definition, and draws the original stair. Continuing through the file, the pen is next directed to translate, then draw an instance of *stair*. To instance, the browser retrieves the saved definition of *stair* and the pen draws it. The rest of the file repeats this sequence, translating and drawing instances of *stair* over and over to build the staircase.

Understanding the DEF Syntax

To define an original node for use in instancing, precede the node with the word "**DEF**" and a node name.

SYNTAX **DEF**

```
DEF node_name node...
```

A node name is any convenient sequence of characters, such as the name *stair* used in the earlier example. Node names may include letters, numbers, and underscores. Names should not start with a number or include other punctuation characters, and may not include spaces, tabs, or carriage-returns. To create multiword names, use underscores between words. For example, the following are legal node names:

```
stair     chair     space_shuttle   Pats_Cafe
Indy500   bedroom   truck           Kitchen_Design_12
```

Node names are case-sensitive. For example, the names "ABC" and "abc" are considered to be different by the VRML browser.

TIP *Some VRML browsers allow additional characters in defined names. To ensure that your VRML worlds can be read by* any *VRML browser, limit your names to include only the upper- and lowercase letters, numbers, and the underscore.*

When your VRML browser encounters a **DEF,** the virtual pen is instructed to:

1. Save the node name and original node.
2. Draw the original node.

A VRML file can contain any number of named nodes. You can even use the same name more than once. When you do, the first **DEF** for the name is available for instancing until you define a *second* node that uses the same name. The second **DEF** using that name becomes the original for that name and is available for instancing until a *third* node is defined with that name, and so on.

TIP *Using the same name in more than one* ***DEF*** *can make a VRML file hard to understand.*

TIP *In version 1.0 of VRML, you can define the same name for more than one node. In version 1.1, you will get an error message from your VRML browser if you do this. Defining the same name for more than one node may become an error in later versions.*

Understanding the USE Syntax

To use an instance of an original node, precede the original's name, as defined earlier by a **DEF**, with the word "**USE.**"

SYNTAX **USE**

```
USE node_name
```

A **USE** drawing instruction can be specified anywhere a node can be specified, including within grouping nodes such as **Separator** and **Switch** nodes. When a **USE** instruction is encountered by the VRML browser, the virtual pen is instructed to:

1. Find the saved original node from among the browser's defined nodes.
2. Draw the original node.

When step 2 is finished, the pen continues to read the node after the **USE** instruction.

Experimenting with Instancing

The following examples provide a more detailed examination of the ways in which **USE** and **DEF** can be used and how they interact with nodes we've discussed in previous chapters.

Instancing **Shape** Nodes

Consider again the staircase example shown earlier. A single stair is named and drawn by a flattened **Cube** node. Thereafter, the *stair* node is instanced multiple times, once for each additional stair in the staircase:

```
#VRML V1.0 ascii

# Original stair
DEF stair Cube {
      width  1.0
      height 0.1
      depth  3.0
}
# Second stair
Translation {
      translation -1.0 0.8 0.0
}
USE stair
# Third stair
Translation {
      translation -1.0 0.8 0.0
}
```

Figure 12.2 continues

```
USE stair
# Fourth stair
Translation {
     translation -1.0 0.8 0.0
}
USE stair
```

Figure 12.2 *Instancing a stair to create a staircase.*

Reading the VRML file from top to bottom, the virtual pen is instructed to:

1. Define *stair.*
   a. Save the name *stair* and its associated definition.
   b. Draw the stair cube.

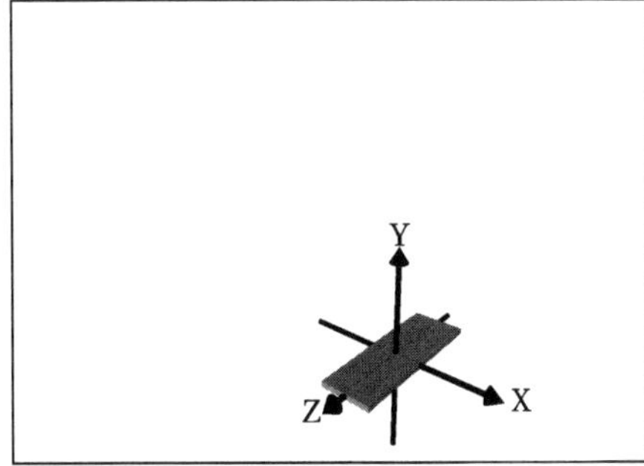

Figure 12.3 *Defining (saving and drawing)* stair.

2. Translate to the next stair's position.

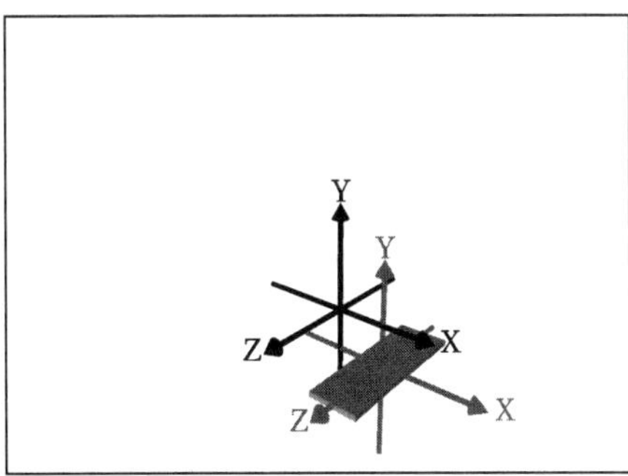

Figure 12.4 *Positioning to prepare to draw the next stair.*

3. Use *stair.*
   a. Find the name and definition of *stair.*
   b. Draw the stair cube.

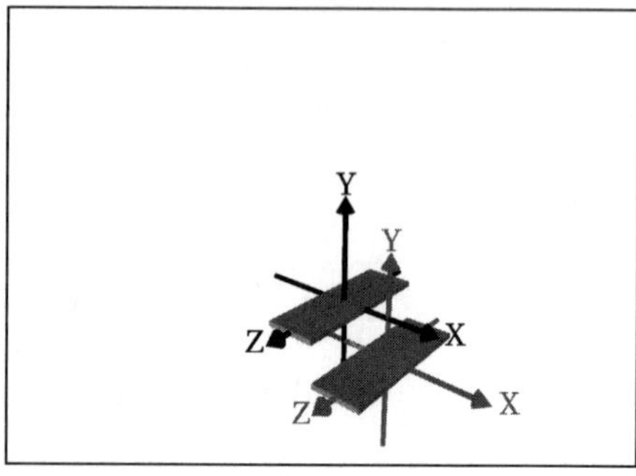

Figure 12.5 *Instancing (using)* stair.

4. Translate to the next stair's position.

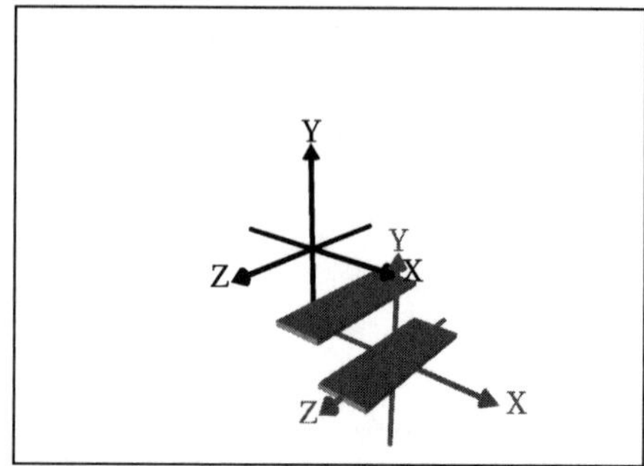

Figure 12.6 *Positioning to prepare to draw the next stair.*

5. Use *stair.*
   a. Find the name and definition of *stair.*
   b. Draw the stair cube.

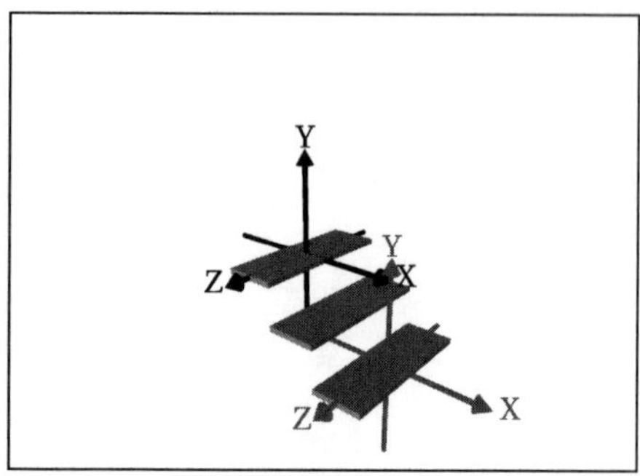

Figure 12.7 *Instancing (using)* stair.

6. Translate to the next stair's position.

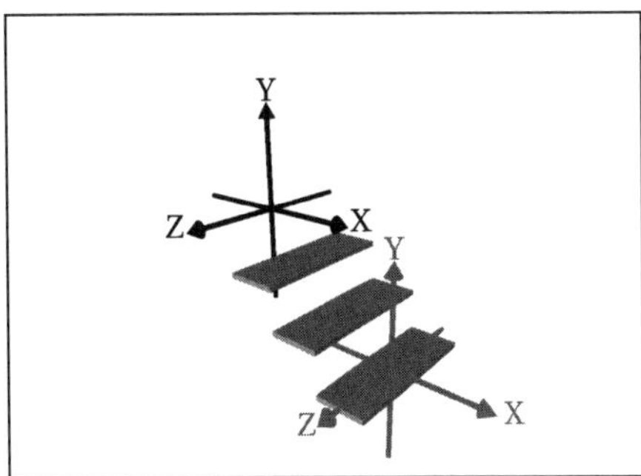

Figure 12.8 *Positioning to prepare to draw the next stair.*

7. Use *stair.*
   a. Find the name and definition of *stair.*
   b. Draw the stair cube.

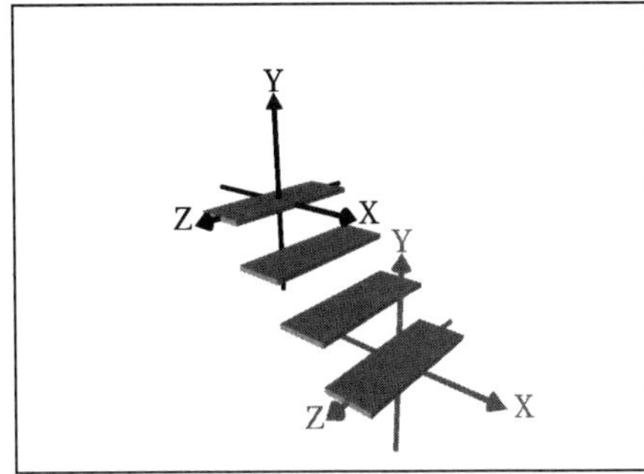

Figure 12.9 *Instancing (using)* stair.

The result is a staircase with four stairs.

Instancing Complex Shapes

You can define a name for any grouping node. Thereafter, each time you use the name, the entire group is instanced. The example text in Figure 12.10 uses a separator group containing the nodes used to build the chair from Chapter 7. The chair is then instanced three times, once on each side of a table.

```
#VRML V1.0 ascii

# Table
Separator {
      # Table base
      Translation {
            translation 0.0 1.25 0.0
      }
```

Figure 12.10 continues

```
        Cylinder {
              height 2.5
              radius 0.25
        }
        # Table top
        Translation {
              translation 0.0 1.25 0.0
        }
        Cube {
              height 0.1
              width 5.0
              depth 7.0
        }
  }
  # First Chair
  Separator {
        # Move to the 1st chair position
        Translation {
              translation 3.0 0.0 0.0
        }
        # Chair
        DEF chair Separator {
              # Scale down the chair to make it match the table
              Scale {
                    scaleFactor 0.5 0.5 0.5
              }
              # Chair seat
              Translation {
                    translation 0.0 3.0 0.0
              }
              Cube {
                    height 0.2
                    width 3.2
                    depth 4.0
              }
              # Chair front legs
              Translation {
                    translation -1.5 -1.5 0.0
              }
              Cube {
                    height 3.0
                    width 0.2
                    depth 4.0
              }
              # Chair back legs and back
              Translation {
                    translation 3.0 2.5 0.0
              }
```

Figure 12.10 continues

```
            Cube {
                  height 8.0
                  width 0.2
                  depth 4.0
            }
      }
}
# Second Chair
Separator {
      # Move to the 2nd chair position
      Translation {
            translation -3.0 0.0 0.0
      }
      Rotation {
            #             Y       +180.0 degrees
            rotation 0.0 1.0 0.0  3.14
      }
      USE chair
}
# Third Chair
Separator {
      # Move to the 3rd chair position
      Translation {
            translation 0.0 0.0 -4.0
      }
      Rotation {
            #             Y       +90.0 degrees
            rotation 0.0 1.0 0.0  1.57
      }
      USE chair
}
# Fourth Chair
Separator {
      # Move to the 4th chair position
      Translation {
            translation 0.0 0.0 4.0
      }
      Rotation {
            #             Y       -90.0 degrees
            rotation 0.0 1.0 0.0  -1.57
      }
      USE chair
}
```

Figure 12.10 *Instancing a chair defined by a* ***Separator*** *node.*

Notice that the *chair* **DEF** occurred within a **Separator** node. **DEF** definitions may occur anywhere, inside or outside any grouping node.

Notice also that the chair's **USE** occurred within a **Separator** node. **USE** may also occur anywhere, inside or outside grouping nodes.

Defining Multiple Names

The same VRML file may contain many shapes with defined names. You can even define a name for a shape that is inside a group when that group is also a defined shape. For example, the VRML text in Figure 12.11 optimizes the staircase example by defining a name for a single stair cube, then another name for a group of two stairs. It then uses the two-stair group to create a staircase of four stairs.

```
#VRML V1.0 ascii

# First and second stairs
DEF two_stairs Separator {
      # Original stair
      DEF stair Cube {
            width 1.0
            height 0.1
            depth 3.0
      }
      # Move to next stair position
      DEF tostair Translation {
            translation -1.0 0.8 0.0
      }
      # Repeat stair
      USE stair
}
# Move to next stair position
USE tostair
USE tostair
# Repeat two stairs
USE two_stairs
```

Figure 12.11 *Optimizing the staircase by defining a group containing a defined shape.*

Defining Named Shapes without Instancing Them

The **DEF** syntax both defines a name for a shape *and* instructs the virtual pen to immediately draw that shape. However there are times when you may not want to draw that shape immediately.

You can use the **Switch** node to instruct the VRML browser to group shapes and define names, but *not* draw them, by using the –1 **whichChild** field value. Recall from Chapter 11 that a **whichChild** field value of –1 indicates that *none* of its children are drawn. This defines the shape names, but skips them after they are defined.

For instance, the example text in Figure 12.12 defines a set of parts to build a fancier staircase, including a stair, a riser, a railing post, and a railing. These parts are then combined together later in the file to create the full staircase.

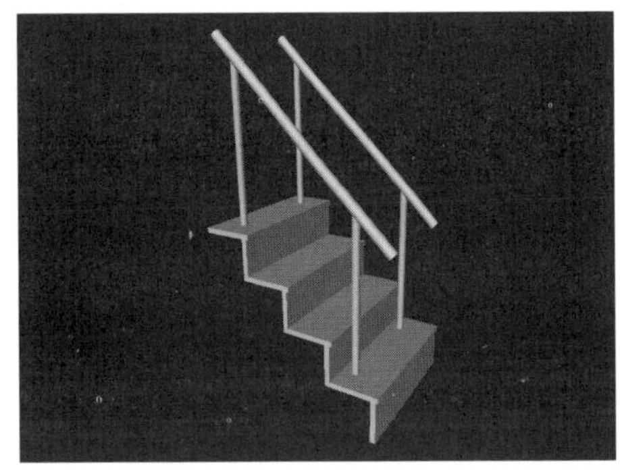

```
#VRML V1.0 ascii

Switch {
      whichChild -1
      # Stair
      DEF stair Cube {
            width 1.0
            height 0.1
            depth 3.0
      }
      # Move to riser
      DEF toriser Translation {
            translation -0.5 0.35 0.0
      }
      # Riser
      DEF riser Cube {
            width 0.1
            height 0.8
            depth 3.0
      }
      # Move to stair
      DEF tostair Translation {
            translation -0.4 0.45 0.0
      }
      # Railing post
      DEF railing_post Cylinder {
            height 3.0
            radius 0.075
      }
      # Railing
      DEF railing TransformSeparator {
            Translation {
                  translation 0.5 1.15 0.0
            }
            USE railing_post
            Translation {
                  translation 2.5 -2.4 0.0
            }
            USE railing_post
            Translation {
                  translation -1.1 2.6 0.0
            }
            Rotation {
                  #                 Z   +46.0 degrees
                  rotation 0.0 0.0 1.0  0.802
            }
            Cylinder {
                  height 5.0
                  radius 0.1
            }
      }
}
# Build a staircase
USE riser USE tostair
```

Figure 12.12 continues

```
USE stair USE toriser
USE riser USE tostair
USE stair USE toriser
USE riser USE tostair
USE stair USE toriser
USE riser USE tostair
USE stair USE toriser
Translation {
      translation 0.0 0.0 -1.4
}
USE railing
Translation {
      translation 0.0 0.0 2.8
}
USE railing
```

Figure 12.12 *Defining shapes in a* ***Switch*** *node and drawing them only as they are needed.*

Extended Examples

The following examples build on the concepts presented in this chapter. They illustrate the worlds you can create by instancing shapes. Try them on your own.

TIP *All of the VRML text in the extended examples throughout this book are available via anonymous ftp from John Wiley & Sons at* `ftp.wiley.com/public/computer_books/vrml` *and from the VRML Repository at* `http://www.sdsc.edu/vrml`.

Caterpillar in Red Shoes

In Figure 12.13 caterpillar's body is instanced as sections. Each section has an instanced leg and an instanced foot. Then the instances of these shapes are grouped into sections.

```
#VRML V1.0 ascii

DEF section Separator {
      DEF leg Separator {
            DEF foot Separator {
                  Material {
                        diffuseColor 1.0 0.0 0.0
                  }
                  Scale {
                        scaleFactor 1.75 0.5 1.0
                  }
                  Sphere {
                  }
            }
```

Figure 12.13 continues

```
                Material {
                    diffuseColor 0.9 0.5 0.4
                }
                Translation {
                    translation 0.5 2.5 0.0
                }
                Cylinder {
                    height 5.0
                    radius 0.25
                }
            }
            Translation {
                translation 0.0 0.0 3.0
            }
            USE leg
            Translation {
                translation 0.0 8.0 -1.5
            }
            Material {
                diffuseColor 0.0 0.5 0.0
            }
            Sphere {
                radius 4.0
            }
            DEF next Transform {
                translation -7.0 -8.0 0.0
                rotation 0.0 1.0 0.0  +0.39
            }
        }
        USE section USE next
        USE section USE next
        USE section USE next
        USE section USE next
        USE section USE next
        USE section USE next
        Translation {
            translation 0.0 11.0 0.0
        }
        Sphere {
            radius 4.0
        }
        Material {
            diffuseColor 1.0 1.0 1.0
        }
        Translation {
            translation -4.0 1.0 -2.0
        }
        Sphere {
        }
        Translation {
            translation 0.0 0.0 3.0
        }
        Sphere {
        }
```

Figure 12.13 continues

```
    Material {
          diffuseColor 0.0 0.0 0.0
    }
    Translation {
          translation -0.8 0.0 0.0
    }
    Sphere {
          radius 0.5
    }
    Translation {
          translation 0.0 0.0 -3.0
    }
    Sphere {
          radius 0.5
    }
    Material {
          diffuseColor 0.9 0.2 0.1
    }
    Translation {
          translation 2.2 -3.0 2.0
    }
    Cylinder {
          height 0.2
    }
```

Figure 12.13 *A caterpillar in red shoes.*

Computer Keyboard

Figure 12.14 illustrates an excellent use for instancing. By instancing the keys of the keyboard, you don't have to create each one individually.

```
#VRML V1.0 ascii

# Define some standard nodes
Switch {
      whichChild -1
      # White
      DEF white Material {
            diffuseColor 0.8 0.8 0.8
      }
      # Gray
      DEF gray Material {
            diffuseColor 0.4 0.4 0.4
      }
      # Small Key
      DEF smallKey Separator {
            USE white
            Translation {
                  translation 1.0 0.0 0.0
            }
```

Figure 12.14 continues

```
            Cube {
            }
        }
        # Medium Key
        DEF mediumKey Separator {
            USE gray
            Translation {
                translation 1.5 0.0 0.0
            }
            Cube {
                width 3.0
            }
        }
        # Big Key
        DEF bigKey Separator {
            USE gray
            Translation {
                translation 2.25 0.0 0.0
            }
            Cube {
                width 4.5
            }
        }
        # Move by 2.5 in X
        DEF x2_5 Translation {
            translation 2.5 0.0 0.0
        }
        # Move by 25.0 in X
        DEF x25 Translation {
            translation 25.0 0.0 0.0
        }
    }
    # Bottom row
    Separator {
        USE mediumKey            # Control
        Translation {
            translation 5.5 0.0 0.0
        }
        USE mediumKey            # Alt
        USE white
        Translation {
            translation 12.0 0.0 0.0
        }
        Cube {
            width 17.0          # Space
        }
        Translation {
            translation 9.0 0.0 0.0
        }
        USE mediumKey            # Alt
```

Figure 12.14 continues

```
        Translation {
              translation 5.5 0.0 0.0
        }
        USE mediumKey            # Control
  }
  # Second row
  DEF nextRow Translation {
        translation 0.0 2.5 0.0
  }
  Separator {
        USE bigKey               # Shift
        Translation {
              translation 5.25 0.0 0.0
        }
        DEF tenSmallKeys Separator {  # Z X C V B N M , . /
              USE smallKey    USE x2_5
              USE smallKey    USE x2_5
              USE smallKey    USE x2_5
              USE smallKey    USE x2_5
              USE smallKey    USE x2_5
              USE smallKey    USE x2_5
              USE smallKey    USE x2_5
              USE smallKey    USE x2_5
              USE smallKey    USE x2_5
              USE smallKey
        }
        Translation {
              translation 25.5 0.0 0.0
        }
        USE bigKey               # Shift
  }
  # Third row
  USE nextRow
  Separator {
        USE mediumKey            # Caps Lock
        Translation {
              translation 4.0 0.0 0.0
        }
        USE tenSmallKeys         # A S D F G H J K L ;
        USE x25
        USE smallKey             # '
        Translation {
              translation 4.5 0.0 0.0
        }
        USE gray
        Cube {
              width 4.0      # Enter
        }
  }
  # Fourth row
  USE nextRow
  Separator {
        USE mediumKey            # Tab
```

Figure 12.14 continues

```
        Translation {
              translation 3.5 0.0 0.0
        }
        USE tenSmallKeys        # Q W E R T Y U I O P
        USE x25
        USE smallKey            # [
        USE x2_5
        USE smallKey            # ]
        USE x2_5
        USE smallKey            # \
}
# Top row
USE nextRow
Separator {
        USE tenSmallKeys        # ` 1 2 3 4 5 6 7 8 9
        USE x25
        USE smallKey            # 0
        USE x2_5
        USE smallKey            # -
        USE x2_5
        USE smallKey            # =
        USE x2_5
        USE mediumKey           # Backspace
}
# Keyboard
Translation {
        translation 18.0 -5.0 -2.0
}
Cube {
        width 40.0
        height 15.0
}
```

Figure 12.14 *A computer keyboard.*

Summary

VRML's **DEF** syntax enables you to define a *name* for any node in a VRML file, including shape, property, and grouping nodes. Later in the file, you can use instances of that same node by specifying the word "**USE**" followed by the node's defined *name*.

By instancing, you can name commonly used shapes, then use those shapes repeatedly throughout your file. Each instance is an exact duplicate of the original, named node. If you change the named node's fields, all the instances change as well.

You can define names anywhere within a VRML file, including within groups. Similarly, you can instance nodes anywhere within a VRML file, including inside groups.

A **DEF** both defines a name for a node *and* immediately draws it. You can avoid this by including **DEF**s within a **Switch** node whose **whichChild** field value is set to –1.

CHAPTER 13

Linking in Your Worlds

Perhaps the most exciting feature of VRML is its ability to link VRML worlds together on the **World Wide Web** (**WWW**, or **the Web**). Using links, you can connect a door in your world to another VRML world described elsewhere on the Web. One of the doors in *that* world can link back to your world or to other worlds. Linking puts the entire Internet at your fingertips, enabling you to explore the network as if wandering through a vast building, stepping through door after door between worlds.

VRML world links are bound, or **anchored**, to specific shapes in your world, such as a door or window. By clicking on an anchor shape, you jump to the world connected by that anchor. You can use any shape as an anchor shape, including doorways, paintings on walls, mouse holes, computer screens, maps, and so on. Any shape you can describe using a series of VRML nodes can be an anchor to another world.

You can also use linking to assemble a world from bits and pieces in different VRML files on your hard disk or on the Web. This technique, known as **inlining**, enables you to build a room using walls from one VRML file, furniture from several others, and so on.

VRML anchors are defined using the **WWWAnchor** node and a **URL** (**Universal Resource Locator**) that specifies the address of a file on the Web. The file specified in the URL is the world to which you jump when you click the anchored shape. VRML inlining is accomplished using the **WWWInline** node and a URL. This URL specifies the address of a VRML file that you want to include in the current world.

Understanding Linking

A link is a connection between one VRML file and another. To link to another file, the link must provide the address of the other file on the Internet, like giving a street address for a house in another city. Internet file addresses are specified as URLs. For example, the URL `http://www.sdsc.edu/vrml` is the Internet file address of the VRML Repository's HTML home page.

You can also use URLs to address files on your own hard disk. The URL `file:stairs.wrl`, for instance, addresses a VRML file named `stairs.wrl` on your hard disk.

TIP *The URL* `file:stairs.wrl` *is equivalent to* `stairs.wrl`*, and they are interpreted the same way by your VRML browser. When we refer to files on your hard disk, we will omit* `file:` *from the address.*

Understanding Anchors

An **anchor** is the description of a link connecting one VRML file to another. An anchor is built from three components:

- *A URL specifying a file to link to, such as* `file:stairs.wrl`
- *A text description of the file you're linking to, such as "My stairway"*
- *A series of VRML nodes describing a shape in your VRML file, such as a door or window*

The shape described for an anchor is called the **anchor shape**. When you click on an anchor shape, you jump by way of that anchor's link to another VRML file, automatically loading it into the browser. While viewing that new file you can click on one of its anchor shapes and jump to yet another file, and so on, bouncing from VRML file to VRML file as you wander the Internet.

The anchor shape is described by one or more nodes in your VRML files. Any shape you can define with a collection of VRML nodes can be used as an anchor shape.

The collection of nodes that make up an anchor shape are contained within an **anchor group** that acts just like a separator group constructed by a **Separator** node. Like separator groups, anchor groups collect together a series of nodes that are drawn by the virtual pen in order from top to bottom. Before drawing the first node in the anchor group, the VRML browser saves all of the pen properties, including the current material, font style, and so on. Upon completing the last node in the anchor group, the pen properties are restored. The only difference between an anchor group and a separator group is that an anchor group contains the anchor's URL link as well as the nodes composing the anchor shape, while a separator group doesn't contain a URL.

You can have any number of anchors within a single VRML file. Each anchor has its own anchor shape (described by an anchor group) and URL.

Understanding Inlining

In each of the examples in previous chapters, you created a shape or shapes within a single VRML file. As you assembled these shapes together to create more complex shapes and worlds, your VRML files got larger and harder to manage. Inlining is a world construction technique that enables you to keep each of the pieces of your VRML worlds in separate, smaller files. To construct a world that uses each of those pieces, you create a VRML file that lists the pieces to assemble into a new world. That list does not include the full text of those pieces. Instead, it specifies only the names of the files. Your VRML browser reads each of the named files and assembles the world for you.

For instance, imagine that you have three VRML files on your hard disk:

`wall.wrl`	A piece of a wall
`door.wrl`	A door
`table.wrl`	A table

To construct a room from these pieces, you can create a new VRML file that inlines the wall, the door, and the table. Each inline is accomplished using a VRML node. The file using these inline nodes builds a room by directing the VRML browser to:

- *Read the file* `wall.wrl` *and draw it.*
- *Read the file* `door.wrl` *and draw it.*
- *Read the file* `table.wrl` *and draw it.*

You can quickly construct very complex VRML worlds by listing the pieces necessary to assemble your new world. By keeping key pieces in separate files, you can also build several different worlds that share the same pieces. For instance, you can construct different rooms by using combinations of your wall, chair, table, door, window, floor, desk, shelf, and lamp shapes.

You can think of an inlined file as describing a shape, just like VRML's built-in **Cube, Cylinder, Cone,** and **Sphere** node shapes. When inlined into your world, the inlined file's collection of nodes makes up an inline shape contained within an inline group. Such a group acts just like a separator group created by a **Separator** node.

Like separator groups, inline groups draw the group's nodes from top to bottom. Before drawing the first node in the inline group, the VRML browser saves all pen properties, including the current material, font style, and so on. Upon completing the last node in the inline group, the saved properties are restored. The difference between an inline group and a separator group is that a separator group lists the nodes explicitly, while an inline group simply names a VRML file that contains the nodes.

Like shapes drawn within a separator group, shapes drawn within an inline group can be transformed using the translation, rotation, and scaling features of VRML. You can also control the font style, color, and other properties used to draw an inline shape. These capabilities enable you to assemble pieces from different files and scale, rotate, translate, and color them appropriately for your own world.

Shapes are inlined using a URL, just like that used for linking anchors. Using URLs, you can construct VRML worlds where the walls come from one site on the Internet, a chair and table from another, paintings on the walls from still other sites, and so on. You construct a VRML world from pieces described at different Internet sites all over the world.

Linking to Other Worlds with Anchors

Anchors that link to shapes and worlds on the Web are created using the VRML **WWWAnchor** node. The example text in Figure 13.1 uses a **WWWAnchor** node to describe a door anchor shape. Clicking on the door directs your VRML browser to jump to the VRML world behind the door. In this case, the door links to a VRML file named `city.wrl` on your hard disk.

TIP *Anchors and inlines refer to files on your hard disk. The examples in this chapter specify fictional names for the VRML files, but you can change them to anything you want.*

```
#VRML V1.0 ascii

# Draw a stretch of wall
Material {
	diffuseColor 0.6 0.55 0.4
}
Cube {
	width 12.0
	height 7.0
	depth 0.25
}
# Draw a door - use it as an anchor to The City
WWWAnchor {
	name "file:city.wrl"
	description "The City"
	Material {
		diffuseColor 0.3 0.2 0.0
	}
	Cube {
		width 3.0
		height 7.01
		depth 0.3
	}
	# Door knob
	Translation {
		translation 1.1 -0.25 0.325
	}
	Material {
		diffuseColor 0.6 0.6 0.0
	}
	Sphere {
		radius 0.2
	}
```

Figure 13.1 continues

```
        # Door name
        Material {
              diffuseColor 0.8 0.8 0.8
        }
        Translation {
              translation -1.1 2.25 -0.1
        }
        FontStyle {
              size 0.6
              style BOLD
        }
        AsciiText {
              string [ "Doorway", "to", "The City" ]
              justification CENTER
        }
}
```

Figure 13.1 *A door linked to a city.*

Notice the structure and order of the VRML file in Figure 13.1. Reading from the top of the file, the drawing color is set to beige and a flattened cube drawn to create one wall for a room. Following the wall, a **WWWAnchor** node creates an anchor group of nodes to draw a door on the wall. The door is described by a flattened cube for the door, a series of nodes to create a doorknob on the door, and a series of nodes to add a sign to the door that reads "Doorway to The City." The entire door, including the doorknob and sign, is an anchor shape linking to the file named `city.wrl` on your hard disk.

Understanding the **WWWAnchor** Node Syntax

The **WWWAnchor** node has three fields: **name, description,** and **map.** The curly braces of a **WWWAnchor** node group together a list of child nodes contained within the anchor group that define an anchor shape.

TIP *In version 1.1 of VRML, URLs may contain an optional camera selection name. To select a camera, you may append a name to the URL using a string of this form:*

`#camera`

where camera *is the name of a camera node in the file to which you are linking.*

SYNTAX **WWWAnchor**

```
WWWAnchor {
   name            ""        # URL
   description     ""        # text string
   map             NONE      # mapping type
}
```

The **name** field specifies a URL for the anchor's link. The URL can lead to any VRML file on the Web or on your hard disk. If the **name** field is an empty string, such as "", then the anchor is disabled. When an anchor is disabled, the anchor shape is still drawn, but you do not jump to a new world when you click on the shape.

The **description** field gives a text description of the world to which you jump if you click on the link.

TIP *Most VRML browsers display the URL of an anchor when you move the cursor over the anchor shape. That URL is usually shown at the top or bottom of the screen in a special part of the browser window. URLs, however, are often long and cryptic and provide little information about the kind of world behind an anchor. The* ***description*** *field is your opportunity to make things clearer by specifying a brief, one-line description of what lies behind an anchor. Some VRML browsers display both the URL and your description, while others display only one or the other. In most cases, if you don't supply a description, only the URL is displayed.*

TIP *Typically, URLs specified within* ***WWWAnchor*** *nodes link to VRML files. Such URLs may also link to files of other types, including* **HTML** *files,* **GIF** *image files,* **AIF** *sound files, and so on. Different VRML browsers handle these files differently. Some browsers load and present those non-VRML files themselves, while others open these files using* **helper applications** *designed specifically to present HTML, GIF, AIF, or other types of files. Check your VRML browser manual to see what method it uses. In this book, we show examples where links lead only to VRML files.*

When you click on an anchor shape, the VRML browser uses the URL in the anchor's **name** field to load a world from across the Internet or from your hard disk. Worlds loaded from the Internet are delivered to you by a **Web server** program running on the **remote host** at the remote Internet site. That Web server looks up the URL of the file you want in the list of files it can deliver.

In sophisticated systems, the URL can name a **mapping program** to run instead of a VRML file to display. That program runs on the remote host, under the control of that site's Web server. The program typically creates a VRML file that is delivered across the Internet and displayed by your VRML browser.

Using this kind of mapping program, you can set up Web servers that automatically compute and deliver different VRML worlds depending on where the anchor shape is clicked. If, for instance, you create an anchor shape that draws the Earth, then clicking on Africa can send Africa's coordinates to the mapping program and the program can return to you a VRML world describing Africa. If you click on Hawaii, the same program can return to you a VRML world describing Hawaii. The world the program delivers to you depends on the coordinates of your mouse click.

The **map** field of the **WWWAnchor** node indicates whether the coordinates of your mouse click on an anchor shape are, or are not, sent to the remote Web server for use by a mapping program. The **map** field has two values:

- ***NONE****—Do not pass coordinate mapping information to the remote Web server.*
- ***POINT****—Pass coordinate mapping information to the remote Web server.*

The **NONE** value is the default. When point mapping is used, a mapping string is created by your VRML browser and appended to the end of the anchor's URL before it sends the URL off to the remote Web server. The mapping string has the form:

```
?x,y,z
```

where *x* is replaced with the X coordinate of the mouse-click location, *y* is replaced with the Y coordinate, and *z* is replaced with the Z coordinate.

TIP *Mapping coordinates appended to a URL are ignored if the URL links to a VRML file, instead of a program managed by a Web server. When a URL links to a program, it is up to that program to decide what to do with the mapping coordinates. It may choose to ignore them.*

TIP *The construction of Web server programs that use mapping coordinates is beyond the scope of this book. Such programs are typically written in the* **Perl scripting language** *and are collectively known as* **CGI scripts** *(***Common Gateway Interface** *scripts). Books describing how to set up a Web server discuss writing CGI scripts.*

A **WWWAnchor** node also defines a group of nodes that draw an anchor shape or shapes. These anchor shapes act like 3-D buttons in your world. By clicking anywhere on one of these shapes, you jump by way of a link to a new world.

TIP *Different VRML browsers provide different ways to select anchor shapes to jump to new worlds. Some use a special mode, while others use a special mouse button. Check your VRML browser manual to see what method it uses. In this book, we assume that you select an anchor by clicking on it with your mouse.*

To group the nodes of an anchor shape, the **WWWAnchor** node acts just like the **Separator** node discussed in Chapter 11. When entering the group, a **WWWAnchor** node directs the VRML browser to save all pen properties, then follow the directions of each of the group's child nodes, in order, from top to bottom. Upon exiting the group, the VRML browser restores the saved properties. Pen property changes made by nodes within the anchor group do not affect how the VRML browser draws shapes following the **WWWAnchor** node in the VRML file.

WWWAnchor nodes may contain nodes of any type as their children, including any of the grouping, shape, or property nodes.

TIP *Some VRML browsers do not allow* ***WWWAnchor*** *nodes to contain children that are, themselves,* ***WWWAnchor*** *nodes. Such children may be treated like* ***Separator*** *nodes rather than anchors.*

TIP *Different VRML browsers have different methods of indicating anchor shapes as you view a world. Some browsers, for instance, highlight anchor shapes when you move your cursor over them. Other browsers change the color of anchor shapes, outline them, or do nothing when you move your cursor over them. Check your VRML browser manual to see what method of indicating anchor shapes it uses.*

Linking to Other Worlds with Inlines

File inlining is accomplished using the VRML **WWWInline** node. The example text in Figure 13.2 uses two **WWWInline** nodes to assemble a table and a desk lamp together in one world, placing the desk lamp on the table. The table is the one you constructed in Chapter 7, and the lamp is the one you constructed in Chapter 11.

TIP *Anchors and inlines refer to files on your hard disk. The examples in this chapter specify fictional names for the VRML files, but you can change them to anything you want.*

```
#VRML V1.0 ascii

# Draw a table
WWWInline {
      name "file:table.wrl"
}
# Draw an adjustable desk lamp
Separator {
      Translation {
            translation 1.5 2.59 -2.0
      }
      Rotation {
            #             Y       -60.0 degrees
            rotation 0.0 1.0 0.0 -1.047
      }
      WWWInline {
            name "file:lamp.wrl"
      }
}
# Draw a desk blotter
Separator {
      Translation {
            translation -1.0 2.6 0.0
      }
      Cube {
            width  2.5
            height 0.01
            depth  3.0
      }
}
```

Figure 13.2 *Inlining a table and a lamp to create one VRML world.*

Notice the structure and order of the VRML file in Figure 13.2. Reading from the top of the file, the first **WWWInline** node directs the VRML browser to use the table shape described in the file `table.wrl` on your hard disk. The next node in the file creates a separator group that translates, rotates, then inlines the lamp shape described in the file `lamp.wrl` on your hard disk. After drawing the desk lamp, the VRML file adds a flattened cube to draw a desk blotter on the table.

Understanding the **WWWInline** Node Syntax

The **WWWInline** node has three fields: **name, bboxSize,** and **bboxCenter.**

SYNTAX **WWWInline node**

```
WWWInline {
   name         ""                  # URL
   bboxSize     0.0 0.0 0.0         # width, height, depth
   bboxCenter   0.0 0.0 0.0         # 3-D coordinate
}
```

The **name** field specifies a URL for a file on the Internet included as a piece of the VRML world. If the URL is an empty string, such as `""`, then no file is inlined into the world.

TIP *Similar to* ***WWWAnchor*** *nodes,* ***WWWInline*** *nodes may link to files other than VRML files. Your browser may display these files, open them using helper applications, or reject the files completely. Check your VRML browser manual to see what method it uses. In this book, we show examples where inline links lead only to VRML files.*

TIP *Different VRML browsers will react differently if a* ***WWWInline*** *node URL names a file or host that cannot be accessed. Some browsers report an error and stop loading the whole VRML world. Other browsers draw a box where the inlined shape should be. Still others do nothing about bad URLs. Check the manual for your VRML browser to see what method it uses.*

Some VRML browsers use bounding boxes to perform render culling of inlined shapes. You can provide the size and location of the bounding box by setting the **bboxSize** and **bboxCenter** fields within a **WWWInline** node. The **bboxSize** field uses three floating-point values to describe the width, height, and depth of a box. The **bboxCenter** field uses three floating-point values for the X, Y, and Z components of a 3-D coordinate describing the center of the bounding box. This bounding box center is *relative to* the current origin location.

If you do not provide a bounding box size and center for an inlined world, the VRML browser computes one for you. To do this, it must read the entire inlined file. If it finds that the bounding box and inlined file's shapes are *not* visible from your current view, it has wasted time reading the inlined file. It can draw your world more quickly if it skips over shapes in inlined files that are not visible in the current view and concentrates on the shapes that are.

By providing a bounding box size and center, you give your browser the information it needs to skip inlined shapes that can't be seen from the current view. If the bounding box indicates that an inlined file's shapes are not visible, the VRML browser skips the inline file completely until you later change your view and make the inlined shapes visible. This saves a lot of time as the VRML browser reads a world, especially if the inlined file is downloaded from the Internet using a slow **modem** connected to your computer.

TIP *Different VRML browsers read inlined files at different times as they load worlds. Some browsers look through a world, find all its inlined files, and load them all before displaying anything on your screen. Others display the world in pieces, loading each inlined file and displaying it as it is read. Check your VRML browser manual to see what method of loading inlined files it uses.*

To group the nodes of an inlined file's shapes, the **WWWInline** node acts just like the **Separator** node discussed in Chapter 11. When entering the inline group, a **WWWInline** node directs the browser to save all pen properties, then follow the directions of each of the inlined file's nodes, in order, from top to bottom. Upon exiting the group, the browser restores the saved properties. Pen property changes made by nodes within the inlined file do not affect how the VRML browser draws shapes following the **WWWInline** node in the VRML file.

An inlined file may contain one or more **WWWInline** nodes to inline further files. This enables you to build up complex hierarchies of shapes. For instance, you can build wall and door shapes, each in separate VRML files. Next, you can construct a new VRML file that builds the side of a room by inlining a door shape and two wall shapes, one on either side of the door. To build the complete room, you can create a new VRML file that inlines the wall-and-door shape file four times, once for each side of a room. That complete room file can be inlined by a house file, the house file inlined within a city file, and so on.

An inlined file may also contain one or more **WWWAnchor** nodes. For instance, you can create a VRML file describing an anchor shape that, when clicked on, displays a *help* file. Then you can inline that same help anchor any number of times in any of your worlds. By clicking on that anchor in any of those worlds, you jump to the help file.

Inlined files may define and use node names using the **DEF** and **USE** syntax described in Chapter 12. The names of nodes, however, are known only within the VRML file that defines them. Imagine you have two VRML files, `stairs.wrl` and `hall.wrl`, and `hall.wrl` inlines `stairs.wrl` to create a stairway within the hall. The `stairs.wrl` file defines and uses names for stair and riser shapes like those in Chapter 12. These stair and riser node names, however, cannot be used within the `hall.wrl` file. Node names can be used only within the file in which they are defined.

Experimenting with Linking

The following examples provide a more detailed examination of the ways in which anchors and inlines can be used and how the **WWWAnchor** and **WWWInline** nodes interact with nodes we've discussed in previous chapters.

Using Anchors to Link Worlds

The example text in Figure 13.3 creates the wall and door shown earlier. The door is drawn within the anchor group of a **WWWAnchor** node. Clicking anywhere on the door, you jump to a VRML file named `city.wrl` on your hard disk.

TIP *Anchors and inlines refer to files on your hard disk. The examples in this chapter specify fictional names for the VRML files, but you can change them to anything you want.*

```
#VRML V1.0 ascii

# Draw a stretch of wall
Material {
      diffuseColor 0.6 0.55 0.4
}
Cube {
      width 12.0
      height 7.0
      depth  0.25
}
# Draw a door - use it as an
# anchor to Pat's Office
WWWAnchor {
      name "file:room1.wrl"
      description "Pat's Office"
      Material {
            diffuseColor 0.3 0.2 0.0
      }
      Cube {
            width  3.0
            height 7.01
            depth  0.3
      }
      # Door knob
      Translation {
            translation 1.1 -0.25 0.325
      }
      Material {
            diffuseColor 0.6 0.6 0.0
      }
```

Figure 13.3 continues

```
		Sphere {
			radius 0.2
		}
		# Door name
		Material {
			diffuseColor 0.8 0.8 0.8
		}
		Translation {
			translation -1.1 2.25 -0.1
		}
		FontStyle {
			size 0.6
			style BOLD
		}
		AsciiText {
			string [ "Pat's", "Office" ]
			justification CENTER
		}
	}
```

Figure 13.3 *By clicking on the door created within a **WWWAnchor** node, you jump to a city.*

Reading from the top of the file, the VRML browser is directed to:

1. Change its color to beige.
2. Draw a wall using a flattened beige cube.
3. Draw the anchor group.
   a. Save all pen properties.
   b. Use the URL `file:city.wrl` if you click on the anchor shape.
   c. Use the description "The City" when displaying anchor information.
   d. Draw a brown door, gold door knob, and white door sign using a series of **Material, Translation, Cube, Sphere, FontStyle,** and **AsciiText** nodes.
   e. Restore all pen properties.

If you click anywhere on the door, door knob, or door sign, the VRML browser jumps to the VRML file `city.wrl`.

Using Inlines to Assemble Worlds

The following example assembles the table and desk lamp shown earlier. The table shape is described by a VRML file `table.wrl` on your hard disk. The desk lamp shape is described by a VRML file `lamp.wrl`, also on your hard disk. You can use the table from Chapter 7 and the adjustable desk lamp from Chapter 11 for these two shapes.

The table and lamp are combined in the VRML file in Figure 13.4 by using a **WWWInline** node for each one. A **Translation** and a **Rotation** node position and orient the desk lamp on the table. Additional nodes in the file create a desk blotter for the table.

```
#VRML V1.0 ascii

# Draw a table
WWWInline {
      name "file:table.wrl"
}
# Draw an adjustable desk lamp
Separator {
      Translation {
            translation 1.5 2.59 -2.0
      }
      Rotation {
               #            Y        -60.0 degrees
               rotation 0.0 1.0 0.0 -1.047
      }
      WWWInline {
            name "file:lamp.wrl"
      }
}
# Draw a desk blotter
Separator {
      Translation {
            translation -1.0 2.6 0.0
      }
      Cube {
            width  2.5
            height 0.01
            depth  3.0
      }
}
```

Figure 13.4 *Creating a table with a lamp and blotter by inlining the table and lamp.*

Reading from the top of the file, the VRML browser is instructed to:

1. Load the file `table.wrl` and draw its shapes. Treat the shapes in the inlined file as if they are within a separator group.
   a. Save all pen properties.
   b. Draw the shapes found in `table.wrl`.
   c. Restore all pen properties.
2. Draw the separator group.
   a. Save all pen properties.
   b. Translate and rotate to position and orient subsequent shapes.

   c. Load the file `lamp.wrl`, and draw its shapes. Treat the shapes in the inlined file as if they are within a separator group:
      i. Save pen properties.
      ii. Draw the shapes found in `lamp.wrl`.
      iii. Restore all pen properties.
   d. Restore all pen properties.
3. Draw the separator group.
   a. Save all pen properties.
   b. Translate and draw a flattened cube to make a desk blotter.
   c. Restore all pen properties.

When this VRML file is read, the VRML browser is instructed to display the inlined table and lamp shapes, as well.

Notice that in this example neither **WWWInline** node provided bounding box size and center values for the table or the lamp. The VRML browser loads both files, unable to perform render culling. You can provide bounding box size and center values for both inlines, as shown in Figure 13.5.

```
#VRML V1.0 ascii

# Draw a table
WWWInline {
     name "file:table.wrl"
     bboxSize 5.0 2.5 7.0
     bboxCenter 0.0 1.5 0.0
}
# Draw an adjustable desk lamp
Separator {
     Translation {
          translation 1.5 2.59 -2.0
     }
     Rotation {
          #            Y       -60.0 degrees
          rotation 0.0 1.0 0.0 -1.047
     }
     WWWInline {
          name "file:lamp.wrl"
          bboxSize 3.0 3.0 3.0
          bboxCenter 0.0 1.5 0.0
     }
}
# Draw a desk blotter
Separator {
     Translation {
          translation -1.0 2.6 0.0
     }
```

Figure 13.5 continues

```
        Cube {
             width
             height 0.01
             depth 3.0
        }
   }
```

Figure 13.5 *Providing bounding box size and center values to optimize how the browser reads and displays the inlined table and lamp.*

Building and Linking Complex Worlds

Using **WWWInline** nodes, you can quickly build complex worlds out of a set of standard pieces, such as walls, doors, tables, and lamps. Each time you use one of these you can make it an anchor shape so that by clicking on different doors in a room you jump to different worlds.

The following examples build a room, piece by piece. The final room has a floor, three walls, three doors, and a table with a lamp and desk blotter on it. Each of the three doors is an anchor for links to other worlds. To build this world, first create each of the individual pieces in separate VRML files. The table, lamp, and desk blotter are described by the VRML file in the previous example. The walls and door are described by the two files that follow and are somewhat different from the wall-and-door example shown earlier.

The following VRML file creates a beige wall in a file named `wall.wrl`.

```
#VRML V1.0 ascii

Material {
     diffuseColor 0.6 0.55 0.4
}
Cube {
     width  8.0
     height 6.0
     depth  0.3
}
```

Figure 13.6 *A beige wall in* `wall.wrl`.

The VRML file in Figure 13.7 creates a brown door with a gold door knob in a file named `door.wrl`.

```
#VRML V1.0 ascii

Translation {
     translation 1.5 0.0 0.0
}
# Door
Material {
     diffuseColor 0.3 0.2 0.0
}
```

Figure 13.7 continues

```
Cube {
      width  3.0
      height 6.0
      depth  0.25
}
# Door knob
Translation {
      translation 1.1 -0.25 0.325
}
Material {
      diffuseColor 0.6 0.6 0.0
}
Sphere {
      radius 0.2
}
```

Figure 13.7 *A brown door with a gold knob in* `door.wrl`.

The table and desk lamp shapes are the same as those used in the earlier example. They are in a file named `dtable.wrl`.

Using these pieces, we can construct a room by inlining each piece and positioning and orienting them within the room. Each door is inlined and drawn with a different door sign and a different anchor URL. The table and desk are inlined last, placing them in the middle of the room.

```
#VRML V1.0 ascii

# Define a few pieces to use
# in building a room
Switch {
      whichChild -1
      # An 8 foot stretch of wall
      DEF wall WWWInline {
            name "wall.wrl"
      }
      # Door opening angle
      DEF doorAngle Rotation {
            #           Y        -30.0 degrees
            rotation 0.0 1.0 0.0 -0.52
      }
      # A 3 foot wide door
      DEF door WWWInline {
            name "door.wrl"
      }
      # White
      DEF white Material {
            diffuseColor 0.8 0.8 0.8
      }
      # Position of sign on door
      DEF toSign Translation {
            translation 1.5 2.0 0.15
      }
```

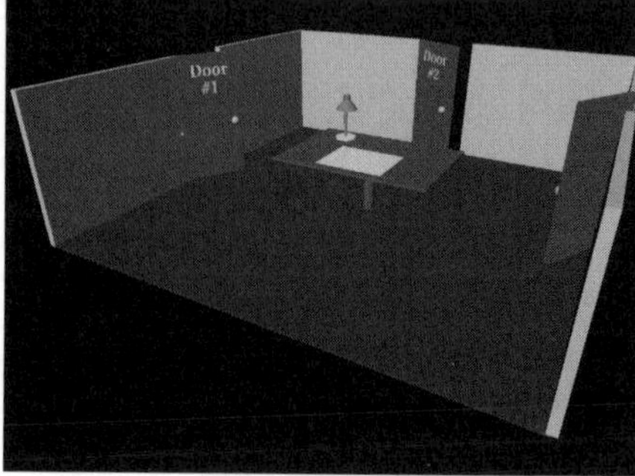

Figure 13.8 continues

```
		# Sign font
		DEF signFont FontStyle {
			size 0.8
			style BOLD
		}
		# Two walls with a door slot between them
		DEF two_walls Separator {
			Translation {
				translation 4.0 0.0 0.0
			}
			USE wall
			Translation {
				translation 11.0 0.0 0.0
			}
			USE wall
		}
		# Move to door
		DEF toDoor Translation {
			translation 8.0 0.0 0.0
		}
	}
	# Build a room
	# Floor
	Separator {
		Translation {
			translation 0.0 -3.0 0.0
		}
		Material {
			diffuseColor 0.15 0.1 0.1
		}
		Cube {
			width 19.0
			height 0.1
			depth 19.0
		}
	}
	# Left wall
	Separator {
		Translation {
			translation -9.5 0.0 9.5
		}
		Rotation {
			#             Y       +90.0 degrees
			rotation 0.0 1.0 0.0  1.57
		}
		USE two_walls
		USE toDoor
```

Figure 13.8 continues

```
        WWWAnchor {
            name "world1.wrl"
            description "Door #1"
            USE doorAngle
            USE door
            USE white
            USE toSign
            USE signFont
            AsciiText {
                string [ "Door", "#1" ]
                justification CENTER
            }
        }
    }
    # Front wall
    Separator {
        Translation {
            translation -9.5 0.0 -9.5
        }
        USE two_walls
        USE toDoor
        WWWAnchor {
            name "world2.wrl"
            description "Door #2"
            USE doorAngle
            USE door
            USE white
            USE toSign
            USE signFont
            AsciiText {
                string [ "Door", "#2" ]
                justification CENTER
            }
        }
    }
    # Right wall
    Separator {
        Translation {
            translation 9.5 0.0 -9.5
        }
        Rotation {
            #            Y       -90.0 degrees
            rotation 0.0 1.0 0.0 -1.57
        }
        USE two_walls
        USE toDoor
```

Figure 13.8 continues

```
        WWWAnchor {
              name "world3.wrl"
              description "Door #3"
              USE doorAngle
              USE door
              USE white
              USE toSign
              USE signFont
              AsciiText {
                    string [ "Door", "#3" ]
                    justification CENTER
              }
        }
}
# Table in the corner
Separator {
      Translation {
            translation 0.0 -3.0 0.0
      }
      Rotation {
            #           Y       +90.0 degrees
            rotation 0.0 1.0 0.0  1.57
      }
      WWWInline {
            name "dtable.wrl"
      }
}
```

Figure 13.8 *A room created by inlining walls with doors and a table and desk lamp; each door jumps to a different, linked VRML world.*

Extended Examples

The following examples build on the concepts we present in this chapter. They illustrate the worlds you can create by linking worlds and using text and primitive shapes, transforms, materials, groups, and instances. Try them on your own.

TIP *All of the VRML text in the extended examples throughout this book are available via anonymous ftp from John Wiley & Sons at* `ftp.wiley.com/public/computer_books/vrml` *and from the VRML Repository at* `http://www.sdsc.edu/vrml`.

A Table with a Computer and Note on It

The example text in Figure 13.9 creates a table with a computer, a book, and a note on it. All of the shapes are created in separate files and inlined into the current world. **Translation** and **Transform** nodes position, orient, and scale before loading each shape into the world.

You created the table with the note on it in Chapter 11. The computer monitor is an example from Chapter 7. The keyboard is created in Chapter 12.

```
#VRML V1.0 ascii

# Draw a table
WWWInline {
      name "file:table.wrl"
}
# Draw a computer on top
Separator {
      Translation {
            translation 0.0 2.9 4.0
      }
      WWWInline {
            name "file:computer2.wrl"
      }
}
# Draw keyboard
Separator {
      Transform {
            translation -1.8 0.5 6.0
            #        X                -90 degrees
            rotation 1.0 0.0 0.0   -1.57
            scaleFactor 0.1 0.1 0.1
      }
      WWWInline {
            name "file:keyboard.wrl"
      }
}
```

Figure 13.9 *A computer and table created by inlining.*

Summary

A link is a connection from one VRML file to another and is specified using a URL: an address for a file on the Internet or on your hard disk.

The **WWWAnchor** node groups nodes to draw an anchor shape that, when clicked, directs the VRML browser to jump to another VRML world. The **name** field of the **WWWAnchor** node specifies the URL of the linked world to which to jump, and the **description** field specifies a simple, one-line text description of that world.

The **map** field of a **WWWAnchor** node can include a 3-D coordinate in a URL. The 3-D coordinate specifies to the remote Web server where on the anchor shape you clicked. That coordinate can be used by the Web server to decide which of many VRML files to return to you.

A **WWWAnchor** field acts just like a **Separator** node. It saves and restores all pen properties and draws the grouped nodes from the top to bottom in order. A **WWWAnchor** node may contain any other node except **WWWAnchor** nodes.

The **WWWInline** node names a VRML file included as a piece of your VRML world. Using inlined shapes, you can quickly build complex VRML worlds using standard pieces, such as walls, doors, tables, and lamps.

The **name** field of a **WWWInline** node specifies the URL of the VRML file to read in and assemble into your world. The **bboxSize** and **bboxCenter** fields describe the size and location of a bounding box large enough to surround all of the shapes of the inlined world. This bounding box is used by your VRML browser to perform render culling when it loads the inlined file.

A **WWWInline** node acts just like a **Separator** node surrounding the nodes of the inlined shape. It saves and restores all pen properties and draws the grouped nodes from top to bottom in order. A **WWWInline** node may address a file that includes **WWWInline** nodes or **WWWAnchor** nodes.

CHAPTER 14

Creating Shapes with Faces, Lines, and Points

The primitive shapes can be used to create tables, chairs, planets, wheels, lamp shades, and so on. They are, however, insufficient when the goal is to create more complex shapes, particularly those with smooth flowing curves. Fortunately, VRML provides a very flexible set of nodes for use in constructing such shapes out of faces, lines, and points.

VRML faces are flat, multisided shapes, like triangles, squares, and octagons. By arranging many adjacent faces, you can construct complex 2-D and 3-D faceted surfaces. The VRML primitive shapes are actually constructed from faces. The **Cube** node creates six adjacent square faces arranged to form a box. The **Cylinder** node creates two circular faces for the top and bottom of the cylinder plus a number of long, thin faces to create the faceted sides of the cylinder. A similar approach is used by the **Sphere** and **Cone** nodes to create those shapes.

Using faces, you can create your own faceted shapes. By using a large number of tiny facets, you can closely approximate any smooth surface. You can create the curved body of a sports car, the rolling hills of a landscape, the rounded shape of a computer mouse, or the smooth curves of a vase.

VRML lines are straight, 2-D segments connecting the vertices of a shape. Using lines, you can draw line plots, curves, and grids. You can use lines to create the grout lines between tiles on a floor, add lines to the side of a building to mark the different building floors, and draw the edges of vents and grill work.

VRML points are simply dots. Using sets of points, you can draw star fields and scatter plots. You can simulate the rows of guide lights of a distant aircraft runway, or create the lights of a sparkling nighttime city skyline.

VRML's **Coordinate3** node and **PointSet** node enable you to create lists of points. The **IndexedLineSet** node, in conjunction with the **Coordinate3** node, enables you to create lists of lines, or **polylines**, to create the outlines of shapes. The **IndexedFaceSet** node, in conjunction with the **Coordinate3** node, enables you to define the faces that make up faceted shapes.

TIP *Throughout the discussions of many-sided objects in this book, we do not use the word polygon. Instead, we use the word face to be consistent with VRML's terminology.*

Understanding Faces

Every face is made up of two components:

- **Vertices**—*The corners of the face. A triangle, for instance, has three vertices, while a square has four.*
- **Edges**—*The lines that connect a face's vertices together to form the perimeter of the face. A triangle has three edges, and a square has four.*

Creating a Face

Creating a face in VRML is like creating a child's connect-the-dots drawing. First you define the locations of the dots, or vertices, of a shape. Next you connect together those vertices, in a particular order, to form the edges of the face.

To create 3-D faces, the locations of a face's vertices are each defined by a 3-D coordinate. Recall from Chapter 2 that a 3-D coordinate is made up of an X, a Y, and a Z value specifying a location measured out from the origin along the X, Y, and Z axes.

A coordinate list specifies the coordinates needed to define a face. For example, the following coordinates define the vertices of a triangle:

Vertex Index	*Coordinate*
0	`0.0 1.0 0.0`
1	`-1.0 0.0 0.0`
2	`1.0 0.0 0.0`

Each vertex in the list is a coordinate numbered with an **index** starting with zero. By indexing them, each coordinate can then be referenced with the index rather than repeating the entire 3-D, X Y Z-coordinate value.

To draw the triangle, connect the vertices together with three edges:

Edge	*Starting Vertex Index*	*Ending Vertex Index*
0	0	1
1	1	2
2	2	0

Each edge is described by specifying the coordinate list indexes for its starting and ending vertices. Edge 0, for instance, connects vertex index 0 to vertex index 1. Edge 1 connects vertex index 1 to vertex index 2. And edge 2 connects vertex index 2 back to vertex index 0.

In the list of vertex coordinates, vertex index 0 is the coordinate `0.0 1.0 0.0` and vertex index 1 is `-1.0 0.0 0.0`. Edge 0 connects these two vertices together and forms the left edge of a triangle. Similarly, edge 1 creates the bottom of the triangle, and edge 2 the right side of the triangle.

Figure 14.1*a* shows the vertices of the triangle. Figure 14.1*b* shows the vertices connected together to form the edges of the triangle.

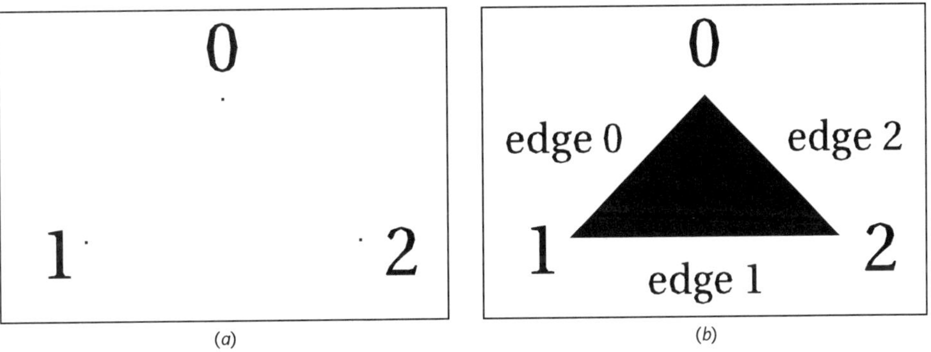

Figure 14.1 *The vertices and edges of a triangle.*

Using Vertex Index Lists

Indexing vertices not only enables you to reference coordinates, but it also enables you to specify the drawing order from one vertex to another. In other words, you can specify the order in which the vertices of a face connect to create its edges.

The edges of any face are strung together in an unbroken chain that forms the perimeter of the face. The ending vertex of the first edge is the starting vertex of the second edge, the ending vertex of the second edge is the starting vertex of the third, and so on. The last edge closes the face by connecting the last vertex back to the starting vertex of the first edge. You can describe a face-edge chain with a list of the vertex indexes used by consecutive edges. For instance, the triangle has this vertex index list:

```
0, 1, 2, 0
```

Using this vertex index list, the edge from vertex 0 to vertex 1 is the first edge drawn, then from vertex 1 to vertex 2, and finally from vertex 2 back to vertex 0. Because faces are always closed, the last vertex in the list is always the same as the first vertex, and you don't have to specify it explicitly. You can then specify the triangle's vertex index list as:

```
0, 1, 2
```

The starting vertex in an index list doesn't matter. It is equally valid to start with vertex 1, instead of vertex 0, and then draw edges from vertex 1 to vertex 2, vertex 2 to vertex 0, and vertex 0 to vertex 1 to form a triangle identical to that preceding. As long as the edges are connected between the same vertices, it doesn't matter what the starting index is. The following three vertex index lists all create the same triangle:

```
0, 1, 2
1, 2, 0
2, 1, 0
```

Starting at vertex 0, there are two possible drawing directions useful for building the vertex index list. For instance, both of these vertex index lists define a triangle starting at vertex 0:

```
0, 1, 2
0, 2, 1
```

The first list connects the edges around the triangle in *counterclockwise* order, while the second list goes in clockwise order. VRML faces should always be described by vertex index lists specified in counterclockwise order, because the order of vertices in a vertex index list can affect how shapes built from faces are shaded. This effect is discussed in a later chapter.

Using Coordinates

Notice that the vertex index lists define a triangle no matter what the actual coordinates, or locations, are for each of the vertices. For instance, the following coordinates for vertices 0, 1, and 2 also create a triangle when connected together using the preceding vertex index lists:

Vertex Index	Coordinate
0	-1.0 1.0 0.0
1	-0.5 -0.25 0.0
2	1.0 -0.5 0.0

The result is the triangle in Figure 14.2. Figure 14.2*a* shows the vertices of the triangle, and Figure 14.2*b*, the triangle built by connecting together those vertices.

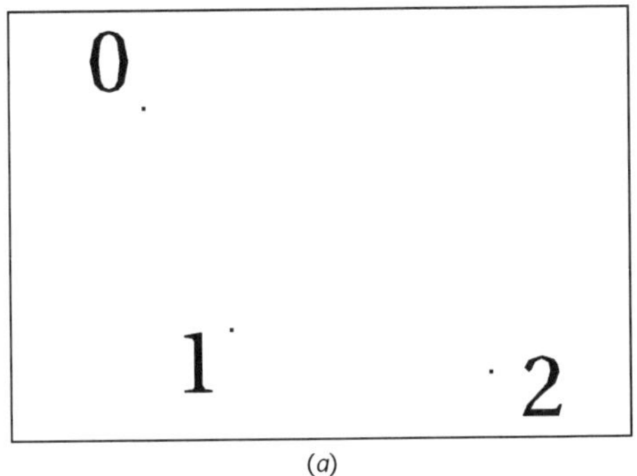

(*a*)

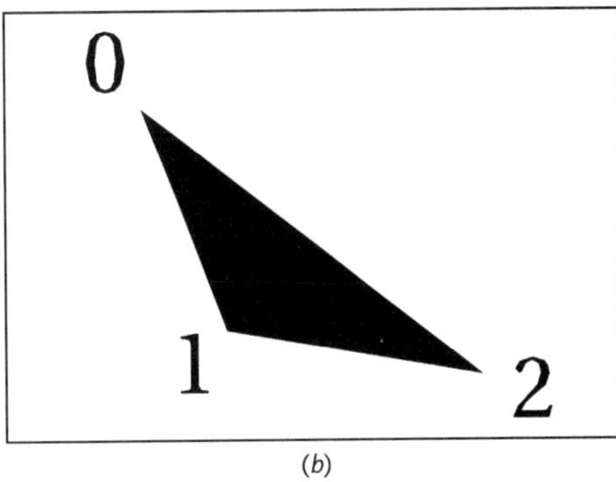

(*b*)

Figure 14.2 *The vertices and triangle drawn by specifying an index list and connecting the vertices.*

The list of vertex *coordinates* defines locations in 3-D space. The vertex *index list* connects these coordinates together to form a shape. Changing the coordinates used changes the locations of the face's vertices, but not the way they are connected together.

One set of coordinates can be used to create different shapes by connecting them differently with different vertex index lists. For example, consider the following four coordinates:

Vertex Index	Coordinate
0	-1.0 1.0 0.0
1	-1.0 -1.0 0.0
2	1.0 -1.0 0.0
3	1.0 1.0 0.0

You can connect these four coordinates together to form a square (shown in Figure 14.3) using this vertex index list.

You can also skip one of the coordinates and create four different triangles using the same coordinate list, but different vertex index lists:

```
0, 1, 2, 3
```

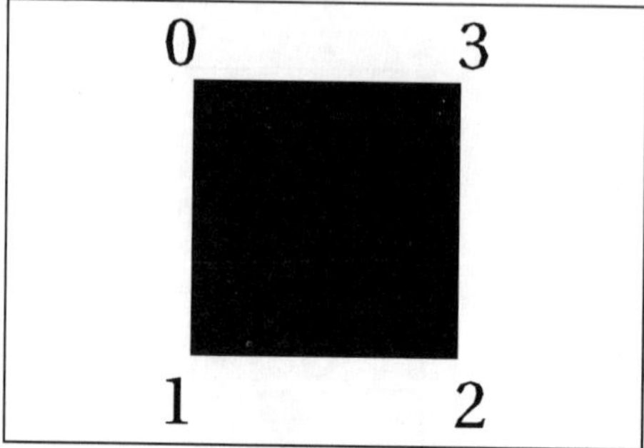

Figure 14.3 *Creating a square using a vertex index list of* `0, 1, 2, 3`.

```
0, 1, 2
```

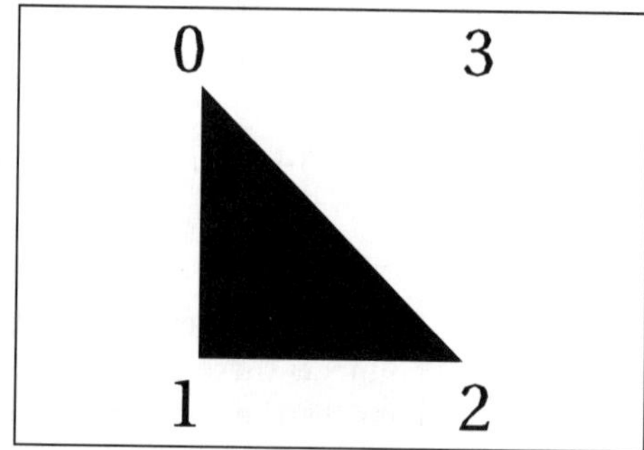

Figure 14.4 *Creating a triangle using a vertex index list of* `0, 1, 2`.

```
0, 1, 3
```

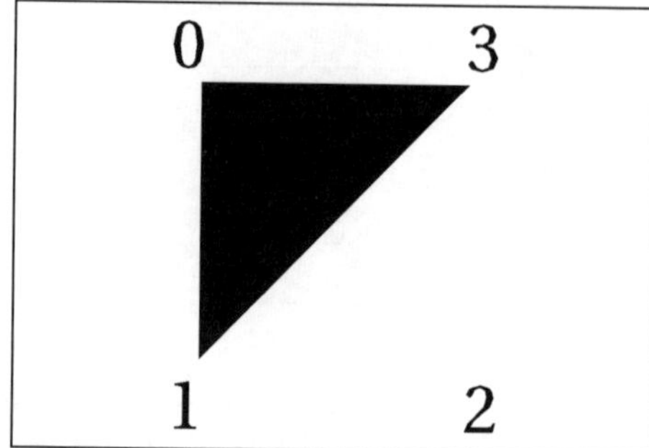

Figure 14.5 *Creating a triangle using a vertex index list of* `0, 1, 3`.

```
0, 2, 3
```

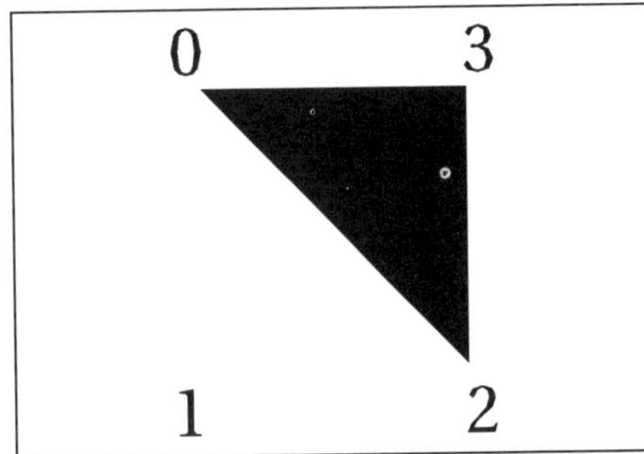

Figure 14.6 *Creating a triangle using a vertex index list of* `0, 2, 3`.

```
1, 2, 3
```

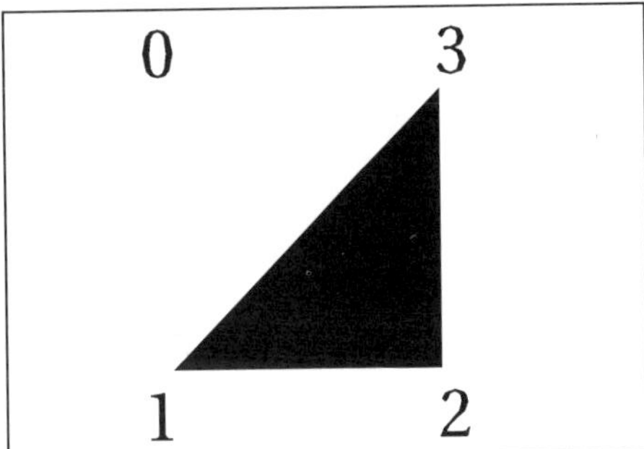

Figure 14.7 *Creating a triangle using a vertex index list of* `1, 2, 3`.

By separating the vertex *coordinates* from the vertex *index list* that connects them, you gain flexibility when defining your own VRML shapes. You can use the same vertex coordinates to define multiple shapes by using different vertex index lists. You can also use the same vertex index list to create multiple shapes using different vertex coordinates.

Dealing with Non-Planar Faces

Mathematically, a **planar** face is one in which all of the vertices lie on a **plane**. In other words, a planar face is flat. If you toss a planar face on a table, it lies flat, and all of its vertices simultaneously touch the tabletop. A triangle, for instance, is always planar.

A **non-planar** face is one in which the vertices *don't* all lie on a plane. If you toss a non-planar face on a table, it does not lie flat, and at least one vertex does not touch the tabletop. For example, while a perfectly flat piece of paper is planar, the same piece of paper is non-planar when one corner of it is lifted.

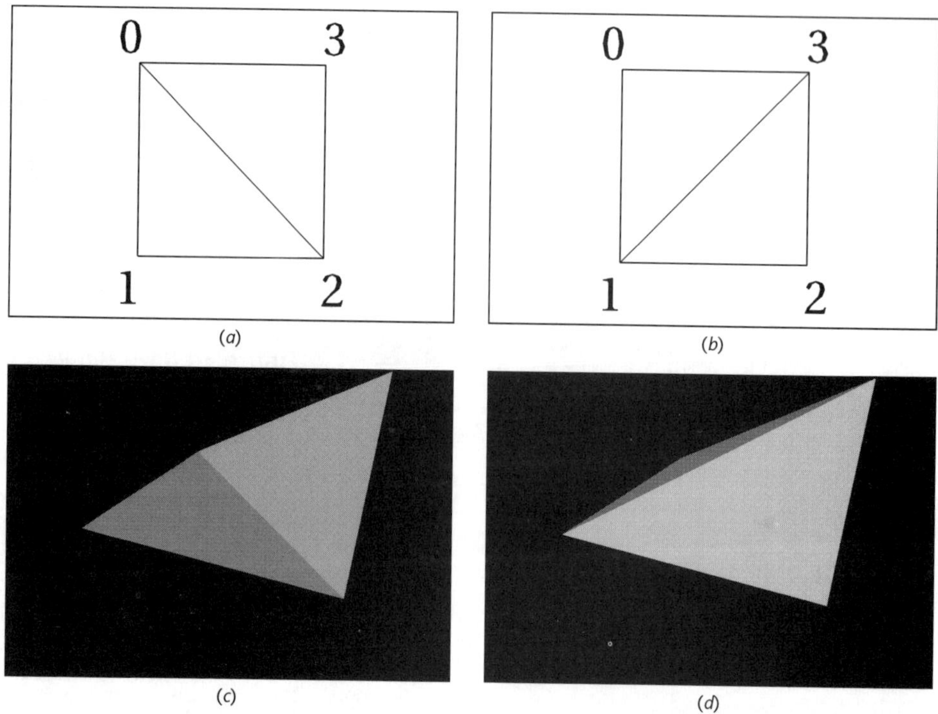

Figure 14.8 *Two different shaded shapes created by splitting the same non-planar square two different ways.*

VRML, similar to most computer graphics hardware and software, can reliably draw only planar faces. To draw non-planar faces, the VRML browser attempts to automatically split non-planar faces into multiple planar faces, typically triangles. This can be a problem, however, because there are always many ways to split any non-planar face.

For example, the following diagrams show a non-planar square face where vertex 3 is pulled up, like lifting one corner of a piece of paper. Figure 14.8*a* and Figure 14.8*b* show top view diagrams of the square illustrating the two ways the square might be split into two planar triangles. Figure 14.8*c* and Figure 14.8*d* show the shaded result from an angled view. Notice that the two ways of splitting the same non-planar square create very different shaded results.

Both of these splits are correct, but the results are very different. If you use non-planar faces, the automatic splitting performed by the VRML browser may create either result. The browser may even split non-planar faces differently depending on your viewpoint. This can make a shape look the way you intended from one angle but look wrong from another angle.

You can't direct the VRML browser to perform one splitting method instead of the other. Instead, you should manually split non-planar faces into triangles. For example, the following coordinates define the vertices of the preceding non-planar square:

Vertex Index	*Coordinate*
0	`-1.0  1.0 0.0`
1	`-1.0 -1.0 0.0`
2	`1.0 -1.0 0.0`
3	`1.0  1.0 1.0`

Using the following vertex list, the VRML browser splits the non-planar square into planar triangles in one of the two ways previously shown:

```
0, 1, 2, 3
```

Manually splitting the non-planar square into two triangles enables you to avoid the unpredictable results of automatic splitting. The following two vertex lists split the square as shown in Figure 14.8*a:*

```
0, 1, 2
0, 2, 3
```

Alternatively, the following two vertex lists split the square into two triangles as shown in Figure 14.8*b:*

```
0, 1, 3
1, 2, 3
```

Creating Complex Faces

The previous examples use only three and four coordinates to make triangles and a square. You can use longer lists of coordinates to create complex faces, such as the silhouette of a person's face or the skyline of a city. Complex faces have one of two forms:

- **Concave faces**—*Faces with inlets, or cavities. The outline of a capital C, for instance, is concave.*
- **Convex faces**—*Faces without inlets, or cavities. The outer perimeter of a capital O is convex.*

Squares, triangles, pentagons, and octagons are all examples of convex faces. The silhouette of a person's face, however, is concave since it dips in and out as it passes over the brow ridge, under the nose, across the lips, and under the chin.

VRML, similar to most computer graphics software, can draw only convex faces. Any concave face can be split up and drawn as multiple convex faces, typically triangles. Figure 14.9, for instance, shows how a concave face silhouette can be split into multiple triangles.

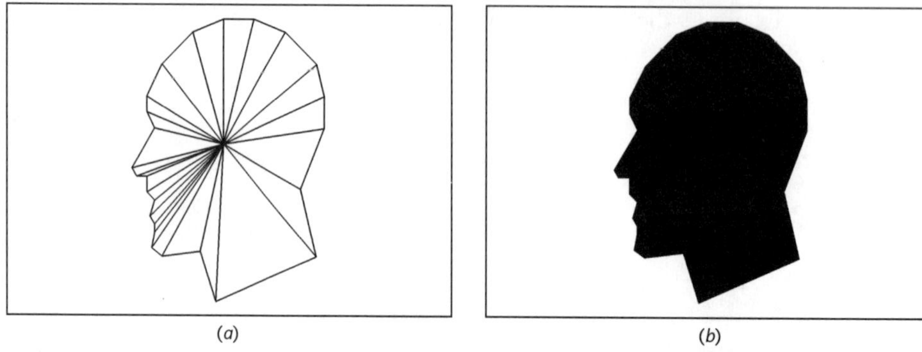

Figure 14.9 *The concave shape of a person's face split into multiple convex triangles.*

Creating 3-D Shapes Using Faces

You can build complex 3-D shapes using adjacent faces. A cube, for instance, can be built from six square faces positioned so that their edges touch. This is, in fact, how VRML creates the primitive cube drawn by a **Cube** node. The vertex coordinates to create a default cube with 2.0 units per side are:

Vertex Index	*Coordinate*
0	-1.0 1.0 1.0
1	1.0 1.0 1.0
2	1.0 1.0 -1.0
3	-1.0 1.0 -1.0
4	-1.0 -1.0 1.0
5	1.0 -1.0 1.0
6	1.0 -1.0 -1.0
7	-1.0 -1.0 -1.0

The vertex index lists to form each of the six faces of the cube are listed in the following table and shown in Figure 14.10.

Face	*Point List*
Top	0, 1, 2, 3
Bottom	4, 7, 6, 5
Front	0, 5, 4, 1
Back	2, 6, 7, 3
Left	3, 7, 4, 0
Right	1, 5, 6, 2

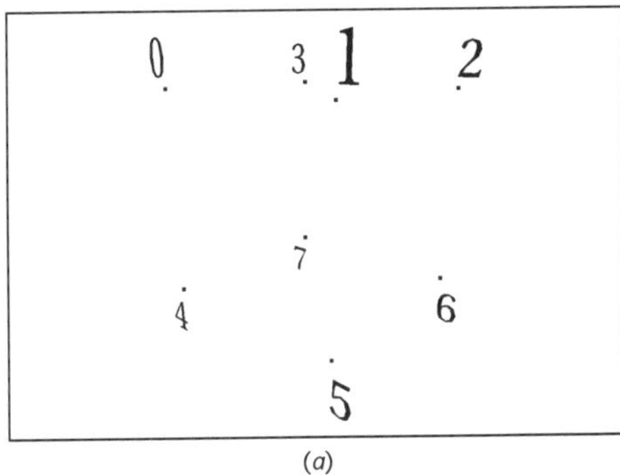

(a)

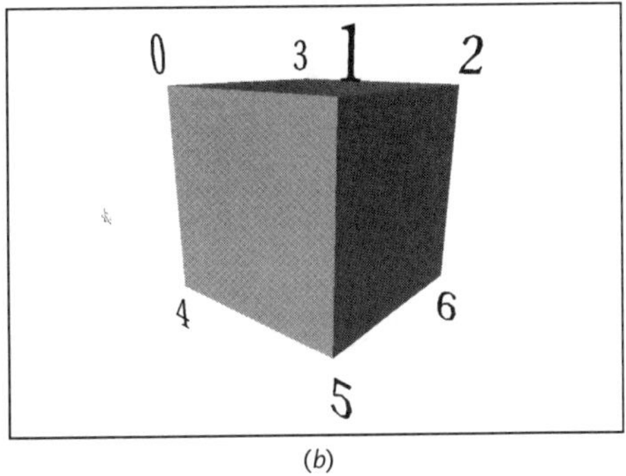

(b)

Figure 14.10 *A cube built from six adjacent square faces.*

Similarly, you can create more complex 3-D shapes. Figures 14.11 through 14.13 illustrate some possibilities.

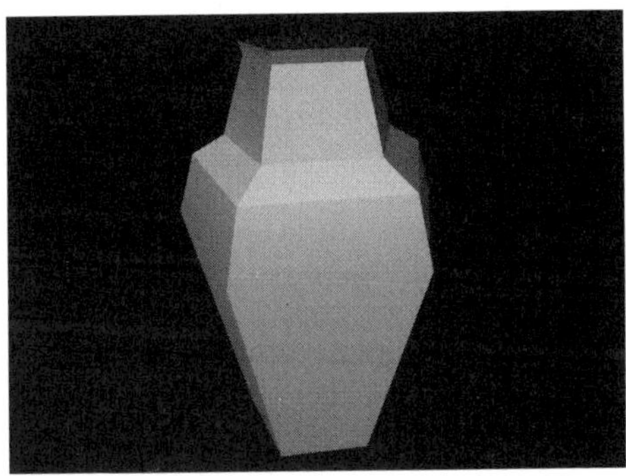

Figure 14.11 *A vase.*

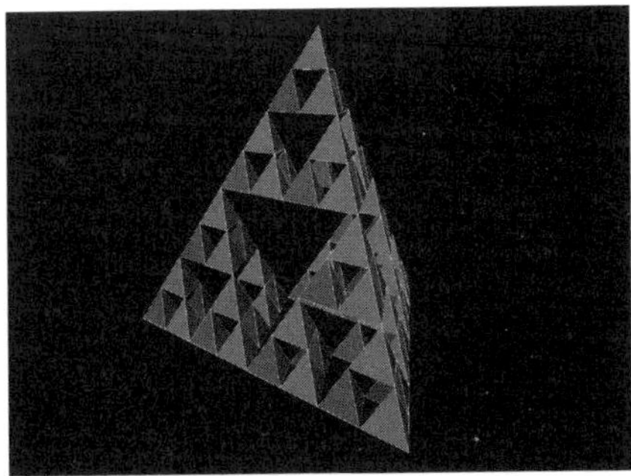

Figure 14.12 *A colored fractal pyramid.*

Figure 14.13 *A model of a hurricane.*

Understanding Lines

A *polyline* is a series of straight line segments, strung together so that the end of one line segment is the beginning of the next. Every polyline is made up of two components:

- **Vertices**—*The end point of each line segment*
- **Segments**—*Each of the straight lines connecting two vertices together*

For example, a polyline that draws a single straight line has one segment and two vertices: one vertex for each end point of the segment. A polyline that draws a capital Z uses four vertices connected together by three line segments.

The construction of polylines is slightly different from the construction of faces. Faces always describe a **closed** shape, like a triangle or square. The ending vertex of a face is automatically connected back to the starting vertex of the face to close it.

Polylines, however, are not automatically closed. The last vertex of a polyline is *not* automatically connected back to the starting vertex. This enables you to use polylines to describe arbitrary, **open** curves whose starting and ending vertices do not connect. A capital Z is an example of an open curve. Other examples include the capital letters W, C, and U, or a plot of a flight path from one city to another.

Creating a Polyline

If face construction is similar to a child's connect-the-dots drawing, polylines are the line segments that connect the dots together.

To create a polyline, define a list of 3-D coordinates to locate in space each of a polyline's vertices. Then connect together those vertices to form the line segments of a polyline.

For example, the following coordinates define the vertices of a capital Z:

Vertex Index	*Coordinate*
0	`-1.0 1.0 0.0`
1	`1.0 1.0 0.0`
2	`-1.0 -1.0 0.0`
3	`1.0 -1.0 0.0`

To draw the capital Z, connect the vertices together with three segments:

Segment	*Starting Vertex Index*	*Ending Vertex Index*
0	0	1
1	1	2
2	2	3

Each line segment is described by specifying the coordinate list indexes for the starting and ending vertices of each segment. Segment 0, for instance, connects vertex index 0 to vertex index 1. Segment 1 connects vertex index 1 to vertex index 2. Segment 2 connects vertex index 2 to vertex index 3.

In the polyline's list of vertex coordinates, vertex index 0 is the coordinate `-1.0 1.0 0.0`, and vertex index 1 is `1.0 1.0 0.0`. Segment 0 connects these two vertices together and forms the top line of the capital Z. Similarly, segment 1 creates the diagonal line of the capital Z, and segment 2 the bottom line of the capital Z.

Figure 14.14*a* shows the vertices of the capital Z. Figure 14.14*b* shows the vertices connected together to form the line segments of a polyline capital Z.

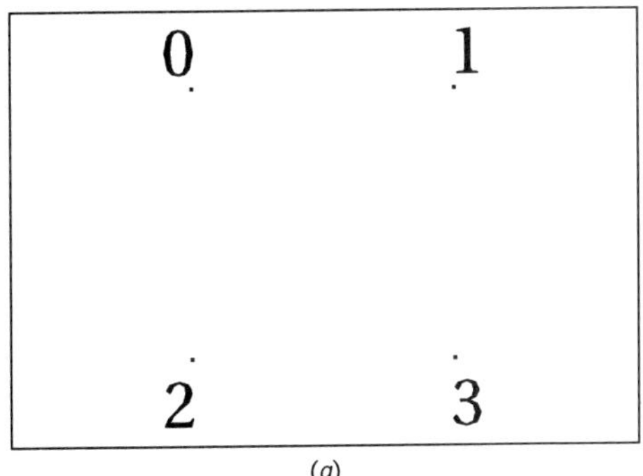

(*a*)

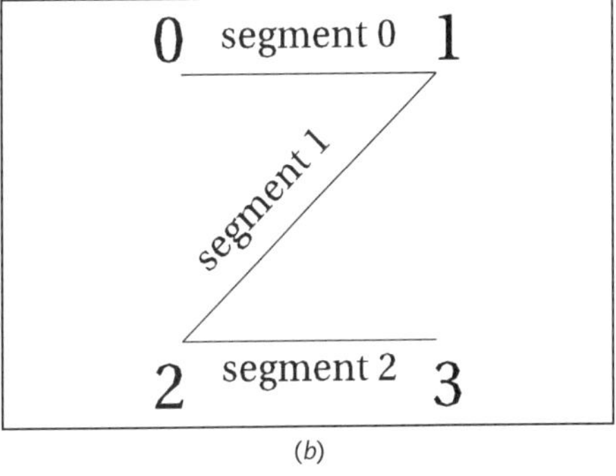

(*b*)

Figure 14.14 *The vertices and line segments creating a polyline capital Z.*

Polyline vertex index lists are similar to face vertex index lists. You can describe a polyline-segment chain with a list of the vertex indexes used by consecutive segments. For instance, the capital Z has this vertex index list:

```
0, 1, 2, 3
```

Using this vertex index list, the line segment from vertex 0 to vertex 1 is the first segment drawn, then from vertex 1 to vertex 2, and finally from vertex 2 to vertex 3. Unlike faces, polylines are *not* automatically closed. No line segment will be automatically drawn between the last vertex, 3, back to the first vertex, 0.

The list of vertex coordinates defines locations in 3-D space. The vertex index list connects these coordinates together to form a line shape. Changing the coordinates used changes the locations of the polyline's vertices, but not the way they are connected together. For instance, using the same vertex index list `0, 1, 2, 3`, with a different set of coordinates you can create a capital N instead of a capital Z as shown in Figure 14.15.

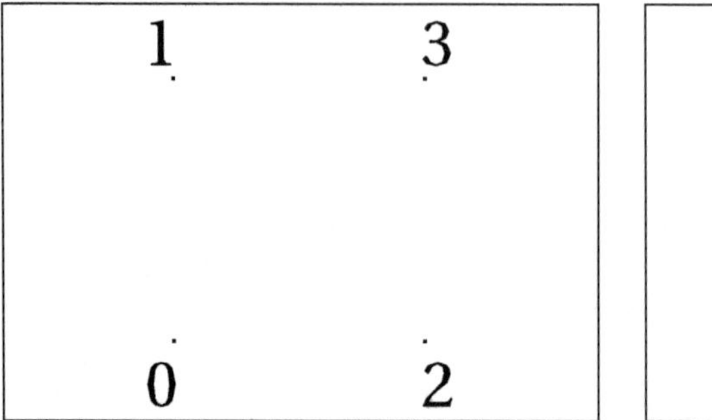

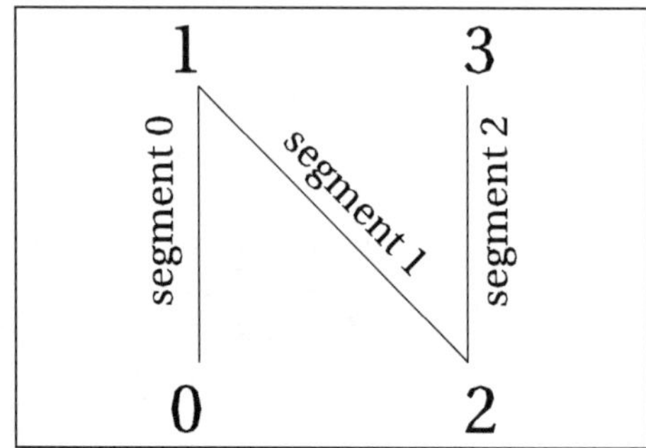

Figure 14.15 *The vertices and line segments used to create a polyline capital N.*

One set of coordinates can be used to create different shapes by connecting them differently with different vertex index lists, like the shapes shown in Figures 14.3 through 14.7.

Creating 3-D Shapes Using Polylines

Using 3-D coordinates, you can connect vertices with line segments to create complex 3-D line shapes. For instance, the vertex coordinates used to create a default cube (shown in Figure 14.16) with 2.0 units per side are:

Vertex Index	*Coordinate*
0	-1.0 1.0 1.0
1	1.0 1.0 1.0
2	1.0 1.0 -1.0
3	-1.0 1.0 -1.0
4	-1.0 -1.0 1.0
5	1.0 -1.0 1.0
6	1.0 -1.0 -1.0
7	-1.0 -1.0 -1.0

The vertex index lists to outline the six faces of the cube are:

Face	*Vertex Index List*
Top	0 1 2 3 0
Bottom	4 7 6 5 4
Front	0 5 4 1 0
Back	2 6 7 3 2
Left	3 7 4 0 3
Right	1 5 6 2 1

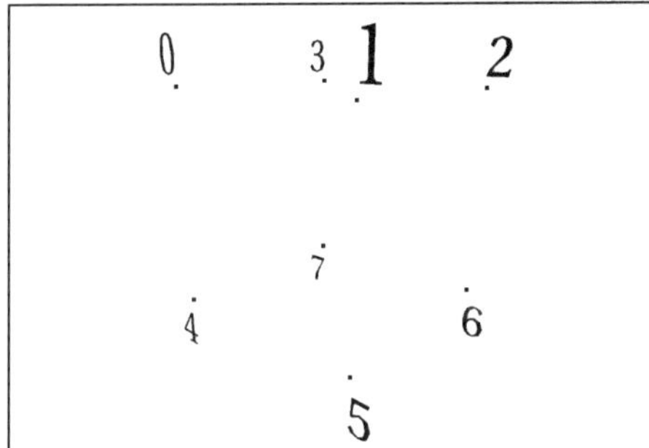

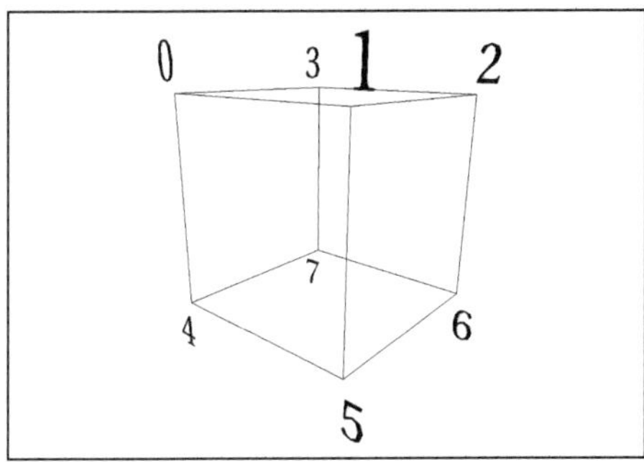

Figure 14.16 *The vertices and line segments used to create a cube.*

Notice that each of the preceding vertex index lists repeats the starting vertex again at the end. For example, the top of the cube is drawn as a polyline that connects vertex 0 to 1, 1 to 2, 2 to 3, and 3 back to 0. This is necessary to close the square.

You can describe complex 3-D shapes using polylines. Figures 14.17 through 14.20 illustrate some possibilities.

Figure 14.17 *A vase.*

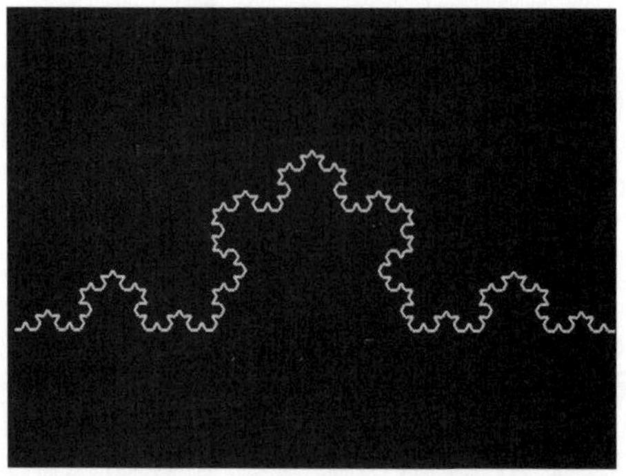

Figure 14.18 *A Koch snowflake.*

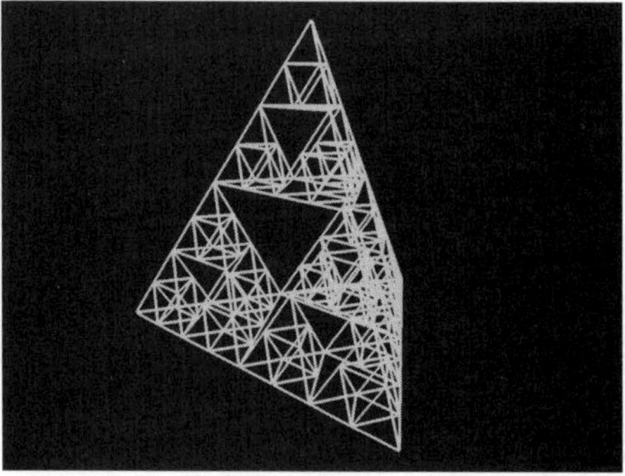

Figure 14.19 *A fractal.*

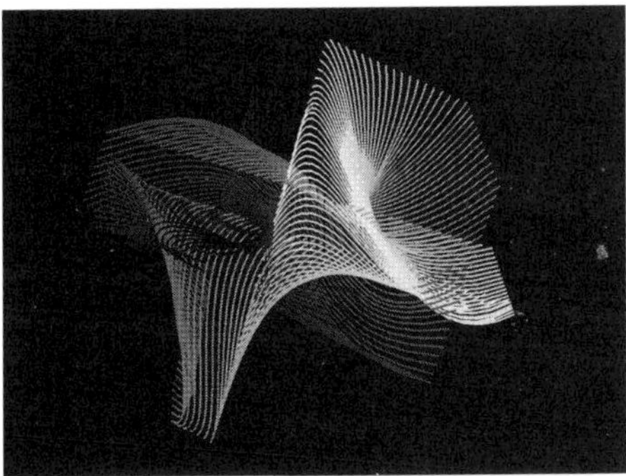

Figure 14.20 *An abstract, string-art-type shape.*

Understanding Points

Think of a vertex as an imaginary dot in space. The vertex's coordinate describes that vertex's location in space. A point drawn at that coordinate is a visible representation of that vertex. It's a dot you can actually see with your browser.

A **point set** is a list of points, each placed at a vertex whose location is described by a 3-D coordinate. A point set draws a dot at each vertex *without* connecting the dots together.

Creating a Point Set

If face construction is similar to a child's connect-the-dots drawing, and polylines are like the line segments that connect the dots together, then point sets are the dots of such a drawing *without* any connecting lines.

To create a point set, define a list of 3-D coordinates to locate in space each point in the set. For example, the following coordinates can be used to put dots at the four corners of a square:

Vertex Index	*Coordinate*
0	`-1.0  1.0 0.0`
1	`-1.0 -1.0 0.0`
2	`1.0 -1.0 0.0`
3	`1.0  1.0 0.0`

To draw a point set using some or all of these coordinates, specify the portion of the coordinate list you wish to draw:

```
start index  0
number of points  4
```

This specifies the point in the list at which to begin drawing (vertex index 0) and how many consecutive coordinates to draw after the starting point (4). In the point set's list of vertex coordinates, vertex index 0 is the coordinate `-1.0 1.0 0.0`. A point in the point set will be placed at this coordinate and at each of the next three coordinates in the list: `-1.0 -1.0 0.0`; `1.0 -1.0 0.0`; and `1.0 1.0 0.0`. This collection of four points describes the four corners of a square.

Figure 14.21*a* shows the vertices of the square. Figure 14.21*b* shows the resulting four points.

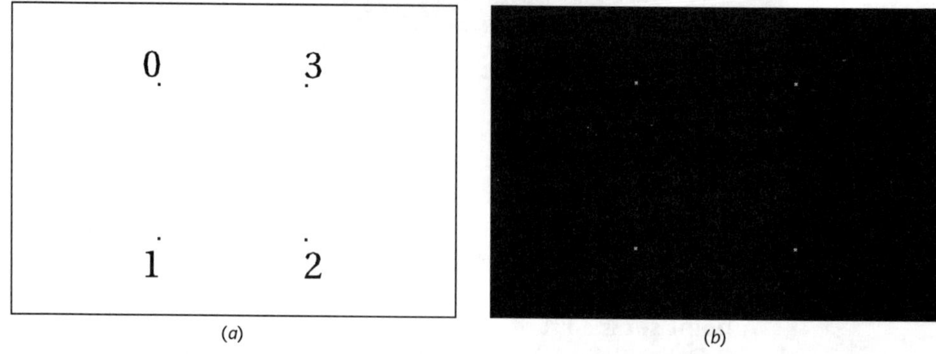

Figure 14.21 *The vertices of a square and the resulting points drawn.*

Changing the locations of the coordinates in the coordinate list changes the positions of the points in a set. For instance, using the same vertex index starting point (0) and number of points (4), but a different set of coordinates, you can create a line of points instead of points at the four corners of a square:

Vertex Index	*Coordinate*
0	`-1.5 0.0 0.0`
1	`-0.5 0.0 0.0`
2	`0.5 0.0 0.0`
3	`1.5 0.0 0.0`

Figure 14.22*a* shows the vertices of the line. Figure 14.22*b* shows the resulting line of four points.

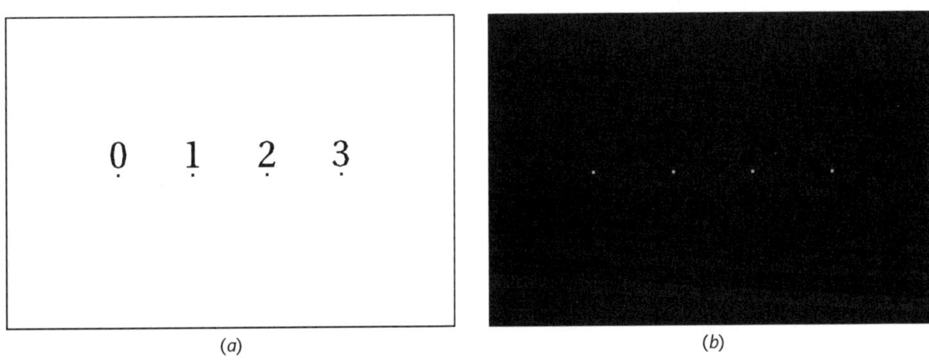

(a) (b)

Figure 14.22 *The vertices of a line and the resulting points drawn.*

The same set of coordinates can also be used to create different point sets by selecting different starting vertices and a different number of points to draw. For instance, you can draw only the first two points in the line:

```
start index  0
number of points  2
```

or only the last two points in the same line:

```
start index  2
number of points  2
```

Creating 3-D Shapes Using Point Sets

Using 3-D coordinates, you can place points to create complex 3-D point shapes. For instance, the vertex coordinates used to create a default cube with 2.0 units per side are:

Vertex Index	*Coordinate*
0	-1.0 1.0 1.0
1	1.0 1.0 1.0
2	1.0 1.0 -1.0
3	-1.0 1.0 -1.0
4	-1.0 -1.0 1.0
5	1.0 -1.0 1.0
6	1.0 -1.0 -1.0
7	-1.0 -1.0 -1.0

The following is a point set to place a point at each corner of the cube shown in Figure 14.23:

```
start index 0
number of points 8
```

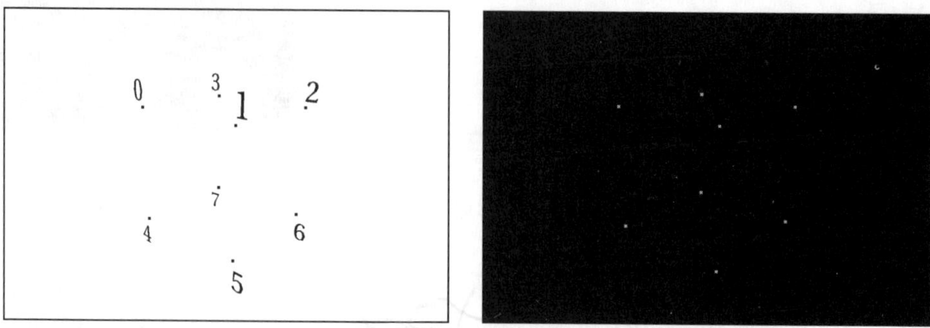

Figure 14.23 *The vertices of a cube and the resulting points drawn.*

You can describe complex 3-D sets of points. Figures 14.24 through 14.26 illustrate some possibilities.

Figure 14.24 *A plot.*

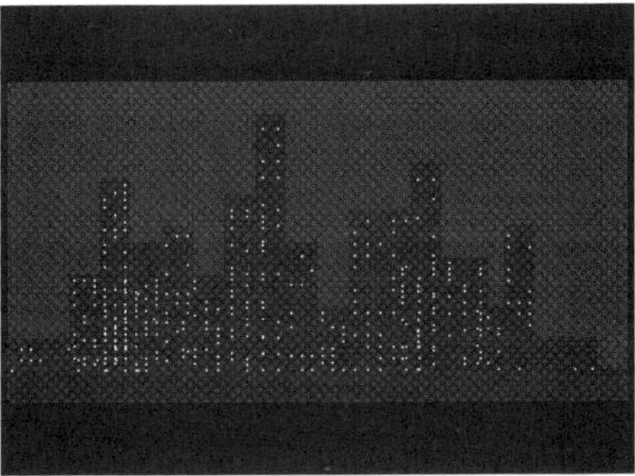

Figure 14.25 *A city skyline.*

Figure 14.26 *Stars.*

Creating a Shape with Faces

VRML's faces are created using two nodes: the **Coordinate3** node and the **IndexedFaceSet** node. The **Coordinate3** node lists the vertex coordinates for a face. The **IndexedFaceSet** node lists the vertex index list used to construct a face from the vertices in a **Coordinate3** node. For instance, the example text in Figure 14.27 creates the triangle shown in Figure 14.1.

```
#VRML V1.0 ascii

# List the vertex coordinates
Coordinate3 {
      point [
              0.0 1.0 0.0,
             -1.0 0.0 0.0,
              1.0 0.0 0.0
      ]
}
```

Figure 14.27 continues

```
# Connect the vertices together to create a face
IndexedFaceSet {
      coordIndex [
            0, 1, 2
      ]
}
```

Figure 14.27 *Coordinate3 and **IndexedFaceSet** nodes creating the triangle shown in Figure 14.1.*

Notice the structure and order of the VRML file in Figure 14.27. Reading from the top of the file, the **Coordinate3** node defines a set of 3-D coordinates to use in subsequent shapes. The **IndexedFaceSet** node that follows directs the virtual pen to draw a face by connecting together vertex indexes 0, 1, and 2 to form a triangle.

Understanding the **Coordinate3** Node Syntax

The **Coordinate3** node has a single **point** field that specifies a list of 3-D coordinates to be used later as vertices to draw a point set, a line, or a face.

SYNTAX **Coordinate3 node**

```
Coordinate3 {
   point [ 0.0 0.0 0.0 ]      # coordinate list
}
```

The **point** field lists the 3-D coordinates that define the vertices of a shape. Each coordinate is specified as three floating-point values, one each for the X, Y, and Z distances from the origin. Coordinates in the **point** field list are separated by commas, and the entire list is enclosed within square brackets.

The coordinates of a **Coordinate3** node set the pen's coordinates property, just as the colors of a **Material** node set the pen's drawing color property. Like all pen properties, the pen's coordinates property is saved and restored by **Separator** nodes.

Understanding the **IndexedFaceSet** Node Syntax

The **IndexedFaceSet** node has four fields: **coordIndex, materialIndex, normalIndex,** and **textureCoordIndex.** All four fields are lists of integer index values.

SYNTAX **IndexedFaceSet node**

```
IndexedFaceSet {
   coordIndex          [0]     # coordinate index list
   materialIndex       -1      # material index list
   normalIndex         -1      # normal index list
   textureCoordIndex   -1      # texture index list
}
```

The **coordIndex** field lists the vertex coordinate indexes that define the edges of a face. Each value is an integer index corresponding to a coordinate in the vertex coordinate list set by a **Coordinate3** node. Indexes in the **coordIndex** field are separated by commas, and the entire list is enclosed within square brackets.

Multiple **IndexedFaceSet** nodes may use the same **Coordinate3** node coordinates. For instance, these two **IndexedFaceSet** nodes create two faces, one connecting vertices 0, 1, and 2, and the other connecting vertices 3, 4, and 5:

```
IndexedFaceSet {
    coordIndex [ 0, 1, 2 ]
}
IndexedFaceSet {
    coordIndex [ 3, 4, 5 ]
}
```

When listing multiple faces, you can combine the **coordIndex** fields of multiple **IndexedFaceSet** nodes, and draw multiple faces at once:

```
IndexedFaceSet
    coordIndex [
        0, 1, 2, -1,
        3, 4, 5
    ]
}
```

When face index lists are combined into a single **coordIndex** field, the special index value of –1 marks the end of one face index list and the beginning of the next. The –1 index is not needed at the end of the entire list; the closing square bracket of the **coordIndex** field indicates the end of the last face's index list.

The **materialIndex** field defines the colors used to shade faces or the individual vertices of a face. Shading and the **materialIndex** field are discussed in a later chapter.

The **normalIndex** field defines a face's **normal**. A normal indicates the direction in which a face points and enables you to control how shapes are shaded. Normals and the **normalIndex** field are discussed in a later chapter.

The **textureCoordIndex** field defines how **textures** are applied to a shape. Textures are like decals or wallpaper applied to a shape. Textures and the **textureCoordIndex** field are discussed in a later chapter.

When the VRML browser reads an **IndexedFaceSet** node, the virtual pen is instructed to draw the face or faces described by the vertex index list in the **coordIndex** field. The pen moves to the first vertex coordinate, draws the perimeter of the face vertex by vertex, and shades the face using the current pen color. When it encounters a –1 index in the index list, the pen completes the face and starts a new one, beginning with the next index in the list. When the last face in the list is completed, the pen returns to the starting origin, ready to draw additional shapes.

Creating a Shape with Lines

VRML polylines are created using two nodes: the **Coordinate3** node and the **IndexedLineSet** node. The **Coordinate3** node lists the vertex coordinates for a polyline. The **IndexedLineSet** node specifies the vertex index list that constructs a polyline from the vertices in a **Coordinate3** node. For instance, the example text in Figure 14.28 creates the capital Z shown in Figure 14.14.

```
#VRML V1.0 ascii

# List the vertex coordinates
Coordinate3 {
      point [
            -1.0  1.0 0.0,
             1.0  1.0 0.0,
            -1.0 -1.0 0.0,
             1.0 -1.0 0.0
      ]
}
# Connect the vertices together to create a polyline Z
IndexedFaceSet {
      coordIndex [
            0, 1, 2, 3
      ]
}
```

Figure 14.28 *A capital Z created with **Coordinate3** and **IndexedLineSet** nodes.*

Notice the structure and order of the VRML file in Figure 14.28. Reading from the top of the file, the **Coordinate3** node defines a set of 3-D coordinates to use in subsequent shapes. The **IndexedLineSet** node that follows directs the virtual pen to draw a polyline by connecting together vertex indexes 0, 1, 2, and 3 to form a capital Z.

Understanding the **IndexedLineSet** Node Syntax

The **IndexedLineSet** node has four fields: **coordIndex, materialIndex, normalIndex,** and **textureCoordIndex.** All four fields are lists of integer index values.

SYNTAX **IndexedLineSet node**

```
IndexedLineSet {
   coordIndex           [0]     # coordinate index list
   materialIndex        -1      # material index list
   normalIndex          -1      # normal index list
   textureCoordIndex    -1      # texture index list
}
```

The **coordIndex** field lists the vertex coordinate indexes that define the line segments of a polyline. Each value is an integer index corresponding to a coordinate in the current vertex coordinate list set by a **Coordinate3** node. Indexes in the **coordIndex** field are separated by commas, and the entire list is enclosed within square brackets.

Multiple **IndexedLineSet** nodes may use the same **Coordinate3** node coordinates. For instance, the following two **IndexedLineSet** nodes create two lines, one connecting vertices 0 and 3, and the other connecting vertices 1 and 2:

```
IndexedLineSet {
   coordIndex [ 0, 3 ]
}
IndexedLineSet {
   coordIndex [ 1, 2 ]
}
```

When listing multiple polylines, you can combine the **coordIndex** fields of multiple **IndexedLineSet** nodes, and draw multiple polylines at once:

```
IndexedLineSet
   coordIndex [
      0, 3, -1,
      1, 2
   ]
}
```

When polyline index lists are combined into a single **coordIndex** field, the special index value of –1 marks the end of one polyline index list and the beginning of the next. The –1 index is not needed at the end of the entire list; the closing square bracket of the **coordIndex** field indicates the end of the last polyline's index list.

The **materialIndex** field defines the colors used to shade polylines or individual vertices of a polyline. Polyline coloring using this field is discussed in a later chapter.

The **normalIndex** field defines the normal to use for polylines or individual vertices of a polyline. A normal indicates the direction in which a polyline faces and enables you to control how polylines are shaded. The use of normals and the **normalIndex** field are discussed in a later chapter.

The **textureCoordIndex** field defines how textures are applied to a polyline. Textures are like decals or wallpaper applied to a share. Texturing and the **textureCoordIndex** field are discussed in a later chapter.

When the VRML browser reads an **IndexedLineSet** node, the virtual pen is instructed to draw the polyline or polylines described by the vertex index list in the **coordIndex** field. The pen moves to the first vertex coordinate then traces out the line segments of the polyline, vertex by vertex, and shades the polyline using the current pen color. When it encounters a –1 index in the index list, the pen finishes tracing the polyline and starts a new one, beginning with the next index in the list. When the last polyline in the list is finished, the pen returns to the starting origin, ready to draw additional shapes.

Creating a Shape with Points

VRML point sets are created using two nodes: the **Coordinate3** node and the **PointSet** node. The **Coordinate3** node lists the vertex coordinates for a point set. The **PointSet** node indicates the range of coordinates from a **Coordinate3** node's coordinate list that are used to draw points. The range is specified with a starting vertex index and a number of points to draw. For instance, the example text in Figure 14.29 creates points at a square's corners.

```
#VRML V1.0 ascii

# List the vertex coordinates
Coordinate3 {
      point [
      -1.0  1.0 0.0,
      -1.0 -1.0 0.0,
       1.0 -1.0 0.0,
       1.0  1.0 0.0,
      ]
}
# Put dots at the corners
PointSet {
      startIndex 0
      numPoints 4
}
```

Figure 14.29 *A square created with points.*

Notice the structure and order of the VRML file in Figure 14.29. Reading from the top of the file, the **Coordinate3** node defines a set of 3-D coordinates to use in subsequent shapes. The **PointSet** node that follows directs the virtual pen to draw points at four vertices starting with vertex 0.

Understanding the **PointSet** Node Syntax

The **PointSet** node has two fields: **startIndex** and **numPoints.**

SYNTAX **PointSet node**

```
PointSet {
   startIndex   0       # coordinate index
   numPoints   -1       # number of points to draw
}
```

The integer **startIndex** field specifies the first vertex coordinate index for a point set. The integer **numPoints** field specifies the number of consecutive coordinates to draw as points, starting with the coordinate indicated by the **startIndex** field. The point set uses coordinates from the pen's coordinates property, previously set by a **Coordinate3** node.

The special value of –1 may be used in the **numPoints** field to indicate that points are to be drawn for all coordinates in the current coordinate list, starting with the **startIndex** coordinate and extending to the end of the coordinate list. Multiple **PointSet** nodes can use the same current coordinates. For instance, the following two **PointSet** nodes create two pairs of dots, one using vertices 0 and 1, and the other using vertices 2 and 3:

```
PointSet {
   startIndex 0
   numPoints 2
}
PointSet {
   startIndex 2
   numPoints 2
}
```

When the VRML browser reads a **PointSet** node, the virtual pen is instructed to draw a point at each vertex coordinate starting with the **startIndex** vertex and continuing for a total of **numPoints** points. The pen moves to each vertex coordinate and draws a point, coloring it using the current pen color. When the last point is drawn, the pen returns to the starting origin, ready to draw additional shapes.

Experimenting with Faces, Lines, and Points

The following examples provide a more detailed examination of the ways in which the **Coordinate3**, **PointSet**, **IndexedLineSet**, and **IndexedFaceSet** nodes can be used and how they interact with nodes we've discussed in previous chapters.

Creating Stars Using 3-D Points

The example text in Figure 14.30 creates a cluster of stars by specifying a list of star coordinates. Each star is drawn as a VRML point in a point set.

```
#VRML V1.0 ascii

Coordinate3 {
      point [
       0.18 -0.53  0.17,
       0.23 -0.12 -0.39,
      -0.37  0.54  0.65,
       0.78  0.15  0.31,
      -0.92  0.40  0.79,
       0.87  0.67  0.58,
      -0.36 -0.83 -0.46,
       0.13 -0.96  0.41,
       0.76  0.03 -0.76,
      -0.59 -0.96 -0.06,
      -0.92  0.12  0.25,
      -0.24 -0.41  0.43,
      -0.38 -0.16  0.70,
      -0.40  0.24 -0.23,
      -0.30  0.04  0.40,
       0.73  0.23  0.97,
       0.43  0.81 -0.28,
      -0.86  0.21 -0.29,
       0.22  0.72 -0.99,
      -0.43  0.86  0.98,
      -0.43 -0.46 -0.99,
       0.60 -0.45  0.08,
      -0.15 -0.94  0.99,
      -0.80  0.38 -0.53,
      -0.59 -0.14  0.71,
      -0.70 -0.96  0.74,
       0.64  0.19 -0.28,
       0.29  0.42 -0.44,
       0.49  0.42 -0.26,
      -0.98 -0.38  0.35,
      ]
}
PointSet {
      startIndex 0
      numPoints 30
}
```

Figure 14.30 *A star field.*

Reading the file from top to bottom, the virtual pen is instructed to:

1. Set its coordinates property to 30 coordinates.
2. Draw a set of 30 points starting at vertex index 0.

The result is a star field. Using your VRML browser, you can fly into the middle of the stars and look about, creating the feel of being within a star field. By specifying many more points you can enhance this effect. You can also arrange the points into bands, clusters, and swirls to simulate other star patterns and structures.

Using Faces, Lines, and Points to Build a 3-D Shape

The example text in Figure 14.31 constructs a cube identical to that created by the default **Cube** node. The eight vertices of the cube are listed within a **Coordinate3** node. The vertex index lists in the **coordIndex** field of the **IndexedFaceSet** node connect the vertices together to construct each of the cube's six faces.

```
#VRML V1.0 ascii

# Vertex coordinates for a cube
Coordinate3 {
      point [
            # Around the top of the cube
            -1.0  1.0  1.0,
             1.0  1.0  1.0,
             1.0  1.0 -1.0,
            -1.0  1.0 -1.0,
            # Around the bottom of the cube
            -1.0 -1.0  1.0,
             1.0 -1.0  1.0,
             1.0 -1.0 -1.0,
            -1.0 -1.0 -1.0
      ]
}
# Vertex index list for a cube
IndexedFaceSet {
      coordIndex [
            0, 1, 2, 3, -1, # Top
            4, 7, 6, 5, -1, # Bottom
            0, 4, 5, 1, -1, # Front
            2, 6, 7, 3, -1, # Back
            3, 7, 4, 0, -1, # Left
            1, 5, 6, 2      # Right
      ]
}
```

Figure 14.31 *A cube drawn using the* ***Coordinate3*** *and* ***IndexedFaceSet*** *nodes.*

Reading the file from top to bottom, the virtual pen is instructed to:

1. Set its coordinates property to eight coordinates.

2. Draw a list of faces.

   a. Draw the top face of the square by connecting the following vertices in this order:

Vertex Index	*Coordinate*
0	-1.0 1.0 1.0
1	1.0 1.0 1.0
2	1.0 1.0 -1.0
3	-1.0 1.0 1-1.0

   b. Draw the bottom face of the square by connecting the following vertices in this order:

Vertex Index	*Coordinate*
4	-1.0 -1.0 1.0
7	-1.0 -1.0 -1.0
6	1.0 -1.0 -1.0
5	1.0 -1.0 1.0

   c. Draw the front face of the square by connecting the following vertices in this order:

Vertex Index	*Coordinate*
0	-1.0 1.0 1.0
4	-1.0 -1.0 1.0
5	1.0 -1.0 1.0
1	1.0 1.0 1.0

   d. Draw the back face of the square by connecting the following vertices in this order:

Vertex Index	*Coordinate*
2	1.0 1.0 -1.0
6	1.0 -1.0 -1.0
7	-1.0 -1.0 -1.0
3	-1.0 1.0 -1.0

e. Draw the left face of the square by connecting the following vertices in this order:

Vertex Index	*Coordinate*
3	`-1.0  1.0 -1.0`
7	`-1.0 -1.0 -1.0`
4	`-1.0 -1.0  1.0`
0	`-1.0  1.0  1.0`

f. Draw the right face of the square by connecting the following vertices in this order:

Vertex Index	*Coordinate*
1	`1.0  1.0  1.0`
5	`1.0 -1.0  1.0`
6	`1.0 -1.0 -1.0`
2	`1.0  1.0 -1.0`

The result is a cube identical to the default cube primitive.

The same cube can be represented with a polyline outline or as a set of points. To create an outline cube like the one shown in Figure 14.32, exchange the **IndexedFaceSet** node in Figure 14.31 for an **IndexedLineSet** node like this one:

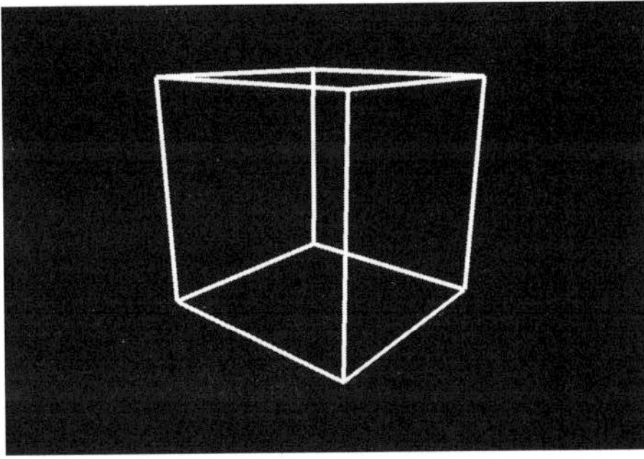

Figure 14.32 *The cube drawn with a polyline.*

```
IndexedLineSet {
    coordIndex [
    0, 1, 2, 3, 0, -1, # Top
    4, 7, 6, 5, 4, -1, # Bottom
    0, 4, 5, 1, 0, -1, # Front
    2, 6, 7, 3, 2, -1, # Back
    3, 7, 4, 0, 3, -1, # Left
    1, 5, 6, 2, 1,     # Right
    ]
}
```

Any shaded shape you can draw with faces, you can also draw as outlines using polylines. Remember, however, that the vertex index lists specified in the **IndexedLineSet** node *must* duplicate the first vertex at the end.

For example, the following two nodes both use a coordinate list to draw a triangle. The **IndexedFaceSet** node draws a shaded triangle, and the **IndexedLineSet** draws a triangular outline:

```
IndexedFaceSet {
   coordIndex [
      0, 1, 2 # No duplicate vertex
   ]
}
IndexedLineSet {
   coordIndex [
      0, 1, 2, 0 # Duplicate first vertex at end
   ]
}
```

If you forget to duplicate the last vertex, then the triangle will not be closed.

TIP *You can include the first vertex at the end of a vertex index list in the **IndexedFaceSet** node. By including a duplicate vertex, you can use the same vertex index lists for both faces and polylines. To switch back and forth between drawing shaded and outline shapes, change the node from an **IndexedFaceSet** node to an **IndexedLineSet** node.*

To create the cube in Figure 14.33 with a point set like the one shown in Figure 14.23, exchange the **IndexedFaceSet** node in Figure 14.31 for a **PointSet** node like this one:

```
PointSet {
   startIndex 0
   numPoints 8
}
```

You can use the cube's coordinate list and a different vertex index list to create other shapes. The example text in Figure 14.34 creates an X using two faces connecting together the same coordinates used to build the cube in Figure 14.31.

Figure 14.33 *The cube drawn with a point set.*

```
#VRML V1.0 ascii

# Vertex coordinates for a cube
Coordinate3 {
      point [
            # Around the top of the cube
            -1.0  1.0  1.0,
             1.0  1.0  1.0,
             1.0  1.0 -1.0,
            -1.0  1.0 -1.0,
            # Around the bottom of the
            # cube
            -1.0 -1.0  1.0,
             1.0 -1.0  1.0,
             1.0 -1.0 -1.0,
            -1.0 -1.0 -1.0
      ]
}
# Vertex index list for an X instead of a cube
IndexedFaceSet {
      coordIndex [
            0, 5, 6, 3, -1, # Upper-left to lower-right
            1, 2, 7, 4      # Upper-right to lower-left
      ]
}
```

Figure 14.34 *An X shape constructed with two overlapping square faces.*

Reading the file from top to bottom, the virtual pen is instructed to:

1. Set its coordinates property to eight coordinates.

2. Draw a list of faces.
   a. Draw a face from upper left to lower right by connecting the following vertices in this order:

Vertex Index	*Coordinate*
0	-1.0 1.0 1.0
5	1.0 -1.0 1.0
6	1.0 -1.0 -1.0
3	-1.0 1.0 -1.0

   b. Draw a face from upper right to lower left by connecting the following vertices in this order:

Vertex Index	*Coordinate*
1	1.0 1.0 1.0
2	1.0 1.0 -1.0
7	-1.0 -1.0 -1.0
4	-1.0 -1.0 1.0

The result is an X made from two intersecting faces.

The same X can be drawn with polylines by exchanging the **IndexedFaceSet** node in Figure 14.34 for the following **IndexedLineSet** node:

```
IndexedLineSet {
   coordIndex [
      0, 5, 6, 3, 0, -1, # Upper-left to lower-right
      1, 2, 7, 4, 1      # Upper-right to lower-left
   ]
}
```

Using Separators

The **Coordinate3** node sets the pen's coordinates property to the list of coordinates specified within the node. Each time an **IndexedFaceSet**, **IndexedLineSet,** or **PointSet** node is encountered, the pen's current coordinates property is used to supply vertex coordinates for faces, lines, or points to be drawn.

You can save and restore the pen's coordinates property using the **Separator** node. The example text in Figure 14.35 draws two squares and a triangle between them. The squares' coordinates are defined by a single **Coordinate3** node at the top of the file. The triangle's coordinates are defined by a second **Coordinate3** node within a **Separator** node. Notice how the squares' coordinates are saved and later restored by the **Separator** node so that coordinate property changes made inside the **Separator** node do not affect shapes drawn after exiting the **Separator** node.

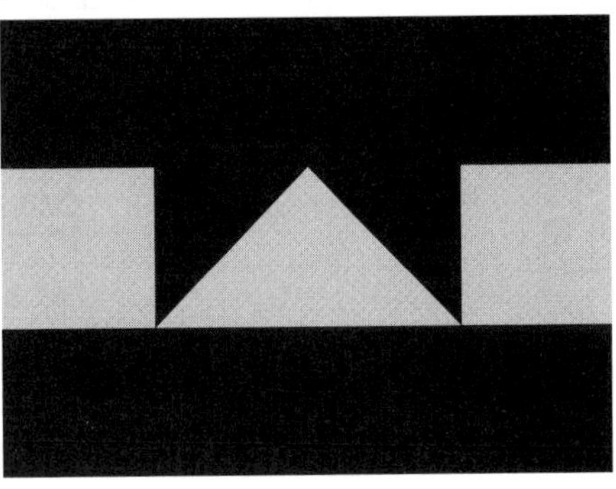

```
#VRML V1.0 ascii

# Coordinates for two squares
Coordinate3 {
	point [
		# Left square
		-2.0 1.0 0.0,
		-2.0 0.0 0.0,
		-1.0 0.0 0.0,
		-1.0 1.0 0.0,
		# Right square
		 1.0 1.0 0.0,
		 1.0 0.0 0.0,
		 2.0 0.0 0.0,
		 2.0 1.0 0.0
	]
}
# Draw left square
IndexedFaceSet {
	coordIndex [
		0, 1, 2, 3
	]
}
Separator {
	# Coordinates for a triangle
	Coordinate3 {
		point [
			 0.0 1.0 0.0,
			-1.0 0.0 0.0,
			 1.0 0.0 0.0
		]
	}
	# Draw middle triangle
	IndexedFaceSet {
		coordIndex [
			0, 1, 2
		]
	}
}
# Draw right square
IndexedFaceSet {
	coordIndex [
		4, 5, 6, 7
	]
}
```

Figure 14.35 *Two square faces and a triangular face constructed with the same **IndexedFaceSet** node and different coordinates.*

Reading the file from top to bottom, the virtual pen is instructed to:

1. Set its coordinates property to eight coordinates.
2. Draw a face using the current coordinates property in the following order:

Vertex Index	*Coordinate*
0	`-2.0 1.0 0.0`
1	`-2.0 0.0 0.0`
2	`-1.0 0.0 0.0`
3	`-1.0 1.0 0.0`

3. Draw the separator group.
   a. Save its properties, including the coordinates property.
   b. Set its coordinates property to three coordinates.
   c. Draw a face using the current coordinates property in the following order:

Vertex Index	*Coordinate*
0	`-2.0 1.0 0.0`
1	`-2.0 0.0 0.0`
2	`-1.0 0.0 0.0`

   d. Restore its properties, including the coordinates property.
4. Draw a face using the current coordinates property in the following order:

Vertex Index	*Coordinate*
4	`1.0 1.0 0.0`
5	`1.0 0.0 0.0`
6	`2.0 0.0 0.0`
7	`2.0 7.0 0.0`

The result is two squares, both drawn using the coordinates set in step 1, and a triangle drawn between the squares using the coordinates set in step 3b.

Constructing More Complex Shapes

Using VRML you can construct much more complex shapes than the cube, the X, the squares, and the triangle shown previously. The example text in Figure 14.36

constructs a vase using 30 coordinates. The coordinates are grouped into six rings that define the lip, neck, body, and base of the vase. An **IndexedFaceSet** node then connects these vertices together to create 26 faces for the faceted sides and bottom of the vase.

```
#VRML V1.0 ascii

Coordinate3 {
      point [
            # ring 0
             0.32 2.00  0.00,
             0.10 2.00  0.30,
            -0.26 2.00  0.19,
            -0.26 2.00 -0.19,
             0.10 2.00 -0.30,
            # ring 1
             0.30 1.95  0.00,
             0.09 1.95  0.29,
            -0.24 1.95  0.18,
            -0.24 1.95 -0.18,
             0.09 1.95 -0.29,
            # ring 2
             0.42 1.60  0.00,
             0.13 1.60  0.40,
            -0.34 1.60  0.25,
            -0.34 1.60 -0.25,
             0.13 1.60 -0.40,
            # ring 3
             0.60 1.50  0.00,
             0.19 1.50  0.57,
            -0.48 1.50  0.35,
            -0.49 1.50 -0.35,
             0.18 1.50 -0.57,
            # ring 4
             0.70 1.20  0.00,
             0.22 1.20  0.67,
            -0.57 1.20  0.41,
            -0.57 1.20 -0.41,
             0.21 1.20 -0.67,
            # ring 5
             0.40 0.00  0.00,
             0.12 0.00  0.38,
            -0.32 0.00  0.24,
            -0.32 0.00 -0.23,
             0.12 0.00 -0.38
      ]
}
```

Figure 14.36 continues

```
IndexedFaceSet {
     coordIndex [
          # ring 0
           0,  1,  6,  5, -1,
           1,  2,  7,  6, -1,
           2,  3,  8,  7, -1,
           3,  4,  9,  8, -1,
           4,  0,  5,  9, -1,
          # ring 1
           5,  6, 11, 10, -1,
           6,  7, 12, 11, -1,
           7,  8, 13, 12, -1,
           8,  9, 14, 13, -1,
           9,  5, 10, 14, -1,
          # ring 2
          10, 11, 16, 15, -1,
          11, 12, 17, 16, -1,
          12, 13, 18, 17, -1,
          13, 14, 19, 18, -1,
          14, 10, 15, 19, -1,
          # ring 3
          15, 16, 21, 20, -1,
          16, 17, 22, 21, -1,
          17, 18, 23, 22, -1,
          18, 19, 24, 23, -1,
          19, 15, 20, 24, -1,
          # ring 4
          20, 21, 26, 25, -1,
          21, 22, 27, 26, -1,
          22, 23, 28, 27, -1,
          23, 24, 29, 28, -1,
          24, 20, 25, 29, -1,
          # base
          25, 26, 27, 28, 29
     ]
}
```

Figure 14.36 *A vase constructed with 30 vertices making 26 faces.*

Complex shapes are constructed using large numbers of faces, often in the thousands. Construction of complex shapes typically requires the use of a computer application that can automatically compute coordinates and vertex indexes. Such applications are called **3-D modelers** or **world editors** and are essential tools for creating complex VRML shapes.

Constructing Mountainous Terrains

You can create mountainous terrains by starting with a flat grid of triangles, like that shown in Figure 14.37. Figure 14.37*a* shows the grid constructed with lines, and Figure 14.37*b* illustrates the same grid drawn as shaded faces.

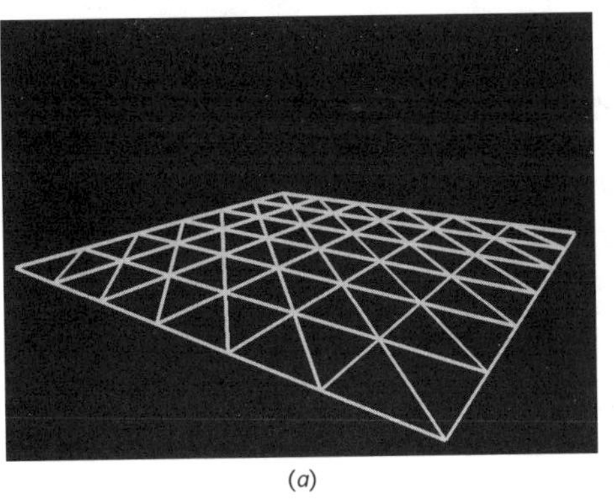

(a)

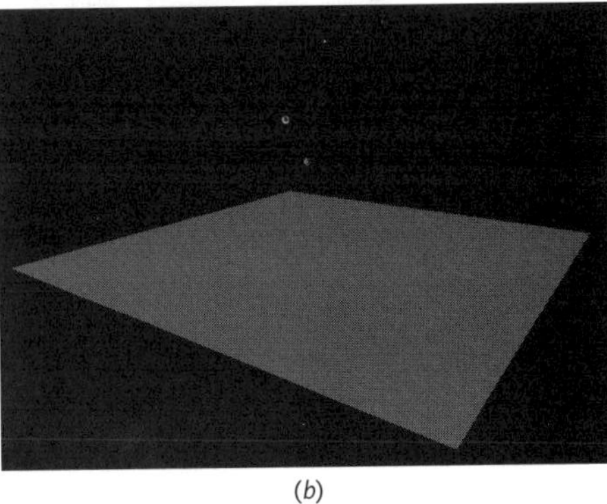

(b)

Figure 14.37 *A flat grid of triangles.*

The X and Z values of each grid coordinate correspond to a location on a plot of land. The Y value of each coordinate specifies the elevation at that location. For instance, you can create a mountain out of the flat grid by selecting a middle grid point and setting its Y coordinate to a high value, like that shown in Figure 14.38.

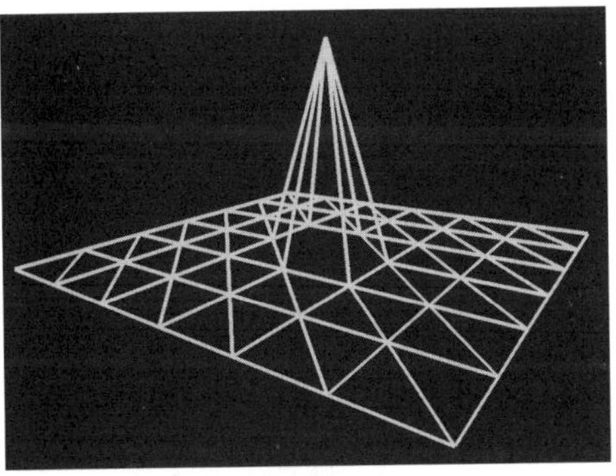

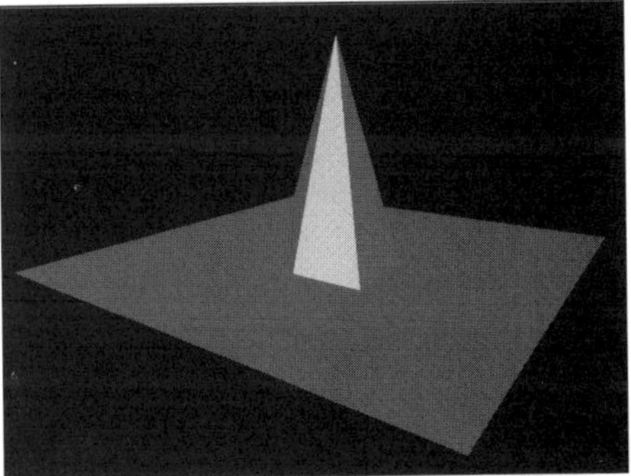

Figure 14.38 *A mountain created by specifying a high Y value for one coordinate in the grid of triangles.*

Continuing this process, you can create arbitrarily bumpy terrains, like that shown in Figure 14.39.

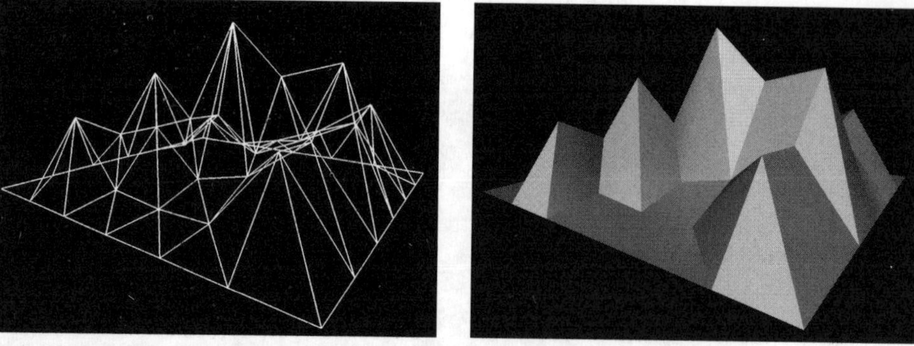

Figure 14.39 *Mountains created with high Y-value coordinates.*

Using Transforms

Using the **Translation, Rotation, Scale, Transform,** and **MatrixTransform** nodes, you can position, rotate, scale, and warp shapes drawn using the **IndexedFaceSet** node. To illustrate, Figures 14.40 through 14.45 build a fractal pyramid.

Fractals are created by defining a shape, then using several copies of the shape to build a larger shape that structurally resembles the original. The larger composite shape is then copied several times to build an even larger shape that resembles the original, and so on.

This fractal technique creates a complex shape that is structurally similar to its components, which in turn are structurally similar to *their* components, and so on down to the base shape. This is known as **self-similarity**.

The following fractal examples start first with the basic triangular shape built using four faces shown in Figure 14.40.

```
#VRML V1.0 ascii

# Triangular base piece
Coordinate3 {
      point [
              0.0  1.5  0.0,
             -0.86 0.0  0.5,
              0.86 0.0  0.5,
              0.0  0.0 -1.0
      ]
}
```

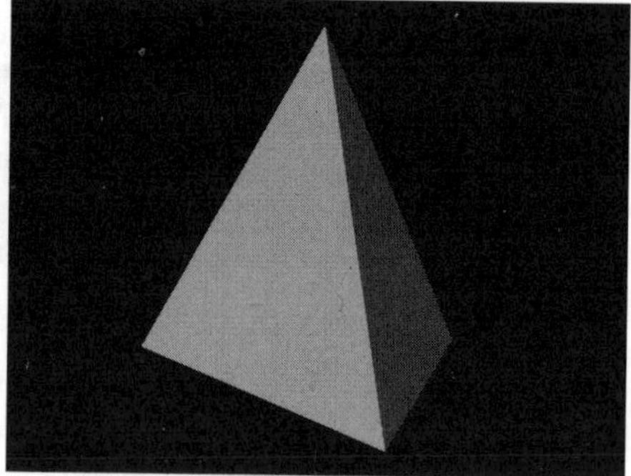

Figure 14.40 continues

```
IndexedFaceSet {
      coordIndex [
            0, 1, 2, -1,
            0, 2, 3, -1,
            0, 3, 1, -1,
            1, 3, 2
      ]
}
```

Figure 14.40 *The basic triangular shape of a fractal.*

To build a larger triangular shape similar to the triangular base shape, combine four base shapes together using **Translation** and **Scale** nodes, like that shown in Figure 14.41.

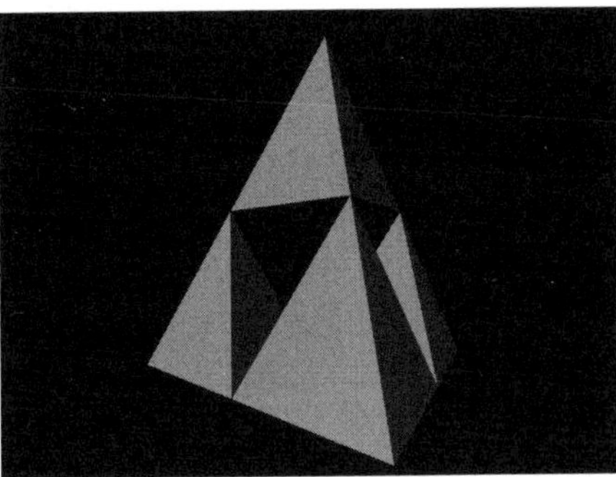

```
#VRML V1.0 ascii

Switch {
      whichChild -1
      # Triangular base piece
      DEF tri Separator {
            Coordinate3 {
                  point [
                         0.0  1.5  0.0,
                        -0.86 0.0  0.5,
                         0.86 0.0  0.5,
                         0.0  0.0 -1.0
                  ]
            }
            IndexedFaceSet {
                  coordIndex [
                        0, 1, 2, -1,
                        0, 2, 3, -1,
                        0, 3, 1, -1,
                        1, 3, 2
                  ]
            }
      }
}
# Four triangular base pieces
DEF tri2 Separator {
      DEF smaller Scale {
            scaleFactor 0.5 0.5 0.5
      }
      DEF left Translation {
            translation -0.86 0.0 0.5
      }
      USE tri
      DEF right Translation {
            translation 1.73 0.0 0.0
      }
```

Figure 14.41 continues

```
        USE tri
        DEF back Translation {
              translation -0.86 0.0 -1.5
        }
        USE tri
        DEF up Translation {
              translation 0.0 1.5 1.0
        }
        USE tri
}
```

Figure 14.41 *A larger fractal built by combining four of the base triangular shapes with **Translation** and **Scale** nodes.*

The preceding example illustrates several techniques to simplify construction of the fractal:

- *The triangular base shape is given a defined name,* tri, *so that the entire shape can be repeatedly instanced later.*
- *The base shape is placed within a **Switch** node, and the **whichChild** field is set to –1 to prevent the base shape from being instanced immediately.*
- *Four instances of the base shape* tri *are combined together to form a larger triangular structure. That structure is enclosed within a **Separator** node to group its pieces together. The **Separator** node is given a defined name,* tri2, *so that it can be instanced later.*
- *Each of the **Scale** and **Translation** nodes used to position the four base shapes is also given a defined name—*left, right, back, *and* up*—so that they, too, can be instanced later.*

You can now continue to build the fractal by reusing the same shapes and transforms to create more complex, self-similar structures. The VRML text shown in Figure 14.42, for instance, is the fractal pyramid extended twice more in complexity.

```
#VRML V1.0 ascii

# Build the fractal pyramid
Switch {
      whichChild 3
      # Triangular base piece
      DEF tri Separator {
            Coordinate3 {
                  point [
                         0.0  1.5  0.0,
                        -0.86 0.0  0.5,
                         0.86 0.0  0.5,
                         0.0  0.0 -1.0
                  ]
            }
```

Figure 14.42 continues

```
        IndexedFaceSet {
            coordIndex [
                0, 1, 2, -1,
                0, 2, 3, -1,
                0, 3, 1, -1,
                1, 3, 2
            ]
        }
}
# Four triangular base pieces
DEF tri2 Separator {
        DEF smaller Scale {
            scaleFactor 0.5 0.5 0.5
        }
        DEF left Translation {
            translation -0.86 0.0 0.5
        }
        USE tri
        DEF right Translation {
            translation 1.73 0.0 0.0
        }
        USE tri
        DEF back Translation {
            translation -0.86 0.0 -1.5
        }
        USE tri
        DEF up Translation {
            translation 0.0 1.5 1.0
        }
        USE tri
}
# Four tri2 pieces
DEF tri3 Separator {
        USE smaller
        USE left
        USE tri2
        USE right
        USE tri2
        USE back
        USE tri2
        USE up
        USE tri2
}
# Four tri3 pieces
DEF tri4 Separator {
        USE smaller
        USE left
        USE tri3
        USE right
        USE tri3
        USE back
```

Figure 14.42 continues

```
                    USE tri3
                    USE up
                    USE tri3
            }
    }
```

Figure 14.42 *Creating a more complex fractal by reusing named shapes and transforms.*

Notice how the named shapes and transforms are repeatedly reused to build each larger structure. The *tri2* structure is built using four *tri* base shapes. The *tri3* structure uses four *tri2* instances. The *tri4* structure uses four *tri3* instances. And so on. You can continue building this kind of structure indefinitely, creating more complex pyramids based on the previous pyramid. By combining all the pyramids into one **Switch** node, you can use the **whichChild** field to select different complexity levels of the fractal pyramid.

Using Multiple Coordinate Lists

You can use any number of **Coordinate3, IndexedFaceSet, IndexedLineSet,** and **PointSet** nodes within the same VRML file. Each use of a **Coordinate3** node sets the pen's coordinate properties. Each use of an **IndexedFaceSet, IndexedLineSet,** or **PointSet** node uses the pen's current coordinate properties to build shapes.

The following series of examples build a self-similar fractal archway from four triangular shapes, each defined with a different **Coordinate3** coordinate list. The base arch looks like that in Figure 14.43.

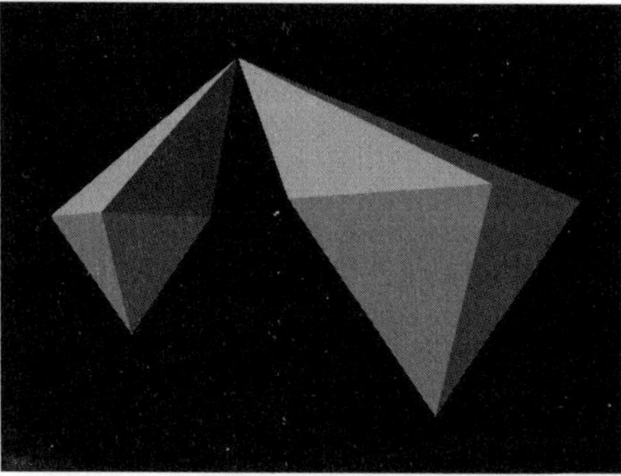

Figure 14.43 *The base shape of an archway.*

To make the fractal, the next-larger arch structure uses three base arches. The first base arch forms a main upper arch, while the second two base arches extend the legs of the main arch, like that in Figure 14.44.

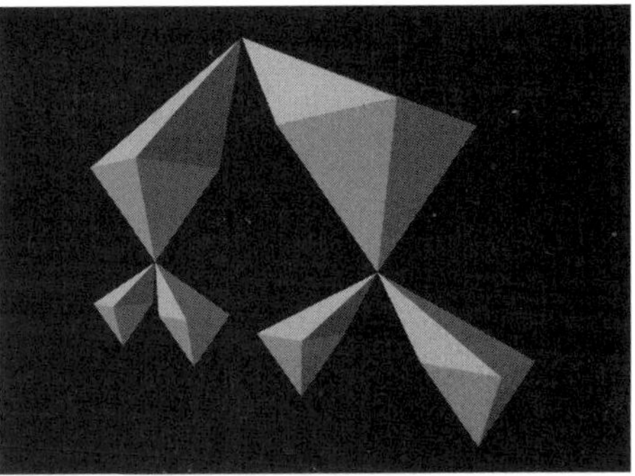

Figure 14.44 *Extend the legs of the base arch using two more base arch shapes.*

Like the pyramid fractal of the previous section, you can extend the fractal archway indefinitely, adding further and further arches beneath each arch leg. Figure 14.45 shows the result.

```
#VRML V1.0 ascii

# Build the fractal archway
Switch {
      whichChild 3
      # Triangular arch base piece
      DEF arch Separator {
            # Left leg
            Coordinate3 {
                  point [
                         0.0 1.0  0.0,
                        -2.0 0.0  0.5,
                        -1.0 0.0  0.5,
                        -1.0 0.0 -0.5,
                        -2.0 0.0 -0.5
                  ]
            }
            IndexedFaceSet {
                  coordIndex [
                        0, 1, 2, -1,
                        0, 2, 3, -1,
                        0, 3, 4, -1,
                        0, 4, 1, -1,
                        1, 4, 3,  2
                  ]
            }
            DEF left Translation {
                  translation -1.5 0.0 0.0
            }
```

Figure 14.45 continues

```
        # Triangular bottom for each arch leg
        DEF base Separator {
              Rotation {
                     #        X             +180 degrees
                     rotation 1.0 0.0 0.0  3.14
              }
              Coordinate3 {
                     point [
                            0.0 1.0  0.0,
                           -0.5 0.0  0.5,
                            0.5 0.0  0.5,
                            0.5 0.0 -0.5,
                           -0.5 0.0 -0.5
                     ]
              }
              IndexedFaceSet {
                     coordIndex [
                            0, 1, 2, -1,
                            0, 2, 3, -1,
                            0, 3, 4, -1,
                            0, 4, 1, -1,
                            1, 4, 3,  2
                     ]
              }
        }
        DEF right Translation {
              translation 1.5 0.0 0.0
        }
        # Right leg
        Coordinate3 {
              point [
                     0.0 1.0  0.0,
                     1.0 0.0  0.5,
                     2.0 0.0  0.5,
                     2.0 0.0 -0.5,
                     1.0 0.0 -0.5
              ]
        }
        IndexedFaceSet {
              coordIndex [
                     0, 1, 2, -1,
                     0, 2, 3, -1,
                     0, 3, 4, -1,
                     0, 4, 1, -1,
                     1, 4, 3,  2
              ]
        }
        USE right
        USE base
}
```

Figure 14.45 continues

```
        # Three arch pieces
        DEF arch2 Separator {
              USE arch
              DEF down Translation {
                    translation 0.0 -1.5 0.0
              }
              Separator {
                    USE left
                    DEF smaller Scale {
                           scaleFactor 0.5 0.5 0.5
                    }
                    USE arch
              }
              Separator {
                    USE right
                    USE smaller
                    USE arch
              }
        }
        # Three arch2 pieces
        DEF arch3 Separator {
              USE arch2
              USE down
              Separator {
                    USE left
                    USE smaller
                    USE arch2
              }
              Separator {
                    USE right
                    USE smaller
                    USE arch2
              }
        }
        # Three arch3 pieces
        DEF arch4 Separator {
              USE arch3
              USE down
              Separator {
                    USE left
                    USE smaller
                    USE arch3
              }
              Separator {
                    USE right
                    USE smaller
                    USE arch3
              }
        }
  }
```

Figure 14.45 *The final arch.*

The preceding example illustrates several techniques to simplify construction of the fractal archway:

- *A base arch shape is constructed and named* arch. *Each arch is built from four shapes:*
  - *A left-leg sloped pyramid.*
  - *A left-leg, upside-down pyramid base.*
  - *A right-leg sloped pyramid.*
  - *A right-leg, upside-down pyramid base.*

  Each of these shapes is constructed using a different ***Coordinate3*** *and* ***IndexedFaceSet*** *node pair.*
- *Several of the transforms used in the archway are given defined names so that they can be instanced later when building larger and larger archways.*
- *Each larger arch is built from three smaller base arches. By instancing both shapes and transforms, the larger arches can be built quickly.* arch2 *uses three* arch *pieces.* arch3 *uses three* arch2 *pieces.* arch4 *uses three* arch3 *pieces.*

Using Transforms with Point Sets

Using the **Translation, Rotation, Scale, Transform,** and **MatrixTransform** nodes, you can position, rotate, scale, and warp sets of points drawn with the **PointSet** node. The example text in Figure 14.46 illustrates this. Start with the star field in Figure 14.30, and then duplicate it repeatedly, in different orientations and at different scale factors, to quickly build up a complex star field that looks like a spiral galaxy.

```
#VRML V1.0 ascii
Coordinate3 {
      point [
        0.18 -0.53  0.17,
        0.23 -0.12 -0.39,
       -0.37  0.54  0.65,
        0.78  0.15  0.31,
       -0.92  0.40  0.79,
        0.87  0.67  0.58,
       -0.36 -0.83 -0.46,
        0.13 -0.96  0.41,
        0.76  0.03 -0.76,
       -0.59 -0.96 -0.06,
       -0.92  0.12  0.25,
       -0.24 -0.41  0.43,
       -0.38 -0.16  0.70,
       -0.40  0.24 -0.23,
       -0.30  0.04  0.40,
        0.73  0.23  0.97,
        0.43  0.81 -0.28,
       -0.86  0.21 -0.29,
        0.22  0.72 -0.99,
       -0.43  0.86  0.98,
```

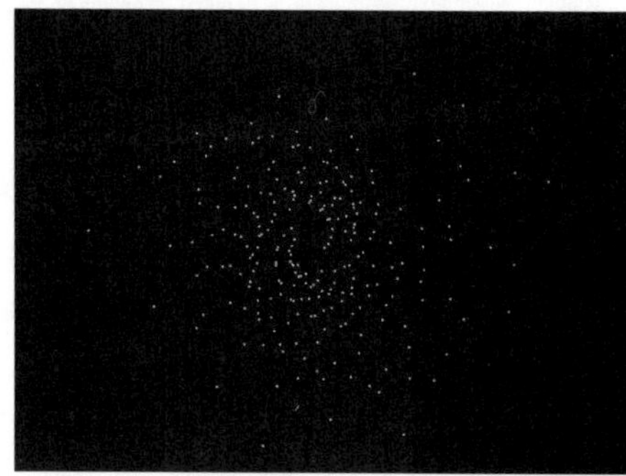

Figure 14.46 continues

```
        -0.43 -0.46 -0.99,
         0.60 -0.45  0.08,
        -0.15 -0.94  0.99,
        -0.80  0.38 -0.53,
        -0.59 -0.14  0.71,
        -0.70 -0.96  0.74,
         0.64  0.19 -0.28,
         0.29  0.42 -0.44,
         0.49  0.42 -0.26,
        -0.98 -0.38  0.35,
        ]
}
DEF stars PointSet {
        startIndex 0
        numPoints -1
}
DEF bigger Scale {
        scaleFactor 1.2 1.2 1.0
}
DEF spin Rotation {
        #                 Z   +20.0 degrees
        rotation 0.0 0.0 1.0  0.349
}
USE stars
USE bigger
USE spin
USE stars
USE bigger
USE spin
USE stars
USE bigger
USE spin
USE stars
USE bigger
USE spin
USE stars
USE bigger
USE spin
USE stars
USE bigger
USE spin
USE stars
```

Figure 14.46 *A spiral star field.*

Using Polylines to Outline Faces

You can combine faces created with **IndexedFaceSet** nodes with polylines created with **IndexedLineSet** nodes. This enables you to outline the edges of shaded faces, making them easier to see. For example, you can draw the fractal pyramid in

Figure 14.42 with each of the triangular pieces shaded with a color and outlined in white.

Like other VRML shapes, faces are drawn the color of the current material properties. When the virtual pen draws the faces of an **IndexedFaceSet** node, each face is drawn using the current pen color. For instance, the fractal pyramid can be drawn in color by inserting **Material** nodes before each instance of the base triangular shape. The result is shown in Figure 14.47.

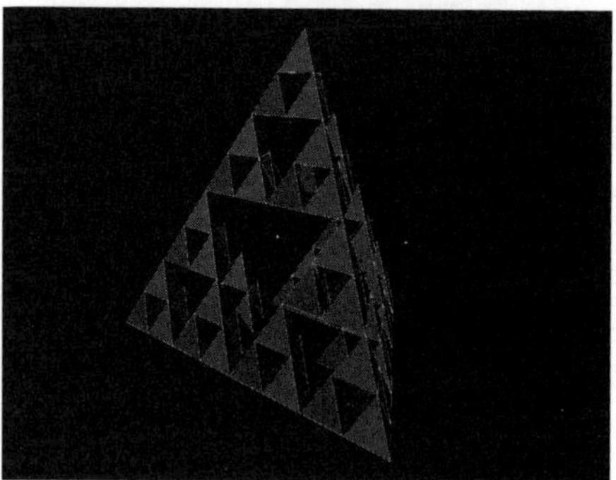

Figure 14.47 *The fractal pyramid with colored faces each outlined in white.*

Extended Examples

The following examples build on the concepts presented in this chapter. They illustrate the worlds you can build using faces, lines, and point sets. Try them on your own.

TIP *All of the VRML text in the extended examples throughout this book are available via anonymous ftp from John Wiley & Sons at* `ftp.wiley.com/public/computer_books/vrml` *and from the VRML Repository at* `http://www.sdsc.edu/vrml`.

A Koch Snowflake Fractal

The example VRML file in Figure 14.48 creates a Koch snowflake fractal using polylines. Notice how the named shapes and transforms are used over and over again to build each larger structure. The *curve1* structure is built using four *base* shapes, the *curve2* structure uses four *curve1* instances, and so on. You can continue building this kind of structure indefinitely, creating more complex zigzags based on the previous zigzag. By combining all your polyline fractals into one **Switch** node, you can use the **whichChild** field to select different complexity levels of the Koch snowflake.

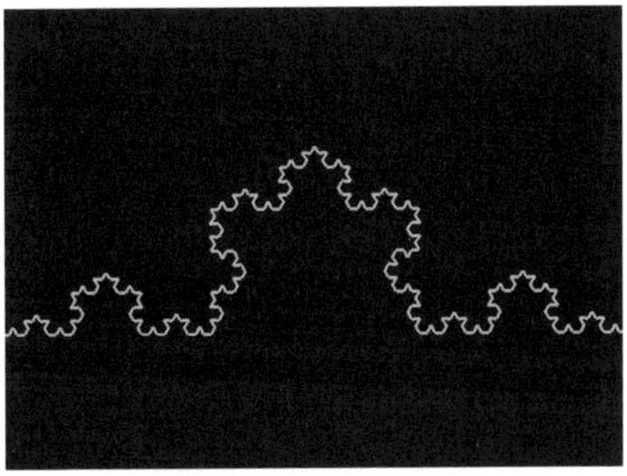

```
#VRML V1.0 ascii

# Zig-zag base piece
Coordinate3 {
      point [
            0.0 0.0 0.0,
            1.0 0.0 0.0,
            1.5 1.0 0.0,
            2.0 0.0 0.0,
            3.0 0.0 0.0
      ]
}
Switch {
      whichChild 3
      # zig-zag base piece
      DEF base IndexedLineSet {
            coordIndex [
                  0, 1, 2, 3, 4
            ]
      }
      # Four base pieces
      DEF curve1 Separator {
            DEF smaller Scale {
                  scaleFactor 0.3333 0.3333 0.3333
            }
            USE base
            DEF right Translation {
                  translation 3.0 0.0 0.0
            }
            DEF turnup Rotation {
                  #                 Z   +60.0 degrees
                  rotation 0.0 0.0 1.0  1.0472
            }
            USE base
            USE right
            DEF turndown Rotation {
                  #                 Z    -120.0 degrees
                  rotation 0.0 0.0 1.0  -2.0944
            }
            USE base
            USE right
            USE turnup
            USE base
      }
      # Four curve1 pieces
      DEF curve2 Separator {
            USE smaller
            USE curve1
            USE right
            USE turnup
            USE curve1
            USE right
            USE turndown
```

Figure 14.48 continues

```
                USE curvel
                USE right
                USE turnup
                USE curvel
          }
          # Four curve2 pieces
          DEF curve3 Separator {
                USE smaller
                USE curve2
                USE right
                USE turnup
                USE curve2
                USE right
                USE turndown
                USE curve2
                USE right
                USE turnup
                USE curve2
          }
    }
```

Figure 14.48 *A Koch snowflake.*

A Guitar

The example text in Figure 14.49 creates a guitar using faces for the guitar body and lines for the guitar strings. You might extend this guitar by creating frets, a bridge, or a pick guard.

```
#VRML V1.0 ascii

# Guitar body, Bridge, Rosette, and Sound Hole
Separator {
      Coordinate3 {
            point [
                  # Front: left end down along the bottom...
                  -1.0  -0.0   0.0,    -1.0  -0.2   0.0,
                  -0.95 -0.5   0.0,    -0.7  -0.8   0.0,
                  -0.55 -0.85  0.0,    -0.2  -0.85  0.0,
                   0.05 -0.75  0.0,     0.3  -0.55  0.0,
                   0.4  -0.5   0.0,     0.55 -0.5   0.0,
                   0.7  -0.58  0.0,     0.85 -0.62  0.0,
                   0.9  -0.65  0.0,     1.2  -0.65  0.0,
                   1.33 -0.6   0.0,     1.45 -0.5   0.0,
                   1.6  -0.2   0.0,     1.6  -0.0   0.0,
                  # ...and up over the top
                   1.6   0.0   0.0,     1.6   0.2   0.0,
                   1.45  0.5   0.0,     1.33  0.6   0.0,
                   1.2   0.65  0.0,     0.9   0.65  0.0,
                   0.85  0.62  0.0,     0.7   0.58  0.0,
                   0.55  0.5   0.0,     0.4   0.5   0.0,
```

Figure 14.49 continues

```
                 0.3   0.55 0.0,     0.05 0.75 0.0,
                -0.2   0.85 0.0,    -0.55 0.85 0.0,
                -0.7   0.8  0.0,    -0.95 0.5  0.0,
                -1.0   0.2  0.0,
                # Back: left end down along the bottom...
                -1.0  -0.0  -0.3,    -1.0  -0.2  -0.3,
                -0.95 -0.5  -0.3,    -0.7  -0.8  -0.3,
                -0.55 -0.85 -0.3,    -0.2  -0.85 -0.3,
                 0.05 -0.75 -0.3,     0.3  -0.55 -0.3,
                 0.4  -0.5  -0.3,     0.55 -0.5  -0.3,
                 0.7  -0.58 -0.3,     0.85 -0.62 -0.3,
                 0.9  -0.65 -0.3,     1.2  -0.65 -0.3,
                 1.33 -0.6  -0.3,     1.45 -0.5  -0.3,
                 1.6  -0.2  -0.3,     1.6  -0.0  -0.3,
                # ...and up over the top
                 1.6   0.0  -0.3,     1.6   0.2  -0.3,
                 1.45  0.5  -0.3,     1.33  0.6  -0.3,
                 1.2   0.65 -0.3,     0.9   0.65 -0.3,
                 0.85  0.62 -0.3,     0.7   0.58 -0.3,
                 0.55  0.5  -0.3,     0.4   0.5  -0.3,
                 0.3   0.55 -0.3,     0.05  0.75 -0.3,
                -0.2   0.85 -0.3,    -0.55  0.85 -0.3,
                -0.7   0.8  -0.3,    -0.95  0.5  -0.3,
                -1.0   0.2  -0.3,
        ]
}
Material {
        diffuseColor 0.6 0.25 0.0
}
IndexedFaceSet {
        coordIndex [
                # Around the perimeter of the front
                 0,  1,  2,  3,  4,  5,  6,  7,  8,
                27, 28, 29, 30, 31, 32, 33, 34, -1,
                 8,  9, 10, 11, 12, 13, 14, 15, 16, 17,
                18, 19, 20, 21, 22, 23, 24, 25, 26, 27, -1,
        ]
}
DEF brown Material {
        diffuseColor 0.22 0.08 0.0
}
IndexedFaceSet {
        coordIndex [
                # Around the perimeter of the back
                69, 68, 67, 66, 65, 64, 63, 62, 61, 62,
                43, 42, 41, 40, 39, 38, 37, 36, 35, -1,
                62, 61, 60, 59, 58, 57, 56, 55, 54, 53, 52,
                51, 50, 49, 48, 47, 46, 45, 44, 43, -1,
```

Figure 14.49 continues

```
                # Sides
                 0, 35, 36,  1, -1,  1, 36, 37,  2, -1,
                 2, 37, 38,  3, -1,  3, 38, 39,  4, -1,
                 4, 39, 40,  5, -1,  5, 40, 41,  6, -1,
                 6, 41, 42,  7, -1,  7, 42, 43,  8, -1,
                 8, 43, 44,  9, -1,  9, 44, 45, 10, -1,
                10, 45, 46, 11, -1, 11, 46, 47, 12, -1,
                12, 47, 48, 13, -1, 13, 48, 49, 14, -1,
                14, 49, 50, 15, -1, 15, 50, 51, 16, -1,
                16, 51, 52, 17, -1, 17, 52, 53, 18, -1,
                18, 53, 54, 19, -1, 19, 54, 55, 20, -1,
                20, 55, 56, 21, -1, 21, 56, 57, 22, -1,
                22, 57, 58, 23, -1, 23, 58, 59, 24, -1,
                24, 59, 60, 25, -1, 25, 60, 61, 26, -1,
                26, 61, 62, 27, -1, 27, 62, 63, 28, -1,
                28, 63, 64, 29, -1, 29, 64, 65, 30, -1,
                30, 65, 66, 31, -1, 31, 66, 67, 32, -1,
                32, 67, 68, 33, -1, 33, 68, 69, 34, -1,
                34, 69, 36,  0, -1,
            ]
        }
        Translation {
            translation -0.4 0.0 0.01
        }
        USE brown
        Cube {
            width 0.15
            height 0.7
            depth 0.01
        }
        Transform {
            translation 1.1 0.0 0.01
            #        X            +90.0 degrees
            rotation 1.0 0.0 0.0  1.57
        }
        Cylinder {
            radius 0.25
            height 0.01
            parts TOP
        }
        Material {
            diffuseColor 0.0 0.0 0.0
        }
        Cylinder {
            radius 0.2
            height 0.02
            parts TOP
        }
}
```

Figure 14.49 continues

```
# Fingerboard and Tuning Pegs
Separator {
      Translation {
            translation 1.9 0.0 0.0
      }
      USE brown
      Cube {
            width 2.0
            height 0.22
            depth 0.08
      }
      Transform {
            translation 1.25 0.0 0.0
            #           Y        +5.0 degrees
            rotation 0.0 1.0 0.0  0.087
            center -0.25 0.0 0.0
      }
      Cube {
            width 0.5
            height 0.3
            depth 0.08
      }
      Translation {
            translation -0.12 0.0 0.0
      }
      # Gold Pegs
      Material {
            diffuseColor 0.32 0.25 0.10
      }
      DEF peg Cylinder {
            height 0.45
            radius 0.025
      }
      DEF right Translation {
            translation 0.12 0.0 0.0
      }
      USE peg
      USE right
      USE peg
}
# Strings
Separator {
      Coordinate3 {
            point [
                  -0.4  0.1  0.05, 3.05  0.075 0.05,
                  -0.4  0.06 0.05, 3.17  0.045 0.05,
                  -0.4  0.02 0.05, 3.29  0.015 0.05,
                  -0.4 -0.02 0.05, 3.29 -0.015 0.05,
                  -0.4 -0.06 0.05, 3.17 -0.045 0.05,
                  -0.4 -0.1  0.05, 3.05 -0.075 0.05,
            ]
      }
```

Figure 14.49 continues

```
        Material {
              diffuseColor 0.5 0.5 0.5
        }
        IndexedLineSet {
              coordIndex [
                    0, 1, -1, 2, 3, -1,  4,  5, -1,
                    6, 7, -1, 8, 9, -1, 10, 11, -1,
              ]
        }
}
```

Figure 14.49 *A guitar.*

Summary

Faces are flat, multisided shapes, like triangles, squares, and octagons. Faces are built from two components: a vertex coordinate list and a vertex index list. The coordinate list provides the 3-D locations of each corner, or vertex, of a face. The vertex index list specifies the order in which the coordinates are to be chained together to form the perimeter, or edges, of a face.

Planar faces are flat, while non-planar faces are twisted and don't lie flat. Non-planar faces are split into planar faces (triangles) by the VRML browser. You should split non-planar faces manually rather than allow the VRML browser to split them.

Concave faces, like the silhouette of a person, have inlets and cavities. Convex faces, like triangles and squares, do not have inlets or cavities. The VRML browser can draw only convex faces. Concave faces must be split manually into multiple convex faces, usually triangles.

A point is a single dot on the screen. A point set is a series of such dots. Points are placed at vertices listed as 3-D coordinates in a coordinate list. The range of coordinates describing the points to draw is defined by specifying a starting vertex in the list and a number of consecutive coordinates to use.

Polylines are lists of straight line segments, strung together in a chain where the end of one is the start of the next. Polylines are built from two components: a vertex coordinate list and a vertex index list. The coordinate list specifies the 3-D locations of each line end point, or vertex, of a polyline. The vertex index list specifies the coordinates to be chained together to form the line segments of a polyline.

The **Coordinate3** node's **point** field specifies a list of 3-D coordinates, each constructed from three floating-point values. The coordinate list is saved as the pen's coordinate property for later use by **PointSet, IndexedLineSet,** and **IndexedFaceSet** nodes.

The **PointSet** node's **startIndex** field selects the vertex index for the first point to draw. The **numPoints** field selects the total number of points to draw. Points will be placed at the starting vertex and at consecutive vertices in the current coordinate list. A value of –1 for the **numPoints** field indicates that points should be drawn for all coordinates from the **startIndex** to the end of the coordinate list.

The **IndexedLineSet** node's **coordIndex** field takes a list of vertex indexes defining the vertices of a polyline to draw. Each vertex index selects a vertex in the pen's current coordinate property. The vertex index list may define multiple polylines at once, each one's vertex list separated by a –1 index.

The **IndexedFaceSet** node's **coordIndex** field specifies a list of vertex indexes defining the vertices of a face. Each vertex index selects a vertex in the pen's current coordinate property. The vertex index list may define multiple faces at once, each one's vertex list separated by a –1 index.

The same 3-D coordinates may be used to make one or more shapes. Likewise, the same vertex index list may be used to connect together different coordinates.

Face, line, and point shapes may be transformed and colored like any VRML shape. Complex fractal structures, for instance, are built by creating a few base shapes, and repeatedly instancing them in larger and larger structures. Such fractal structures are called self-similar, because the large structure is similar to its components, which are in turn similar to their components, and so on.

CHAPTER 15

Binding Materials to Shapes

Using a **Material** node, you can specify a color to shade an entire shape, such as a cube or a set of faces, lines, or points. You may want to shade different parts of the same shape with different colors. For example, you may want to shade the six sides of a cube with six different colors.

A **material binding type** specifies how materials set in a **Material** node are used to shade the individual parts, faces, or vertices of shapes. Up to this point, you have used only the default material binding type that applies a single material to an entire shape all at once. VRML provides additional material binding types which enable you to apply different materials to individual parts, faces, and vertices of a shape.

Using material binding types, you can create a multicolored cube, draw each point in a point set with a different color, or create color gradations across a face. With these features, you can create rainbows, smoothly color the sides of a vase, or shade a mountain terrain.

Material bindings affect how each of the VRML shapes is shaded, including the primitive shapes, faces, lines, and point sets. Using a **MaterialBinding** node, you can selectively **bind** to shapes a list of colors specified in a **Material** node. Using a **materialIndex** field within the **IndexedFaceSet** and **IndexedLineSet** nodes, you can bind particular materials to different faces, lines, or vertices of a shape.

Understanding Material Binding

Shapes are built from several components. A cylinder, for instance, is built from three parts: the top, the bottom, and the sides. Each of these parts is, in turn, built from several components. The sides of the cylinder, for instance, are a series of thin faces like those you can create with an **IndexedFaceSet** node. Each of these faces is built from a series of vertices connected together to form a face. Table 15.1 summarizes this component hierarchy of VRML shapes.

Table 15.1 The Hierarchy of Shape Components

Component	*Description*
Overall shape	The entire shape, built from parts
Parts	Major pieces of a shape, each built from faces
Faces	Faces of a shape, each built from vertices
Vertices	The corners of faces

Some shapes have all of these component levels, such as a cylinder. Other shapes skip some of the component levels. A point set, for instance, has vertices, but no faces or parts. A sphere has vertices and faces, but it is constructed of only one part.

Binding Materials to Shapes and Shape Components

To bind different materials to different components of a shape, you must:

1. List the materials.
2. Describe how you want those materials bound to shape components.

A **material list** specifies a series of material attributes, such as an RGB diffuse color, an RGB emissive color, and a transparency factor:

Material Index	*Diffuse Color*	*Emissive Color*	*Transparency*
0	1.0 0.0 0.0	0.0 0.5 0.5	0.0
1	0.0 1.0 0.0	0.5 0.0 0.5	0.5
2	0.0 0.0 1.0	0.5 0.5 0.0	0.0

Each material in the material list has a **material index**. The first material has a material index of 0, the second a material index of 1, and so on. Using the material index, you can later refer to a particular material in the list without explicitly specifying the diffuse color, emissive color, and transparency of the material.

Using an indexed material list, you can direct the VRML browser to bind each material in the list to a different component of subsequent shapes. Different material binding types determine how materials are bound: to the overall shape, on a per-part basis, on a per-face basis, or on a per-vertex basis. You can, for instance, bind material index 0 to the entire shape, only to the first part of the shape, to the first face of the first part of the shape, or to the first vertex of the first face of the first part of the shape. This gives you maximum flexibility to control how you want a shape shaded.

The material binding type you choose is a property, just like the current font style, coordinates, materials, and other properties. Like all properties, you specify the material binding type before you draw, and it remains in effect until you change it again later in the file.

VRML supports four main types of material bindings:

- **Overall**—*Bind a single material to the entire shape*
- **Per-part**—*Bind a different material to each part of the shape*
- **Per-face**—*Bind a different material to each face of the shape*
- **Per-vertex**—*Bind a different material to each vertex of the shape*

For example, if you use an *overall* material binding type, the entire shape is shaded with the same color. Using a *per-part* material binding type, you can shade the sides, top, and bottom of a cylinder with different colors. With a *per-face* material binding type, you can shade each face in an indexed face set with a different color.

Using a *per-vertex* material binding type, you can shade each vertex in a face, line, or point set with a different color. This enables you to create dramatic or subtle color variations across the front of a face, along the length of a line, or from point to point in a point set. For instance, if you create a triangular face with red at one vertex, green at a second, and blue at the third, the face will be shaded with a rainbow as it varies from red to green to blue across the triangle.

When you specify *per-part*, *per-face*, and *per-vertex* material binding types, the materials in the material list are used in order, one for each part, face, or vertex. For example, a cylinder is made up of these parts:

Part Index	*Part*
0	SIDES
1	TOP
2	BOTTOM

Using a *per-part* material binding type, material index 0 is bound to part 0 (sides), material index 1 to part 1 (top), and material index 2 to part 2 (bottom).

Materials are bound in a similar way when a *per-face* material binding type is specified for faces in an indexed face set. The first face in the set uses material index 0, the second uses material index 1, and so on. Similarly, when you specify a *per-vertex* material binding type, the materials are bound in order for each of the vertices listed in an **IndexedFaceSet** node, an **IndexedLineSet** node, or a **PointSet** node.

The *overall* material binding type always binds only the *first* material in a material list, regardless of the length of the material list or the number of parts, faces, or vertices in a shape. Everything in the shape is shaded with the first material.

Binding Materials to Indexed Shape Components

VRML supports three additional types of material binding to enable you to bind materials to indexed components of shapes:

- **Per-part indexed**—*Bind a different material to each part of the shape, specified by index*
- **Per-face indexed**—*Bind a different material to each face of the shape, specified by index*
- **Per-vertex indexed**—*Bind a different material to each vertex of the shape, specified by index*

For each part, face, or vertex in your shape, you can specify a material index corresponding to a material in a material list. This enables you to specify, for instance, that the 14th material be bound to the 1st face of a shape, the 5th material be bound to the 2nd face, and so on.

For example, using a *per-vertex indexed* material binding type, you can construct a triangle with an **IndexedFaceSet** node and bind a different material to each vertex with a material index list like this:

```
2, 0, 1
```

This material index list binds material index 2 to the first vertex, material index 0 to the second, and material index 1 to the third.

Binding Materials to Shapes

Using the **MaterialBinding** node you can specify how materials from a material list are bound to the parts, faces, or vertices of all subsequent shapes drawn by the VRML browser. For instance, the example text in Figure 15.1 specifies a *per-part* material binding type to color the sides, top, and bottom of a cylinder with different colors.

```
#VRML V1.0 ascii

Material {
      diffuseColor [
            1.0 0.0 0.0,
            0.0 1.0 0.0,
            0.0 0.0 1.0
      ]
}
MaterialBinding {
      value PER_PART
}
Cylinder {
}
```

Figure 15.1 *Binding a different color to each of the three parts of a cylinder.*

Notice the structure and order of the VRML file in Figure 15.1. Reading from the top of the file, the **Material** node lists three colors: red, green, and blue. The **MaterialBinding** node specifies the *per-part* material binding type. And the **Cylinder** node draws a cylinder, shading each of the cylinder's parts with a different color from the **Material** node's color list. In this case, the sides of the cylinder are shaded red, the top green, and the bottom blue.

Understanding the Extended **Material** Node Syntax

Up to this point, you've used **Material** nodes with only a single RGB color in the **diffuseColor** and **emissiveColor** fields and a single transparency factor in the **transparency** field. The same fields, however, can also specify a list of values by enclosing the list within square brackets and separating the values in the list with commas. This creates a material list for use during material binding.

SYNTAX **Material node**

```
Material {
    diffuseColor  0.8 0.8 0.8        # RGB color list
    emissiveColor 0.0 0.0 0.0        # RGB color list
    transparency  0.0                # transparency factor
    ambientColor  0.2 0.2 0.2        # RGB color list
    specularColor 0.0 0.0 0.0        # RGB color list
    shininess     0.2                # shininess factor
}
```

For instance, the previous example creates a list of three colors like this:

```
Material {
    diffuseColor [
        1.0 0.0 0.0,
        0.0 1.0 0.0,
        0.0 0.0 1.0
    ]
}
```

The entire material list is included in the material property. **Separator** nodes save and restore the whole material list, and shape nodes use the material list to bind different materials to different parts, faces, or vertices of a shape.

All fields in a **Material** node can specify lists of values. Value lists for each of the fields need not all be the same length. Typically, the **diffuseColor** field is specified using a list of RGB colors, but the **transparency** and other fields are specified with only a single value.

The VRML browser interprets **Material** node value lists differently if the lists are all the same or of different lengths.

Interpreting Field Value Lists of the Same Length

The following **Material** node specifies three diffuse colors, three emissive colors, and three transparency values with the indicated indices:

```
Material {
   diffuseColor [   # Diffuse color index
      1.0 0.0 0.0, # 0
      0.0 1.0 0.0, # 1
      0.0 0.0 1.0  # 2
   ]
   emissiveColor [ # Emissive color index
      0.0 0.5 0.5, # 0
      0.5 0.0 0.5, # 1
      0.5 0.5 0.0  # 2
   ]
   transparency [ # Transparency factor index
      0.0,         # 0
      0.5,         # 1
      0.0          # 2
   ]
}
```

Based on this indexed materials list, material index 0 comprises diffuse color index 0, emissive color index 0, and transparency factor index 0. Similarly material index 1 comprises diffuse color index 1, emissive color index 1, and transparency factor index 1. And so on, like this:

Material Index	*Diffuse Color*	*Emissive Color*	*Transparency*
0	0	0	0
1	1	1	1
2	2	2	2

If the VRML browser needs more materials than those listed, it picks materials by starting over from the beginning of the list. In the preceding example, if more than three materials are necessary, the browser reuses material index 0 for the third, material index 1 for the fourth, material index 2 for the fifth, material index 0 for the sixth, and so on, like this:

Material Index	*Diffuse Color*	*Emissive Color*	*Transparency*
3 (reuses 0)	0	0	0
4 (reuses 1)	1	1	1
5 (reuses 2)	2	2	2
6 (reuses 0)	0	0	0

Interpreting a Single Field Value List

Typically, only the **diffuseColor** field specifies a field value list. The remaining **Material** node fields are set to a single value. For instance, the following example sets three diffuse colors, but only one transparency and emissive color value:

```
Material {
   diffuseColor [   # Diffuse color index
      1.0 0.0 0.0, # 0
      0.0 1.0 0.0, # 1
      0.0 0.0 1.0  # 2
   ]
   emissiveColor 0.0 0.5 0.0 # Emissive color index 0
   transparency 0.0 # Transparency factor index 0
}
```

When the VRML browser looks up materials in this list, material index 0 comprises diffuse color index 0, emissive color index 0, and transparency factor index 0. Material index 1 comprises diffuse color index 1, emissive color index 0, and transparency factor index 0. Since there is only one value for the emissive and transparency fields, they are reused, like this:

Material Index	*Diffuse Color*	*Emissive Color*	*Transparency*
0	0	0	0
1	1	0 (reuse 0)	0 (reuse 0)
2	2	0 (reuse 0)	0 (reuse 0)

If the VRML browser needs more materials than those listed, it again picks materials by starting over from the beginning of the list, reusing values as necessary.

Interpreting Field Value Lists of Different Lengths

This is uncommon, but the VRML browser will handle field value lists of different lengths. For instance, the following **Material** node specifies three diffuse colors, two emissive colors, and one transparency factor:

```
Material {
   diffuseColor [   # Diffuse color index
      1.0 0.0 0.0, # 0
      0.0 1.0 0.0, # 1
      0.0 0.0 1.0  # 2
   ]
   emissiveColor [ # Emissive color index
      0.0 0.5 0.5, # 0
      0.5 0.0 0.5  # 1
   ]
   transparency 0.25 # Transparency factor index 0
}
```

Given the preceding material list, material index 0 comprises diffuse color index 0, emissive color index 0, and transparency factor index 0. Material index 1 comprises diffuse color index 1, emissive color index 1, and transparency factor index 0, which is reused.

Material index 2 comprises diffuse color index 2, emissive color index 1, and transparency factor index 0, reusing the emissive color and transparency factor, like this:

Material Index	*Diffuse Color*	*Emissive Color*	*Transparency*
0	0	0	0
1	1	1	0 (reuse 0)
2	2	1 (reuse 1)	0 (reuse 0)

If the VRML browser needs more materials than those listed, it again picks materials by starting over from the beginning of the list, reusing values as necessary, like this:

Material Index	*Diffuse Color*	*Emissive Color*	*Transparency*
3 (reuse 0)	0	0	0
4 (reuse 1)	1	1	0 (reuse 0)
5 (reuse 2)	2	1 (reuse 1)	0 (reuse 0)
6 (reuse 0)	0	0	0

TIP *This index cycling through value lists of different lengths can be confusing. Typically, this feature is not used. Most VRML files using material lists either specify equal length value lists for all **Material** node fields or set some fields to a single value and the others to value lists of equal length.*

TIP *In version 1.1 of VRML, material cycling and reuse may no longer be supported. Instead, you will provide one material for each material index you use.*

Understanding the **MaterialBinding** Node Syntax

The **MaterialBinding** node has a single **value** field whose value specifies the material binding type to use:

- **DEFAULT**—*Bind appropriately for the shape.*
- **OVERALL**—*Bind a single material to the entire shape.*
- **PER_PART**—*Bind a different material to each part of the shape.*
- **PER_FACE**—*Bind a different material to each face of the shape.*

- **PER_VERTEX**—*Bind a different material to each vertex of the shape.*
- **PER_PART_INDEXED**—*Bind a different material to each part of the shape, specified by index.*
- **PER_FACE_INDEXED**—*Bind a different material to each face of the shape, specified by index.*
- **PER_VERTEX_INDEXED**—*Bind a different material to each vertex of the shape, specified by index.*

SYNTAX **MaterialBinding node**

```
MaterialBinding {
    value DEFAULT       # binding type
}
```

The **OVERALL** material binding type uses the first material in the current material list and applies it to the entire shape. All of the examples in the previous chapters use an **OVERALL** material binding type.

The **PER_PART, PER_FACE,** and **PER_VERTEX** material binding types specify consecutive materials in the current material list and apply them to shape parts, faces, and vertices, in order. Material index 0 is bound to part, face, or vertex 0; material index 1 is bound to part, face, or vertex 1; and so on.

The **PER_PART_INDEXED, PER_FACE_INDEXED,** and **PER_VERTEX_INDEXED** material binding types specify particular material indexes from the current material list and apply them to shape parts, faces, and vertices. Material indexes are specified using the **materialIndex** field of **IndexedFaceSet** and **IndexedLineSet** nodes.

Each of the different shape nodes in VRML have their own default material binding type. When the **DEFAULT** material binding type is specified in a **MaterialBinding** node, the VRML browser uses the shape node's default material binding type. In most cases, this default is the same as the **OVERALL** material binding type. Each of the shape nodes is discussed in a later section along with their default material binding types.

Binding Materials to Primitive Shapes

Each of the primitive shapes responds somewhat differently to the different material binding types of a **MaterialBinding** node.

Cube Nodes

- ***DEFAULT***—*Same as* ***OVERALL****.*
- ***OVERALL***—*One material is bound to the entire cube.* If no material list was previously defined by a **Material** node, the default material list is

used. The default material list contains a single material with a diffuse color of white (`0.8 0.8 0.8`).

- ***PER_PART****—Materials are bound to the six faces one by one in this order:*

Index	*Part*
0	Front (+Z)
1	Back (–Z)
2	Left (–X)
3	Right (+X)
4	Top (+Y)
5	Bottom (–Y)

If no material list was previously defined by a **Material** node, the default material list is used. The default material list contains a single material with a diffuse color of white (`0.8 0.8 0.8`).

- ***PER_PART_INDEXED****—Same as* ***PER_PART.***
- ***PER_FACE****—Same as* ***PER_PART.***
- ***PER_FACE_INDEXED****—Same as* ***PER_PART.***
- ***PER_VERTEX****—Not applicable. Defaults to* **OVERALL.**
- ***PER_VERTEX_INDEXED****—Not applicable. Defaults to* **OVERALL.**

Cone Nodes

- ***DEFAULT****—Same as* **OVERALL.**
- **OVERALL***—One material is bound to the entire cone.* If no material list was previously defined by a **Material** node, the default material list is used. The default material list contains a single material with a diffuse color of white (`0.8 0.8 0.8`).
- ***PER_PART—Materials*** *are bound to the sides and bottom one by one in this order:*

Index	*Part*
0	Sides
1	Bottom

If no material list is currently defined by a **Material** node, the default material list is used. The default material list contains a single material with a diffuse color of white (`0.8 0.8 0.8`).

- ***PER_PART_INDEXED****—Same as* ***PER_PART.***
- ***PER_FACE****—Not applicable. Defaults to* **OVERALL.**

- ***PER_FACE_INDEXED**—Not applicable. Defaults to* **OVERALL.**
- ***PER_VERTEX**—Not applicable. Defaults to* **OVERALL.**
- ***PER_VERTEX_INDEXED**—Not applicable. Defaults to* **OVERALL.**

Cylinder Nodes

- ***DEFAULT**—Same as* **OVERALL.**
- ***OVERALL**—One material is bound to the entire cylinder.* If no material list was previously defined by a **Material** node, the default material list is used. The default material list contains a single material with a diffuse color of white (`0.8 0.8 0.8`).
- ***PER_PART**—Materials are bound to the sides, top, and bottom one by one in this order:*

Index	*Part*
0	Sides
1	Top
2	Bottom

  If no material list was previously defined by a **Material** node, the default material list is used. The default material list contains a single material with a diffuse color of white (`0.8 0.8 0.8`).
- ***PER_PART_INDEXED**—Same as* **PER_PART.**
- ***PER_FACE**—Not applicable. Defaults to* **OVERALL.**
- ***PER_FACE_INDEXED**—Not applicable. Defaults to* **OVERALL.**
- ***PER_VERTEX**—Not applicable. Defaults to* **OVERALL.**
- ***PER_VERTEX_INDEXED**—Not applicable. Defaults to* **OVERALL.**

Sphere Nodes

- ***DEFAULT**—Same as* **OVERALL.**
- ***OVERALL**—One material is bound to the entire sphere.* If no material list was previously defined by a **Material** node, the default material list is used. The default material list contains a single material with a diffuse color of white (`0.8 0.8 0.8`).
- ***PER_PART**—Not applicable. Defaults to* **OVERALL.**
- ***PER_PART_INDEXED**—Not applicable. Defaults to* **OVERALL.**
- ***PER_FACE**—Not applicable. Defaults to* **OVERALL.**
- ***PER_FACE_INDEXED**—Not applicable. Defaults to* **OVERALL.**
- ***PER_VERTEX**—Not applicable. Defaults to* **OVERALL.**
- ***PER_VERTEX_INDEXED**—Not applicable. Defaults to* **OVERALL.**

Notice that many of the material binding types are not applicable to some or all of the primitive shapes. A sphere, for instance, has no parts, so **PER_PART** and **PER_PART_INDEXED** material binding types do not apply to it. All of the primitive shapes use faces to generate their parts, but only the **Cube** node recognizes the **PER_FACE** and **PER_FACE_INDEXED** material binding types to color each of those faces differently.

VRML does not allow you to specify **PER_FACE** or **PER_FACE_INDEXED** material binding types on the cylinder, cone, and sphere primitive shapes, because the number of faces used to construct the primitive shapes varies from VRML browser to VRML browser, and possibly from computer to computer. On a slower computer, your VRML browser may choose to use fewer faces to speed up drawing. On a faster computer, a browser may use many faces to make shapes smoother. Since the number of faces varies from situation to situation, it is impossible for you to reliably specify each face and shade it a particular color.

Notice that none of the primitive shapes use the **PER_VERTEX** and **PER_VERTEX_INDEXED** material binding types. These types are used only when shading shapes created with the **IndexedFaceSet**, **IndexedLineSet,** and **PointSet** nodes. This is because the VRML browser may use more or fewer faces when building cylinders, cones, and spheres. If it uses more faces, it requires more vertices. With less faces, it requires fewer vertices. Since the actual number of vertices used to build a shape varies from VRML browser to VRML browser, and from computer to computer, it isn't possible for you to predict the number of vertices and reliably shade each one with a specific color.

The **PER_PART_INDEXED** and **PER_FACE_INDEXED** material binding types are designed for use with the **IndexedFaceSet** and **IndexedLineSet** nodes. For the primitive shapes, each of these material binding types is identical to the **PER_PART** and **PER_FACE** types, respectively.

When you bind materials to primitive shapes, you typically follow one of two approaches:

- *Shade all the parts of a primitive shape using the first color in the current material list.* This is the easiest and most common approach. Leave the material binding type set to **DEFAULT,** and don't specify a **MaterialBinding** node. All of the primitive shapes created in previous chapters use this approach.
- *Provide your own material for every shape part.* Set the material binding type to **PER_PART** with a **MaterialBinding** node. List the materials in a **Material** node, one per part, and arranged to correspond with the ordering of parts particular to that shape node. The first material is bound to the first part, the second is bound to the second part, and so on. Then let the VRML browser color each part with the appropriate material.

Binding Materials to Text Shapes

Text shapes created with the **AsciiText** node are always shaded with a single overall material, regardless of the current material binding type:

- *DEFAULT—Same as* **OVERALL.**
- *OVERALL—One material is bound to the entire block of text.* If no material list was previously defined by a **Material** node, the default material list is used. The default material list contains a single material with a diffuse color of white (`0.8 0.8 0.8`).
- *PER_PART—Not applicable. Defaults to* **OVERALL.**
- *PER_PART_INDEXED—Not applicable. Defaults to* **OVERALL.**
- *PER_FACE—Not applicable. Defaults to* **OVERALL.**
- *PER_FACE_INDEXED—Not applicable. Defaults to* **OVERALL.**
- *PER_VERTEX—Not applicable. Defaults to* **OVERALL.**
- *PER_VERTEX_INDEXED—Not applicable. Defaults to* **OVERALL.**

Binding Materials to Point Sets

The individual points of a **PointSet** node may be shaded differently based on the material binding type:

- *DEFAULT—Same as* **OVERALL.**
- *OVERALL—One material is bound to the entire set of points.* If no material list was previously defined by a **Material** node, the default material list is used. The default material list contains a single material with a diffuse color of white (`0.8 0.8 0.8`). The material in the current material list corresponding to the value of the **startIndex** field is used to color all points in the point set. If no material list was previously defined by a **Material** node, the default material list is used. The default material list contains a single material with a diffuse color of white (`0.8 0.8 0.8`). The material in the current material list corresponding to the value of the **startIndex** field is used to color all points in the point set. The second vertex is shaded with the material at **startIndex**+1, the third at **startIndex**+2, and so on.
- *PER_PART—Same as* **PER_VERTEX.**
- *PER_PART_INDEXED—Same as* **PER_VERTEX.**
- *PER_FACE—Same as* **PER_VERTEX.**
- *PER_FACE_INDEXED—Same as* **PER_VERTEX.**
- *PER_VERTEX—A different material is bound to each point vertex in the point set.*
- *PER_VERTEX_INDEXED—Same as* **PER_VERTEX.**

When you bind materials to point sets, you typically follow one of two approaches:

- *Shade all the points of a point set using the first color in the current material list.* This is the easiest and most common approach. Leave the material binding type set to **DEFAULT**, don't specify a **MaterialBinding** node, and provide only one material in a **Material** node. All of the point sets created in previous chapters use this approach.

- *Provide your own material for every vertex.* Set the material binding type to **PER_VERTEX** a **MaterialBinding** node. List the materials in a **Material** node, one per vertex, arranged to correspond with the vertex coordinates of the current coordinates property. The first material is bound to the first vertex, the second is bound to the second vertex, and so on. The browser then uses the **startIndex** field for coordinates and their associated materials.

Binding Materials to Shapes Using Material Indexing

Using material indexing, you can bind specific materials to each face or line in an **IndexedFaceSet** node or an **IndexedLineSet** node. To specify material indexes for these components, use the **materialIndex** field of both of these nodes. For instance, the text in Figure 15.2 uses a **PER_FACE_INDEXED** material binding type to bind a different color to each triangular face in a face set.

```
#VRML V1.0 ascii

Coordinate3 {
	point [
		 0.0 1.0 0.0,
		-1.0 0.0 0.0,
		-0.2 0.0 0.0,
		 0.2 0.0 0.0,
		 1.0 0.0 0.0
	]
}
Material {
	diffuseColor [
		1.0 0.0 0.0,
		0.0 1.0 0.0,
		0.0 0.0 1.0,
		1.0 1.0 0.0,
		0.0 1.0 1.0,
		1.0 0.0 1.0,
		1.0 1.0 1.0,
		0.5 0.5 0.5,
		0.1 0.1 0.1
	]
}
MaterialBinding {
	value PER_FACE_INDEXED
}
```

Figure 15.2 continues

```
IndexedFaceSet {
      coordIndex [
            0, 1, 2, -1,  # Triangle 1
            0, 3, 4       # Triangle 2
      ]
      materialIndex [
            3,            # Triangle 1
            7             # Triangle 2
      ]
}
```

Figure 15.2 *Binding a different color to each face in a set.*

Notice the structure and order of the VRML file in Figure 15.2. Reading from the top of the file, the **Coordinate3** node lists four vertices and the **Material** node lists nine materials. The **MaterialBinding** node specifies the **PER_FACE_INDEXED** material binding type. Finally, the **IndexedFaceSet** node draws two triangles, shading the first one with material index 3, and the second with material index 7. The first triangle is drawn in yellow and the second in gray.

Understanding the Extended IndexedFaceSet Node Syntax

The **IndexedFaceSet** node has four fields: **coordIndex, materialIndex, normalIndex,** and **textureCoordIndex.**

SYNTAX **IndexedFaceSet node**

```
IndexedFaceSet {
   coordIndex           [0]    # coordinate index list
   materialIndex        -1     # material index list
   normalIndex          -1     # normal index list
   textureCoordIndex    -1     # texture index list
}
```

The **coordIndex** field is discussed in Chapter 14 and works the same when using material binding.

The **normalIndex** and **textureCoordIndex** fields are discussed in later chapters.

The **materialIndex** field specifies a list of material indexes, listed within square brackets and separated by commas. Each material index specifies a color from the current material list. A material index of 0, for instance, specifies the first material in the current material list. Material index 1 specifies the second, and so on.

Materials and material indexes are used differently depending on the material binding type chosen for the face set.

- ***DEFAULT****—Same as* ***OVERALL****.*
- ***OVERALL****—One material is bound to the entire set of faces.* If no material list was previously defined by a **Material** node, the default material list is used. The default material list contains a single material with a diffuse color

of white (`0.8 0.8 0.8`). All faces in the face set are shaded using the first material in the current material list. The **materialIndex** field is unused.

- ***PER_PART***—*Same as* ***PER_FACE.***
- ***PER_PART_INDEXED***—*Same as* ***PER_FACE_INDEXED.***
- ***PER_FACE***—*A different material is bound to each face in the face set.* If no material list was previously defined by a **Material** node, the default material list is used. The default material list contains a single material with a diffuse color of white (`0.8 0.8 0.8`).

  The first material in the current material list is bound to the first face, the second material is bound to the second face, and so on. The **materialIndex** field is unused.
- ***PER_FACE_INDEXED***—*A different material, specified by a material index, is bound to each face in the face set.* If no material list was previously defined by a **Material** node, the default material list is used. The default material list contains a single material with a diffuse color of white (`0.8 0.8 0.8`). Material indexes in the **materialIndex** field specify a material from the current material list to bind to each face of the face set. The first index in the field specifies the material bound to the first face, the second index bound to the second face, and so on. If the **materialIndex** field is not set, the coordinate indexes of the **coordIndex** field are used instead. The first coordinate index specifies the material for the first face, the second coordinate index for the second face, and so on.
- ***PER_VERTEX***—*A different material is bound to each vertex in the face set.* If no material list was previously defined by a **Material** node, the default material list is used. The default material list contains a single material with a diffuse color of white (`0.8 0.8 0.8`). The first material in the current material list is bound to the first vertex, the second material is bound to the second vertex, and so on. The **materialIndex** field is unused.
- ***PER_VERTEX_INDEXED***—*A different material, specified by a material index, is bound to each vertex in the face set.* If no material list was previously defined by a **Material** node, the default material list is used. The default material list contains a single material with a diffuse color of white (`0.8 0.8 0.8`). Material indexes in the **materialIndex** field specify a material from the current material list to bind to each vertex of each face of the face set. The first index in the field specifies the material bound to the first vertex, the second index bound to the second vertex, and so on. A material index must correspond with each vertex and each -1 face divider value in the vertex list. If the **materialIndex** field is not set, the coordinate indexes of the **coordIndex** field are used instead. The first coordinate index specifies the material for the first vertex, the second coordinate index specifies the material for the second vertex, and so on.

TIP *When you use **DEFAULT, PER_PART_INDEXED, PER_FACE_INDEXED,** and **PER_VERTEX_INDEXED** material binding types, material indexes are specified in the **materialIndex** field, one for each face or vertex. If there are more faces or vertices in the **IndexedFaceSet** node than material indexes in the **materialIndex** field, unpredictable results may occur. Some VRML browsers detect this problem and report an error. Others do not. If you are using materials and material indexing, be sure you specify at least one material index for each face or vertex in the **IndexedFaceSet** node, depending on the material binding type you are using.*

TIP *When you use **DEFAULT** and **PER_VERTEX_INDEXED** material binding types, you must specify a material index in the **materialIndex** field for each vertex, including the –1 value indexes used to mark the end of one face's vertices and the start of the next face's vertices.*

Notice that the **DEFAULT, PER_PART_INDEXED, PER_FACE_INDEXED,** and **PER_VERTEX_INDEXED** material binding types can all use the coordinate indexes in the **coordIndex** field as material indexes if you don't provide explicit material indexes in the **materialIndex** field. This is convenient when you create shaded shapes that have a unique material in a **Material** node for each vertex of the shape described in a corresponding **Coordinate3** node.

TIP *Using the **coordIndex** field's values as material indexes with the **PER_PART_INDEXED** and **PER_FACE_INDEXED** material binding types may cause unexpected results. The first **coordIndex** field value specifies the material for the first face. The second **coordIndex** field value specifies the material for the second face, even though that **coordIndex** field value is actually the second vertex of the first face. When using materials and these material binding types, include explicit material indexes for each face within the **materialIndex** field.*

When you bind materials to face sets, you typically follow one of three approaches:

- *Shade all the faces of a face set using the first color in the current material list.* This is the easiest approach. Leave the material binding type set to **DEFAULT,** don't specify a **MaterialBinding** node, and provide only one material in a **Material** node. All of the face sets created in previous chapters have used this approach.
- *Provide your own material for every vertex.* Set the material binding type to **PER_VERTEX_INDEXED** with a **MaterialBinding** node. List the materials in a **Material** node, one per vertex, arranged to correspond with the vertex coordinates in a neighboring **Coordinate3** node. The first material is bound to the first vertex, the second is bound to the second vertex, and so on. Don't specify values the **materialIndex** field of the **IndexedFaceSet** node, and let the VRML browser use the **coordIndex** field to specify both coordinates and their associated materials.

- *Provide your own material for every vertex.* Set the material binding type to **PER_VERTEX_INDEXED** with a **MaterialBinding** node. List the materials in a **Material** node in any order, then specify in the **materialIndex** field of the **IndexedFaceSet** node the appropriate material to bind to each vertex. Be sure to include one material index for every coordinate in the **coordIndex** field, including –1 face divider coordinate indexes.

Typically, the **PER_PART, PER_PART_INDEXED, PER_FACE,** and **PER_FACE_INDEXED** material binding types are rarely used. Instead, use a **PER_VERTEX** or **PER_VERTEX_INDEXED** material binding type to provide a different color for each vertex of each face in the face set.

Understanding the Extended **IndexedLineSet** Node Syntax

The **IndexedLineSet** node has four fields: **coordIndex, materialIndex, normalIndex,** and **textureCoordIndex.**

SYNTAX **IndexedLineSet node**

```
IndexedLineSet {
   coordIndex          [0]       # coordinate index list
   materialIndex       -1        # material index list
   normalIndex         -1        # normal index list
   textureCoordIndex   -1        # texture index list
}
```

The **coordIndex** field is discussed in Chapter 14 and works the same when using material binding.

The **normalIndex** and **textureCoordIndex** fields are discussed in later chapters.

The **materialIndex** field specifies a list of material indexes, listed within square brackets and separated by commas. Each material index specifies a color from the current material list. A material index of 0, for instance, specifies the first material in the current material list. Material index 1 specifies the second, and so on.

Materials and material indexes are used differently depending on the material binding type chosen for the line set:

- ***DEFAULT****—Same as* **OVERALL.**
- ***OVERALL****—One material is bound to the entire set of lines.* If no material list was previously defined by a **Material** node, the default material list is used. The default material list contains a single material with a diffuse color of white (`0.8 0.8 0.8`). All lines in the line set are shaded using the first material in the current material list. The **materialIndex** field is unused.
- ***PER_PART****—A different material is bound to each line segment in the line set.* If no material list was previously defined by a **Material** node, the

default material list is used. The default material list contains a single material with a diffuse color of white (`0.8 0.8 0.8`). The first material in the current material list is bound to the first line segment, the second material is bound to the second line segment, and so on. The **materialIndex** field is unused.

- *PER_PART_INDEXED—A different material, specified by a material index, is bound to each line segment in the line set.* If no material list was previously defined by a **Material** node, the default material list is used. The default material list contains a single material with a diffuse color of white (`0.8 0.8 0.8`). Material indexes in the **materialIndex** field specify a material from the current material list for each line segment of the line set. The first index in the field specifies the material bound to the first line segment, the second index bound to the second line segment, and so on. If the **materialIndex** field is not set, the coordinate indexes of the **coordIndex** field are used instead. The first coordinate index specifies the material for the first line segment, the second coordinate index for the second line segment, and so on.
- *PER_FACE—A different material is bound to each polyline in the line set.* If no material list was previously defined by a **Material** node, the default material list is used. The default material list contains a single material with a diffuse color of white (`0.8 0.8 0.8`). The first material in the current material list is bound to the first polyline (including all of its line segments), the second material is bound to the second polyline, and so on. The **materialIndex** field is unused.
- *PER_FACE_INDEXED—A different material, specified by a material index, is bound to each polyline in the line set.* If no material list was previously defined by a **Material** node, the default material list is used. The default material list contains a single material with a diffuse color of white (`0.8 0.8 0.8`). Material indexes in the **materialIndex** field specify a material from the current material list for each polyline (including all of its line segments) of the line set. The first index in the field specifies the material bound to for the first polyline, the second index bound to for the second polyline, and so on. If the **materialIndex** field is not set, the coordinate indexes of the **coordIndex** field are used instead. The first coordinate index specifies the material for the first polyline, the second coordinate index for the second polyline, and so on.
- *PER_VERTEX—A different material is bound to each vertex in the line set.* If no material list was previously defined by a **Material** node, the default material list is used. The default material list contains a single material with a diffuse color of white (`0.8 0.8 0.8`). The first material in the current material list is bound to the first vertex, the second material is bound to the second vertex, and so on. The **materialIndex** field is unused.

- ***PER_VERTEX_INDEXED—A different material, specified by a material index, is bound to each vertex in the line set.*** If no material list was previously defined by a **Material** node, the default material list is used. The default material list contains a single material with a diffuse color of white (`0.8 0.8 0.8`). Material indexes in the **materialIndex** field specify a material from the current material list for each vertex of each polyline of the line set. The first index in the field specifies the material for the first vertex, the second index for the second vertex, and so on. A material index is needed to match each vertex and each –1 polyline divider value in the vertex list. If the **materialIndex** field is not set, the coordinate indexes of the **coordIndex** field are used instead. The first coordinate index specifies the material for the first vertex, the second coordinate index for the second vertex, and so on.

TIP *When you use **DEFAULT, PER_PART_INDEXED, PER_FACE_INDEXED,** and **PER_VERTEX_INDEXED** material binding types, material indexes are specified in the **materialIndex** field, one for each polyline or vertex. If there are more line segments or vertices in the **IndexedLineSet** node than material indexes in the **materialIndex** field, unpredictable results may occur. Some VRML browsers detect this problem and report an error. Others do not. If you are using materials and material indexing, be sure you specify at least one material index for each polyline or vertex in the **IndexedLineSet** node, depending on the material binding type you are using.*

TIP *When you use **DEFAULT** and **PER_VERTEX_INDEXED** material binding types, you must specify a material index in the **materialIndex** field for each vertex, including the –1 value indexes used to mark the end of one polyline's vertices and the start of the next polyline's vertices.*

Notice that the **DEFAULT, PER_PART_INDEXED, PER_FACE_INDEXED,** and **PER_VERTEX_INDEXED** material binding types can all use the coordinate indexes in the **coordIndex** field as material indexes if you don't provide explicit material indexes in the **materialIndex** field. This is convenient when you create shaded shapes that have a unique material in a **Material** node for each vertex of the shape described in a corresponding **Coordinate3** node.

TIP *Using the **coordIndex** field's values as material indexes with the **PER_PART_INDEXED** and **PER_FACE_INDEXED** material binding types may cause unexpected results. The first **coordIndex** field value specifies the material for the first polyline. The second **coordIndex** field value specifies the material for the second polyline, even though that **coordIndex** field value is actually the second vertex of the first face. When using materials and these material binding types, include explicit material indexes for each line segment within the **materialIndex** field.*

When you bind materials to face sets, you typically follow one of three approaches:

- *Shade all the lines of a line set using the first color in the current material list.* This is the easiest approach. Leave the material binding type set to **DEFAULT**, don't specify a **MaterialBinding** node, and provide only one material in a **Material** node. All of the line sets created in previous chapters use this approach.
- *Provide your own material for every vertex.* Set the material binding type to **PER_VERTEX_INDEXED** with a **MaterialBinding** node. List the materials in a **Material** node, one per vertex, arranged to correspond with the vertex coordinates in a neighboring **Coordinate3** node. The first material is bound to the first vertex, the second is bound to the second vertex, and so on. Don't specify values in the **materialIndex** field of the **IndexedLineSet** node, and let the VRML browser use the **coordIndex** field to specify both coordinates and their associated materials.
- *Provide your own material for every vertex.* Set the material binding type to **PER_VERTEX_INDEXED** with a **MaterialBinding** node. List the materials in a **Material** node in any order, then specify in the **materialIndex** field of the **IndexedLineSet** node the correct material indexes so that the appropriate material is bound to each vertex. Be sure to include one material index for every coordinate in the **coordIndex** field, including –1 polyline divider coordinate indexes.

Typically, the **PER_PART, PER_PART_INDEXED, PER_FACE,** and **PER_FACE_INDEXED** material binding types are rarely used. Use a single color and an **OVERALL** material binding type, or use a **PER_VERTEX** or **PER_VERTEX_INDEXED** material binding type in order to provide a different color for each vertex of each line in the line set.

Experimenting with Material Binding and Material Indexing

The following examples provide a more detailed examination of the ways in which material binding and material indexing features can be used and how they interact with nodes we've discussed in previous chapters.

Coloring the Parts of a Cylinder

The example text in Figure 15.3 colors the sides, top, and bottom of a cylinder with different colors by using a **PER_PART** material binding type.

```
#VRML V1.0 ascii

Material {
      diffuseColor [
            1.0 0.0 0.0,
            0.0 1.0 0.0,
            0.0 0.0 1.0
      ]
}
MaterialBinding {
      value PER_PART
}
Cylinder {
}
```

Figure 15.3 *A cylinder with each of its parts colored differently.*

Reading from the top of the file, the VRML browser is directed to:

1. Set the materials property to three materials.
2. Specify **PER_PART** material binding.
3. Draw a cylinder using the current material binding type and materials list.
   a. Shade the sides of the cylinder with material index 0 (red).
   b. Shade the top of the cylinder with material index 1 (green).
   c. Shade the bottom of the cylinder with material index 2 (blue).

Coloring the Parts of a Cube

Using the same approach used for the cylinder, you can shade each side of a cube differently. The example text in Figure 15.4 uses a **PER_PART** material binding type and a list of six colors.

```
#VRML V1.0 ascii

Material {
      diffuseColor [
            0.0 0.0 0.6, # for front
            0.8 0.8 0.8, # for back
            0.0 0.6 0.0, # for left
            0.8 0.8 0.0, # for right
            0.7 0.0 0.0, # for top
            1.0 0.2 0.0  # for bottom
      ]
}
MaterialBinding {
      value PER_PART
}
Cube {
}
```

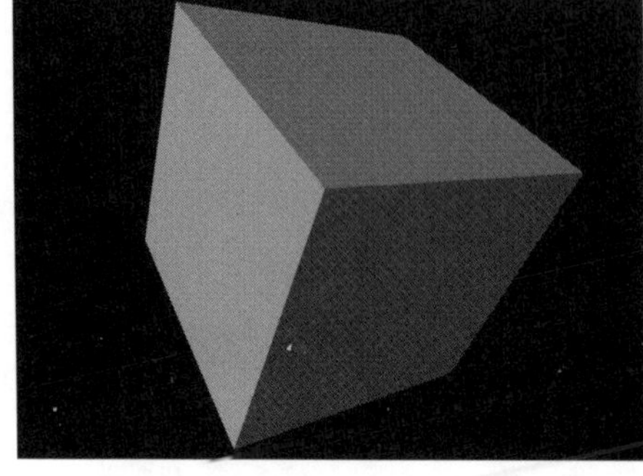

Figure 15.4 *A cube drawn with each part a different color.*

Reading from the top of the file, the VRML browser is directed to:

1. Set the materials property to six materials.
2. Specify **PER_PART** material binding.
3. Draw a cube using the current material binding type and materials list.
   a. Shade the front with material index 0 (blue).
   b. Shade the back with material index 1 (white).
   c. Shade the left side with material index 2 (green).
   d. Shade the right side with material index 3 (yellow).
   e. Shade the top with material index 4 (red).
   f. Shade the bottom with material index 5 (orange).

Coloring More Than One Shape's Parts

The material binding type specified within a **MaterialBinding** node applies until it is changed by another **MaterialBinding** node. While the material binding type is in effect, you can color the parts of more than one shape. For instance, using the same materials, material binding type, and cube, you can add a cone and shade its sides and bottom using different colors. The result is shown in Figure 15.5 and in color plate 2*d*.

```
#VRML V1.0 ascii

Material {
        diffuseColor [
                0.0 0.0 0.6, # for front
                0.8 0.8 0.8, # for back
                0.0 0.6 0.0, # for left
                0.8 0.8 0.0, # for right
                0.7 0.0 0.0, # for top
                1.0 0.2 0.0  # for bottom
        ]
}
MaterialBinding {
        value PER_PART
}
Cube {
}
Translation {
        translation 2.0 0.0 0.0
}
Cone {
}
```

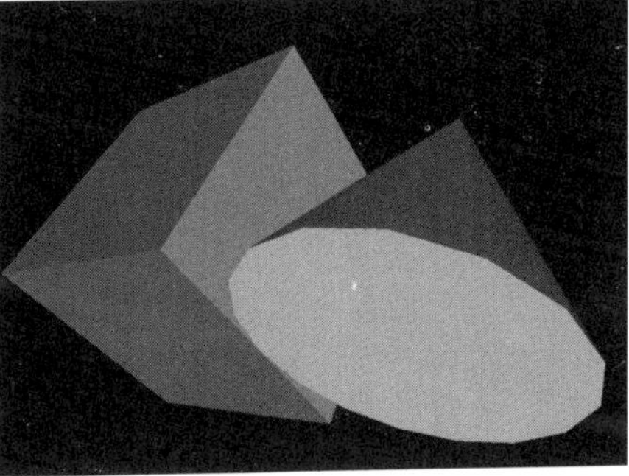

Figure 15.5 *A cube and cone, each with all sides colored differently.*

Coloring Points in a Point Set

Using a **PER_VERTEX** material binding type, you can color differently each of the points of the star field from Chapter 14, as shown in Figure 15.6.

```
#VRML V1.0 ascii
Coordinate3 {
      point [
            0.18 -0.53  0.17,
            0.23 -0.12 -0.39,
           -0.37  0.54  0.65,
            0.78  0.15  0.31,
           -0.92  0.40  0.79,
            0.87  0.67  0.58,
           -0.36 -0.83 -0.46,
            0.13 -0.96  0.41,
            0.76  0.03 -0.76,
           -0.59 -0.96 -0.06,
           -0.92  0.12  0.25,
           -0.24 -0.41  0.43,
           -0.38 -0.16  0.70,
           -0.40  0.24 -0.23,
           -0.30  0.04  0.40,
            0.73  0.23  0.97,
            0.43  0.81 -0.28,
           -0.86  0.21 -0.29,
            0.22  0.72 -0.99,
           -0.43  0.86  0.98,
           -0.43 -0.46 -0.99,
            0.60 -0.45  0.08,
           -0.15 -0.94  0.99,
           -0.80  0.38 -0.53,
           -0.59 -0.14  0.71,
           -0.70 -0.96  0.74,
            0.64  0.19 -0.28,
            0.29  0.42 -0.44,
            0.49  0.42 -0.26,
           -0.98 -0.38  0.35,
      ]
}
Material {
      diffuseColor [
            1.0 0.0 0.0,
            0.0 1.0 0.0,
            0.0 0.0 1.0
      ]
}
MaterialBinding {
      value PER_VERTEX
}
```

Figure 15.6 continues

```
PointSet {
      startIndex 0
      numPoints 30
}
```

Figure 15.6 *A colored star field.*

Notice that while there are 30 points in the point set, there are only three materials in the material list. The VRML browser assigns the three materials to the first three points, then starts the material list again from the beginning and assigns the three materials to the second three points, then the third three points, and so on.

Using this colored star field, you can create a swirling galactic cluster by instancing the same colored star pattern repeatedly, as shown in Chapter 14. The result is shown in Figure 15.7.

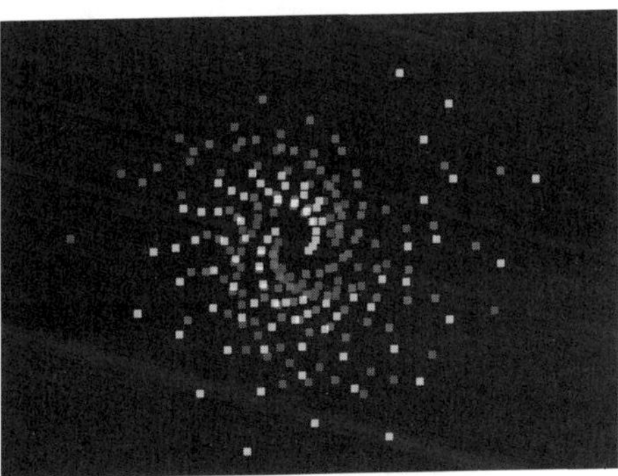

Figure 15.7 *A swirling multicolored star field.*

Using Separators with Material Binding Types

Using a **Separator** node, you can save and restore the current material binding type. For instance, the example text in Figure 15.8 draws two cubes side by side. The first cube is drawn within a **Separator** node with an **OVERALL** material binding type. The second cube is drawn outside the **Separator** node with a **PER_PART** material binding type, which is set *before* the **Separator** node. Because the **Separator** node saves and restores the material binding type, the type chosen before the separator also applies to nodes following the **Separator** node.

```
#VRML V1.0 ascii

Material {
	diffuseColor [
		0.0 0.0 0.6, # for front
		0.8 0.8 0.8, # for back
		0.0 0.6 0.0, # for left
		0.8 0.8 0.0, # for right
		0.7 0.0 0.0, # for top
		1.0 0.2 0.0  # for bottom
	]
}
MaterialBinding {
	value PER_PART
}
Separator {
	MaterialBinding {
		value OVERALL
	}
	Cube {
	}
}
Translation {
	translation 3.0 0.0 0.0
}
Cube {
}
```

Figure 15.8 *Two cubes drawn with different material binding types by using a **Separator** node.*

The first cube is drawn using an **OVERALL** material binding type. So, only the first material is used and the entire cube is drawn in the first material's color: blue. The second cube is drawn using a **PER_PART** material binding type, creating the multicolored cube again.

Changing the Material Binding Type More Than Once

You can change the material binding type any number of times within the same VRML file. The example text in Figure 15.9, for instance, creates a book from a cube and labels the book with text. Using a **PER_PART** material binding type for the cube, the front, back, and left side of the cube are shaded brown to form the cover of the book. The remaining cube sides are shaded beige to form the page edges. Once the book is complete, the material binding type is set back to **DEFAULT** and two **AsciiText** nodes are used to add the book's front cover and spine titles. The resulting book is shown in Figure 15.9.

```
#VRML V1.0 ascii

# Book
Separator {
      Material {
            diffuseColor [
                  0.2 0.1 0.0, # Front
                  0.2 0.1 0.0, # Back
                  0.2 0.1 0.0, # Left
                  0.8 0.6 0.3, # Right
                  0.8 0.6 0.3, # Top
                  0.8 0.6 0.3, # Bottom
            ]
      }
      MaterialBinding {
            value PER_PART
      }
      Cube {
            width 0.6
            height 1.0
            depth 0.15
      }
}
# Cover
Material {
      diffuseColor 0.8 0.8 0.8
}
MaterialBinding {
      value DEFAULT
}
Separator {
      Translation {
            translation 0.0 0.31 0.08
      }
      FontStyle {
            size 0.1
            family SANS
            style ITALIC
      }
      AsciiText {
            string [ "The", "VRML", "Sourcebook" ]
            spacing 1.2
            justification CENTER
      }
}
# Binding
Separator {
      Translation {
            translation -0.31 0.0 -0.02
      }
```

Figure 15.9 continues

```
        Rotation {
              #          X            +90.0 degrees
              rotation 1.0 0.0 0.0  1.57
        }
        Rotation {
              #               Y       -90.0 degrees
              rotation 0.0 1.0 0.0 -1.57
        }
        FontStyle {
              size 0.07
              family SANS
              style ITALIC
        }
        AsciiText {
              string "The VRML Sourcebook"
              justification CENTER
        }
  }
```

Figure 15.9 *A book created from a multicolored cube.*

Coloring Two Triangles in Various Ways

The next series of examples all use two triangles to illustrate several material binding types for the **IndexedFaceSet** and **IndexedLineSet** nodes.

Coloring Faces in a Face Set

Using **PER_FACE** and **PER_FACE_INDEXED** material binding types, you can color each of the individual faces in a face set. For example, using two triangles, each triangle can be shaded a different color, as shown in Figure 15.10.

```
#VRML V1.0 ascii

Coordinate3 {
      point [
             0.0 1.0 0.0,
            -1.0 0.0 0.0,
            -0.2 0.0 0.0,
             0.2 0.0 0.0,
             1.0 0.0 0.0
      ]
}
Material {
      diffuseColor [
            1.0 0.0 0.0,
            0.0 1.0 0.0,
            0.0 0.0 1.0,
            1.0 1.0 0.0,
            0.0 1.0 1.0,
            1.0 0.0 1.0,
```

Figure 15.10 continues

```
                1.0 1.0 1.0,
                0.5 0.5 0.5,
                1.0 0.2 0.1
        ]
}
MaterialBinding {
        value PER_FACE
}
IndexedFaceSet {
        coordIndex [
                0, 1, 2, -1, # Triangle 1
                0, 3, 4 # Triangle 2
        ]
}
```

Figure 15.10 *Two triangular faces, each shaded differently.*

Reading from the top of the file, the VRML browser is directed to:

1. Set the coordinates property to five coordinates.
2. Set the materials property to nine materials.
3. Specify the **PER_FACE** material binding type.
4. Draw a list of faces using the current material binding type and materials list.
   a. Draw a face with vertices 0, 1, and 2 using material index 0 (red).
   b. Draw a face with vertices 0, 3, and 4 using material index 1 (green).

The result is two triangles as shown in color plate 2*e*.

When you use a **PER_FACE** material binding type, the VRML browser always uses the first material for the first face, the second material for the second face, and so forth. You can, instead, choose specific materials for each face by using a **PER_FACE_INDEXED** material binding type. Material indexes for the faces are specified in a **materialIndex** field in the **IndexedFaceSet** node.

The example text in Figure 15.11 shades the first triangle with material index 3, and the second with material index 7.

```
#VRML V1.0 ascii

Coordinate3 {
        point [
                 0.0 1.0 0.0,
                -1.0 0.0 0.0,
                -0.2 0.0 0.0,
                 0.2 0.0 0.0,
                 1.0 0.0 0.0
        ]
}
```

Figure 15.11 continues

```
Material {
      diffuseColor [
            1.0 0.0 0.0,
            0.0 1.0 0.0,
            0.0 0.0 1.0,
            1.0 1.0 0.0,
            0.0 1.0 1.0,
            1.0 0.0 1.0,
            1.0 1.0 1.0,
            0.5 0.5 0.5,
            1.0 0.2 0.1
      ]
}
MaterialBinding {
      value PER_FACE_INDEXED
}
IndexedFaceSet {
      coordIndex [
            0, 1, 2, -1, # Triangle 1
            0, 3, 4      # Triangle 2
      ]
      materialIndex [
            3,           # Triangle 1
            7            # Triangle 2
      ]
}
```

Figure 15.11 *Two triangles shaded differently.*

Reading from the top of the file, the VRML browser is directed to:

1. Set the coordinates property to five coordinates.
2. Set the materials property to nine materials.
3. Specify the **PER_FACE_INDEXED** material binding type.
4. Draw a list of faces using the current material binding type and materials list.
   a. Draw a face with vertices 0, 1, and 2 using material index 3 (yellow).
   b. Draw a face with vertices 0, 3, and 4 using material index 7 (gray).

The result is again two triangles as shown in color plate 2*f*.

Coloring Vertices in a Face Set

Using **PER_VERTEX** and **PER_VERTEX_INDEXED** material binding types, you can color each of the vertices in a face set. When the vertices of a single face have different colors, the VRML browser automatically creates a color gradation that smoothly varies from one vertex color to the next across the face. This can create interesting rainbow effects when the vertex colors are dramatically different.

For example, each triangle vertex can be shaded a different color, as shown in Figure 15.12.

```
#VRML V1.0 ascii

Coordinate3 {
        point [
                 0.0 1.0 0.0,
                -1.0 0.0 0.0,
                -0.2 0.0 0.0,
                 0.2 0.0 0.0,
                 1.0 0.0 0.0
        ]
}
Material {
        diffuseColor [
                1.0 0.0 0.0,
                0.0 1.0 0.0,
                0.0 0.0 1.0,
                1.0 1.0 0.0,
                0.0 1.0 1.0,
                1.0 0.0 1.0,
                1.0 1.0 1.0,
                0.5 0.5 0.5,
                1.0 0.2 0.1
        ]
}
MaterialBinding {
        value PER_VERTEX
}
IndexedFaceSet {
        coordIndex [
                0, 1, 2, -1, # Triangle 1
                0, 3, 4      # Triangle 2
        ]
}
```

Figure 15.12 *Two triangles with each vertex shaded a different color.*

Reading from the top of the file, the VRML browser is directed to:

1. Set the coordinates property to five coordinates.
2. Set the materials property to nine materials.
3. Specify the **PER_VERTEX** material binding type.
4. Draw a list of faces using the current material binding type and materials list.
   a. Draw a face with vertices 0, 1, and 2. Bind to vertex 0 material index 0, to vertex 1 material index 1, and to vertex 2 material index 2.
   b. Draw a face with vertices 0, 3, and 4. Bind to vertex 0 material index 3, to vertex 3 material index 4, and to vertex 4 material index 5.

The result is two triangles shown in Figure 15.12 and in color plate 2g. The first triangle uses the first three materials for its three vertices: red, green, and blue. The VRML browser creates a color gradation across the triangle and creates a red, green, and blue rainbow effect. The second triangle uses the next three materials for its three vertices: yellow, cyan, magenta. Again, the VRML browser creates a color gradation across the triangle.

Using **PER_VERTEX** material binding type, the VRML browser always binds the first material to the first vertex, the second material to the second vertex, and so on. You can also use specific materials for each vertex by specifying the **PER_VERTEX_INDEXED** material binding type. Material indexes for the vertices are specified in the **materialIndex** field of an **IndexedFaceSet** node.

In the example text in Figure 15.13, the first triangle's vertices are shaded with material indexes 3, 5, and 1, and the second triangle's vertices are shaded with material indexes 7, 8, and 2.

```
#VRML V1.0 ascii

Coordinate3 {
      point [
            0.0 1.0 0.0,
           -1.0 0.0 0.0,
           -0.2 0.0 0.0,
            0.2 0.0 0.0,
            1.0 0.0 0.0
      ]
}
Material {
      diffuseColor [
            1.0 0.0 0.0,
            0.0 1.0 0.0,
            0.0 0.0 1.0,
            1.0 1.0 0.0,
            0.0 1.0 1.0,
            1.0 0.0 1.0,
            1.0 1.0 1.0,
            0.5 0.5 0.5,
            1.0 0.2 0.1
      ]
}
MaterialBinding {
      value PER_VERTEX_INDEXED
}
```

Figure 15.13 continues

```
IndexedFaceSet {
      coordIndex [
            0, 1, 2, -1, # Triangle 1
            0, 3, 4      # Triangle 2
      ]
      materialIndex [
            3, 5, 1, 0,  # Triangle 1
            7, 8, 2      # Triangle 2
      ]
}
```

Figure 15.13 *Specifying particular materials for each vertex of two triangles.*

Reading from the top of the file, the VRML browser is directed to:

1. Set the coordinates property to five coordinates.
2. Set the materials property to nine materials.
3. Specify the **PER_VERTEX_INDEXED** material binding type.
4. Draw a list of faces using the current material binding type and materials list.
   a. Draw a face with vertices 0, 1, and 2. Bind to vertex 0 material index 3, to vertex 1 material index 5, and to vertex 2 material index 1.
   b. Draw a face with vertices 0, 3, and 4. Bind to vertex 0 material index 7, to vertex 3 material index 8, and to vertex 4 material index 2.

The result is two triangles as shown in Figure 15.13 and in color plate 2*h*. The first triangle uses materials 3, 5, and 1 for its three vertices: yellow, magenta, and green. The second triangle uses materials 7, 8, and 2 for its vertices: gray, orange, and blue. For both triangles, the VRML browser smoothly varies the colors across the face of the triangle.

Coloring Line Segments in a Line Set

Using **PER_PART** and **PER_PART_INDEXED** material binding types, you can color the individual line segments in a line set. For example, using the same two triangles from the previous examples, the triangles are now drawn as polylines, and each line segment is shaded a different color, as shown in Figure 15.14.

```
#VRML V1.0 ascii

Coordinate3 {
      point [
             0.0 1.0 0.0,
            -1.0 0.0 0.0,
            -0.2 0.0 0.0,
             0.2 0.0 0.0,
             1.0 0.0 0.0
      ]
}
```

Figure 15.14 continues

```
Material {
     diffuseColor [
          1.0 0.0 0.0,
          0.0 1.0 0.0,
          0.0 0.0 1.0,
          1.0 1.0 0.0,
          0.0 1.0 1.0,
          1.0 0.0 1.0,
          1.0 1.0 1.0,
          0.5 0.5 0.5,
          1.0 0.2 0.1
     ]
}
MaterialBinding {
     value PER_PART
}
IndexedFaceSet {
     coordIndex [
          0, 1, 2, 0, -1, # Triangle 1
          0, 3, 4, 0      # Triangle 2
     ]
}
```

Figure 15.14 *Two triangular polylines with each line segment a different color.*

Reading from the top of the file, the VRML browser is directed to:

1. Set the coordinates property to five coordinates.
2. Set the materials property to nine materials.
3. Specify the **PER_PART** material binding type.
4. Draw a list of lines using the current material binding type and materials list.
   a. Draw a polyline with vertices 0, 1, 2, and back to 0. Shade the first line segment with material index 0, the second line segment with material index 1, and the third with material index 2.
   b. Draw a polyline with vertices 0, 3, 4, and back to 0. Shade the first line segment with material index 3, the second line segment with material index 4, and the third with material index 5.

The result is two outlined triangles shown in Figure 15.14. The first triangle's line segments are colored using materials 0, 1, and 2: red, green, and blue. The second triangle's line segments are colored using materials 3, 4, and 5: yellow, cyan, magenta.

Using a **PER_PART** material binding type, the VRML browser always uses the first material for the first line segment, the second material for the second line segment, and so on. You can also specify particular materials for each line segment by using a **PER_PART_INDEXED** material binding type. Material indexes for the line segments are specified in the **materialIndex** field of an **IndexedLineSet** node.

The example text in Figure 15.15 shades the line segments of the first triangle with material indexes 3, 5, and 1, and those of the second triangle with material index 7, 8, and 2.

```
#VRML V1.0 ascii

Coordinate3 {
      point [
             0.0 1.0 0.0,
            -1.0 0.0 0.0,
            -0.2 0.0 0.0,
             0.2 0.0 0.0,
             1.0 0.0 0.0
      ]
}
Material {
      diffuseColor [
             1.0 0.0 0.0,
             0.0 1.0 0.0,
             0.0 0.0 1.0,
             1.0 1.0 0.0,
             0.0 1.0 1.0,
             1.0 0.0 1.0,
             1.0 1.0 1.0,
             0.5 0.5 0.5,
             1.0 0.2 0.1
      ]
}
MaterialBinding {
      value PER_PART_INDEXED
}
IndexedFaceSet {
      coordIndex [
             0, 1, 2, 0, -1, # Triangle 1
             0, 3, 4, 0      # Triangle 2
      ]
      materialIndex [
             3, 5, 1,        # Triangle 1
             7, 8, 2         # Triangle 2
      ]
}
```

Figure 15.15 *Specifying particular materials for each line segment of two triangles.*

Reading from the top of the file, the VRML browser is directed to:

1. Set the coordinates property to five coordinates.
2. Set the materials property to nine materials.
3. Specify the **PER_PART_INDEXED** material binding type.
4. Draw a list of lines using the current material binding type and materials list.

a. Draw a polyline with vertices 0, 1, 2, and back to 0. Shade the first line segment with material index 3, the second line segment with material index 5, and the third with material index 1.
b. Draw a polyline with vertices 0, 3, 4, and back to 0. Shade the first line segment with material index 7, the second line segment with material index 8, and the third with material index 2.

The result is two outlined triangles shown in Figure 15.15. The first triangle's line segments are colored using materials 3, 5, and 1. The second triangle's line segments are colored using materials 7, 8, and 2.

Coloring Polylines in a Line Set

Using a nearly identical approach to that for **IndexedFaceSet** nodes, you can shade differently the individual polylines of a line set by using **PER_FACE** or **PER_FACE_INDEXED** material binding types. The example text in Figure 15.16 draws outlines of the same two triangles used in the preceding examples, shading each one with a different color.

```
#VRML V1.0 ascii

Coordinate3 {
      point [
             0.0 1.0 0.0,
            -1.0 0.0 0.0,
            -0.2 0.0 0.0,
             0.2 0.0 0.0,
             1.0 0.0 0.0
      ]
}
Material {
      diffuseColor [
             1.0 0.0 0.0,
             0.0 1.0 0.0,
             0.0 0.0 1.0,
             1.0 1.0 0.0,
             0.0 1.0 1.0,
             1.0 0.0 1.0,
             1.0 1.0 1.0,
             0.5 0.5 0.5,
             1.0 0.2 0.1
      ]
}
MaterialBinding {
      value PER_FACE
}
```

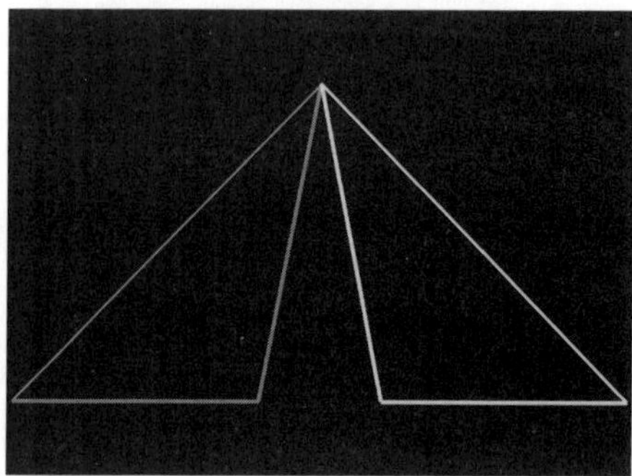

Figure 15.16 continues

```
IndexedLineSet {
      coordIndex [
            0, 1, 2, 0, -1, # Triangle 1
            0, 3, 4, 0      # Triangle 2
      ]
}
```

Figure 15.16 *Two triangles outlined in two different colors.*

The result is two triangle outlines, shown in Figure 15.16. The first triangle is outlined with material index 0 (red), and the second with material index 1 (green).

Similarly, you can provide individual material indexes for each polyline by using a **PER_FACE_INDEXED** material binding type and setting the material indexes in a **materialIndex** field for the **IndexedLineSet** node, as shown in Figure 15.17.

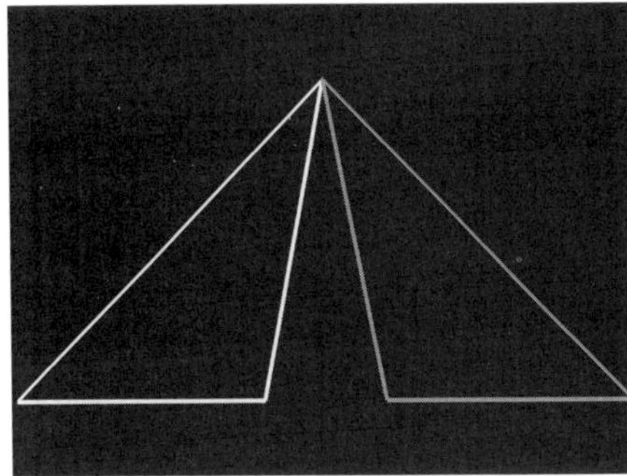

```
#VRML V1.0 ascii

Coordinate3 {
      point [
             0.0 1.0 0.0,
            -1.0 0.0 0.0,
            -0.2 0.0 0.0,
             0.2 0.0 0.0,
             1.0 0.0 0.0
      ]
}
Material {
      diffuseColor [
            1.0 0.0 0.0,
            0.0 1.0 0.0,
            0.0 0.0 1.0,
            1.0 1.0 0.0,
            0.0 1.0 1.0,
            1.0 0.0 1.0,
            1.0 1.0 1.0,
            0.5 0.5 0.5,
            1.0 0.2 0.1
      ]
}
MaterialBinding {
      value PER_FACE_INDEXED
}
```

Figure 15.17 continues

```
IndexedLineSet {
      coordIndex [
             0, 1, 2, 0, -1, # Triangle 1
             0, 3, 4, 0      # Triangle 2
      ]
      materialIndex [
             3, # Triangle 1
             7  # Triangle 2
      ]
}
```

Figure 15.17 *Two triangles outlined with two different colors.*

The result is again two triangle outlines, as shown in Figure 15.17. The first triangle is outlined with material index 3 (yellow), and the second with material index 7 (gray).

Coloring Vertices in a Line Set

Applying different materials to the vertices of a line set is nearly identical to applying different materials to the vertices of a face set. When vertices of a line segment have different colors, the VRML browser creates a smooth color gradation from the color at one vertex to that at the next vertex. For example, outlines of the same two triangles can again be drawn, this time using different colors for each vertex, as shown in Figure 15.18.

```
#VRML V1.0 ascii

Coordinate3 {
      point [
             0.0 1.0 0.0,
            -1.0 0.0 0.0,
            -0.2 0.0 0.0,
             0.2 0.0 0.0,
             1.0 0.0 0.0
      ]
}
Material {
      diffuseColor [
             1.0 0.0 0.0,
             0.0 1.0 0.0,
             0.0 0.0 1.0,
             1.0 1.0 0.0,
             0.0 1.0 1.0,
             1.0 0.0 1.0,
             1.0 1.0 1.0,
             0.5 0.5 0.5,
             1.0 0.2 0.1
      ]
}
```

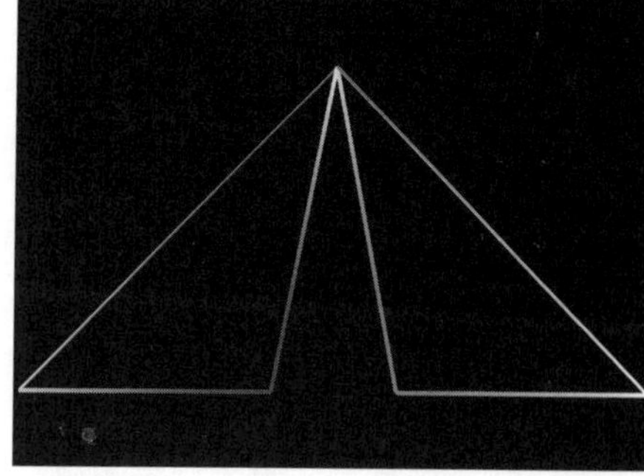

Figure 15.18 continues

```
MaterialBinding {
      value PER_VERTEX
}
IndexedLineSet {
      coordIndex [
            0, 1, 2, 0, -1, # Triangle 1
            0, 3, 4, 0      # Triangle 2
      ]
}
```

Figure 15.18 *Two triangular polylines with different colored vertices.*

The result is the two triangles shown in Figure 15.18. The first vertex of the first triangle is bound to material index 0. The second vertex to material index 1, the third to material index 2, and the fourth to material index 3. Likewise, the first vertex of the second triangle is bound to material index 4, the second to material index 5, the third to material index 6, and the fourth to material index 7. The VRML browser draws each line segment using a smooth gradation from vertex color to vertex color. The first line segment, for instance, smoothly varies from red to green. The second varies from green to blue. And so on.

You can specify material indexes to use for each vertex along the polyline by using a **PER_VERTEX_INDEXED** material binding type and setting the material indexes to use in the **materialIndex** field of the **IndexedLineSet** node, as demonstrated in Figure 15.19.

```
#VRML V1.0 ascii

Coordinate3 {
      point [
             0.0 1.0 0.0,
            -1.0 0.0 0.0,
            -0.2 0.0 0.0,
             0.2 0.0 0.0,
             1.0 0.0 0.0
      ]
}
Material {
      diffuseColor [
            1.0 0.0 0.0,
            0.0 1.0 0.0,
            0.0 0.0 1.0,
            1.0 1.0 0.0,
            0.0 1.0 1.0,
            1.0 0.0 1.0,
            1.0 1.0 1.0,
            0.5 0.5 0.5,
            1.0 0.2 0.1
      ]
}
```

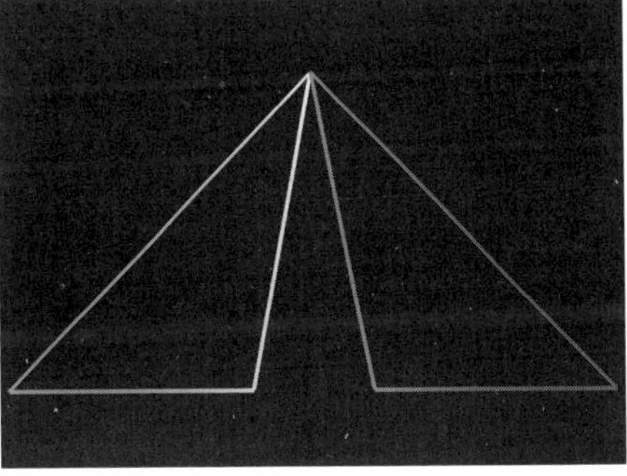

Figure 15.19 continues

```
MaterialBinding {
      value PER_VERTEX_INDEXED
}
IndexedLineSet {
      coordIndex [
             0, 1, 2, 0, -1, # Triangle 1
             0, 3, 4, 0      # Triangle 2
      ]
      materialIndex [
             3, 5, 1, 3, 0,  # Triangle 1
             7, 8, 2, 7      # Triangle 2
}
```

Figure 15.19 *Two triangular polylines with different colored vertices.*

The resulting triangles are shown in Figure 15.19. The first vertex of the first triangle is bound to material index 3. The second vertex to material index 5, the third to material index 1, and the fourth to material index 3. Likewise, the first vertex of the second triangle is bound to material index 7, the second to material index 8, the third to material index 2, and the fourth to material index 7. The VRML browser draws each triangle line segment using a smooth gradation from vertex color to vertex color. The first line segment, for instance, smoothly varies from yellow to magenta. The second varies from magenta to green. And so on.

Coloring More Complicated Line Shapes

Material binding and indexed materials are particularly powerful when shading shapes more complicated than a pair of triangles. The following example shades a 2-D starburst pattern of lines in a line set. Each line extending out of the starburst is shaded from yellow at the center of the starburst to red at the outer tip. To create this effect, a **PER_VERTEX_INDEXED** material binding type is specified with a series of **materialIndex** values in the **IndexedLineSet** node. This is illustrated in Figure 15.20.

```
#VRML V1.0 ascii

Coordinate3 {
      point [
            0.0   0.0  0.0,
            1.00  0.00 0.0,
            0.92  0.38 0.0,
            0.71  0.71 0.0,
            0.38  0.92 0.0,
            0.00  1.00 0.0,
           -0.38  0.92 0.0,
           -0.71  0.71 0.0,
           -0.92  0.38 0.0,
           -1.00  0.00 0.0,
           -0.92 -0.38 0.0,
           -0.71 -0.71 0.0,
           -0.38 -0.92 0.0,
            0.00 -1.00 0.0,
            0.38 -0.92 0.0,
            0.71 -0.71 0.0,
            0.92 -0.38 0.0,
      ]
}
Material {
      diffuseColor [
            1.0 1.0 0.0, # burst center
            1.0 0.0 0.0  # burst ends
      ]
}
MaterialBinding {
      value PER_VERTEX
}
IndexedLineSet {
      coordIndex [
            0,  1, -1,
            0,  2, -1,
            0,  3, -1,
            0,  4, -1,
            0,  5, -1,
            0,  6, -1,
            0,  7, -1,
            0,  8, -1,
            0,  9, -1,
            0, 10, -1,
            0, 11, -1,
            0, 12, -1,
            0, 13, -1,
            0, 14, -1,
            0, 15, -1,
            0, 16, -1,
      ]
}
```

Figure 15.20 *A starburst shaded with a color gradient from the center outward.*

You can create a 3-D starburst by replicating the same 2-D starburst repeatedly, rotated about the Y axis, as shown in Figure 15.21.

```
#VRML V1.0 ascii

Coordinate3 {
      point [
              0.0   0.0  0.0,
              1.00  0.00 0.0,
              0.92  0.38 0.0,
              0.71  0.71 0.0,
              0.38  0.92 0.0,
              0.00  1.00 0.0,
             -0.38  0.92 0.0,
             -0.71  0.71 0.0,
             -0.92  0.38 0.0,
             -1.00  0.00 0.0,
             -0.92 -0.38 0.0,
             -0.71 -0.71 0.0,
             -0.38 -0.92 0.0,
              0.00 -1.00 0.0,
              0.38 -0.92 0.0,
              0.71 -0.71 0.0,
              0.92 -0.38 0.0,
      ]
}
Material {
      diffuseColor [
            1.0 1.0 0.0, # burst center
            1.0 0.0 0.0  # burst ends
      ]
}
MaterialBinding {
      value PER_VERTEX
}
```

Figure 15.21 continues

```
Switch {
      whichChild -1
      DEF burst IndexedLineSet {
            coordIndex [
                  0,  1, -1,
                  0,  2, -1,
                  0,  3, -1,
                  0,  4, -1,
                  0,  5, -1,
                  0,  6, -1,
                  0,  7, -1,
                  0,  8, -1,
                  0,  9, -1,
                  0, 10, -1,
                  0, 11, -1,
                  0, 12, -1,
                  0, 13, -1,
                  0, 14, -1,
                  0, 15, -1,
                  0, 16, -1,
            ]
      }
      DEF yspin Rotation {
            #             Y        +22.5 degrees
            rotation 0.0 1.0 0.0  0.392
      }
}
DEF burst4 Separator {
      USE yspin    USE burst
      USE yspin    USE burst
      USE yspin    USE burst
      USE yspin    USE burst
}
USE burst4
USE burst4
USE burst4
```

Figure 15.21 *A 3-D color starburst.*

Letting Material Indexes Reuse Materials

Using a **PER_FACE** material binding type, the VRML browser will automatically generate consecutive material indexes for each face within a face set. If you specify more faces than colors in the material list, the material indexes are reused, starting again from the beginning of the material list. The example text in Figure 15.22 creates a checkerboard with ten faces, but only two colors are specified in the material list.

```
#VRML V1.0 ascii

Coordinate3 {
      point [
            -2.0 0.0 0.0,
            -1.0 0.0 0.0,
             0.0 0.0 0.0,
             1.0 0.0 0.0,
             2.0 0.0 0.0,
             3.0 0.0 0.0,
            -2.0 0.0 1.0,
            -1.0 0.0 1.0,
             0.0 0.0 1.0,
             1.0 0.0 1.0,
             2.0 0.0 1.0,
             3.0 0.0 1.0,
            -2.0 0.0 2.0,
            -1.0 0.0 2.0,
             0.0 0.0 2.0,
             1.0 0.0 2.0,
             2.0 0.0 2.0,
             3.0 0.0 2.0,
      ]
}
Material {
      diffuseColor [
            0.1 0.1 0.1,
            1.0 1.0 1.0
      ]
}
MaterialBinding {
      value PER_FACE
}
IndexedFaceSet {
      coordIndex [
            # Back row
             0,  6,  7,  1, -1,
             1,  7,  8,  2, -1,
             2,  8,  9,  3, -1,
             3,  9, 10,  4, -1,
             4, 10, 11,  5, -1,
            # Front row
             6, 12, 13,  7, -1,
             7, 13, 14,  8, -1,
             8, 14, 15,  9, -1,
             9, 15, 16, 10, -1,
            10, 16, 17, 11, -1,
      ]
}
```

Figure 15.22 *A checkerboard created by specifying ten faces and only two colors in the material list.*

Using a **PER_FACE** material binding type, the VRML browser generates ten material indexes, 0 through 9, for the ten faces in the face set. Face 0's material index is 0, face 1's is 1, face 2's is 2, and so forth. However, there are only two materials in the material index list. So, while face 0 is bound to material 0, and face 1 is bound to material 1, face 2 must reuse material 0. Similarly, face 3 reuses material 1, face 4 reuses material 0, and so on, like this:

Face	*Generated Material I*	*Material Chosen*
0	0	0
1	1	1
2	2	0 (reuse)
3	3	1 (reuse)
4	4	0 (reuse)
5	5	1 (reuse)
etc.		

Alternating between material 0 and material 1 creates the checkerboard effect. This technique can be used to create checks on any multifaced shape. You can reuse indexes in material lists of any length, not just two-item lists.

Coloring More Complicated Face Shapes

You can shade complex 3-D shapes using a different material for each vertex of each face. The example text in Figure 15.23 shades each face of a vase to create a white, pink, and blue finish. The result is shown in Figure 15.23 and in color plate 3*a*.

```
#VRML V1.0 ascii

Coordinate3 {
      point [
            # ring 0
            0.32 2.00  0.00,
            0.10 2.00  0.30,
           -0.26 2.00  0.19,
           -0.26 2.00 -0.19,
            0.10 2.00 -0.30,
            # ring 1
            0.30 1.95  0.00,
            0.09 1.95  0.29,
           -0.24 1.95  0.18,
           -0.24 1.95 -0.18,
            0.09 1.95 -0.29,
            # ring 2
            0.42 1.60  0.00,
            0.13 1.60  0.40,
           -0.34 1.60  0.25,
           -0.34 1.60 -0.25,
            0.13 1.60 -0.40,
            # ring 3
            0.60 1.50  0.00,
            0.19 1.50  0.57,
           -0.48 1.50  0.35,
           -0.49 1.50 -0.35,
            0.18 1.50 -0.57,
            # ring 4
            0.70 1.20  0.00,
            0.22 1.20  0.67,
           -0.57 1.20  0.41,
           -0.57 1.20 -0.41,
            0.21 1.20 -0.67,
            # ring 5
            0.40 0.00  0.00,
            0.12 0.00  0.38,
           -0.32 0.00  0.24,
           -0.32 0.00 -0.23,
            0.12 0.00 -0.38
      ]
}
Material {
      diffuseColor [
            1.0 1.0 1.0, # white
            1.0 0.1 0.8, # pink
            0.0 0.3 1.0, # blue
      ]
}
MaterialBinding {
      value PER_VERTEX_INDEXED
}
```

Figure 15.23 continues

```
IndexedFaceSet {
     coordIndex [
          # ring 0
           0,  1,  6,  5, -1,
           1,  2,  7,  6, -1,
           2,  3,  8,  7, -1,
           3,  4,  9,  8, -1,
           4,  0,  5,  9, -1,
          # ring 1
           5,  6, 11, 10, -1,
           6,  7, 12, 11, -1,
           7,  8, 13, 12, -1,
           8,  9, 14, 13, -1,
           9,  5, 10, 14, -1,
          # ring 2
          10, 11, 16, 15, -1,
          11, 12, 17, 16, -1,
          12, 13, 18, 17, -1,
          13, 14, 19, 18, -1,
          14, 10, 15, 19, -1,
          # ring 3
          15, 16, 21, 20, -1,
          16, 17, 22, 21, -1,
          17, 18, 23, 22, -1,
          18, 19, 24, 23, -1,
          19, 15, 20, 24, -1,
          # ring 4
          20, 21, 26, 25, -1,
          21, 22, 27, 26, -1,
          22, 23, 28, 27, -1,
          23, 24, 29, 28, -1,
          24, 20, 25, 29, -1,
          # base
          25, 26, 27, 28, 29
     ]
     materialIndex [
          # ring 0
          0, 0, 0, 0, 0,
          0, 0, 0, 0, 0,
          0, 0, 0, 0, 0,
          0, 0, 0, 0, 0,
          0, 0, 0, 0, 0,
          # ring 1
          0, 0, 2, 2, 0,
          0, 0, 2, 2, 0,
          0, 0, 2, 2, 0,
          0, 0, 2, 2, 0,
          0, 0, 2, 2, 0,
```

Figure 15.23 continues

```
                # ring 2
                2, 2, 1, 1, 0,
                2, 2, 1, 1, 0,
                2, 2, 1, 1, 0,
                2, 2, 1, 1, 0,
                2, 2, 1, 1, 0,
                # ring 3
                1, 1, 1, 1, 0,
                1, 1, 1, 1, 0,
                1, 1, 1, 1, 0,
                1, 1, 1, 1, 0,
                1, 1, 1, 1, 0,
                # ring 4
                1, 1, 0, 0, 0,
                1, 1, 0, 0, 0,
                1, 1, 0, 0, 0,
                1, 1, 0, 0, 0,
                1, 1, 0, 0, 0,
                # base
                0, 0, 0, 0, 0
            ]
    }
```

Figure 15.23 *A pink, white, and blue vase.*

Using the same technique, you can create shaded mountainous terrains. Start with a mountain grid, and assign each grid vertex a material color based on the height of that vertex. Low grid vertices are shaded green, midheight vertices brown, higher vertices dark mountain green, and the highest vertices white. Figure 15.24 shows a simple grid mountain.

Figure 15.24 *A mountainous terrain.*

Using the Same Material Indexes with Different Material Lists

Material indexes in a **materialIndex** field refer to the current material list set by a **Material** node. If the current material list's values change, the material indexes refer to new colors. You can take advantage of this feature by defining a shape once, with its material indexes, and later instance that shape using a different set of materials each time. This enables you to create multiple variations of the same shape that differ only in color.

The example text in Figure 15.25 creates a thistle-like flower in a bed of leaves with a starburst of lines representing the flower. Only a single leaf shape is defined using an **IndexedFaceSet** node. The same leaf is then instanced to create the bed of leaves. To add variation to the leaves, three different material lists are defined, each with a slightly different set of greens for the vertices of the leaf. Each time the leaf is instanced, a different material list is used. Though the leaf's material indexes remain the same, the leaves themselves are drawn in different colors each time. The resulting flower is shown in Figure 15.25. The starburst is inlined from the file `burst.wrl`.

```
#VRML V1.0 ascii

##############
# Build a bed of leaves for a flower
# Define some shapes, colors, and transforms
Switch {
      whichChild -1
      DEF green1 Material {
            diffuseColor [
                  0.0 0.1 0.0, # dark green
                  0.1 0.4 0.0, # lighter green
                  0.0 0.5 0.0, # lightest green
                  0.0 0.2 0.0, # lighter green
            ]
      }
      DEF green2 Material {
            diffuseColor [
                  0.0 0.1 0.0, # dark green
                  0.0 0.3 0.0, # lighter green
                  0.2 0.3 0.0, # lightest green
                  0.0 0.4 0.0, # lighter green
            ]
      }
      DEF green3 Material {
            diffuseColor [
                  0.0 0.1 0.0, # dark green
                  0.0 0.4 0.0, # lighter green
                  0.1 0.2 0.0, # lightest green
                  0.0 0.3 0.0, # lighter green
            ]
      }
```

Figure 15.25 continues

```
        DEF leaf IndexedFaceSet {
              coordIndex [
                    0, 1, 3, -1,
                    0, 3, 2, -1,
                    4, 7, 5, -1,
                    4, 6, 7
              ]
              materialIndex [
                    0, 1, 2, 0,
                    0, 2, 3, 0,
                    0, 2, 1, 0,
                    0, 3, 2
              ]
        }
        DEF yturn1 Rotation {
              #             Y       +72.0 degrees
              rotation 0.0 1.0 0.0  1.257
        }
        DEF yturn2 Rotation {
              #             Y       +52.0 degrees
              rotation 0.0 1.0 0.0  0.908
        }
        DEF zturn Rotation {
              #             Y       +20.0 degrees
              rotation 0.0 0.0 1.0  0.349
        }
        DEF smaller Scale {
              scaleFactor 0.8 1.2 0.8
        }
        DEF up Translation {
              translation 0.0 0.2 0.0
        }
  }
  Coordinate3 {
        point [
              0.0  0.0    0.0,
              0.4  0.1    0.2,
              0.4  0.1   -0.2,
              1.0  0.2    0.0,
              0.0 -0.001  0.0,
              0.4  0.099  0.2,
              0.4  0.099 -0.2,
              1.0  0.199  0.0
        ]
  }
  MaterialBinding {
        value PER_VERTEX_INDEXED
  }
```

Figure 15.25 continues

```
# Build a bed of leaves
Separator {
      DEF leaf_bed Separator {
                        USE green1   USE leaf
            USE yturn1  USE green2   USE leaf
            USE yturn2  USE green1   USE leaf
            USE yturn1  USE green3   USE leaf
            USE yturn2  USE green2   USE leaf
            USE yturn2  USE green3   USE leaf
      }
      USE yturn2   USE smaller  USE leaf_bed
      USE yturn2   USE smaller  USE leaf_bed
}
#############
# Build a short stem
MaterialBinding {
      value OVERALL
}
Material {
      diffuseColor 0.0 0.1 0.0
}
Cylinder {
      height 0.8
      radius 0.015
}
#############
# Add the star burst as a thistle-like flower
Translation {
      translation 0.0 0.4 0.0
}
Scale {
      scaleFactor 0.25 0.25 0.25
}
WWWInline {
      name "burst.wrl"
}
```

Figure 15.25 *A flower whose leaves are many shades of green.*

The preceding example illustrates several techniques to simplify the construction of the flower:

- *A **Switch** node is used to define multiple materials, shapes, and transforms for instancing later in the file.*
- *A single leaf shape is defined, and instanced repeatedly. A different material list is applied to each instance to achieve slight variations in the leaf colors.*
- *After the bed of leaves is completed, the material binding type is set back to **OVERALL** before drawing a cylinder for the flower stem.*

- *The starburst from Figure 15.21 is scaled down and positioned for the thistle-like flower above the leaf bed. When the starburst is used, the material binding type is changed to* ***PER_VERTEX*** *before drawing the starburst lines.*

Extended Example

The following example builds on the concepts presented in this chapter. Try it on your own.

Flames

The flames in the example text in Figure 15.26 use the **PER_VERTEX_INDEXED** binding type to shade each flame triangle. One flame is instanced many times at different scales and in different positions. This creates an overall, random flame effect on the log.

```
#VRML V1.0 ascii

# Flames
Separator {
	Coordinate3 {
		point [
			-0.7 0.0 0.0,   -0.8 1.5 0.0,   -1.0 0.0 0.0,
			-0.5 0.0 0.01,  -0.7 1.2 0.01,  -0.9 0.0 0.01,
			-0.1 0.0 0.0,   -0.2 1.6 0.0,   -0.4 0.0 0.0,
			 0.3 0.0 0.01,   0.2 1.0 0.01,   0.0 0.0 0.0,
		]
	}
	MaterialBinding {
		value PER_VERTEX_INDEXED
	}
	Material {
		diffuseColor [
			1.0 0.0 0.0, 1.0 0.5 0.0, 1.0 0.1 0.0,
			0.8 0.0 0.0, 1.0 0.9 0.0, 1.0 0.0 0.0,
		]
	}
	DEF flames IndexedFaceSet {
		coordIndex [
			0, 1, 2, -1, 3,  4,  5, -1,
			6, 7, 8, -1, 9, 10, 11, -1,
		]
		materialIndex [
			3, 4, 5, -1, 0, 1, 2, -1,
			3, 4, 5, -1, 0, 1, 2, -1,
		]
	}
```

Figure 15.26 continues

```
        Transform {
            translation 0.8 0.0 0.02
            scaleFactor 1.0 1.3 1.0
        }
        USE flames
        Transform {
            translation 0.3 0.0 0.02
            scaleFactor 1.0 0.5 1.0
        }
        USE flames
        Transform {
            translation -1.4 0.0 0.02
            scaleFactor  1.0 1.1 1.0
        }
        USE flames
        Transform {
            translation 0.2 0.0 0.02
            scaleFactor 1.0 0.4 1.0
        }
        USE flames
        Transform {
            translation 0.9 0.0 0.02
            scaleFactor 1.0 1.1 1.0
        }
        USE flames
    }
    # A simple log
    Transform {
        translation 0.0 -0.4 0.0
        rotation    0.0  0.0 1.0 -1.57
    }
    Material {
        diffuseColor 0.5 0.15 0.0
    }
    Cylinder {
        height 2.9
        radius 0.4
    }
```

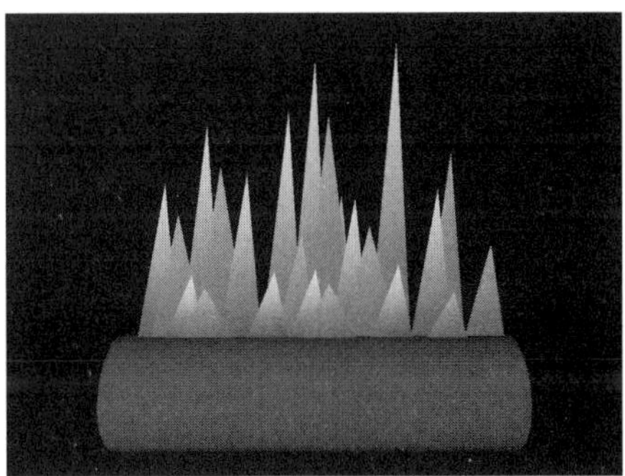

Figure 15.26 *A flaming log.*

Summary

Different materials can be bound to each part, face, or vertex of a shape by specifying a material binding type with the **MaterialBinding** node. The material binding type is a property that is saved and restored by **Separator** nodes, and remains in effect until changed again by another **MaterialBinding** node.

The **OVERALL** material binding type shades entire shapes with a single material.

The **PER_PART** and **PER_PART_INDEXED** material binding types shade each part of a shape with a different material. The primitive-shape parts include those like the sides, top, and bottom of a cylinder. Line set parts are the individual line segments of polylines. Face set parts are the individual faces in the set.

The **PER_FACE** and **PER_FACE_INDEXED** material binding types shade each face or polyline with a different material.

The **PER_VERTEX** and **PER_VERTEX_INDEXED** material binding types shade each face, line, or point vertex with a different material. When vertices of the same face have different colors, the VRML browser creates a smooth gradation from color to color across the face. Similarly, when vertices of the same line segment have different colors, the VRML browser creates a smooth variation from the color at one end of the line to the color at the other end.

The **DEFAULT** material binding type for a shape depends on the shape, but is usually the same as **OVERALL.**

To shade a shape using multiple materials, specify a list of materials using the **Material** node. Each field of the **Material** node can include a list of values, each separated by commas and all enclosed within square brackets. Materials in such a list are referenced with a material index. The first material in the list has an index of 0, the second an index of 1, and so on.

Material indexes are automatically generated by the VRML browser for **PER_PART, PER_FACE,** and **PER_VERTEX** material binding types with **IndexedFaceSet** and **IndexedLineSet** nodes. The first part, face, or vertex will have a material index of 0. The second will have a material index of 1. And so on.

Material indexes for **PointSet** nodes start with the index value in the **startIndex** field and increment by one for each subsequent point in the point set.

Explicit material indexes can be used with **PER_PART_INDEXED, PER_FACE_INDEXED,** and **PER_VERTEX_INDEXED** material binding types. Material indexes for each part, face, or vertex of a shape are specified in the **materialIndex** field of **IndexedFaceSet** and **IndexedLineSet** nodes.

When listing material indexes per vertex, a material index is needed to match each vertex *and* the –1 face or polyline separator flag in the **coordIndex** field of a **IndexedFaceSet** or **IndexedLineSet** node.

CHAPTER 16

Advanced Shading Techniques

The brightness of a face on a VRML shape depends on how much it is lit by light in the virtual world. The more a face is oriented toward a light, the more brightly it is shaded by the VRML browser. A face that is oriented directly away from a light is shaded dark.

To decide whether a face is oriented toward or away from a light, the VRML browser computes a **normal** for the face. You can think of a normal as an arrow that points straight out from the face, perpendicular to the face. If the face is oriented toward the right, then its normal arrow points to the right. If the face is oriented upward, then its normal arrow points upward.

If a face's normal points directly at a light, the face is oriented toward the light as well, and the VRML browser shades it bright. If a face's normal points away from a light, the face is shaded darker. Computing this normal is usually the task of the VRML browser. For instance, in all of the examples in the previous chapters, we let the VRML browser automatically compute normals for every face. You can, however, compute normals yourself and specify them with the **Normal** node. Then, as with materials, you can bind normals to specific parts, faces, or vertices of a shape by choosing a **normal binding type** with a **NormalBinding** node.

By computing your own normals you can create interesting shading effects. The most useful effect is **smooth shading**. This effect creates normals for each vertex of each face on a complex 3-D shape. By intentionally computing normals differently than those automatically computed by the VRML browser, you can make a faceted shape appear smooth. The flower vase used in previous chapters, for instance, can be shaded so that it appears smooth and rounded instead of faceted. This smoothing technique can help you dramatically reduce the number of faces you use to build curved shapes and decrease the time your VRML browser takes to draw a world.

TIP *Computing normals is a time-consuming process best left to a computer program. Most of this chapter assumes that you have access to such a program or wish to write your own.*

Understanding Normals

A normal is a way of indicating the orientation of a face. A face that is oriented to the right has a normal that points to the right. A face that is oriented upward has a normal that points upward, and so forth. In this chapter's diagrams, normals are indicated with arrows that point outward from a face or vertex. For instance, Figure 16.1 shows a cube and the normals for each of its six faces.

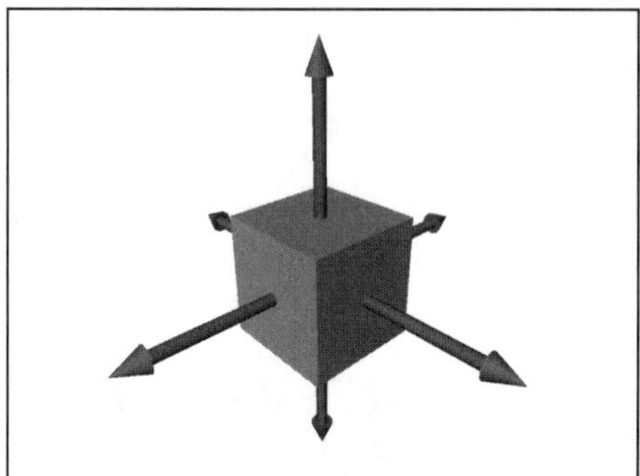

Figure 16.1 *A cube with its normals indicated with arrows.*

Shading Based on Normal Directions

Recall from Chapter 10 that the VRML browser always creates a headlight to illuminate your VRML worlds. That headlight, as the name implies, is positioned on your head in the world. As you move about the world, the light moves with you and always illuminates whatever you can see at the moment, as shown in Figure 16.2.

To shade a face, the VRML browser measures the angle between a face's normal and an imaginary line pointing from the face straight at a light. With the headlight, for instance, the imaginary line always points from a face straight at you and your headlight.

When a face is facing you and your headlight, the angle between the face's normal and the light line is small, and the face is shaded brightly. As a face turns away from you, its normal points increasingly away from you and your headlight. Since your headlight illuminates the face less when it is turned edge-on, the VRML browser shades the face darker. Faces that are oriented directly away from you and your headlight are shaded darkest.

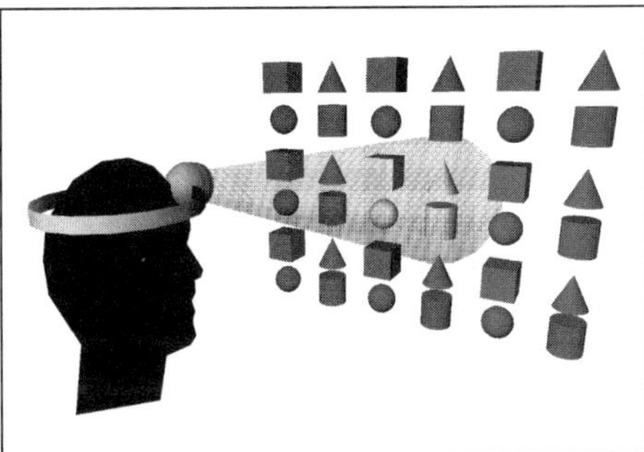

Figure 16.2 *Your headlight.*

Notice that as the face points more away from you, the face is shaded darker, and *the angle between the normal and the light line increases.* This link between shading darkness and the normal angle is what your VRML browser uses when it computes shading for your world. You can use this same link by computing your own normals to create specific shading effects.

Figure 16.3 shows square face and how it is shaded as it is turned to face toward, and then away from, a light. In Figure 16.3*a*, the face is directly facing you and your headlight, so the face is shaded brightly. In Figure 16.3*b* the face is turned a bit to the right. Since it no longer directly faces you and your headlight, it is a bit darker. Figures 16.3*c* through 16.3*i* continue to turn the face away from you bit by bit. At each stage the face is shaded more and more darkly. As you walk about within your virtual world, you see this effect, sometimes viewing faces from the front and shaded brightly, and sometimes viewing them edge-on and shaded darker.

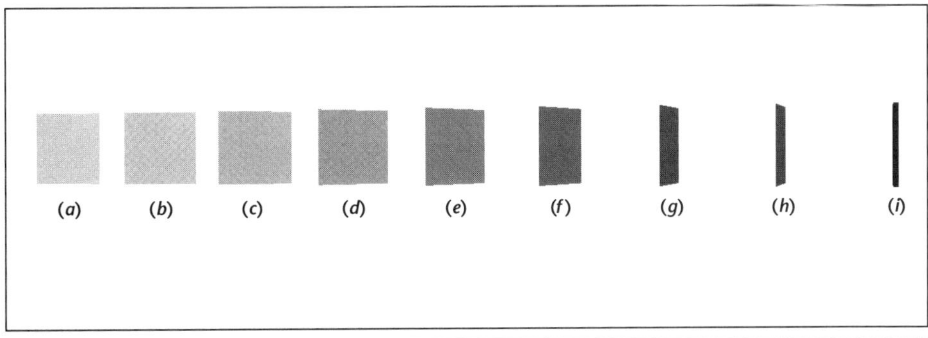

Figure 16.3 *A face shaded based on its orientation toward or away from a light source.*

To further illustrate this shading effect, consider the top view diagram in Figure 16.4, showing a single face, viewed edge-on from above. Pointing out from the face is a normal arrow. The starburst indicates a light in the world, such as your headlight. Finally, a light line is drawn from the face to the light. We are most interested in the angle between the normal arrow and this light line.

Imagine swiveling the face so that it faces the light or faces away from it. Figure 16.4 shows the face at a 45.0 degree angle away from the light. As the face swivels, it is shaded brighter or darker depending on whether it faces the light or not. In the figure, a shaded square is shown next to the diagram and indicates how bright the face is shaded at the current swivel angle if we view the face from directly in front of it. In this case, the face shown is turned 45.0 degrees away from the light and is shaded medium bright.

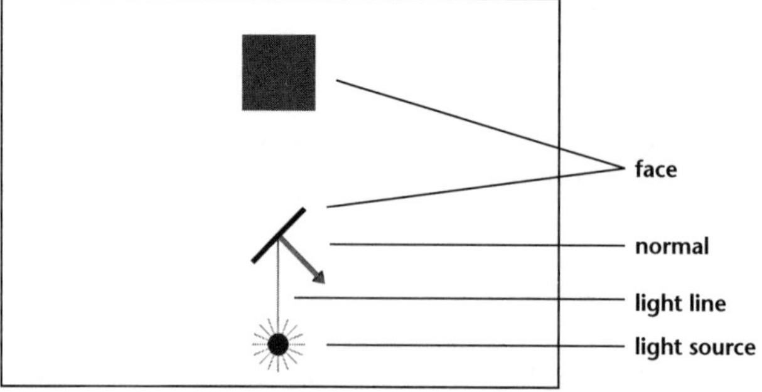

Figure 16.4 *A medium-bright shaded face with its normal, a light source, and a light line.*

Figure 16.5 shows a series of diagrams like those in Figure 16.4. The first shows the face directly facing the light. The next shows the face turned slightly away from the light, and so on until the last shows the face oriented 90.0 degrees away from the light. The shaded squares next to each diagram show the face's brightness at that rotation

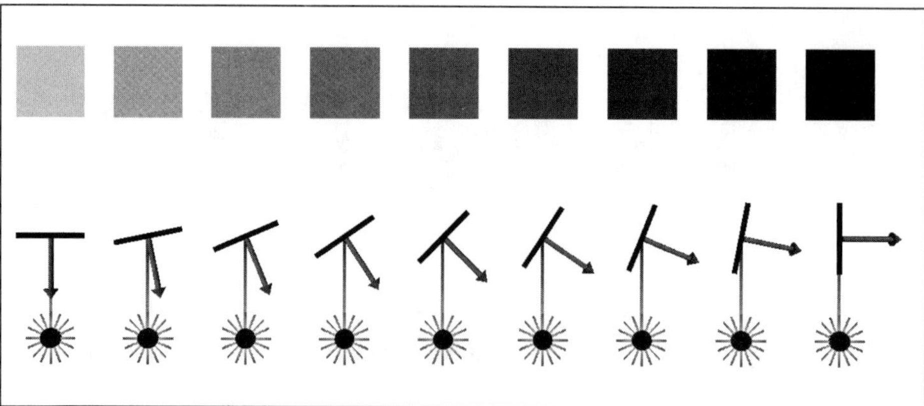

Figure 16.5 *Shading variations based on the face's orientation toward the light source.*

angle. The first shades the face the brightest, while the last shades it entirely black since the face is aimed away from the light.

Notice that as the angle between the normal and the face-to-light line increases, the brightness of the face decreases.

Figure 16.6 continues this diagram series by swiveling the face entirely around from an initial position facing the light, to one facing directly away, and then back again. Notice that the face is shaded black for all positions where the face is edge-on or facing away from the light. The face is only shaded lighter when it faces the light at least a little bit.

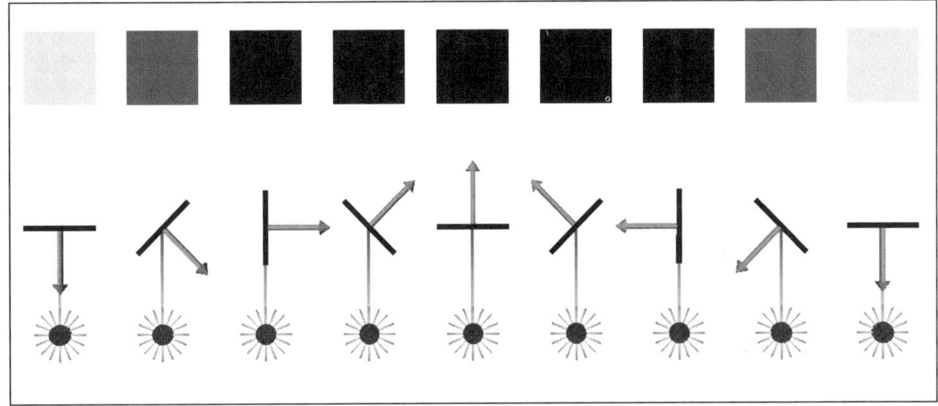

Figure 16.6 *Shading variations.*

As these diagrams illustrate, the normal of a face is the key to understanding how the VRML browser shades faces. If the normal points towards a light, the face is shaded brightly. If it points away from a light, it is shaded dark.

Determining Normal Directions

Typically, the VRML browser computes normals for you. Once computed, it uses them to determine how bright a face should be shaded. You can override the VRML browser's normal computation by providing your own normals. This enables you to create special shading effects the VRML browser would not normally perform.

The normal direction for a face is computed by looking at the order in which vertices are specified to trace out the perimeter of a face. Consider the triangle in Figure 16.7 as an example.

```
#VRML V1.0 ascii

Coordinate3 {
   point [
       0.0 1.0 0.0,
      -1.0 0.0 0.0,
       1.0 0.0 0.0
   ]
}
IndexedFaceSet {
   coordIndex [
      0, 1, 2
   ]
}
```

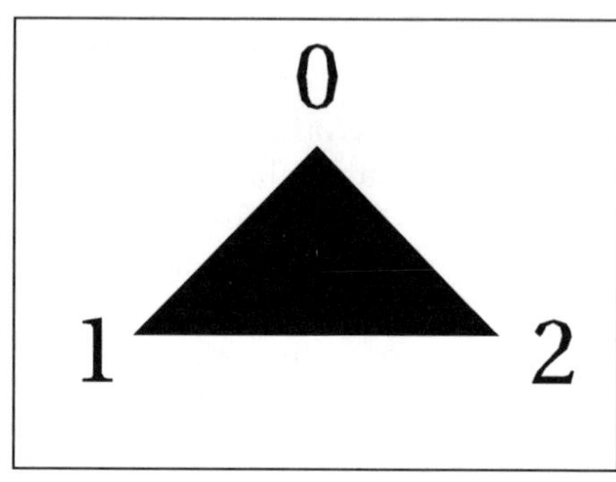

Figure 16.7 *A triangle described by an indexed face set.*

The vertices for this triangle trace out a face perimeter starting at the top, then drawing to the left, to the right, and back again to the top of the triangle. The vertex order used in the **IndexedFaceSet** node above is a *counterclockwise* circuit about the triangle's perimeter. If you spin this triangle around to look at the opposite side, the vertices now appear ordered *clockwise.* VRML defines that the side where vertices appear ordered counterclockwise is the *front* of the face. The opposite side is the *back* of the face. The normal for the face always points outwards from the face's front.

One way to remember how the order of vertices indicates the normal direction is to use the right-hand rule explaining rotation directions in Chapter 6. To use the rule for normals, imagine that the fingers of your right hand are curling about the perimeter of a face, following the vertices in the order specified in an **IndexedFaceSet** node. Stick your thumb out, as if hitchhiking, and your thumb will point in the direction of the normal for the face. Figure 16.8 shows the right-hand rule applied to the above triangle.

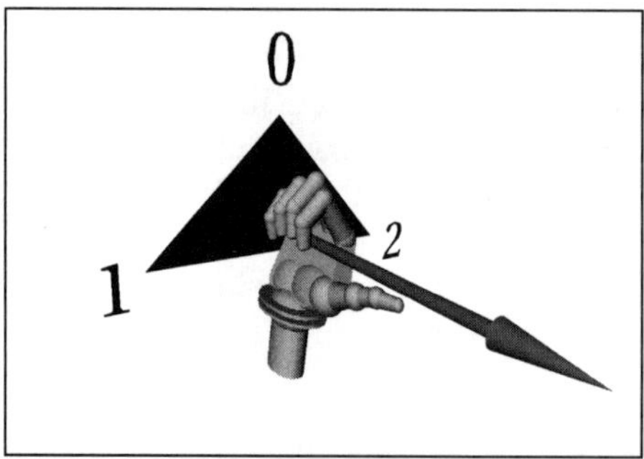

Figure 16.8 *The right-hand rule for normals.*

You can view the same triangle from the back and again curl your fingers around the perimeter following the order in which vertices are specified in the **IndexedFaceSet** node. Figure 16.9 shows the result.

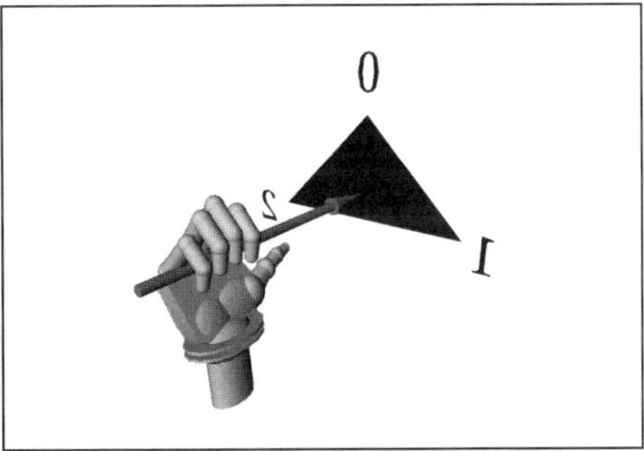

Figure 16.9 *The right-hand rule from the back of the face.*

Notice that no matter which side of the triangle you view, if you curl your fingers using the right-hand rule, your thumb always points out the front of the triangle.

The same right-hand rule applies for any face with any number of vertices. Figure 16.10 shows the rule applied to a more complicated face.

Figure 16.10 *Applying the right-hand rule to a more complex shape.*

Using the right-hand rule, the VRML browser determines which side of a face is the front and which general direction a face's normal points. To compute the exact shade of a face, however, the VRML browser needs an exact normal direction to measure the exact angle between the normal and a line from the face to a light. Using that angle, the VRML browser then computes the brightness of the face and shades it.

TIP *The exact mathematics used to compute the angle between a normal and a light line to determine the shading brightness of a face is beyond the scope of this book. Any of the graphics textbooks listed in Appendix C are excellent resources for learning about lighting equations.*

Computing Normals

Computing exact normals is a time-consuming process best left to computer programs. If, however, you wish to compute normals yourself, or you are writing a program to do it, here's how.

A normal for a face is computed using three consecutive vertices around the perimeter of a face. For the triangle above, the first three (and only three) vertices are:

Vertex Index	*Coordinate*
0	`0.0 1.0 0.0`
1	`-1.0 0.0 0.0`
2	`1.0 0.0 0.0`

To compute a normal, start by computing two **vectors**, one from vertex 0 to vertex 1, and the other from vertex 1 to vertex 2. A vector is an arrow pointing from a starting point to an ending point. It is represented as three X, Y, and Z values computed as the difference between the ending and starting X values of the arrow's points, the ending and starting Y values, and the ending and starting Z values. So, the vector from vertex 0 to vertex 1 of the triangle is this:

```
0 to 1 = (-1.0 - 0.0,
           0.0 - 1.0,
           0.0 - 0.0)           = (-1.0, -1.0, 0.0)
```

The vector from vertex 1 to vertex 2 of the triangle is this:

```
1 to 2 = (1.0 - -1.0,
          0.0 -  0.0,
          0.0 -  0.0)           = (2.0, 0.0, 0.0)
```

You can think of a vector as a translation distance in X, Y, and Z directions to take you from a starting point to an ending point. The vector from vertex 0 to vertex 1 above indicates a translation in X by –1.0 unit, in Y by –1.0 unit, and in Z by 0.0 units. Figure 16.11 shows the two vectors computed above.

The normal we want to compute is also a vector. The direction of that vector tells us how a face is oriented and thus how to shade it.

We can be more generic when computing vectors from vertex to vertex by using a bit of algebra and labeling the X, Y, and Z components of each of the three vertices with letters:

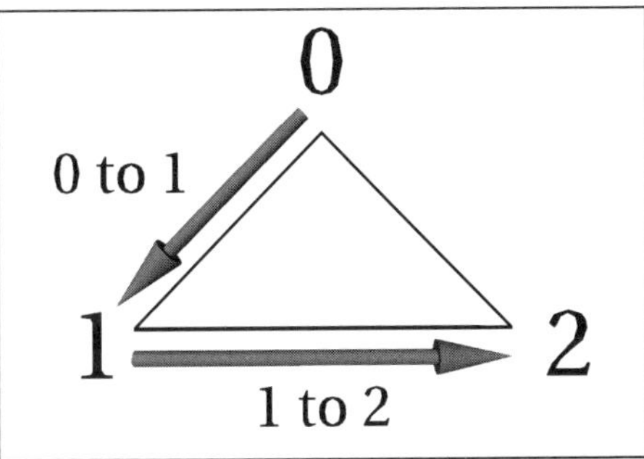

Figure 16.11 *Two vectors computed for the triangle.*

Vertex Index	*Coordinate*
0	X_0, Y_0, Z_0
1	X_1, Y_1, Z_1
2	X_2, Y_2, Z_2

The two vectors we need, V and W, are computed and shown in Figure 16.12.

$$V = (X_1 - X_0,\ Y_1 - Y_0,\ Z_1 - Z_0) = (X_v, Y_v, Z_v) = (-1.0, -1.0, 0.0)$$

$$W = (X_2 - X_1,\ Y_2 - Y_1,\ Z_2 - Z_1) = (X_w, Y_w, Z_w) = (\ 2.0, 0.0, 0.0)$$

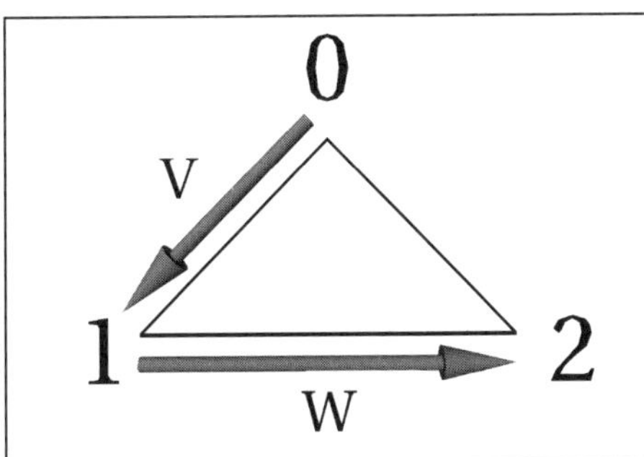

Figure 16.12 *Computing the two vectors.*

Vector V is the vector from vertex 0 to vertex 1, and vector W is the vector from vertex 1 to vertex 2. Using these two vectors, the face's normal vector, N, is computed by calculating the **cross-product** of the two vectors. A cross-product multiplies two vectors together to get a third vector and is computed like this:

$$N = (Y_V * Z_W - Z_V * Y_W,\; Z_V * X_W - X_V * Z_W,\; X_V * Y_W - Y_V * X_W)$$

The cross-product computes a vector that points directly outward from the face. That outward-pointing vector is the normal.

For example, using the two vectors computed for the triangle above, the normal, N, is computed as follows and shown in Figure 16.13.

```
N = (-1.0 * 0.0 -  0.0 * 0.0,
      0.0 * 2.0 - -1.0 * 0.0,
     -1.0 * 0.0 - -1.0 * 2.0) = (0.0, 0.0, 2.0)
```

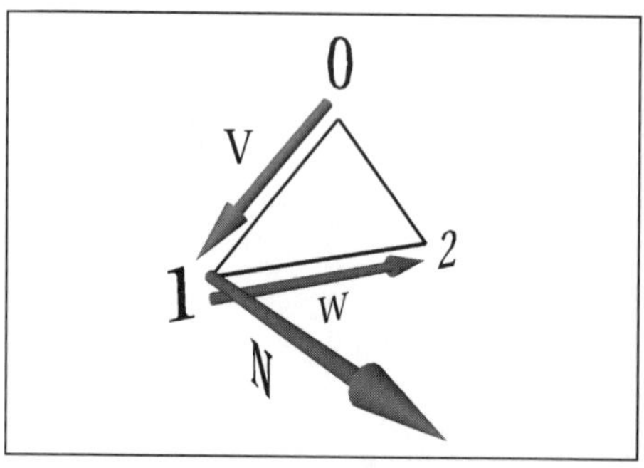

Figure 16.13 *The normal for the triangle.*

The normal, N, is a vector just like V and W. If you think of N as a translation distance, then the N above is a translation straight out the Z axis. Recall that the triangle we started with lies flat with a Z value of 0.0 for all three vertices. This normal N, then, points straight out from the front face of the triangle. This is the exact normal necessary to compute the brightness of the triangle.

You can compute normals for any face oriented in any direction. For example, imagine a triangle with these vertex coordinates:

Vertex Index	*Coordinate*	
0	X_0, Y_0, Z_0	0.0 0.0 -1.0
1	X_1, Y_1, Z_1	-1.0 0.0 0.0
2	X_2, Y_2, Z_2	1.0 0.0 0.0

This triangle, with all three Y values 0.0, lies flat and faces straight up the Y axis. Its normal, then, should point straight up. You can compute the normal by using the approach used for the previous triangle. The result is shown in Figure 16.14.

$$V = (X_1 - X_0,\ Y_1 - Y_0,\ Z_1 - Z_0) = (X_v,\ Y_v,\ Z_v) = (-1.0,\ 0.0,\ 1.0)$$
$$W = (X_2 - X_1,\ Y_2 - Y_1,\ Z_2 - Z_1) = (X_w,\ Y_w,\ Z_w) = (\ 2.0,\ 0.0,\ 0.0)$$
$$N = (Y_v * Z_w - Z_v * Y_w,\ Z_v * X_w - X_v * Z_w,\ X_v * Y_w - Y_v * X_w) = (0.0,\ 2.0,\ 0.0)$$

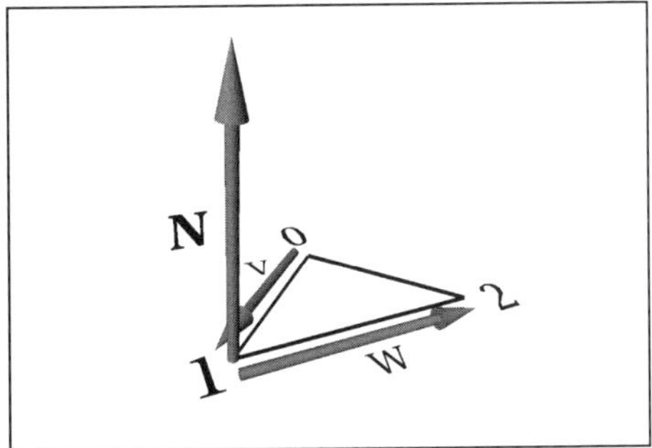

Figure 16.14 *Computing the normal for a second triangle.*

The computed normal for this triangle points straight up the Y axis.

TIP *In some graphics software, normal vectors are expected to be* **unit vectors** *such that the sum of the X, Y, and Z values is 1.0. The above normal, however, sums to 0.0 + 2.0 + 0.0 = 2.0 and is not such a unit vector. Fortunately, in VRML, a normal need not be a unit vector; any vector of any length will do.*

The normal computed using the three triangle vertices 0, 1, and 2 can be used for the entire triangle face, or just for the single vertex in the middle of this list: vertex 1. If, instead, you use vertices 1, 2, and then 0, you are computing the normal at vertex 2. Finally, if you use triangle vertices 2, 0, and 1, you are computing the normal at vertex 0. For a flat triangle, all three vertex normals are the same. For a curved surface, however, the normal at each vertex may be different.

Using the above approach you can compute normals for any face, with any number of vertices and oriented in any direction. Typically, such normals are computed using a computer program. Once you have normals, however, you can associate them with specific parts, faces, or vertices in a VRML face set, line set, or point set.

Binding Normals

To bind different normals to different components of a shape, you need to:

1. Specify a list of normals.
2. Select how you want those normals bound to shape components.

A normal list specifies a series of normals, each described by an X, Y, and Z value, like a translation distance:

Normal Index	*Normal*
0	`0.0 0.0 2.0`
1	`0.0 2.0 0.0`
2	`2.0 0.0 0.0`

Each normal in the normal list has a **normal index**. The first normal has a normal index of 0, the second a normal index of 1, and so on. Using the normal index, you can later refer to a specific normal in the list without explicitly specifying again the X, Y, and Z components of the normal.

Using such a normal list, you can direct the VRML browser to bind each normal in the list to a different component of subsequent shapes. Different normal binding types select whether you want normals bound to the *overall* shape, or on a *per-part* basis, a *per-face* basis, or a *per-vertex* basis. You can, for instance, bind normal index 0 to the entire shape, to the first face of the shape, or to the first vertex of the first face of the shape. This gives you flexibility to control how you want a shape to be shaded.

The normal binding type you choose is a property, just like the current material binding, font style, coordinates, materials, and others. Like all properties, you select the normal binding type before you draw and it remains in effect until you change it again later in the file.

VRML supports four main types of normal bindings:

- **Overall**—*Bind a single normal to the entire shape.*
- **Per part**—*Bind a different normal to each part of the shape.*
- **Per face**—*Bind a different normal to each face of the shape.*
- **Per vertex**—*Bind a different normal to each vertex of the shape.*

For example, if you use an *overall* normal binding type, the entire shape is shaded using the same normal. This is, however, very uncommon.

Using a *per face* normal binding type, you can shade each face in an **IndexedFaceSet** node using a different normal.

Using a *per vertex* normal binding type, you can shade each vertex of a face, line, or point set using a different normal. It is this normal binding type that is the most common and that gives you the greatest control over how the VRML browser shades your shapes. Using the *per vertex* normal binding type, you can create smooth shading effects that obscure the faceted nature of your shapes. This shading technique is discussed in detail later in this chapter.

Using the **per-part**, **per-face**, and **per-vertex** normal binding types, the normals in the normal list are automatically used in order, one for each part, face, or vertex. For example, using a *per face* normal binding type and a set of faces in an **IndexedFaceSet** node, the first normal index is bound to face 0, the second normal index to face 1, and so on. Similarly, when using a *per vertex* normal binding type, the normals are used in order for each of the vertices listed by an **IndexedFaceSet** node, an **IndexedLineSet** node, or a **PointSet** node.

The *overall* normal binding type always uses only the first normal in a normal list, regardless of the length of the normal list or the number of parts, faces, or vertices in a shape. Everything in the shape is shaded using the first normal.

Indexing Normals

Using an approach similar to material binding, you can select specific normals from a normal list and bind them to the parts, faces, or vertices of a shape. This enables you to use, for instance, the 8th normal for the 1st face of a shape, the 12th normal for the 2nd face, and so on.

VRML supports three additional types of normal binding to perform normal indexing:

- **Per part indexed**—*Bind a different normal to each part of the shape, specified by index.*
- **Per face indexed**—*Bind a different normal to each face of the shape, specified by index.*
- **Per vertex indexed**—*Bind a different normal to each vertex of the shape, specified by index.*

For example, by specifying the *per vertex indexed* binding type, you can construct a triangle with an **IndexedFaceSet** node and bind a different normal to each vertex with a normal index list like this:

```
8, 12, 1
```

This normal index list binds normal index 8 to the first vertex, normal index 12 to the second, and normal index 1 to the third.

Binding Normals to Shapes

Using the **NormalBinding** node you can select how normals from a normal list are bound to the parts, faces, or vertices of all subsequent shapes drawn by the VRML browser. For instance, the example text in Figure 16.15 uses a *per vertex indexed* normal binding type to bind a different normal to each vertex of four rectangles.

```
#VRML V1.0 ascii

Coordinate3 {
   point [
      -2.00  3.00 0.00,
      -2.00 -3.00 0.00,
      -1.41  3.00 1.41,
      -1.41 -3.00 1.41,
       0.00  3.00 2.00,
       0.00 -3.00 2.00,
       1.41  3.00 1.41,
       1.41 -3.00 1.41,
       2.00  3.00 0.00,
       2.00 -3.00 0.00,
   ]
}
Normal {
   vector [
      -1.00 0.00 0.00,
      -0.71 0.00 0.71,
       0.00 0.00 1.00,
       0.71 0.00 0.71,
       1.00 0.00 0.00,
   ]
}
NormalBinding {
   value PER_VERTEX_INDEXED
}
IndexedFaceSet {
   coordIndex [
       0, 1, 3, 2, -1,
       2, 3, 5, 4, -1,
       4, 5, 7, 6, -1,
       6, 7, 9, 8, -1,
   ]
   normalIndex [
       0, 0, 1, 1,  0,
       1, 1, 2, 2,  0,
       2, 2, 3, 3,  0,
       3, 3, 4, 4,  0,
   ]
}
```

Figure 16.15 *Binding normals to vertices with the* per vertex indexed *binding type.*

Notice the structure and order of the VRML file in Figure 16.15. Reading from the top of the file, the **Coordinate3** node lists ten vertices. The **Normal** node that follows lists five normal vectors. The **NormalBinding** node specifies the *per vertex indexed* normal binding type. The **IndexedFaceSet** node draws four rectangles, shading each of the faces with a different normal bound to each vertex. Normal indexes for each vertex are specified by the **normalIndex** field of the **IndexedFaceSet** node and specific normals in the **Normal** node's normal list.

Understanding the **Normal** Node Syntax

The **Normal** node has a single **vector** field whose value is a list of normal vectors, enclosed within square brackets and separated by commas. Each normal vector is comprised of an X, a Y, and a Z value. The **Normal** node defines a normal list for use later by VRML's normal binding features.

SYNTAX **Normal node**

```
Normal {
   vector 0.0 0.0 1.0      # X, Y, Z distance
}
```

The entire normal list is included in the **normal property**. **Separator** nodes save and restore the whole normal list, and shape nodes use the normal list to bind different normals to different parts, faces, or vertices of a shape.

Understanding the **NormalBinding** Node Syntax

The **NormalBinding** node has a single **value** field that selects the normal binding type to use:

- ***DEFAULT***—*Bind appropriately for the shape.*
- ***OVERALL***—*Bind a single normal to the entire shape.*
- ***PER_PART***—*Bind a different normal to each part of the shape.*
- ***PER_FACE***—*Bind a different normal to each face of the shape.*
- ***PER_VERTEX***—*Bind a different normal to each vertex of the shape.*
- ***PER_PART_INDEXED***—*Bind a different normal to each part of the shape, specified by index.*
- ***PER_FACE_INDEXED***—*Bind a different normal to each face of the shape, specified by index.*
- ***PER_VERTEX_INDEXED***—*Bind a different normal to each vertex of the shape, specified by index.*

SYNTAX **NormalBinding node**

```
NormalBinding {
   value DEFAULT      # Binding type
}
```

An **OVERALL** normal binding type applies the first normal in the current normal list and applies it to the entire shape.

The **PER_PART**, **PER_FACE**, and **PER_VERTEX** normal binding types apply consecutive normals in the current normal list to shape parts, faces, and vertices, in order. Normal index 0 is bound to part, face, or vertex 0. Normal index 1 is bound to part, face, or vertex 1. And so forth.

The **PER_PART_INDEXED**, **PER_FACE_INDEXED**, and **PER_VERTEX_INDEXED** normal binding types apply specific normal indexes in the current normal list to shape parts, faces, and vertices. Normal indexes are specified using the **normalIndex** field of **IndexedFaceSet** and **IndexedLineSet** nodes discussed later.

Each of the shape node types in VRML have their own **DEFAULT** normal binding type. The shape nodes are discussed in later sections, along with their default normal binding types.

Understanding the Extended **IndexedFaceSet** Node Syntax

The **IndexedFaceSet** node has four fields: **coordIndex**, **materialIndex**, **normalIndex**, and **textureCoordIndex**.

SYNTAX **IndexedFaceSet node**

```
IndexedFaceSet {
   coordIndex        [0]      # Coordinate index list
   materialIndex     -1       # Material index list
   normalIndex       -1       # Normal index list
   textureCoordIndex -1       # Texture index list
}
```

The **coordIndex** field is discussed in Chapter 14 and the **materialIndex** field in Chapter 15. Both fields work as described in those chapters when using normal binding.

The **textureCoordIndex** field is discussed in a later chapter.

The **normalIndex** field specifies a list of normal indexes, enclosed within square brackets and separated by commas. Each normal index specifies a normal from the current normal list. A normal index of 0, for instance, specifies the first normal in the current normal list. Normal index 1 specifies the second, and so on.

Understanding the Extended **IndexedLineSet** Node Syntax

The **IndexedLineSet** node has four fields: **coordIndex**, **materialIndex**, **normalIndex**, and **textureCoordIndex**.

SYNTAX **IndexedLineSet node**

```
IndexedLineSet {
coordIndex         [0]     # Coordinate index list
materialIndex      -1      # Material index list
normalIndex        -1      # Normal index list
textureCoordIndex  -1      # Texture index list
}
```

The **coordIndex** field is discussed in Chapter 14 and the **materialIndex** field in Chapter 15. Both fields work as described in those chapters when using normal binding.

The **textureCoordIndex** field is discussed in a later chapter.

The **normalIndex** field specifies a list of normal indexes, enclosed within square brackets and separated by commas. Each normal index specifies a normal from the current normal list. A normal index of 0, for instance, specifies the first normal in the current normal list. Normal index 1 selects the second, and so on.

Understanding Normal Binding with Primitive Shapes

Each of the primitive shapes computes its own normals internally. The **Normal** and **NormalBinding** nodes have no effect on how **Cube**, **Cone**, **Cylinder**, and **Sphere** shapes are shaded.

Understanding Normal Binding with Text Shapes

Text shapes created with the **AsciiText** node compute their own normals internally. The **Normal** and **NormalBinding** nodes have no effect when shading text shapes.

Understanding Normal Binding with Point Sets

Normals and normal indexes are used differently depending on the normal binding type chosen for the point set:

- *OVERALL—One normal is bound to the entire set of points.* If no normal list is currently defined by a **Normal** node, then the default normal list is used containing the single normal: `0.0, 0.0, 1.0`. The value of the **startIndex** field is used as a normal index selecting the normal in the current normal list to be used to shade all points in the point set.
- *PER_PART—Same as PER_VERTEX.*
- *PER_PART_INDEXED—Same as PER_VERTEX.*
- *PER_FACE—Same as PER_VERTEX.*
- *PER_FACE_INDEXED—Same as PER_VERTEX.*

- ***PER_VERTEX***—*A different normal is bound to each vertex in the point set.* If no normal list is currently defined by a **Normal** node, then the default normal list is used containing the single normal: `0.0, 0.0, 1.0`. The value of the **startIndex** field is used as a normal index selecting the normal in the current normal list to be used for the first vertex. The second vertex is shaded with the normal at **startIndex**+1, the third at **startIndex**+2, and so on.
- ***PER_VERTEX_INDEXED***—*Same as* ***PER_VERTEX***.
- ***DEFAULT***—*No normals are used when shading points in the point set.* Every point is shaded as if it were face-on to a light, regardless of its orientation to a light. Values in the current normal list are unused.

TIP *For all normal binding types except* ***DEFAULT****, if you don't set the current normal list with a* ***Normal*** *node, the VRML browser uses a default normal list containing a single normal:* `0.0, 0.0, 1.0`*. Do not rely on this default normal list. If you are using normals, and have set the normal binding type using a* ***NormalBinding*** *node, set the current normal list using a* ***Normal*** *node before drawing with a* ***PointSet*** *node.*

TIP *All normal binding types index the current normal list to specify normals for each vertex. If there are more normal indexes than there are normals in the current normal list, unpredictable results may occur. Some VRML browsers detect this problem and report an error. Others do not. If you are using normals, be sure you specify one normal for each normal index.*

TIP *Technically, a point has no normal since it doesn't have a front, back, or any 3-D dimensions. VRML extends the notion of a point by considering it to be a tiny face. A normal for the point's tiny face controls the shading of that point just as if the point were a 3-D shape with a front and back. So, a point with a normal pointing directly at a light is shaded brightly. A point with a normal pointing directly away from a light is shaded dark.*

When you bind normals to point sets, you typically follow one of two approaches:

- *Shade points without normals, as if they are face-on to a light.* This is the easiest and most common approach. Leave the normal binding type set to **DEFAULT**, don't specify a **Normal** node, and don't specify a **NormalBinding** node. All of the point sets created in previous chapters use this approach.
- *Provide your own normal for every vertex.* Set the normal binding type with a **NormalBinding** node to **PER_VERTEX**. List the normals in a **Normal** node, one per vertex, arranged to correspond with the vertex coordinates in a neighboring **Coordinate3** node. The first normal is bound to the first vertex, the second is bound to the second vertex, and

so on. The VRML browser then uses the **startIndex** field for coordinates and their associated normals.

Typically, points are not shaded based on normals. The normal binding type is left set to **DEFAULT** and no normals are provided.

Understanding Normal Binding with Face Sets

Normals and normal indexes are used differently depending on the normal binding type chosen for the face set:

- ***OVERALL****—One normal is bound to the entire set of faces.* If no normal list is currently defined by a **Normal** node, then the default normal list is used containing the single normal: `0.0, 0.0, 1.0`. All faces in the face set are shaded using the first normal in the current normal list. The **normalIndex** field is unused.
- ***PER_PART****—Same as* ***PER_FACE****.*
- ***PER_PART_INDEXED****—Same as* ***PER_FACE_INDEXED****.*
- ***PER_FACE****—A different normal is bound to each face in the face set.* If no normal list is currently defined by a **Normal** node, then the default normal list is used containing the single normal: `0.0, 0.0, 1.0`. The first normal in the current normal list binds to the first face, the second normal to the second face, and so on. The **normalIndex** field is unused.
- ***PER_FACE_INDEXED****—A different normal, selected by a normal index, is bound to each face in the face set.* If no normal list is currently defined by a **Normal** node, then the default normal list is used containing the single normal: `0.0, 0.0, 1.0`. Normal indexes in the **normalIndex** field specify a normal from the current normal list for each face of the face set. The first index in the field specifies the normal to bind to the first face, the second index for the second face, and so on. If the **normalIndex** field is not set, the coordinate indexes of the **coordIndex** field are used instead. The first coordinate index specifies the normal to bind to the first face, the second coordinate index for the second face, and so on.
- ***PER_VERTEX****—A different normal is bound to each vertex in the face set.* If no normal list is currently defined by a **Normal** node, then the default normal list is used containing the single normal: `0.0, 0.0, 1.0`. The first normal in the current normal list binds to the first vertex, the second normal to the second vertex, and so on. The **normalIndex** field is unused.
- ***PER_VERTEX_INDEXED****—A different normal, selected by a normal index, is bound to each vertex in the face set.* If no normal list is currently defined by a **Normal** node, then the default normal list is used containing the single normal: `0.0, 0.0, 1.0`. Normal indexes in the **normalIndex** field specify a normal from the current normal list for each vertex of the

face set. The first index in the field specifies the normal to bind to the first vertex, the second index for the second vertex, and so on. A normal index must correspond each vertex and each –1 face divider value in the vertex list. If the **normalIndex** field is not set, the coordinate indexes of the **coordIndex** field are used instead. The first coordinate index specifies the normal to bind to the first vertex, the second coordinate index for the second vertex, and so on.

- *DEFAULT—Similar to* **PER_VERTEX_INDEXED** *except that if no normal list is currently defined by a* **Normal** *node, then normals are automatically generated for each vertex of each face in the face set.* Values in the **normalIndex** field are overridden by this automatic normal binding.

TIP *For all normal binding types except* ***DEFAULT****, if you don't set the current normal list with a* ***Normal*** *node, the VRML browser will use a default normal list containing a single normal:* `0.0, 0.0, 1.0`*. It is virtually never a good idea to rely on this default normal list. If you are using normals, and have set the normal binding type using a* ***NormalBinding*** *node, set the current normal list using a* ***Normal*** *node before drawing with an* ***IndexedFaceSet*** *node.*

TIP *All normal binding types index the current normal list to specify normals for each part, face, or vertex. If there are more normal indexes than there are normals in the current normal list, unpredictable results may occur. Some VRML browsers detect this problem and report an error. Others do not. If you are using normals, be sure you specify one normal for each normal index.*

TIP *For the* ***DEFAULT****,* ***PER_PART_INDEXED****,* ***PER_FACE_INDEXED****, and* ***PER_VERTEX_INDEXED*** *normal binding types, normal indexes are used from the* ***normalIndex*** *field, one for each face or vertex. If there are more faces or vertices in the* ***IndexedFaceSet*** *node than there are normal indexes in its* ***normalIndex*** *field, unpredictable results may occur. Some VRML browsers detect this problem and report an error. Others do not. If you are using normals and normal indexing, you should be sure to have at least one normal index for each face or vertex in the* ***IndexedFaceSet*** *node, depending on the normal binding type you are using.*

TIP *For the* ***DEFAULT*** *and* ***PER_VERTEX_INDEXED*** *normal binding types, a normal index from the* ***normalIndex*** *field must correspond to each vertex, including –1 valued indexes used to mark the end of one face's vertices and the start of the next face's vertices.*

Notice that the **DEFAULT**, **PER_PART_INDEXED**, **PER_FACE_INDEXED**, and **PER_VERTEX_INDEXED** normal binding types can all use the coordinate indexes in the **coordIndex** field as normal indexes if you don't provide explicit normal indexes in a **normalIndex** field. This is very convenient when creating shaded shapes that have a unique computed normal in a **Normal** node for each vertex of the shape described in a corresponding **Coordinate3** node.

TIP *When used with the **PER_PART_INDEXED** and **PER_FACE_INDEXED** normal binding types, using the **coordIndex** field's values as normal indexes can produce unexpected results. For each of these types, the first **coordIndex** field value selects the normal for the* first face. *The second **coordIndex** field value selects the normal for the* second face, *even though that **coordIndex** field value is actually the second vertex of the* first face. *To avoid these problems, include explicit normal indexes for each face using the **normalIndex** field.*

When you bind normals to face sets, you typically follow one of three approaches:

- *Let the VRML browser compute normals for you.* This is the easiest and most common approach. Leave the normal binding type set to **DEFAULT**, don't specify a **Normal** node, don't specify a **NormalBinding** node, and don't fill in the **normalIndex** field of the **IndexedFaceSet** node. All of the face sets created in previous chapters use this approach.
- *Provide your own normal for every vertex.* Set the normal binding type with a **NormalBinding** node to **PER_VERTEX_INDEXED**. List the normals in a **Normal** node, one per vertex, and arranged to correspond with the vertex coordinates in a neighboring **Coordinate3** node. The first normal is bound to the first vertex, the second is bound to the second vertex, and so on. Don't fill in the **normalIndex** field of the **IndexedFaceSet** node, and let the VRML browser use the **coordIndex** field for both coordinates and their associated normals.
- *Provide your own normal for every vertex.* Set the normal binding type with a **NormalBinding** node to **PER_VERTEX_INDEXED**. List the normals in a **Normal** node in any order, then specify in the **normalIndex** field of the **IndexedFaceSet** node the appropriate normal to bind to each vertex. Be sure to include one normal index for every coordinate in the **coordIndex** field, including –1 face divider coordinate indexes.

Typically, the **PER_PART**, **PER_PART_INDEXED**, **PER_FACE**, and **PER_FACE_INDEXED** normal binding types are rarely used. If you compute your own normals, do so on a vertex-by-vertex basis. This enables you to achieve the smoothing effects discussed later in this chapter.

Understanding Normal Binding with Line Sets

Normals and normal indexes are used differently depending on the normal binding type chosen for the line set. These features are very similar to those for indexed face sets.

- ***OVERALL**—One normal is bound to the entire set of lines.* If no normal list is currently defined by a **Normal** node, then the default normal list is used containing the single normal: `0.0, 0.0, 1.0`. All lines in the line set are shaded using the first normal in the current normal list. The **normalIndex** field is unused.
- ***PER_PART**—A different normal is bound to each line segment in the line set.* If no normal list is currently defined by a **Normal** node, then the default normal list is used containing the single normal: `0.0, 0.0, 1.0`. The first normal in the current normal list binds to the first line segment, the second normal to the second line segment, and so on. The **normalIndex** field is unused.
- ***PER_PART_INDEXED**—A different normal, selected by a normal index, is bound to each line segment in the line set.* If no normal list is currently defined by a **Normal** node, then the default normal list is used containing the single normal: `0.0, 0.0, 1.0`. Normal indexes in the **normalIndex** field specify a normal from the current normal list for each line segment of the line set. The first index in the field specifies the normal to bind to the first line segment, the second index for the second line segment, and so on. If the **normalIndex** field is not set, the coordinate indexes of the **coordIndex** field are used instead. The first coordinate index specifies the normal to bind to the first line segment, the second coordinate index for the second line segment, and so on.
- ***PER_FACE**—A different normal is bound to each polyline in the line set.* If no normal list is currently defined by a **Normal** node, then the default normal list is used containing the single normal: `0.0, 0.0, 1.0`. The first normal in the current normal list binds to the first polyline (including all of its line segments), the second normal to the second polyline, and so on. The **normalIndex** field is unused.
- ***PER_FACE_INDEXED**—A different normal, selected by a normal index, is bound to each polyline in the line set.* If no normal list is currently defined by a **Normal** node, then the default normal list is used containing the single normal: `0.0, 0.0, 1.0`. Normal indexes in the **normalIndex** field specify a normal from the current normal list for each polyline (including all of its line segments) of the line set. The first index in the field specifies the normal to bind to the first polyline, the second index for the second polyline, and so on. If the **normalIndex** field is not set, the coordinate indexes of the **coordIndex** field are used instead. The first coordinate index specifies the normal to bind to the first polyline, the second coordinate index for the second polyline, and so on.
- ***PER_VERTEX**—A different normal is bound to each vertex in the line set.* If no normal list is currently defined by a **Normal** node, then the default normal list is used containing the single normal: `0.0, 0.0, 1.0`. The first normal in the current normal list binds to the first vertex, the second normal to the second vertex, and so on. The **normalIndex** field is unused.

- ***PER_VERTEX_INDEXED****—A different normal, selected by a normal index, is bound to each vertex in the line set.* If no normal list is currently defined by a **Normal** node, then the default normal list is used containing the single normal: `0.0, 0.0, 1.0`. Normal indexes in the **normalIndex** field specify a normal from the current normal list for each vertex of the line set. The first index in the field specifies the normal to bind to the first vertex, the second index for the second vertex, and so on. If the **normalIndex** field is not set, the coordinate indexes of the **coordIndex** field are used instead. The first coordinate index specifies the normal to bind to the first vertex, the second coordinate index for the second vertex, and so on.
- ***DEFAULT****—Similar to* ***PER_VERTEX_INDEXED*** *except that if no normal list is currently defined by a* ***Normal*** *node, the polylines in the line set are not shaded.* Instead, every polyline is shaded as if it were face-on to a light regardless of its orientation to a light. Values in the **normalIndex** field are overridden by this effect.

All of the cautionary notes discussed for indexed face sets also apply to indexed line sets.

When you bind normals to line set, you typically follow one of three approaches.

- *Shade polylines without normals, exactly as if they are face-on to a light.* This is the easiest and most common approach. Leave the normal binding type set to **DEFAULT**, don't specify a **Normal** node, and don't specify a **NormalBinding** node. All of the line sets created in previous chapters use this approach.

- *Provide your own normal for every vertex.* Set the normal binding type with a **NormalBinding** node to **PER_VERTEX_INDEXED**. List the normals in a **Normal** node, one per vertex, and arranged to correspond with the vertex coordinates in a neighboring **Coordinate3** node. The first normal is bound to the first vertex, the second is bound to the second vertex, and so on. Don't fill in the **normalIndex** field of the **IndexedLineSet** node and let the VRML browser use the **coordIndex** field for both coordinates and their associated normals.

- *Provide your own normal for every vertex.* Set the normal binding type with a **NormalBinding** node to **PER_VERTEX_INDEXED**. List the normals in a **Normal** node in any order, then fill in the **normalIndex** field of the **IndexedLineSet** node. Be sure to include one normal index for every coordinate in the **coordIndex** field, including –1 polyline divider coordinate indexes.

Typically, lines are shaded as if they were face-on to a light using the first approach, previously described. Using your own normals to control line shading is not as common as it is for face sets.

Experimenting with Normal Binding and Normal Indexing

The following examples provide a more detailed examination of the ways in which normal binding and normal indexing features can be used and how they interact with nodes we've discussed in previous chapters.

Shading Using Your Own Normals

By default, the VRML browser computes vertex normals for you for all of your shapes. By overriding this default normal computation you can apply your own normals and achieve non-standard shading effects.

To illustrate, the examples that follow all draw four rectangles arranged as facets around half of a column. Figure 16.16 shows outlines of the four rectangles, and Figure 16.17 shows a top view showing the half column's facets.

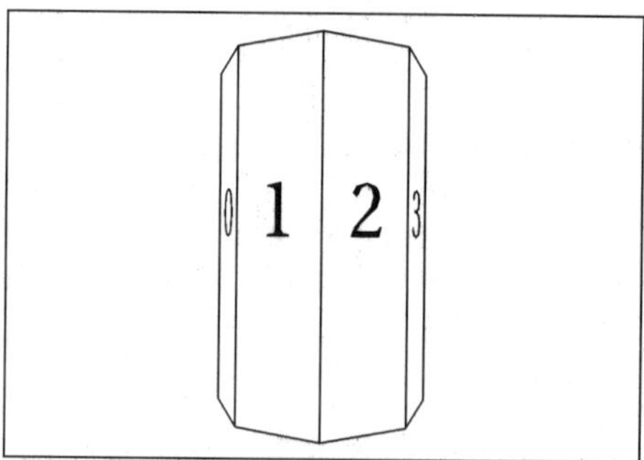

Figure 16.16 *Outlines of the four rectangles composing the half-column's facets.*

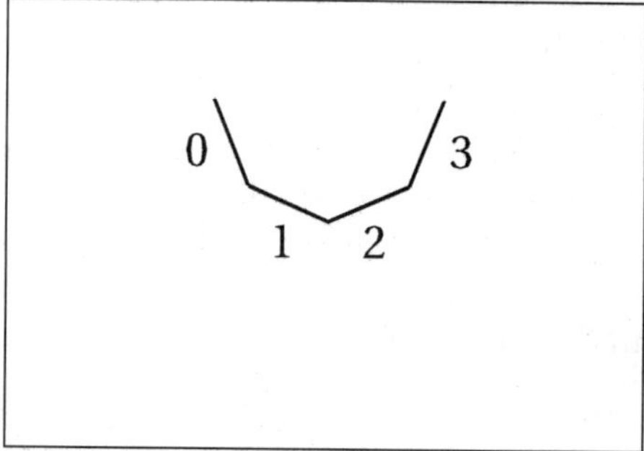

Figure 16.17 *A top view of the half-column's faces.*

The example text in Figure 16.18 draws and shades this column using normals automatically computed by the VRML browser.

```
#VRML V1.0 ascii

Coordinate3 {
   point [
      -2.00  3.00 0.00,
      -2.00 -3.00 0.00,
      -1.41  3.00 1.41,
      -1.41 -3.00 1.41,
       0.00  3.00 2.00,
       0.00 -3.00 2.00,
       1.41  3.00 1.41,
       1.41 -3.00 1.41,
       2.00  3.00 0.00,
       2.00 -3.00 0.00,
   ]
}
IndexedFaceSet {
   coordIndex [
      0, 1, 3, 2, -1,
      2, 3, 5, 4, -1,
      4, 5, 7, 6, -1,
      6, 7, 9, 8, -1,
   ]
}
```

Figure 16.18 *The shaded half-column.*

Since this example doesn't explicitly set the normal binding type, it remains at its initial **DEFAULT** value and the VRML browser automatically computes normals for each vertex of each face in the face set. Using these normals, the half-column is shaded and clearly reveals its faceted structure.

Imagine you want to create the appearance of a smoothly rounded half-column. The most direct approach is to use more rectangles to more closely approximate a rounded surface. The images in Figure 16.19 show the use of four (a), five (b), six (c), and seven (d) rectangular facets to approximate the curved surface of a rounded half-column. As the number of facets increases, the shading of the half-column makes it look more and more round.

Unfortunately, using more rectangular faces means the VRML browser has more to draw, and it takes longer to draw your world. If you use large numbers of faces throughout your world to simulate smooth surfaces, you can end up with so many faces that your VRML browser takes many seconds, or even minutes, to draw the world.

Using your own normals, however, you can create the smooth shading of a rounded half-column, or other curved surface, but use only a few faces and avoid slowing your VRML browser. To do this, you shade a flat face *as if it were curved*. This technique is called smooth shading.

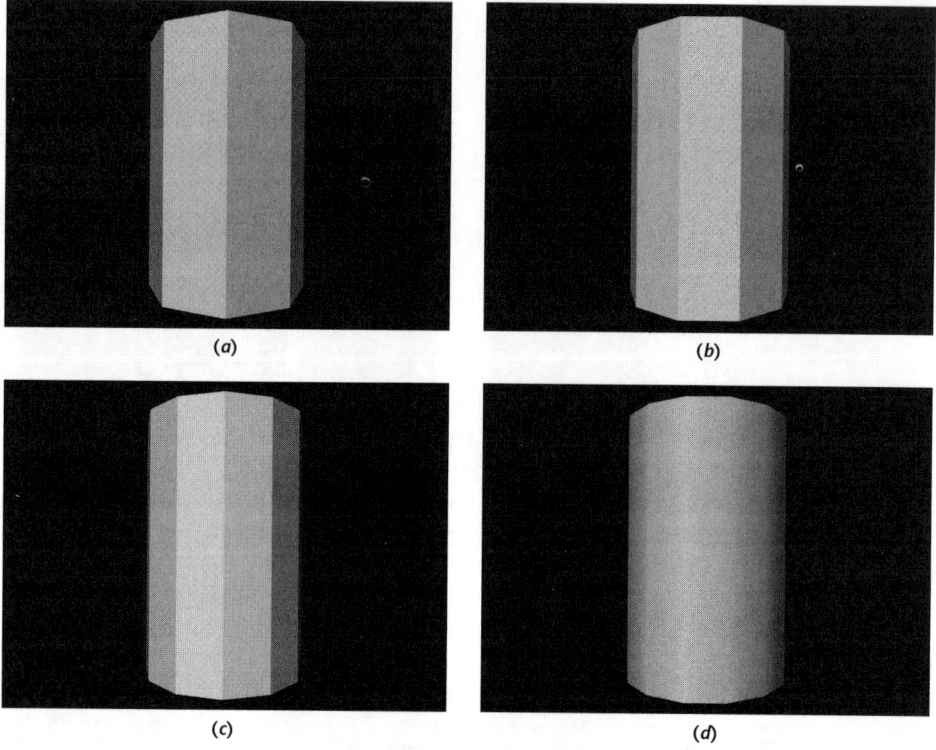

Figure 16.19 *Using more facets to create smoother shading: (a) four facets, (b) five facets, (c) six facets, and (d) seven facets.*

The example text in Figure 16.20 draws the same four rectangles of the half-column, but shades the rectangles as if they were curved surfaces. This illustrates the effect of the smooth shading technique. To do this, specially computed normals are bound to each vertex of each face.

```
#VRML V1.0 ascii

Coordinate3 {
   point [
      -2.00  3.00 0.00,
      -2.00 -3.00 0.00,
      -1.41  3.00 1.41,
      -1.41 -3.00 1.41,
       0.00  3.00 2.00,
       0.00 -3.00 2.00,
       1.41  3.00 1.41,
       1.41 -3.00 1.41,
       2.00  3.00 0.00,
       2.00 -3.00 0.00,
   ]
}
```

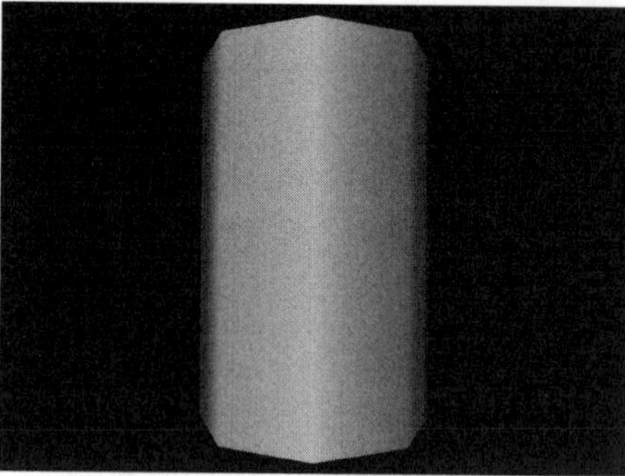

Figure 16.20 continues

```
Normal {
   vector [
      -1.00 0.00 0.00,
      -0.71 0.00 0.71,
       0.00 0.00 1.00,
       0.71 0.00 0.71,
       1.00 0.00 0.00,
   ]
}
NormalBinding {
   value PER_VERTEX_INDEXED
}
IndexedFaceSet {
   coordIndex [
      0, 1, 3, 2, -1,
      2, 3, 5, 4, -1,
      4, 5, 7, 6, -1,
      6, 7, 9, 8, -1,
   ]
   normalIndex [
      0, 0, 1, 1,  0,
      1, 1, 2, 2,  0,
      2, 2, 3, 3,  0,
      3, 3, 4, 4,  0,
   ]
}
```

Figure 16.20 *The smooth shading effect.*

Reading from the top of the file, the VRML browser is directed to:

1. Set the coordinates property to ten coordinates.
2. Set the normals property to five normal vectors.
3. Select a **PER_VERTEX_INDEXED** normal binding type.
4. Draw a list of faces.
   a. Draw a face with vertices 0, 1, 3, and 2 using normals 0, 0, 1, and 1, respectively.
   b. Draw a face with vertices 2, 3, 5, and 4 using normals 1, 1, 2, and 2, respectively.
   c. Draw a face with vertices 4, 5, 7, and 6 using normals 2, 2, 3, and 3, respectively.
   d. Draw a face with vertices 6, 7, 9, and 8 using normals 3, 3, 4, and 4, respectively.

Notice that a normal index is specified in the **normalIndex** field for each vertex in the **coordIndex** field, *including* the –1 index used to mark the end of one face's vertex list and the start of the next face's vertex list.

Using the smooth shading technique, the same four rectangles are shaded so that they more closely approximate a smoothly rounded half-column. Only by looking at the top and bottom edges of the faces is it obvious that the column is made of only four rectangles.

Understanding Smooth Shading

Performing smooth shading, as in the previous example, is the principal reason the **Normal** and **NormalBinding** nodes are available in VRML. Using this technique, you can shade simple faceted shapes so that they look like smoothly curved surfaces.

A faceted shape, like the half-column, approximates (rather poorly) the curved surface of a rounded half-column. Figure 16.21 shows a top view of the four facets, while Figure 16.22 shows a top view of a rounded half-column we'd like to approximate.

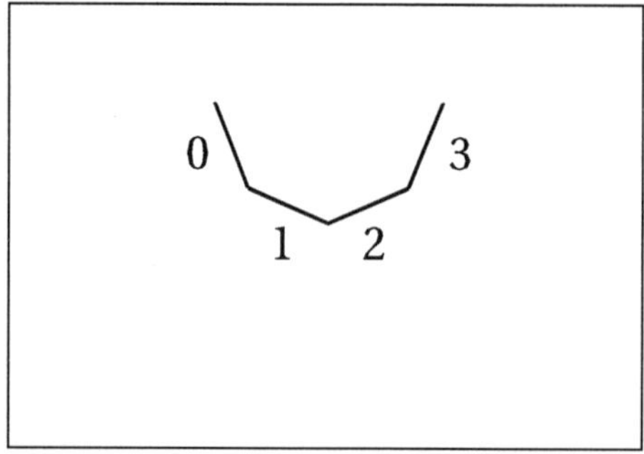

Figure 16.21 *Top view of four facets.*

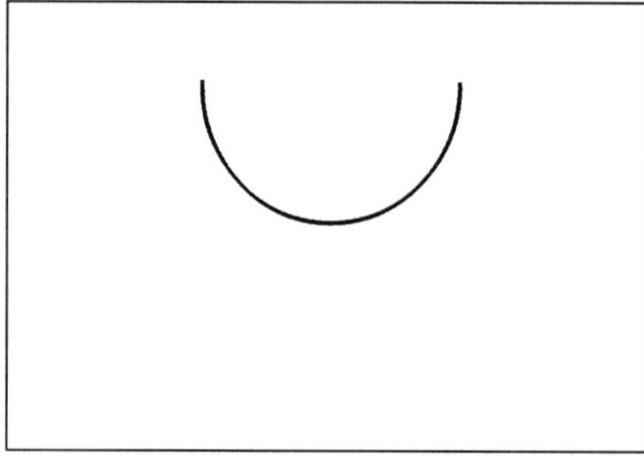

Figure 16.22 *Top view of smoothly rounded half-column.*

When the VRML browser automatically computes normals, it aims a normal straight out each face in the faceted column. Figure 16.23 shows a top view of the faceted column with normal arrows pointing out from each face. If you compute a perfectly smooth column, however, the normal at any point on the column points outward as if extending straight out from the center point of the column, such as those in Figure 16.24.

Figure 16.25 overlays the diagrams of the faceted column and the curved column. The normals at the centers of each face on the faceted column coincide perfectly with those of the curved column. But what about at the vertices of each face?

The VRML browser's automatic normal computation usually creates a single normal for each face in a shape. All of the vertices of a face share this normal. Figure 16.26 shows the faceted column top view again, but this time each face's normal arrow is shown pointing out of each vertex of each face.

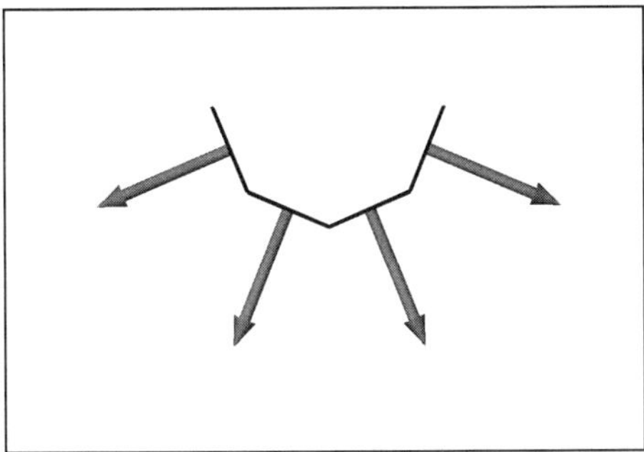

Figure 16.23 *Normals pointing straight out from each facet of the column.*

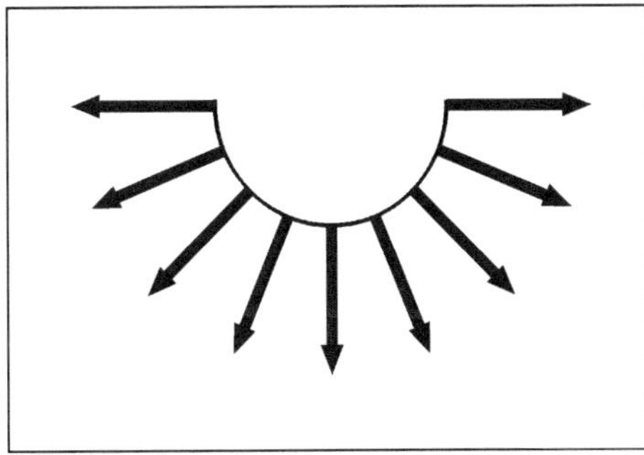

Figure 16.24 *Normals point out from the center of a perfectly smooth column.*

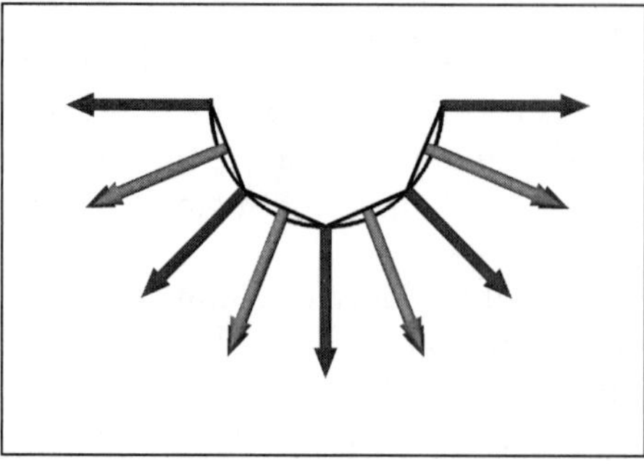

Figure 16.25 *Comparing facets with face normals to a smooth curve.*

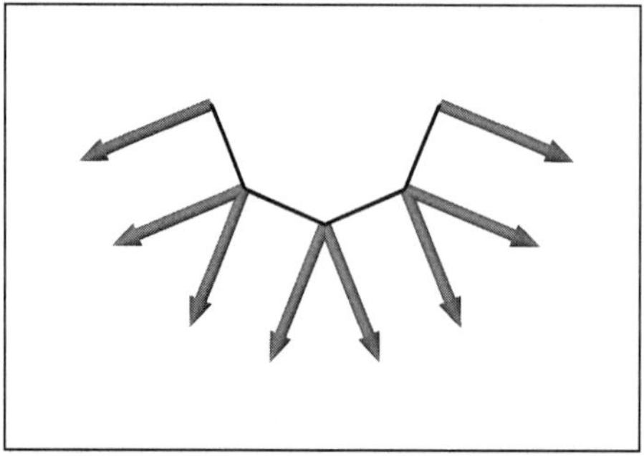

Figure 16.26 *Top view of normals pointing out from each vertex of each face.*

TIP *VRML can also compute a different normal for each vertex of a shape if you give it hints on how to do so. This feature of VRML is discussed in a later chapter in the discussion of the* ***ShapeHints*** *node.*

Figure 16.27 lays this new faceted column diagram over the curved column diagram. Notice that the normals used at the vertices for the faceted column are wrong. The true curved column normals point straight out from the center of the column, but the faceted column's vertex normals point off in one direction or another.

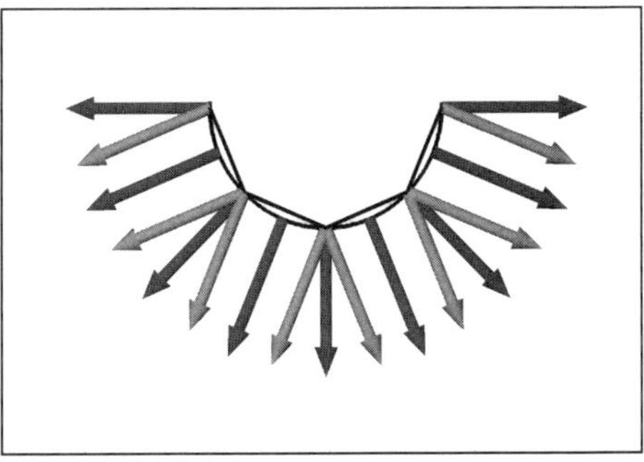

Figure 16.27 *Comparing facets with vertex normals to a smooth curve.*

Notice also that when a vertex is shared between two adjacent faces, it is assigned a different normal for each face on the faceted column. The shared vertex, however, represents a single point on the approximated curved column and should have only one normal, not two.

It is this series of problems with normals that leads to the faceted shading you see when using the VRML browser's automatic normal computation. The normals used do not accurately reflect the normals of the curved surface we are trying to approximate with facets.

Because the VRML browser doesn't know what kind of shape it is computing normals for, normal calculations typically compute a single face's vertex normals without knowing if the face is a facet that is supposed to approximate a smooth column or if the face is for the flat top of a table.

If the VRML browser always computed normals assuming that faces were approximating curved surfaces, then a face for a tabletop would be shaded as if it were bowed in the middle. If, however, the browser always computed normals assuming faces were flat, then the facets approximating curved surfaces would look flat when shaded. The latter choice is that made by the VRML browser. By choosing to assume that faces are flat, it enables you to correctly draw flat surfaces like tables, floors, walls, and so forth. This same choice, however, means that curved surfaces approximated by faces have incorrect normals and look faceted.

You can override the normal computations of the VRML browser and supply your own normals for each vertex. This smooth shading technique is needed to make the faceted half-column appear curved when shaded.

TIP *The next chapter discusses ways of tuning the VRML browser so that it can, in some cases, automatically compute normals as if a surface were curved.*

To smoothly shade the faceted half-column, compute vertex normals based on the true normals of the curved half-column we're trying to approximate. Figure 16.28 shows the corrected normals pointing outward from each vertex of the faceted half-column.

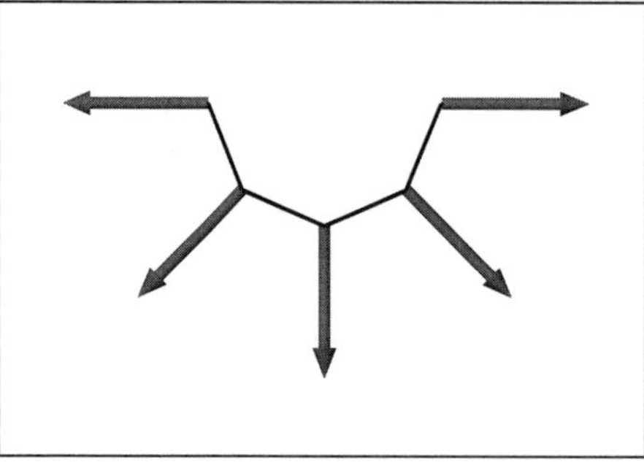

Figure 16.28 *Normals pointing out from each face's vertex.*

Using these new normals, the VRML browser can shade each face, gradually varying the face brightness from one edge to the other. Such shading closely approximates the shading that occurs on the smoothly rounded half-column, but uses only the four faces of the faceted half-column. Figure 16.29*a* shows the original faceted half column, Figure 16.29*b* the smoothly shaded, faceted half-column, and Figure 16.29*c* the ideal smoothly rounded half-column. The shading of Figures 16.29*b* and 16.29*c* are quite close, and yet the half-column has only four facets and will be drawn considerably quicker than the smoothly rounded half-column.

Calculating normals for facets depends on the smooth surface you are trying to approximate. All of the previous examples have approximated a half-column. The normals for such a surface always point straight out the half-column's radius. Other curved shapes, however, may require more complicated normal computations. Figure 16.30, for instance, shows the normal arrows for a sideways S shape (a sine wave).

You can compute normals for curved shapes like these using several techniques. When a shape is known to be curved based on a mathematical equation, such as the outline of a circle or the sine wave shown here, then the easiest approach is to use that same curve equation to generate the normals. For each vertex along the shape, compute a normal vector that is orthogonal (crosses the shape line at a 90.0-degree angle) at that vertex. For a circle, like the half-column used in the previous examples, the normal always points straight out along a radius line from the circle's center point.

In other cases, the curved surface you are trying to approximate with facets isn't based on a mathematical equation. To compute curve normals for a surface like this, follow the steps on 422.

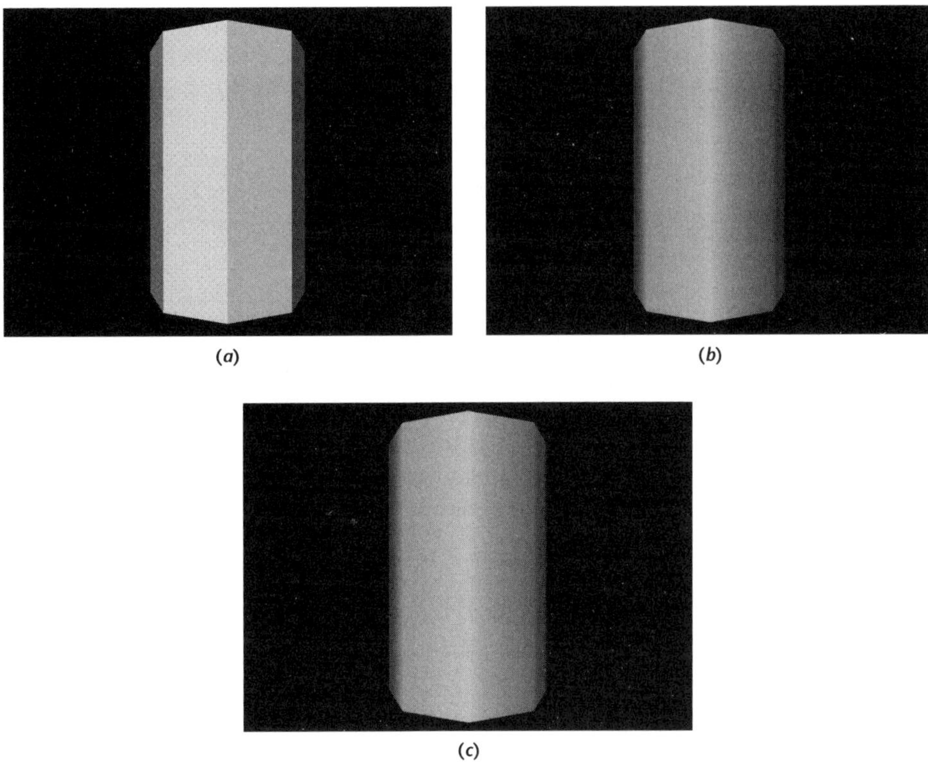

Figure 16.29 *Comparing half-column shading:* (a) *faceted,* (b) *smoothly shaded and faceted, and* (c) *smoothly rounded.*

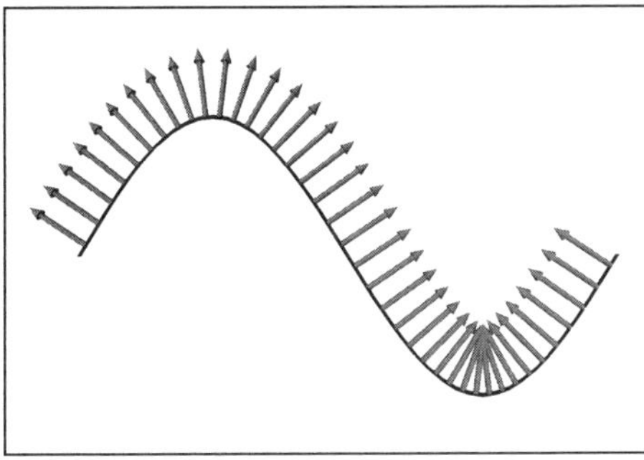

Figure 16.30 *The normals for a sine wave.*

1. Compute normals for each vertex of each shape face using the vector and cross-product calculations explained earlier.
2. Look at adjacent faces on your shape. If there are two side-by-side faces with an edge in common, they must share at least two vertices: one at each end of the common edge. At each shared vertex you calculated multiple normals in step 1, one normal for each face that shares that vertex. Average those normals together to get a single normal for each vertex.
3. Use the average vertex normals calculated in step 2 as the smooth shading vertex normals for your shape.

As we noted earlier, calculating normals is a time-consuming process and is best left to computer programs. Computing average normals, or normals based on curve equations, can be done with relatively simple programs, often written in scripting languages such as Perl. The normals for all of the examples presented in this chapter were computed using Perl scripts of less than a dozen lines.

Smoothly Shading Complex Shapes

Using the smooth shading technique, you can smoothly shade any shape. The example text in Figure 16.31 shades a vase.

```
#VRML V1.0 ascii

Coordinate3 {
   point [
       # ring 0
       0.32 2.00  0.00,
       0.10 2.00  0.30,
      -0.26 2.00  0.19,
      -0.26 2.00 -0.19,
       0.10 2.00 -0.30,
       # ring 1
       0.30 1.95  0.00,
       0.09 1.95  0.29,
      -0.24 1.95  0.18,
      -0.24 1.95 -0.18,
       0.09 1.95 -0.29,
       # ring 2
       0.42 1.60  0.00,
       0.13 1.60  0.40,
      -0.34 1.60  0.25,
      -0.34 1.60 -0.25,
       0.13 1.60 -0.40,
       # ring 3
       0.60 1.50  0.00,
       0.19 1.50  0.57,
      -0.48 1.50  0.35,
      -0.49 1.50 -0.35,
       0.18 1.50 -0.57,
```

Figure 16.31 continues

```
        # ring 4
        0.70  1.20  0.00,
        0.22  1.20  0.67,
       -0.57  1.20  0.41,
       -0.57  1.20 -0.41,
        0.21  1.20 -0.67,
        # ring 5
        0.40  0.00  0.00,
        0.12  0.00  0.38,
       -0.32  0.00  0.24,
       -0.32  0.00 -0.23,
        0.12  0.00 -0.38,
    ]
}
Normal {
    vector [
        # ring 0
        1.00  0.00  0.00,
        0.31  0.00  0.95,
       -0.81  0.00  0.59,
       -0.81  0.00 -0.59,
        0.31  0.00 -0.95,
        # ring 1
        1.00 -0.60  0.00,
        0.31 -0.60  0.95,
       -0.81 -0.60  0.59,
       -0.81 -0.60 -0.59,
        0.31 -0.60 -0.95,
        # ring 2
        1.00  1.00  0.00,
        0.31  1.00  0.95,
       -0.81  1.00  0.59,
       -0.81  1.00 -0.59,
        0.31  1.00 -0.95,
        # ring 3
        1.00  0.60  0.00,
        0.31  0.60  0.95,
       -0.81  0.60  0.59,
       -0.81  0.60 -0.59,
        0.31  0.60 -0.95,
        # ring 4
        1.00  0.00  0.00,
        0.31  0.00  0.95,
       -0.81  0.00  0.59,
       -0.81  0.00 -0.59,
        0.31  0.00 -0.95,
        # ring 5
        1.00 -1.00  0.00,
        0.31 -1.00  0.95,
       -0.81 -1.00  0.59,
       -0.81 -1.00 -0.59,
        0.31 -1.00 -0.95,
    ]
}
```

Figure 16.31 continues

```
NormalBinding {
   value PER_VERTEX_INDEXED
}
IndexedFaceSet {
   coordIndex [
      # ring 0
       0,  1,  6,  5, -1,
       1,  2,  7,  6, -1,
       2,  3,  8,  7, -1,
       3,  4,  9,  8, -1,
       4,  0,  5,  9, -1,
      # ring 1
       5,  6, 11, 10, -1,
       6,  7, 12, 11, -1,
       7,  8, 13, 12, -1,
       8,  9, 14, 13, -1,
       9,  5, 10, 14, -1,
      # ring 2
      10, 11, 16, 15, -1,
      11, 12, 17, 16, -1,
      12, 13, 18, 17, -1,
      13, 14, 19, 18, -1,
      14, 10, 15, 19, -1,
      # ring 3
      15, 16, 21, 20, -1,
      16, 17, 22, 21, -1,
      17, 18, 23, 22, -1,
      18, 19, 24, 23, -1,
      19, 15, 20, 24, -1,
      # ring 4
      20, 21, 26, 25, -1,
      21, 22, 27, 26, -1,
      22, 23, 28, 27, -1,
      23, 24, 29, 28, -1,
      24, 20, 25, 29, -1,
      # base
      25, 26, 27, 28, 29
   ]
}
```

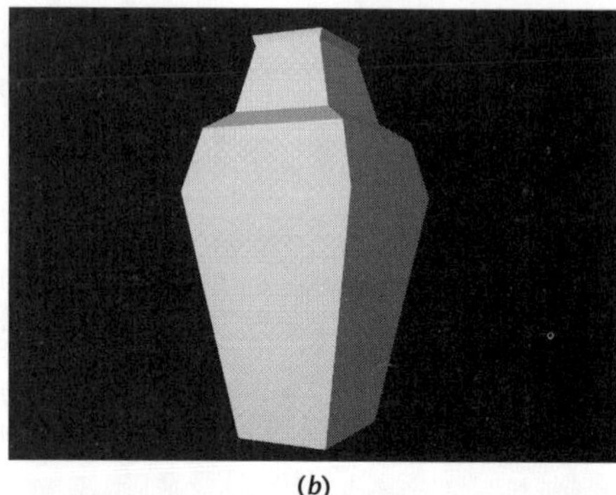

(*b*)

(*c*)

Figure 16.31 *The vase: (b) faceted and (c) smoothly shaded*

Figure 16.31*b* shows the smoothly shaded vase, while Figure 16.31*c* shows the original faceted vase.

Notice that the preceding example uses a unique normal computed for each vertex in the vase. These normals are listed in a **Normal** node in the same order as their associated coordinates in the **Coordinate3** node. Because the order is the same, the normal for the first vertex is the first in the normal list, the normal for the second vertex is the second in the list, and so on. The same coordinate index that selects a coordinate from the coordinate list can, then, be used as the normal index to select the associated normal from the normal list. Since the indexes are the same, the **normalIndex** field of the **IndexedFaceSet** node need not be set and the VRML browser automatically uses the coordIndex value as a normal index as well as for a coordinate index. This technique reduces the VRML file's size and saves a bit of typing.

Smoothly Shading and Coloring Shapes

You can use **Material** nodes to control the shading color while you control the shading brightness with normals in a **Normal** node. The following example combines the white, blue, and pink flower vase coloring from Chapter 15 with the smooth shading normals mentioned here. The resulting vase is shown in Figure 16.32.

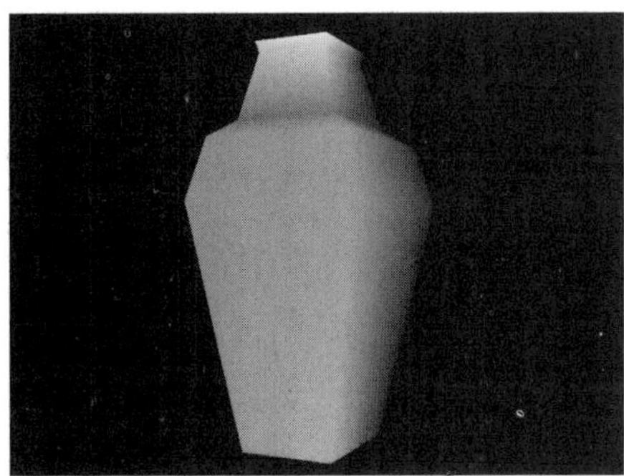

```
#VRML V1.0 ascii

Coordinate3 {
    point [
        # ring 0
        0.32 2.00  0.00,
        0.10 2.00  0.30,
       -0.26 2.00  0.19,
       -0.26 2.00 -0.19,
        0.10 2.00 -0.30,
        # ring 1
        0.30 1.95  0.00,
        0.09 1.95  0.29,
       -0.24 1.95  0.18,
       -0.24 1.95 -0.18,
        0.09 1.95 -0.29,
        # ring 2
        0.42 1.60  0.00,
        0.13 1.60  0.40,
       -0.34 1.60  0.25,
       -0.34 1.60 -0.25,
        0.13 1.60 -0.40,
        # ring 3
        0.60 1.50  0.00,
        0.19 1.50  0.57,
       -0.48 1.50  0.35,
       -0.49 1.50 -0.35,
        0.18 1.50 -0.57,
        # ring 4
        0.70 1.20  0.00,
        0.22 1.20  0.67,
       -0.57 1.20  0.41,
       -0.57 1.20 -0.41,
        0.21 1.20 -0.67,
```

Figure 16.32 continues

```
            # ring 5
            0.40  0.00  0.00,
            0.12  0.00  0.38,
           -0.32  0.00  0.24,
           -0.32  0.00 -0.23,
            0.12  0.00 -0.38,
        ]
    }
    Normal {
        vector [
            # ring 0
            1.00  0.00  0.00,
            0.31  0.00  0.95,
           -0.81  0.00  0.59,
           -0.81  0.00 -0.59,
            0.31  0.00 -0.95,
            # ring 1
            1.00 -0.60  0.00,
            0.31 -0.60  0.95,
           -0.81 -0.60  0.59,
           -0.81 -0.60 -0.59,
            0.31 -0.60 -0.95,
            # ring 2
            1.00  1.00  0.00,
            0.31  1.00  0.95,
           -0.81  1.00  0.59,
           -0.81  1.00 -0.59,
            0.31  1.00 -0.95,
            # ring 3
            1.00  0.60  0.00,
            0.31  0.60  0.95,
           -0.81  0.60  0.59,
           -0.81  0.60 -0.59,
            0.31  0.60 -0.95,
            # ring 4
            1.00  0.00  0.00,
            0.31  0.00  0.95,
           -0.81  0.00  0.59,
           -0.81  0.00 -0.59,
            0.31  0.00 -0.95,
            # ring 5
            1.00 -1.00  0.00,
            0.31 -1.00  0.95,
           -0.81 -1.00  0.59,
           -0.81 -1.00 -0.59,
            0.31 -1.00 -0.95,
        ]
    }
```

Figure 16.32 continues

COLOR PLATE 1

These color swatch charts illustrate only a few of the many colors you can create in VRML. To specify one of these colors in your VRML file: **1.** Locate the color on one of the color swatch charts: **2.** Make a note of the row number and column letter corresponding to the swatch. **3.** Find the corresponding RGB color table in Appendix B, and locate the red (R), green (G), and blue (B) values corresponding to the row number and column letter of the color swatch. **4.** Use the red, green, and blue color values in your **Material** node.

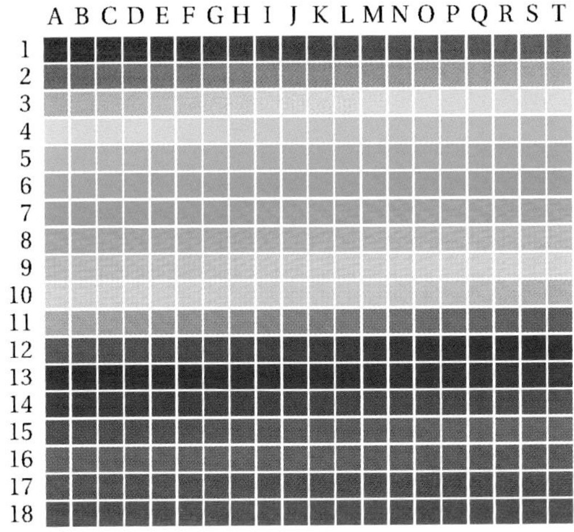

1a *Vivid colors (see Appendix B, Table B.1)*

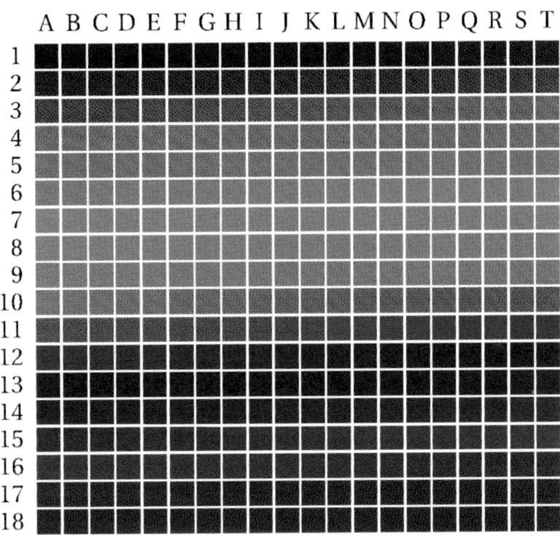

1b *Dark colors (see Appendix B, Table B.2)*

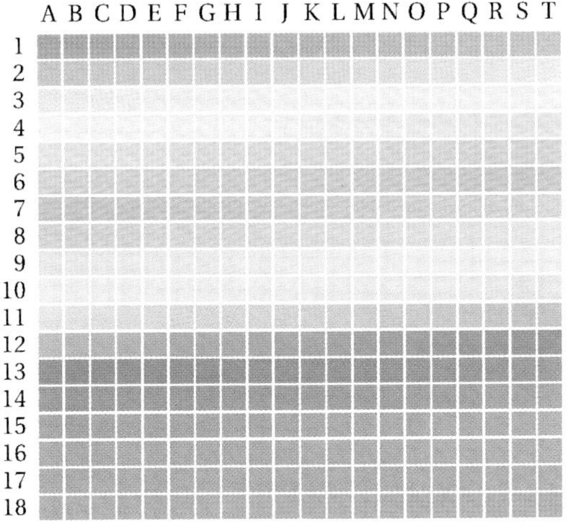

1c *Pastel colors (see Appendix B, Table B.3)*

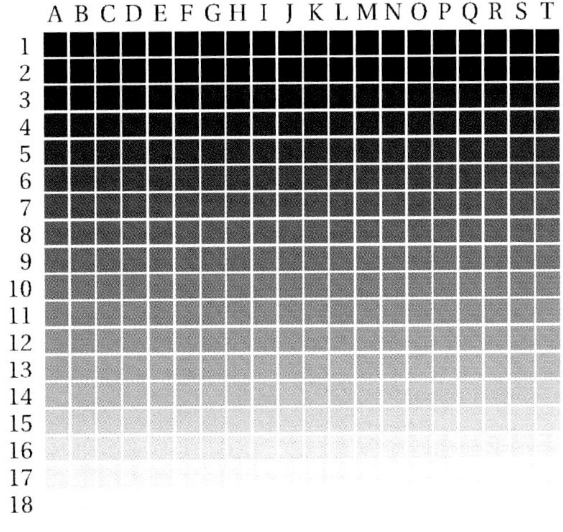

1d *Shades of gray (see Appendix B, Table B.4)*

COLOR PLATE 2

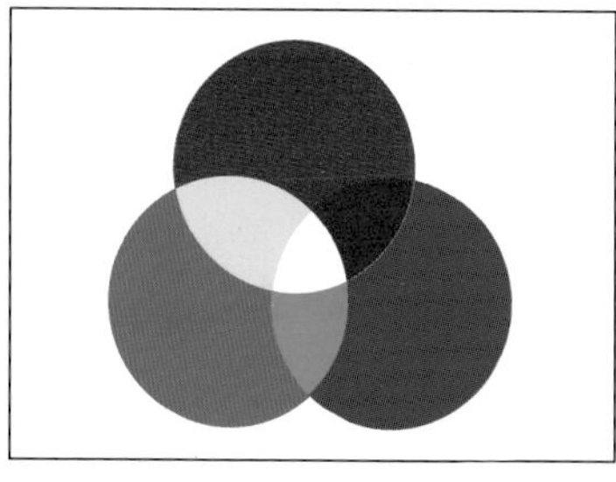

2a *Spots created by three colored flashlights (one red, one green, one blue) on a white wall (see text Figure 10.1).*

2b *Using emissive color and turning* off *shading to create a glowing light bulb (see text Figure 10.8).*

2c *Turbine with each blade a different color (see text Figure 10.11).*

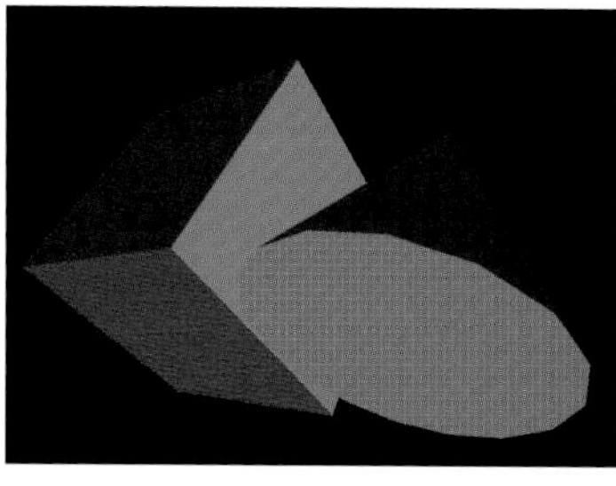

2d *Setting the material binding type and coloring a cube, then resetting the material binding and coloring a cone (see text Figure 15.5).*

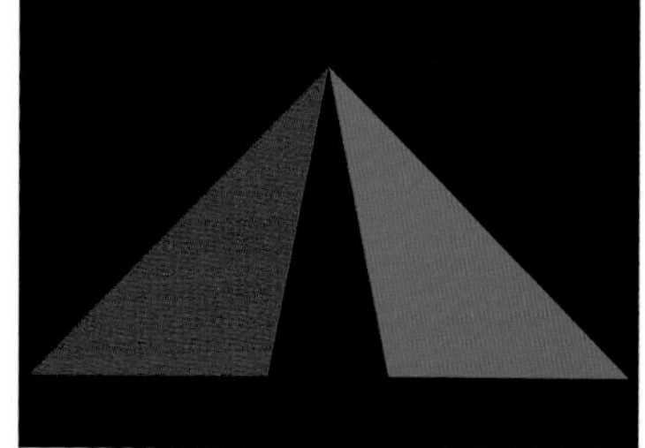

2e *Coloring* per face *the faces of two triangles (see text Figure 15.10)—compare to Color Plate 2f.*

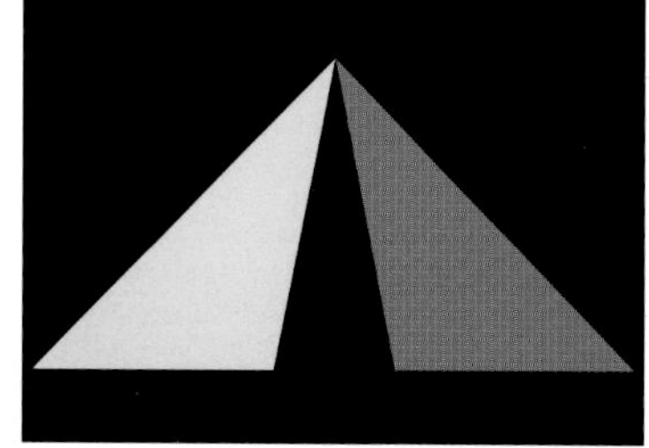

2f *Coloring* per face indexed *the faces of two triangles (see text Figure 15.11)—compare to Color Plate 2e.*

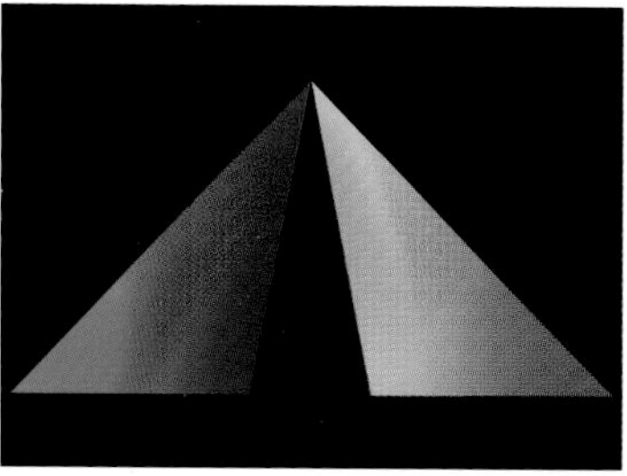

2g *Coloring* per vertex *the faces of two triangles (see text Figure 15.12)—compare to Color Plate 2h.*

2h *Coloring* per vertex indexed *the faces of two triangles (see text Figure 15.13)—compare to Color Plate 2g.*

COLOR PLATE 3

3a *A vase shaded with a pink, blue, and white color gradient (see text Figure 15.23).*

3b *A small cottage with no textures (see text Figure 18.1a)—compare to Color Plate 3c.*

3c *A small cottage with textures applied (see text Figure 18.1b)—compare to Color Plate 3b.*

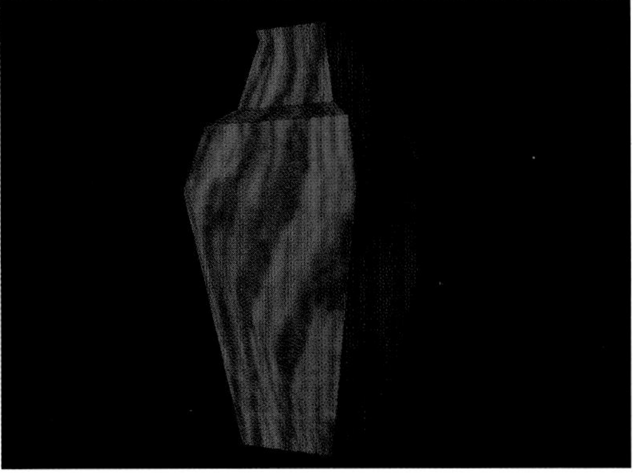

3d *A vase with a wood texture (see text Figure 18.39).*

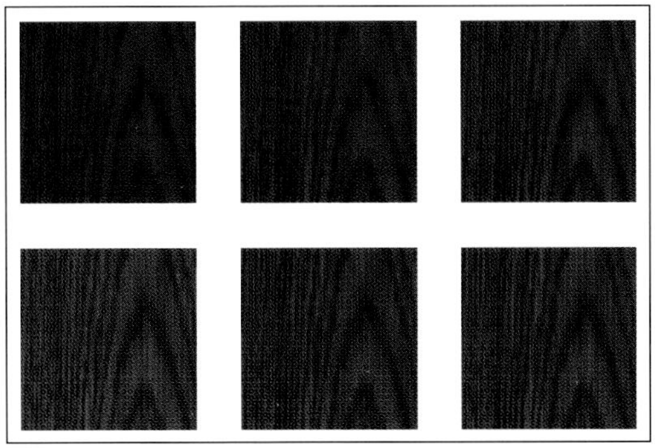

3e *Six different wood textures created by applying color to a grayscale texture (see text Figure 18.42).*

COLOR PLATE 4

White Light
Red Light
Green Light
Blue Light

4a *The effects of shining white, red, green, and blue light on different colored spheres (see text Figure 19.4).*

4b *Using point lights to create colored lights (see text Figure 19.21).*

4c *A hallway of meshes illustrating lighting effects (see text Figure 19.22).*

4d *A dungeon (see text Figure 21.1).*

```
NormalBinding {
   value PER_VERTEX_INDEXED
}
Material {
   diffuseColor [
      1.0 1.0 1.0, # white
      1.0 0.1 0.8, # pink
      0.0 0.3 1.0, # blue
   ]
}
MaterialBinding {
   value PER_VERTEX_INDEXED
}
IndexedFaceSet {
   coordIndex [
      # ring 0
       0,  1,  6,  5, -1,
       1,  2,  7,  6, -1,
       2,  3,  8,  7, -1,
       3,  4,  9,  8, -1,
       4,  0,  5,  9, -1,
      # ring 1
       5,  6, 11, 10, -1,
       6,  7, 12, 11, -1,
       7,  8, 13, 12, -1,
       8,  9, 14, 13, -1,
       9,  5, 10, 14, -1,
      # ring 2
      10, 11, 16, 15, -1,
      11, 12, 17, 16, -1,
      12, 13, 18, 17, -1,
      13, 14, 19, 18, -1,
      14, 10, 15, 19, -1,
      # ring 3
      15, 16, 21, 20, -1,
      16, 17, 22, 21, -1,
      17, 18, 23, 22, -1,
      18, 19, 24, 23, -1,
      19, 15, 20, 24, -1,
      # ring 4
      20, 21, 26, 25, -1,
      21, 22, 27, 26, -1,
      22, 23, 28, 27, -1,
      23, 24, 29, 28, -1;
      24, 20, 25, 29, -1,
      # base
      25, 26, 27, 28, 29
   ]
```

Figure 16.32 continues

```
        materialIndex [
            # ring 0
            0, 0, 0, 0, 0,
            0, 0, 0, 0, 0,
            0, 0, 0, 0, 0,
            0, 0, 0, 0, 0,
            0, 0, 0, 0, 0,
            # ring 1
            0, 0, 2, 2, 0,
            0, 0, 2, 2, 0,
            0, 0, 2, 2, 0,
            0, 0, 2, 2, 0,
            0, 0, 2, 2, 0,
            # ring 2
            2, 2, 1, 1, 0,
            2, 2, 1, 1, 0,
            2, 2, 1, 1, 0,
            2, 2, 1, 1, 0,
            2, 2, 1, 1, 0,
            # ring 3
            1, 1, 1, 1, 0,
            1, 1, 1, 1, 0,
            1, 1, 1, 1, 0,
            1, 1, 1, 1, 0,
            1, 1, 1, 1, 0,
            # ring 4
            1, 1, 0, 0, 0,
            1, 1, 0, 0, 0,
            1, 1, 0, 0, 0,
            1, 1, 0, 0, 0,
            1, 1, 0, 0, 0,
            # base
            0, 0, 0, 0, 0
        ]
    }
```

Figure 16.32 *A colored, smoothly shaded vase.*

Smoothly Shading Line Sets

The flower vase can be shaded using lines instead of faces by changing the **IndexedFaceSet** node to an **IndexedLineSet** node, and adding a closing polyline coordinate to each polyline vertex list. Figure 16.33*b* shows the smoothly shaded line-drawn vase, while Figure 16.33*a* shows the original line-drawn vase.

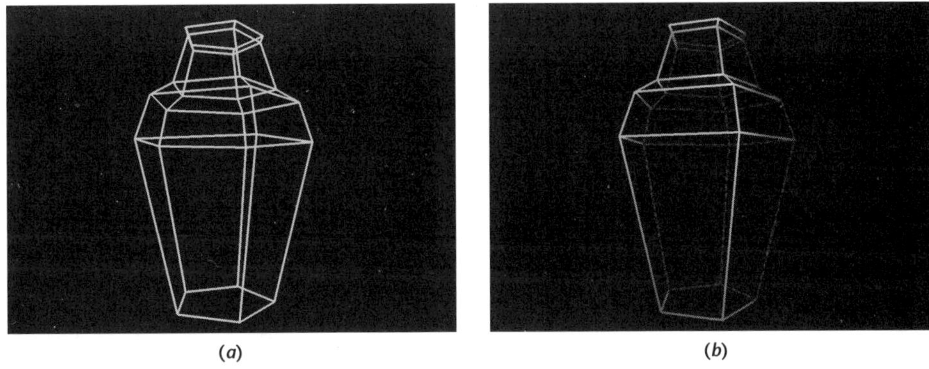
(a) (b)

Figure 16.33 *A line-drawn vase:* (a) *default and* (b) *smoothly shaded.*

Recall that, by default, polylines are drawn *unshaded,* appearing lit as if they were face-on to a light regardless of their actual orientation. When you bind your own normals to polylines, however, you can create shading effects like those previously shown. The lines outlining faces at the front of the vase are brightly lit because they face the headlight. The lines to the side and back of the vase, however, face away from the headlight and are drawn dark. In this case, this creates an odd black-vase-in-a-dark-room kind of effect.

Consider, however, combining smoothly shaded lines with smoothly shaded faces, each of a different color. Figure 16.34*a* shows the smoothly shaded vase with *unshaded* polylines outlining each vase face. Figure 16.34*b* shows the same smoothly shaded vase, but this time with *smooth shaded* polylines outlining the vase faces. Notice that when the outlines are unshaded, they appear to glow and look odd. By smoothly shading the polylines, you ensure that dark faces of the vase are outlined with dark polylines and the whole appearance is more natural.

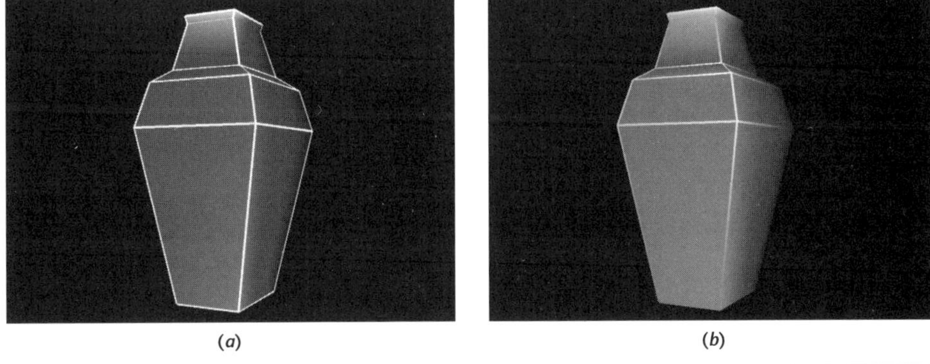
(a) (b)

Figure 16.34 *Smoothly shaded vase* (a) *without smoothly shaded polylines and* (b) *with smoothly shaded polylines.*

Smoothly Shading Point Sets

You can also bind your own normals to individual points in a point set. The example text in Figure 16.35 uses the points to create an interesting effect. A normal that points in a different direction binds to each point. As you walk around the point set, the points that face you in your current orientation are shaded brightly while others are darker. As your orientation changes, the points appear to alternately glow on and off. If you stop moving, however, the points stop changing and are shaded based on your current stationary position. Using a technique like this, you can create a simple star twinkle effect.

```
#VRML V1.0 ascii

Coordinate3 {
   point [
       0.18 -0.53  0.17,
       0.23 -0.12 -0.39,
      -0.37  0.54  0.65,
       0.78  0.15  0.31,
      -0.92  0.40  0.79,
       0.87  0.67  0.58,
      -0.36 -0.83 -0.46,
       0.13 -0.96  0.41,
       0.76  0.03 -0.76,
      -0.59 -0.96 -0.06,
      -0.92  0.12  0.25,
      -0.24 -0.41  0.43,
      -0.38 -0.16  0.70,
      -0.40  0.24 -0.23,
      -0.30  0.04  0.40,
       0.73  0.23  0.97,
       0.43  0.81 -0.28,
      -0.86  0.21 -0.29,
       0.22  0.72 -0.99,
      -0.43  0.86  0.98,
      -0.43 -0.46 -0.99,
       0.60 -0.45  0.08,
      -0.15 -0.94  0.99,
      -0.80  0.38 -0.53,
      -0.59 -0.14  0.71,
      -0.70 -0.96  0.74,
       0.64  0.19 -0.28,
       0.29  0.42 -0.44,
       0.49  0.42 -0.26,
      -0.98 -0.38  0.35,
   ]
}
NormalBinding {
   value PER_VERTEX
}
```

Figure 16.35 continues

```
Normal {
   vector [
      -1.0  0.0  0.0,
       1.0  0.0  0.0,
       0.0 -1.0  0.0,
       0.0  1.0  0.0,
       0.0  0.0 -1.0,
       0.0  0.0  1.0,
      -1.0  0.0  0.0,
       1.0  0.0  0.0,
       0.0 -1.0  0.0,
       0.0  1.0  0.0,
       0.0  0.0 -1.0,
       0.0  0.0  1.0,
      -1.0  0.0  0.0,
       1.0  0.0  0.0,
       0.0 -1.0  0.0,
       0.0  1.0  0.0,
       0.0  0.0 -1.0,
       0.0  0.0  1.0,
      -1.0  0.0  0.0,
       1.0  0.0  0.0,
       0.0 -1.0  0.0,
       0.0  1.0  0.0,
       0.0  0.0 -1.0,
       0.0  0.0  1.0,
   ]
}
PointSet {
   startIndex 0
   numPoints 30
}
```

Figure 16.35 *Creating a twinkling star effect.*

Using Separators with Normals

Using a **Separator** node you can save and restore the current normal binding type and normal list. For instance, the example text in Figure 16.36 draws two copies of the half-column, one stacked on top of the other. The top one is smoothly shaded, while the bottom one is faceted by the VRML browser's default normal computation.

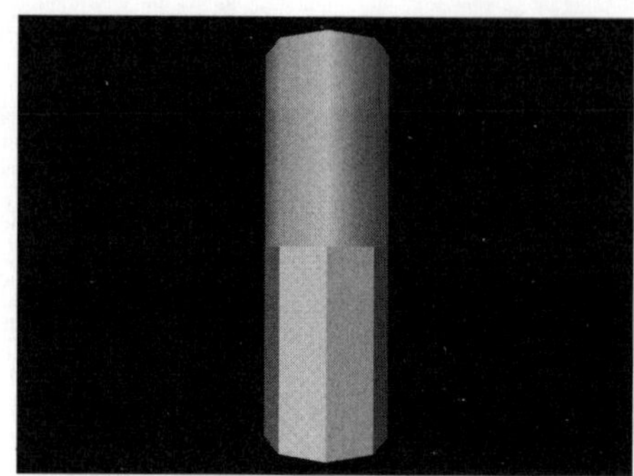

```
#VRML V1.0 ascii

Coordinate3 {
   point [
      -2.00  3.00 0.00,
      -2.00 -3.00 0.00,
      -1.41  3.00 1.41,
      -1.41 -3.00 1.41,
       0.00  3.00 2.00,
       0.00 -3.00 2.00,
       1.41  3.00 1.41,
       1.41 -3.00 1.41,
       2.00  3.00 0.00,
       2.00 -3.00 0.00,
   ]
}
# Smooth half-column
Separator {
   Normal {
      vector [
         -1.00 0.00 0.00,
         -0.71 0.00 0.71,
          0.00 0.00 1.00,
          0.71 0.00 0.71,
          1.00 0.00 0.00,
      ]
   }
   NormalBinding {
      value PER_VERTEX_INDEXED
   }
   DEF half_column IndexedFaceSet {
      coordIndex [
         0, 1, 3, 2, -1,
         2, 3, 5, 4, -1,
         4, 5, 7, 6, -1,
         6, 7, 9, 8, -1,
      ]
      normalIndex [
         0, 0, 1, 1,  0,
         1, 1, 2, 2,  0,
         2, 2, 3, 3,  0,
         3, 3, 4, 4,  0,
      ]
   }
}
# Faceted half-column
Separator {
   Translation {
      translation 0.0 -6.0 0.0
   }
   USE half_column
}
```

Figure 16.36 *Using separators with normal binding.*

Reading from the top of the file, the VRML browser is directed to:

1. Set the coordinates property to ten coordinates.
2. Draw the separator group:
   a. Specify all the properties, including the current normal binding type (**DEFAULT**) and current normal list (empty).
   b. Set the normals property to five normal vectors.
   c. Select a **PER_VERTEX_INDEXED** normal binding type.
   d. Draw a list of faces.
      i. Draw a face with vertices 0, 1, 3, and 2 using normals 0, 0, 1, and 1, respectively.
      ii. Draw a face with vertices 2, 3, 5, and 4 using normals 1, 1, 2, and 2, respectively.
      iii. Draw a face with vertices 4, 5, 7, and 6 using normals 2, 2, 3, and 3, respectively.
      iv. Draw a face with vertices 6, 7, 9, and 8 using normals 3, 3, 4, and 4, respectively.
   e. Restore all the properties.
3. Draw the separator group:
   a. Save all the properties, including the current normal binding type (**DEFAULT**) and current normal list (empty).
   b. Translate –6.0 units down the Y axis.
   c. Draw a list of faces.
      i. Draw a face with vertices 0, 1, 3, and 2 using automatically computed normals.
      ii. Draw a face with vertices 2, 3, 5, and 4 using automatically computed normals.
      iii. Draw a face with vertices 4, 5, 7, and 6 using automatically computed normals.
      iv. Draw a face with vertices 6, 7, 9, and 8 using automatically computed normals.
   d. Restore all the properties.

Notice that each half-column is drawn within its own **Separator** node but both use a common set of coordinates set by a **Coordinate3** node outside both separator groups. The first half-column is drawn with a **PER_VERTEX_INDEXED** normal binding type and a specific normal list designed for smooth shading. Both the normal binding type, and the normals are specified within the first half-column's separator group. When the separator group is exited, the normal binding type is returned to its initial **DEFAULT** value, and the current normal list restored to its initial empty state.

The second half-column is also drawn within its own separator group. Since that group doesn't change the normal binding type, it remains at its **DEFAULT** value. Additionally, since that group doesn't set the current normal list, the VRML browser automatically computes default normals for the half-column, shading it faceted. Note also that since the **DEFAULT** normal binding type causes normals to be computed automatically, the normalIndex values in the instanced **IndexedFaceSet** node are ignored.

TIP *Always include normals and normal binding types within* ***Separator*** *nodes to ensure that each shape gets the appropriate normals. This also enables you to turn on and off default normal computations. For instance, if you didn't use the first* ***Separator*** *node in the preceding example, the normal list set by the* ***Normal*** *node would apply to both* ***IndexedFaceSet*** *nodes. Changing the normal binding type explicitly to a* ***DEFAULT*** *value for the second face set does not, in itself, force the VRML browser to automatically compute normals. The normal binding type must be* ***DEFAULT*** and *the normal list must be empty. Since there is no way in VRML to explicitly specify an empty normal list, you must rely instead on preserving its initial empty state by setting normals only within separator groups. Each time you exit a group, the normal list is again set to its initial empty state, and you can use this to force shapes to be drawn with automatically computed normals. This is the approach used in the preceding example.*

Extended Examples

The following examples build on the concepts presented in this chapter. Try them on your own.

A Half-Dome

The example text in Figure 16.37 specifies normals to smooth the faceted dome. Notice that it is easy to calculate normals on a sphere. Each vertex on the sphere has a normal that points outward from the sphere's center through that vertex. This enables you to use the vertex coordinates as the normal vector values.

```
#VRML V1.0 ascii

# Half-dome smoothly shaded by using normals
Coordinate3 {
     point [
             1.0000 0.0000 0.0000,     0.7071 0.0000 0.7071,
             0.0000 0.0000 1.0000,    -0.7071 0.0000 0.7071,
            -1.0000 0.0000 0.0000,     0.9239 0.3827 0.0000,
             0.6533 0.3827 0.6533,     0.0000 0.3827 0.9239,
            -0.6533 0.3827 0.6533,    -0.9239 0.3827 0.0000,
```

```
                0.7071 0.7071 0.0000,    0.5000 0.7071 0.5000,
                0.0000 0.7071 0.7071,   -0.5000 0.7071 0.5000,
               -0.7071 0.7071 0.0000,    0.3827 0.9239 0.0000,
                0.2706 0.9239 0.2706,    0.0000 0.9239 0.3827,
               -0.2706 0.9239 0.2706,   -0.3827 0.9239 0.0000,
                0.0000 1.0000 0.0000,
        ]
}
Normal {
        vector [
                1.0000 0.0000 0.0000,    0.7071 0.0000 0.7071,
                0.0000 0.0000 1.0000,   -0.7071 0.0000 0.7071,
               -1.0000 0.0000 0.0000,    0.9239 0.3827 0.0000,
                0.6533 0.3827 0.6533,    0.0000 0.3827 0.9239,
               -0.6533 0.3827 0.6533,   -0.9239 0.3827 0.0000,
                0.7071 0.7071 0.0000,    0.5000 0.7071 0.5000,
                0.0000 0.7071 0.7071,   -0.5000 0.7071 0.5000,
               -0.7071 0.7071 0.0000,    0.3827 0.9239 0.0000,
                0.2706 0.9239 0.2706,    0.0000 0.9239 0.3827,
               -0.2706 0.9239 0.2706,   -0.3827 0.9239 0.0000,
                0.0000 1.0000 0.0000,
        ]
}
NormalBinding {
        value PER_VERTEX_INDEXED
}
IndexedFaceSet {
        coordIndex [
                 0,  5,  6,  1, -1,  1,  6,  7,  2, -1,
                 2,  7,  8,  3, -1,  3,  8,  9,  4, -1,
                 5, 10, 11,  6, -1,  6, 11, 12,  7, -1,
                 7, 12, 13,  8, -1,  8, 13, 14,  9, -1,
                10, 15, 16, 11, -1, 11, 16, 17, 12, -1,
                12, 17, 18, 13, -1, 13, 18, 19, 14, -1,
                15, 20, 16, -1, 16, 20, 17, -1,
                17, 20, 18, -1, 18, 20, 19, -1,
        ]
}
```

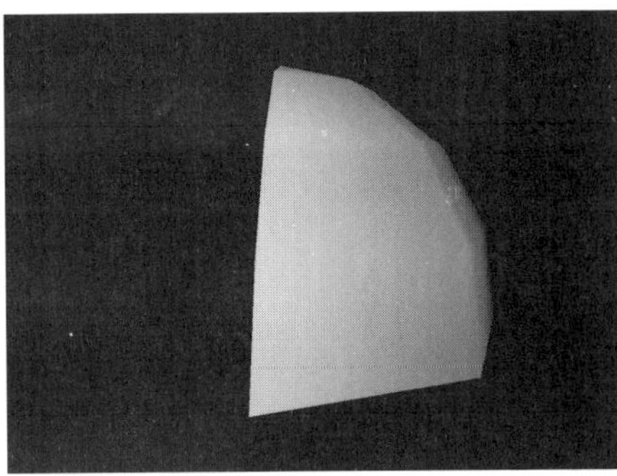

Figure 16.37 *A half-dome.*

A Dome City

The example text in Figure 16.38 inlines the VRML text from halfdome.wrl (Figure 16.37) and halftube.wrl (Figure 16.20) to create a dome city. Two half-domes are set up back to back to create a full dome, or hemisphere, used for the city domes. The shaded column is used for the half-tubes between the city domes.

```
#VRML V1.0 ascii

# Dome and tube parts
Switch {
	whichChild -1
	DEF full_dome Separator {
		DEF dome_color Material {
			diffuseColor 0.5 0.5 0.5
		}
		DEF half_dome WWWInline {
			name "halfdome.wrl"
		}
		Rotation {
			#               Y        +180.0 degrees
			rotation 0.0 1.0 0.0  3.14
		}
		USE half_dome
	}
	DEF short_tube Separator {
		DEF tube_color Material {
			diffuseColor 0.2 0.2 0.2
		}
		Transform {
			#         X              -90.0 degrees
			rotation 1.0 0.0 0.0 -1.57
			scaleFactor 0.1 0.20 0.1
		}
		DEF half_tube WWWInline {
			name "halftube.wrl"
		}
	}
	DEF long_tube Separator {
		USE tube_color
		Transform {
			#         X              -90.0 degrees
			rotation 1.0 0.0 0.0 -1.57
			scaleFactor 0.1 0.4 0.1
		}
		USE half_tube
	}
}
# Ground
Cube {
	width 10.0
	height 0.05
	depth 10.0
}
```

Figure 16.38 continues

```
# Tower
DEF tower Separator {
      Translation {
            translation 0.0 1.15 0.0
      }
      USE tube_color
      Cylinder {
            height 0.5
            radius 0.2
      }
      Transform {
            translation 0.0 0.4 0.0
            #        X           +180.0 degrees
            rotation 1.0 0.0 0.0  3.14
            scaleFactor 0.5 0.2 0.5
      }
      USE dome_color USE full_dome USE tube_color
      Cylinder {
            height 0.3
            radius 1.7
      }
      Transform {
            translation 0.0 -0.2 0.0
            #        X           +180.0 degrees
            rotation 1.0 0.0 0.0  3.14
            scaleFactor 1.5 1.5 1.5
      }
      USE dome_color
      USE full_dome
      Cylinder {
            height 6.0
            radius 0.04
      }
}
# Central dome and arms
Separator {
      USE full_dome
      Separator {
            Transform {
                  translation 1.0 0.0 1.0
                  #           Y        +45.0 degrees
                  rotation 0.0 1.0 0.0  0.785
            }
            USE short_tube
            DEF short_to_dome Transform {
                  translation 0.0 0.0 1.0
                  scaleFactor 0.5 0.5 0.5
            }
            USE full_dome
      }
```

Figure 16.38 continues

```
        Separator {
            Translation {
                translation 0.0 0.0 2.0
            }
            USE long_tube
            DEF long_to_dome Transform {
                translation 0.0 0.0 1.5
                scaleFactor 0.5 0.5 0.5
            }
            USE full_dome USE tower
        }
        Separator {
            Transform {
                translation -1.3 0.0 0.0
                #               Y       -90.0 degrees
                rotation 0.0 1.0 0.0 -1.57
            }
            USE short_tube USE short_to_dome USE full_dome
            Transform {
                translation -2.0 0.0 0.0
                #               Y       -90.0 degrees
                rotation 0.0 1.0 0.0 -1.57
                scaleFactor 2.0 2.0 2.0
            }
            USE short_tube USE short_to_dome USE full_dome
        }
        Separator {
            Transform {
                translation 1.3 0.0 -1.3
                #               Y       +135.0 degrees
                rotation 0.0 1.0 0.0 2.36
            }
            USE long_tube USE long_to_dome USE full_dome
            USE tower
        }
}
# Landing pads
Separator {
    Translation {
        translation 3.0 0.025 3.0
    }
    USE tube_color
    DEF pad Cylinder {
        height 0.05
        radius 0.5
    }
    DEF pad_right Translation {
        translation 0.0 0.0 -1.2
    }
    USE pad USE pad_right USE pad
}
```

Figure 16.38 *A city of domes.*

Summary

A normal indicates the orientation of a face and is used by the VRML browser to determine how brightly to shade a face. Normals are drawn as arrows pointing out the front of a face. The more a normal arrow points at a light, such as the headlight, the brighter the face is shaded. Faces that are oriented directly toward a light have normals that point straight at the light and are shaded the brightest, while faces whose normals point away from a light are shaded darker.

The front of a face is the side where the vertices of its perimeter appear ordered in a counterclockwise fashion. You can use the right-hand rule to determine which direction a normal will point: Curl the fingers of your right hand in the same direction as vertices are ordered around a face's perimeter, then stick your thumb out as if hitchhiking. Your thumb will point in the direction of the face's normal.

The normal for a vertex or face is computed using three consecutive vertices: 0, 1, and 2. Compute two vectors, one as the difference between vertices 1 and 0, and the other as the difference between vertices 2 and 1 Next, compute the cross-product of the two vectors to get a third vector pointing outward from the face. This is the normal for the face at vertex 1.

Different normals can be bound to each part, face, or vertex of a shape by selecting a normal binding type with the **NormalBinding** node. The normal binding type is a property that is saved and restored by **Separator** nodes, and remains in effect until changed by another **NormalBinding** node.

The **OVERALL** normal binding type shades entire shapes using a single normal. This is very uncommon.

The **PER_PART** and **PER_PART_INDEXED** normal binding types shade each part of a shape using a different normal. Line set parts are the individual line segments of every polyline. Face set parts are the individual faces in the set.

The **PER_FACE** and **PER_FACE_INDEXED** normal binding types shade each face or polyline using a different normal.

The **PER_VERTEX** and **PER_VERTEX_INDEXED** normal binding types shade each face, line, or point vertex using a different normal. These normal binding types enable you to bind your own normals to shape vertices in order to create smooth shading effects. Such smooth shading creates flat faces that look as if they are curved, enabling you to create the appearance of a smoothly curved shape using only a few faces. This reduces the number of faces the VRML browser has to draw and decreases the time it takes to draw your world.

The **DEFAULT** normal binding type for a shape depends on the shape. For point sets and line sets, the **DEFAULT** normal binding type shades shapes as if they are always facing directly toward a light, regardless of their actual orientation. The **DEFAULT** normal binding type for face sets automatically computes normals for all faces.

To shade a shape using your own normals, specify a list of normals using the **Normal** node. Each field of the **Normal** node includes a list of values, enclosed within square brackets and separated by commas. Normals in a list are referred to by a normal index. The first normal in the list has an index of 0, the second an index of 1, and so on.

Normal indexes are automatically generated by the VRML browser for **PER_PART**, **PER_FACE**, and **PER_VERTEX** normal binding types with **IndexedFaceSet** and **IndexedLineSet** nodes. The first part, face, or vertex has a normal index of 0, the second has a normal index of 1, and so on.

Normal indexes for **PointSet** nodes start with the index value in the **startIndex** field, and increment by one for each subsequent point in the point set.

Explicit normal indexes can be used with **PER_PART_INDEXED**, **PER_FACE_INDEXED**, and **PER_VERTEX_INDEXED** normal binding types with **IndexedFaceSet** and **IndexedLineSet** nodes. Normal indexes for each part, face, or vertex of a shape are specified in the **normalIndex** field of the **IndexedFaceSet** and **IndexedLineSet** nodes.

When listing normal indexes *per vertex*, a normal index must correspond to each vertex, *and* the –1 face or polyline divider flag in the **coordIndex** field of a **IndexedFaceSet** or **IndexedLineSet** node.

CHAPTER 17

Optimizing How VRML Draws Faces (Advanced)

When drawing faces defined by an **IndexedFaceSet** node, the VRML browser implements one of several approaches for optimizing how faces are drawn depending on characteristics of the faces it is drawing. For instance, **convex** faces can be drawn more quickly than **concave** faces. Convex faces require that the VRML browser split the concave faces into convex faces first. If you indicate ahead of time that all faces in a face set are convex, the browser doesn't waste time checking for concave faces, and instead just draws.

Optimizing drawing like this enables the VRML browser to draw your worlds more quickly. To optimize, however, you need to provide **hints** to the browser to let it know that certain sets of faces are all convex and not concave. These hints are specified within a **ShapeHints** node.

Using shape hints, the VRML browser can draw face sets more quickly. Shape hints can also be used to indicate that face sets define facets approximating a curved surface. Using hints like this, the VRML browser can compute smooth shading normals for face sets, similar to those you computed in Chapter 16. This enables you to quickly create smoothly shaded shapes without the extra work of computing your own normals.

Understanding Shape Drawing Hints

Shape hints help a VRML browser choose among ways to optimize drawing special types of faces in an **IndexedFaceSet** node. Since optimizing can significantly speed up the drawing of your world, it is generally worth the extra effort to provide such hints to the browser.

The shape hints you specify are properties, just like the current material binding, font style, coordinates, normals, materials, and others. Like all properties, you set the shape hints before you draw, and they remain in effect until you change them later in the file.

There are four categories of shape hints that you can provide to the browser:

- *Face type*
- *Shape type*
- *Vertex ordering*
- *Crease angle*

Hinting at the Face Type

The **face type** shape hint enables you to control the VRML browser's **face tessellation** abilities. Recall from Chapter 14 that there are two face types:

- **Concave faces**—*Faces with inlets, or cavities. The outline of a capital C, for instance, is concave.*
- **Convex faces**—*Faces without inlets, or cavities. The outer perimeter of a capital O is convex.*

Recall also that any concave face can be split into multiple convex faces. Splitting faces in this way is known as face tessellation. The VRML browser can perform face tessellation, but it is time consuming. By default, the VRML browser assumes that all faces specified in a face set are convex and do not require tessellation. If you must use concave faces, you can direct the VRML browser to perform face tessellation by using the *face type* shape hint.

Hinting at the Shape Type and Vertex Ordering

The **shape type** and **vertex ordering** shape hints combine to let you control two types of VRML browser optimization:

- **Backface culling**
- **Two-sided lighting**

Faces in a face set describe one of two types of shapes:

- *Solid shapes*
- *Open shapes*

Solid shapes, like a cube or a sphere, entirely enclose a volume. No matter how you turn a solid shape, you can't see inside it. If you fill a solid shape with water, no water leaks from it, no matter how you turn the shape.

Open shapes are any shapes that do *not* entirely enclose a volume. The vase from past chapters, for instance, is an open shape. If you fill the vase with water and turn it upside down, the water will spill out. If, however, you close off the top of the vase with another face, it becomes a solid shape and holds water without leaking.

The outsides of solid and open shapes are described by faces in a face set. All such faces have a front and a back, and the VRML browser may need to be draw both faces. Solid shapes, however, have an interesting characteristic. The back sides of faces used to construct a solid shape can never be seen.

Consider a cube and its six faces. A cube is a solid shape, since its faces entirely enclose a volume that can hold water without leaking. No matter how you turn the cube, you can't see the back side of any of its faces. The front side of some other face or faces of the cube is always in the way. The only way to see the back side of a cube face is to open up the cube and look inside. However, opening the cube "lets the water out," and the cube is no longer a solid shape.

Open shapes do not share this characteristic of solid shapes. The back sides of faces describing open shapes are often visible. Consider the vase again. If you tilt the vase down and look inside, you can easily see the back sides of the faces that describe the vase's outer surface.

By default, the VRML browser doesn't assume that shapes are solid. It draws all faces of a face set, front and back. If the face set does describe a solid shape, the browser wastes time drawing the back sides of faces that you never see.

To avoid wasting time, you can hint to the VRML browser that a face set describes a solid shape. Using this hint, the browser can skip drawing the back sides of faces in the face set and speed the drawing process. This process of *not* drawing back faces is known as **backface culling** and is a key optimization you can control using the *shape type* shape hint.

To perform backface culling, however, the VRML browser must have reliable information about the orientation of a face. Only when the face is facing away from you—its back hidden from you—is it a candidate for backface culling. When a face instead faces you, it should not be culled.

To determine whether a face faces you or not, the VRML browser computes a face normal direction as discussed in Chapter 16. That normal direction, however, is based in part on the order of vertices specified to describe the perimeter of a face. Recall that vertices can be ordered in *clockwise* order or *counterclockwise* order. While counterclockwise order is preferred (and used in all examples in this book), there are cases where clockwise ordering may be used.

By default, the VRML browser cannot assume that all faces in a face set specify clockwise or counterclockwise vertex ordering. Without knowing this, the VRML browser cannot perform backface culling, even when the *shape type* hint indicates that the faces describe a solid shape. To perform backface culling, the browser needs to know both that the shape is a solid *and* that the vertices of faces in a face set are all specified in a clockwise order or are all specified in a counterclockwise order. You can provide this additional information by using the *vertex ordering* shape hint.

Combining the *shape type* shape hint and the *vertex ordering* shape hint, the VRML browser can decide whether to perform backface culling using one of these rules:

- *If the shape is solid, and all vertices are ordered clockwise, then perform backface culling.*

- *If the shape is solid, and all vertices are ordered counterclockwise, then perform backface culling.*
- *Otherwise, do not perform backface culling.*

You can also control *shape type* and *vertex ordering* shape hints. By default, the VRML browser shades only the front of any face. A face that is brightly lit when viewed from the front is completely dark when you look at it from the back.

You can direct the VRML browser to light both sides of faces by specifying two-sided lighting. This is convenient when debugging complex face shapes. It does, however, cause the VRML browser to do more work and slows drawing, sometimes quite a bit. Use two-sided lighting sparingly.

Turning on two-sided lighting for solid shapes is a waste of time, since they never expose the back sides of their faces. Whenever the *shape type* shape hint indicates that a shape is solid, two-sided lighting is automatically turned off.

When the *shape type* shape hint indicates a shape is not solid, then the *vertex ordering* shape hint can enable or disable two-sided lighting using one of these rules:

- *If the shape is solid, then do not perform two-sided lighting.*
- *If the shape is not solid, and vertices are ordered clockwise, then perform two-sided lighting. If the shape is not solid, and vertices are ordered counterclockwise, then perform two-sided lighting. Otherwise, do not perform two-sided lighting.*

Hinting at the Crease Angle

In Chapter 16 you used specially computed normals to achieve a smooth shading effect that obscured the facets of a shape. In essence, you smoothed the creases, or sharp facet edges, in the shape. You did this because the VRML browser's automatic normal computations wouldn't. Using the **crease angle** shape hint, you can direct the VRML browser to perform crease smoothing for you.

By default, the VRML browser assumes that the faces of a face set describe a faceted shape and that the creases in the shape are intentional. When you use the **DEFAULT** normal binding type, the VRML browser automatically computes normals assuming that it cannot smooth the creases in your shape.

You can direct the VRML browser to selectively smooth over creases by specifying a maximum *crease angle.* Any shape creases that are sharper than this angle are left as creases. Any shape creases that are shallower than this angle are smoothed by calculating smooth shading normals like those we computed in Chapter 16.

Optimizing How Faces Are Drawn

You provide shape drawing hints to the VRML browser using the **ShapeHints** node. The example text in Figure 17.1 draws the half-column from Chapter 16, without custom normals, and adjusts the crease angle so that the VRML browser can automatically generate normals for a smooth shading effect.

```
#VRML V1.0 ascii

Coordinate3 {
      point [
            -2.00  3.00 0.00,
            -2.00 -3.00 0.00,
            -1.41  3.00 1.41,
            -1.41 -3.00 1.41,
             0.00  3.00 2.00,
             0.00 -3.00 2.00,
             1.41  3.00 1.41,
             1.41 -3.00 1.41,
             2.00  3.00 0.00,
             2.00 -3.00 0.00,
      ]
}
ShapeHints {
      creaseAngle 0.8
}
IndexedFaceSet {
      coordIndex [
            0, 1, 3, 2, -1,
            2, 3, 5, 4, -1,
            4, 5, 7, 6, -1,
            6, 7, 9, 8, -1,
      ]
}
```

Figure 17.1 *A smoothed half-column.*

Notice the structure and order of the VRML file in Figure 17.1. Reading from the top of the file, the **Coordinate3** node lists ten vertices. The **ShapeHint** node sets the crease angle to 0.8 radians (about 45.8 degrees). The **IndexedFaceSet** node draws four rectangles, shading with automatically generated normals. Because the crease angle is set to be larger than the angle between any two faces on the half-column, the VRML browser automatically computes normals to achieve a smooth shading effect.

Understanding the **ShapeHints** Node Syntax

The **ShapeHints** node has four fields: **vertexOrdering, shapeType, faceType,** and **creaseAngle**. The **vertexOrdering** field can have one of three values:

- ***UNKNOWN_ORDERING****—The ordering of face vertices is unknown. It could be either clockwise or counterclockwise.*
- ***CLOCKWISE****—The ordering of face vertices is clockwise, as viewed from the front of the face.*

- **COUNTERCLOCKWISE**—*The ordering of face vertices is counterclockwise, as viewed from the front of the face.*

The default value for the **vertexOrdering** field is **UNKNOWN_ORDERING**.

The **shapeType** field can have one of two values:

- **UNKNOWN_SHAPE_TYPE**—*The shape described by a face set may be solid or open. Neither type can be assumed.*
- **SOLID**—*The shape described by a face set is a solid; it encloses a volume and therefore the back sides of faces are never visible.*

The default value for the **shapeType** field is **UNKNOWN_SHAPE_TYPE.**

The **faceType** field can have one of two values:

- **UNKNOWN_FACE_TYPE**—*Each face in a face set may be concave or convex. Neither type can be assumed.*
- **CONVEX**—*Each face in a face set is convex (without cavities) and does not need to be tessellated.*

The default value for the **faceType** field is **CONVEX**.

The **creaseAngle** field is a floating-point value specifying an angle, in radians. Creases in shapes defined by a face set will be smoothed if the angle between adjacent facets is less than the crease angle. The default value is 0.5 radians (about 28.6 degrees).

SYNTAX **ShapeHints node**

```
ShapeHints {
      vertexOrdering    UNKNOWN_ORDERING      # Ordering type
      shapeType         UNKNOWN_SHAPE_TYPE    # Shape type
      faceType          CONVEX                # Face type
      creaseAngle       0.5                   # Angle
}
```

TIP *In version 1.1 of VRML, the default shape hints values may change to specify a **shapeType** of **SOLID** and a **vertexOrdering** of **COUNTERCLOCKWISE**. Your VRML browser will provide better performance for typical shapes with these default values.*

The shape hints are included in the shape hints property. **Separator** nodes save and restore the shape hints.

Using different values for the shape hints, you can turn on and off backface culling, two-sided lighting, and face tessellation features of the VRML browser.

Backface Culling:

	shapeType	
vertexOrdering	SOLID	UNKNOWN_SHAPE_TYPE
CLOCKWISE	off	on
COUNTERCLOCKWISE	off	on
UNKNOWN_ORDERING	off	off

Two-Sided Lighting:

	shapeType	
vertexOrdering	SOLID	UNKNOWN_SHAPE_TYPE
CLOCKWISE	off	on
COUNTERCLOCKWISE	off	on
UNKNOWN_ORDERING	off	off

Face Tessellation:

faceType	
CONVEX	off
UNKNOWN_FACE_TYPE	on

TIP *For maximum performance when drawing face sets that describe solid shapes, turn* on *backface culling, turn* off *two-sided lighting, and turn* off *face tessellation.*

TIP *For maximum performance when drawing face sets that do not describe solid shapes, turn* off *backface culling, turn* off *two-sided lighting, and turn* off *face tessellation.*

TIP *Enabling two-sided lighting can significantly slow your browser's drawing speed.*

Experimenting with Shape Hints

The following examples provide a more detailed examination of the ways in which shape hints can be used.

Optimizing Solid Shapes

In Chapter 14 we built a fractal pyramid out of a repeated triangular base piece. We can use the **ShapeHints** node to let the VRML browser know that the base shape is solid, enabling the browser to perform backface culling to speed up its drawing, as shown in Figure 17.2.

```
#VRML V1.0 ascii

Coordinate3 {
      point [
            0.0  1.5  0.0,
           -0.86 0.0  0.5,
            0.86 0.0  0.5,
            0.0  0.0 -1.0
      ]
}
ShapeHints {
      vertexOrdering COUNTERCLOCKWISE
      shapeType      SOLID
}
IndexedFaceSet {
      coordIndex [
            0, 1, 2, -1,
            0, 2, 3, -1,
            0, 3, 1, -1,
            1, 3, 2
      ]
}
```

Figure 17.2 *Speeding how the fractal is drawn.*

Reading from the top of the file, the VRML browser is directed to:

1. Set the coordinates property to four coordinates.
2. Set the shape hints property to indicate that shapes are **SOLID** and that faces are described with a **COUNTERCLOCKWISE** vertex order.
3. Draw a list of faces.
   a. Draw a face with vertices 0, 1, and 2.
   b. Draw a face with vertices 0, 2, and 3.
   c. Draw a face with vertices 0, 3, and 1.
   d. Draw a face with vertices 1, 3, and 2.

The result is the same triangular base piece used in Chapter 14. With the **ShapeHints** node added, however, the VRML browser draws the base shape and the entire fractal pyramid more quickly.

Enabling Two-Sided Lighting

By default, faces are drawn with only one side illuminated by lights in the world, such as your headlight. Two-sided lighting forces both sides of a shape to be illuminated and is often used to help debug complex worlds. The example text in Figure 17.3 uses a **ShapeHints** node to enable two-sided lighting while drawing a square.

```
#VRML V1.0 ascii

Coordinate3 {
      point [
            -1.0  1.0 0.0,
            -1.0 -1.0 0.0,
             1.0 -1.0 0.0,
             1.0  1.0 0.0,
      ]
}
ShapeHints {
      vertexOrdering COUNTERCLOCKWISE
      shapeType      UNKNOWN_SHAPE_TYPE
}
IndexedFaceSet {
      coordIndex [
            0, 1, 2, 3
      ]
}
```

Figure 17.3 *Lighting both sides of a shape with two-sided lighting.*

If you turn the face, you see that both the front *and the back* of the face are now illuminated. You can achieve this same effect by applying the shape hint to text drawn with the **AsciiText** node, as shown in Figure 17.4.

```
#VRML V1.0 ascii

ShapeHints {
      vertexOrdering COUNTERCLOCKWISE
      shapeType      UNKNOWN_SHAPE_TYPE
}
AsciiText {
      string "Qwerty"
}
```

Figure 17.4 *Lighting the front and back of a text shape.*

Similarly, you can enable two-sided lighting to shapes drawn with the primitive shape nodes, such as the cylinder shown in Figure 17.5.

```
#VRML V1.0 ascii

ShapeHints {
      vertexOrdering COUNTERCLOCKWISE
      shapeType      UNKNOWN_SHAPE_TYPE
}
Cylinder {
      parts SIDES
}
```

Figure 17.5 *Lighting the inside of a cylinder.*

Drawing Concave Faces

By default, the VRML browser does not draw concave faces (faces with ins and outs like the perimeter of a capital C). Such faces must be tessellated by hand before they are entered into a VRML file and drawn by the browser. You can, however, direct the VRML browser to tessellate concave faces for you by setting the **faceType** field of a **ShapeHint** node to **UNKNOWN_FACE_TYPE**. The example text in Figure 17.6, for instance, draws a capital C using an **IndexedFaceSet** node.

```
#VRML V1.0 ascii

Coordinate3 {
      point [
            # Outer circle
             1.62  1.18 0.00,
             0.62  1.90 0.00,
            -0.62  1.90 0.00,
            -1.62  1.18 0.00,
            -2.00  0.00 0.00,
            -1.62 -1.18 0.00,
            -0.62 -1.90 0.00,
             0.62 -1.90 0.00,
             1.62 -1.18 0.00,
            # Inner circle
             1.21  0.88 0.00,
             0.46  1.43 0.00,
            -0.46  1.43 0.00,
            -1.21  0.88 0.00,
            -1.50  0.00 0.00,
            -1.21 -0.88 0.00,
            -0.46 -1.43 0.00,
             0.46 -1.43 0.00,
             1.21 -0.88 0.00,
      ]
}
```

Figure 17.6 continues

```
ShapeHints {
      faceType UNKNOWN_FACE_TYPE
}
IndexedFaceSet {
      coordIndex [
            0, 1, 2, 3, 4, 5, 6, 7, 8,
            17, 16, 15, 14, 13, 12, 11, 10, 9
      ]
}
```

Figure 17.6 *Drawing a capital letter C.*

Smooth Shading Using the Crease Angle

By specifying custom normals in a **Normal** node and the **PER_VERTEX_INDEXED** normal binding type in a **NormalBinding** node in Chapter 16, you create a smooth shading technique that shades flat faces as if they are curved. The VRML browser automatic normals always create faceted shading.

In fact, the VRML browser's automatic normal calculations can achieve approximately the same smooth shading effect. For faceted shapes, like the half-column in Chapter 16, the VRML browser can compute smooth shading normals for all adjacent faces if the angle between the faces is less than a crease angle set within a **ShapeHints** node. The example text in Figure 17.7 draws the half-column from Chapter 16 without specially computed normals. Instead, a **ShapeHints** node sets the crease angle to about 45.8 degrees, a value just slightly larger than the largest angle between adjacent half-column faces. Using this crease angle shape hint, the VRML browser's own automatic normal computations create smooth shading normals identical to those we computed in Chapter 16.

```
#VRML V1.0 ascii

Coordinate3 {
      point [
           -2.00  3.00 0.00,
           -2.00 -3.00 0.00,
           -1.41  3.00 1.41,
           -1.41 -3.00 1.41,
            0.00  3.00 2.00,
            0.00 -3.00 2.00,
            1.41  3.00 1.41,
            1.41 -3.00 1.41,
            2.00  3.00 0.00,
            2.00 -3.00 0.00,
      ]
}
ShapeHints {
      creaseAngle 0.8 #  45.6 degrees
}
```

Figure 17.7 continues

```
IndexedFaceSet {
      coordIndex [
            0, 1, 3, 2, -1,
            2, 3, 5, 4, -1,
            4, 5, 7, 6, -1,
            6, 7, 9, 8, -1,
      ]
}
```

Figure 17.7 *Smoothly shading the half-column using a crease angle.*

Using the crease angle shape hint you can direct the VRML browser to smoothly shade any faceted surface. While very handy, the crease angle approach to smooth shading is not a substitute for computing your own normals using the techniques in Chapter 16. The browser's automatic computations apply the same crease angle to the entire set of faces in a face set. Using your own normal calculations, you have the control to compute smooth shading normals for only some parts of a shape, while other parts remain faceted.

Consider, for instance, a mountain scene. You might wish to use smooth shading to smooth out the lower valleys, but leave on faceted shading for the craggy peaks. Using the **ShapeHints** node's **creaseAngle** field, you must specify a single crease angle that works for all faces in a face set. This might inappropriately smooth some faces, while leaving others faceted. So, the crease angle shape hint is very useful, but it is not always a substitute for computing your own normals.

Using Separators with Shape Hints

Using a **Separator** node, you can save and restore the current shape hints. For instance, the example text in Figure 17.8 draws two copies of the half-column, one stacked on the other. The top one is smoothly shaded using a crease angle of 0.8 radians (45.8 degrees), while the bottom one is shaded with obvious facets by using the default crease angle of 0.5 radians (28.6 degrees).

```
#VRML V1.0 ascii

Coordinate3 {
      point [
            -2.00  3.00 0.00,
            -2.00 -3.00 0.00,
            -1.41  3.00 1.41,
            -1.41 -3.00 1.41,
             0.00  3.00 2.00,
             0.00 -3.00 2.00,
             1.41  3.00 1.41,
             1.41 -3.00 1.41,
             2.00  3.00 0.00,
             2.00 -3.00 0.00,
      ]
}
```

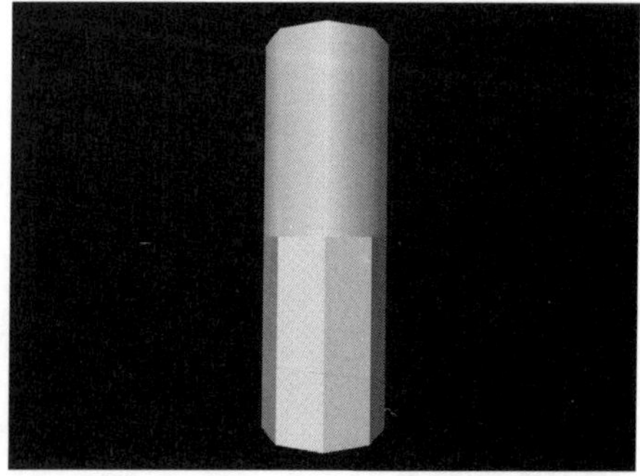

Figure 17.8 continues

```
# Smooth half-column
Separator {
	ShapeHints {
		creaseAngle 0.8 # 45.6 degrees
	}
	IndexedFaceSet {
		coordIndex [
			0, 1, 3, 2,   -1,
			2, 3, 5, 4,   -1,
			4, 5, 7, 6,   -1,
			6, 7, 9, 8,   -1,
		]
	}
}
# Faceted half-column
Translation {
	translation 0.0 -6.0 0.0
}
IndexedFaceSet {
	coordIndex [
		0, 1, 3, 2,   -1,
		2, 3, 5, 4,   -1,
		4, 5, 7, 6,   -1,
		6, 7, 9, 8,   -1,
	]
}
```

Figure 17.8 *Saving and restoring shape hints with a **Separator** node.*

Reading from the top of the file, the VRML browser is directed to:

1. Set the coordinates property to ten coordinates.
2. Draw the separator group:
   a. Save all the properties, including the current shape hints (default values).
   b. Set the shape hints property to a crease angle of 0.8 radians (45.6 degrees).
   c. Draw a list of faces using automatically generated smooth shading normals:
      i. Draw a face with vertices 0, 1, 3, and 2.
      ii. Draw a face with vertices 2, 3, 5, and 4.
      iii. Draw a face with vertices 4, 5, 7, and 6.
      iv. Draw a face with vertices 6, 7, 9, and 8.
   d. Restore all the properties.

3. Translate –6.0 units down the Y axis.
4. Draw a list of faces using automatically generated faceted shading normals:
   a. Draw a face with vertices 0, 1, 3, and 2.
   b. Draw a face with vertices 2, 3, 5, and 4.
   c. Draw a face with vertices 4, 5, 7, and 6.
   d. Draw a face with vertices 6, 7, 9, and 8.

The first half-column is drawn within its own **Separator** node with a **ShapeHints** node that sets the crease angle to 0.8 radians (45.6 degrees). Since this crease angle is larger than the largest angle between adjacent faces on the half-column, the normals automatically computed by the VRML browser create a smooth shading effect. When the separator group is finished, the shape hints crease angle is restored to its original default value of 0.5 radians (28.6 degrees).

The second half-column is drawn using the default crease angle. Since this angle is less than the angle between adjacent faces on the half-column, the normals automatically computed by the VRML browser create a faceted shading effect.

Extended Example

The following example builds on the concepts presented in this chapter. Try it on your own.

A Scroll

The two VRML files shown in Figure 17.9 are used together to create a scroll. The first file, (*a*) `curl.wrl`, creates the curled end of a half-open scroll. The curl is used twice, once for each end of the scroll, in the VRML file describing the scroll (*b*). A flat face is used to connect the two curls, and text is added to the front of the face. Because the scroll is drawn as a flat face, by default only one side of it is lit. To light both sides, the **ShapeHints** node is used to turn on two-sided lighting. To obscure the faceted construction of the scroll curls, the **ShapeHints** node also sets a crease angle which generates normals to smooth out the shading on the curls.

```
#VRML V1.0 ascii

Coordinate3 {
      point [
            2.00  0.35  0.20, -2.00  0.35  0.20,
            2.00  0.39 -0.01, -2.00  0.39 -0.01,
            2.00  0.32 -0.21, -2.00  0.32 -0.21,
            2.00  0.15 -0.34, -2.00  0.15 -0.34,
            2.00 -0.05 -0.36, -2.00 -0.05 -0.36,
            2.00 -0.22 -0.27, -2.00 -0.22 -0.27,
            2.00 -0.32 -0.11, -2.00 -0.32 -0.11,
            2.00 -0.32  0.08, -2.00 -0.32  0.08,
            2.00 -0.22  0.23, -2.00 -0.22  0.23,
            2.00 -0.06  0.30, -2.00 -0.06  0.30,
            2.00  0.10  0.28, -2.00  0.10  0.28,
            2.00  0.23  0.18, -2.00  0.23  0.18,
            2.00  0.28  0.03, -2.00  0.28  0.03,
            2.00  0.24 -0.12, -2.00  0.24 -0.12,
            2.00  0.14 -0.22, -2.00  0.14 -0.22,
            2.00  0.00 -0.25, -2.00  0.00 -0.25,
            2.00 -0.13 -0.20, -2.00 -0.13 -0.20,
            2.00 -0.21 -0.10, -2.00 -0.21 -0.10,
            2.00 -0.22  0.02, -2.00 -0.22  0.02,
            2.00 -0.17  0.13, -2.00 -0.17  0.13,
            2.00 -0.07  0.19, -2.00 -0.07  0.19,
      ]
}
IndexedFaceSet {
      coordIndex [
             2,  3,  1,  0, -1,  4,  5,  3,  2, -1,
             6,  7,  5,  4, -1,  8,  9,  7,  6, -1,
            10, 11,  9,  8, -1, 12, 13, 11, 10, -1,
            14, 15, 13, 12, -1, 16, 17, 15, 14, -1,
            18, 19, 17, 16, -1, 20, 21, 19, 18, -1,
            22, 23, 21, 20, -1, 24, 25, 23, 22, -1,
            26, 27, 25, 24, -1, 28, 29, 27, 26, -1,
            30, 31, 29, 28, -1, 32, 33, 31, 30, -1,
            34, 35, 33, 32, -1, 36, 37, 35, 34, -1,
            38, 39, 37, 36, -1,
      ]
}
```

(*a*)

```
#VRML V1.0 ascii

# The scroll's paper
Separator {
      ShapeHints {
            shapeType       UNKNOWN_SHAPE_TYPE
            vertexOrdering  COUNTERCLOCKWISE
            #               45.0 degrees
            creaseAngle     0.785
      }
```

Figure 17.9 continues

```
          # Top curl
          Material {
               diffuseColor 0.8 0.55 0.3
          }
          DEF curl WWWInline {
               name "curl.wrl"
          }
          # Exposed sheet of paper
          Coordinate3 {
               point [
                    2.00 0.35 0.20, -2.00 0.35 0.20,
                    2.00 -0.35 3.80, -2.00 -0.35 3.80,
               ]
          }
          IndexedFaceSet {
               coordIndex [
                    0, 1, 3, 2,
               ]
          }
          # Bottom curl
          Transform {
               translation 0.0 0.0 4.0
               rotation 0.0 0.0 1.0 3.14
          }
          Rotation {
               rotation 0.0 1.0 0.0 3.14
          }
          USE curl
     }
     # Words on the paper
     Separator {
          Transform {
               translation 0.0 0.40 0.0
               #       X              -79.03 degrees
               rotation 1.0 0.0 0.0  -1.379
          }
          Material {
               diffuseColor 0.0 0.0 0.0
          }
          Translation {
               translation -0.1 -0.5 0.0
          }
          # Title
          FontStyle {
               family SANS
               style (BOLD|ITALIC)
               size 0.4
          }
          AsciiText {
               string [ "Declaration of", "Independence" ]
               justification CENTER
          }
```

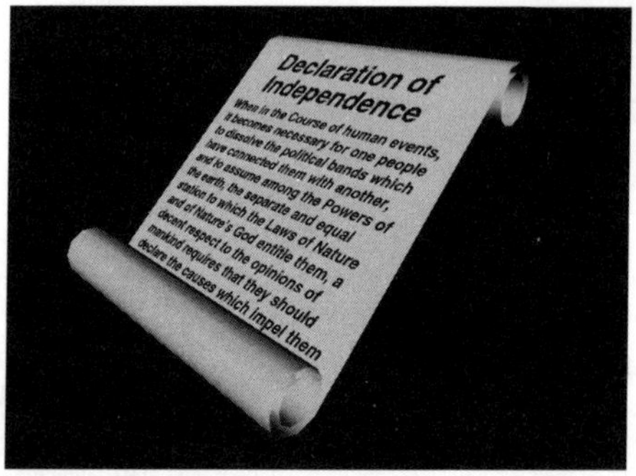

Figure 17.9 continues

```
        # Body text
        Translation {
              translation -1.7 -0.75 0.0
        }
        FontStyle {
              family SANS
              style (BOLD|ITALIC)
              size 0.2
        }
        AsciiText {
              string [
                    "When in the Course of human events,",
                    "it becomes necessary for one people",
                    "to dissolve the political bands which",
                    "have connected them with another,",
                    "and to assume among the Powers of",
                    "the earth, the separate and equal",
                    "station to which the Laws of Nature",
                    "and of Nature's God entitle them, a",
                    "decent respect to the opinions of",
                    "mankind requires that they should",
                    "declare the causes which impel them",
                    "to the separation."
              ]
              spacing 1.2
        }
  }
```

(*b*)

Figure 17.9 *A scroll with curled ends.*

Summary

The **ShapeHints** node gives you control over four shape hints that, in turn, enable or disable browser features and optimize drawing.

The **faceType** field selects whether faces are assumed to be **CONVEX** or of an **UNKNOWN_FACE_TYPE**. When the field value is **UNKNOWN_FACE_TYPE**, the VRML browser tessellates all concave faces into convex faces. This can slow the browser's drawing of your world. The default field value is **CONVEX**, which disables automatic face tessellation.

The **shapeType** field specifies whether shapes drawn by faces in a face set are **SOLID** or of an **UNKNOWN_SHAPE_TYPE**. Solid shapes entirely enclose a volume, leaving no way to see inside shape's perimeter. The default field value is **UNKNOWN_SHAPE_TYPE**.

The **vertexOrdering** field selects whether vertices of faces are ordered in **CLOCKWISE** or **COUNTERCLOCKWISE** order when viewed from the front of the face. The field default value is **UNKNOWN_ORDERING**, indicating to the VRML browser that neither clockwise nor counterclockwise vertex ordering can be assumed.

When the **shapeType** is **SOLID** and the **vertexOrdering** is either **CLOCKWISE** or **COUNTERCLOCKWISE**, the VRML browser can use backface culling to skip drawing faces that face away from you.

When the **shapeType** is **UNKNOWN_SHAPE_TYPE** and the **vertexOrdering** is either **CLOCKWISE** or **COUNTERCLOCKWISE**, the VRML browser enables two-sided lighting to illuminate both the front and back sides of all faces.

The **creaseAngle** field enables you to specify a maximum angle allowed between two adjacent faces to smooth the crease between them with smooth-shading normals computed by the VRML browser.

CHAPTER 18

Mapping Textures

The real world is filled with an extraordinary amount of visual detail. Consider a tree, for instance. From a distance a tree appears to be a large greenish blob. As you near it, it resolves into a trunk and leafy canopy. Come closer still and branches and clumps of leaves are visible, then the individual leaves, the veins on the leaves, and, with a microscope, the cells between the veins, and even their cellular structure. With all this detail, how can you create a tree shape or any other shape from the real world, using VRML and its relatively simple ability to draw shapes? How far must you go to simulate the real world and make your VRML world look fairly believable?

In computer graphics, this visual detail is called **texture**. Creating extraordinarily detailed shapes for every branch, leaf, vein, or cell is impractical. Instead, VRML enables you to simply take a picture of anything in the real world, then "paint" it on any shape in your VRML world. This technique **maps** a picture of real-world textures onto a shape and is known as **texture mapping**.

Texture mapping saves a lot of time, since you no longer need to create shapes for every leaf on a tree, every brick in a building, every blade of grass in a lawn, and so on. Instead, take a picture of a tree, a brick wall, a grassy lawn, or anything else, scan it into your computer, and map it to a simple shape, like a square. If you look closely at the texture-mapped shape, it does not look like a tree, a brick wall, or a grassy lawn. It looks like a square painted with a picture of those things. However, when you step back a bit in your VRML world, the tree, brick wall, or lawn texture-mapped squares look surprisingly realistic.

The **Texture2**, **TextureCoordinate2**, and **Texture2Transform** nodes map textures to any shape you can create in VRML, including primitive shapes, text shapes, face sets, line sets, and point sets. Each of these shapes responds somewhat differently to the mapping of textures. **IndexedFaceSet** and **IndexedLineSet** nodes also have an additional **textureCoordIndex** field to control the way textures are mapped to faces and lines.

TIP *Texture-mapped shapes usually take longer to draw than non-texture-mapped shapes. On some computers, texture mapping may be so slow that it's not practical to use. Check your graphics hardware manual to see if your hardware has the ability to texture-map. Check your VRML browser manual to see if your browser optimizes texture mapping.*

Understanding Texture Mapping

Texture mapping is a technique used to add detail to a world without creating shapes for every brick, leaf, blade of grass, cloud, and so on. Figure 18.1*a* and *b* show a small cottage built using VRML shapes. Figure 18.1*a* shows the cottage shaded without textures. Figure 18.1*b* shows the same cottage texture-mapped to add bricks to the walls, shutter detail to the window shutters, grass to the lawn, and clouds in the sky. Color plates 3*b* and 3*c* show the same two cottages in color.

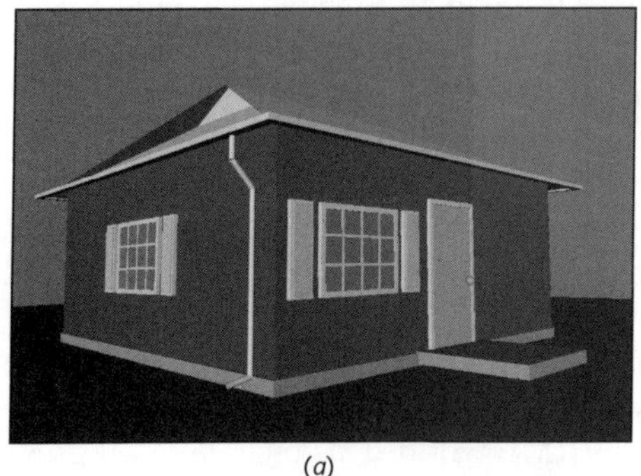

(a)

(b)

Figure 18.1 *A small cottage* (a) *without and* (b) *with textures.*

Any VRML shape can be texture-mapped. The brick-covered cottage walls in the preceding figure are faces in a face set. The windows are flattened cubes with a cloudy-sky texture applied. The sky in the background is the inside of a giant sphere with the same cloudy sky texture-mapped to it.

To texture-map a shape you must specify:

- *The texture image you want mapped onto the shape.*
- *What portions of the texture are to be bound to what portions of the shape.*
- *Whether you want the texture to repeat over and over across a shape or to occur only once.*
- *How the texture should be translated, rotated, or scaled to fit the dimensions of your shape.*

Understanding Texture Images

A texture image is any image stored in a file. Figure 18.2 shows the four texture images used to texture-map the cottage: bricks, window shutters, grass, and sky.

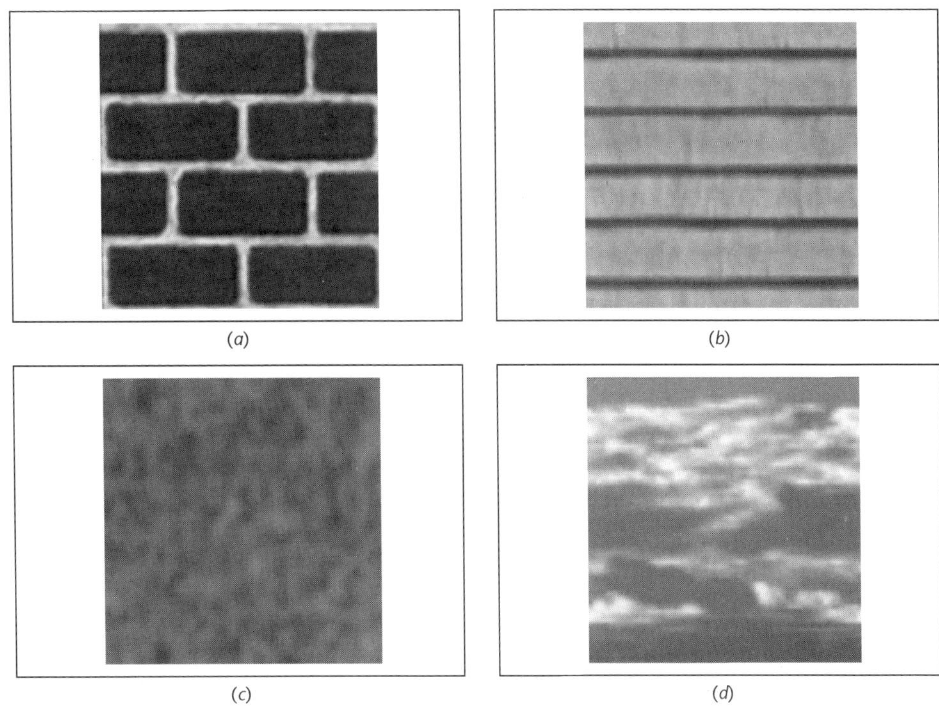

Figure 18.2 *The images used to texture-map the cottage:* (a) *brick,* (b) *shutters,* (c) *grass, and* (d) *sky.*

You can use any image you like as a texture. For instance, we could just as easily have used alternative texture images on the cottage to achieve a different, bizarre effect, as shown in Figure 18.3.

Figure 18.3 *The small cottage texture-mapped strangely.*

You can think of a texture image as a 2-D grid, like a piece of graph paper, with each grid square colored a different color. The grid squares of the image are called **pixels**, which is an abbreviation for **picture element**. The size of an image is specified as the number of pixels the image is in width and height. While texture images can be any size in VRML, typically, texture images are quite small, usually 128 by 128 pixels, 64 by 64 pixels, or smaller. In comparison, your computer screen is 640 by 480 pixels or larger.

TIP *Some graphics hardware can accelerate texture mapping by storing texture images in RAM (random access memory) on the graphics board. Since the amount of texture RAM is usually limited, you may not be able to use large texture images in your VRML worlds. Additionally, if you want to use multiple-texture images, say for brick, lawn, sky, leaves, and so forth, then you must load all of those texture images into your hardware's texture RAM all at once in order to achieve maximum performance. Keep both the number and the size of texture images you use to a minimum. This is not a severe constraint. Using small textures, you can dramatically increase the realism of your worlds.*

You can specify a texture image file with a URL, just like those used to specify inlined VRML files. Using a URL for a texture image file enables you to select texture images from anywhere on the Internet or from your own hard disk.

TIP *Loading a texture image file from the Internet via a modem can be very slow. When building your own VRML worlds, it is more convenient to refer to texture images on your own hard disk.*

The texture image file, like a material or font style, is a property that is saved and restored by **Separator** nodes. This enables you to use different texture images at different places within your VRML file. One shape can be textured with bricks, while another uses clouds, and another uses grass.

Understanding Texture Coordinates

Texture mapping selects a portion of a texture image and maps it to the face of a shape. You can think of this as using a cookie cutter to stamp out a piece of a texture image, then using glue to attach that piece of the image to the shape.

In Chapter 14 you used 3-D coordinates to describe the perimeter of faces in an indexed face set. Using the same idea, you use 2-D **texture coordinates** to describe the perimeter of a texture cookie cutter. For instance, if you define a square with texture coordinates, you'll stamp out square pieces of texture images.

Texture image pieces are then mapped to shapes by *binding* to each shape vertex the corresponding vertex of the cut-out piece of texture image. If your shape face has four corners, then your piece of the texture image will have four corners as well.

The shape of a texture cookie cutter is described by a list of 2-D texture coordinates that trace out the perimeter of the cookie cutter. Each 2-D texture coordinate is a pair of values, called the S and the T values. The S value specifies a location left-to-right on a texture image, while the T value specifies a location bottom-to-top. Figure 18.4 shows the S and T directions applied to the texture image of a person's head.

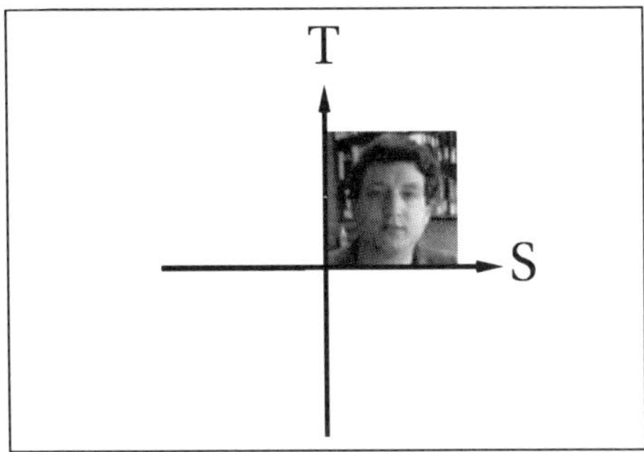

Figure 18.4 *The S and T directions of a texture image.*

S values start with 0.0 at the left edge of a texture image and extend to 1.0 at the right edge. Similarly, T values start with 0.0 at the bottom edge of a texture image and extend up to 1.0 at the top edge. Notice that this range of S and T values across a texture image is always from 0.0 to 1.0, regardless of the width or height, in pixels, of the texture image. A texture coordinate of `0.0 0.0` specifies the lower-left corner of the texture image, and `1.0 1.0` specifies the upper-right corner.

To cut a square piece of the texture image, define a square shape using a list of 2-D texture coordinates, such as these:

Texture Coordinate Index	*2-D Texture Coordinate*
0	`0.0 1.0`
1	`0.0 0.0`
2	`1.0 0.0`
3	`1.0 1.0`

Texture coordinate index 0 specifies the upper-left corner of the full texture image, 1 the lower-left corner, and so on around the entire texture image.

To texture-map this square piece of texture, map it to a shape. Following are the 3-D coordinates for a square face constructed using an **IndexedFaceSet** node.

Shape Coordinate Index	*3-D Shape Coordinate*
0	`-1.0  1.0 0.0`
1	`-1.0 -1.0 0.0`
2	`1.0 -1.0 0.0`
3	`1.0  1.0 0.0`

Coordinate index 0 is the upper-left corner of the square, 1 is the lower-left corner, and so on.

To map the square piece of texture to the square shape, you *bind* each texture coordinate to a shape coordinate, one by one, around the shape. You can, for instance, bind the upper-left corner of the square piece of texture to the upper-left corner of the square shape, the lower-left texture corner to the lower-left shape corner, and so on around the square shape. The following coordinate index lists create such a binding:

Shape Coordinate Index	*Texture Coordinate Index*
0	0
1	1
2	2
3	3

Figure 18.5 shows the mapping that results from this binding.

Figure 18.5 *Mapping a texture to a square, corner for corner.*

You can use any texture-to-shape coordinate binding you like. For instance, you can turn the cut-out piece of texture on its side by binding the texture to the shape, like this:

Texture Coordinate Index	*Shape Coordinate Index*
3	0
0	1
1	2
2	3

In this example, texture coordinate index 3 (upper right of image) is bound to shape coordinate index 0 (upper left of square). Similarly, texture coordinate index 0 (upper left of image) is bound to shape coordinate index 1 (lower left of square), and so on around the square. This binding results in the texture image mapping sideways on the square, as shown in Figure 18.6.

Figure 18.6 *A texture mapped sideways on a square.*

You can use any binding you like to indicate which texture coordinate to associate with each shape vertex. For instance, you can turn the texture image upside down using a binding, as shown in Figure 18.7.

Texture Coordinate Index	*Shape Coordinate Index*
1	0
0	1
3	2
2	3

Notice that for each of these different bindings, the same texture coordinates describing the same cut-out piece of texture are used. All that changes for each one is the *binding* that specifies which texture coordinate to bind to which shape coordinate. This separation of texture coordinates and texture bindings enables you to flexibly cut and bind textures to shapes. This is the same kind of flexibility you have when binding different materials in a material list or different normals in a normal list to individual shape coordinates.

Texture coordinates, like 3-D shape coordinates, are properties that are saved and restored by **Separator** nodes. This enables you to use different texture coordinates in different places within your VRML file. One shape may use one set of texture coordinates to control its texture mapping, while another shape uses a different set of texture coordinates.

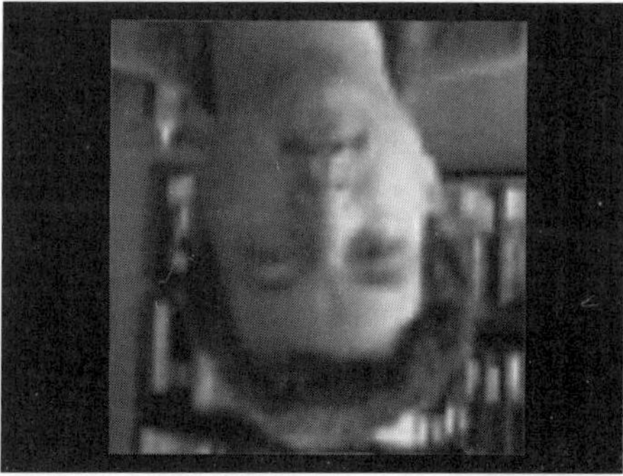

Figure 18.7 *A texture mapped upside down on a square.*

Using Portions of a Texture Image

The previous examples used a square piece of texture that extends edge to edge across the entire texture image. You can also select smaller portions of the texture image by changing the size and position of your texture cookie cutter. This enables you to select any specific part of a texture image and map it to a shape.

For example, the following texture coordinates select the center part of the head texture image.

Texture Coordinate Index	*2-D Texture Coordinate*
0	0.2 0.8
1	0.2 0.2
2	0.8 0.2
3	0.8 0.8

Figure 18.8 shows the full head texture image with a white square around this selected portion. Figure 18.9 shows this portion of the texture image mapped to the square. The binding used binds texture coordinate index 0 to shape coordinate index 0, 1 to 1, and so on around the square shape.

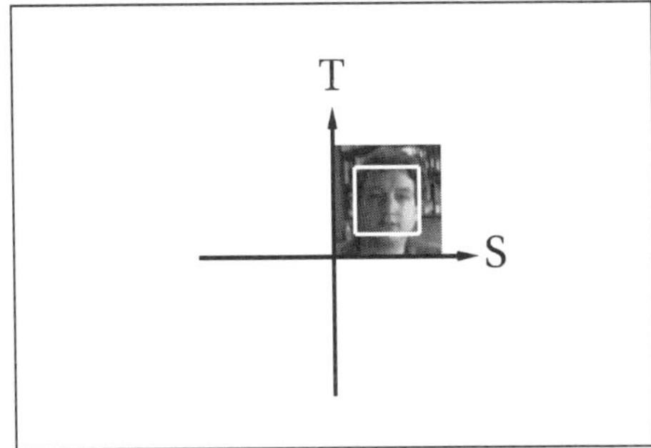

Figure 18.8 *A smaller piece of the texture image.*

Figure 18.9 *The smaller piece of texture mapped to the square, corner for corner.*

If you select a non-square portion of a texture image and map it to the square shape, the texture image stretches, warping to fit the square. For example, Figure 18.10 shows a rectangular portion of the head texture image and Figure 18.11 shows that portion stretched to fit the square.

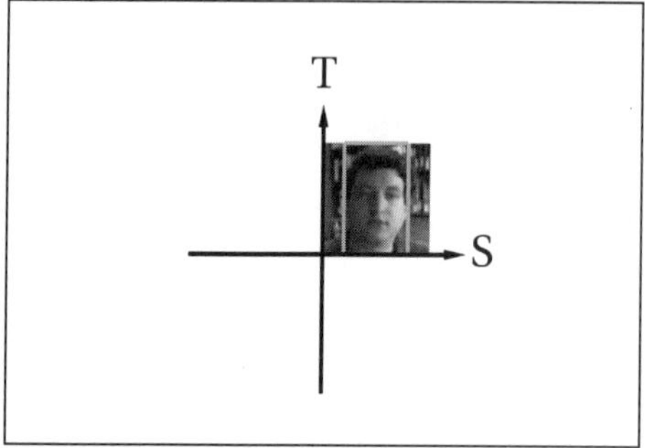

Figure 18.10 *A rectangular piece of the texture image.*

Figure 18.11 *The rectangular piece of texture warped to map to the square.*

You can also create warped texturing effects by mapping a square portion of a texture image to a non-square shape. For example, Figure 18.12 shows the head texture image mapped to a wide rectangle.

Figure 18.12 *The square-shaped head texture warped to map to a wide rectangle.*

Wrapping Texture Coordinates

Recall that a texture image always extends from 0.0 to 1.0 in the S direction and from 0.0 to 1.0 in the T direction. Each of the previous examples has used texture coordinates to select a region *within* those coordinates of the texture image. You can also use texture coordinates to select regions *outside* of the texture image, beyond the left, right, top, or bottom edges of the image. When you do so, your texture coordinates are repeated, or **wrapped**, so that coordinates above the top of an image, wrap to the bottom of the image. Likewise, texture coordinates below the bottom edge wrap to the top of the texture image. Texture coordinates to the left of the left edge wrap to the right edge, and texture coordinates to the right of the right edge wrap to the left edge.

You can think of the original texture image as repeating endlessly left-to-right, bottom-to-top in a giant sheet of texture images. As you move to the left off the left edge of the original texture image, you move onto a copy of the image placed to the left. If you move off the right edge, you move onto a copy of the image placed to the right, and so on. Figure 18.13 shows a brick texture image. Figure 18.14 shows the same brick texture image and several of its duplicate neighbors surrounding it. Each of those neighbors has duplicate neighbors, and so on.

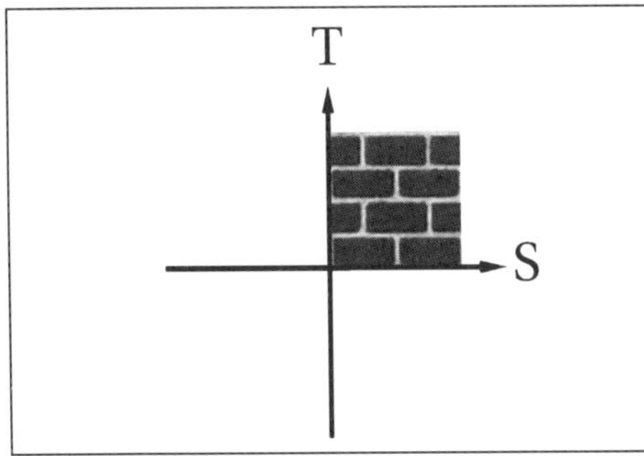

Figure 18.13 *A brick texture image.*

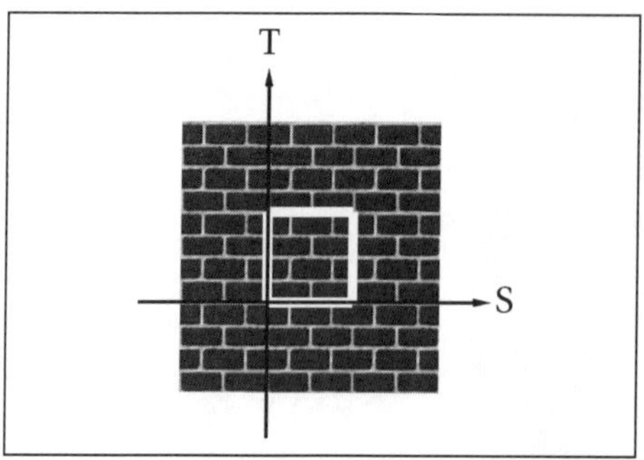

Figure 18.14 *The repeating nature of the brick texture image.*

For example, a texture coordinate of `1.0 0.0` specifies a point on the right edge of the original texture image. A coordinate further to the right, such as `1.2 0.0`, moves past the right edge of the original texture image and specifies a point on the left side of the duplicate neighbor just to the right.

You can think of this infinite series of duplicate texture images as describing a giant sheet of repeating texture images. Using your texture cookie cutter, you can stamp out a texture of any size from this sheet. For example, the following texture coordinates select a portion of this sheet containing nine copies of the original texture image: three from side to side and three from bottom to top.

Texture Coordinate Index	*2-D Texture Coordinate*
0	`0.0 3.0`
1	`0.0 0.0`
2	`3.0 0.0`
3	`3.0 3.0`

Figure 18.15 shows this large, multi-image texture selection mapped to a square.

Figure 18.15 *A repeated texture wrapped using texture coordinates to a square.*

You can use texture coordinate wrapping to create repeating patterns across shapes, like the brick wall of the cottage. For each shape, select an appropriately large portion of the infinitely repeating texture image sheet and map it to the shape.

You can use wrapping texture coordinates to select portions of an infinite sheet built from any texture image. Figure 18.16, for instance, shows the head texture image repeated.

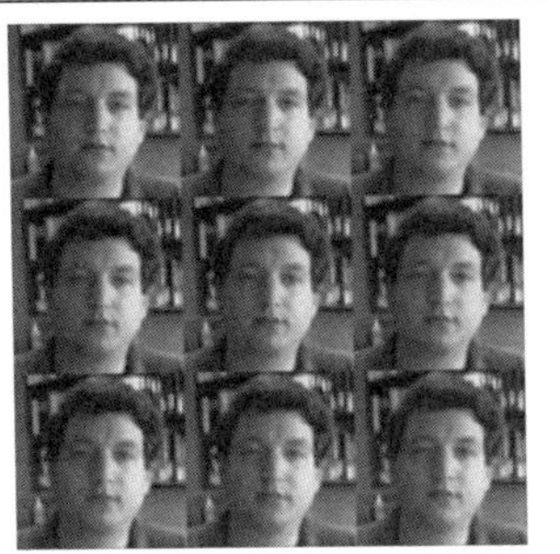

Figure 18.16 *Repeated head texture.*

TIP *Some texture images work well repeated, and others do not. The brick texture, for instance, repeats well but the head texture does not. The brick texture image has been processed with a painting application program so that each edge will neatly butt against its opposite edge without a seam. Many painting and image-processing application programs have features to help you create repeatable texture images like these from scanned images. You can also find repeatable texture images on the Internet or purchase them.*

Clamping Texture Coordinates

By **clamping** texture coordinates, you can prevent them from repeating, like those in the previous examples. You can use clamped texture coordinates to ensure that a texture image occurs just once on a shape, instead of repeating it over and over, like the brick wall.

You can clamp in the S direction, in the T direction, or in both directions at once. When you clamp in the S direction, S texture coordinate values less than 0.0 (the left edge of the texture image) or greater than 1.0 (the right edge) are pulled back, or clamped, to those edges. So, for instance, a texture coordinate like `2.5 0.0` beyond the right edge of the texture image will be clamped back to the right edge at `1.0 0.0`. A texture coordinate like `-1.3 0.5` beyond the left edge will be clamped back to the left edge at `0.0 0.5`.

Clamping in the T direction works in the same way. T-texture coordinate values less than 0.0 (the bottom edge) or greater than 1.0 (the top edge) are clamped back to those edges.

You can think of clamping as restricting the infinite sheet of texture images in the S, T, or both directions. Instead of repeating the texture image over and over in those directions, only the *edges* of the texture image are repeated infinitely. This creates a smearing effect that wipes the texture image's left edge infinitely to the left, the right edge infinitely to the right, bottom to the bottom, and top to the top.

For example, Figure 18.17 shows the head texture image placed in the middle of a square, and with its texture coordinates clamped instead of wrapped. Figure 18.18 shows the same effect with the brick texture image.

Figure 18.17 *The head texture clamped to a square.*

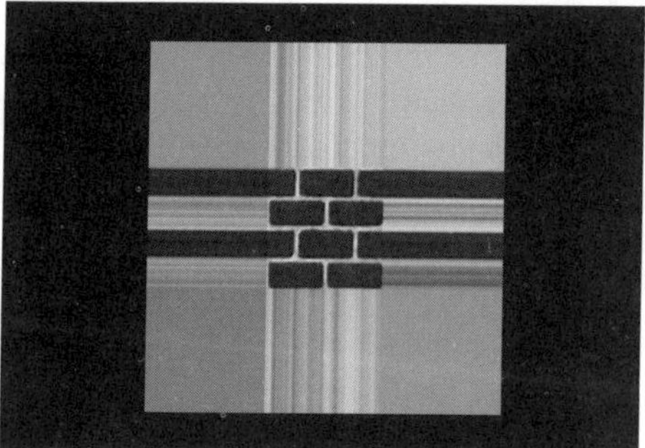

Figure 18.18 *The brick texture clamped to a square.*

TIP *You can reduce these smearing effects by adding a solid-color border to your texture image. Then, when the edges of the texture image are smeared across a shape, like those preceding, it will be the border pixels that are smeared. If you create a solid red border, for instance, the smear will be a solid red. This prevents the striped smear effect shown in the preceding images.*

Transforming Texture Coordinates

You can translate, rotate, and scale 2-D texture coordinates using texture transforms. This enables you to slide a texture around on a shape, positioning it, orienting it, and even shrinking or enlarging it as it is mapped to the shape.

Texture transforms apply only to 2-D texture coordinates, just as the traditional shape transforms (**Translate**, **Rotate**, etc.) apply only to 3-D shape coordinates. If you think of texture coordinates as defining the shape of a texture cookie cutter, then the texture transforms translate, rotate, and scale that cookie cutter before it cuts out a texture for mapping to a shape.

Texture coordinate translations are specified as distances measured in the S and T directions across a texture image. Translating texture coordinates to the right by, say, 0.5 units slides the texture cookie cutter to the right by 0.5 units before stamping out a texture piece and mapping it to a shape.

Figure 18.19 shows a square mapped with head texture images. Figure 18.20 shows the same square with its texture coordinates translated to the right by 0.5

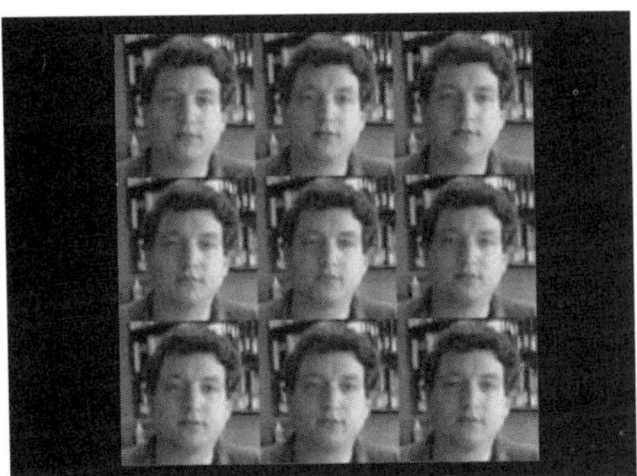

Figure 18.19 *The head texture mapped to the square.*

Figure 18.20 *The head texture's coordinates translated to the right by 0.5 units and mapped to the square.*

units first. Since the texture cookie cutter is moved to the right, it stamps out a piece farther to the right than the original, and the effect is one of sliding the texture images to the right on the square shape.

Texture coordinate rotations spin the texture cookie cutter around before it stamps out a piece of the texture mapped to the square. Figure 18.21 shows the square with its texture coordinates rotated by 45.0 degrees first. The effect is one of spinning the texture image around on the square shape.

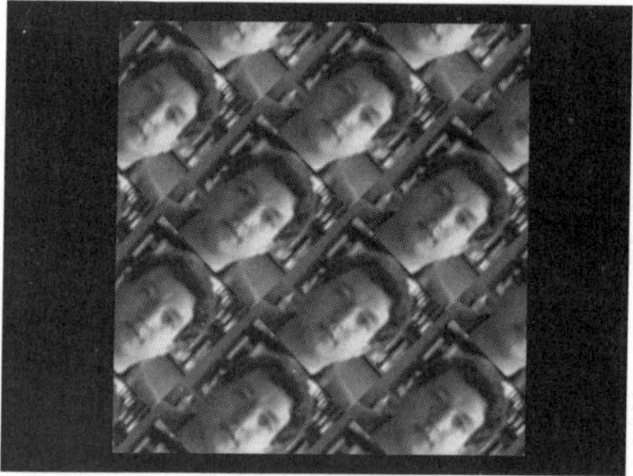

Figure 18.21 *The head texture's coordinates rotated 45 degrees and mapped to the square.*

Texture coordinate scaling increases, or decreases, the size of the texture cookie cutter before it stamps out a piece of the texture for mapping. If you scale up the texture cookie cutter, it stamps out a larger piece of the texture image sheet. When using repeating textures, that larger stamped-out piece will include a larger number of repeats of the original texture. In the same way, when you scale down the texture cookie cutter, it stamps out a smaller piece of texture that includes a smaller number of texture repeats from the original texture. For example, Figure 18.22 scales up by 2.0 the texture coordinates of the head texture image. Figure 18.23 scales down by 0.5.

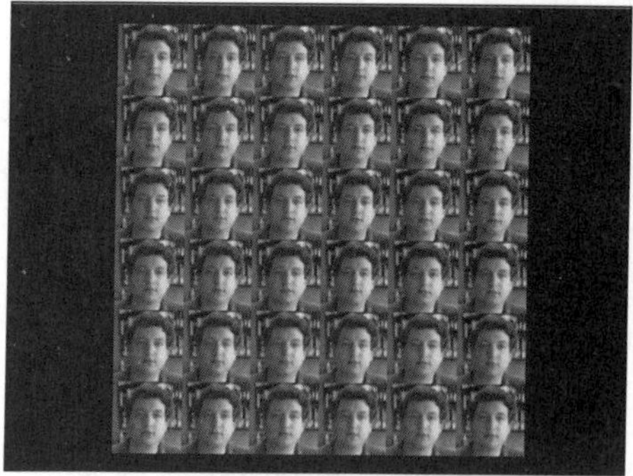

Figure 18.22 *The head texture coordinates scaled by 2.0.*

Figure 18.23 *The head texture coordinates scaled by 0.5.*

You can use all of these texture coordinate transforms to help you position, orient, and size texture images you map to shapes in your world. Texture transforms, like 3-D shape transforms, are properties that are saved and restored by **Separator** nodes. Texture transforms are not, however, saved and restored by **TransformSeparator** nodes.

Mapping Textures to Shapes

The example text in Figure 18.24 maps a texture image, edge to edge, to a square shape drawn by an **IndexedFaceSet** node. The texture image is specified by a **Texture2** node, and the texture coordinates are specified by a **TextureCoordinate2** node.

```
#VRML V1.0 ascii

Coordinate3 {
      point [
            0.0 1.0 0.0,
            0.0 0.0 0.0,
            1.0 0.0 0.0,
            1.0 1.0 0.0,
      ]
}
Texture2 {
      filename "brick.gif"
}
TextureCoordinate2 {
      point [
            0.0 1.0,
            0.0 0.0,
            1.0 0.0,
            1.0 1.0,
      ]
}
```

Figure 18.24 continues

```
IndexedFaceSet {
        coordIndex [
                0, 1, 2, 3
        ]
        textureCoordIndex [
                0, 1, 2, 3
        ]
}
```

Figure 18.24 *Mapping a texture to a square.*

Notice the structure and order of the VRML file in Figure 18.24. Reading from the top of the file, the **Coordinate3** node defines four coordinates for the four corners of a square. The **Texture** node specifies an image texture named `brick.gif` to be mapped to subsequent shapes. The **TextureCoordinate2** node defines four texture coordinates for the corresponding four corners of a texture cookie cutter. The **IndexedFaceSet** node draws the square, using the brick texture, and binds texture coordinates to shape coordinates, one by one.

Understanding the **Texture2** Node Syntax

The Texture2 node has four fields: **filename**, **image**, **wrapS**, and **wrapT**.

SYNTAX **Texture2 node**

```
Texture2 {
        filename    ""          # URL
        wrapS       REPEAT      # Texture wrap type
        wrapT       REPEAT      # Texture wrap type
        image       0 0 0       # Raw image pixels
}
```

The **filename** field value is a URL specifying a texture image to be mapped to subsequent shapes. If you specify nothing or the empty string, "", no texture is mapped to subsequent shapes.

TIP *There are literally hundreds of different ways of storing images in files. Each storage method uses a different structure for the data inside an image file. Common image file formats include TIFF, GIF, JPEG, PCX, TGA, and SGI files. Different VRML browsers will support different image file formats, though most support JPEG and GIF. Check your browser manual to see what texture image file formats it supports.*

The **image** field can be used to provide raw image pixels instead of using an image file. In practice, this field is rarely used and is not discussed in this book. The interested reader is encouraged to explore this feature of VRML by reading its description in the official VRML specification.

The **wrapS** and **wrapT** fields enable you to turn on or off texture coordinate clamping. Both fields have two available values:

- *REPEAT—Allow texture coordinates to wrap, repeating a texture image over and over across a shape.*
- *CLAMP—Clamp texture coordinates to the edges of the texture image, preventing a texture image from repeating.*

The default value for both of these fields is **REPEAT**, which causes texture coordinates to wrap and create repeating texture image effects.

The **Texture2** node sets the texture property and enables texture mapping for all subsequent shapes. **Separator** nodes save and restore the current texture, and shape nodes use the texture to color the faces of shapes.

TIP *The exact method used to color shape faces based on a texture varies from VRML browser to VRML browser and among computer graphics boards. One common method is to use the RGB texture color values and multiply them by the current RGB material color previously set by a **Material** node. The brighter the material color, the more vivid the texture is when it is mapped onto the shape. For the most vivid texture mapping, use bright white diffuse or emissive color values.*

Understanding the **TextureCoordinate2** Node Syntax

The **TextureCoordinate2** node has a single **point** field whose value is a list of 2-D texture coordinates, enclosed within square brackets and separated by commas. Each texture coordinate is composed of an S and a T component. The S value specifies a horizontal location within the texture image, while the T value specifies a vertical location.

The **TextureCoordinate2** node defines a texture coordinate list for use by VRML's texture-mapping features.

SYNTAX **TextureCoordinate2 node**

```
TextureCoordinate2 {
     point 0.0 0.0       # S, T texture coordinate
}
```

The entire texture coordinate list is included in the texture coordinate property. **Separator** nodes save and restore the whole texture coordinate list, and shape nodes use the texture coordinate list to bind different texture coordinates to different vertices of a shape.

Understanding the **Texture2Transform** Node Syntax

The **Texture2Transform** node has four fields, all similar to those of the shape **Transform** node.

SYNTAX **Texture2Transform node**

```
Texture2Transform {
      translation 0.0 0.0        # S, T distance
      rotation    0              # Rotation amount
      scaleFactor 1 1            # S, T scale factors
      center      0 0            # S, T texture coordinate
}
```

The **translation** field contains two floating-point values specifying translation distances in the S and T texture coordinate directions. S translations move horizontally on the texture image in the positive and negative directions. T translations move vertically in the positive and negative directions. S and T values may be used in combination to move the texture cookie cutter diagonally across the texture image.

The **rotation** field contains a rotation amount, measured in radians, that specifies by how much to rotate texture coordinates. Positive rotation amounts turn texture coordinates counterclockwise, and negative amounts clockwise.

The **scaleFactor** field specifies two scale factors for S and T texture coordinate scaling. The S scale factor scales texture coordinates horizontally, while the T scale factor scales them vertically. S and T scale factors may be the same or different.

The **center** field specifies the distance to a center point for scaling, similar to the **center** field for the **Transform** node. Using a scale center point, you can enlarge or shrink texture coordinates with respect to a specified location within the texture image.

Texture transforms are relative to the current texture transform. If you use two consecutive **Texture2Transform** nodes, the effects of the second transform are relative to the first. This relative transform effect is identical to that observed when ordering shape transforms to translate, rotate, and scale before drawing shapes.

The **Texture2Transform** node affects the texture transform property. **Separator** nodes save and restore the texture transform, and shape nodes use the texture transform to transform texture coordinates before selecting a region of the current texture image for mapping to a shape.

TIP *If you think of texture mapping as using a cookie cutter to stamp out pieces of a texture image, then the **Texture2Transform** node affects the location, orientation, and size of that cookie cutter. The order of operations on the texture cookie cutter by the **Texture2Transform** node is always to translate to a texture location, rotate at that location, scale up or down from that rotated location, and then stamp out a texture piece. This is the same order used by the **Transform** node for applying transforms before drawing shapes.*

Understanding the Extended **IndexedFaceSet** Node Syntax

The **IndexedFaceSet** node has four fields: **coordIndex**, **materialIndex**, **normalIndex**, and **textureCoordIndex**.

SYNTAX **IndexedFaceSet node**

```
IndexedFaceSet {
      coordIndex           [0]      # Coordinate index list
      materialIndex        -1       # Material index list
      normalIndex          -1       # Normal index list
      textureCoordIndex    -1       # Texture index list
}
```

The **coordIndex** field is discussed in Chapter 14, the **materialIndex** field in Chapter 15, and the **normalIndex** field in Chapter 16. All three of these fields work as described in those chapters even when using texture mapping.

The **textureCoordIndex** field specifies a list of texture coordinate indexes, enclosed within square brackets and separated by commas. Each texture coordinate index corresponds to a texture coordinate from the current texture coordinate list. A texture coordinate index of 0, for instance, corresponds to the first texture coordinate in the current texture coordinate list. Texture coordinate index 1 corresponds to the second coordinate, and so on.

TIP *Texture coordinate indexes, like material, normal, and vertex indexes, are numbered from 0. So, the first texture coordinate in a texture coordinate list has an index of 0, the second an index of 1, and so forth.*

Understanding the Extended **IndexedLineSet** Node Syntax

The **IndexedLineSet** node has four fields: **coordIndex**, **materialIndex**, **normalIndex**, and **textureCoordIndex**.

SYNTAX **IndexedLineSet node**

```
IndexedLineSet {
      coordIndex           [0]      # Coordinate index list
      materialIndex        -1       # Material index list
      normalIndex          -1       # Normal index list
      textureCoordIndex    -1       # Texture index list
}
```

The **coordIndex** field is discussed in Chapter 14, the **materialIndex** field in Chapter 15, and the **normalIndex** field in Chapter 16. All three of these fields work as described in those chapters, even when using texture mapping.

The **textureCoordIndex** field specifies a list of texture coordinate indexes, enclosed within square brackets and separated by commas. Each texture coordinate index corresponds to a texture coordinate from the current texture coordinate list. A texture coordinate index of 0, for instance, corresponds to the first texture coordinate in the current texture coordinate list. Texture coordinate index 1 corresponds to the second coordinate, and so on.

TIP *Texture coordinate indexes, like material, normal, and vertex indexes, are numbered from 0. The first texture coordinate in a texture coordinate list has an index of 0, the second an index of 1, and so forth.*

Understanding Texture Binding

Like material binding, texture binding affects different kinds of shapes differently. For example, textures map to primitive shapes differently than to shapes described by points, lines, or faces. Textures bind differently *among* the primitive shapes, also.

Binding Textures to Primitive Shapes

Each of the primitive shapes can be texture-mapped, but each handles textures differently. They all compute their own texture coordinates internally, so any values set by a **TextureCoordinate2** are ignored. The internally computed texture coordinates are affected by **Texture2Transform** nodes.

Binding Textures to Cubes

The current texture image is mapped individually to each face of the cube. Texturing uses internally generated texture coordinates for each face that initially extend from `0.0 0.0` at the lower-left corner of a face to `1.0 1.0` at the upper-right corner. The current texture transform translates, rotates, or scales these texture coordinates before a texture is mapped to the cube's faces.

Texture images are mapped to cube faces like this:

- *The texture image appears right side up on the front, back, left, and right sides of a cube if you view each face with the cube's top pointing upward along the positive Y axis.*
- *On the top of a cube, the texture image appears right side up if you tilt the top of the cube down to face you while keeping the left face pointing to the left and the right face pointing to the right.*
- *On the bottom of a cube, the texture image will appear right side up if you tilt the bottom of the cube up to face you while keeping the left face pointing to the left and the right face pointing to the right.*

Binding Textures to Cylinders

The current texture image is mapped individually to the sides, top, and bottom of the cylinder. On the top and bottom, a circle is cut out of a square texture image and applied to the face. Internally generated texture coordinates for the square extend from `0.0 0.0` at the lower-left corner of a face to `1.0 1.0` at the upper-right corner. The current texture transform translates, rotates, or scales these texture coordinates before a texture is mapped to the cylinder's top and bottom.

Texture images are mapped to the cylinder top and bottom like this:

- *On the top of a cylinder, the texture image will appear right side up if you tilt the top of the cylinder down to face you without turning the cylinder along its axis.*
- *On the bottom of a cylinder, the texture image will appear right side up if you tilt the bottom of the cylinder up to face you without turning the cylinder along its axis.*

On the sides of a cylinder, the texture is wrapped around front to back. The seam where the left and right edges of the texture image join runs vertically along the back of the cylinder. Internally generated texture coordinates for the cylinder sides extend from `0.0 0.0` at the back bottom, around the front, and to the back `1.0 0.0` at the back bottom. Similarly, texture coordinates extend from `0.0 1.0` at the back top, around the front, and to the back at `1.0 1.0` at the back top. The current texture transform translates, rotates, or scales these texture coordinates before a texture is mapped to the cylinder's sides.

Binding Textures to Cones

The current texture image is mapped individually to the sides and bottom of the cone. On the bottom, a circle is cut out of a square texture image and applied to the face. Internally generated texture coordinates for the square extend from `0.0 0.0` at the lower-left corner of a face to `1.0 1.0` at the upper-right corner. The current texture transform translates, rotates, or scales these texture coordinates before a texture is mapped to the cone's bottom.

Texture images are mapped to the cone bottom like this:

- *On the bottom of a cone, the texture image appears right side up if you tilt the bottom of the cone up to face you without turning the cylinder along its axis.*

On the sides of a cone, the texture is wrapped around front to back. The seam where the left and right edges of the texture image join runs vertically along the back of the cone. Internally generated texture coordinates for the cone sides extend from `0.0 0.0` at the back bottom, around the front, and to the back `1.0 0.0` at the back bottom. Texture coordinates `0.0 1.0` and `1.0 1.0` both map to the tip of the cone, thereby causing the texture image to be pinched tighter and tighter as it approaches the cone tip. The current texture transform translates, rotates, or scales these texture coordinates before a texture is mapped to the cone's sides.

Binding Textures to Spheres

The current texture image is mapped to the sides of the sphere, wrapping it around front to back. The seam where the left and right edges of the texture image join runs vertically along the back of the sphere. Internally generated texture coordinates for the sphere sides map both `0.0 0.0` and `1.0 0.0` to the bottom pole of the sphere, and `0.0 1.0` and `1.0 1.0` the top pole of the sphere. This causes the texture image to be pinched tighter and tighter as it approaches either sphere pole. The current texture transform translates, rotates, or scales these texture coordinates before a texture is mapped to the sphere's sides.

Binding Textures to Text Shapes

Text shapes can be texture-mapped. Each text character cuts out its own character-shaped texture from the current texture image. All text characters compute their own texture coordinates internally, so any values set by a **TextureCoordinate2** are thus ignored. The internally computed texture coordinates are affected by **Texture2Transform** nodes.

Each character shape in a font is defined within a character **cell** that is square in shape and has a width and height equal to the font size. For the default font, for instance, the character cell is 10.0 units wide and 10.0 units high. Characters are defined within their cells so that they all sit on a common **baseline**, an imaginary horizontal line like a ruled line on notebook paper. The bottoms of all capital letters and most lowercase letters sit on the baseline. The tallest capital letter reaches up towards the top of the cell, while the lowest point of a "g," "j," or "y" extends down past the baseline and just touches the bottom of the cell.

Internally generated texture coordinates for text are based on the character cell. For each character in a string, a new set of texture coordinates is generated that extend from `0.0 0.0` at the lower-left corner of the character's cell to `1.0 1.0` at the upper-right corner of the cell. The character shape itself, then, cuts out a character-shaped texture from the square area of the texture image defined by this character cell. The effect is to texture each character in a string individually, as if it were its own shape rather than part of the larger text string shape.

The current texture transform translates, rotates, or scales each character's texture coordinates before a texture is mapped to the character shape.

Binding Textures to Point Sets

Texturing points in a **PointSet** node is controlled by texture coordinates from a **TextureCoordinate2** node. A different texture coordinate is bound to each vertex in the point set. The value of the **startIndex** field in the point set is used as a texture coordinate index specifying the coordinate in the current texture coordinate list to be used for the first vertex. The second vertex is shaded using the texture coordinate at **startIndex**+1, the third at **startIndex**+2, and so on.

If no texture coordinate list is currently defined by a **TextureCoordinate2** node, then texture coordinates are automatically generated as follows:

1. The VRML browser computes a bounding box for the point set. The box is a 3-D rectangle whose center is at the center of the point set, and whose width, height, and depth are just large enough to encompass the entire point set.

2. The longest edge of the bounding box is used to define the S direction for mapping textures to the points. The value of the S texture coordinate index varies from 0.0 to 1.0 at the two opposite ends of this longest edge.
3. The second-longest edge of the bounding box is used to define the T direction for mapping textures to the points. The value of the T-texture coordinate index varies from 0.0 to *n* at the two opposite ends of this second longest edge. The value *n* is computed as the length of the longest edge of the box divided by the length of the second-longest edge.

TIP *Allowing your VRML browser to compute point set texture coordinates may produce unexpected results. To avoid this, provide a* ***TextureCoordinate2*** *node with one texture coordinate for each point in the point set before texture mapping a* ***PointSet*** *node.*

Whether you use your own texture coordinates or rely on the VRML browser's default texture coordinate computations, the texture coordinates are transformed by the current texture transform before the texture is mapped to each point.

TIP *The point set uses the* ***startIndex*** *field value, and consecutive values thereafter, to index into the current texture coordinate list and specify a texture coordinate for each point vertex. If there are more points than there are texture coordinates in the current texture coordinate list, unpredictable results may occur. Some VRML browsers may detect this problem and report an error. Others do not. To avoid this, specify one texture coordinate for each point.*

Binding Textures to Face Sets

Texturing of faces in an **IndexedFaceSet** node is controlled by texture coordinates specified in a **TextureCoordinate2** node. A different texture coordinate, specified by a texture coordinate index, is bound to each vertex in the face set.

Texture coordinate indexes in the **textureCoordIndex** field specify a texture coordinate from the current texture coordinate list for each vertex of each face of the face set. The first index in the field specifies the texture coordinate for the first vertex, the second index for the second vertex, and so on. A texture coordinate index is needed to match each vertex *and* each –1 face divider value in the vertex list.

If the **textureCoordIndex** field is not set, the coordinate indexes of the **coordIndex** field are used instead. The first coordinate index specifies the texture coordinate index for the first vertex, the second coordinate index for the second vertex, and so on. This is very convenient when creating textured shapes that have a unique computed texture coordinate in a **TextureCoordinate2** node for each vertex of the shape described in a corresponding **Coordinate3** node. This is the most common way in which texture coordinates are bound to face vertices.

If no texture coordinate list is currently defined by an earlier **TextureCoordinate2** node, then texture coordinates are automatically generated. The method is the same as that for point sets, previously described. The point-set cautions previously stated also apply to face sets.

Binding Textures to Line Sets

Texturing of lines in an **IndexedLineSet** node is controlled by texture coordinates specified in a **TextureCoordinate2** node. A different texture coordinate, specified by the texture coordinate index, is bound to each vertex in the line set.

Texture coordinate indexes in the **textureCoordIndex** field specify a texture coordinate from the current texture coordinate list for each vertex of each line of the line set. The first index in the field specifies the texture coordinate for the first vertex, the second index for the second vertex, and so on. A texture coordinate index is needed to match each vertex *and* each –1 polyline divider value in the vertex list.

If the **textureCoordIndex** field is not set, the coordinate indexes of the **coordIndex** field are used instead. The first coordinate index specifies the texture coordinate index for the first vertex, the second coordinate index for the second vertex, and so on. This is very convenient when creating textured shapes that have a unique computed texture coordinate in a **TextureCoordinate2** node for each vertex of the shape described in a corresponding **Coordinate3** node. This is the most common way in which texture coordinates are bound to line vertices.

If no texture coordinate list is currently defined by an earlier **TextureCoordinate2** node, then texture coordinates are automatically generated. The method is the same as that for point sets, previously described. The point-set cautions previously stated also apply to line sets.

Experimenting with Texture Mapping

The following examples provide a more detailed examination of the ways in which texture mapping can be used.

Many of the examples that follow use one of these texture images: (Figure 18.25) brick, (Figure 18.26) wood, (Figure 18.27) head, and (Figure 8.28) graffiti.

Figure 18.25 *Brick texture image.*

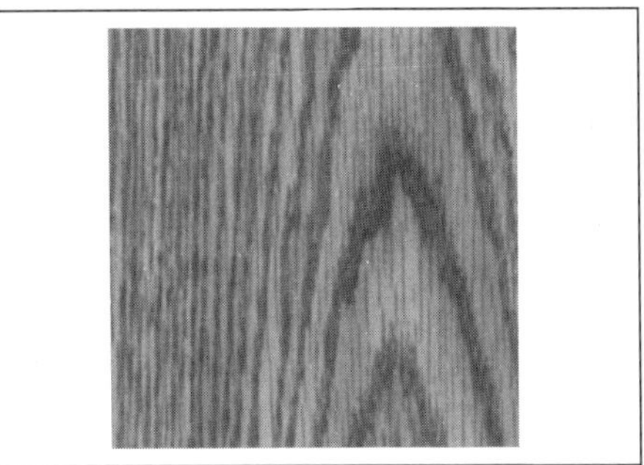

Figure 18.26 *Wood texture image.*

Figure 18.27 *Head texture image.*

Figure 18.28 *Graffiti paint texture image.*

You can use any image you like when trying these examples for yourself. Interesting images can be found throughout the Internet or as part of clip-art CD-ROMs and Kodak PhotoCDs. You can create your own texture images using any painting application program or any of several texture-generation applications available for your computer. You can also scan photos and images to be used as texture maps or use pictures taken with a digital camera.

Texture-Mapping Primitive Shapes

The following examples map a texture image to the sides of a cube (Figure 18.29), a cylinder (Figure 18.30), a cone (Figure 18.31), and a sphere (Figure 18.32). Notice how the texture image is stretched to fit around the circumference of a cylinder, cone, or sphere, and how it is oriented when mapped to different parts of a cube, cylinder, or cone. Notice also how the texture image is pinched at the top of a cone and at the top and bottom poles of a sphere.

```
#VRML V1.0 ascii

Texture2 {
      filename "paint.gif"
}
Cube {
}
```

Figure 18.29 *A texture-mapped cube.*

```
#VRML V1.0 ascii

Texture2 {
      filename "paint.gif"
}
Cylinder {
}
```

Figure 18.30 *A texture-mapped cylinder.*

```
#VRML V1.0 ascii

Texture2 {
      filename "paint.gif"
}
Cone {
}
```

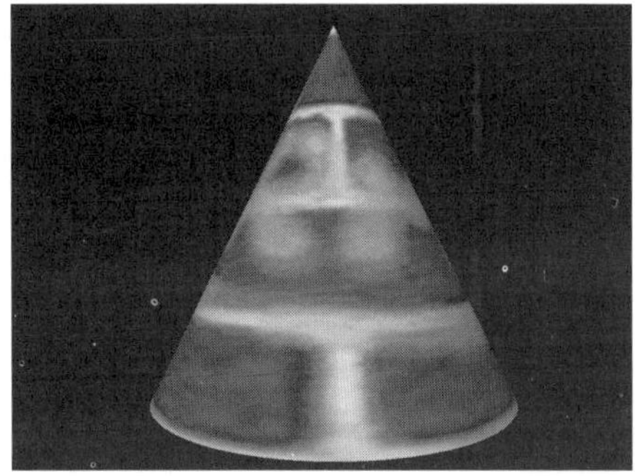

Figure 18.31 *A texture-mapped cone.*

```
#VRML V1.0 ascii

Texture2 {
      filename "paint.gif"
}
Sphere {
}
```

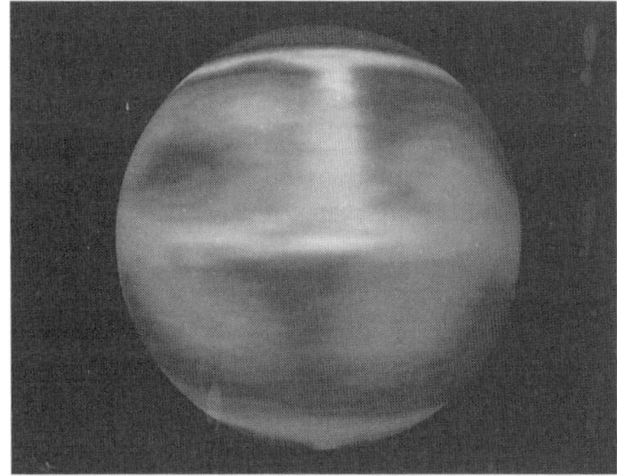

Figure 18.32 *A texture-mapped sphere.*

Using texture-mapped primitives, you can create a number of useful shapes without computing your own texture coordinates for indexed face sets. The example text in Figure 18.36 uses three texture images for the top (Figure 18.33), bottom (Figure 18.34), and sides (Figure 18.35) of a soft drink can and maps them to the top, bottom, and sides of three cylinders, one at a time.

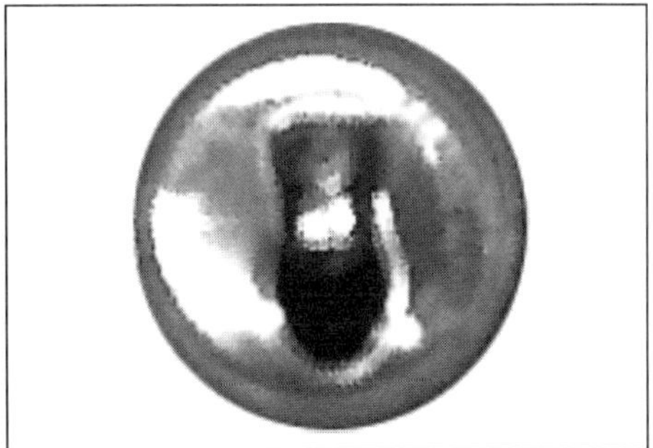

Figure 18.33 *The can top texture image.*

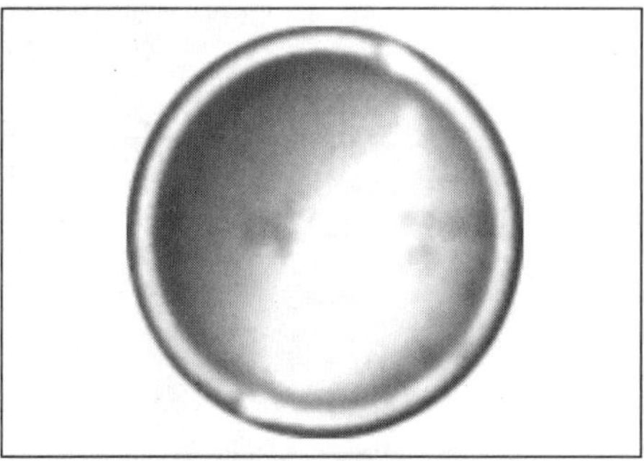

Figure 18.34 *The can bottom texture image.*

Figure 18.35 *The can label texture image.*

```
#VRML V1.0 ascii

# Can top
Texture2 {
      filename "cantop.gif"
}
Cylinder {
      parts TOP
      height 2.7
}
# Can bottom
Texture2 {
      filename "canbot.gif"
}
Cylinder {
      parts BOTTOM
      height 2.7
}
# Can sides
Texture2 {
      filename "canlabel.gif"
}
```

Figure 18.36 continues

```
Cylinder {
      parts SIDES
      height 2.8
}
```

Figure 18.36 *The final, texture-mapped cylinder.*

Texture-Mapping Text Shapes

The example text in Figure 18.37 maps a texture image to text shapes drawn by an **AsciiText** node. Notice how the texture image is mapped individually, one at a time, to each text shape.

```
#VRML V1.0 ascii

Texture2 {
      filename "paint.gif"
}
FontStyle {
      style BOLD
}
AsciiText {
      string [ "Qwerty", "0123" ]
}
```

Figure 18.37 *Texture-mapped text.*

Texture-Mapping Face Sets

Mapping textures to shapes defined by face sets is the most common use of texture mapping. You can map textures to face sets describing any arbitrary shape. All of the examples in the first part of this chapter mapped a texture to a simple square, as shown in Figure 18.38

```
#VRML V1.0 ascii

Coordinate3 {
      point [
            0.0 1.0 0.0,
            0.0 0.0 0.0,
            1.0 0.0 0.0,
            1.0 1.0 0.0,
      ]
}
Texture2 {
      filename "brick.gif"
}
```

Figure 18.38 continues

```
TextureCoordinate2 {
      point [
            0.0 1.0,
            0.0 0.0,
            1.0 0.0,
            1.0 1.0,
      ]
}
IndexedFaceSet {
      coordIndex [
            0, 1, 2, 3
      ]
      textureCoordIndex [
            0, 1, 2, 3
      ]
}
```

Figure 18.38 *Texture-mapping a square defined by an indexed face set.*

Reading from the top of the file, the VRML browser is directed to:

1. Set the coordinate property to four coordinates.
2. Set the texture image property to the texture image in `brick.gif`.
3. Set the texture coordinate property to four coordinates.
4. Draw a face set.
   a. Draw a face with coordinate indexes 0, 1, 2, and 3. Bind texture coordinate index 0 to coordinate index 0, and bind texture coordinate index 1 to coordinate index 1, 2 to 2, and 3 to 3.

You can use this same approach to texture-map any arbitrary collection of faces within a face set. The example text in Figure 18.39 maps a wood texture to a vase. Color plate 3*d* shows the textured vase.

```
#VRML V1.0 ascii

Coordinate3 {
      point [
            # ring 0
             0.32 2.00  0.00,
             0.10 2.00  0.30,
            -0.26 2.00  0.19,
            -0.26 2.00 -0.19,
             0.10 2.00 -0.30,
            # ring 1
             0.30 1.95  0.00,
             0.09 1.95  0.29,
            -0.24 1.95  0.18,
            -0.24 1.95 -0.18,
             0.09 1.95 -0.29,
```

Figure 18.39 continues

```
                # ring 2
                 0.42 1.60  0.00,
                 0.13 1.60  0.40,
                -0.34 1.60  0.25,
                -0.34 1.60 -0.25,
                 0.13 1.60 -0.40,
                # ring 3
                 0.60 1.50  0.00,
                 0.19 1.50  0.57,
                -0.48 1.50  0.35,
                -0.49 1.50 -0.35,
                 0.18 1.50 -0.57,
                # ring 4
                 0.70 1.20  0.00,
                 0.22 1.20  0.67,
                -0.57 1.20  0.41,
                -0.57 1.20 -0.41,
                 0.21 1.20 -0.67,
                # ring 5
                 0.40 0.00  0.00,
                 0.12 0.00  0.38,
                -0.32 0.00  0.24,
                -0.32 0.00 -0.23,
                 0.12 0.00 -0.38
        ]
}
Texture2 {
        filename "wood.gif"
}
TextureCoordinate2 {
        point [
                # ring 0
                0.8 1.0,
                0.6 1.0,
                0.4 1.0,
                0.2 1.0,
                0.0 1.0,
                # ring 1
                0.8 0.975,
                0.6 0.975,
                0.4 0.975,
                0.2 0.975,
                0.0 0.975,
                # ring 2
                0.8 0.8,
                0.6 0.8,
                0.4 0.8,
                0.2 0.8,
                0.0 0.8,
```

Figure 18.39 continues

```
                    # ring 3
                    0.8 0.75,
                    0.6 0.75,
                    0.4 0.75,
                    0.2 0.75,
                    0.0 0.75,
                    # ring 4
                    0.8 0.6,
                    0.6 0.6,
                    0.4 0.6,
                    0.2 0.6,
                    0.0 0.6,
                    # ring 5
                    0.8 0.0,
                    0.6 0.0,
                    0.4 0.0,
                    0.2 0.0,
                    0.0 0.0,
                ]
        }
        IndexedFaceSet {
                coordIndex [
                    # ring 0
                     0,  1,  6,  5, -1,
                     1,  2,  7,  6, -1,
                     2,  3,  8,  7, -1,
                     3,  4,  9,  8, -1,
                     4,  0,  5,  9, -1,
                    # ring 1
                     5,  6, 11, 10, -1,
                     6,  7, 12, 11, -1,
                     7,  8, 13, 12, -1,
                     8,  9, 14, 13, -1,
                     9,  5, 10, 14, -1,
                    # ring 2
                    10, 11, 16, 15, -1,
                    11, 12, 17, 16, -1,
                    12, 13, 18, 17, -1,
                    13, 14, 19, 18, -1,
                    14, 10, 15, 19, -1,
                    # ring 3
                    15, 16, 21, 20, -1,
                    16, 17, 22, 21, -1,
                    17, 18, 23, 22, -1,
                    18, 19, 24, 23, -1,
                    19, 15, 20, 24, -1,
                    # ring 4
                    20, 21, 26, 25, -1,
                    21, 22, 27, 26, -1,
                    22, 23, 28, 27, -1,
                    23, 24, 29, 28, -1,
                    24, 20, 25, 29, -1,
```

Figure 18.39 continues

```
            # base
            25, 26, 27, 28, 29
        ]
    }
```

Figure 18.39 *A wood-textured vase.*

Notice there is one texture coordinate in the **TextureCoordinate2** node for each shape coordinate in the **Coordinate3** node. Because of this one-to-one correspondence, there is no need to specify **textureCoordIndex** field values. Instead, the VRML browser defaults to the **coordIndex** field's values both as coordinate indexes *and* as texture coordinate indexes.

Texture-Mapping Line Sets

While less common than face texture mapping, line texture mapping can also be useful. You can create dotted lines of any style by mapping to the lines a checkerboard or any other regular pattern. The example text in Figure 18.40 maps the brick texture image to the radial starburst example from Chapter 15. Notice that the texture coordinates in the **TextureCoordinate2** node are just the X and Y components from the **Coordinate3** node.

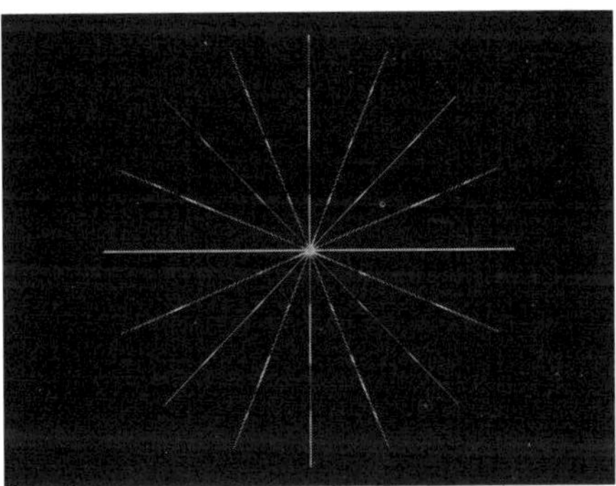

```
#VRML V1.0 ascii

Texture2 {
    filename "brick.gif"
}
Coordinate3 {
    point [
         0.0   0.0  0.0,
         1.00  0.00 0.0,
         0.92  0.38 0.0,
         0.71  0.71 0.0,
         0.38  0.92 0.0,
         0.00  1.00 0.0,
        -0.38  0.92 0.0,
        -0.71  0.71 0.0,
        -0.92  0.38 0.0,
        -1.00  0.00 0.0,
        -0.92 -0.38 0.0,
        -0.71 -0.71 0.0,
        -0.38 -0.92 0.0,
         0.00 -1.00 0.0,
         0.38 -0.92 0.0,
         0.71 -0.71 0.0,
         0.92 -0.38 0.0,
    ]
}
```

Figure 18.40 continues

```
TextureCoordinate2 {
      point [
             0.0   0.0,
             1.00  0.00,
             0.92  0.38,
             0.71  0.71,
             0.38  0.92,
             0.00  1.00,
            -0.38  0.92,
            -0.71  0.71,
            -0.92  0.38,
            -1.00  0.00,
            -0.92 -0.38,
            -0.71 -0.71,
            -0.38 -0.92,
             0.00 -1.00,
             0.38 -0.92,
             0.71 -0.71,
             0.92 -0.38,
      ]
}
IndexedLineSet {
      coordIndex [
            0,  1, -1,
            0,  2, -1,
            0,  3, -1,
            0,  4, -1,
            0,  5, -1,
            0,  6, -1,
            0,  7, -1,
            0,  8, -1,
            0,  9, -1,
            0, 10, -1,
            0, 11, -1,
            0, 12, -1,
            0, 13, -1,
            0, 14, -1,
            0, 15, -1,
            0, 16, -1,
      ]
}
```

Figure 18.40 *A brick-textured starburst.*

Using Color and Texture at the Same Time

Texture image RGB colors are usually multiplied by the current material RGB color to obtain an RGB color with which to shade a shape. This has the effect of **colorizing** the texture image as it is applied to your shape.

Texture image colorizing is most effective when applied to **grayscale** textures to achieve a colored texture. You can, for instance, use a single grayscale wood texture, like that in Figure 18.41, and colorize it differently to get different shades of wood, like those in Figure 18.42. The colorized versions of this wood texture are also shown in color plate 3*e*.

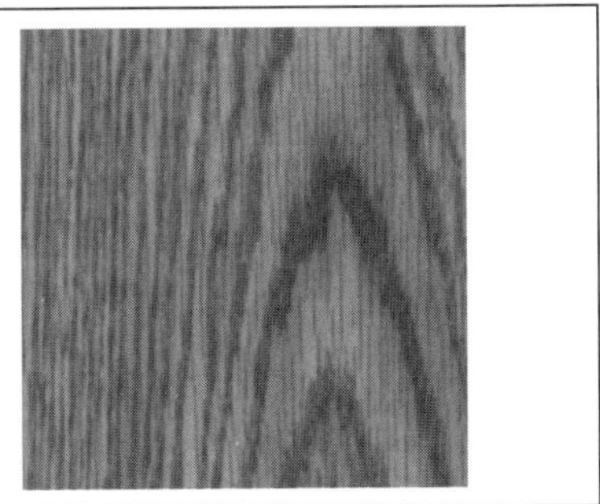

Figure 18.41 *A wood texture.*

Figure 18.42 *Six different wood colors created by colorizing a grayscale texture.*

The colorized wood swatches shown in Figure 18.42 are created using a series of square faces, each one preceded by a **Material** node to specify a color of yellow or orange to colorize the grayscale wood texture, as shown in Figure 18.43.

```
#VRML V1.0 ascii

Coordinate3 {
      point [
            0.0 1.0 0.0,
            0.0 0.0 0.0,
            1.0 0.0 0.0,
            1.0 1.0 0.0,
      ]
}
```

Figure 18.43 continues

```
Texture2 {
     filename "woodg.gif"
}
TextureCoordinate2 {
     point [
          0.0 1.0,
          0.0 0.0,
          1.0 0.0,
          1.0 1.0,
     ]
}
# Top row
Separator {
     Material {
          diffuseColor 1.0 0.35 0.23
     }
     DEF square IndexedFaceSet {
          coordIndex [
               0, 1, 2, 3
          ]
     }
     Translation {
          translation 1.25 0.0 0.0
     }
     Material {
          diffuseColor 1.0 0.45 0.23
     }
     USE square
     Translation {
          translation 1.25 0.0 0.0
     }
     Material {
          diffuseColor 1.0 0.55 0.23
     }
     USE square
}
Translation {
     translation 0.0 -1.25 0.0
}
# Bottom row
Separator {
     Material {
          diffuseColor 1.0 0.65 0.53
     }
     DEF square IndexedFaceSet {
          coordIndex [
               0, 1, 2, 3
          ]
     }
     Translation {
          translation 1.25 0.0 0.0
     }
```

Figure 18.43 continues

```
        Material {
              diffuseColor 1.0 0.55 0.43
        }
        USE square
        Translation {
              translation 1.25 0.0 0.0
        }
        Material {
              diffuseColor 1.0 0.55 0.53
        }
        USE square
}
```

Figure 18.43 *The VRML text used to colorize the grayscale wood texture.*

Wrapping and Clamping Texture Coordinates

Recall that wrapping texture coordinates enables you to select large areas on a sheet of infinitely repeating texture images. That selection is then mapped to a shape face to create a repeating pattern across that face. You can use this effect to repeatedly map a single-texture image, such as bricks, across a larger shape, such as a wall. The example text in Figure 18.44 uses the brick texture and maps it repeatedly to a square by using wrapping texture coordinates.

```
#VRML V1.0 ascii

Coordinate3 {
      point [
            0.0 1.0 0.0,
            0.0 0.0 0.0,
            1.0 0.0 0.0,
            1.0 1.0 0.0,
      ]
}
Texture2 {
      filename "brick.gif"
}
TextureCoordinate2 {
      point [
            0.0 3.0,
            0.0 0.0,
            3.0 0.0,
            3.0 3.0,
      ]
}
Material {
      emissiveColor 1.0 1.0 1.0
}
```

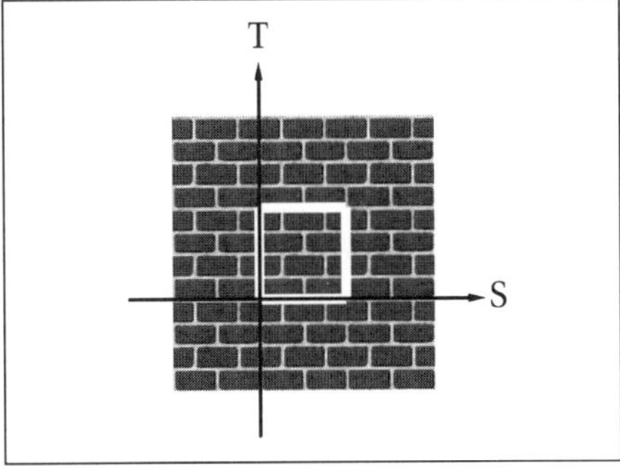

Figure 18.44 continues

```
IndexedFaceSet {
      coordIndex [
            0, 1, 2, 3
      ]
}
```

Figure 18.44 *Repeating a brick texture to cover a wall.*

You can clamp the texture coordinates for this same example by setting the **wrapS** and **wrapT** fields of the **Texture2** node to **CLAMP**, as shown in Figure 18.45.

```
#VRML V1.0 ascii

Coordinate3 {
      point [
            0.0 1.0 0.0,
            0.0 0.0 0.0,
            1.0 0.0 0.0,
            1.0 1.0 0.0,
      ]
}
Texture2 {
      filename "brick.gif"
      wrapS CLAMP
      wrapT CLAMP
}
TextureCoordinate2 {
      point [
            0.0 3.0,
            0.0 0.0,
            3.0 0.0,
            3.0 3.0,
      ]
}
Material {
      emissiveColor 1.0 1.0 1.0
}
IndexedFaceSet {
      coordIndex [
            0, 1, 2, 3
      ]
}
```

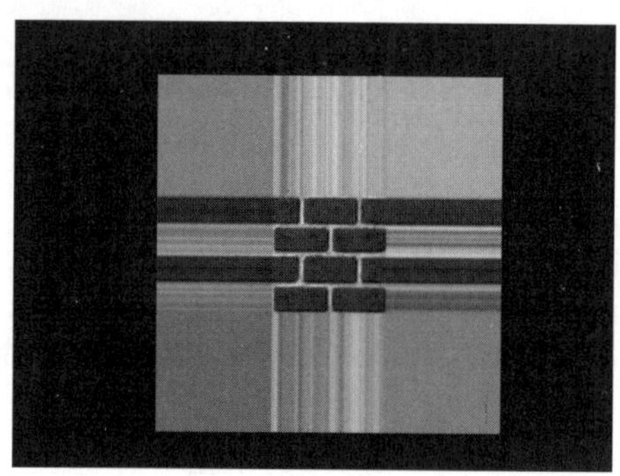

Figure 18.45 *Clamping the brick texture to the wall.*

Translating, Rotating, and Scaling Texture Coordinates

Using the **Texture2Transform** node, you can transform texture coordinates before they are used to texture-map a shape. The following examples, for instance, translate (Figure 18.46), rotate (Figure 18.47), or scale (Figure 18.48) the texture coordinates used to map the head texture image to a square.

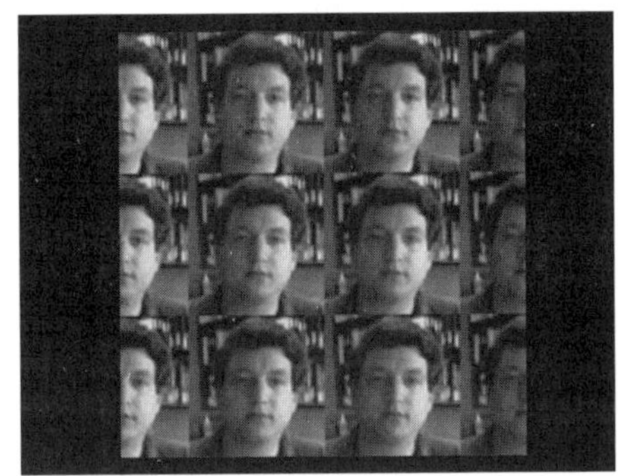

```
#VRML V1.0 ascii

Coordinate3 {
      point [
            0.0 1.0 0.0,
            0.0 0.0 0.0,
            1.0 0.0 0.0,
            1.0 1.0 0.0,
      ]
}
Texture2 {
      filename "head.gif"
}
TextureCoordinate2 {
      point [
            -1.0  2.0,
            -1.0 -1.0,
             2.0 -1.0,
             2.0  2.0,
      ]
}
Texture2Transform {
      translation 0.5 0.0
}
Material {
      emissiveColor 1.0 1.0 1.0
}
IndexedFaceSet {
      coordIndex [
            0, 1, 2, 3
      ]
}
```

Figure 18.46 *Translating before texture mapping.*

```
#VRML V1.0 ascii

Coordinate3 {
      point [
            0.0 1.0 0.0,
            0.0 0.0 0.0,
            1.0 0.0 0.0,
            1.0 1.0 0.0,
      ]
}
Texture2 {
      filename "head.gif"
}
```

Figure 18.47 continues

```
TextureCoordinate2 {
      point [
            -1.0  2.0,
            -1.0 -1.0,
             2.0 -1.0,
             2.0  2.0,
      ]
}
Texture2Transform {
      #        45.0 degrees
      rotation 0.785
}
Material {
      emissiveColor 1.0 1.0 1.0
}
IndexedFaceSet {
      coordIndex [
            0, 1, 2, 3
      ]
}
```

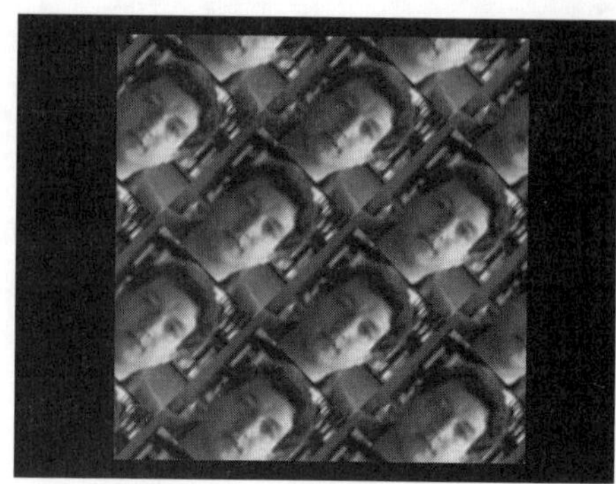

Figure 18.47 *Rotating before texture mapping.*

```
#VRML V1.0 ascii

Coordinate3 {
      point [
            0.0 1.0 0.0,
            0.0 0.0 0.0,
            1.0 0.0 0.0,
            1.0 1.0 0.0,
      ]
}
Texture2 {
      filename "head.gif"
}
TextureCoordinate2 {
      point [
            -1.0  2.0,
            -1.0 -1.0,
             2.0 -1.0,
             2.0  2.0,
      ]
}
Texture2Transform {
      scaleFactor 2.0 2.0
}
Material {
      emissiveColor 1.0 1.0 1.0
}
```

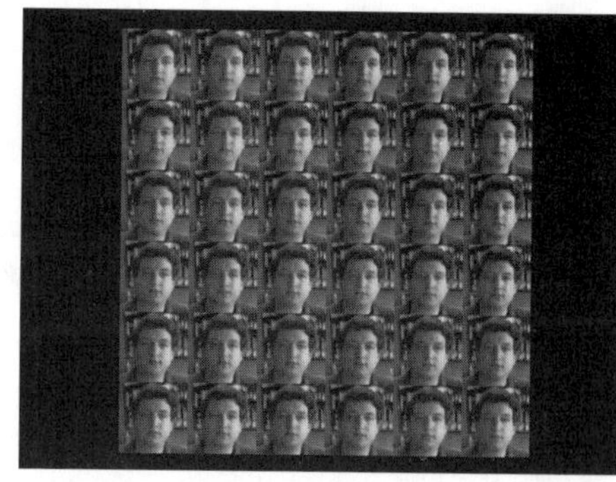

Figure 18.48 continues

```
IndexedFaceSet {
      coordIndex [
            0, 1, 2, 3
      ]
}
```

Figure 18.48 *Scaling before texture mapping.*

You can also apply texture transforms to the internally generated texture coordinates of primitive and text shapes. The example text in Figure 18.49 scales and rotates texture coordinates used by a cylinder node to texture-map the brick texture.

```
#VRML V1.0 ascii

Texture2 {
      filename "brick.gif"
}
Texture2Transform {
      #        45.0 degrees
      rotation 0.785
      scaleFactor 2.0 2.0
}
Cylinder {
}
```

Figure 18.49 *Rotating and scaling before texture mapping text.*

Texture transforms, like shape transforms, are relative so that if you use more than one, the second transforms relative to the first, the third relative to the second, and so on. The example text in Figure 18.50 uses three **Texture2Transform** nodes. The first turns the texture coordinates (the cookie cutter) 45.0 degrees counterclockwise. The second transform then scales the texture coordinates (cookie cutter) up in the T direction by a factor of 1.4. The third texture transform turns the resulting warped texture coordinates (diagonally stretched cookie cutter) 45.0 degrees clockwise. This process stretches the texture image along a diagonal from the lower-left corner to the upper-right corner, creating a diamond-shaped texture image when mapped to the square shape.

```
#VRML V1.0 ascii

Coordinate3 {
      point [
            0.0 1.0 0.0,
            0.0 0.0 0.0,
            1.0 0.0 0.0,
            1.0 1.0 0.0,
      ]
}
```

Figure 18.50 continues

```
Texture2 {
      filename "head.gif"
}
TextureCoordinate2 {
      point [
            0.0 1.0,
            0.0 0.0,
            1.0 0.0,
            1.0 1.0,
      ]
}
Texture2Transform {
      #         45.0 degrees
      rotation 0.785
}
Texture2Transform {
      scaleFactor 1.0 1.4
}
Texture2Transform {
      #         45.0 degrees
      rotation  0.785
}
Material {
      emissiveColor 1.0 1.0 1.0
}
IndexedFaceSet {
      coordIndex [
            0, 1, 2, 3
      ]
}
```

Figure 18.50 *Creating a diamond-shaped texture by transforming the cookie cutter.*

Using Separators with Texture Mapping

Using a **Separator** node you can save and restore the current texture image, texture transform, and texture coordinate list. For instance, the example text in Figure 18.51 draws three cubes side by side. A brick texture is specified and the first cube drawn. A separator then encloses the second cube and its wood-grain texture. The third cube is drawn after the close of the separator group and defaults back to the brick texture specified before the separator group was entered.

```
#VRML V1.0 ascii

# Brick cube
Texture2 {
      filename "brick.gif"
}
Cube {
}
```

Figure 18.51 continues

```
# Wood cube
Translation {
      translation 3.0 0.0 0.0
}
Separator {
      Texture2 {
            filename "wood.gif"
      }
      Cube {
      }
}
# Brick cube
Translation {
      translation 3.0 0.0 0.0
}
Cube {
}
```

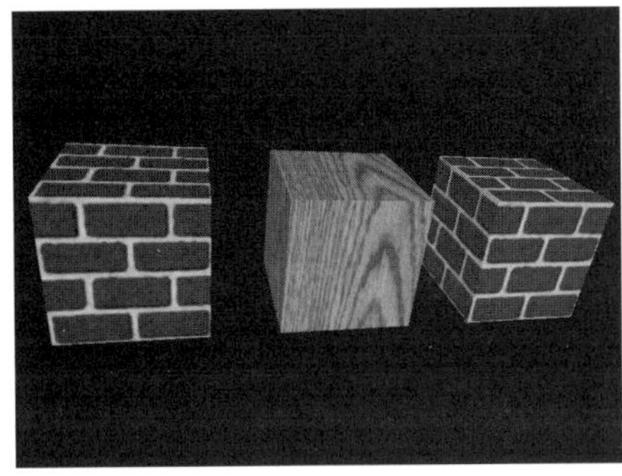

Figure 18.51 *Texture mapping using separators.*

Reading from the top of the file, the VRML browser is directed to:

1. Set the texture image property to the texture image in `brick.gif`.
2. Draw a cube with a brick texture.
3. Translate along the X axis by 3.0 units.
4. Draw the separator group:
   a. Save all the properties, including the current texture choice, texture transform, and texture coordinate list.
   b. Set the texture image property to the texture image in `wood.gif`.
   c. Draw a cube with a wood texture.
   d. Restore all the properties.
5. Translate along the X axis by 3.0 units.
6. Draw a cube with a brick texture.

Extended Examples

The following examples build on the concepts presented in this chapter. Try them on your own.

Creating a Computer Monitor

The example text in Figure 18.52 applies to the computer monitor from Chapter 7 a texture image that is **captured** from an actual computer screen. All computers have some utility built in, or available as shareware, to take a snapshot of part or all of the screen and store it in an image file. Try setting up windows on your computer screen, capturing the screen in an image file, then mapping it to this computer monitor's screen.

```
#VRML V1.0 ascii

Rotation {
	#        X               -5.0 degrees
	rotation 1.0 0.0 0.0  -0.087
}
Scale {
	scaleFactor 1.0 1.0 0.25
}
# Rounded screen:
Separator {
	Texture2 {
		filename "screen.gif"
		wrapS CLAMP
		wrapT CLAMP
	}
	Texture2Transform {
		scaleFactor 4.0 2.5
		center 0.5 0.5
	}
	Sphere {
		radius 2.0
	}
}
Scale {
	scaleFactor 1.0 1.0 4.0
}
Translation {
	translation 1.707 0.0 0.0
}
# Screen border:
Cube {
	width 0.586
	height 4.0
	depth 1.0
}
Translation {
	translation -3.414 0.0 0.0
}
Cube {
	width 0.586
	height 4.0
	depth 1.0
}
Translation {
	translation 1.707 1.707 0.0
}
```

Figure 18.52 continues

```
Cube {
      width 4.0
      height 0.586
      depth 1.0
}
Translation {
      translation 0.0 -3.414 0.0
}
Cube {
      width 4.0
      height 0.586
      depth 1.0
}
Translation {
      translation 0.0 1.707 -1.914
}
# Body:
Cube {
      width 2.828
      height 2.828
      depth 2.828
}
Rotation {
      #        X              +5.0 degrees
      rotation 1.0 0.0 0.0  0.087
}
Translation {
      translation 0.0 -1.5 0.0
}
# Base:
Cone {
      bottomRadius 1.5
}
Translation {
      translation 0.0 -0.875 0.0
}
Cube {
      width 3.0
      height .25
      depth 3.0
}
```

Figure 18.52 *Texture mapping a screen capture to a computer monitor.*

Creating a Window

Windows, from the outside, partially reflect the sky. If the sky is dark, house windows reflect dark grays. If the sky is light blue with a few clouds, then those are reflected in the window. You can create convincing windows for a house by mapping a cloudy-sky texture to a cube or rectangular face that represents the window.

The example text in Figure 18.55 builds the window and shutters from the cottage shown on page 460. Two texture images are used, one for the sky (Figure 18.53) and one for a window shutter texture (Figure 18.54).

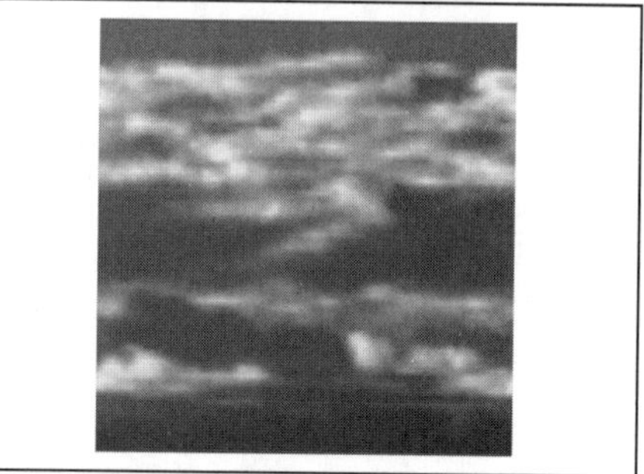

Figure 18.53 *The sky texture.*

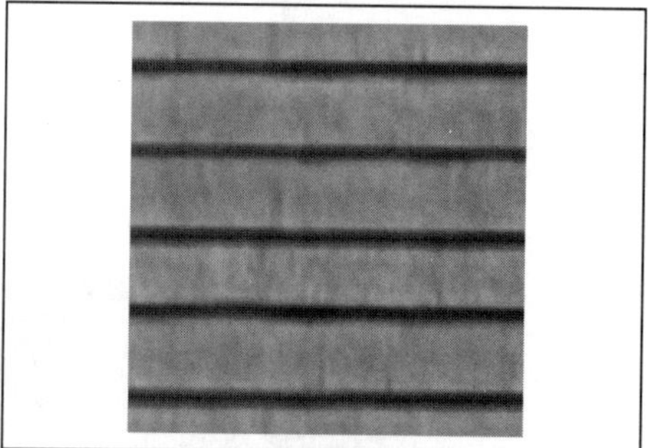

Figure 18.54 *The shutters texture.*

Notice that the shutter texture image creates a simple, somewhat uneven horizontal set of stripes. When repeated up and down the window shutters, it adds a slightly uneven pattern that makes the shutters look more realistic. A similar approach can be used for the window frame and shutter frames. For instance, try taking a picture of a bit of peeling paint from a real weathered window frame and mapping it to these parts of the window.

```
#VRML V1.0 ascii

# Window trim color
Material {
      diffuseColor 0.8 0.8 0.8
}
```

Figure 18.55 continues

```
# Window with sky texture applied
Separator {
      Texture2 {
            filename "sky.gif"
      }
      Material {
            emissiveColor 1.0 1.0 1.0
      }
      Cube {
            width  4.0
            height 3.0
            depth  0.25
      }
}
# Window pane dividers
Separator {
      Separator {
            Translation {
                  translation -1.0 0.0 0.0
            }
            DEF pane_div Cube {
                  height 3.2
                  width  0.1
                  depth  0.3
            }
            Translation {
                  translation 1.0 0.0 0.0
            }
            USE pane_div
            Translation {
                  translation 1.0 0.0 0.0
            }
            USE pane_div
      }
      Separator {
            Translation {
                  translation 0.0 0.5 0.0
            }
            DEF pane_div2 Cube {
                  width  4.2
                  height 0.1
                  depth  0.3
            }
            Translation {
                  translation 0.0 -1.0 0.0
            }
            USE pane_div2
      }
}
```

Figure 18.55 continues

```
# Window frame
Separator {
      Separator {
            Translation {
                  translation -2.0 0.0 0.0
            }
            Cube {
                  width  0.2
                  height 3.2
                  depth  0.35
            }
      }
      Separator {
            Translation {
                  translation 2.0 0.0 0.0
            }
            Cube {
                  width  0.2
                  height 3.2
                  depth  0.35
            }
      }
      Separator {
            Translation {
                  translation 0.0 1.5 0.0
            }
            Cube {
                  height 0.2
                  width  4.2
                  depth  0.35
            }
      }
      Separator {
            Translation {
                  translation 0.0 -1.5 0.0
            }
            Cube {
                  height 0.2
                  width  4.2
                  depth  0.35
            }
      }
}
# Window shutters
Separator {
      # Left shutter
      Translation {
            translation -3.0 0.0 0.0
      }
```

Figure 18.55 continues

```
        DEF shutter Separator {
            # Shutter frame
            Cube {
                width  1.0
                height 3.2
                depth  0.35
            }
            # Shutter center
            Texture2 {
                filename "shutters.gif"
            }
            Texture2Transform {
                scaleFactor 1.0 4.0
            }
            Material {
                emissiveColor 1.0 1.0 1.0
            }
            Cube {
                width  0.8
                height 3.0
                depth  0.45
            }
        }
        # Right shutter
        Translation {
            translation 6.0 0.0 0.0
        }
        USE shutter
    }
```

Figure 18.55 *A realistic window reflecting the sky.*

Summary

Texture mapping maps an image of a real-world texture, such as brick, to the faces of shapes. This technique enables you to add realistic detail to a VRML world without creating individual shapes for every brick, shingle, or tree leaf.

A texture for mapping is selected by the **Texture2** node, which has a **filename** field whose value is a URL corresponding to a texture image on your hard disk or on the Internet.

Texture images are mapped by selecting a portion of the texture image and mapping it to a shape. Think of it as using a cookie cutter to stamp out a portion of the texture image before gluing it to the shape. The perimeter of the texture cookie cutter is described by a list of texture coordinates.

Texture coordinates are a pair of values called S and T. The S value specifies a horizontal location on a texture image, and the T value specifies a vertical location. The texture coordinate `0.0 0.0` is the lower-left corner of the texture image, and `1.0 1.0` is in the upper-right corner.

Texture coordinates can be wrapped or clamped by setting the **wrapS** and **wrapT** fields of the **Texture2** node to either **REPEAT**, for wrapping, or **CLAMP** for clamping. When clamping, texture coordinates outside of the range 0.0 to 1.0 will be clamped back to this range. When wrapping, texture coordinates outside of this range repeat. By wrapping coordinates, you can map a repeating pattern on the side of a shape.

The **Texture2Transform** node applies translation, rotation, and scale transforms to texture coordinates. Think of translation as moving the texture cookie cutter before it stamps out a texture to map. Rotation orients that cookie cutter, and scaling increases or decreases the size of the cookie cutter.

Each of the primitive shapes and text shapes compute their own texture coordinates internally and use them, after being transformed by the current texture transform, to map texture images. A cube shape maps a separate copy of the current texture image to each of its faces. A cylinder shape maps a separate copy to the top and bottom faces and a third copy stretched around the sides. A cone shape maps a copy to the bottom face and another stretched around its sides, pinched up at the cone tip. A sphere shape maps a single copy around its sides, pinched at the top and bottom poles. A copy of the texture is mapped to each character shape in a text shape as if stamping out a character-shaped cookie in the texture image.

Textures are mapped to vertex-based shapes, such as point sets, line sets, and face sets, using texture coordinates defined within a **TextureCoordinate2** node. There should be one texture coordinate for each vertex in the point set, line set, or face set.

The current texture, texture transform, and list of texture coordinates are all properties saved and restored by **Separator** nodes.

CHAPTER 19

Lighting Your Worlds (Advanced)

Lights in a VRML world serve the same purpose as lights in the real world: they brighten a scene and highlight points of interest. Until now you have used only the headlight, a light automatically created by your VRML browser and attached to your current view point. You can also create additional lights and place them anywhere you like within your VRML world.

VRML supports three node types to control lighting: **PointLight, DirectionalLight,** and **SpotLight.** Using these light nodes, you can brighten a dark room corner, highlight a picture on a wall, or add a stage spotlight. Creative lighting can add tremendously to the realism of any world.

Understanding Lights

A VRML light illuminates shapes in your world. As we saw in Chapter 16 when discussing shape normals, the more a shape face faces a light, the more brightly it is shaded. In all of the previous chapters you have used only the headlight, always positioned by the VRML browser to shine from your current view point in the world. Using the headlight, shapes that face you are brightly lit, while shapes that face away are darker.

Using VRML you can create additional lights in your world, placing them at specific locations, and aiming them in specific directions. Shape faces are then shaded based on whether they face any of these additional lights, as well as whether they face you and your headlight.

TIP *Most VRML browsers have a feature in one of their menus to turn off the headlight. While working with lights, you may want the headlight off so that* *you see only the lighting caused by your additional lights, and not that caused by the headlight.*

TIP *VRML lights have no form or shape. They describe how to light a world, but not what the shape of an actual light is, like a lamp or a sun. Since VRML lights have no shape, you will not be able to see them when they are placed in a world. You see only their lighting effects on the world.*

VRML supports three types of lights, each mimicking the attributes of real world lights: **point lights**, **directional lights**, and **spot lights**.

Understanding Point Lights

A **point light** is a light located in your world that emanates light radially in all directions, as if the light rays were all coming from a single point. In the real world, a lamp with its shade removed acts like a point light.

Figure 19.1 shows the effects of a point light placed in the middle of a world with four spheres. The sides of the spheres that face the point light are illuminated, while the sides that face away are not. The arrows in Figure 19.1 show how the light rays of a point light emanate radially in all directions from its location.

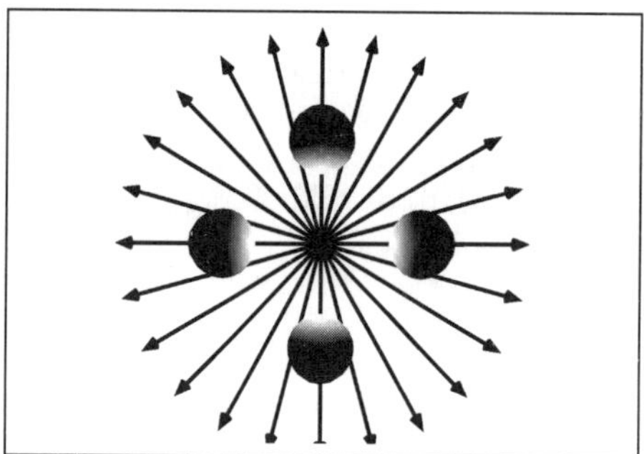

Figure 19.1 *The rays from a point light radiate out from it in all directions.*

In VRML, a point light is created by specifying its 3-D location in your world, its intensity, and its color. Light intensities can be varied from 0.0 (off), to 1.0 (full on), as if turning a dimmer knob on a real light. You can also use intensity values greater than 1.0 to create extra-bright lights.

TIP *Most graphics boards and VRML browsers also support using* negative *light intensities. This enables you to create* **anti-lights** *that actually suck light out of a scene, thereby darkening regions instead of illuminating them. You can use negative* *lights to add dark gloomy corners to a dungeon or to more subtly adjust a room's lighting to highlight foreground features by darkening backgrounds and corners.*

The color of a light is controlled by an RGB color, just like that used to set a material color. A red light, for instance, gives a red glow to a world. You can use this to light up a fireplace or a photographic darkroom. You can similarly use green, blue, or any other shade of light for other lighting effects.

Understanding Directional Lights

A **directional light** is a light aimed at your world from infinitely far away so that all of its light rays are parallel and point in the same direction. In the real world, the sun is essentially a directional light. It is so far away that by the time the sun's rays reach the Earth, they are nearly parallel.

Figure 19.2 shows a directional light whose parallel light rays shine from left to right on a world with four spheres. The sides of the spheres that face the directional light are illuminated, while the sides that face away are not. The arrows in Figure 19.2 show how the light rays of the directional light all project in the same direction.

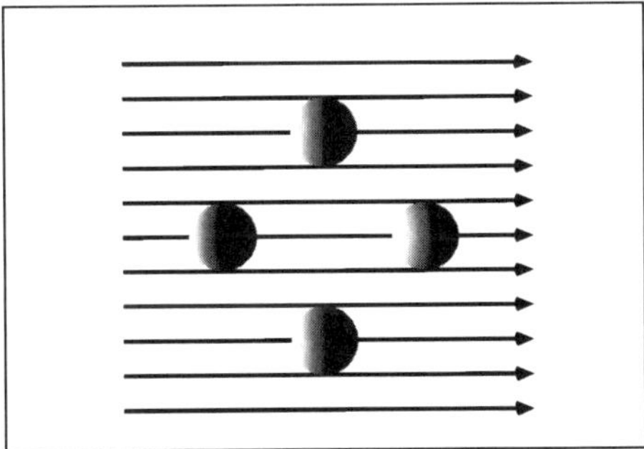

Figure 19.2 *The rays from a directional light all project in the same direction.*

In VRML, a directional light is created by specifying an **aim direction** for the light. You define an aim direction in the same way you define rotation axes. Imagine a line drawn between two points, one always at the origin `0.0 0.0 0.0` and the other under your control. As you move the second point around, the line between the origin and your second point changes directions. For instance, if you place your second point at `1.0 0.0 0.0`, then the line drawn between the origin and your point is a horizontal line pointing to the right. This is an aim direction that aims to the right.

Aim directions can point a directional light in any direction. To point a light straight up the Y axis use an aim direction of `0.0 1.0 0.0`. To point straight down the negative Z axis, use an aim direction of `0.0 0.0 -1.0`. You can also use diagonal aim directions, for instance, to aim a directional light 45.0 degrees in the positive X, Y, and Z directions at once by using `1.0 1.0 1.0`.

VRML directional lights also have an intensity and a color, just like point lights.

Understanding Spot Lights

A **spot light** is a light placed at a location in your world, aimed in a specific direction, and constrained so that its rays emanate within a **light cone**. Shapes that fall within that cone of light are illuminated by the spot light, and others are not.

Figure 19.3 shows the effects of a spot light placed in the middle of a world with four spheres, and aimed to the right at the right-most sphere. The spot light's cone is tightened to hit only the right sphere and light up its left side. The remaining three spheres in the world are outside of the spot light's cone of light and are shaded dark. The arrows in Figure 19.3 show how the spot light's cone of light rays emanate from it.

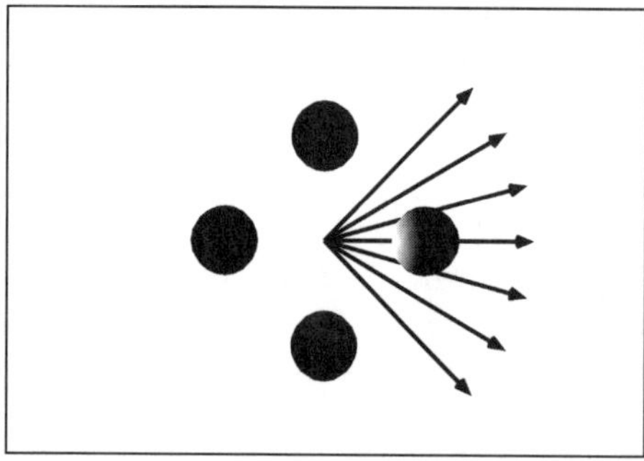

Figure 19.3 *The rays of a spot light radiate within a strictly defined area.*

In VRML, a spot light is created by specifying its 3-D location in your world, an aim direction, and two values to control the size and edge sharpness of the light cone: the cutoff angle and the drop-off rate. The cutoff angle is the angular spread of the cone of light. A smaller angle makes the light cone narrower, and a larger angle makes the light cone wider. The drop-off rate controls how gradually the light's intensity drops off toward the edges of the light cone. A low value makes the drop-off rapid at the edges, and a high value makes it gradual.

VRML spot lights also have an intensity and a color, just like point lights.

Coloring Lights

You may recall from physics classes that white light is made up of all colors of light. When white light shines on a colored surface, some colors of light are absorbed by the surface, while others are reflected. Absorbed light turns into heat, and reflected light bounces off the surface and may, eventually, reach your eye.

The colors of light that are absorbed and reflected by a surface are determined by that surface's color. A blue surface, for instance, reflects blue light and absorbs the rest. So, when a white light shines on a blue surface, the blue components of that white light are reflected, and the remainder is absorbed. What you see when you look at such a surface is the reflected light. White surfaces reflect all colors of light, and black surfaces absorb all colors of light.

In VRML, you set the color of shapes using the **Material** node. When white light from the headlight shines on those colored shapes, each shape reflects back some of the colors in the light. A blue shape reflects blue light, a red shape reflects red light, and so on. Lighting in VRML, then, works the same way as lighting in the real world.

The headlight is a white light and cannot be colored. Point lights, directional lights, and spot lights that you add to your world may, however, be colored lights. Unlike white light, colored light contains only a narrow range of colors of light. When a colored light shines on a white surface, the only light colors available for reflection are those that are present in the colored light. For instance, a white surface illuminated by a red light will look red since the only reflected light is red light. A white surface lit by a green light will look green, and so on. The **apparent color** of a shape, then, depends on both its color, set by a **Material** node, and the color of light that shines on it.

The situation is trickier when you shine a colored light on a colored surface. A blue surface, for instance, can reflect only blue light. A red light, however, has no blue light in it. So, a blue surface illuminated by a red light appears *black* since there is no blue light to reflect off of it. Similarly, a blue surface lit by a green light appears black. A blue surface lit by a blue light, however, appears blue.

Figure 19.4 and color plate 4*a* show four rows of spheres illuminated, row by row, by a white light, a red light, a green light, and a blue light. The first sphere in each row of spheres has a white material color set by a **Material** node. The remaining spheres on the row have red, yellow, green, cyan, blue, and purple material colors.

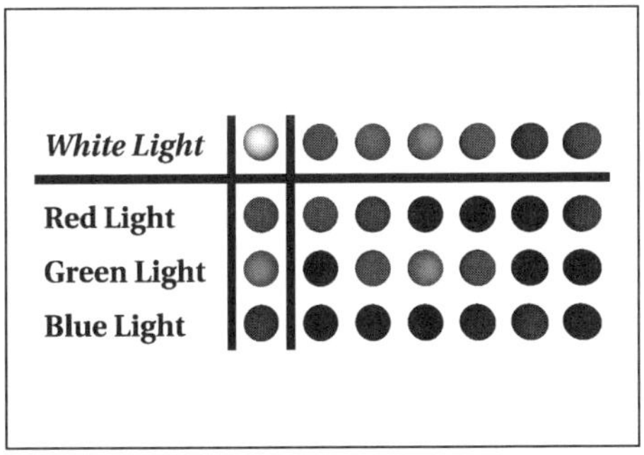

Figure 19.4 *The effects of white, red, green, and blue light on different colored spheres.*

Notice that when a white light shines on one of the colored spheres, the sphere's own material color is apparent. A red sphere, for instance, reflects the red components in the white light and the sphere is seen as red.

When a red light shines on each of the colored spheres, only those spheres with some amount of red in their material color are bright. The green, cyan, and blue spheres, for instance, are all black when illuminated by a red light. A similar effect occurs when the green and blue lights shine on the colored spheres.

In VRML, you can set the light color for any point light, directional light, and spot light. Using colored lights, you can specify creative lighting effects. You can give a room a warm glow by using a yellowish light. You can make a world seem cold and harsh by using a light with a slight blue tinge to it.

Creating Shadows

In the real world, shapes cast shadows when they block light rays. In VRML, however, shapes do not cast shadows. Shadow computation is a complicated and time-consuming operation that cannot easily be performed interactively. Since VRML shapes do not cast shadows, a light can illuminate a shape even if the shape is behind another shape. VRML light travels straight through shapes, unhindered.

Shadows in the real world tell us much about the solidity and positioning of shapes. Without shadows, VRML worlds can look odd and ambiguous. It is sometimes difficult, for instance, to tell whether one shape sits directly on top of another, or whether it is hovering above it. Without a shadow cast by the hovering shape, it is difficult to determine where it actually is.

You can compensate for this lack of shadows in VRML worlds by creating your own fake shadows. For any shape, look at how it would block light and where it should cast a shadow. Then, create a face using, say, an indexed face set, color it black and semitransparent, then place it where the shadow should be. While not a perfect representation of shadows, the effect is close, easy to do, and can make a huge difference in the realism of your world. Figure 19.5, for instance, shows the texture-mapped cottage from Chapter 18 (Figure 19.5*a*) with a few fake shadows added behind the house (Figure 19.5*b*) to simulate the effects of a low sun on the horizon to the right.

Restricting Lights

VRML lights define lighting properties that are saved and restored by **Separator** nodes. A light defined within a separator group sets the lighting properties used to illuminate all shapes drawn after the light. Later, at the end of the separator group, the original lighting properties are restored, canceling any further effects of the light defined within the group. Shapes drawn after the separator group are not lit by the light within the group.

You can use this light restriction ability to illuminate only specific shapes in your world. You can, for instance, use a light to brighten a feature of interest, such

(a)

(b)

Figure 19.5 *Creating the effect of shadows.*

as a wall painting, sign, or important doorway, without that light also brightening everything else in your world. To achieve this effect, create a separator group and place the light definition inside the group along with the nodes that draw the shapes you want to highlight. Place the rest of your world outside that group. Shapes inside the group will be brightly lit by your light, while shapes outside the group will not be.

Transforming Lights

Lights, like shapes, can be translated, rotated, and scaled by the standard shape transform nodes: **Translation, Rotation, Scale, Transform,** and **MatrixTransform.** This enables you to position a light within a world, move it about with a translation, or move both it and a group of shapes it illuminates using any transform.

Using Multiple Lights

You can define multiple lights in your VRML world. Each new light definition is *added* to the current lighting properties. For instance, if you define a light, then define a second light immediately after it, then *both* lights are part of the lighting properties and both will be used to illuminate your world.

You can use multiple lights to give you very flexible control over the lighting of your world. To prevent all of your lights from illuminating all of your shapes, you can use separator groups to restrict some lights to one part of your world, and other lights to other parts of your world.

TIP *3-D graphics boards usually support only a limited number of simultaneous lights in a world. This limit may be as low as just one, for the headlight, but is typically eight or more. Using more lights in your world than your graphics board can support may cause noticeable slowing, or may cause some lights to be skipped when drawing* *your world. Check the manuals for your graphics board and your VRML browser to see what light limitations they each have.*

Lighting Flat Shapes

Intuitively, aiming a spot light at the center of a large cube's face should create a bright spot in the middle of that face. The actual effect, however, may vary with the VRML browser and graphics hardware you are using.

Typical graphics hardware and software computes the effect of lighting only at the vertices of a shape, such as the corners of a cube's faces. Using those computed vertex lighting values, the hardware or software then shades from one vertex's value to the next as it shades across the face of the shape. You use a similar shading effect in Chapter 15 when you assign a different material color to each vertex of a face and let the VRML browser smoothly vary colors from one to the next across the face.

Now, imagine that you aim a spot light straight at the center of a square and draw the square using typical graphics hardware or software. Each of the four corners of the square is the same distance from the spot light and has the same computed illumination intensity from the light. Using these four identical values at the four corners of the square, the graphics hardware or software will smoothly vary from one to the next across the face. But since all four vertex values are identical, no variation occurs and the entire square is drawn at the same brightness. The spot light's bright spot that should have been drawn at the center of the square is completely missed.

Properly computing the effects of spot lights aimed like the one previously described requires sophisticated graphics hardware that is out of the price range of most individuals. Graphics software can properly compute this type of lighting, but at such a cost in drawing time that it is usually impractical for interactive graphics. As a result, shapes lit by spot lights, and point lights in a VRML world will not always show the exact lighting effects you'd expect from observing the real world.

One way to compensate for these lighting limitations is to create **meshed** shapes that use a kind of mesh or gridwork of vertices and small faces to create a surface. You used this kind of approach when you created faceted shapes in previous chapters. You can use a mesh even when creating flat shapes.

If you aim a spot light at the center of a meshed square, lighting is be computed at every vertex in the mesh. Each tiny facet will be shaded independently. Facets near the center of the square mesh and closer to the spot light will be shaded bright. Those farther away at the edges of the square mesh will be shaded dark. The effect is to create a bright spot in the center of the square mesh where the spot light's light strikes the surface. The limitations of graphics hardware have thus been overcome by using a mesh instead of a single square face on a cube.

Smooth shapes such as cylinders, cones, and spheres are usually already meshed in this way to create their faceted shapes. Cubes, however, are not meshed. You can create your own meshed flat or curved surfaces using **IndexedFaceSet** nodes.

TIP *While meshing a shape does compensate for lighting problems inherent in typical graphic hardware and software, it also drastically increases the number of vertices in a shape* and *the time it takes your computer to draw the shape. Meshing a flat shape should be done only when you must have proper lighting effects on that shape. The rest of your shapes should be left unmeshed in order to achieve maximum drawing performance.*

Lighting Shapes

The example text in Figure 19.6 uses a single point light placed in the middle of a field of spheres.

```
#VRML V1.0 ascii

PointLight {
      location 3.75 3.75 0.0
}
DEF balls TransformSeparator {
      DEF ball Sphere {
            radius 0.5
      }
      DEF up Translation {
            translation 0.0 1.5 0.0
      }
      USE ball
      USE up      USE ball
      USE up      USE ball
      USE up      USE ball
      USE up      USE ball
}
DEF right Translation {
      translation 1.5 0.0 0.0
}
USE balls
USE right    USE balls
USE right    USE balls
USE right    USE balls
USE right    USE balls
```

Figure 19.6 *A point light placed in a field of spheres.*

Notice the structure and order of the VRML file in Figure 19.6. At the top, a **PointLight** node defines a point light to illuminate the subsequent shapes. Following the light, a column of six spheres is defined within a transform separator, and the entire column is repeated six times. The result is a rectangular grid of spheres, all illuminated by the point light.

Understanding the **PointLight** Node Syntax

The **PointLight** node has four fields: **on, intensity, color,** and **location.**

SYNTAX **PointLight node**

```
PointLight {
      on            TRUE             # "True" or "false"
      intensity     1                # Light intensity
      color         1.0 1.0 1.0      # RGB color
      location      0.0 0.0 0.0      # X, Y, Z, coordinate
}
```

The **on** field turns on the light with a **TRUE** value, or turns it off with a **FALSE** value. By default, lights are on. You can turn them off by either removing the node from your file or setting the **on** field to **FALSE.** This gives you a quick way to test out different lighting variations without having to do lots of editing of your VRML file.

The **intensity** field controls the brightness of the light. A value of 0.0 turns it dark, while 1.0 turns it to full brightness. Intensities greater than 1.0 create extra-bright lights, while negative intensities create anti-lights that actually darken a world.

The **color** field provides an RGB color for the light. The default values create a white light.

The **location** field specifies a 3-D coordinate for the light. A value of `0.0 0.0 0.0` places the light at the current origin. Light locations are transformed by shape transforms such as **Translation, Rotation,** and **Scale** nodes.

TIP *In version 1.1 of VRML, lighting may no longer be a property that can be saved and restored by **Separator** nodes. As a result, you may not be able to position a **PointLight** node in a VRML file so that it only illuminates a particular part of your world. Instead, lights may always illuminate all shapes in a world.*

Understanding the **DirectionalLight** Node Syntax

The **DirectionalLight** node has four fields: **on, intensity, color,** and **direction.**

SYNTAX **DirectionalLight node**

```
DirectionalLight {
      on            TRUE             # "True" or "false"
      intensity     1                # Light intensity
      color         1.0 1.0 1.0      # RGB color
      direction     0.0 0.0 0.0      # X, Y, Z, coordinate
}
```

The **on, intensity,** and **color** fields are identical to the same fields in a **PointLight** node.

The **direction** field specifies an aim direction for the directional light. The aim direction is specified as X, Y, and Z directions from the current origin. An aim direction of `1.0 0.0 0.0` for instance, aims the directional light straight to the right. Light aim directions are transformed by shape transforms like **Translation, Rotation,** and **Scale** nodes.

TIP *In version 1.1 of VRML, lighting may no longer be a property that can be saved and restored by **Separator** nodes. As a result, you may not be able to position a **DirectionalLight** node in a VRML file so that it only illuminates a particular part of your world. Instead, lights may always illuminate all shapes in a world.*

Understanding the **SpotLight** Node Syntax

The **SpotLight** node has seven fields. The **on, intensity, color, location,** and **direction** fields are the same as for **PointLight** and **DirectionalLight** nodes. The additional **dropOffRate** and **cutOffAngle** fields control the spot light's cone of illumination.

SYNTAX **SpotLight node**

```
SpotLight {
      on            TRUE               # "True" or "false"
      intensity     1                  # Light intensity
      color         1.0 1.0  1.0       # RGB color
      location      0.0 0.0  0.0       # X, Y, Z, coordinate
      direction     0.0 0.0 -1.0       # X, Y, Z, coordinate
      dropOffRate   0                  # Drop-off factor
      cutOffAngle   0.785              # Cone angle
}
```

The **on, intensity, color,** and **location** fields are identical to the same fields in a **PointLight** node. The **direction** field is identical to the same field in the **Directional-Light** node.

The **cutOffAngle** field gives the spread angle, in radians, of the spot light's illumination cone. (See Appendix A for a discussion of radians vs. degrees and a table of common conversions.) The default angle of 0.785 radians creates a cone with a spread of 45.0 degrees. Shapes outside this cone of light are not lit by the spot light, while shapes within are. Smaller cutoff angles narrow the cone into a tighter light beam, while larger cutoff angles spread the beam out to illuminate more of the world.

The **dropOffRate** field controls how quickly the spot light's light diminishes in intensity as it illuminates shapes toward the edges of the light cone. The default value of 0.0 evenly illuminates all shapes within the cone, then abruptly drops the illumination to a 0.0 intensity at the cone's edges and beyond. Higher drop-off rates create a more gradual change from full intensity along the center axis of the cone to 0.0 intensity at the cone's edges.

You can think of the drop-off rate of a spot light as controlling the focus of a spot light projecting a circular spot on a wall. A low drop-off rate creates an evenly lit circular spot with sharp edges. Higher drop-off rates blur the edges and create a more gradual change from full intensity at the center of the spot to zero intensity at the spot's edges.

TIP *In version 1.1 of VRML, lighting may no longer be a property that can be saved and restored by* ***Separator*** *nodes. As a result, you may not be able to position a* ***SpotLight*** *node in a VRML file so that it only illuminates a particular part of your world. Instead, lights may always illuminate all shapes in a world.*

Experimenting with Lighting

The following examples provide a more detailed examination of the ways in which lighting can be used. For all of these examples, be sure to turn off the headlight on your VRML browser so you can clearly see the effects of the point lights, directional lights, and spot lights you add yourself.

Lighting Shapes

The example text in Figure 19.7 draws the field of spheres shown earlier. A point light located in the middle of the field illuminates all of the spheres.

```
#VRML V1.0 ascii

PointLight {
      location 3.75 3.75 0.0
}
DEF balls TransformSeparator {
      DEF ball Sphere {
            radius 0.5
      }
      DEF up Translation {
            translation 0.0 1.5 0.0
      }
      USE ball
      USE up USE ball
      USE up USE ball
      USE up USE ball
      USE up USE ball
}
DEF right Translation {
      translation 1.5 0.0 0.0
}
USE balls
USE right    USE balls
USE right    USE balls
USE right    USE balls
USE right    USE balls
```

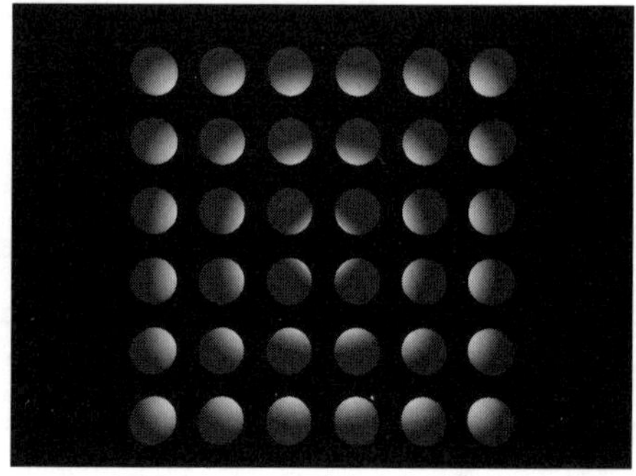

Figure 19.7 *A field of spheres with a point light in the middle.*

Reading from the top of the file, the VRML browser is directed to:

1. Add to the current lighting property a point light at 3.75 units along the X axis, 3.75 units along the Y axis, and 0.0 units along the Z axis away from the current origin.
2. Draw a transform separator group, giving it the defined name *ball.*
   a. Save the transform properties.
   b. Draw a sphere and give it a defined name of *ball.*
   c. Translate up 1.5 units.
   d. Draw *ball,* translate up again, draw *ball,* and so forth, to create a column of six balls.
   e. Restore the transform properties.
3. Translate 1.5 units to the right.
4. Draw *balls,* translate right again, draw *balls,* and so forth to create six columns.

Notice that since the point light is defined before any shapes were drawn, all shapes that follow are lit by the point light.

You can illuminate the same field of spheres using a directional light, as shown in Figure 19.8.

```
#VRML V1.0 ascii

DirectionalLight {
      direction 1.0 0.0 0.0
}
DEF balls TransformSeparator {
      DEF ball Sphere {
            radius 0.5
      }
      DEF up Translation {
            translation 0.0 1.5 0.0
      }
      USE ball
      USE up      USE ball
      USE up      USE ball
      USE up      USE ball
      USE up      USE ball
}
DEF right Translation {
      translation 1.5 0.0 0.0
}
USE balls
      USE right   USE balls
      USE right   USE balls
      USE right   USE balls
      USE right   USE balls
```

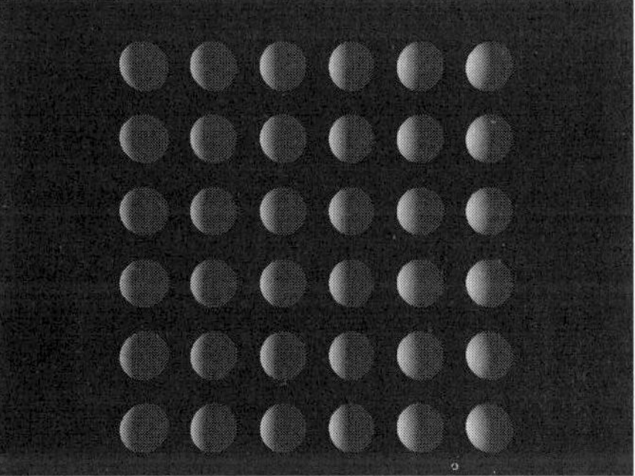

Figure 19.8 *The field of spheres lit by a directional light.*

The directional light is aimed to the right along the X axis and thus illuminates the left side of each of the spheres in the field.

Again, using the same field of spheres, you can illuminate some of them using a spot light aimed to the right, as shown in Figure 19.9

```
#VRML V1.0 ascii

SpotLight {
      location 3.75 3.75 0.0
      direction 1.0 0.0 0.0
      dropOffRate 0.0
      cutOffAngle 0.785   #  45.0 degrees
}
DEF balls TransformSeparator {
      DEF ball Sphere {
            radius 0.5
      }
      DEF up Translation {
            translation 0.0 1.5 0.0
      }
      USE ball
      USE up      USE ball
      USE up      USE ball
      USE up      USE ball
      USE up      USE ball
}
DEF right Translation {
      translation 1.5 0.0 0.0
}
USE balls
USE right   USE balls
USE right   USE balls
USE right   USE balls
USE right   USE balls
```

Figure 19.9 *The field of spheres lit by a spot light.*

The spot light is located at the center of the field and aimed to the right. Its cone of illumination is narrowed to 45.0 degrees, and only the spheres within that cone are illuminated. The remaining spheres are left dark.

Lighting Part of a World

A light illuminates only those shapes drawn after it. The example text in Figure 19.10, for instance, draws the same field of spheres as those previously drawn, but defines a point light after the third column of spheres has been drawn. All spheres drawn before the light is defined are unlit. Only the spheres that follow the light's definition are illuminated by it.

```
#VRML V1.0 ascii

DEF balls TransformSeparator {
      DEF ball Sphere {
            radius 0.5
      }
      DEF up Translation {
            translation 0.0 1.5 0.0
      }
      USE ball
      USE up      USE ball
      USE up      USE ball
      USE up      USE ball
      USE up      USE ball
}
DEF right Translation {
      translation 1.5 0.0 0.0
}
USE balls
USE right USE balls
PointLight {
      location 0.75 3.75 0.0
}
USE right    USE balls
USE right    USE balls
USE right    USE balls
```

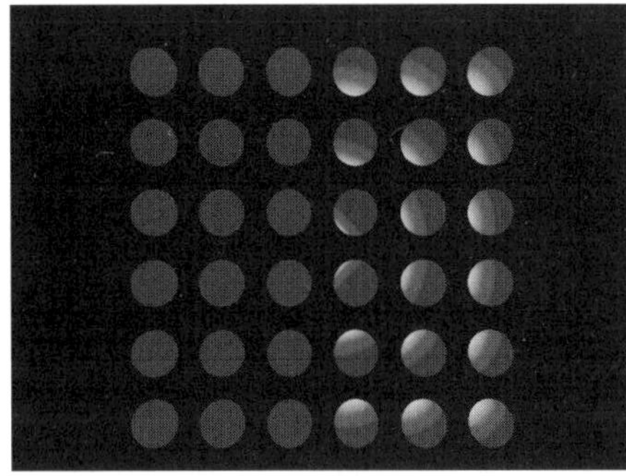

Figure 19.10 *Only the spheres drawn after the light source is defined are lit.*

You can also restrict the range of shapes a light illuminates by placing both the light and the shapes it should illuminate into a separator group, as shown in Figure 19.11. The group restricts the range of world shapes the light illuminates, allowing it to light those shapes drawn after it and within the group. For instance, using the sphere field again, a point light and two columns of the field are drawn within a separator group. The first two columns of spheres are drawn before the separator, and the last two columns are drawn after it. Notice that only the middle two columns drawn following the point light and within the separator group are illuminated by the point light.

```
#VRML V1.0 ascii

DEF balls TransformSeparator {
      DEF ball Sphere {
            radius 0.5
      }
      DEF up Translation {
            translation 0.0 1.5 0.0
      }
      USE ball
      USE up      USE ball
      USE up      USE ball
      USE up      USE ball
      USE up      USE ball
}
```

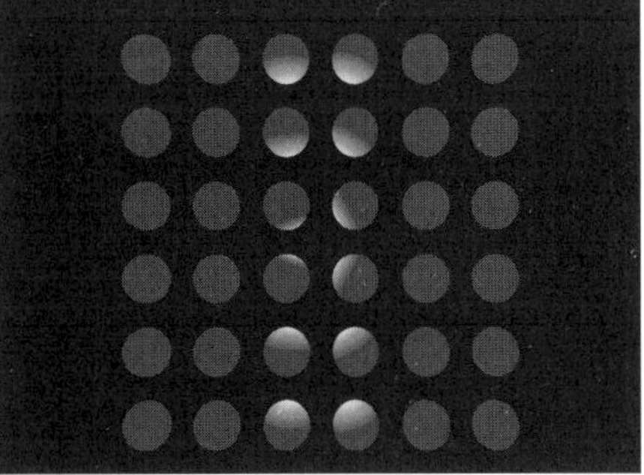

Figure 19.11 continues

```
DEF right Translation {
      translation 1.5 0.0 0.0
}
USE balls
Separator {
      PointLight {
            location 1.75 3.75 0.0
      }
      USE right    USE balls
      USE right    USE balls
}
USE right
USE right
USE right    USE balls
USE right    USE balls
```

Figure 19.11 *Only the spheres drawn after the light and within the separator are lit.*

Creating a Flat Mesh

As noted earlier, lighting calculations are typically performed only for the vertices of a shape. This can cause some lighting effects, particularly those created by spot and point lights, to be missed completely by the VRML browser as it shades a shape. One way to correct this problem is to create a fine mesh of faces instead of using one large face. Such a mesh can be created using an **IndexedFaceSet** node and coordinates within a **Coordinate3** node. The example text in Figure 19.12 is a square mesh with five columns and five rows of vertices connected together to create a mesh of 16 squares.

```
#VRML V1.0 ascii

# Center the mesh
Translation {
      translation -0.5 -0.5 0.0
}
Material {
      diffuseColor 1.0 1.0 1.0
}
Coordinate3 {
      point [
            0.0 0.0 0.0,
            0.2 0.0 0.0,
            0.4 0.0 0.0,
            0.6 0.0 0.0,
            0.8 0.0 0.0,
            1.0 0.0 0.0,
            0.0 0.2 0.0,
            0.2 0.2 0.0,
            0.4 0.2 0.0,
            0.6 0.2 0.0,
```

Figure 19.12 continues

```
                0.8 0.2 0.0,
                1.0 0.2 0.0,
                0.0 0.4 0.0,
                0.2 0.4 0.0,
                0.4 0.4 0.0,
                0.6 0.4 0.0,
                0.8 0.4 0.0,
                1.0 0.4 0.0,
                0.0 0.6 0.0,
                0.2 0.6 0.0,
                0.4 0.6 0.0,
                0.6 0.6 0.0,
                0.8 0.6 0.0,
                1.0 0.6 0.0,
                0.0 0.8 0.0,
                0.2 0.8 0.0,
                0.4 0.8 0.0,
                0.6 0.8 0.0,
                0.8 0.8 0.0,
                1.0 0.8 0.0,
                0.0 1.0 0.0,
                0.2 1.0 0.0,
                0.4 1.0 0.0,
                0.6 1.0 0.0,
                0.8 1.0 0.0,
                1.0 1.0 0.0,
        ]
}
IndexedFaceSet {
        coordIndex [
                 0,  1,  7,  6, -1,
                 1,  2,  8,  7, -1,
                 2,  3,  9,  8, -1,
                 3,  4, 10,  9, -1,
                 4,  5, 11, 10, -1,
                 6,  7, 13, 12, -1,
                 7,  8, 14, 13, -1,
                 8,  9, 15, 14, -1,
                 9, 10, 16, 15, -1,
                10, 11, 17, 16, -1,
                12, 13, 19, 18, -1,
                13, 14, 20, 19, -1,
                14, 15, 21, 20, -1,
                15, 16, 22, 21, -1,
                16, 17, 23, 22, -1,
                18, 19, 25, 24, -1,
                19, 20, 26, 25, -1,
                20, 21, 27, 26, -1,
                21, 22, 28, 27, -1,
                22, 23, 29, 28, -1,
                24, 25, 31, 30, -1,
                25, 26, 32, 31, -1,
```

Figure 19.12 continues

```
                26, 27, 33, 32, -1,
                27, 28, 34, 33, -1,
                28, 29, 35, 34, -1,
        ]
}
```

Figure 19.12 *A mesh created to better show point and spot light effects.*

You can use a similar approach to create a mesh of arbitrary size and density. For many of the examples that follow, we use a mesh with 11 columns and 11 rows of vertices to create 100 squares. This mesh is referenced in the examples by inlining it from a file `wall.wrl` using a **WWWInline** node. You can generate a similar fine mesh yourself, or use the preceding more coarse mesh.

Lighting a Mesh

You can see the effects of a point light clearly when you illuminate a mesh. The example text in Figure 19.13 draws a mesh wall with a point light placed very close and at the center of the mesh. The center of the mesh, then, is illuminated brightly by the close-by point light, while the more distant corners of the mesh are less brightly lit.

```
#VRML V1.0 ascii

PointLight {
        location 0.0 0.0 0.1
}
WWWInline {
        name "wall.wrl"
}
```

Figure 19.13 *The mesh lit by a point light placed very close to the mesh.*

You can use the same mesh to examine the effects of a spot light, as shown in Figure 19.14.

```
#VRML V1.0 ascii

SpotLight {
      location 0.0 0.0 1.0
      direction 1.0 0.0 0.0
      dropOffRate 0.0
      cutOffAngle 0.785 #  45.0 degrees
}
WWWInline {
      name "wall.wrl"
}
```

Figure 19.14 *The effects of a spot light shining on a mesh wall.*

The preceding spot light uses a drop-off rate of 0.0 to create a sharp edge to the spot. Figures 19.15 through 19.18 vary this drop-off rate, showing values of 0.25, 0.5, 0.75, and 1.0 on the same mesh wall with the same spot light position, direction, and cutoff angle.

Figure 19.15 *Spot light drop-off rate of 0.25.*

Figure 19.16 *Spot light drop-off rate of 0.5.*

Figure 19.17 *Spot light drop-off rate of 0.75.*

Figure 19.18 *Spot light drop-off rate of 1.0.*

You can also vary the spot light's cutoff angle to narrow or widen the cone of illumination. Figures 19.19 and 19.20 vary the cutoff angle from 60.0 degrees to 75.0 degrees on the same mesh wall with the same spot light position, and direction, and a drop-off rate of 0.0.

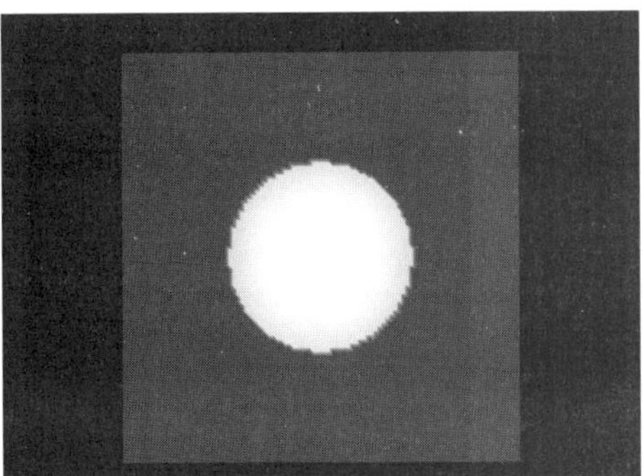

Figure 19.19 *Spot light cutoff angle of 60.0 degrees.*

Figure 19.20 *Spot light cutoff angle of 75.0 degrees.*

Using More Than One Light

Using more than one light, you can create realistic lighting effects. The example text in Figure 19.21 uses five point lights, each a different color, to create a chain of colored bulbs. The bulbs are presented on a mesh like that used in the previous examples. Color plate 4*b* and Figure 19.21 illustrate the result.

```
#VRML V1.0 ascii

# Set up some standard shapes and transforms
Switch {
      whichChild -1
      # Light bulb
      DEF bulb Separator {
            Translation {
                  translation 0.0 -1.9 0.0
            }
            Sphere {
                  radius 1.0
            }
            Material {
                  diffuseColor 0.4 0.4 0.4
            }
            Translation {
                  translation 0.0 1.4 0.0
            }
            Cylinder {
                  height 1.0
                  radius 0.5
            }
      }
      # Wire
      DEF wire Separator {
            Material {
                  diffuseColor 0.1 0.1 0.1
            }
            Rotation {
                  #                 Z    -90.0 degrees
                  rotation 0.0 0.0 1.0  -1.57
            }
            Translation {
                  translation 0.0 2.0 0.0
            }
            Cylinder {
                  height 4.0
                  radius 0.05
            }
      }
      # Floor
      DEF floor Separator {
            Translation {
                  translation 8.0 -2.0 -1.0
            }
            Scale {
                  scaleFactor 20.0 10.0 1.0
            }
            WWWInline {
                  name "wall.wrl"
            }
      }
```

Figure 19.21 continues

```
        # Standard right move
        DEF right Translation {
              translation 4.0 0.0 0.0
        }
        # Standard rotate up
        DEF up Rotation {
              #                Z   +10.0 degrees
              rotation 0.0 0.0 1.0  0.17
        }
        # Standard rotate down
        DEF down Rotation {
              #                Z    -10.0 degrees
              rotation 0.0 0.0 1.0  -0.17
        }
  }
  # Point lights for each light bulb
  TransformSeparator {
        Translation {
              translation 0.0 -1.9 0.0
        }
        PointLight {
              location 0.0 0.0 0.0
              color    1.0 0.0 0.0
        }
        USE right    USE up
        PointLight {
              location 0.0 0.0 0.0
              color    0.0 0.0 1.0
        }
        USE right    USE down
        PointLight {
              location 0.0 0.0 0.0
              color    1.0 1.0 0.0
        }
        USE right    USE down
        PointLight {
              location 0.0 0.0 0.0
              color    1.0 0.0 0.0
        }
        USE right    USE down
        PointLight {
              location 0.0 0.0 0.0
              color    0.0 1.0 0.0
        }
  }
  # Light bulbs
  TransformSeparator {
        Material {
              emissiveColor 1.0 0.0 0.0
              diffuseColor  0.0 0.0 0.0
        }
```

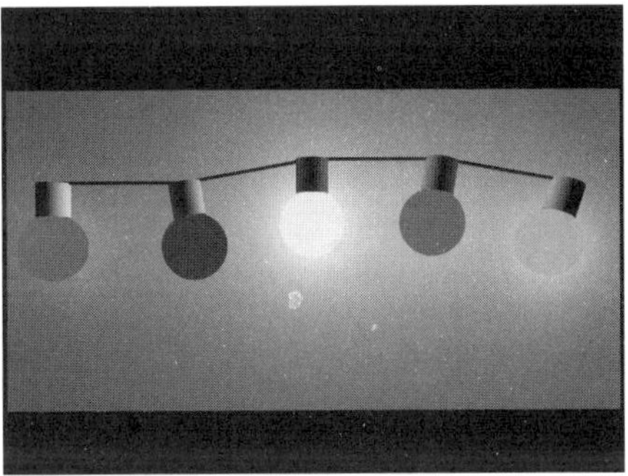

Figure 19.21 continues

```
        USE bulb    USE wire    USE right    USE up
        Material {
              emissiveColor 0.0 0.0 1.0
              diffuseColor  0.0 0.0 0.0
        }
        USE bulb    USE wire    USE right    USE down
        Material {
              emissiveColor 1.0 1.0 0.0
              diffuseColor  0.0 0.0 0.0
        }
        USE bulb    USE wire    USE right    USE down
        Material {
              emissiveColor 1.0 0.0 0.0
              diffuseColor  0.0 0.0 0.0
        }
        USE bulb    USE wire    USE right    USE down
        Material {
              emissiveColor 0.0 1.0 0.0
              diffuseColor  0.0 0.0 0.0
        }
        USE bulb
}
# Floor
USE floor
```

Figure 19.21 *Colored lights created with point lights.*

Several advanced techniques are used to make this string of colored light bulbs:

- *Several standard shapes and transforms are set up and given defined names within a* ***Switch*** *node at the top of the file. This technique allows you to create a library of shapes and transforms, from which to construct your world. In this case, a light bulb shape, a wire shape, the floor mesh, and a few transforms are named and placed within the* ***Switch*** *node.*
- *Each of the five point lights for the world is defined* before *any of the shapes in the world are drawn. This ensures that all of the shapes are lit by all of the lights.*
- *A color is specified for each point light by setting its* ***color*** *field.*
- *All of the point lights are defined with a location of* `0.0 0.0 0.0` *(the origin). However, between the point lights are* ***Translation*** *and* ***Rotation*** *transforms to place and orient each light individually.*
- *Each light bulb shape is positioned and oriented using exactly the same sequence of* ***Translation*** *and* ***Rotation*** *nodes as the sequence used to position and orient the point lights. This ensures that the light bulbs and the point lights line up to make the image more realistic. Using exactly the same transforms is made easy by defining names for each one in the* ***Switch*** *node earlier.*

- *Each light bulb shape appears to glow, because the **emissiveColor** field of a **Material** node is set for that bulb. The emissive colors are the same as those specified for the point light at the same location.*
- *The floor mesh is positioned behind the string of lights. The mesh, and all of the light bulbs, are illuminated by the five colored point lights.*

The point lights, and the light bulb shapes are completely separate and independent. Point lights don't have any visible shape of their own. Only their lighting effects are apparent. The light bulb shapes are not causing the lighting efforts. You can delete these, and the mesh would still be colored the same. You could even change the colors of the light bulb shapes so that, say, a red point light is apparently shining out of a yellow light bulb shape. This ability to separate lights from light bulb shapes gives you tremendous power to design realistic or completely impossible lighting effects.

You can use multiple lights to create subtle, realistic lighting. Figure 19.22 and color plate 4*c* show a hallway made of meshes. The floor, lower portions of each wall, and the door in the distance are all texture-mapped Along the upper-right-hand wall are four slightly yellow point lights to illuminate the hall with a warm glow. The wall mountings used around each light are created using spheres drawn with a high emissive color to make them appear to glow.

```
#VRML V1.0 ascii

Switch {
      whichChild -1
      DEF wall1_base Separator {
            Material {
                  diffuseColor 0.3 0.3 0.3
            }
            WWWInline {
                  name "hwall2.wrl"
            }
      }
      DEF wall2_base Separator {
            Material {
                  diffuseColor 1.0 1.0 1.0
            }
            WWWInline {
                  name "hwall2.wrl"
            }
      }
      DEF wall1_wainscot Separator {
            # trim at top of wainscot
            Separator {
                  Translation {
                        translation 0.0 3.2 0.0
                  }
                  Material {
                        diffuseColor 0.4 0.3 0.2
                  }
```

Figure 19.22 continues

```
          Coordinate3 {
                point [
                       0.0 0.3 0.0,
                       0.0 0.0 0.0,
                      21.0 0.0 0.0,
                      21.0 0.3 0.0,
                ]
          }
          IndexedFaceSet {
                coordIndex [ 0, 1, 2, 3 ]
          }
    }
    # trim at bottom of wainscot
    Separator {
          Translation {
                translation 0.0 0.0 0.1
          }
          Material {
                diffuseColor 0.4 0.3 0.2
          }
          Coordinate3 {
                point [
                       0.0 0.3 0.0,
                       0.0 0.0 0.0,
                      21.0 0.0 0.0,
                      21.0 0.3 0.0,
                ]
          }
          IndexedFaceSet {
                coordIndex [ 0, 1, 2, 3 ]
          }
    }
    Texture2 {
          filename "wood8.gif"
    }
    Texture2Transform {
          scaleFactor 20.0 1.0
    }
    Scale {
          scaleFactor 1.0 0.4 1.0
    }
    Material {
          diffuseColor 0.6 0.6 0.6
    }
    WWWInline {
          name "hwall2.wrl"
    }
}
```

Figure 19.22 continues

```
DEF wall2_wainscot Separator {
      # trim at top of wainscot
      Separator {
            Translation {
                  translation 0.0 3.2 0.0
            }
            Material {
                  diffuseColor 0.8 0.6 0.4
            }
            Coordinate3 {
                  point [
                         0.0 0.3 0.0,
                         0.0 0.0 0.1,
                        21.0 0.0 0.1,
                        21.0 0.3 0.0,
                  ]
            }
            IndexedFaceSet {
                  coordIndex [ 0, 1, 2, 3 ]
            }
      }
      # trim at bottom of wainscot
      Separator {
            Translation {
                  translation 0.0 0.0 0.1
            }
            Material {
                  diffuseColor 0.7 0.5 0.3
            }
            Coordinate3 {
                  point [
                         0.0 0.3 0.0,
                         0.0 0.0 0.05,
                        21.0 0.0 0.05,
                        21.0 0.3 0.0,
                  ]
            }
            IndexedFaceSet {
                  coordIndex [ 0, 1, 2, 3 ]
            }
      }
      Texture2 {
            filename "wood8.gif"
      }
      Texture2Transform {
            scaleFactor 20.0 1.0
      }
      Scale {
            scaleFactor 1.0 0.4 1.0
      }
```

Figure 19.22 continues

```
        Material {
              diffuseColor 1.0 1.0 1.0
              emissiveColor 0.3 0.3 0.3
        }
        WWWInline {
              name "hwall2.wrl"
        }
  }
  DEF wall1 Separator {
        USE wall1_base
        Translation {
              translation 0.0 0.0 0.01
        }
        USE wall1_wainscot
  }
  DEF wall2 Separator {
        USE wall2_base
        Translation {
              translation 0.0 0.0 0.01
        }
        USE wall2_wainscot
  }
  DEF floor Separator {
        Rotation {
              rotation 1.0 0.0 0.0 -1.57
        }
        Texture2 {
              filename "floor5.gif"
        }
        Texture2Transform {
              scaleFactor 12.6 12.6
        }
        Material {
              diffuseColor 1.0 1.0 1.0
        }
        WWWInline {
              name "hfloor.wrl"
        }
  }
  DEF cieling Separator {
        Translation {
              translation 0.0 0.0 -5.0
        }
        Texture2 {
              filename "acoustic.gif"
        }
        Texture2Transform {
              scaleFactor 12.6 12.6
              scaleFactor 6.3 6.0
        }
        Rotation {
              rotation 1.0 0.0 0.0 1.57
        }
```

Figure 19.22 continues

```
            Material {
                  diffuseColor 1.0 1.0 1.0
                  emissiveColor 0.15 0.15 0.15
            }
            WWWInline {
                  name "hfloor.wrl"
            }
      }
      DEF door Separator {
            WWWInline {
                  name "door.wrl"
            }
      }
      DEF hall_light TransformSeparator {
            Translation {
                  translation 0.0 6.9 0.0
            }
            PointLight {
                  location 0.0 0.0 0.0
                  color 1.0 0.9 0.5
                  intensity 0.5
            }
            Translation {
                  translation 0.0 0.0 -0.4
            }
            Material {
                  emissiveColor 0.9 0.9 0.8
                  diffuseColor 0.0 0.0 0.0
                  ambientColor 0.0 0.0 0.0
            }
            Sphere {
                  radius 0.4
            }
            Material {
                  emissiveColor 0.0 0.0 0.0
                  diffuseColor  0.5 0.5 0.5
                  ambientColor  0.0 0.0 0.0
            }
            Cylinder {
                  parts SIDES
                  height 0.2
                  radius 0.7
            }
            Cylinder {
                  parts SIDES
                  height 0.2
                  radius 0.9
            }
      }
}
```

Figure 19.22 continues

```
# Lights
TransformSeparator {
      Translation {
            translation 3.0 0.0 -4.6
      }
      USE hall_light
      Translation {
            translation 6.0 0.0 0.0
      }
      USE hall_light
      Translation {
            translation 6.0 0.0 0.0
      }
      USE hall_light
      Translation {
            translation 4.0 0.0 0.0
      }
      USE hall_light
}
# Hall itself
Separator {
      # Floor
      USE floor
      # Cieling
      Separator {
            Translation {
                  translation 0.0 8.0 0.0
            }
            USE cieling
      }
      # Wall 2 (right)
      Separator {
            Translation {
                  translation 0.0 0.0 -5.0
            }
            USE wall2
      }
      # Wall 1 (left)
      Separator {
            Translation {
                  translation 21.0 0.0 0.0
            }
            Rotation {
                  rotation 0.0 1.0 0.0 3.1415
            }
            USE wall1
      }
      # Door
      Separator {
            Translation {
                  translation 0.0 4.0 0.0
            }
```

Figure 19.22 continues

```
            Rotation {
                 rotation 0.0 1.0 0.0 1.57
            }
            USE door
     }
}
```

Figure 19.22 *A hallway of meshes designed to illustrate lighting affects.*

Extended Example

The following example builds on the concepts presented in this chapter. Try it on your own.

An Adjustable Lamp

The example text in Figure 19.23 is modified from the adjustable desk lamp shown in Chapter 11 to add a spot light within the lamp. A directional light is used at the top of the file to add a gentle ambient light to the world. Without this light, most of the lamp body would be dark, since it is outside the spot light's illumination cone.

The spot light is positioned and oriented using the same set of transforms later used to position and orient the arms and lamp shade of the lamp. Using this technique, the lamp and the spot light move together. The table is drawn using the `wall.wrl` mesh used in previous examples, but it is texture-mapped with a tablecloth image. Using the mesh ensures that the spot light's lighting effect is clearly visible.

Notice that the spot light uses a drop-off rate that causes a gentle drop-off from the center to the edges, like a real lamp.

```
#VRML V1.0 ascii

# General lighting
DirectionalLight {
      intensity 0.5
      direction 1.0 -0.2 1.0
}
# Lamp light
TransformSeparator {
      # First lamp arm
      DEF arm1_rot Rotation {
            #       X              -30.0 degrees
            rotation 1.0 0.0 0.0  -0.523
      }
      DEF arm1_trans Translation {
            translation 0.0 0.75 0.0
      }
```

Figure 19.23 continues

```
        USE arm1_trans
        TransformSeparator {
            # Second lamp arm
            DEF arm2_rot Rotation {
                #       X           +90.0 degrees
                rotation 1.0 0.0 0.0  1.57
            }
            DEF arm2_trans Translation {
                translation 0.0 0.75 0.0
            }
            USE arm2_trans
            TransformSeparator {
                # Lamp shade
                DEF shade_rot Rotation {
                    #       X           -60.0 degrees
                    rotation 1.0 0.0 0.0  -1.05
                }
                DEF shade_trans Translation {
                    translation 0.0 -0.15 0.0
                }
                USE shade_trans
                # Light bulb
                DEF light_trans Translation {
                    translation 0.0 -0.15 0.0
                }
                SpotLight {
                    location 0.0 0.0 0.0
                    direction 0.0 -1.0 0.0
                    intensity 1.0
                    color 1.0 1.0 0.8
                    dropOffRate 0.1
                    #           45.0 degrees
                    cutOffAngle 0.785
                }
            }
        }
    }
    # Lamp
    Separator {
        # Lamp base
        Cylinder {
            height 0.08
            radius 0.5
        }
        Separator {
            # First lamp arm
            USE arm1_rot
            USE arm1_trans
            Material {
                diffuseColor 1.0 0.0 0.0
            }
```

Figure 19.23 continues

```
                DEF arm Cylinder {
                      height 1.5
                      radius 0.07
                }
                USE arm1_trans
                DEF joint Sphere {
                      radius 0.08
                }
                Separator {
                      # Second lamp arm
                      USE arm2_rot
                      USE arm2_trans
                      USE arm
                      USE arm2_trans
                      USE joint
                      Separator {
                            # Lamp shade
                            USE shade_rot
                            USE shade_trans
                            Cylinder {
                                  height 0.3
                                  radius 0.15
                                  parts (SIDES|TOP)
                            }
                            USE shade_trans
                            Cone {
                                  height 0.6
                                  bottomRadius 0.5
                                  parts SIDES
                            }
                            # Light bulb
                            USE light_trans
                            Material {
                                  diffuseColor 0.0 0.0 0.0
                                  emissiveColor 1.0 1.0 1.0
                            }
                            Sphere {
                                  radius 0.2
                            }
                      }
                }
          }
    }
    # Mesh table
    Separator {
          Transform {
                translation 0.0 -0.04 0.0
                #       X             -90.0 degrees
                rotation 1.0 0.0 0.0  -1.57
                scaleFactor 4.0 4.0 4.0
          }
```

Figure 19.23 continues

```
        Texture2 {
            filename "cloth.gif"
        }
        Texture2Transform {
            scaleFactor 4.0 4.0
        }
        WWWInline {
            name "wall.wrl"
        }
}
```

Figure 19.23 *An adjustable desk lamp.*

Summary

By default, the VRML browser creates only a single light in a world: the headlight. The headlight is a white light attached to your current viewpoint that moves as you move and always points straight ahead into the world.

You can add additional lights to the world with one or more **PointLight, DirectionalLight,** and **SpotLight** nodes. Point lights are lights in the world whose rays emanate radially in all directions, like a lamp's light bulb when the shade is removed. Directional lights are lights that aim in a single direction with all of their light rays parallel, like those of the distant sun. Spot lights are lights that aim in a specific direction from one point in the world and illuminate only those shapes within a cone of light emanating from the spot light.

All three light nodes have an **on** field for turning the light on and off, an **intensity** field for setting the light's brightness with values from 0.0 (off) to 1.0 (full on), and a **color** field for setting the light's RGB color.

PointLight and **SpotLight** nodes are positioned in your world using their **location** field, which specifies an X, Y, Z coordinate relative to the current origin.

DirectionalLight and **SpotLight** nodes are aimed in a specific direction using their **direction** field, which specifies an X, Y, Z distance between the current origin and an imaginary point. A line between the origin and this point defines the direction along which the directional light or spot light should aim.

Shape transforms, such as translation, rotation, and so on, move and orient lights as well as shapes.

SpotLight nodes have two additional fields. The **cutOffangle** field sets the spread angle, in radians, of the spot light's illumination cone. A small angle narrows the cone down to a tight beam, while a large angle spreads the light cone out. The **dropOffRate** field sets how quickly the spot light's light diminishes in intensity as it illuminates shapes toward the edges of the light cone.

Lights only illuminate shapes drawn after them in the world.

All lighting nodes affect the current lighting properties, saved and restored by **Separator** nodes. Lights defined within a separator group only illuminate shapes drawn after them within a **Separator** node.

Each light node adds another light to the current set of lights in the lighting property. This enables you to create many lights in a world at once.

CHAPTER 20

Shading Shapes with Advanced Materials

Using a **Material** node and its **diffuseColor** field, you control the color used to shade shapes. Whether lit by your headlight or by additional lights, your shapes have so far appeared as if they are made out of a dull, matte material. Using additional fields in the **Material** node, you can direct the VRML browser to draw *shiny* shapes and simulate plastics, metals, and other shiny materials.

In addition to creating shiny shapes, you can also set the basic, **ambient** illumination used to shade shapes. This creates a minimum lighting for a shape and can reduce the stark appearance of shading.

All of these effects are controlled by fields of the **Material** node, including the **shininess** and **specularColor** fields, used to control how shiny shapes are drawn, and the **ambientColor** field, which sets a basic lighting level for a shape.

Understanding Advanced Materials

The **Material** node introduced in Chapter 10 has a number of additional fields for controlling more advanced shading properties of shapes drawn by the VRML browser. These advanced features are effective when you include one or more point lights, directional lights, or spot lights in your world.

Understanding Light Reflection

In the real world, when light rays strike a surface, some are absorbed by it, some are reflected off it, and some are transmitted through the surface. For example, a window transmits most light rays, and reflects and absorbs the rest. A table, wall, or door, however, transmits no light and reflects or absorbs all of the light that shines on it. In any case, the light that reflects or is transmitted through a surface continues into the world, bouncing from surface to surface to illuminate the scene.

The real-world physics of lighting is very complex. The way light reflects off a real-world surface depends on the surface's material, how rough it is, what temperature it is, and what its electrical properties are. All of these surface properties may even vary for different colors of light up and down the spectrum. Computer programs written to simulate some or all of these lighting effects can draw astonishingly realistic images of virtual worlds. They also can take hours to draw a single image.

To draw virtual worlds quickly, VRML uses a simplified method of simulating real-world lighting. Light transmission, such as that through windows, is simulated using the **transparency** field of a **Material** node, described in Chapter 10. The **transparency** field controls what percentage of incoming light rays is transmitted through a surface.

VRML's simulation of real-world light reflection occurs in two ways: **diffuse reflection** and **specular reflection**. These two reflection types mimic the way light reflects off shapes in the real world. Using them, you can create fairly realistic imagery, usually drawn by your VRML browser in less than a second.

Diffuse reflection bounces light off a surface in random directions, scattering it about. Since each ray striking the surface bounces in a different random direction, the overall effect is one of a gentle *diffuse* lighting on a shape. There are no glints, sparkles, or highlights. Instead, a shape drawn based only on diffuse reflection computations will look dull, or matte, as if painted with flat house paint.

Figure 20.1 shows a VRML sphere shaded using only diffuse reflection. All of the shapes you've drawn using the **Material** node features discussed in Chapter 10 are shaded this way. The **diffuseColor** field of the **Material** node controls the color of the light reflected by diffuse reflection.

Specular reflection bounces light off a surface in a mathematically predictable way. Specifically, if light comes in at one angle, it bounces off at the same angle. Specular reflection makes shiny surfaces reflect the world around them. A mirror,

Figure 20.1 *A sphere shaded using diffuse reflection.*

for instance, bounces incoming light back out so that you see a perfect reflection of yourself. Glossy bowling balls and shiny dinner plates similarly reflect the world in their surfaces due to specular reflection.

Real-world shiny surfaces reflect other shapes in the world, such as a chrome bumper reflecting the sky, ground, and other cars nearby. Such reflections are very time consuming to compute. VRML simplifies the simulation of real-world lighting by skipping shape reflections and concentrating on light-source reflections. In other words, shiny surfaces in VRML can reflect point light sources, directional light sources, and spot light sources in the world, but not shapes. This is sufficient to create many realistic scenes. In the real world, the reflection of light sources causes glints, sparkles, and highlights on shiny surfaces. By simulating these same light-source reflections, VRML enables you to draw shiny surfaces as well as the diffuse, dull surfaces drawn using only the **diffuseColor** field of a **Material** node.

Figure 20.2 shows a VRML sphere shaded using specular reflection. Notice the highlight on the sphere. The highlight is a reflection of a point light source above and to the right of the sphere.

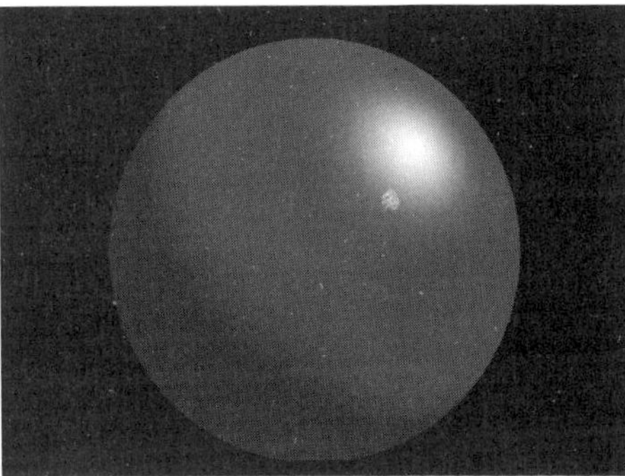

Figure 20.2 *A sphere shaded using specular reflection.*

Recall that point light sources, directional light sources, and spot light sources have no actual shape. How, then, are they reflected by a shiny shape in VRML? The highlight on this sphere is, in a sense, faked. This kind of fakery is essential in computer graphics, because computing a perfect simulation of the real world is very time consuming. Because such time-consuming computations are impractical, computer graphics software and its users perform a lot of fakery. For example, texture mapping enables you to fake detail in a world. Instead of using VRML shapes to draw every brick on a building, you map a picture of bricks to a shape. You can fake shadows by creating black faces and putting them where shadows should be. Specially computed normals enable you to fake curved shapes while using faceted shapes. This kind of fakery is essential in order to make computer graphics computation practical.

Similar fakery enables you to simulate real-world specular reflections. The highlight on this VRML sphere is a bright spot that reflects a distant light source *as if* the light source had a tiny dot as its shape. For point light sources and spot light sources, the tiny dot is located at the light source's location. For directional light sources, the dot is located infinitely far away in the direction from which the light's rays are coming.

Real-world surfaces rarely exhibit just diffuse reflection or just specular reflection. Most surfaces exhibit a little of each characteristic. Dull surfaces exhibit diffuse reflection but only a little specular reflection. Dull surfaces have no shiny highlight reflecting a distant light source.

Shiny surfaces exhibit some diffuse reflection and more specular reflection. A slightly shiny surface has a broad highlight showing the reflection of a light source. A somewhat more shiny surface will have a more focused highlight, while a very shiny surface will have a very focused highlight. Figure 20.3 shows a range of VRML spheres, all lit by a point light source above and to the right. The sphere in the upper left is somewhat shiny and has no highlight. The sphere in the upper right is more shiny, the one in the lower left more so, and the sphere in the lower right the shiniest. The shinier spheres have tighter, more focused highlights.

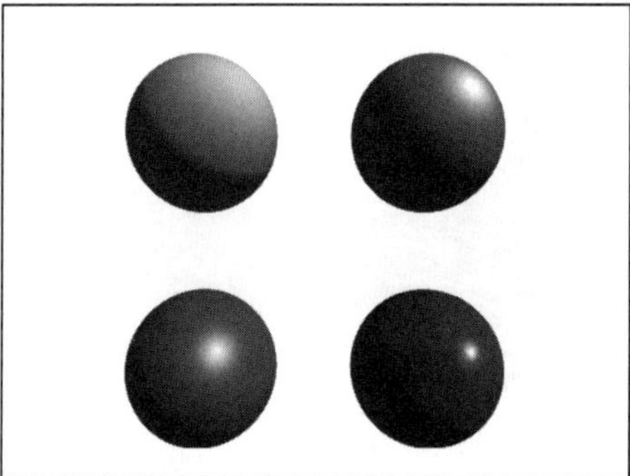

Figure 20.3 *Spheres illustrating a range of specular highlights.*

VRML provides you control over the amount of diffuse reflection and specular reflection exhibited by any shape. You can control the size of the specular reflection highlight to simulate shiny or dull shapes.

The color of a real-world specular reflection highlight on a real-world shiny surface depends partly on the surface material and partly on the color of the light being reflected. Some surfaces, like shiny plastics, reflect white lights as white highlights. Other surfaces, such as metals, reflect white lights as gold-, silver-, or copper-colored highlights.

Computation of real-world colored highlight effects take too long to compute for interactive graphics software like VRML. Instead VRML enables you to set the color of a specular reflection highlight yourself. By choosing the color of the highlight, you can simulate plastics and metals.

Understanding Ambient Lighting

In the real world, surfaces are lit by light sources shining on them directly *and* by light that has bounced off other surfaces. Living room lamps, for instance, frequently aim straight up at the ceiling, and the light that bounces off the ceiling gives the living room a gentle wash of light.

Light in the real world may bounce from surface to surface many times. At each surface, the light reflects by diffuse or specular reflection, or a mix of both. All of this light reflection creates a general, overall brightening of a room called **ambient lighting**.

A room at night, lit only by a flashlight, has a very low ambient-light level. This creates stark light and dark areas. During the day, however, light from windows reflects off of walls, ceiling, floor, and furniture to flood a room with light and create a high ambient-light level. This creates more gentle lighting effects that look more natural.

VRML simulates ambient lighting on a per-shape basis. This gives you tremendous flexibility to control your worlds' appearance. Using a high ambient-light level, your worlds seem like they are lit by a wash of light, like a room lit during the day with sunlight. Using a low ambient-light level, you can create dark environments, like lighting the same room by flashlight at night. You can combine ambient lighting with a few point light sources, directional light sources, or spot light sources to create very realistic environments.

Seeing Specular and Ambient Lighting Effects

Ambient light effectively fills in the dark corners of a world, brightening everything a bit. Shapes are then further brightened by diffuse and specular reflection of light sources in the world, such as point-light sources, directional-light sources, spot-light sources, and the default headlight. Figure 20.4 shows a VRML sphere shaded by all three lighting effects for a point-light source above and to the right of the sphere.

Figure 20.4 *A sphere showing the effects of specular, diffuse, and ambient lighting.*

If you use only the default headlight, it is difficult to see ambient and specular lighting effects. Figure 20.5 shows the same ball illuminated by the headlight at the current viewpoint.

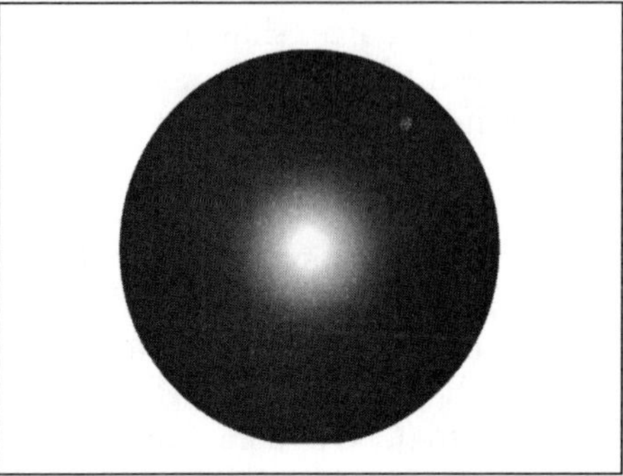

Figure 20.5 *A sphere showing the effects of specular and diffuse lighting.*

With the headlight always positioned at your current viewpoint, you never see the dark sides of shapes. Since ambient lighting's purpose is to brighten up those dark sides, you can't see the effects of ambient lighting using your headlight.

Similarly, with your headlight, its light aims straight into the scene, striking objects and bouncing straight back. On a sphere, like that in Figure 20.5, this creates a specular reflection highlight in the middle of the front of the sphere. The shininess of the shape is less obvious.

Ambient and specular lighting effects are most useful when you turn off your headlight and turn on one or more point light sources, directional light sources, and spot light sources in your world. This creates more realistic lighting effects that are less stark than those apparent using only the headlight.

Shading a Shape with Advanced Materials

The example text in Figure 20.6 creates a shiny gray sphere by setting the specular color to white and controlling the shininess of the material.

```
#VRML V1.0 ascii

PointLight {
     location 3.0 3.0 3.0
}
```

Figure 20.6 continues

```
Material {
      ambientColor  0.15 0.15 0.15
      diffuseColor  0.25 0.25 0.25
      specularColor 0.70 0.70 0.70
      shininess 0.2
}
Sphere {
}
```

Figure 20.6 *A shiny gray sphere with a white specular highlight.*

Notice the structure and order of the VRML text in Figure 20.6. The **PointLight** node places a point light source 3.0 units to the right, up, and forward of the origin. The **Material** node selects shading colors for ambient, diffuse, and specular lighting and sets the shininess to 0.2 (fairly shiny). The **Sphere** node then directs the VRML browser to draw a shiny sphere.

Understanding the Extended **Material** Node Syntax

The **Material** node has six fields: **ambientColor, diffuseColor, specularColor, emissiveColor, shininess,** and **transparency.** All of the color fields specify an RGB color, while the **shininess** and **transparency** fields use floating-point shininess and transparency factors.

SYNTAX **Material node**

```
Material {
      ambientColor       0.2 0.2 0.2       # RGB color
      diffuseColor       0.8 0.8 0.8       # RGB color
      specularColor      0.0 0.0 0.0       # RGB color
      emissiveColor      0.0 0.0 0.0       # RGB color
      shininess          0.2               # shininess factor
      transparency       0.0               # transparency factor
}
```

The **ambientColor** field specifies the RGB color of ambient light that lights subsequent shapes drawn by the VRML browser. The default ambient light is dark gray. Higher values brighten shapes as if lit with a wash of light. Lower values make lighting seem darker.

The **diffuseColor** field specifies the RGB color of light reflected off a shape by diffuse reflection. The diffuse color is what you generally perceive as the main color of a shape. A blue diffuse color makes a shape blue, a red diffuse color makes a shape red, and so on. The **diffuseColor** field was discussed in Chapter 10 when **Material** nodes were first introduced.

Typically the ambient and diffuse colors are the same general color but a different brightness. For instance, a blue shape will have a bright blue diffuse color, but a dark blue ambient color.

The **specularColor** field specifies the RGB color of light reflected off a shape by specular reflection. This controls the color of the highlight on shiny shapes. For many real-world materials, the specular color is white. For metals, however, the specular color tends more towards the color of the material. For realistic metal shading, try using a specular color that is white with a slight tinge of color the same as that in the **diffuseColor** field.

The **shininess** field is a floating-point **shininess factor** controlling how shiny subsequent shapes are drawn. A value of 0.0 makes shapes dull and matte. Higher values make shapes appear more and more shiny. The visual effect reduces the size of the specular reflection highlight when specifying higher values of shininess. Typical values are between 0.0 and 0.5. When the **shininess** field value is 0.0, the **specularColor** field is ignored.

The **emissiveColor** field specifies the RGB color that creates the effect of a glowing shape. Using the emissive color, along with diffuse and specular colors, you can direct the VRML browser to shade shapes so that they are dull or shiny *and* glow a little or a lot. The more a shape glows, however, the more it washes out the effects of diffuse and specular reflection. The **emissiveColor** field is discussed in Chapter 10.

The **transparency** field is a floating-point **transparency factor** that varies the transparency amount of shapes. A value of 0.0 draws opaque shapes, while higher values increase their transparency. A value of 1.0 draws completely transparent shapes, making them invisible. The **transparency** field is discussed in Chapter 10.

All **Material** node fields specify lists of values that can be used in material binding operations discussed in Chapter 15.

All fields in the **Material** node specify the material properties of the VRML browser and are saved and restored by **Separator** nodes.

Experimenting with Advanced Materials

The following examples provide a more detailed examination of the ways in which advanced materials can be used. While trying these examples, turn off your VRML browser's the headlight so you can clearly see the specular highlights caused by your point light sources, directional light sources, and spot light sources.

Making a Shape Shiny

The example text in Figure 20.7 draws a shiny gray sphere illuminated by a white point light source above and to the right of the sphere.

```
#VRML V1.0 ascii

PointLight {
     location 3.0 3.0 3.0
}
```

Figure 20.7 continues

```
Material {
      ambientColor 0.15 0.15 0.15
      diffuseColor 0.25 0.25 0.25
      specularColor 0.70 0.70 0.70
      shininess 0.2
}
Sphere {
}
```

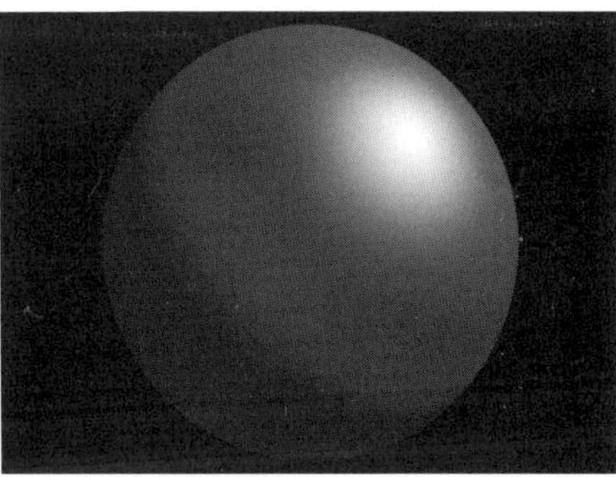

Figure 20.7 *A shiny gray sphere with a white specular highlight.*

Several techniques are used in combination to make the sphere appear shiny:

- *Real-world shiny shapes have a distinct, focused highlight.* The shinier the shape, the more focused the highlight. In VRML, the highlight focus is controlled by the **shininess** field in the **Material** node. This example uses a value of 0.2, which creates a fairly focused highlight. A higher value creates a smaller highlight and makes the shape appear more shiny.
- *Real-world shiny shapes have a bright specular color but a dim diffuse color.* Matte shapes, however, have a brighter diffuse color and a dim specular color. This example uses a medium-bright white for the specular color and a medium-dark gray for the diffuse color. For the best results, when you use a high **shininess** field value, also use a bright specular color and a dim diffuse color. If you use a low **shininess** field value, use a dim specular color and a bright diffuse color.
- *Real-world shiny shapes reflect ambient light by diffuse reflection (random scattering of light rays)*. In VRML, use a dim ambient color whenever the diffuse color is dim. In this example, the ambient color is set to a dark gray. The ambient color is generally a darker version of the diffuse color. Making the ambient color too bright washes out the shape and reduces the apparent shininess.

Using these techniques, you can create a range of shiny spheres by varying the **shininess, ambientColor, diffuseColor,** and **specularColor** fields appropriately.

The example text in Figure 20.8 shades four spheres, each lighted by a point light source above and to the right of the sphere. The upper-left sphere is shaded with a dull, matte material. The upper-right sphere is somewhat shiny. The lower-left sphere is fairly shiny and is the sphere from the previous example. The lower-right sphere is very shiny Its highlight is tightly focused, its specular color is high, and its diffuse and ambient colors are low.

```
#VRML V1.0 ascii

# Matte ball
Separator {
      Material {
            ambientColor 0.20 0.20 0.20
            diffuseColor 0.80 0.80 0.80
            specularColor 0.00 0.00 0.00
            shininess 0.05
      }
      DEF ball_and_light Group {
            PointLight {
                  location 3.0 3.0 3.0
            }
            Sphere {
            }
      }
}
# Slightly shiny ball
Translation {
      translation 3.0 0.0 0.0
}
Separator {
      Material {
            ambientColor 0.20 0.20 0.20
            diffuseColor 0.40 0.40 0.40
            specularColor 0.60 0.60 0.60
            shininess 0.1
      }
      USE ball_and_light
}
# Fairly shiny ball
Translation {
      translation -3.0 -3.0 0.0
}
Separator {
      Material {
            ambientColor 0.15 0.15 0.15
            diffuseColor 0.25 0.25 0.25
            specularColor 0.70 0.70 0.70
            shininess 0.2
      }
      USE ball_and_light
}
# Very shiny ball
Translation {
      translation 3.0 0.0 0.0
}
```

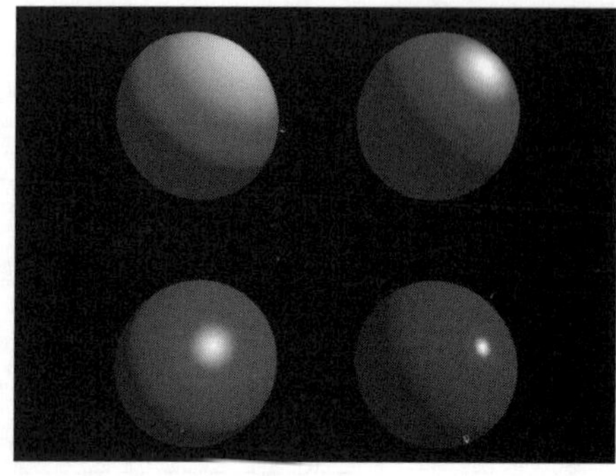

Figure 20.8 continues

```
Separator {
      Material {
            ambientColor 0.15 0.15 0.15
            diffuseColor 0.15 0.15 0.15
            specularColor 0.90 0.90 0.90
            shininess 1.0
      }
      USE ball_and_light
}
```

Figure 20.8 *Four spheres of varying shininess levels.*

Making Shiny Metallic and Plastic Shapes

In the real world, metal shapes reflect different colors of light differently. This has the effect of coloring the highlight on shiny metal shapes. Copper, for instance, has a slightly orange highlight, while gold has a somewhat yellow one. Aluminum's highlight is slightly blue. Colored metals have colored specular highlights as well.

Shiny plastics reflect light the same for all colors of light. A shiny plastic shape has a white specular highlight no matter what color the plastic is.

Figure 20.9 shows a series of six shiny vases illuminated by two white point light sources in front and to the right of each vase. The top row of vases are shaded as if they were gold, aluminum, and copper. The first two vases in the second row are shaded with colored metals. The third vase in the second row is shaded as if it was a shiny blue plastic.

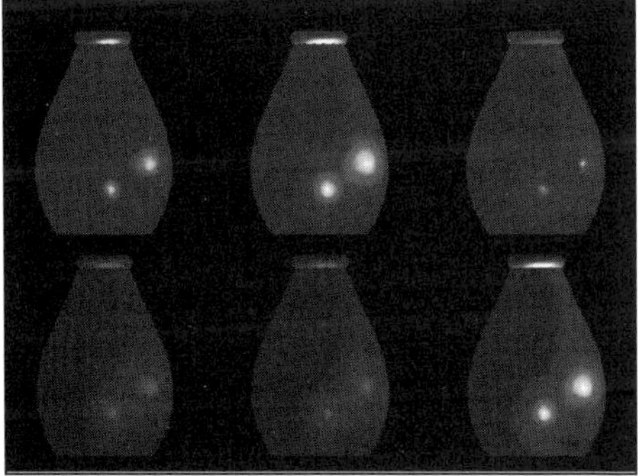

Figure 20.9 *Six vases of different metal and plastic materials.*

The **Material** nodes used for each of these six vases are as follows.

Gold vase:

```
Material {
      ambientColor 0.57 0.40 0.00
      diffuseColor 0.22 0.15 0.00
      specularColor 0.71 0.70 0.56
      shininess 0.16
}
```

Aluminum vase:

```
Material {
      ambientColor 0.30 0.30 0.35
      diffuseColor 0.30 0.30 0.50
      specularColor 0.70 0.70 0.80
      shininess 0.09
}
```

Copper vase:

```
Material {
      ambientColor 0.33 0.26 0.23
      diffuseColor 0.50 0.11 0.00
      specularColor 0.95 0.73 0.00
      shininess 0.93
}
```

Metalic purple vase:

```
Material {
      ambientColor 0.25 0.17 0.19
      diffuseColor 0.10 0.03 0.22
      specularColor 0.64 0.00 0.98
      shininess 0.08
}
```

Metallic red vase:

```
Material {
      ambientColor 0.25 0.15 0.15
      diffuseColor 0.27 0.00 0.00
      specularColor 0.61 0.13 0.18
      shininess 0.12
}
```

Plastic blue vase:

```
Material {
      ambientColor 0.10 0.11 0.79
      diffuseColor 0.30 0.30 0.71
      specularColor 0.83 0.83 0.83
      shininess 0.12
}
```

Extended Example

The following example builds on the concepts presented in this chapter. Try it on your own.

A Treasure Chest

The example text in Figure 20.10 creates a treasure chest. The chest is texture-mapped with a wood texture and shaded using a diffuse color. Two point lights are used to illuminate the outside of the chest, and the inside is lit with a yellow glow.

The brass bands and the lock plate on the chest are created with face sets and cubes, then shaded with a brass material. The brass has a yellow specular color and a medium dark yellow diffuse color. Point lights are placed at the front and right side of the chest to give the bands and lock a shine.

```
#VRML V1.0 ascii

# Treasure chest box
Separator {
      # General lighting for the outside of the chest
      PointLight {
            location 1.4 0.6 1.1
            intensity 1.1
            color 1.0 1.0 0.0
      }
      # A glow for the inside of the chest
      PointLight {
            location -0.9 0.6 -0.4
            intensity 5.0
            color 1.0 1.0 0.0
      }
      Material {
            diffuseColor 1.0 1.0 0.0
      }
      ShapeHints {
            shapeType       UNKNOWN_SHAPE_TYPE
            vertexOrdering COUNTERCLOCKWISE
      }
```

Figure 20.10 continues

```
        Coordinate3 {
            point [
                # Around the top
                -1.0  0.5  -0.5,    -1.0  0.5   0.5,
                 1.0  0.5   0.5,     1.0  0.5  -0.5,
                # Around the bottom
                -1.0 -0.5  -0.5,    -1.0 -0.5   0.5,
                 1.0 -0.5   0.5,     1.0 -0.5  -0.5,
                # Left and right sides
                -1.0  0.75  0.2,    -1.0  0.75 -0.2,
                 1.0  0.75  0.2,     1.0  0.75 -0.2,
            ]
        }
        Texture2 {
            filename "knoty.gif"
        }
        TextureCoordinate2 {
            point [
                1.0 1.0,  0.0 1.0,  0.0  0.0,  1.0  0.0,
                1.0 0.0,  1.0 1.0,  0.25 0.6,  0.25 0.4,
            ]
        }
        # Chest
        IndexedFaceSet {
            coordIndex [
                0, 4, 5, 1, -1,      1, 5, 6, 2, -1,
                2, 6, 7, 3, -1,      3, 7, 4, 0, -1,
                7, 6, 5, 4, -1,
            ]
            textureCoordIndex [
                0, 1, 2, 3, -1,      0, 1, 2, 3, -1,
                0, 1, 2, 3, -1,      0, 1, 2, 3, -1,
                0, 1, 2, 3, -1,
            ]
        }
        DEF hinge Transform {
            #        X              -30.0 degrees
            rotation 1.0 0.0 0.0  -0.523
            center   0.0 0.5 -0.5
        }
        # Top
        IndexedFaceSet {
            coordIndex [
                0, 1,  8,  9, -1,      2, 3, 11, 10, -1,
                8, 1,  2, 10, -1,      9, 8, 10, 11, -1,
                0, 9, 11,  3, -1,
            ]
            textureCoordIndex [
                4, 5, 6, 7, -1,      4, 5, 6, 7, -1,
                0, 1, 2, 3, -1,      0, 1, 2, 3, -1,
                0, 1, 2, 3, -1,
            ]
        }
    }
```

Figure 20.10 continues

```
# Point lights to give the brass a shine
PointLight {
      location -0.3 0.6 0.7
      intensity 2.0
      color 1.0 1.0 1.0
}
PointLight {
      location 1.1 0.6 -0.1
      intensity 2.0
      color 1.0 1.0 1.0
}
# Brass bands
Separator {
      DEF brass Material {
            ambientColor  0.00 0.00 0.00
            diffuseColor  0.22 0.15 0.00
            specularColor 0.91 0.90 0.36
            shininess     0.16
      }
      Coordinate3 {
            point [
                  # Left and right bands, front
                  -0.4    0.5    0.505,      -0.4   -0.5   0.505,
                  -0.325 -0.5    0.505,      -0.325  0.5   0.505,
                   0.325  0.5    0.505,       0.325 -0.5   0.505,
                   0.4   -0.5    0.505,       0.4    0.5   0.505,
                  # Left and right bands, back
                  -0.325  0.5   -0.505,      -0.325 -0.5  -0.505,
                  -0.4   -0.5   -0.505,      -0.4    0.5  -0.505,
                   0.4    0.5   -0.505,       0.4   -0.5  -0.505,
                   0.325 -0.5   -0.505,       0.325  0.5  -0.505,
                  # Left and right bands, top
                  -0.4    0.755  0.2, -0.4    0.755 -0.2,
                  -0.325  0.755  0.2, -0.325  0.755 -0.2,
                   0.325  0.755 -0.2,  0.325  0.755  0.2,
                   0.4    0.755 -0.2,  0.4    0.755  0.2,
                  # Left and right bands, bottom
                  -0.4   -0.505  0.505,      -0.4   -0.505 -0.505,
                  -0.325 -0.505 -0.505,      -0.325 -0.505  0.505,
                   0.325 -0.505  0.505,       0.325 -0.505 -0.505,
                   0.4   -0.505 -0.505,       0.4   -0.505  0.505,
                  # Side band, left and right
                  -1.005 -0.505 -0.0375,     -1.005 -0.505  0.0375,
                  -1.005  0.5    0.0375,     -1.005  0.5   -0.0375,
                   1.005  0.5   -0.0375,      1.005  0.5    0.0375,
                   1.005 -0.505  0.0375,      1.005 -0.505 -0.0375,
                  # Side band, left and right top
                  -1.005  0.5   -0.0375,     -1.005  0.5    0.0375,
                  -1.005  0.755  0.0375,     -1.005  0.755 -0.0375,
                   1.005  0.755 -0.0375,      1.005  0.755  0.0375,
                   1.005  0.5    0.0375,      1.005  0.5   -0.0375,
            ]
      }
```

Figure 20.10 continues

```
        # Bands on box
        IndexedFaceSet {
            coordIndex [
                 0,  1,  2,  3, -1,  4,  5,  6,  7, -1,
                 8,  9, 10, 11, -1, 12, 13, 14, 15, -1,
                24, 25, 26, 27, -1, 28, 29, 30, 31, -1,
                32, 33, 34, 35, -1, 36, 37, 38, 39, -1,
                39, 38, 33, 32, -1,
            ]
        }
        USE hinge
        # Bands on top
        IndexedFaceSet {
            coordIndex [
                 0,  3, 18, 16, -1, 16, 18, 19, 17, -1,
                17, 19,  8, 11, -1,  4,  7, 23, 21, -1,
                21, 23, 22, 20, -1, 20, 22, 12, 15, -1,
                40, 41, 42, 43, -1, 44, 45, 46, 47, -1,
                43, 42, 45, 44, -1,
            ]
        }
    }
    # Brass lock hardware
    Separator {
        USE brass
        Translation {
            translation 0.0 0.4 0.52
        }
        Cube {
            width 0.2
            height 0.23
            depth 0.03
        }
        Material {
            ambientColor 0.0 0.0 0.0
            diffuseColor 0.0 0.0 0.0
        }
        Separator {
            Transform {
                translation 0.0 0.02 0.0
                #          X             +90.0 degrees
                rotation   1.0 0.0 0.0  1.57
            }
            Cylinder {
                height 0.035
                radius 0.015
                parts  TOP
            }
            Translation {
                translation 0.0 0.0 0.035
            }
```

Figure 20.10 continues

```
            Cube {
                  width 0.015
                  height 0.035
                  depth 0.05
            }
      }
      Translation {
            translation 0.0 -0.4 -0.53
      }
      USE hinge
      Transform {
            translation 0.0 0.55 0.48
            #        X              -50.2 degrees
            rotation 1.0 0.0 0.0  -0.876
      }
      USE brass
      Cube {
            width 0.2
            height 0.145
            depth 0.03
      }
}
```

Figure 20.10 *A treasure chest.*

Summary

Real-world light reflection is simulated in VRML using two types of reflection: diffuse reflection and specular reflection. Diffuse reflection scatters light randomly as it reflects off a shape. Specular reflection bounces light in a regular predictable way, like a mirror. The highlight on a shiny shape is a specular reflection of a light source.

The **diffuseColor** field of a **Material** node controls the color of reflected light from diffuse reflection.

The **specularColor** field controls the color of reflected light from specular reflection. For plastics, this is the same color as the light in the scene (usually white). For metals, this is the metal's color, such as a bright yellow for gold or a bright orange for copper.

The **shininess** field controls how shiny a shape is by varying the focus of the highlight on a shape. A **shininess** field value of 0.0 creates dull, matte shapes, while higher values create shinier shapes with more focused highlights.

The **ambientColor** field controls the brightness of the overall lighting in a world. Low values make a world seem dark, while higher values wash a world with light.

CHAPTER 21

Controlling Detail (Advanced)

As you add more detail to your worlds, your VRML browser takes longer to draw them, and they seem less interactive. You are forced to strike a balance between wanting lots of detail for maximum realism and also wanting quick drawing for maximum interactivity.

One technique that can help control world detail is to take advantage of the fact that shapes farther away from you in the world need not be drawn with as much detail as those close to you. Shapes very distant need not be drawn at all since you can hardly see them anyway. By reducing the detail of distant shapes, you give your VRML browser less to draw, and thus increase interactivity. You can control these different **levels of detail** using the VRML **LOD** node, which is an acronym for *Level Of Detail.*

Understanding Detail Control

The level of detail technique comes from computer graphics flight simulators used to train aircraft pilots. In such a simulator, the pilot flies a simulated plane over a simulated landscape, practicing takeoff, landing, and other flight maneuvers. Realism is important, but so is interactivity.

To make a flight simulator feel realistic, the terrain needs lots of detail, including shapes for buildings, streets, cars, trees, and so on. Since the aircraft can fly anywhere over a large terrain, that same detail is needed throughout. With trees, buildings, and so on, in close proximity and far away, the realism of the simulator is great, but the interactivity is poor. Drawing all the detail slows down the system.

To increase the speed of the system, flight simulator designers noted that less detail is needed for distant terrain, than for that directly below the aircraft. Drawing each individual tree for a distant forest is a waste of time since the aircraft pilot can't see that far away anyway. By replacing distant trees with simpler shapes, such as a single green face for the entire forest, the flight simulator can draw the world more quickly and increase interactivity. Only when the aircraft flies close to the forest does the simulator replace the green face with individual tree shapes.

This same technique can be used for buildings, cars, streets, and so on. Each shape is created in multiple versions, typically with high, medium, and low detail. The high-detail version is used only when the aircraft is in close proximity. The medium-detail version is used when the aircraft is farther away, and the low-detail version is used when the aircraft is far away. For greater control, there can be more detail levels, though typically two or three is enough.

You can use this same detail control technique when designing your own VRML worlds. For complex shapes, create two or three versions. The high-detail version has all the detail needed for realism, but it is used only when the viewer is close to the shape. The medium-detail version has only the essential components of the shape and is used when the viewer is farther away. The low-detail version has very few components, providing only the basic parts necessary when the shape is seen from far away.

Understanding Graphics Performance

When designing different detail versions of a shape, it can help to understand a little about what can be drawn quickly, and what cannot. When reducing the detail of a shape, you want to leave out the components that are slow to draw, and include only those that are quick to draw.

The exact drawing speed of different VRML features is dependent on the type of graphics hardware and the VRML browser you are using. In general, however, drawing any shape goes through the following steps:

1. Split concave faces into convex faces.
2. Transform.
   a. Translate, rotate, and scale all coordinates for a face.
   b. If the face is behind the viewer, skip drawing it.
   c. Translate, rotate, and scale all normals for a face.
   d. If the face is aimed away from the viewer, and backface culling is on, skip drawing it.
   e. Translate, rotate, and scale all texture coordinates for a face.
3. Fill.
   a. Get a normal vector for each face coordinate.
   b. Get a color for each face coordinate.

c. Get a texture coordinate for each face coordinate.
d. Walk across a face, filling in each pixel on the screen.
    i. Compute an intensity at this pixel.
    ii. Compute a color at this pixel.
    iii. Compute a texture color at this pixel.
    iv. Combine the intensity, color, and texture color together.
    v. Save the computed color for this pixel into screen memory.

TIP *The order of these steps may vary from system to system. You can read more about graphics systems in any of the graphics books listed in Appendix C.*

When designing efficient shapes, you want the VRML browser to take the smallest amount of time necessary in each of the preceding steps. A high-detail version of a shape may use time-consuming VRML features, but a low-detail version should avoid them.

To help your VRML draw shapes as quickly as possible, follow these tips:

- *Use only convex faces.*
- *Use the fewest coordinates possible.*
- *Minimize the number of lights in a world.*
- *Minimize the use of texture mapping.*

The following sections describe in detail the preceding steps and tips.

Split Concave Faces into Convex Faces

You can create faces that are concave (have inlets) or convex (have no inlets). Concave faces must be split into convex faces by the VRML browser or graphics hardware before they can be drawn. This takes time. If, however, you are careful to use only convex faces (typically triangles), the browser can skip this step entirely.

Using convex faces exclusively speeds drawing for any detail level of a shape. You can hint to your browser that this is the case by using the **ShapeHints** node discussed in Chapter 17.

Transform

Before drawing a face, the graphics system translates, rotates, and scales each coordinate of the face. If the face has lots of coordinates, this step takes longer than if it has only a few coordinates. A cylinder, for instance, typically has 32 or more coordinates describing the circular top and bottom. A cube has only 8 coordinates. A cube, then, is four times faster to process in this step than a cylinder. A sphere may have 60 or more coordinates, and a complex curved surface hundreds, or even thousands. So smooth shapes take more time to transform than angular, chunky shapes.

When designing shapes, keep the number of coordinates to a minimum to speed drawing for any detail level of a shape. A smooth car body, for instance, can be made chunkier for a medium-detail shape. A low-detail version of a car can be drawn as a simple 2-D cutout using only a few coordinates.

Texture coordinates also must be translated, rotated, and scaled before they can be used to texture-map a face. Since there is one texture coordinate for each face coordinate, simpler texture-mapped faces are quicker to draw than those with many coordinates. Additionally, a face drawn without texture mapping does not require that any texture coordinates be transformed.

When creating shapes, keep the use of texture mapping to a minimum to speed up drawing. For the low-detail version of a shape, turn off texture mapping entirely. While this reduces the realism of that shape, it is viewed only from a long distance, so the loss of realism will hardly be noticed.

Fill

After a face's coordinates have all been transformed, the face is drawn, pixel by pixel, into computer video memory (VRAM) used by video circuitry to drive your monitor. Since each pixel covered by a face must be filled in, the more pixels that are covered, the longer it takes. A face that covers only a single pixel will be much quicker to draw than one that fills the entire screen.

Because of perspective, the closer you get to a shape, the bigger it gets and the larger it appears on the screen. Moving around your world causes shapes to fill your screen sometimes though they are tiny at other times. The only thing you can easily control to speed drawing is the length of time it takes to draw a single pixel. If this drawing time is reduced, it has a huge effect when filling thousands of pixels for a close shape.

For most graphics hardware and software, it takes much longer to fill in a pixel for a face that is texture-mapped than for one that is not. To help your browser draw more quickly, keep the number of texture-mapped shapes to a minimum. As noted earlier, for low-detail shapes, turn off texture mapping.

Most graphics hardware and software also take longer to fill a pixel if there is more than one light source. Keep lighting down to the single default headlight for the maximum performance.

Finally, there are three standard ways in which the intensity of a face can be computed based on normals:

- **Flat shading** *computes one intensity for an entire face using one face normal. That intensity is used for all pixels filled by the face.*
- **Gouraud shading** *(pronounced "Go-row") computes an intensity at each face coordinate using coordinate normals. That intensity is then* **interpolated** *(smoothly blended) across the face to draw each pixel.*
- **Phong shading** *interpolates the normal itself across the face to get a custom normal for each pixel filled by the face. Each pixel normal is then used to compute an intensity value for that pixel.*

The choice of shading method is up to your VRML browser. Some browsers include a menu option to select between flat, Gouraud, or Phong shading.

Flat shading is the quickest, but the least realistic. Gouraud shading is fairly realistic and fairly quick. This is the shading method used by most interactive graphics hardware and software. Phong shading is slower to draw, but handles certain lighting conditions more accurately. For most cases, Phong and Gouraud shading of the same world look virtually identical. For this reason Phong shading is frequently not supported, or at least not the default.

Understanding Level of Detail

High-detail versions of a shape typically use many coordinates and textures to create smooth, realistic shapes. Medium-detail versions of a shape can use fewer coordinates and fewer textures. Low-detail versions can use only a few coordinates and no textures.

After creating several different versions of a shape in varying levels of detail, you can enclose them within a level-of-detail group and direct your VRML browser to automatically switch between them based on how far away you are from them. This distance between you and a shape is called the **range**. If you have *three* different detail versions of a shape, then you need to specify to the browser *two* different range values that direct the browser when to switch from one detail version to the next.

Imagine you designed a car and create three different versions of it: high-, medium-, and low-detail. When the viewer is close, within 20 units of the shape, the high-detail version is drawn. When the viewer is a medium distance away, between 20 units and 50 units, the medium-detail version is drawn. Finally, when the viewer is more than 50 units away, the low-detail version is drawn. Notice that, while there are three versions of your car, there are only two range values needed: 20 units and 50 units.

The range is a measure of a distance between the viewer and the center of your shape. By default, shapes are assumed to be at the current origin (the tip of the VRML virtual pen). If you've designed your shape to be centered somewhere other than the origin, you can tell the browser, and it correctly computes viewer-to-shape-center ranges.

Controlling Level of Detail

The example text in Figure 21.1 uses an **LOD** node to select among three different versions of a shape (in this case, a torch for a dungeon room).

```
#VRML V1.0 ascii

# Switch between torch versions
LOD {
      range [ 15.0, 25.0 ]
      center 0.0 0.0 0.0
      WWWInline {
            name "dtorch1.wrl"
            bboxSize   0.8 3.0 0.8
            bboxCenter 0.0 0.0 0.0
      }
      WWWInline {
            name "dtorch2.wrl"
            bboxSize   0.8 3.0 0.8
            bboxCenter 0.0 0.0 0.0
      }
      WWWInline {
            name "dtorch3.wrl"
            bboxSize   0.8 3.0 0.8
            bboxCenter 0.0 0.0 0.0
      }
}
```

Figure 21.1 *Switching among torches created at different levels of detail.*

Notice the structure and order of the VRML file in Figure 21.1. The LOD node creates a level-of-detail group containing three children, each one a **WWWInline** node that loads a different version of a shape. The **range** and **center** fields of the **LOD** node specify range values for switching among the three children and specify the center of the shape.

Understanding the **LOD** Node Syntax

The **LOD** node has two fields, **range** and **center,** used to control the selection of detail level. The curly braces of an **LOD** node group together the list of child nodes contained within the level-of-detail group.

SYNTAX **LOD node**

```
LOD {
      range         [ ]                  # range list
      center         0.0 0.0 0.0         # X, Y, Z coordinate
}
```

The **center** field provides the X, Y, Z coordinate of the center of the shape. By default, this is the origin.

TIP *The shape is assumed to be at the coordinate specified in the* ***center*** *field. It will not be moved there. If the center point you give is wrong, the browser's range computations will be incorrect and level-of-detail switching will not operate properly.*

The **range** field provides a list of viewer-to-shape distances at which the browser is to switch from one level of detail to another. If there are *N* different detail versions of a shape, specify *N*–1 range values. You can specify any number of range values and detail versions you like, though typically there are just two or three versions of varying levels of detail and one or two range values.

While drawing your world, the browser computes the distance between the viewer and the **center** field coordinate. That distance is then compared with each value in the **range** field's list. When the distance is less than the first range value, the VRML browser is directed to draw the first child of the **LOD** node. When the distance is larger than the first range, but smaller than the second, the VRML browser is directed to draw the second child, and so on.

TIP *List range values in increasing order, and specify them as positive values. Unordered and negative ranges may cause your VRML browser to incorrectly compute which level of detail to use.*

TIP *If there are* N *children in the* ***LOD*** *node, then there should be* N–1 *range values. If there are fewer range values than children, then the last few children will never be drawn. If there are more range values than children, the last child is used repeatedly for each of the extra range values.*

The **center** field coordinate and each of the **range** field values are transformed by translation, rotation, scale, and other transforms.

The **LOD** node creates a level-of-detail group similar to that created by the **Group** node. Property changes made by children within a level-of-detail group affect how nodes following the **LOD** node draw shapes.

TIP *In version 1.1 of VRML, the* ***LOD*** *node may be changed so that it saves and restores all properties upon entry to and exit from the group. This will make it similar to a* ***Separator*** *group.*

Experimenting with Level of Detail

The following examples provide a more detailed examination of the ways in which level of detail can be controlled. These examples build a simple dungeon environment consisting of a room, a door in the room, and a second room behind the door. Along the walls are occasional flaming torches. The walls, floor, ceiling, and door are all texture-mapped. Figure 21.2 and color plate 4*d* show the end result.

Figure 21.2 *The final dungeon.*

Creating Multiple Detail Versions of a Shape

Before building the walls, floor, and ceiling of the dungeon, we build a flaming torch to put on the dungeon's walls. When close to the torch, it has enough detail to look realistic. When farther away, the torch is drawn with less detail. When far away, the torch can be reduced to only very basic shapes. After designing these three versions of the torch, we use a **LOD** node to switch among them.

The example text in Figure 21.3 creates the high-detail version of the torch. It uses two cylinders and a few faces to create the fire pot at the head of the torch. The torch handle is an upside-down cone. The bracket to hold the torch to the wall is created using a cylinder and a cube. Flames within the torch's fire pot are triangular faces of varying orange and red colors. Additional flame triangles are drawn so that the flames are apparent from any viewing angle.

```
#VRML V1.0 ascii

# Torch - high detail
# Two rings around fire pot
Material {
      ambientColor 0.2 0.2 0.2
      diffuseColor 0.2 0.2 0.2
      specularColor 0.7 0.7 0.7
}
Separator {
      Cylinder {
            parts SIDES
            height 0.10
            radius 0.40
      }
      Translation {
            translation 0.0 0.2 0.0
      }
```

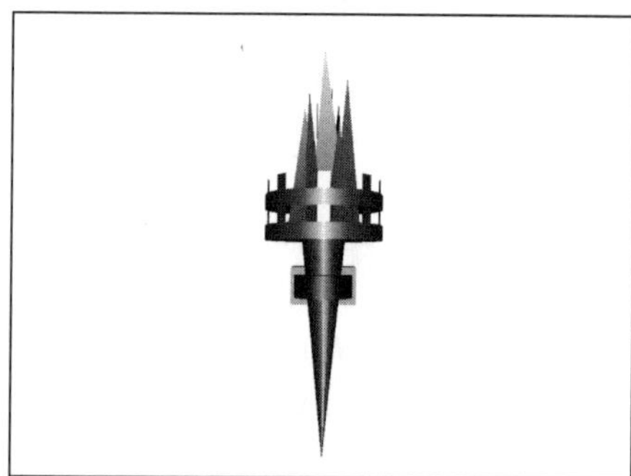

Figure 21.3 continues

```
      Cylinder {
            parts SIDES
            height 0.10
            radius 0.40
      }
}
# Vertical bars on fire pot
Separator {
      Coordinate3 {
            point [
                   0.04 0.00 0.38,
                   0.04 0.35 0.38,
                  -0.04 0.35 0.38,
                  -0.04 0.00 0.38
            ]
      }
      Rotation {
            #             Y         -90.0 degrees
            rotation 0.0 1.0 0.0  -1.57
      }
      DEF bar IndexedFaceSet {
            coordIndex [
                  0, 1, 2, 3
            ]
      }
      DEF rot Rotation {
            #             Y        +45.0 degrees
            rotation 0.0 1.0 0.0  0.785
      }
      USE bar USE rot
      USE bar USE rot
      USE bar USE rot
      USE bar
}
# Torch handle
Separator {
      Translation {
            translation 0.0 -0.75 0.0
      }
      Rotation {
            #        X             +180.0 degrees
            rotation 1.0 0.0 0.0  3.14
      }
      Cone {
            height 1.5
            bottomRadius 0.15
      }
}
```

Figure 21.3 continues

```
# Torch mounting bracket
Separator {
      Material {
            ambientColor 0.0 0.0 0.0
            diffuseColor 0.0 0.0 0.0
            specularColor 0.6 0.6 0.6
      }
      Translation {
            translation 0.0 -0.35 0.0
      }
      Cylinder {
            height 0.15
            radius 0.20
      }
      Translation {
            translation 0.0 0.0 -0.2
      }
      Cube {
            width 0.45
            height 0.25
            depth 0.39
      }
}
# Fire
Separator {
      MaterialBinding {
            value PER_VERTEX_INDEXED
      }
      Coordinate3 {
            point [
                   0.25 0.0 0.00,
                   0.15 1.0 0.10,
                   0.05 0.0 0.15,
                   0.18 0.0 0.05,
                   0.00 1.2 0.05,
                  -0.10 0.0 0.05,
                  -0.00 0.0 0.15,
                  -0.13 0.8 0.10,
                  -0.25 0.0 0.00,
            ]
      }
      Material {
            diffuseColor [
                  1.0 0.0 0.0,
                  0.9 0.5 0.0,
                  1.0 0.0 0.0,
                  0.9 0.3 0.0,
                  1.0 1.0 0.0,
                  0.9 0.3 0.0,
                  0.7 0.1 0.2,
                  0.9 0.8 0.0,
                  1.0 0.0 0.0,
            ]
      }
```

Figure 21.3 continues

```
        DEF flames IndexedFaceSet {
            coordIndex [
                0, 1, 2, -1,
                3, 4, 5, -1,
                6, 7, 8, -1,
            ]
        }
        # Additional flames
        Separator {
            Transform {
                #          Y        +90.0 degrees
                rotation 0.0 1.0 0.0  1.57
                scaleFactor 0.9 0.9 1.0
            }
            USE flames
        }
        Separator {
            Transform {
                #          Y        -90.0 degrees
                rotation 0.0 1.0 0.0  -1.57
                scaleFactor 0.9 0.9 1.0
            }
            USE flames
        }
    }
```

Figure 21.3 *High-detail torch.*

You can get a rough idea of the complexity of the high-detail torch by counting the number of coordinates used by all of its shapes. Each cylinder in the fire pot and in the mounting bracket contains about 32 coordinates, for a total of 96 coordinates. The cone handle uses another 17 coordinates. The cube on the mounting bracket, and the vertical bars on the fire pot add another 28 coordinates. Finally, the flame requires another 28 coordinates. The total complexity of the high-detail torch is, then, about 168 coordinates. While this is by no means a perfect measure of how hard this shape is to draw for the VRML browser, it is at least a partial measure and something you can look at when trying to reduce the shape's detail to create medium- and low-detail versions.

When the torch is some distance from the viewer, some of the detail can be dropped without the viewer noticing. In particular, the fire pot at the head of the torch can be drawn more simply by eliminating the vertical faces. The wall-mounting bracket also can be skipped. These two simplifications reduce the shape's coordinate count by 60 coordinates—about a 36 percent reduction from the original shape.

The example text in Figure 21.4 creates this medium-detail version of the torch.

```
#VRML V1.0 ascii

# Torch - medium detail
# Two rings around fire pot
Material {
      ambientColor 0.2 0.2 0.2
      diffuseColor 0.2 0.2 0.2
      specularColor 0.7 0.7 0.7
}
Separator {
      Cylinder {
            parts SIDES
            height 0.10
            radius 0.40
      }
      Translation {
            translation 0.0 0.2 0.0
      }
      Cylinder {
            parts SIDES
            height 0.10
            radius 0.40
      }
}
# Vertical bars on fire pot
# None
# Torch handle
Separator {
      Translation {
            translation 0.0 -0.75 0.0
      }
      Rotation {
            #        X            +180.0 degrees
            rotation 1.0 0.0 0.0  3.14
      }
      Cone {
            height 1.5
            bottomRadius 0.15
      }
}
# Torch mounting bracket
# None
# Fire
Separator {
      MaterialBinding {
            value PER_VERTEX_INDEXED
      }
```

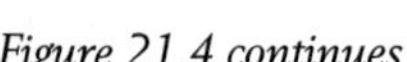

Figure 21.4 continues

```
Coordinate3 {
      point [
             0.25 0.0 0.00,
             0.15 1.0 0.10,
             0.05 0.0 0.15,
             0.18 0.0 0.05,
             0.00 1.2 0.05,
            -0.10 0.0 0.05,
            -0.00 0.0 0.15,
            -0.13 0.8 0.10,
            -0.25 0.0 0.00,
      ]
}
Material {
      diffuseColor [
            1.0 0.0 0.0,
            0.9 0.5 0.0,
            1.0 0.0 0.0,
            0.9 0.3 0.0,
            1.0 1.0 0.0,
            0.9 0.3 0.0,
            0.7 0.1 0.2,
            0.9 0.8 0.0,
            1.0 0.0 0.0,
      ]
}
DEF flames IndexedFaceSet {
      coordIndex [
            0, 1, 2, -1,
            3, 4, 5, -1,
            6, 7, 8, -1,
      ]
      materialIndex [
            0, 1, 2, -1,
            3, 4, 5, -1,
            6, 7, 8, -1,
      ]
}
# Additional flames
Separator {
      Transform {
            #          Y       +90.0 degrees
            rotation 0.0 1.0 0.0  1.57
            scaleFactor 0.9 0.9 1.0
      }
      USE flames
}
```

Figure 21.4 continues

```
        Separator {
            Transform {
                #               Y         -90.0 degrees
                rotation 0.0 1.0 0.0  -1.57
                scaleFactor 0.9 0.9 1.0
            }
            USE flames
        }
    }
```

Figure 21.4 *Medium-detail torch.*

Finally, when the torch is quite distant, the shape can be simplified considerably. The cylinders for the fire pot can be drawn as simple 2-D faces. Similarly, the torch handle can be changed to a downward-pointing 2-D triangle face. The flames can be reduced to a single orange triangle. The resulting shape uses only 14 coordinates, about a 92 percent reduction from the original shape.

The example text in Figure 21.5 creates the low-detail version of the torch.

```
#VRML V1.0 ascii

# Torch - low detail
# Two rings around fire pot
Material {
    ambientColor 0.2 0.2 0.2
    diffuseColor 0.3 0.3 0.3
    specularColor 0.0 0.0 0.0
}
Separator {
    # Just use a single flat face for each
    Coordinate3 {
        point [
            # Flattened ring 1
            -0.40  0.05 0.1,
            -0.40 -0.05 0.1,
             0.40 -0.05 0.1,
             0.40  0.05 0.1,
            # Flattened ring 2
            -0.40  0.25 0.1,
            -0.40  0.15 0.1,
             0.40  0.15 0.1,
             0.40  0.25 0.1,
        ]
    }
    IndexedFaceSet {
        coordIndex [
            0, 1, 2, 3, -1,
            4, 5, 6, 7
        ]
    }
}
```

Figure 21.5 continues

```
# Vertical bars on fire pot
# None
# Torch handle
Separator {
      # Just use a single flat face
      Coordinate3 {
            point [
                  -0.15  0.0 0.0,
                   0.00 -1.5 0.0,
                   0.15  0.0 0.0
            ]
      }
      IndexedFaceSet {
            coordIndex [
                  0, 1, 2
            ]
      }
}
# Torch mounting bracket
# None
# Fire
Separator {
      # Just one flame point and just one color
      Coordinate3 {
            point [
                   0.18 0.0 0.05,
                   0.00 1.2 0.05,
                  -0.18 0.0 0.05,
            ]
      }
      Material {
            diffuseColor 0.9 0.3 0.0
      }
      IndexedFaceSet {
            coordIndex [
                  0, 1, 2,
            ]
      }
      # Additional flames
      # None
}
```

Figure 21.5 *Low-detail torch.*

Switching Among Detailed Shapes

The example text in Figure 21.6 draws the three torch versions side by side.

```
#VRML V1.0 ascii

# All three torches, side-by-side
# Torch 1 - high detail
Separator {
      Translation {
            translation -1.0 0.0 0.0
      }
      WWWInline {
            name "dtorch1.wrl"
            bboxSize   0.8 3.0 0.8
            bboxCenter 0.0 0.0 0.0
      }
}
# Torch 2 - medium detail
Separator {
      WWWInline {
            name "dtorch2.wrl"
            bboxSize   0.8 3.0 0.8
            bboxCenter 0.0 0.0 0.0
      }
}
# Torch 3 - low detail
Separator {
      Translation {
            translation 1.0 0.0 0.0
      }
      WWWInline {
            name "dtorch3.wrl"
            bboxSize   0.8 3.0 0.8
            bboxCenter 0.0 0.0 0.0
      }
}
```

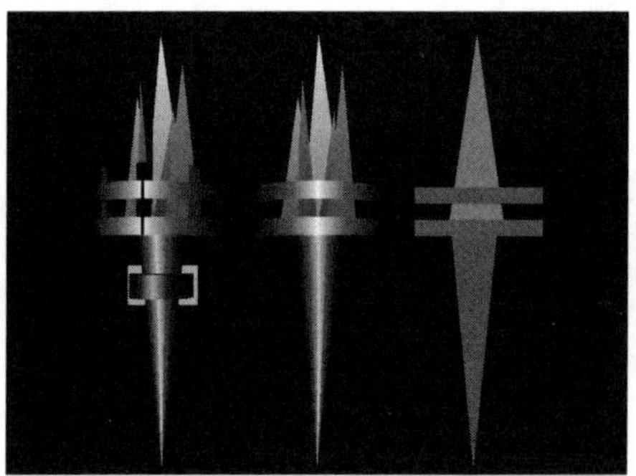

Figure 21.6 *The three torches side by side.*

The high-detail version of the shape is read in from the file `dtorch1.wrl` by a **WWWInline** node. Similarly, the medium- and low-detail versions are read in from `dtorch2.wrl` and `dtorch3.wrl`. Notice that bounding boxes have been set for all three **WWWInline** nodes using the **bboxSize** and **bboxCenter** fields. Since all three torch files define the same shape, though at different detail levels, they all have the same bounding box.

Eventually, we'll use an **LOD** node to direct the VRML browser to automatically switch between the torch versions based on a range from the viewer to the torch. You can use the preceding three-torch file to help you decide what range to specify for each torch version. Using your browser, start with all three torches close up, then gradually move back in the world. Stop moving when the high- and medium-detail torches appear approximately the same. Since you can no longer see the added detail of the high-detail torch, this distance is a good point to switch from the high- to medium-detail torch. Many VRML browsers have a menu item to show you the current viewpoint position. Jot down this position.

Now move farther away from the torches until the medium- and low-detail versions of the torches look approximately the same. Jot down this viewpoint position.

Ranges of 15.0 and 25.0 units work well for switching among the three torch versions. Using these ranges, you can now place all three torches within an **LOD** node to direct your VRML browser to switch among them automatically. The example text in Figure 21.7 shows the file `dtorch.wrl`.

```
#VRML V1.0 ascii

# Switch between torch versions
LOD {
        range [ 15.0, 25.0 ]
        center 0.0 0.0 0.0
        WWWInline {
                name "dtorch1.wrl"
                bboxSize   0.8 3.0 0.8
                bboxCenter 0.0 0.0 0.0
        }
        WWWInline {
                name "dtorch2.wrl"
                bboxSize   0.8 3.0 0.8
                bboxCenter 0.0 0.0 0.0
        }
        WWWInline {
                name "dtorch3.wrl"
                bboxSize   0.8 3.0 0.8
                bboxCenter 0.0 0.0 0.0
        }
}
```

Figure 21.7 *Switching among torches.*

The **LOD** node groups together the three versions of the torch, listed from high detail to low detail within the group. The **range** field is set to the two range switch points determined by the previous experiment: 15.0 units and 25.0 units. Since the torch was built centered at the origin, the **center** field of the **LOD** node is set to `0.0 0.0 0.0`.

Using your VRML browser, you can experiment to confirm that the range values are right and tweak them if they are not. Start close to the torch. The high-detail torch version is drawn, since the distance between you and the torch is less than the first range value. Slowly move back away from the torch. At 15.0 units away, the torch is switched from the high-detail version to the medium-detail version. At 25.0 units away the torch is switched again, this time from the medium-detail version to the low-detail version. As you move still farther away, the low-detail version will dwindle in size but not change again. The low-detail version remains in use at any farther distances.

You can use this kind of detail switching to change automatically among different versions of any shape. On a city street, for instance, cars in the distance can be drawn with low detail, while those nearby are drawn with high detail. Street signs near you can include **AsciiText** nodes for the sign text, while those farther away can be drawn only as blank sign shapes.

Simple Animation Using Detail Levels

While the **LOD** node is not designed for animation, it can be used to create simple animation effects. You can, for instance, make several versions of a shape, each rotated, translated, or scaled slightly differently. Then, using an **LOD** node to switch among them, the shapes appear to animate as you move closer to them.

You can use this animation effect to cause a door in a room to gradually open as you approach. The example text in Figure 21.8 starts by creating a door to animate. The door is drawn as a texture-mapped face, followed by a set of faces to draw a door handle.

```
#VRML V1.0 ascii

# Dungeon door
Separator {
      Material {
            ambientColor 0.8 0.8 0.8
            diffuseColor 0.8 0.8 0.8
            emissiveColor 0.4 0.4 0.4
      }
      Coordinate3 {
            point [
                   1.50 0.00 0.01,
                   1.50 4.50 0.01,
                   1.39 5.07 0.01,
                   1.06 5.56 0.01,
                   0.57 5.89 0.01,
                   0.00 6.00 0.01,
                  -0.57 5.89 0.01,
                  -1.06 5.56 0.01,
                  -1.39 5.07 0.01,
                  -1.50 4.50 0.01,
                  -1.50 0.00 0.00
            ]
      }
      Texture2 {
            filename "wood8.gif"
      }
```

Figure 21.8 continues

```
        TextureCoordinate2 {
              point [
                     1.50 0.00,
                     1.50 4.50,
                     1.39 5.07,
                     1.06 5.56,
                     0.57 5.89,
                     0.00 6.00,
                    -0.57 5.89,
                    -1.06 5.56,
                    -1.39 5.07,
                    -1.50 4.50,
                    -1.50 0.00,
              ]
        }
        Texture2Transform {
              scaleFactor 0.22 0.15
        }
        IndexedFaceSet {
              coordIndex [
                     0, 1, 2, 3, 4, 5, 6, 7, 8, 9, 10
              ]
        }
  }
  # Dungeon door handle
  Separator {
        Material {
              ambientColor 0.2 0.2 0.2
              diffuseColor 0.2 0.2 0.2
              specularColor 0.5 0.5 0.5
        }
        Coordinate3 {
              point [
                    # Door plate
                    1.30 2.20 0.02,
                    1.30 3.20 0.02,
                    0.90 3.20 0.02,
                    0.90 2.20 0.02,
```

Figure 21.8 continues

```
                    # Door handle
                    1.20 3.10 0.02,
                    1.20 2.90 0.20,
                    1.20 2.50 0.20,
                    1.20 2.30 0.02,
                    1.20 3.00 0.02,
                    1.20 2.90 0.10,
                    1.20 2.50 0.10,
                    1.20 2.40 0.02,
                    1.00 3.10 0.02,
                    1.00 2.90 0.20,
                    1.00 2.50 0.20,
                    1.00 2.30 0.02,
                    1.00 3.00 0.02,
                    1.00 2.90 0.10,
                    1.00 2.50 0.10,
                    1.00 2.40 0.02,
              ]
        }
        IndexedFaceSet {
              coordIndex [
                    # Plate
                     0,  1,  2,  3, -1,
                    # Handle top
                     4, 12, 13,  5, -1,
                     5, 13, 14,  6, -1,
                     6, 14, 15,  7, -1,
                    # Handle right side
                     8,  4,  5,  9, -1,
                     9,  5,  6, 10, -1,
                    10,  6,  7, 11, -1,
                    # Handle left side
                    16, 17, 13, 12, -1,
                    17, 18, 14, 13, -1,
                    18, 19, 15, 14, -1,
              ]
        }
  }
```

Figure 21.8 *A texture-mapped dungeon door.*

Using the door, you can create three versions: one fully open, one half open, and one closed. These are grouped as children of an **LOD** node, and the **range** field is set to select the closed door when you are far away, the half-open door when you are somewhat close, and the fully open door when you are very close. Moving toward the door opens the door for you.

The example text in Figure 21.9 shows the **LOD** node switching among these three door versions. The original door is inlined from the file `ddoor.wrl`.

```
#VRML V1.0 ascii

# Dungeon doorway
LOD {
      range [ 9.0, 10.0 ]
      # Open door
      Separator {
            Transform {
                  #            Y        +90.0 degrees
                  rotation 0.0 1.0 0.0  1.57
                  center -1.5 0.0 0.0
            }
            DEF door WWWInline {
                  name "ddoor.wrl"
            }
      }
      # Half-open door
      Separator {
            Transform {
                  #            Y        +45.0 degrees
                  rotation 0.0 1.0 0.0  0.785
                  center -1.5 0.0 0.0
            }
            USE door
      }
      # Closed door
      USE door
}
```

Figure 21.9 *Switching among versions of the door.*

The door can now be integrated into a room by building walls, floor, and ceiling and then inlining the door itself. To create a dungeon-like effect, a rock wall texture is used for the walls, floor, and ceiling.

The example text in Figure 21.10, saved in file `dwall.wrl`, creates a blank wall for the dungeon.

```
#VRML V1.0 ascii

# Dungeon room wall
Material {
      ambientColor 0.8 0.8 0.8
      diffuseColor 0.8 0.8 0.8
      emissiveColor 0.4 0.4 0.4
}
```

Figure 21.10 continues

```
Coordinate3 {
      point [
            -5.0 7.0 0.0,
            -5.0 0.0 0.0,
             5.0 0.0 0.0,
             5.0 7.0 0.0,
      ]
}
Texture2 {
      filename "rockface.gif"
}
TextureCoordinate2 {
      point [
            0.0 2.0,
            0.0 0.0,
            2.0 0.0,
            2.0 2.0,
      ]
}
IndexedFaceSet {
      coordIndex [
            0, 1, 2, 3,
      ]
}
```

Figure 21.10 *The dungeon wall.*

The example text in Figure 21.11, saved in file `dwalldr.wrl`, defines a second wall that contains an archway for a door. Notice how a series of simple faces, each with a warped bit of rock-wall texture, are used to create the keystone archway for the door.

```
#VRML V1.0 ascii

# Dungeon wall with a doorway arch in the middle
# Dungeon wall
Material {
      ambientColor 0.8 0.8 0.8
      diffuseColor 0.8 0.8 0.8
      emissiveColor 0.4 0.4 0.4
}
Coordinate3 {
      point [
            # Left side of doorway
            -5.0 7.0 0.0,
            -5.0 0.0 0.0,
            -2.0 0.0 0.0,
            -2.0 7.0 0.0,
            # Right side of doorway
             2.0 7.0 0.0,
             2.0 0.0 0.0,
             5.0 0.0 0.0,
             5.0 7.0 0.0,
```

Figure 21.11 continues

```
                # Left triangular filler
                -2.0 4.5 0.0,
                -1.0 6.0 0.0,
                -2.0 6.0 0.0,
                # Right triangular filler
                 2.0 4.5 0.0,
                 2.0 6.0 0.0,
                 1.0 6.0 0.0,
                # Above the door
                -2.0 6.0 0.0,
                 2.0 6.0 0.0,
                 2.0 7.0 0.0,
                -2.0 7.0 0.0,
          ]
}
Texture2 {
      filename "rockface.gif"
}
TextureCoordinate2 {
      point [
            # Left side of doorway
            0.0 2.0,
            0.0 0.0,
            0.6 0.0,
            0.6 2.0,
            # Right side of doorway
            0.4 2.0,
            0.4 0.0,
            1.0 0.0,
            1.0 2.0,
            # Left triangular filler
            0.6 0.286,
            0.8 0.715,
            0.6 0.715,
            # Right triangular filler
            0.4 0.286,
            0.4 0.715,
            0.2 0.715,
            # Above the door
            0.6 0.715,
            1.4 0.715,
            1.4 1.0,
            0.6 1.0,
      ]
}
IndexedFaceSet {
      coordIndex [
             0,  1,  2,  3, -1,
             4,  5,  6,  7, -1,
             8,  9, 10, -1,
            11, 12, 13, -1,
            14, 15, 16, 17
      ]
}
```

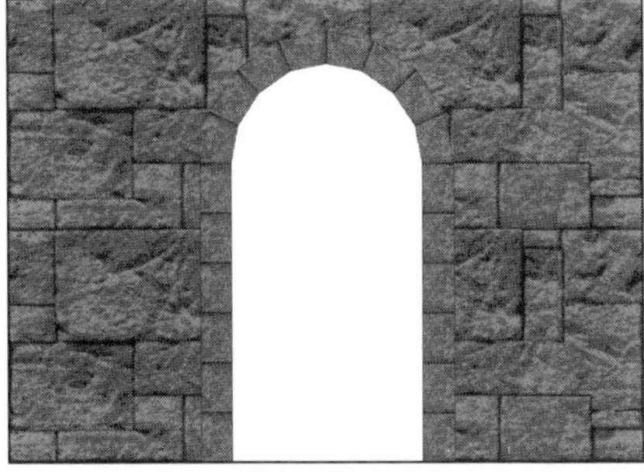

Figure 21.11 continues

```
# Dungeon door archway
Material {
      ambientColor 0.7 0.7 0.7
      diffuseColor 0.7 0.7 0.7
      emissiveColor 0.3 0.3 0.3
}
Coordinate3 {
      point [
             # Inside of arch, next to door
             1.50 0.00 0.01,
             1.50 4.50 0.01,
             1.39 5.07 0.01,
             1.06 5.56 0.01,
             0.57 5.89 0.01,
             0.00 6.00 0.01,
            -0.57 5.89 0.01,
            -1.06 5.56 0.01,
            -1.39 5.07 0.01,
            -1.50 4.50 0.01,
            -1.50 0.00 0.01,
            # Outside of arch
             2.00 0.00 0.01,
             2.00 4.50 0.01,
             1.85 5.27 0.01,
             1.41 5.91 0.01,
             0.77 6.35 0.01,
             0.00 6.50 0.01,
            -0.77 6.35 0.01,
            -1.41 5.91 0.01,
            -1.85 5.27 0.01,
            -2.00 4.50 0.01,
            -2.00 0.00 0.01,
      ]
}
Texture2 {
      filename "rock.gif"
}
TextureCoordinate2 {
      point [
             0.0 0.0,
             1.0 0.0,
             1.0 1.0,
             0.0 1.0,
             1.0 6.0,
             0.0 6.0,
      ]
}
```

Figure 21.11 continues

```
IndexedFaceSet {
	coordIndex [
		0, 11, 12, 1, -1,
		1, 12, 13, 2, -1,
		2, 13, 14, 3, -1,
		3, 14, 15, 4, -1,
		4, 15, 16, 5, -1,
		5, 16, 17, 6, -1,
		6, 17, 18, 7, -1,
		7, 18, 19, 8, -1,
		8, 19, 20, 9, -1,
		9, 20, 21, 10, -1,
	]
	textureCoordIndex [
		0, 1, 4, 5, -1,
		0, 1, 2, 3, -1,
		0, 1, 2, 3, -1,
		0, 1, 2, 3, -1,
		0, 1, 2, 3, -1,
		0, 1, 2, 3, -1,
		0, 1, 2, 3, -1,
		0, 1, 2, 3, -1,
		0, 1, 2, 3, -1,
		0, 1, 4, 5, -1,
	]
}
```

Figure 21.11 *All wall with a doorway in it.*

The example text in Figure 21.12, saved in file `dfloor.wrl`, defines a floor and a ceiling, both drawn with a dark repeating rock-block texture.

```
#VRML V1.0 ascii

# Dungeon room floor and ceiling
Coordinate3 {
	point [
		-5.0 0.0 -5.0,
		-5.0 0.0  5.0,
		 5.0 0.0  5.0,
		 5.0 0.0 -5.0,
		-5.0 7.0 -5.0,
		-5.0 7.0  5.0,
		 5.0 7.0  5.0,
		 5.0 7.0 -5.0
	]
}
Texture2 {
	filename "rock.gif"
}
```

Figure 21.12 continues

```
TextureCoordinate2 {
      point [
             0.0 8.0,
             0.0 0.0,
             8.0 0.0,
             8.0 8.0,
      ]
}
# Floor
Material {
      ambientColor 0.5 0.5 0.5
      diffuseColor 0.8 0.8 0.8
      emissiveColor 0.2 0.2 0.2
}
IndexedFaceSet {
      coordIndex [
            0, 1, 2, 3
      ]
      textureCoordIndex [
            0, 1, 2, 3
      ]
}
# Ceiling
Material {
      ambientColor 0.3 0.3 0.3
      diffuseColor 0.8 0.8 0.8
      emissiveColor 0.2 0.2 0.2
}
IndexedFaceSet {
      coordIndex [
            7, 6, 5, 4
      ]
      textureCoordIndex [
            0, 1, 2, 3
      ]
}
```

Figure 21.12 *The dungeon floor and ceiling.*

Finally, you can put all these pieces together to build a dungeon. The floor, ceiling, left, and right walls use the room pieces given before. The room's back wall is built from the wall with the arch in it. The animated door is added, along with two copies of the torch. The example text in Figure 21.13, saved in file `droom.wrl`, is the result.

```
#VRML V1.0 ascii

# Dungeon room
# Room floor and ceiling
DEF floor WWWInline {
     name "dfloor.wrl"
}
```

Figure 21.13 continues

```
# Left wall
Separator {
      Transform {
            translation -5.0 0.0 0.0
            rotation 0.0 1.0 0.0  1.57
      }
      DEF wall WWWInline {
            name "dwall.wrl"
      }
}
# Right wall
Separator {
      Transform {
            translation 5.0 0.0 0.0
            rotation 0.0 1.0 0.0 -1.57
      }
      USE wall
}
# Back wall
Separator {
      Translation {
            translation 0.0 0.0 -5.0
      }
      DEF wall WWWInline {
            name "dwalldr.wrl"
      }
      DEF door WWWInline {
            name "ddoorway.wrl"
      }
      Translation {
            translation -3.5 4.5 0.4
      }
      DEF torch WWWInline {
            name "dtorch.wrl"
      }
      Translation {
            translation 7.0 0.0 0.0
      }
      USE torch
}
```

Figure 21.13 *The final room with opening door and torches.*

Figure 21.13 shows the room from far away, closer, and very close. Notice how the door swings open ahead of you as you approach. Notice also that both torches switch their detail level when you move closer or farther away.

Turning Shapes On and Off Automatically

A room, like the dungeon room previously described, is typically just one part of a much larger, more complex world. The room by itself is already relatively complex. As you add more and more rooms, the number of shapes to draw increases and the VRML browser can slow when trying to draw all of them.

Notice, however, that while inside one room, all further rooms need not be drawn since they are on the other side of opaque walls. The VRML browser can't optimize in this way automatically. While drawing a room described early in a VRML file, it does not know if there will be any walls drawn later in the file that will block the view of that room. Since the browser doesn't know whether the room will or will not be blocked from view, it is forced to draw the entire room.

You can optimize in this way using the **LOD** node. Consider, for example, that each room can have two detail versions. The high-detail version contains a full description of a room and is used only when the room is visible to the viewer, such as when the viewer is in it. The low-detail version of a room contains nothing: no walls, floor, ceiling, door, or anything. It is a completely empty list of nodes and is to be used only when the room is not visible to the viewer, such as when it is on the other side of an opaque wall.

Using these two versions of a room, switch between them with an **LOD** node. Set the node's **range** field to select the full room when the viewer walks through a door, and select the empty room when the viewer is on the other side of the door.

For example, you can create a second room on the other side of the first room's door. Draw the second room only when the animated door first opens. When the door is closed, don't draw the second room.

The example text in Figure 21.14 draws the two rooms, each one contained in the file `droom.wrl`.

```
#VRML V1.0 ascii

# Two dungeon rooms
# First room
LOD {
      range [ 15.0 ]
      center 0.0 0.0 0.0
      # When close, draw the room
      DEF room WWWInline {
            name "droom.wrl"
      }
      # When far, do nothing
      Separator {
      }
}
# Second room
Translation {
      translation 0.0 0.0 -10.0
}
```

Figure 21.14 continues

```
LOD {
        range [ 15.0 ]
        center 0.0 0.0 0.0
        # When close, draw the room
        USE room
        # When far, do nothing
        Separator {
        }
}
```

Figure 21.14 *Two dungeon rooms.*

This example places both rooms in **LOD** nodes. The second room is drawn only when the first room's door opens. The first room, however, is drawn only while you are in it or near it. After you move into the second room, the first room disappears. This is more obvious if you move into the second room, then turn around and look back. If you are far into the second room when you look back, the first room will not be there. That side of the second room will be empty. As you move back toward the first room again, it reappears.

Notice that the torches automatically switch between detail versions as you move between the two rooms. Also notice that the second room's door animates open as you approach, just like in the first room, but independent of the first room.

These examples create a simple two-room dungeon. You can extend these examples to add a front wall to both rooms, some thickness to the walls, additional doors, more rooms, hallways, furniture, and so forth. You can also experiment with lighting by adding point lights located at each torch. You may want to convert each wall to a mesh in order to get a good lighting effect.

You can also try making three copies of each room, all within a **LOD** node. For the first copy, add a bright point light in the center of the room. For the second, add a dim point light. For the third, use a very dim point light. Now, as you move towards the room through the door, the light in the room brightens as the browser switches from the dim version of the room to the brighter versions.

When building a long hallway with doors down the walls, try making a version of the door for use when the door is very far away. For the far door, use the same description shown earlier, but turn off texture mapping and set the door color to approximately the same wood color as used on a textured door. Without texture mapping, this far-away door is drawn more quickly. Since it is distant, the lack of texturing will likely go unnoticed by the viewer of the hallway.

Summary

The more detail you add to a world, the longer it takes the VRML browser to draw it. To maintain both high realism and high interactivity, you can control the detail level at which the VRML browser draws shapes by using **LOD** nodes.

For key shapes in your world, create multiple versions, typically high-, medium-, and low-detail versions. For the high-detail version, include all the detail needed to make the shape look realistic when you're near it. For the medium-detail version, delete some of the extra detail to simplify the shape for viewing from medium distances. For the low-detail version, reduce the shape to the bare essentials needed to make the shape look right from far away.

Collect together each of the detail versions of a shape and place them within a level of detail group managed by an **LOD** node. The **center** field of the **LOD** node indicates the center of the shape. The **LOD** node's **range** field provides a list of viewer-to-shape-center distances at which a switch from a higher- to a lower-detail version is to be made. When the viewer is closer than the first range value, the first detail version in the group will be drawn. When the viewer is farther away than the first range value, but closer than the second, the second detail version in the group will be drawn. And so on. For N different versions of a shape, there should be $N-1$ range values indicating where to switch from one to the next.

Using **LOD** nodes, you can switch between different detail versions of the same shape, perform simple animation by switching between different transformations of the same shape, and turn entire groups of shapes on and off based on their proximity.

CHAPTER 22

Using Cameras

In previous chapters, you used your VRML browser to "walk" around within a world and view it from different positions and orientations. At each new viewpoint, the browser snaps a picture, as if using a virtual camera, and displays the picture on your screen. Your movements in the world continually position and orient that camera.

It is often convenient to set up a predefined camera position in a world. Each time that world's VRML file is loaded, the browser automatically positions your viewpoint at that predefined camera position. From there, you can move around in the world and view it from additional positions and orientations.

VRML provides two node types for setting up predefined camera positions: **PerspectiveCamera** and **OrthographicCamera.**

Understanding Cameras

There are two types of cameras: **perspective cameras** and **orthographic cameras**. Each is used for different purposes and has slightly different features you can control.

Understanding Perspective Cameras

Perspective is a feature of the real world that makes things appear smaller as they get farther away. Railroad tracks, for instance, appear smaller and closer together as they recede into the distance, as in Figure 22.1.

Figure 22.1 *Railroad tracks receding into the distance.*

A **perspective camera** computes a perspective view of your VRML world. Such cameras provide a natural and realistic way of viewing worlds. In fact, the default camera for all VRML browsers is a perspective camera.

In the real world, you use different camera lenses to control how much of the world in front of you can be seen by the camera. A wide-angle lens, for instance, enables you to see a broad expanse of the world, while a telephoto lens focuses instead on a small part of the world.

The name *wide-angle lens* comes from the real-world camera lens' ability to see a wide area of the world, measured as an angle from the left edge to the right edge of what the camera sees. This viewing angle is sometimes called a **field-of-view angle** or, in VRML, a **height angle**. For VRML perspective cameras, a large height angle describes a camera lens with a tall and wide view of the world, like a real-world wide-angle lens. A smaller height angle focuses the VRML camera down to see a smaller portion of the world, like a real-world telephoto lens.

The range of the world that is visible to a VRML camera can be illustrated by a tapered box with the narrow end at the camera and the wide end at the horizon. Any shape that falls within the box is visible, while those outside of the box are beyond your peripheral vision or behind your back. As you decrease the height angle, you taper the box to make it more narrow and decrease the range of the world that is visible to the camera. If you widen the height angle, you widen the box and increase the range of the world visible to the camera.

Mathematicians call such a tapered box a **frustrum**. A frustrum that describes the range of the world visible to a camera is called a **viewing-volume frustrum**. A VRML camera uses a viewing volume like this to select the range of the VRML world that is visible from the current camera position and orientation. The VRML browser draws only those shapes that fall within the camera's viewing volume.

Figure 22.2 shows two viewing-volume frustrums, one (*a*) with a narrow height angle of 30.0 degrees, and the other (*b*) with a normal height angle of 45.0 degrees.

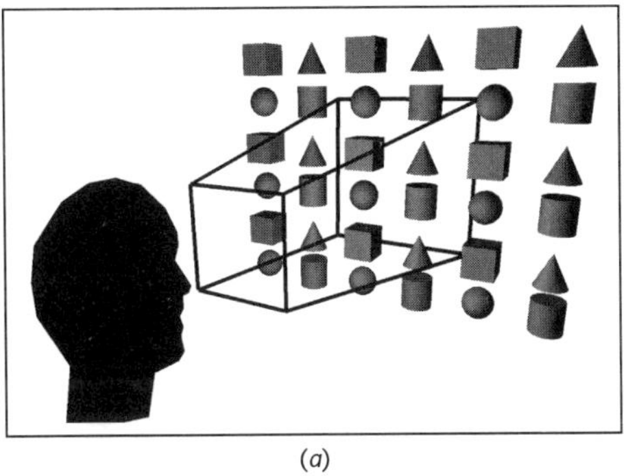

(a)

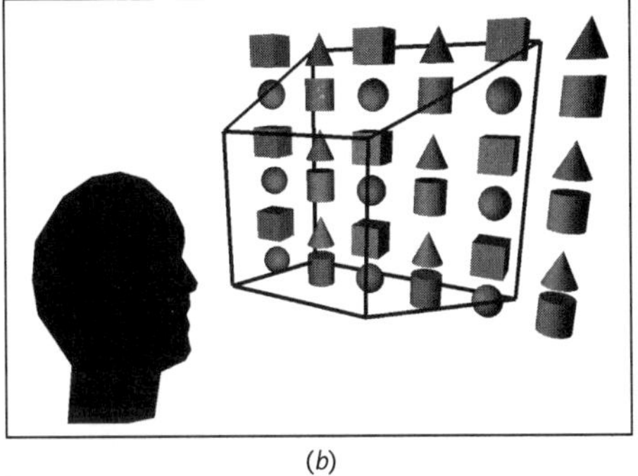

(b)

Figure 22.2 *Two viewing-volume frustrums, one with a narrow height angle (a) and one with a normal height angle (b).*

In Figure 22.2, notice that the 45.0-degree height-angle frustrum describes a taller and wider visible range of the world than the narrower 30.0-degree frustrum. If you enlarge the frustrum even further, the camera sees even more of the world. A very tall and wide frustrum with a large height angle creates an unnaturally broad view of the world like a real-world fish-eye lens.

TIP *The VRML height angle actually controls only the vertical spread angle from top to bottom of the viewing-volume frustrum. The horizontal spread angle from left to right is computed by your VRML browser based on the height angle and the size of the browser's window on your screen. If you have a perfectly square window, the vertical and horizontal spread angles are equal. If you widen the window, the horizontal spread angle increases. If you make the window thinner, the horizontal spread angle decreases.*

With many browsers, you can also control the range of shapes from front to back that are visible to a camera by changing the **near distance** to the near end of the frustrum, and the **far distance** to the far end of the frustrum. Any shape closer than the near distance or farther away than the far distance will be clipped off at the near and far boundaries of the viewing-volume frustrum.

Because the near and far distances define the distances to near and far planes that **clip** near and far shapes, they are also known as **near clipping planes** and **far clipping planes**. As you move the near clipping plane away from you into your world by increasing the near distance, you clip more and more of the nearby shapes. Similarly, if you move the far clipping plane closer to you by decreasing the far distance, you clip more and more of the further shapes. Only the band of shapes between the near and far clipping planes are drawn by the VRML browser.

Figure 22.3*a* shows a viewing volume with the near clipping plane very close, and the far clipping plane far away. Figure 22.3*b* shows the near clipping plane moved farther away, shrinking the viewing volume. Figure 22.3*c* shows the far clipping plane moved closer, which also shrinks the viewing volume. Figure 22.3*d* shows both the near and the far clipping planes moved, constricting the viewing volume so that the browser draws only a narrow slice of the world.

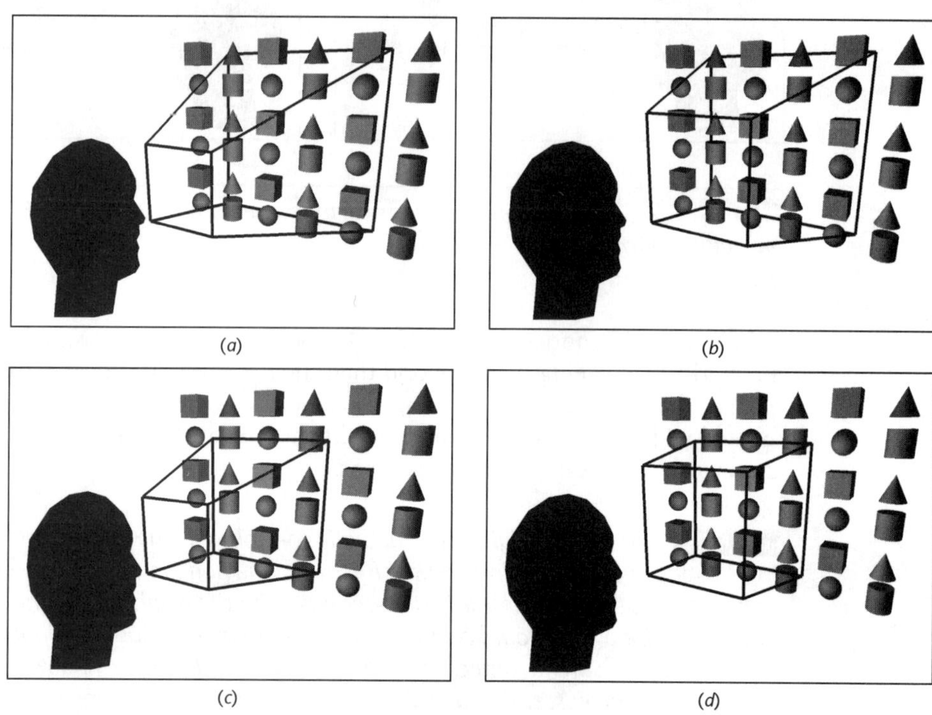

Figure 22.3 *Various viewing-volume frustrums with clipping planes moved closer and farther away.*

These near and far clipping features enable you to cut out extraneous detail nearby or far away, or even to cut away the front of a shape and look inside. This can be very helpful as you debug a complex world. Simply move the near and far clipping planes so that they are on either side of the problem area in your world. Since the VRML browser skips drawing all of the shapes outside of this narrow area, its drawing is quicker. Additionally, clipping all the extra detail in front of or behind your problem area makes it easier to see and fix the problem.

Understanding Orthographic Cameras

An **orthographic camera** draws the world without perspective so that shapes are always drawn the same size whether they are close to you or not. Figure 22.4 shows a set of railroad tracks extending into the distance. Notice, however, that they don't appear any smaller when far away.

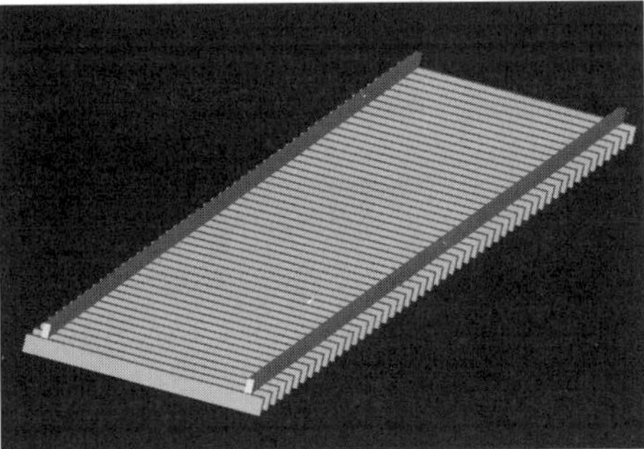

Figure 22.4 *Railroad tracks viewed with an orthographic camera.*

Visually, orthographic camera views look strange and warped. They don't mimic the real-world perspective we are used to. They are useful, however, and are commonly used to create blueprints, like those used in architectural and engineering applications. The advantage of orthographic cameras is that you can accurately compare the size of shapes using the image or blueprint. Shapes that are the same size are always drawn the same size, regardless of their distance from the orthographic camera.

When performing drafting work, such as designing a house, orthographic cameras are essential. They enable you to view your work and accurately compare sizes without the shrinking effect caused by perspective. Typically, shapes are viewed from the front, right side, and top using orthographic cameras, and then viewed with a perspective camera to add a natural view of the shape. Figure 22.5 shows such views of a simple cottage.

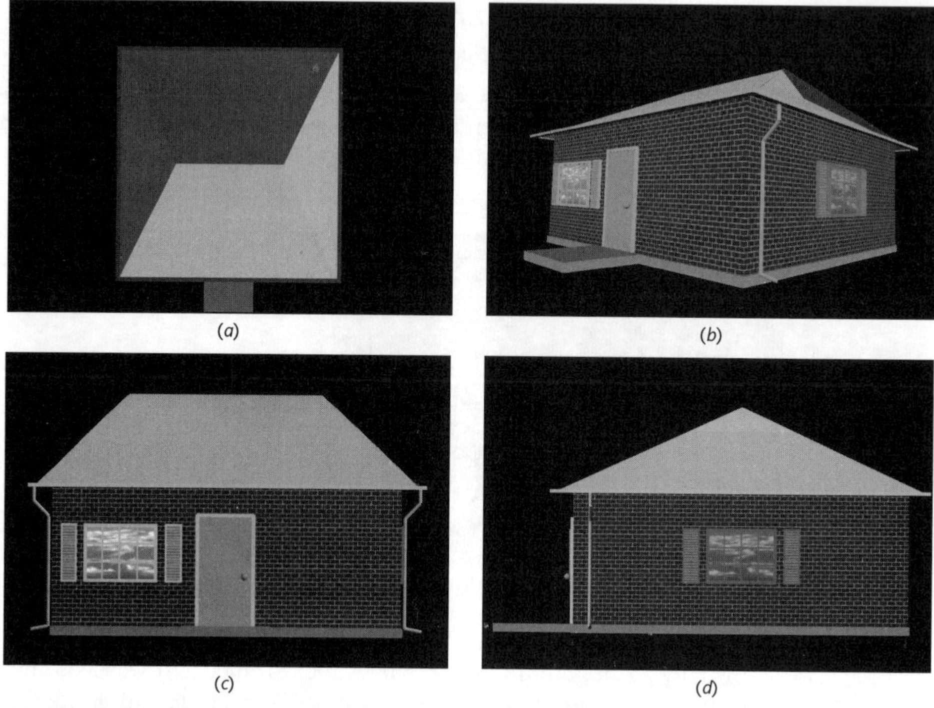

Figure 22.5 *Orthographic and perspective views of a cottage: (a) top view, (b) using a perspective camera, (c) front view, and (d) side view.*

Like perspective cameras, orthographic cameras view the world's shapes through a viewing volume. However, where a perspective camera's viewing volume is a frustrum, an orthographic camera's viewing volume is a rectangular block with parallel sides. The height of this block controls the size of the viewing volume, and thus the range of world shapes visible to the camera. Only those shapes enclosed by the orthographic camera's viewing volume are drawn.

Figure 22.6 shows two orthographic viewing volumes, (a) one with a small height and (b) a second with a larger height.

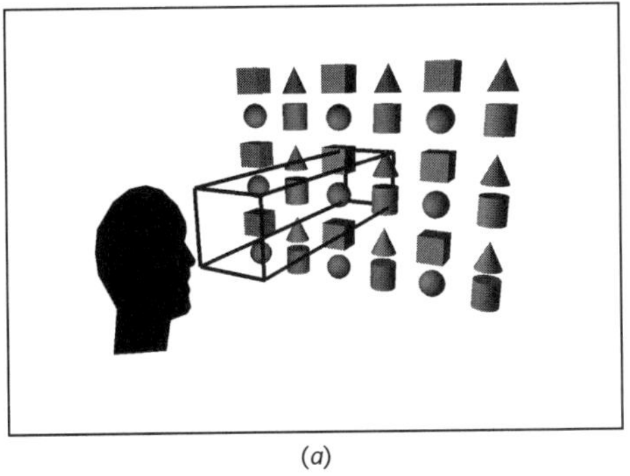

(a)

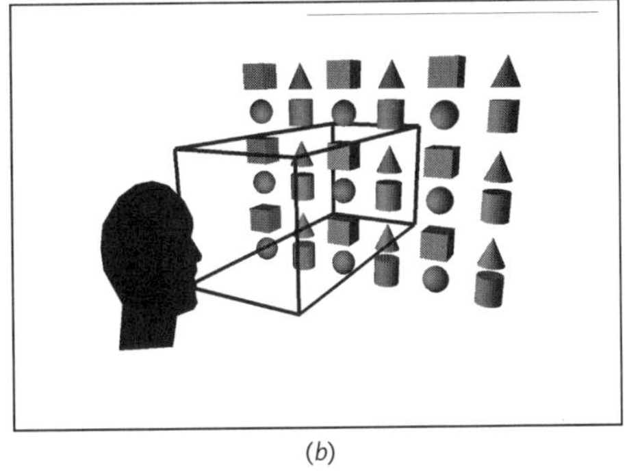

(b)

Figure 22.6 *Two orthographic viewing volumes, (a) one with a small height and (b) one with a larger height.*

TIP *The VRML height for an orthographic camera actually controls only the vertical size of the viewing volume. The horizontal size of the viewing volume is computed by your VRML browser based on the height and the size of the browser's window on your screen. If you have a perfectly square window, the vertical and horizontal sizes will be the same. If you widen the window, the horizontal viewing-volume size will increase. If you make the window thinner, the horizontal viewing-volume size will decrease.*

With many browsers, you can control the clipping planes when using orthographic cameras.

Creating Your Own Cameras

Perspective and orthographic cameras are controlled by VRML **PerspectiveCamera** and **OrthographicCamera** nodes placed at the top of any VRML file. The example text in Figure 22.7 uses a **PerspectiveCamera** node to control a camera viewing a world created by the inlined VRML file `dungeon.wrl`.

```
#VRML V1.0 ascii

PerspectiveCamera {
      position 0.0 3.5 12.0
      orientation 0.0 0.0 1.0 0.0
}
WWWInline {
      name "dungeon.wrl"
}
```

Figure 22.7 *Using a perspective camera to control world viewing.*

Notice the structure and order of the VRML file in Figure 22.7. The **PerspectiveCamera** node defines the position and orientation of a perspective camera. The **WWWInline** node that follows inlines a VRML world from the file `dungeon.wrl` and draws it from the point of view of the perspective camera.

Understanding the **PerspectiveCamera** Node Syntax

The **PerspectiveCamera** node has six fields: **position, orientation, heightAngle, focalDistance, nearDistance,** and **farDistance.**

SYNTAX **PerspectiveCamera node**

```
PerspectiveCamera {
      position      0.0 0.0 1.0       # X, Y, Z coordinate
      orientation   0.0 0.0 1.0 0.0   # Rotation axis and amount
      focalDistance 5                 # Distance
      heightAngle   0.785             # Angle
      nearDistance  0.01              # Distance
      farDistance   5.0               # Distance
}
```

The **position** field value is a 3-D coordinate describing the position of the camera relative to the current position. The **orientation** field value is a rotation axis and rotation amount, in radians, to aim the camera. Both the position and orientation of the camera are relative to the current origin.

When orienting a camera, a rotation about the X axis tilts the camera up (positive angle) and down (negative angle). A rotation about the Y axis turns the camera left (positive angle) and right (negative angle). A rotation about the Z axis tilts the camera counterclockwise (positive angle) and clockwise (negative angle). All of these rotations follow the right-hand rule discussed in Chapter 6.

The **heightAngle** field value is an angle, in radians, that indicates the vertical spread angle, from top to bottom, of the camera's viewing-volume frustrum. A large angle creates a wide-angle camera affect, while a small angle creates a telephoto camera affect. The default 45.0-degree (0.785-radian) angle is appropriate for most VRML worlds. It is sometimes effective to use a larger angle, around 65.0 degrees (1.13 radians), to exaggerate the perspective of a world, making it seem larger. This is particularly effective in rooms, such as the dungeon from Chapter 21.

TIP ***heightAngle*** *field values over 90.0 degrees create severe visual distortions, like looking through a fish-eye lens. Angles greater than 180.0 degrees are unusable. Different VRML browsers handle very large angles differently. Some browsers constrain the range of values allowed for a* ***heightAngle*** *field, typically limiting them to 180.0 degrees or less. Other browsers allow angles larger than 180.0 degrees, but draw strange jumbled views. Check your VRML browser manual to see how it handles large* ***heightAngle*** *field values.*

TIP *The VRML **heightAngle** controls only the vertical spread angle of the viewing-volume frustrum. The horizontal spread angle is computed by your VRML browser based on the height angle and the size of the browser's window on your screen.*

The **focalDistance** field value is a distance measured from the camera to the focus of attention in the world.

TIP *The **focalDistance** field is not used by most VRML browsers. Those browsers that use the field define its value to be the distance from the camera to the center of the world. When in certain viewing modes, typically called examiner viewers, the world is made to rotate about that center when the user moves the mouse. Check your VRML browser manual to see how it uses **focalDistance** field values.*

The **nearDistance** and **farDistance** fields set the location of near and far clipping planes. Both field values are a distance measured from the camera to the near or the far plane. These planes form the near and far ends of the viewing-volume frustrum. Typically, the **nearDistance** field is set to slightly more than 0.0 units (such as 0.01 units), while the **farDistance** field is set to the maximum distance from one extreme edge of your world to the other. Using these values, you can move anywhere within the world without shapes clipping at the front or back by these planes. Setting the **nearDistance** field to a higher value clips the front of the world, as viewed from your current position. Setting the **farDistance** field to a lower value clips the back of the world.

TIP *Some browsers do not handle **nearDistance** values of exactly 0.0 units. Such browsers may draw a blank screen, or quit with an error. To be safe, always use a **nearDistance** slightly larger than 0.0 units, such as 0.01 units.*

TIP *Many VRML browsers set both near and far clipping plane distances so that they never clip the world. To force clipping to occur, you may need to select a special browser option on one of its menus. Check your VRML browser manual to see how it handles near and far clipping planes.*

TIP *The **nearDistance** and **farDistance** fields may not be supported by all VRML browsers. Check your VRML browser manual to see if it supports them.*

TIP *In version 1.1 of VRML, the **nearDistance** and **farDistance** fields will be added to the **PerspectiveCamera** node. These fields set the location of near and far clipping planes. Both field values are a distance measured from the camera to the near or the far plane. These planes form the near and far ends of the viewing frustrum.*

*Typically, the **nearDistance** field is set to slightly more than 0.0 units (such as 0.01 units), while the **farDistance** field is set to the maximum distances from one extreme edge of your world to the other. Using these values, you can move anywhere within your world without shapes clipping at the front or back by these planes. Setting the **nearDis-***

***tance** field to a higher value clips the front of the world, as viewed from your current position. Setting the **farDistance** field to a lower value clips the back of the world.*

TIP *Specify at most one **PerspectiveCamera** or **OrthographicCamera** node in your VRML files. Different VRML browsers react differently if more than one camera is found while drawing the world. Some may ignore the extra camera nodes, while others may quit with an error.*

TIP *Place camera nodes at the top of your VRML file, before any nodes that draw shapes. Some VRML browsers will draw shapes found before the first camera, while others will not, or will quit with an error. If shapes before the camera are drawn, they may not be drawn as you expect.*

Understanding the **OrthographicCamera** Node Syntax

The **OrthographicCamera** node has six fields: **position, orientation, height, focal Distance, nearDistance,** and **farDistance.**

SYNTAX **OrthographicCamera node**

```
OrthographicCamera {
      position       0.0 0.0 1.0       # X, Y, Z coordinate
      orientation    0.0 0.0 1.0 0.0   # Rotation axis and amount
      focalDistance  5                 # Distance
      height         2                 # Height
      nearDistance   0.01              # Distance
      farDistance    5.0               # Distance
}
```

The **position, orientation, focalDistance, nearDistance,** and **farDistance** fields of an **OrthographicCamera** node are identical to those in a **PerspectiveCamera** node. They control the camera's position and orientation, as well as the distance to the focus of attention, to the near clipping plane, and to the far clipping plane.

The **height** field value specifies the height of the orthographic camera's rectangular-block viewing volume. A larger height increases the size of the viewing volume and increases the range of the world seen by the camera. Typically, the **height** field is set to be somewhat taller than the height of your world, or of a shape you are viewing with the camera.

TIP *The VRML height for an orthographic camera controls only the vertical size of the viewing volume. The horizontal size of the viewing volume is automatically computed by your VRML browser based on the height and the size of the browser's window on your screen.*

The notes and cautions at the end of the Perspective Camera section also apply to orthographic cameras.

Experimenting with Cameras

The following examples provide a more detailed examination of the ways in which cameras can be used. All of the examples inline the file `dungeon.wrl` containing the dungeon rooms created in Chapter 21.

Positioning a Camera

Cameras are positioned by setting the **position** field in **PerspectiveCamera** and **OrthographicCamera** nodes. Figures 22.8 through 22.11 each set the position of a perspective camera to view the dungeon from different positions. The camera position is set relative to the current origin, so a positive X, Y, or Z value positions the camera along the positive directions of the X, Y, or Z axes. Similarly, negative positions place the camera along the negative directions of the X, Y, or Z axes.

Figure 22.8 shows the first room of the dungeon.

```
#VRML V1.0 ascii

PerspectiveCamera {
      position 0.0 3.5 12.0
      orientation 0.0 0.0 1.0 0.0
}
WWWInline {
      name "dungeon.wrl"
}
```

Figure 22.8 *Starting view of the dungeon.*

Figure 22.9 shows the dungeon door opening and a bit of the second room.

```
#VRML V1.0 ascii

PerspectiveCamera {
      position 0.0 3.5 4.0
      orientation 0.0 0.0 1.0 0.0
}
WWWInline {
      name "dungeon.wrl"
}
```

Figure 22.9 *A viewing position closer to the door.*

Figure 22.10 shows a view from the doorway between the dungeon rooms.

```
#VRML V1.0 ascii

PerspectiveCamera {
      position 0.0 3.5 -4.0
      orientation 0.0 0.0 1.0 0.0
}
WWWInline {
      name "dungeon.wrl"
}
```

Figure 22.10 *A viewing position in the doorway.*

Figure 22.11 shows a close-up of a torch.

```
#VRML V1.0 ascii

PerspectiveCamera {
      position 3.25 4.35 -1.0
      orientation 0.0 0.0 1.0 0.0
}
WWWInline {
      name "dungeon.wrl"
}
```

Figure 22.11 *A close-up view of a torch.*

Orienting a Camera

The **orientation** field of a camera node aims the camera. The following examples turn the camera with positive and negative rotation angles around the X, Y, and Z axes.

An X-axis rotation tilts the camera, pitching it up or down, as shown in Figures 22.12 and 22.13.

```
#VRML V1.0 ascii

PerspectiveCamera {
      position 0.0 3.5 4.0
      #           X            +10.0 degrees
      orientation 1.0 0.0 0.0  0.17
}
WWWInline {
      name "dungeon.wrl"
}
```

Figure 22.12 *Positive X-axis camera rotation.*

```
#VRML V1.0 ascii

PerspectiveCamera {
      position 0.0 3.5 4.0
      #           X            -10.0 degrees
      orientation 1.0 0.0 0.0  -0.17
}
WWWInline {
      name "dungeon.wrl"
}
```

Figure 22.13 *Negative X-axis camera rotation.*

A Y-axis rotation turns the camera left and right, as shown in Figures 22.14 and 22.15.

```
#VRML V1.0 ascii

PerspectiveCamera {
      position 0.0 3.5 4.0
      #                Y         +10.0 degrees
      orientation 0.0 1.0 0.0  0.17
}
WWWInline {
      name "dungeon.wrl"
}
```

Figure 22.14 *Positive Y-axis camera rotation.*

```
#VRML V1.0 ascii

PerspectiveCamera {
      position 0.0 3.5 4.0
      #                Y         -10.0 degrees
      orientation 0.0 1.0 0.0  -0.17
}
WWWInline {
      name "dungeon.wrl"
}
```

Figure 22.15 *Negative Y-axis camera rotation.*

A Z-axis rotation tilts the camera, rolling it counterclockwise or clockwise, as shown in Figures 22.16 and 22.17.

```
#VRML V1.0 ascii

PerspectiveCamera {
      position 0.0 3.5 4.0
      #                  Z   +10.0 degrees
      orientation 0.0 0.0 1.0  0.17
}
WWWInline {
      name "dungeon.wrl"
}
```

Figure 22.16 *Positive Z-axis camera rotation.*

```
#VRML V1.0 ascii

PerspectiveCamera {
      position 0.0 3.5 4.0
      #                  Z   -10.0 degrees
      orientation 0.0 0.0 1.0  -0.17
}
WWWInline {
      name "dungeon.wrl"
}
```

Figure 22.17 *Negative Z-axis camera rotation.*

Changing a Perspective Camera's Height Angle

The **heightAngle** field of a **PerspectiveCamera** node varies the spread of the viewing-volume frustrum, creating wide-angle, normal, and telephoto lens effects. The examples in Figures 22.18 through 22.21 vary the **heightAngle** from a small angle to a large angle, while keeping the camera position and orientation the same. Notice that a very large **heightAngle** creates a severely distorted image, like that through a fish-eye lens. A small **heightAngle** acts like a telephoto lens, zooming in on the world.

```
#VRML V1.0 ascii

PerspectiveCamera {
      position 0.0 3.5 4.0
      orientation 0.0 0.0 1.0  0.0
      #            25.0 degrees
      heightAngle 0.44
}
WWWInline {
      name "dungeon.wrl"
}
```

Figure 22.18 *A small height angle.*

```
#VRML V1.0 ascii

PerspectiveCamera {
      position 0.0 3.5 4.0
      orientation 0.0 0.0 1.0  0.0
      #            45.0 degrees
      heightAngle 0.785
}
WWWInline {
      name "dungeon.wrl"
}
```

Figure 22.19 *A medium height angle.*

```
#VRML V1.0 ascii

PerspectiveCamera {
      position 0.0 3.5 4.0
      orientation 0.0 0.0 1.0  0.0
      #            65.0 degrees
      heightAngle 1.13
}
WWWInline {
      name "dungeon.wrl"
}
```

Figure 22.20 *A large height angle.*

```
#VRML V1.0 ascii

PerspectiveCamera {
      position 0.0 3.5 4.0
      orientation 0.0 0.0 1.0  0.0
      #            120.0 degrees
      heightAngle 2.09
}
WWWInline {
      name "dungeon.wrl"
}
```

Figure 22.21 *A very large height angle.*

Using an Orthographic Camera

Orthographic cameras, like perspective cameras, are positioned and oriented using their **position** and **orientation** fields. The **height** field controls the vertical size of the orthographic camera's rectangular-block viewing volume. Typically the **height** field is set to be somewhat taller than the height of your world or of a shape you are viewing with the camera.

The example text in Figure 22.22 uses an **OrthographicCamera** node to view the front room of the dungeon. Since the dungeon wall is 7.0 units high, the camera's **height** is set a bit larger: 9.0 units.

```
#VRML V1.0 ascii

OrthographicCamera {
      position 0.0 3.5 12.0
      orientation 0.0 0.0 1.0 0.0
      height 9.0
}
WWWInline {
      name "dungeon.wrl"
}
```

Figure 22.22 *Viewing the dungeon with an orthographic camera.*

Switching between Cameras

Normally, you should never put more than one camera node into a VRML world. However, you can use a **Switch** node to group together several cameras for the same world, then use the **whichChild** field to select which single camera to use. Since the

VRML browser will see only the single camera selected by the **whichChild** field and ignore the rest of the cameras in the **Switch** node, there will be no drawing problems caused by having more than one camera in the same file.

Some VRML browsers will look for a **Switch** node with the defined name *Cameras* in order to find a list of your cameras for the world. That list is then added to a menu from which you can quickly select one camera or another. So that each camera has a name appearing in the menu, define a name for each camera in the **Switch** node.

Using this feature of some VRML browsers, you can set up a list of cameras, each one aimed at a particular point of interest in your world. This gives viewers of your world tips on good things to look at. Check the manual for your VRML browser to see if it supports the *Cameras* **Switch** node.

The example text in Figure 22.23 combines some of the previous cameras together into a **Switch** node named *Cameras*. Each camera node has its own defined name that describes the view the camera sees. The **whichChild** field of the **Switch** node is set to select the camera to be used as the initial view when the VRML file is first loaded by the VRML browser.

```
#VRML V1.0 ascii

# Select among several camera views
DEF Cameras Switch {
      whichChild 0
      DEF first_room PerspectiveCamera {
            position 0.0 3.5 12.0
            orientation 0.0 0.0 1.0 0.0
      }
      DEF open_door PerspectiveCamera {
            position 0.0 3.5 4.0
            orientation 0.0 0.0 1.0 0.0
      }
      DEF second_room PerspectiveCamera {
            position 0.0 3.5 -4.0
            orientation 0.0 0.0 1.0 0.0
      }
      DEF torch PerspectiveCamera {
            position 3.25 4.35 -1.0
            orientation 0.0 0.0 1.0 0.0
      }
      DEF warped_view PerspectiveCamera {
            position -3.5 3.5 3.5
            #                Y       -30.0 degrees
            orientation 0.0 1.0 0.0  -0.5
            #           120.0 degrees
            heightAngle 2.09
      }
```

Figure 22.23 continues

```
      DEF ortho_view OrthographicCamera {
            position 0.0 3.5 12.0
            orientation 0.0 0.0 1.0 0.0
            height 9.0
      }
}
WWWInline {
      name "dungeon.wrl"
}
```

Figure 22.23 *Using a **Switch** node to define many camera views.*

Summary

PerspectiveCamera and **OrthographicCamera** nodes define how a virtual camera views your world. Using the **position** field and the **orientation** field of either nodes, you can position and orient either camera.

PerspectiveCamera nodes compute a perspective view of the world, like that in the real world. Shapes near the camera are drawn large, while those far away are drawn smaller. The range of the world seen by a perspective camera is defined by a viewing-volume frustrum: a tapered box with the small end at the camera and the large end at the horizon. The **PerspectiveCamera** node's **heightAngle** field controls the spread of the frustrum so that a large height angle creates a wide-angle lens effect, while a small height angle creates a telephoto lens effect. The **nearDistance** and **farDistance** fields set the distance to the front and back of the frustrum, clipping near and far shapes that fall outside the frustrum.

OrthographicCamera nodes compute a view of the world without perspective. Shapes near or far from the camera are drawn the same size. The range of the world seen by an orthographic camera is defined by a rectangular-block viewing volume. The **OrthographicCamera** node's **height** field controls the height of the viewing volume. The **nearDistance** and **farDistance** fields set the distance to the front and back of the block, clipping off near and far shapes that fall outside the block.

The **focalDistance** field of both camera nodes specifies the distance between the camera and a center of interest in the world. This field is unused by most VRML browsers.

Camera nodes should be placed at the top of a VRML file with no shapes drawn before them. There should be at most one camera node in a VRML file, unless they are enclosed within a **Switch** node. Some VRML browsers will look for a **Switch** node with the defined name *Cameras* to find a list of cameras to place in a menu.

CHAPTER 23

Providing Information about Your Worlds

After completing a world, it's time to title it and sign it. You can, and should, include this information as comments in any VRML file you write. You can also include this information within special **Info** nodes. Unlike comments, the information you put in **Info** nodes can be easily extracted by your VRML browser and, optionally, displayed to a user of your world. This enables you to title and sign your work, and lets others see your title and signature as they view your world.

Info nodes can also be used to turn on and off custom features supported by your VRML browser. This provides a convenient way to access the special abilities of your browser that are not yet standard in the VRML specification.

Understanding Information Strings

VRML information strings are arbitrary messages surrounded by quotation marks. They can be any length and include any characters, just like strings used for **AsciiText** nodes.

Information strings are *not* drawn as shapes in your world, and have no color, position, or font style. You can include any number of information strings in your file, placed anywhere. They do not affect any of your browser's drawing functions.

Information strings are used to create special comments that can be extracted by your VRML browser. The information your browser extracts can be used or displayed in any way it needs. Title and signature information, for instance, is typically displayed by browsers when you choose a *Document Info* menu item.

Other types of information turn on and off internal features of the browser and are never displayed.

Providing Information about Your Worlds

The VRML **Info** node is a generic node for providing information strings in your VRML file. The example text in Figure 23.1 adds title and scene information **Info** nodes to describe a VRML file.

```
#VRML V1.0 ascii

DEF Title Info {
      string "Crystal Empire"
}
DEF SceneInfo Info {
      string "by Pat Doe, 1995"
}
WWWInline {
      name "empire.wrl"
}
```

Figure 23.1 *Adding a title and scene information to a VRML file.*

Understanding the **Info** Node Syntax

The **Info** node has a single **string** field containing any message you want to include. **Info** nodes do not draw anything and have no effect on how the VRML browser draws subsequent shapes.

SYNTAX **Info node**

```
Info {
      string "<Undefined info>" # String
}
```

Many VRML browsers look for **Info** nodes with particular defined names, extract their information strings, and use them to determine the title and signature for the world or to turn on and off custom features of the browser. The specific **Info** node names recognized by a browser vary from browser to browser. Check your VRML browser manual for a list of **Info** node names and a description of how your browser is affected by them.

A few **Info** node names have become commonly supported by many browsers and are listed as follows:

Defined Name	*Description*
Title	The title of your world
SceneInfo	Information about your world, such as your name, when you created it, why you created it, and how you can be reached by other users of your world
BackgroundColor	The RGB color to use for the background

TIP *The preceding **Info** node names are commonly supported, but are not part of the VRML specification. These features may not work on some VRML browsers.*

TIP *In version 1.1 of VRML the **BackgroundColor** mechanism for specifying a background color may become part of the standard.*

Experimenting with Information Strings

The following examples provide a more detailed examination of the ways in which **Info** nodes can be used.

Titling and Signing Your Worlds

The example text in Figure 23.2 creates a simple VRML file that provides a title and signature for a world that is inlined from the file `empire.wrl`.

```
#VRML V1.0 ascii

DEF Title Info {
      string "Crystal Empire"
}
DEF SceneInfo Info {
      string "by Pat Doe, 1995"
}
WWWInline {
      name "empire.wrl"
}
```

Figure 23.2 *Titling and signing your world at the beginning of the file.*

The preceding **Info** nodes provide information about your VRML file. The **Info** node named **Title** may be recognized by your VRML browser and its information extracted and used as the title of the world. Similarly, the **Info** node named **SceneInfo** may be recognized and its information extracted and used as information about your world. How a VRML browser uses this information, if at all, depends on your browser. Check your VRML browser manual for information about how it supports this information.

Info nodes like these can be placed anywhere in your file, though they are typically placed at the top of the file. The example text in Figure 23.3 instead places them at the end and in a different order.

```
#VRML V1.0 ascii

WWWInline {
      name "empire.wrl"
}
DEF SceneInfo Info {
      string "by Pat Doe, 1995"
}
DEF Title Info {
      string "Crystal Empire"
}
```

Figure 23.3 *Signing and titling your world at the end of the file.*

Setting the Background Color

The background color is the color of the "page" on which your world is drawn. Different VRML browsers use different default background colors, though a black background is the most common. Some browsers recognize an **Info** node with the defined name **BackgroundColor** and use its information string to select the RGB background color to use. Check your VRML browser manual for information about its default and if and how to set it.

The example text in Figure 23.4 sets the background color to red, then draws a cube.

```
#VRML V1.0 ascii

DEF BackgroundColor Info {
      string "1.0 0.0 0.0"
}
Cube {
}
```

Figure 23.4 *Setting the background color in your world.*

Summary

Info nodes provide generic information strings that can be used to set the title of a world and give credit information about who created it, when, and why. Some VRML browsers also use information strings to enable you to turn on and off custom features of the browser, such as controlling the background color.

APPENDIX A

Radians and Degrees

Several of VRML's nodes have fields whose values include an angle measured in **radians**. For instance, an angle is used by the **Rotation** node to determine how far to rotate the virtual pen before drawing subsequent shapes. Other nodes that use angles include the **Transform, Texture2Transform, PerspectiveCamera, OrthographicCamera, SpotLight,** and **ShapeHints** nodes.

Most people find it easier to measure angles using **degrees** rather than radians. This means you'll probably be converting a lot from degrees to radians, and back again, as you create your VRML worlds.

In degrees, an angle measures the size of an arc from 0.0 degrees to 360.0 degrees, counterclockwise around a full circle. Halfway around the circle is 180.0 degrees, and a quarter of the way is 90.0 degrees. On a clock face, for instance, if 0.0 degrees is at 12 o'clock, then 9 o'clock is 90.0 degrees counterclockwise around the clock face. 6 o'clock is 180.0 degrees around, and 3 o'clock is 270.0 degrees around.

In radians, an angle measures the same arc but instead varies from 0.0 radians to $2\pi = 6.283$ radians full circle. Halfway around the circle is $\pi = 3.142$ radians, and a quarter of the way is $0.5\pi = 1.571$ radians. Figure A.1 shows the correspondence between degrees and radians as they measure out points around a circle.

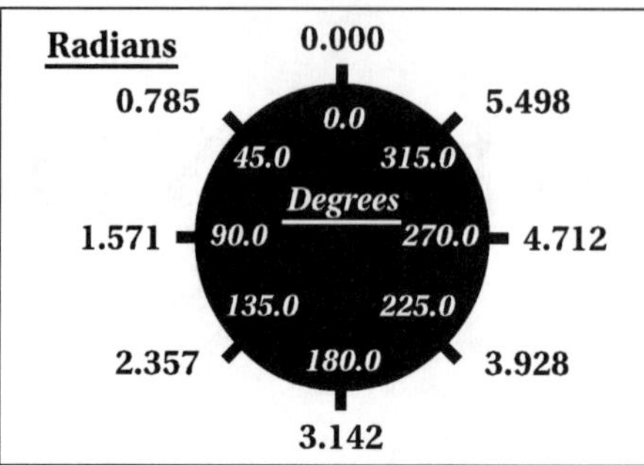

Figure A.1 *Degrees and radians and their correspondence to each other and a clock face.*

Radians are convenient for computer computations, while degrees are more convenient for people. To convert from an angle in degrees to one in radians, use this simple formula:

$$rad = deg \div 180.0 \times 3.142$$

For instance, 30.0 degrees is 0.524 radians:

$$0.524 = 30.0 \div 180 \times 3.142$$

To convert from radians back to degrees, use the reverse formula:

$$deg = rad \div 3.142 \times 180.0$$

For instance, 0.785 radians is 45.0 degrees:

$$45.0 = 0.785 \div 3.142 \times 180.0$$

Table A.1 provides the degree and radian values for several common angles.

Table A.1 Common Angles in Degrees Converted to Radian Values

Degrees	*Radians*
0.0	0.000
1.0	0.017
2.0	0.035
5.0	0.087
10.0	0.175
20.0	0.349
30.0	0.524
45.0	0.785
90.0	1.571
180.0	3.142
270.0	4.712
360.0	6.283

APPENDIX B

RGB Color Table

The following tables correspond to the RGB color swatch charts shown in color plate 1. They provide the red, green, and blue values necessary to create the colors shown in each swatch. Use the red, green, and blue values in these tables to specify field values in your VRML text. The **Material** node is the most likely candidate for RGB color specification: the **ambientColor, diffuseColor, emissiveColor,** and **specularColor** fields. You may also specify RGB colors in the **DirectionalLight, PointLight,** and **SpotLight** nodes.

To specify an RGB color in your VRML file:

1. Locate the color on one of the color swatch charts in color plate 1: (*a*) vivid colors, (*b*) dark colors, (*c*) pastel colors, or (*d*) shades of gray.
2. Make a note of the row number and column letter corresponding to the swatch.
3. Find the RGB color in the table of this appendix that corresponds to the color swatch chart in color plate 1: vivid colors in Table B.1 (see color plate 1*a*), dark colors in Table B.2 (see color plate 1*b*), pastel colors in Table B.3 (see color plate 1*c*), or shades of gray in Table B.4 (see color plate 1*d*).
4. Locate the red (R), green (G), and blue (B) values in the table corresponding to the row number and column letter of the color swatch.
5. Use the red, green, and blue color values in your **Material** node.

Table B.1 Vivid Colors (See color plate 1*a*)

	A	*B*	*C*	*D*	*E*	*F*	*G*	*H*	*I*	*J*	*K*	*L*	*M*	*N*	*O*	*P*	*Q*	*R*	*S*	*T*	
1	1.00	0.00	0.00	1.00	0.02	0.00	1.00	0.03	0.00	1.00	0.05	0.00	1.00	0.07	0.00	1.00	0.08	0.00	1.00	0.10	R
	0.00	0.00	1.00	0.02	0.00	1.00	0.03	0.00	1.00	0.05	0.00	1.00	0.07	0.00	1.00	0.08	0.00	1.00	0.10	0.00	G
	0.00	1.00	0.02	0.00	1.00	0.03	0.00	1.00	0.05	0.00	1.00	0.07	0.00	1.00	0.08	0.00	1.00	0.10	0.00	1.00	B
2	0.00	1.00	0.12	0.00	1.00	0.13	0.00	1.00	0.15	0.00	1.00	0.17	0.00	1.00	0.18	0.00	1.00	0.20	0.00	1.00	R
	1.00	0.12	0.00	1.00	0.13	0.00	1.00	0.15	0.00	1.00	0.17	0.00	1.00	0.18	0.00	1.00	0.20	0.00	1.00	0.22	G
	0.12	0.00	1.00	0.13	0.00	1.00	0.15	0.00	1.00	0.17	0.00	1.00	0.18	0.00	1.00	0.20	0.00	1.00	0.22	0.00	B
3	0.22	0.00	1.00	0.23	0.00	1.00	0.25	0.00	1.00	0.27	0.00	1.00	0.28	0.00	1.00	0.30	0.00	1.00	0.32	0.00	R
	0.00	1.00	0.23	0.00	1.00	0.25	0.00	1.00	0.27	0.00	1.00	0.28	0.00	1.00	0.30	0.00	1.00	0.32	0.00	1.00	G
	1.00	0.23	0.00	1.00	0.25	0.00	1.00	0.27	0.00	1.00	0.28	0.00	1.00	0.30	0.00	1.00	0.32	0.00	1.00	0.33	B
4	1.00	0.33	0.00	1.00	0.35	0.00	1.00	0.37	0.00	1.00	0.38	0.00	1.00	0.40	0.00	1.00	0.42	0.00	1.00	0.43	R
	0.33	0.00	1.00	0.35	0.00	1.00	0.37	0.00	1.00	0.38	0.00	1.00	0.40	0.00	1.00	0.42	0.00	1.00	0.43	0.00	G
	0.00	1.00	0.35	0.00	1.00	0.37	0.00	1.00	0.38	0.00	1.00	0.40	0.00	1.00	0.42	0.00	1.00	0.43	0.00	1.00	B
5	0.00	1.00	0.45	0.00	1.00	0.47	0.00	1.00	0.48	0.00	1.00	0.50	0.00	1.00	0.52	0.00	1.00	0.53	0.00	1.00	R
	1.00	0.45	0.00	1.00	0.47	0.00	1.00	0.48	0.00	1.00	0.50	0.00	1.00	0.52	0.00	1.00	0.53	0.00	1.00	0.55	G
	0.45	0.00	1.00	0.47	0.00	1.00	0.48	0.00	1.00	0.50	0.00	1.00	0.52	0.00	1.00	0.53	0.00	1.00	0.55	0.00	B
6	0.55	0.00	1.00	0.57	0.00	1.00	0.58	0.00	1.00	0.60	0.00	1.00	0.62	0.00	1.00	0.63	0.00	1.00	0.65	0.00	R
	0.00	1.00	0.57	0.00	1.00	0.58	0.00	1.00	0.60	0.00	1.00	0.62	0.00	1.00	0.63	0.00	1.00	0.65	0.00	1.00	G
	1.00	0.57	0.00	1.00	0.58	0.00	1.00	0.60	0.00	1.00	0.62	0.00	1.00	0.63	0.00	1.00	0.65	0.00	1.00	0.67	B
7	1.00	0.67	0.00	1.00	0.68	0.00	1.00	0.70	0.00	1.00	0.72	0.00	1.00	0.73	0.00	1.00	0.75	0.00	1.00	0.77	R
	0.67	0.00	1.00	0.68	0.00	1.00	0.70	0.00	1.00	0.72	0.00	1.00	0.73	0.00	1.00	0.75	0.00	1.00	0.77	0.00	G
	0.00	1.00	0.68	0.00	1.00	0.70	0.00	1.00	0.72	0.00	1.00	0.73	0.00	1.00	0.75	0.00	1.00	0.77	0.00	1.00	B
8	0.00	1.00	0.78	0.00	1.00	0.80	0.00	1.00	0.82	0.00	1.00	0.83	0.00	1.00	0.85	0.00	1.00	0.87	0.00	1.00	R
	1.00	0.78	0.00	1.00	0.80	0.00	1.00	0.82	0.00	1.00	0.83	0.00	1.00	0.85	0.00	1.00	0.87	0.00	1.00	0.88	G
	0.78	0.00	1.00	0.80	0.00	1.00	0.82	0.00	1.00	0.83	0.00	1.00	0.85	0.00	1.00	0.87	0.00	1.00	0.88	0.00	B
9	0.88	0.00	1.00	0.90	0.00	1.00	0.92	0.00	1.00	0.93	0.00	1.00	0.95	0.00	1.00	0.97	0.00	1.00	0.98	0.00	R
	0.00	1.00	0.90	0.00	1.00	0.92	0.00	1.00	0.93	0.00	1.00	0.95	0.00	1.00	0.97	0.00	1.00	0.98	0.00	1.00	G
	1.00	0.90	0.00	1.00	0.92	0.00	1.00	0.93	0.00	1.00	0.95	0.00	1.00	0.97	0.00	1.00	0.98	0.00	1.00	1.00	B
10	1.00	1.00	0.00	0.98	1.00	0.00	0.97	1.00	0.00	0.95	1.00	0.00	0.93	1.00	0.00	0.92	1.00	0.00	0.90	1.00	R
	1.00	0.00	0.98	1.00	0.00	0.97	1.00	0.00	0.95	1.00	0.00	0.93	1.00	0.00	0.92	1.00	0.00	0.90	1.00	0.00	G
	0.00	0.98	1.00	0.00	0.97	1.00	0.00	0.95	1.00	0.00	0.93	1.00	0.00	0.92	1.00	0.00	0.90	1.00	0.00	0.88	B
11	0.00	0.88	1.00	0.00	0.87	1.00	0.00	0.85	1.00	0.00	0.83	1.00	0.00	0.82	1.00	0.00	0.80	1.00	0.00	0.78	R
	0.88	1.00	0.00	0.87	1.00	0.00	0.85	1.00	0.00	0.83	1.00	0.00	0.82	1.00	0.00	0.80	1.00	0.00	0.78	1.00	G
	1.00	0.00	0.87	1.00	0.00	0.85	1.00	0.00	0.83	1.00	0.00	0.82	1.00	0.00	0.80	1.00	0.00	0.78	1.00	0.00	B
12	1.00	0.00	0.77	1.00	0.00	0.75	1.00	0.00	0.73	1.00	0.00	0.72	1.00	0.00	0.70	1.00	0.00	0.68	1.00	0.00	R
	0.00	0.77	1.00	0.00	0.75	1.00	0.00	0.73	1.00	0.00	0.72	1.00	0.00	0.70	1.00	0.00	0.68	1.00	0.00	0.67	G
	0.77	1.00	0.00	0.75	1.00	0.00	0.73	1.00	0.00	0.72	1.00	0.00	0.70	1.00	0.00	0.68	1.00	0.00	0.67	1.00	B
13	0.67	1.00	0.00	0.65	1.00	0.00	0.63	1.00	0.00	0.62	1.00	0.00	0.60	1.00	0.00	0.58	1.00	0.00	0.57	1.00	R
	1.00	0.00	0.65	1.00	0.00	0.63	1.00	0.00	0.62	1.00	0.00	0.60	1.00	0.00	0.58	1.00	0.00	0.57	1.00	0.00	G
	0.00	0.65	1.00	0.00	0.63	1.00	0.00	0.62	1.00	0.00	0.60	1.00	0.00	0.58	1.00	0.00	0.57	1.00	0.00	0.55	B
14	0.00	0.55	1.00	0.00	0.53	1.00	0.00	0.52	1.00	0.00	0.50	1.00	0.00	0.48	1.00	0.00	0.47	1.00	0.00	0.45	R
	0.55	1.00	0.00	0.53	1.00	0.00	0.52	1.00	0.00	0.50	1.00	0.00	0.48	1.00	0.00	0.47	1.00	0.00	0.45	1.00	G
	1.00	0.00	0.53	1.00	0.00	0.52	1.00	0.00	0.50	1.00	0.00	0.48	1.00	0.00	0.47	1.00	0.00	0.45	1.00	0.00	B
15	1.00	0.00	0.43	1.00	0.00	0.42	1.00	0.00	0.40	1.00	0.00	0.38	1.00	0.00	0.37	1.00	0.00	0.35	1.00	0.00	R
	0.00	0.43	1.00	0.00	0.42	1.00	0.00	0.40	1.00	0.00	0.38	1.00	0.00	0.37	1.00	0.00	0.35	1.00	0.00	0.33	G
	0.43	1.00	0.00	0.42	1.00	0.00	0.40	1.00	0.00	0.38	1.00	0.00	0.37	1.00	0.00	0.35	1.00	0.00	0.33	1.00	B
16	0.33	1.00	0.00	0.32	1.00	0.00	0.30	1.00	0.00	0.28	1.00	0.00	0.27	1.00	0.00	0.25	1.00	0.00	0.23	1.00	R
	1.00	0.00	0.32	1.00	0.00	0.30	1.00	0.00	0.28	1.00	0.00	0.27	1.00	0.00	0.25	1.00	0.00	0.23	1.00	0.00	G
	0.00	0.32	1.00	0.00	0.30	1.00	0.00	0.28	1.00	0.00	0.27	1.00	0.00	0.25	1.00	0.00	0.23	1.00	0.00	0.22	B
17	0.00	0.22	1.00	0.00	0.20	1.00	0.00	0.18	1.00	0.00	0.17	1.00	0.00	0.15	1.00	0.00	0.13	1.00	0.00	0.12	R
	0.22	1.00	0.00	0.20	1.00	0.00	0.18	1.00	0.00	0.17	1.00	0.00	0.15	1.00	0.00	0.13	1.00	0.00	0.12	1.00	G
	1.00	0.00	0.20	1.00	0.00	0.18	1.00	0.00	0.17	1.00	0.00	0.15	1.00	0.00	0.13	1.00	0.00	0.12	1.00	0.00	B
18	1.00	0.00	0.10	1.00	0.00	0.08	1.00	0.00	0.07	1.00	0.00	0.05	1.00	0.00	0.03	1.00	0.00	0.02	1.00	0.00	R
	0.00	0.10	1.00	0.00	0.08	1.00	0.00	0.07	1.00	0.00	0.05	1.00	0.00	0.03	1.00	0.00	0.02	1.00	0.00	0.00	G
	0.10	1.00	0.00	0.08	1.00	0.00	0.07	1.00	0.00	0.05	1.00	0.00	0.03	1.00	0.00	0.02	1.00	0.00	0.00	1.00	B

Table B.2 Dark Colors (See color plate 1*b*)

	A	*B*	*C*	*D*	*E*	*F*	*G*	*H*	*I*	*J*	*K*	*L*	*M*	*N*	*O*	*P*	*Q*	*R*	*S*	*T*	
1	0.50	0.00	0.00	0.50	0.01	0.00	0.50	0.02	0.00	0.50	0.03	0.00	0.50	0.03	0.00	0.50	0.04	0.00	0.50	0.05	R
	0.00	0.00	0.50	0.01	0.00	0.50	0.02	0.00	0.50	0.03	0.00	0.50	0.03	0.00	0.50	0.04	0.00	0.50	0.05	0.00	G
	0.00	0.50	0.01	0.00	0.50	0.02	0.00	0.50	0.03	0.00	0.50	0.03	0.00	0.50	0.04	0.00	0.50	0.05	0.00	0.50	B
2	0.00	0.50	0.06	0.00	0.50	0.07	0.00	0.50	0.08	0.00	0.50	0.08	0.00	0.50	0.09	0.00	0.50	0.10	0.00	0.50	R
	0.50	0.06	0.00	0.50	0.07	0.00	0.50	0.08	0.00	0.50	0.08	0.00	0.50	0.09	0.00	0.50	0.10	0.00	0.50	0.11	G
	0.06	0.00	0.50	0.07	0.00	0.50	0.08	0.00	0.50	0.08	0.00	0.50	0.09	0.00	0.50	0.10	0.00	0.50	0.11	0.00	B
3	0.11	0.00	0.50	0.12	0.00	0.50	0.12	0.00	0.50	0.13	0.00	0.50	0.14	0.00	0.50	0.15	0.00	0.50	0.16	0.00	R
	0.00	0.50	0.12	0.00	0.50	0.12	0.00	0.50	0.13	0.00	0.50	0.14	0.00	0.50	0.15	0.00	0.50	0.16	0.00	0.50	G
	0.50	0.12	0.00	0.50	0.12	0.00	0.50	0.13	0.00	0.50	0.14	0.00	0.50	0.15	0.00	0.50	0.16	0.00	0.50	0.17	B
4	0.50	0.17	0.00	0.50	0.17	0.00	0.50	0.18	0.00	0.50	0.19	0.00	0.50	0.20	0.00	0.50	0.21	0.00	0.50	0.22	R
	0.17	0.00	0.50	0.17	0.00	0.50	0.18	0.00	0.50	0.19	0.00	0.50	0.20	0.00	0.50	0.21	0.00	0.50	0.22	0.00	G
	0.00	0.50	0.17	0.00	0.50	0.18	0.00	0.50	0.19	0.00	0.50	0.20	0.00	0.50	0.21	0.00	0.50	0.22	0.00	0.50	B
5	0.00	0.50	0.22	0.00	0.50	0.23	0.00	0.50	0.24	0.00	0.50	0.25	0.00	0.50	0.26	0.00	0.50	0.27	0.00	0.50	R
	0.50	0.22	0.00	0.50	0.23	0.00	0.50	0.24	0.00	0.50	0.25	0.00	0.50	0.26	0.00	0.50	0.27	0.00	0.50	0.28	G
	0.22	0.00	0.50	0.23	0.00	0.50	0.24	0.00	0.50	0.25	0.00	0.50	0.26	0.00	0.50	0.27	0.00	0.50	0.28	0.00	B
6	0.28	0.00	0.50	0.28	0.00	0.50	0.29	0.00	0.50	0.30	0.00	0.50	0.31	0.00	0.50	0.32	0.00	0.50	0.33	0.00	R
	0.00	0.50	0.28	0.00	0.50	0.29	0.00	0.50	0.30	0.00	0.50	0.31	0.00	0.50	0.32	0.00	0.50	0.33	0.00	0.50	G
	0.50	0.28	0.00	0.50	0.29	0.00	0.50	0.30	0.00	0.50	0.31	0.00	0.50	0.32	0.00	0.50	0.33	0.00	0.50	0.33	B
7	0.50	0.33	0.00	0.50	0.34	0.00	0.50	0.35	0.00	0.50	0.36	0.00	0.50	0.37	0.00	0.50	0.38	0.00	0.50	0.38	R
	0.33	0.00	0.50	0.34	0.00	0.50	0.35	0.00	0.50	0.36	0.00	0.50	0.37	0.00	0.50	0.38	0.00	0.50	0.38	0.00	G
	0.00	0.50	0.34	0.00	0.50	0.35	0.00	0.50	0.36	0.00	0.50	0.37	0.00	0.50	0.38	0.00	0.50	0.38	0.00	0.50	B
8	0.00	0.50	0.39	0.00	0.50	0.40	0.00	0.50	0.41	0.00	0.50	0.42	0.00	0.50	0.42	0.00	0.50	0.43	0.00	0.50	R
	0.50	0.39	0.00	0.50	0.40	0.00	0.50	0.41	0.00	0.50	0.42	0.00	0.50	0.42	0.00	0.50	0.43	0.00	0.50	0.44	G
	0.39	0.00	0.50	0.40	0.00	0.50	0.41	0.00	0.50	0.42	0.00	0.50	0.42	0.00	0.50	0.43	0.00	0.50	0.44	0.00	B
9	0.44	0.00	0.50	0.45	0.00	0.50	0.46	0.00	0.50	0.47	0.00	0.50	0.47	0.00	0.50	0.48	0.00	0.50	0.49	0.00	R
	0.00	0.50	0.45	0.00	0.50	0.46	0.00	0.50	0.47	0.00	0.50	0.47	0.00	0.50	0.48	0.00	0.50	0.49	0.00	0.50	G
	0.50	0.45	0.00	0.50	0.46	0.00	0.50	0.47	0.00	0.50	0.47	0.00	0.50	0.48	0.00	0.50	0.49	0.00	0.50	0.50	B
10	0.50	0.50	0.00	0.49	0.50	0.00	0.48	0.50	0.00	0.47	0.50	0.00	0.47	0.50	0.00	0.46	0.50	0.00	0.45	0.50	R
	0.50	0.00	0.49	0.50	0.00	0.48	0.50	0.00	0.47	0.50	0.00	0.47	0.50	0.00	0.46	0.50	0.00	0.45	0.50	0.00	G
	0.00	0.49	0.50	0.00	0.48	0.50	0.00	0.47	0.50	0.00	0.47	0.50	0.00	0.46	0.50	0.00	0.45	0.50	0.00	0.44	B
11	0.00	0.44	0.50	0.00	0.43	0.50	0.00	0.43	0.50	0.00	0.42	0.50	0.00	0.41	0.50	0.00	0.40	0.50	0.00	0.39	R
	0.44	0.50	0.00	0.43	0.50	0.00	0.43	0.50	0.00	0.42	0.50	0.00	0.41	0.50	0.00	0.40	0.50	0.00	0.39	0.50	G
	0.50	0.00	0.43	0.50	0.00	0.43	0.50	0.00	0.42	0.50	0.00	0.41	0.50	0.00	0.40	0.50	0.00	0.39	0.50	0.00	B
12	0.50	0.00	0.38	0.50	0.00	0.38	0.50	0.00	0.37	0.50	0.00	0.36	0.50	0.00	0.35	0.50	0.00	0.34	0.50	0.00	R
	0.00	0.38	0.50	0.00	0.38	0.50	0.00	0.37	0.50	0.00	0.36	0.50	0.00	0.35	0.50	0.00	0.34	0.50	0.00	0.33	G
	0.38	0.50	0.00	0.38	0.50	0.00	0.37	0.50	0.00	0.36	0.50	0.00	0.35	0.50	0.00	0.34	0.50	0.00	0.33	0.50	B
13	0.33	0.50	0.00	0.32	0.50	0.00	0.32	0.50	0.00	0.31	0.50	0.00	0.30	0.50	0.00	0.29	0.50	0.00	0.28	0.50	R
	0.50	0.00	0.32	0.50	0.00	0.32	0.50	0.00	0.31	0.50	0.00	0.30	0.50	0.00	0.29	0.50	0.00	0.28	0.50	0.00	G
	0.00	0.32	0.50	0.00	0.32	0.50	0.00	0.31	0.50	0.00	0.30	0.50	0.00	0.29	0.50	0.00	0.28	0.50	0.00	0.28	B
14	0.00	0.28	0.50	0.00	0.27	0.50	0.00	0.26	0.50	0.00	0.25	0.50	0.00	0.24	0.50	0.00	0.23	0.50	0.00	0.22	R
	0.28	0.50	0.00	0.27	0.50	0.00	0.26	0.50	0.00	0.25	0.50	0.00	0.24	0.50	0.00	0.23	0.50	0.00	0.22	0.50	G
	0.50	0.00	0.27	0.50	0.00	0.26	0.50	0.00	0.25	0.50	0.00	0.24	0.50	0.00	0.23	0.50	0.00	0.22	0.50	0.00	B
15	0.50	0.00	0.22	0.50	0.00	0.21	0.50	0.00	0.20	0.50	0.00	0.19	0.50	0.00	0.18	0.50	0.00	0.18	0.50	0.00	R
	0.00	0.22	0.50	0.00	0.21	0.50	0.00	0.20	0.50	0.00	0.19	0.50	0.00	0.18	0.50	0.00	0.18	0.50	0.00	0.17	G
	0.22	0.50	0.00	0.21	0.50	0.00	0.20	0.50	0.00	0.19	0.50	0.00	0.18	0.50	0.00	0.18	0.50	0.00	0.17	0.50	B
16	0.17	0.50	0.00	0.16	0.50	0.00	0.15	0.50	0.00	0.14	0.50	0.00	0.13	0.50	0.00	0.12	0.50	0.00	0.12	0.50	R
	0.50	0.00	0.16	0.50	0.00	0.15	0.50	0.00	0.14	0.50	0.00	0.13	0.50	0.00	0.12	0.50	0.00	0.12	0.50	0.00	G
	0.00	0.16	0.50	0.00	0.15	0.50	0.00	0.14	0.50	0.00	0.13	0.50	0.00	0.12	0.50	0.00	0.12	0.50	0.00	0.11	B
17	0.00	0.11	0.50	0.00	0.10	0.50	0.00	0.09	0.50	0.00	0.08	0.50	0.00	0.07	0.50	0.00	0.07	0.50	0.00	0.06	R
	0.11	0.50	0.00	0.10	0.50	0.00	0.09	0.50	0.00	0.08	0.50	0.00	0.07	0.50	0.00	0.07	0.50	0.00	0.06	0.50	G
	0.50	0.00	0.10	0.50	0.00	0.09	0.50	0.00	0.08	0.50	0.00	0.07	0.50	0.00	0.07	0.50	0.00	0.06	0.50	0.00	B
18	0.50	0.00	0.05	0.50	0.00	0.04	0.50	0.00	0.03	0.50	0.00	0.03	0.50	0.00	0.02	0.50	0.00	0.01	0.50	0.00	R
	0.00	0.05	0.50	0.00	0.04	0.50	0.00	0.03	0.50	0.00	0.03	0.50	0.00	0.02	0.50	0.00	0.01	0.50	0.00	0.00	G
	0.05	0.50	0.00	0.04	0.50	0.00	0.03	0.50	0.00	0.03	0.50	0.00	0.02	0.50	0.00	0.01	0.50	0.00	0.00	0.50	B

Table B.3 Pastel Colors (See color plate 1*c*)

	A	*B*	C	*D*	*E*	*F*	*G*	*H*	*I*	*J*	*K*	*L*	*M*	*N*	O	*P*	*Q*	*R*	*S*	*T*	
1	1.00	0.50	0.50	1.00	0.51	0.50	1.00	0.52	0.50	1.00	0.53	0.50	1.00	0.53	0.50	1.00	0.54	0.50	1.00	0.55	R
	0.50	0.50	1.00	0.51	0.50	1.00	0.52	0.50	1.00	0.53	0.50	1.00	0.53	0.50	1.00	0.54	0.50	1.00	0.55	0.50	G
	0.50	1.00	0.51	0.50	1.00	0.52	0.50	1.00	0.53	0.50	1.00	0.53	0.50	1.00	0.54	0.50	1.00	0.55	0.50	1.00	B
2	0.50	1.00	0.56	0.50	1.00	0.57	0.50	1.00	0.57	0.50	1.00	0.58	0.50	1.00	0.59	0.50	1.00	0.60	0.50	1.00	R
	1.00	0.56	0.50	1.00	0.57	0.50	1.00	0.57	0.50	1.00	0.58	0.50	1.00	0.59	0.50	1.00	0.60	0.50	1.00	0.61	G
	0.56	0.50	1.00	0.57	0.50	1.00	0.57	0.50	1.00	0.58	0.50	1.00	0.59	0.50	1.00	0.60	0.50	1.00	0.61	0.50	B
3	0.61	0.50	1.00	0.62	0.50	1.00	0.62	0.50	1.00	0.63	0.50	1.00	0.64	0.50	1.00	0.65	0.50	1.00	0.66	0.50	R
	0.50	1.00	0.62	0.50	1.00	0.62	0.50	1.00	0.63	0.50	1.00	0.64	0.50	1.00	0.65	0.50	1.00	0.66	0.50	1.00	G
	1.00	0.62	0.50	1.00	0.62	0.50	1.00	0.63	0.50	1.00	0.64	0.50	1.00	0.65	0.50	1.00	0.66	0.50	1.00	0.67	B
4	1.00	0.67	0.50	1.00	0.68	0.50	1.00	0.68	0.50	1.00	0.69	0.50	1.00	0.70	0.50	1.00	0.71	0.50	1.00	0.72	R
	0.67	0.50	1.00	0.68	0.50	1.00	0.68	0.50	1.00	0.69	0.50	1.00	0.70	0.50	1.00	0.71	0.50	1.00	0.72	0.50	G
	0.50	1.00	0.68	0.50	1.00	0.68	0.50	1.00	0.69	0.50	1.00	0.70	0.50	1.00	0.71	0.50	1.00	0.72	0.50	1.00	B
5	0.50	1.00	0.72	0.50	1.00	0.73	0.50	1.00	0.74	0.50	1.00	0.75	0.50	1.00	0.76	0.50	1.00	0.77	0.50	1.00	R
	1.00	0.72	0.50	1.00	0.73	0.50	1.00	0.74	0.50	1.00	0.75	0.50	1.00	0.76	0.50	1.00	0.77	0.50	1.00	0.78	G
	0.72	0.50	1.00	0.73	0.50	1.00	0.74	0.50	1.00	0.75	0.50	1.00	0.76	0.50	1.00	0.77	0.50	1.00	0.78	0.50	B
6	0.78	0.50	1.00	0.78	0.50	1.00	0.79	0.50	1.00	0.80	0.50	1.00	0.81	0.50	1.00	0.82	0.50	1.00	0.82	0.50	R
	0.50	1.00	0.78	0.50	1.00	0.79	0.50	1.00	0.80	0.50	1.00	0.81	0.50	1.00	0.82	0.50	1.00	0.82	0.50	1.00	G
	1.00	0.78	0.50	1.00	0.79	0.50	1.00	0.80	0.50	1.00	0.81	0.50	1.00	0.82	0.50	1.00	0.82	0.50	1.00	0.83	B
7	1.00	0.83	0.50	1.00	0.84	0.50	1.00	0.85	0.50	1.00	0.86	0.50	1.00	0.87	0.50	1.00	0.88	0.50	1.00	0.88	R
	0.83	0.50	1.00	0.84	0.50	1.00	0.85	0.50	1.00	0.86	0.50	1.00	0.87	0.50	1.00	0.88	0.50	1.00	0.88	0.50	G
	0.50	1.00	0.84	0.50	1.00	0.85	0.50	1.00	0.86	0.50	1.00	0.87	0.50	1.00	0.88	0.50	1.00	0.88	0.50	1.00	B
8	0.50	1.00	0.89	0.50	1.00	0.90	0.50	1.00	0.91	0.50	1.00	0.92	0.50	1.00	0.93	0.50	1.00	0.93	0.50	1.00	R
	1.00	0.89	0.50	1.00	0.90	0.50	1.00	0.91	0.50	1.00	0.92	0.50	1.00	0.93	0.50	1.00	0.93	0.50	1.00	0.94	G
	0.89	0.50	1.00	0.90	0.50	1.00	0.91	0.50	1.00	0.92	0.50	1.00	0.93	0.50	1.00	0.93	0.50	1.00	0.94	0.50	B
9	0.94	0.50	1.00	0.95	0.50	1.00	0.96	0.50	1.00	0.97	0.50	1.00	0.97	0.50	1.00	0.98	0.50	1.00	0.99	0.50	R
	0.50	1.00	0.95	0.50	1.00	0.96	0.50	1.00	0.97	0.50	1.00	0.97	0.50	1.00	0.98	0.50	1.00	0.99	0.50	1.00	G
	1.00	0.95	0.50	1.00	0.96	0.50	1.00	0.97	0.50	1.00	0.97	0.50	1.00	0.98	0.50	1.00	0.99	0.50	1.00	1.00	B
10	1.00	1.00	0.50	0.99	1.00	0.50	0.98	1.00	0.50	0.97	1.00	0.50	0.97	1.00	0.50	0.96	1.00	0.50	0.95	1.00	R
	1.00	0.50	0.99	1.00	0.50	0.98	1.00	0.50	0.97	1.00	0.50	0.97	1.00	0.50	0.96	1.00	0.50	0.95	1.00	0.50	G
	0.50	0.99	1.00	0.50	0.98	1.00	0.50	0.97	1.00	0.50	0.97	1.00	0.50	0.96	1.00	0.50	0.95	1.00	0.50	0.94	B
11	0.50	0.94	1.00	0.50	0.93	1.00	0.50	0.93	1.00	0.50	0.92	1.00	0.50	0.91	1.00	0.50	0.90	1.00	0.50	0.89	R
	0.94	1.00	0.50	0.93	1.00	0.50	0.93	1.00	0.50	0.92	1.00	0.50	0.91	1.00	0.50	0.90	1.00	0.50	0.89	1.00	G
	1.00	0.50	0.93	1.00	0.50	0.93	1.00	0.50	0.92	1.00	0.50	0.91	1.00	0.50	0.90	1.00	0.50	0.89	1.00	0.50	B
12	1.00	0.50	0.88	1.00	0.50	0.88	1.00	0.50	0.87	1.00	0.50	0.86	1.00	0.50	0.85	1.00	0.50	0.84	1.00	0.50	R
	0.50	0.88	1.00	0.50	0.88	1.00	0.50	0.87	1.00	0.50	0.86	1.00	0.50	0.85	1.00	0.50	0.84	1.00	0.50	0.83	G
	0.88	1.00	0.50	0.88	1.00	0.50	0.87	1.00	0.50	0.86	1.00	0.50	0.85	1.00	0.50	0.84	1.00	0.50	0.83	1.00	B
13	0.83	1.00	0.50	0.82	1.00	0.50	0.82	1.00	0.50	0.81	1.00	0.50	0.80	1.00	0.50	0.79	1.00	0.50	0.78	1.00	R
	1.00	0.50	0.82	1.00	0.50	0.82	1.00	0.50	0.81	1.00	0.50	0.80	1.00	0.50	0.79	1.00	0.50	0.78	1.00	0.50	G
	0.50	0.82	1.00	0.50	0.82	1.00	0.50	0.81	1.00	0.50	0.80	1.00	0.50	0.79	1.00	0.50	0.78	1.00	0.50	0.78	B
14	0.50	0.78	1.00	0.50	0.77	1.00	0.50	0.76	1.00	0.50	0.75	1.00	0.50	0.74	1.00	0.50	0.73	1.00	0.50	0.72	R
	0.78	1.00	0.50	0.77	1.00	0.50	0.76	1.00	0.50	0.75	1.00	0.50	0.74	1.00	0.50	0.73	1.00	0.50	0.72	1.00	G
	1.00	0.50	0.77	1.00	0.50	0.76	1.00	0.50	0.75	1.00	0.50	0.74	1.00	0.50	0.73	1.00	0.50	0.72	1.00	0.50	B
15	1.00	0.50	0.72	1.00	0.50	0.71	1.00	0.50	0.70	1.00	0.50	0.69	1.00	0.50	0.68	1.00	0.50	0.68	1.00	0.50	R
	0.50	0.72	1.00	0.50	0.71	1.00	0.50	0.70	1.00	0.50	0.69	1.00	0.50	0.68	1.00	0.50	0.68	1.00	0.50	0.67	G
	0.72	1.00	0.50	0.71	1.00	0.50	0.70	1.00	0.50	0.69	1.00	0.50	0.68	1.00	0.50	0.68	1.00	0.50	0.67	1.00	B
16	0.67	1.00	0.50	0.66	1.00	0.50	0.65	1.00	0.50	0.64	1.00	0.50	0.63	1.00	0.50	0.62	1.00	0.50	0.62	1.00	R
	1.00	0.50	0.66	1.00	0.50	0.65	1.00	0.50	0.64	1.00	0.50	0.63	1.00	0.50	0.62	1.00	0.50	0.62	1.00	0.50	G
	0.50	0.66	1.00	0.50	0.65	1.00	0.50	0.64	1.00	0.50	0.63	1.00	0.50	0.62	1.00	0.50	0.62	1.00	0.50	0.61	B
17	0.50	0.61	1.00	0.50	0.60	1.00	0.50	0.59	1.00	0.50	0.58	1.00	0.50	0.57	1.00	0.50	0.57	1.00	0.50	0.56	R
	0.61	1.00	0.50	0.60	1.00	0.50	0.59	1.00	0.50	0.58	1.00	0.50	0.57	1.00	0.50	0.57	1.00	0.50	0.56	1.00	G
	1.00	0.50	0.60	1.00	0.50	0.59	1.00	0.50	0.58	1.00	0.50	0.57	1.00	0.50	0.57	1.00	0.50	0.56	1.00	0.50	B
18	1.00	0.50	0.55	1.00	0.50	0.54	1.00	0.50	0.53	1.00	0.50	0.53	1.00	0.50	0.52	1.00	0.50	0.51	1.00	0.50	R
	0.50	0.55	1.00	0.50	0.54	1.00	0.50	0.53	1.00	0.50	0.53	1.00	0.50	0.52	1.00	0.50	0.51	1.00	0.50	0.50	G
	0.55	1.00	0.50	0.54	1.00	0.50	0.53	1.00	0.50	0.53	1.00	0.50	0.52	1.00	0.50	0.51	1.00	0.50	0.50	1.00	B

Table B.4 Shades of Gray (See color plate 1*d*)

	A	*B*	*C*	*D*	*E*	*F*	*G*	*H*	*I*	*J*	*K*	*L*	*M*	*N*	*O*	*P*	*Q*	*R*	*S*	*T*	
1	0.00	0.00	0.00	0.00	0.00	0.00	0.01	0.01	0.01	0.01	0.01	0.01	0.01	0.01	0.01	0.01	0.01	0.01	0.02	0.02	R
	0.00	0.00	0.00	0.00	0.00	0.01	0.01	0.01	0.01	0.01	0.01	0.01	0.01	0.01	0.01	0.01	0.01	0.02	0.02	0.02	G
	0.00	0.00	0.00	0.00	0.01	0.01	0.01	0.01	0.01	0.01	0.01	0.01	0.01	0.01	0.01	0.01	0.02	0.02	0.02	0.02	B
2	0.02	0.02	0.02	0.02	0.02	0.02	0.02	0.03	0.03	0.03	0.03	0.03	0.03	0.03	0.03	0.03	0.03	0.03	0.03	0.04	R
	0.02	0.02	0.02	0.02	0.02	0.02	0.03	0.03	0.03	0.03	0.03	0.03	0.03	0.03	0.03	0.03	0.03	0.03	0.04	0.04	G
	0.02	0.02	0.02	0.02	0.02	0.03	0.03	0.03	0.03	0.03	0.03	0.03	0.03	0.03	0.03	0.03	0.03	0.04	0.04	0.04	B
3	0.04	0.04	0.04	0.04	0.04	0.04	0.04	0.04	0.04	0.04	0.04	0.05	0.05	0.05	0.05	0.05	0.05	0.05	0.05	0.05	R
	0.04	0.04	0.04	0.04	0.04	0.04	0.04	0.04	0.04	0.04	0.05	0.05	0.05	0.05	0.05	0.05	0.05	0.05	0.05	0.06	G
	0.04	0.04	0.04	0.04	0.04	0.04	0.04	0.04	0.04	0.05	0.05	0.05	0.05	0.05	0.05	0.05	0.05	0.05	0.06	0.06	B
4	0.06	0.06	0.06	0.06	0.06	0.06	0.06	0.06	0.06	0.06	0.06	0.06	0.07	0.07	0.07	0.07	0.07	0.07	0.07	0.07	R
	0.06	0.06	0.06	0.06	0.06	0.06	0.06	0.06	0.06	0.06	0.06	0.07	0.07	0.07	0.07	0.07	0.07	0.07	0.07	0.07	G
	0.06	0.06	0.06	0.06	0.06	0.06	0.06	0.06	0.06	0.06	0.07	0.07	0.07	0.07	0.07	0.07	0.07	0.07	0.07	0.07	B
5	0.07	0.07	0.07	0.07	0.08	0.08	0.08	0.08	0.08	0.08	0.08	0.08	0.08	0.09	0.09	0.09	0.09	0.09	0.09	0.09	R
	0.07	0.07	0.07	0.08	0.08	0.08	0.08	0.08	0.08	0.08	0.08	0.08	0.09	0.09	0.09	0.09	0.09	0.09	0.09	0.09	G
	0.07	0.07	0.08	0.08	0.08	0.08	0.08	0.08	0.08	0.08	0.08	0.09	0.09	0.09	0.09	0.09	0.09	0.09	0.09	0.09	B
6	0.09	0.09	0.09	0.09	0.09	0.10	0.10	0.10	0.10	0.10	0.10	0.10	0.10	0.10	0.11	0.11	0.11	0.11	0.11	0.11	R
	0.09	0.09	0.09	0.09	0.10	0.10	0.10	0.10	0.10	0.10	0.10	0.10	0.10	0.11	0.11	0.11	0.11	0.11	0.11	0.11	G
	0.09	0.09	0.09	0.10	0.10	0.10	0.10	0.10	0.10	0.10	0.10	0.10	0.11	0.11	0.11	0.11	0.11	0.11	0.11	0.11	B
7	0.11	0.11	0.11	0.11	0.11	0.11	0.12	0.12	0.12	0.12	0.12	0.12	0.12	0.12	0.12	0.12	0.12	0.12	0.13	0.13	R
	0.11	0.11	0.11	0.11	0.11	0.12	0.12	0.12	0.12	0.12	0.12	0.12	0.12	0.12	0.12	0.12	0.12	0.13	0.13	0.13	G
	0.11	0.11	0.11	0.11	0.12	0.12	0.12	0.12	0.12	0.12	0.12	0.12	0.12	0.12	0.12	0.12	0.13	0.13	0.13	0.13	B
8	0.13	0.13	0.13	0.13	0.13	0.13	0.13	0.14	0.14	0.14	0.14	0.14	0.14	0.14	0.14	0.14	0.14	0.14	0.14	0.15	R
	0.13	0.13	0.13	0.13	0.13	0.13	0.14	0.14	0.14	0.14	0.14	0.14	0.14	0.14	0.14	0.14	0.14	0.14	0.15	0.15	G
	0.13	0.13	0.13	0.13	0.13	0.14	0.14	0.14	0.14	0.14	0.14	0.14	0.14	0.14	0.14	0.14	0.14	0.15	0.15	0.15	B
9	0.15	0.15	0.15	0.15	0.15	0.15	0.15	0.15	0.16	0.16	0.16	0.16	0.16	0.16	0.16	0.16	0.16	0.16	0.16	0.16	R
	0.15	0.15	0.15	0.15	0.15	0.15	0.15	0.16	0.16	0.16	0.16	0.16	0.16	0.16	0.16	0.16	0.16	0.16	0.16	0.17	G
	0.15	0.15	0.15	0.15	0.15	0.15	0.16	0.16	0.16	0.16	0.16	0.16	0.16	0.16	0.16	0.16	0.16	0.16	0.17	0.17	B
10	0.17	0.17	0.17	0.17	0.17	0.17	0.17	0.17	0.17	0.17	0.17	0.17	0.18	0.18	0.18	0.18	0.18	0.18	0.18	0.18	R
	0.17	0.17	0.17	0.17	0.17	0.17	0.17	0.17	0.17	0.17	0.17	0.18	0.18	0.18	0.18	0.18	0.18	0.18	0.18	0.18	G
	0.17	0.17	0.17	0.17	0.17	0.17	0.17	0.17	0.17	0.17	0.18	0.18	0.18	0.18	0.18	0.18	0.18	0.18	0.18	0.19	B
11	0.18	0.19	0.19	0.19	0.19	0.19	0.19	0.19	0.19	0.19	0.19	0.19	0.19	0.20	0.20	0.20	0.20	0.20	0.20	0.20	R
	0.19	0.19	0.19	0.19	0.19	0.19	0.19	0.19	0.19	0.19	0.19	0.19	0.20	0.20	0.20	0.20	0.20	0.20	0.20	0.20	G
	0.19	0.19	0.19	0.19	0.19	0.19	0.19	0.19	0.19	0.19	0.19	0.20	0.20	0.20	0.20	0.20	0.20	0.20	0.20	0.20	B
12	0.20	0.20	0.21	0.21	0.21	0.21	0.21	0.21	0.21	0.21	0.21	0.21	0.21	0.21	0.22	0.22	0.22	0.22	0.22	0.22	R
	0.20	0.21	0.21	0.21	0.21	0.21	0.21	0.21	0.21	0.21	0.21	0.21	0.21	0.22	0.22	0.22	0.22	0.22	0.22	0.22	G
	0.21	0.21	0.21	0.21	0.21	0.21	0.21	0.21	0.21	0.21	0.21	0.21	0.22	0.22	0.22	0.22	0.22	0.22	0.22	0.22	B
13	0.22	0.22	0.22	0.23	0.23	0.23	0.23	0.23	0.23	0.23	0.23	0.23	0.23	0.23	0.23	0.24	0.24	0.24	0.24	0.24	R
	0.22	0.22	0.23	0.23	0.23	0.23	0.23	0.23	0.23	0.23	0.23	0.23	0.23	0.23	0.24	0.24	0.24	0.24	0.24	0.24	G
	0.22	0.23	0.23	0.23	0.23	0.23	0.23	0.23	0.23	0.23	0.23	0.23	0.23	0.24	0.24	0.24	0.24	0.24	0.24	0.24	B
14	0.24	0.24	0.24	0.24	0.24	0.24	0.24	0.25	0.25	0.25	0.25	0.25	0.25	0.25	0.25	0.25	0.26	0.26	0.26	0.26	R
	0.24	0.24	0.24	0.24	0.24	0.24	0.25	0.25	0.25	0.25	0.25	0.25	0.25	0.25	0.25	0.26	0.26	0.26	0.26	0.26	G
	0.24	0.24	0.24	0.24	0.24	0.25	0.25	0.25	0.25	0.25	0.25	0.25	0.25	0.25	0.26	0.26	0.26	0.26	0.26	0.26	B
15	0.26	0.26	0.26	0.26	0.26	0.26	0.26	0.26	0.27	0.27	0.27	0.27	0.27	0.27	0.27	0.27	0.27	0.28	0.28	0.28	R
	0.26	0.26	0.26	0.26	0.26	0.26	0.26	0.27	0.27	0.27	0.27	0.27	0.27	0.27	0.27	0.27	0.28	0.28	0.28	0.28	G
	0.26	0.26	0.26	0.26	0.26	0.26	0.27	0.27	0.27	0.27	0.27	0.27	0.27	0.27	0.27	0.28	0.28	0.28	0.28	0.28	B
16	0.28	0.28	0.28	0.28	0.28	0.28	0.28	0.28	0.28	0.29	0.29	0.29	0.29	0.29	0.29	0.29	0.29	0.29	0.29	0.29	R
	0.28	0.28	0.28	0.28	0.28	0.28	0.28	0.28	0.29	0.29	0.29	0.29	0.29	0.29	0.29	0.29	0.29	0.29	0.29	0.29	G
	0.28	0.28	0.28	0.28	0.28	0.28	0.28	0.29	0.29	0.29	0.29	0.29	0.29	0.29	0.29	0.29	0.29	0.29	0.29	0.30	B
17	0.29	0.30	0.30	0.30	0.30	0.30	0.30	0.30	0.30	0.30	0.31	0.31	0.31	0.31	0.31	0.31	0.31	0.31	0.31	0.31	R
	0.30	0.30	0.30	0.30	0.30	0.30	0.30	0.30	0.30	0.31	0.31	0.31	0.31	0.31	0.31	0.31	0.31	0.31	0.31	0.31	G
	0.30	0.30	0.30	0.30	0.30	0.30	0.30	0.30	0.31	0.31	0.31	0.31	0.31	0.31	0.31	0.31	0.31	0.31	0.31	0.31	B
18	0.31	0.31	0.32	0.32	0.32	0.32	0.32	0.32	0.32	0.32	0.32	0.33	0.33	0.33	0.33	0.33	0.33	0.33	0.33	0.33	R
	0.31	0.32	0.32	0.32	0.32	0.32	0.32	0.32	0.32	0.32	0.33	0.33	0.33	0.33	0.33	0.33	0.33	0.33	0.33	0.33	G
	0.32	0.32	0.32	0.32	0.32	0.32	0.32	0.32	0.32	0.33	0.33	0.33	0.33	0.33	0.33	0.33	0.33	0.33	0.33	0.33	B

APPENDIX C

Recommended Resources

The Wiley Web Site and FTP Site

Using your HTML Web browser you can retrieve any of the examples used in this book by going to the John Wiley & Sons Web site at:

```
http://www.wiley.com/compbooks/
```

Or you can go directly to the Wiley ftp site at:

```
ftp://ftp.wiley.com/public/computer_books/vrml
```

This site includes all of the VRML examples in the book, all of the texture image files used in the texture-mapping examples, as well as additional VRML examples and texture images that are not in the book.

Also included at the Wiley Web site is the *errata* list for this book, as well as notes on additions and changes made to the VRML specification since this book was printed.

The VRML Repository

The VRML Repository is the principle Internet site for information about VRML. Using your HTML Web browser, you can browse through the VRML Repository's archives at:

```
http://www.sdsc.edu/vrml
```

The VRML Repository is maintained by SDSC (the San Diego Supercomputer Center). The repository includes a tremendous amount of well-organized information about the VRML specification, examples using VRML, images for VRML texture mapping, and information about free and commercial software supporting VRML.

Recommended Reading

As the popularity of computer graphics and virtual reality has grown, dozens of books have become available. Providing a comprehensive list of computer graphics texts is not practical. In this section we instead list some of our favorite texts. All of them are available in most technical and university bookstores.

Introduction to Computer Graphics

Readers interested in learning more about the field of computer graphics are encouraged to read any of several introductory texts:

Angel, Edward, *Computer Graphics,* Reading, MA: Addison-Wesley, 1990.

Foley, James D., van Dam, Andries, Feiner, Stephen K., Hughes, John F., and Phillips, Richard L., *Introduction to Computer Graphics,* Reading, MA: Addison-Wesley, 1994.

Glassner, Andrew S., *3D Computer Graphics: A User's Guide for Artists and Designers,* Design Press, 1989.

Pokorny, Cornel K., and Gerald, Curtis F., *Computer Graphics: The Principles Behind the Art and Science,* Franklin, Beedle & Associates, 1989.

Watt, Alan, *3D Computer Graphics,* Reading, MA: Addison-Wesley, 1993.

Of these texts, *3D Computer Graphics: A User's Guide for Artists and Designers* is a particularly easy-to-read and informative introductory book designed specifically for readers without mathematics and computer programming backgrounds. The remaining books in the list are written for the computer programmer and are frequently used as textbooks for university courses on computer graphics.

Advanced Computer Graphics

The following books provide more advanced information on computer graphics:

Glassner, Andrew S., *Principles of Digital Image Synthesis, volumes one and two,* San Mateo, CA: Morgan Kaufmann, 1995.

Graphics Gems, Andrew S. Glassner, ed., San Diego, CA: Academic Press, 1990.

Foley, James D., van Dam, Andries, Feiner, Stephen K., Hughes, John F., and Phillips, Richard L., *Computer Graphics: Principles and Practice,* Reading, MA: Addison-Wesley, 1995.

Graphics Gems II, James Arvo, ed., San Diego, CA: Academic Press, 1991.

Graphics Gems III, David Kirk, ed., San Diego, CA: Academic Press, 1992.

Graphics Gems IV, Paul S. Heckbert, ed., San Diego, CA: Academic Press, 1994.

Watt, Alan, and Watt, Mark, *Advanced Animation and Rendering Techniques, Theory and Practice,* Reading, MA: Addison-Wesley, 1992.

Advanced Animation and Rendering Techniques, Theory and Practice and *Computer Graphics: Principles and Practice* cover computer graphics topics in depth. The latter text is generally considered the principle technical reference used by computer graphics professionals.

Principles of Digital Image Synthesis is a two-volume set that covers the underlying physics and mathematics behind computer graphics. *Principles of Digital Image Synthesis* requires a good foundation in mathematics and physics.

The *Graphics Gems* series of books provides dozens of algorithmic shortcuts, tricks, and techniques for computer graphics programmers.

Open Inventor

VRML was originally based on the Open Inventor software library developed by Silicon Graphics Inc. (SGI) and available for most computer platforms. Several of the VRML browsers currently available are written using Open Inventor. The following three books are the definitive reference on Open Inventor. All of these books are written for the computer programmer adept at C++.

Open Inventor C++ Reference Manual, Silicon Graphics Inc., Reading, MA: Addison-Wesley, 1994.

Wernecke, Josie, *The Inventor Mentor,* Reading, MA: Addison-Wesley, 1994.

Wernecke, Josie, *The Inventor Toolmaker,* Reading, MA: Addison-Wesley, 1994.

Geometric Modeling

VRML's **IndexedFaceSet** node provides a flexible way to define complex faceted shapes. However, it is often more intuitive to work with mathematically defined surfaces, such as those created by *splines.* Most geometric modeling done in the computer graphics industry is based on splines or similar mathematical surfaces. The following texts cover geometric modeling techniques. All include a fair amount of mathematics and are written for the computer programmer.

Bartels, Richard H., Beatty, John C., and Barsky, Brian A., *An Introduction to Splines for Use in Computer Graphics & Geometric Modeling,* San Mateo, CA: Morgan Kaufmann, 1987.

Farin, Gerald, *Curves and Surfaces for Computer Aided Geometric Design,* second edition, San Diego, CA: Academic Press, 1990.

Mortenson, Michael E., *Geometric Modeling,* New York, NY: John Wiley & Sons, 1985.

Virtual Reality

The following texts each discuss development techniques for writing virtual reality software and working with virtual reality hardware, such as head-mount displays (HMDs), 3-D trackers, and so forth. All are written for the computer programmer.

Burdea, Grigore, and Coiffet, Philippe, *Virtual Reality Technology,* New York, NY: John Wiley & Sons, 1994.

Gradecki, Joe, *The Virtual Reality Construction Kit,* New York, NY: John Wiley & Sons, 1994.

Gradecki, Joe, *The Virtual Reality Programmer's Kit,* New York, NY: John Wiley & Sons, 1994.

Watkins, Christopher, and Marenka, Stephen R., *Virtual Reality ExCursions with Programs in* C, San Diego, CA: Academic Press, 1994.

APPENDIX D

The VRML Specification

The **VRML specification** is an official document available at the VRML Repository that details the features available in VRML and the syntax to invoke those features. This specification is used by software developers when writing VRML browsers and other applications, and it is this specification on which this book is based.

The VRML specification was written *by* computer graphics programmers *for* computer graphics programmers. It uses technical jargon and assumes the reader has a strong background in computer graphics. Both of these can be barriers to you, a reader interested in authoring VRML worlds.

The VRML Sourcebook was designed to lower these barriers by minimizing the use of programmer jargon and by explaining the concepts and techniques that form the basis of the computer graphics field. We have chosen to develop in you an informal and intuitive understanding of computer graphics concepts rather than delve into the underlying mathematics and computer programming.

Because of the jargon-free approach used by this book, readers interested in reading the VRML specification itself may find that some of the specification's jargon and technical points appear unfamiliar. This appendix provides a brief explanation of the jargon used by the specification, discussing each technical term in the context of concepts introduced in the body of this book.

Understanding the VRML Specification

The following sections discuss technical jargon and computer graphics background ideas used by the VRML specification.

The VRML specification is a rapidly evolving document and therefore is not included in this appendix. We encourage you to consult the VRML Repository for the latest information on the specification. The repository's URL is:

```
http://www.sdsc.edu/vrml
```

Understanding the VRML Scene Graph

People tend to organize information into tree-like structures, such as family trees, company organization charts, and computer directory trees. These trees all have a branching structure connecting information into a hierarchy from a parent to the parent's children, to their children, and so on, toward the bottom of the tree.

You can think of a VRML file as a tree-like organization of information. Grouping nodes, such as the **Separator** node, act as parents for their child nodes, each of which may act as a parent for their children, and so on.

This tree-like organization of scene information is sometimes called a **scene tree**. Instancing of nodes using the DEF and USE syntax enables you to connect more than one parent to the same child, creating cross connections between distant branches of the tree. These cross connections turn the scene tree into what mathematicians call a **graph**. For this reason, the VRML Specification often refers to the structure of a VRML file as a **scene graph**.

Understanding the Bottom-to-Top Reading Style

In this book we have advocated a top-to-bottom style of reading VRML files. Using this style, each VRML node is seen as an instruction that directs a **virtual pen** with which the VRML browser draws shapes. For instance, the following VRML text translates in X by 4.0 units, scales up the drawing size by a factor of 2.0 in X, and Z, and 1.0 in Y, then draws a sphere:

```
Translation {
   translation 4.0 0.0 0.0
}
Scale {
   scaleFactor 2.0 1.0 2.0
}
Sphere {
}
```

Computer graphics professionals sometimes find it more convenient to read VRML files in a bottom-to-top style. The VRML specification occasionally uses this reading style when discussing transform order.

Using a bottom-to-top reading style, the preceding file is read like this:

1. Create a sphere.
2. Scale it up by a factor of 2.0 in X and Z, and by 1.0 in Y.
3. Move the sphere in X by 4.0 units.

This style of reading VRML files can be very intuitive when working with transforms. A bottom-to-top reading style becomes confusing, however, when nodes are added to change a material color or any other drawing property. Consider, for instance, the following VRML text to change the drawing color to blue, then to red, then draw a sphere:

```
Material {
   diffuseColor 0.0 0.0 1.0
}
Material {
   diffuseColor 1.0 0.0 0.0
}
Sphere {
}
```

Using a top-to-bottom reading style, like that in this book, it is clear that the pen color in effect when drawing the sphere is the second one, so the sphere will be drawn in red.

Using a bottom-to-top reading style, the preceding file would be read like this:

1. Create a sphere.
2. Color it red.
3. Color it blue.

Using a bottom-to-top style to interpret the VRML files provides incorrect information in this case. As intuitive as it is when working with transforms, this reading style is incorrect when interpreting property changes. For this reason, this book uses the top-to-bottom reading style throughout.

Understanding MIME Types

A **MIME type** is a set of two words, separated by a slash, that indicate the type of information a web server is delivering to your web browser. Typically, only your Web browser ever sees incoming MIME type information.

The VRML Specification states that the official MIME type for VRML information is:

```
x-world/x-vrml
```

This MIME type may be used when you first configure your HTML Web browser to recognize VRML information and deliver it to your VRML browser. Check your HTML and VRML browser manuals for instructions about configuring them to work with each other.

Understanding Node Field-Value Data Types

In computer programming, each piece of data must be stored in memory if it is to be used again later. Different types of data require different amounts of memory and may be handled differently when performing mathematical operations. For instance, a floating-point number, such as 42.0, typically takes 4 bytes of memory, while a character string such as "Albatross" takes 1 byte per character, plus 1 extra byte to mark the end.

The VRML Specification defines names for each type of data that can be specified within a VRML node field. Each of these **field-value data types** is defined as follows with examples of the types of nodes in which they are used.

SFBitMask

A **bit** is a single on or off value. A **bit mask** is a collection of bits, each one used to turn on or off a specific feature.

SFBitMask values are used in VRML to turn on the different parts of primitive shape nodes, like a **Cylinder** node's **TOP, BOTTOM,** and **SIDES.** Bit masks are also used to select **BOLD, ITALIC,** or both styles in a **FontStyle** node.

VRML bit values have names. **TOP** and **BOLD,** for instance, are bit value names. To turn on a single feature in a bit mask, specify a single bit value name as a node's field value. For instance, you can direct the VRML browser to draw only the **SIDES** of a cylinder like this:

```
Cylinder {
   parts SIDES
}
```

To turn on more than one bit mask feature, specify multiple bit value names, separated by vertical bars, and surrounded by parenthesis. For instance, the following **FontStyle** node directs the VRML browser to draw text that is both **BOLD** and **ITALIC:**

```
FontStyle {
   style ( BOLD | ITALIC )
}
```

SFBool

The term **bool** is short for **Boolean**. A Boolean value can be either **TRUE** or **FALSE.** These are also sometimes called **logical** values.

SFBool values are used in VRML to turn on or off lights, including the **DirectionalLight, PointLight,** and **SpotLight** nodes. For instance, the following node turns on a point light:

```
PointLight {
   on TRUE
}
```

SFColor

A VRML color value is a collection of three floating-point values controlling the amounts of red, green, and blue to mix together to form a desired color. Because these colors are a mixture of red, green, and blue, they are also known as **RGB colors**.

The three floating-point values forming an RGB color are specified one after the other, separated by spaces. Each red, green, or blue value ranges from 0.0 to 1.0.

SFColor values are used by the light nodes to select the light's color. For instance, the following node sets the color of a point light to red:

```
PointLight {
   color 1.0 0.0 0.0
}
```

SFEnum

The term **enum** is short for **enumerated type**. An enum is a type of data that can be only one of a short list of possible values, each with a name.

SFEnum values are used by the **AsciiText** node to select among justification types, by the **FontStyle** node to select among font families, by the **MaterialBinding** and **NormalBinding** nodes to select binding types, and so on. For instance, the following **AsciiText** node draws the string "Albatross" using **RIGHT** justification:

```
AsciiText {
   string "Albatross"
   justification RIGHT
}
```

SFFloat

A **float** is a **floating-point value**. Float values are large or small, positive or negative values with decimal points. For instance, 88.5, 3.1415, and –489.398 are all float values.

SFFloat values are used to select line spacing in an **AsciiText** node, the width, height, depth, or radius of the primitive shapes, the intensity of the lights created by the lighting nodes, and so forth. For instance, the following **Cube** node uses three SFFloat values for its **width, height,** and **depth** fields:

```
Cube {
   width 10.0
   height 20.0
   depth 30.0
}
```

SFImage

An **image value** is a digital image stored as a rectangular grid of pixel values. SFImage values are used only by the **Texture2** node to set a texture image.

SFLong

The term **long** is short for **long integer**. Long integer values are large or small, positive or negative values without a decimal point. For instance, 42, 182, and –37 are all long integer values.

SFLong values are used by the **PointSet** node to select the starting coordinate index and the number of coordinate indexes for drawing points, and by the **Switch** node to choose which of its children should be drawn by the VRML browser. For instance, the following **PointSet** node draws points for coordinates starting at 0 and extending for 18 coordinates:

```
PointSet {
    startIndex 0
    numPoints 18
}
```

SFMatrix

A **matrix** is a rectangular grid of 16 floating-point values arranged in four rows and four columns. Matrix values are transformation matrices used by the VRML browser to translate, rotate, scale, shear, and taper before drawing subsequent shapes. Each of the values in the matrix is specified one after the other, separated by spaces.

SFMatrix values are only used by the **MatrixTransform** node. For instance, the following node creates a translation matrix that moves the browser's virtual pen 7.5 units to the right along the X axis:

```
MatrixTransform {
    matrix  1.0 0.0 0.0 0.0
            0.0 1.0 0.0 0.0
            0.0 0.0 1.0 0.0
            7.5 0.0 0.0 1.0
}
```

SFRotation

A **rotation** is a group of four floating-point values. The first three values define a rotation axis, while the last value is a rotation amount measured in radians. The four values of a rotation value are given one after the other, separated by spaces.

SFRotation values are used by the camera nodes to select a camera orientation, and by the **Rotation** and **Transform** nodes to direct the VRML browser to rotate its virtual pen before drawing shapes. For instance, the following **Rotation** node rotates by 45.0 degrees (0.785 radians) around the Y axis:

```
Rotation {
    rotation 0.0 1.0 0.0 0.785
}
```

SFString

A **string** is a list of ascii characters surrounded by quotation marks. Any characters, including carriage returns, may appear within a character string. To include a quotation mark character, precede it with a backslash.

SFString values are only used by the **Info** node to specify an information string. For instance, the following node provides the information string "Albatross":

```
Info {
   string "Albatross"
}
```

SFVec2f

The term **vec** is short for **vector** and refers to a group of values. A **vec2f** is a group of two floating-point values. The values of a vector group are specified one after the other, separated by spaces.

SFVec2f values are only used by the **Texture2Transform** node to select translation, scaling, or a center point for transforming texture coordinates. For instance, the following node transforms texture coordinates by translating in the S direction by 0.5 units:

```
Texture2Transform {
   translation 0.5 0.0
}
```

SFVec3f

A **vec3f** is a group of three floating-point values specified one after the other, separated by spaces.

SFVec3f values are used by the lighting nodes to select a direction or location, by the camera nodes to select a position, by the **Scale** and **Transform** nodes to set X, Y, and Z scale factors, and so on. For instance, the following node scales by a factor of 2.0 in X and by a factor of 3.5 in Y and Z:

```
Scale {
   scaleFactor 2.0 3.5 3.5
}
```

MFColor

An MFColor value is *multiple* SFColor values arranged in a list, separated by commas, and enclosed within square brackets. A comma following the last value in the list is optional.

MFColor values are only used by the **Material** node to set a list of ambient, diffuse, emissive, or specular colors. For instance, the following **Material** node specifies three RGB colors for the **diffuseColor** field:

```
Material {
   diffuseColor [
      1.0 0.0 0.0,
      0.0 1.0 0.0,
      0.0 0.0 1.0
   ]
}
```

MFLong

An MFLong value is *multiple* SFLong values arranged in a list, separated by commas, and enclosed within square brackets. A comma following the last value in the list is optional.

MFLong values are used by the **IndexedFaceSet** and **IndexedLineSet** nodes to specify coordinate indexes. For instance, the following **IndexedFaceSet** node draws a triangle using coordinates 0, 1, and 2:

```
IndexedFaceSet {
   coordIndex [
      0, 1, 2
   ]
}
```

MFString

An MFString value is *multiple* SFString values arranged in a list, separated by commas, and enclosed within square brackets. A comma following the last value in the list is optional.

MFString values are only used by the **AsciiText** node to provide a list of strings to draw. For instance, the following node draws three centered strings:

```
AsciiText {
   string [
      "The",
      "VRML",
      "Sourcebook"
   ]
}
```

MFVec2f

An MFVec2f value is *multiple* SFVec2f values arranged in a list, separated by commas, and enclosed within square brackets. A comma following the last value in the list is optional.

MFVec2f values are only used by the **TextureCoordinate2** node to specify a list of 2-D coordinates. For instance, the following node specifies three 2-D texture coordinates:

```
TextureCoordinate2 {
   point [
      0.0 0.0,
      1.0 0.0,
      1.0 1.0
   ]
}
```

MFVec3f

An MFVec3f value is *multiple* SFVec3f values arranged in a list, separated by commas, and enclosed within square brackets. A comma following the last value in the list is optional.

MFVec3f values are used by the **Coordinate3** and **Normal** nodes to specify lists of 3-D coordinates and normal vectors, respectively. For instance, the following node specifies three 3-D coordinates:

```
Coordinate3 {
   point [
       0.0 0.0 0.0,
      -1.0 1.0 0.0,
      -1.0 0.0 0.0
   ]
}
```

Index

Bold page numbers refer to pages containing Syntax boxes.